:: studysync®

Reading & Writing Companion

GRADE 7

UNITS 1–6

∷studysync

studysync.com

ISBN 978-1-94-973917-6
MHID 1-94-973917-1

8 9 10 11 12 13 14 SWI 26 25 24 23 22

D

Contents

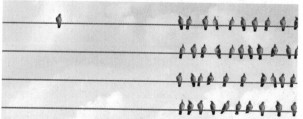

Reading & Writing Companion

iii

Student Guide

Getting Started

Welcome to the StudySync Reading & Writing Companion! In this book, you will find a collection of readings based on the theme of the unit you are studying. As you work through the readings, you will be asked to answer questions and perform a variety of tasks designed to help you closely analyze and understand each text selection. Read on for an explanation of each

Close Reading and Writing Routine

In each unit, you will read texts that share a common theme, despite their different genres, time periods, and authors. Each reading encourages a closer look through questions and a short writing assignment.

Rikki-Tikki-Tavi

FICTION
Rudyard Kipling
1894

Introduction   studysync●

"Rikki-Tikki-Tavi" is one of the most famous tales from *The Jungle Book*, a collection of short stories published in 1894 by English author Rudyard Kipling (1865–1936). The stories in *The Jungle Book* feature animal characters with anthropomorphic traits and are intended to be read as fables, each illustrating a moral lesson. In this story, Rikki-tikki-tavi is a courageous young mongoose adopted as a pet by a British family living in 19th-century colonial India.

① Introduction

An Introduction to each text provides historical context for your reading as well as information about the author. You will also learn about the genre of the text and the year in which it was written.

② Notes

Many times, while working through the activities after each text, you will be asked to **annotate** or **make annotations** about what you are reading. This means that you should highlight or underline words in the text and use the "Notes" column to make comments or jot down any questions you have. You may also want to note any unfamiliar vocabulary words here.

You will also see sample student annotations to go along with the Skill lesson for that text.

Rikki-Tikki-Tavi

"Rikki-tikki held on with his eyes shut, for now he was quite sure he was dead."

This is the story of the great war that Rikki-tikki-tavi fought single-handed, through the bath-rooms of the big bungalow in Segowlee cantonment. Darzee, the Tailorbird, helped him, and Chuchundra, the musk-rat, who never comes out into the middle of the floor, but always creeps round by the wall, gave him advice, but Rikki-tikki did the real fighting.

He was a mongoose, rather like a little cat in his fur and his tail, but quite like a weasel in his head and his habits. His eyes and the end of his restless nose were pink. He could scratch himself anywhere he pleased with any leg, front or back, that he chose to use. He could fluff up his tail till it looked like a bottle brush, and his war cry as he scuttled through the long grass was: "Rikk-tikk-tikki-tikki-tchk!"

One day, a high summer flood washed him out of the burrow where he lived with his father and mother, and carried him, kicking and clucking, down a roadside ditch. He found a little wisp of grass floating there, and clung to it till he lost his senses. When he revived, he was lying in the hot sun on the middle of a garden path, very draggled indeed, and a small boy was saying, "Here's a dead mongoose. Let's have a funeral."

"No," said his mother, "let's take him in and dry him. Perhaps he isn't really dead."

They took him into the house, and a big man picked him up between his finger and thumb and said he was not dead but half choked. So they wrapped him in cotton wool, and warmed him over a little fire, and he opened his eyes and sneezed.

"Now," said the big man (he was an Englishman who had just moved into the bungalow), "don't frighten him, and we'll see what he'll do."

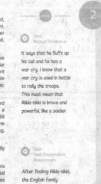

Skill: Textual Evidence

It says that he fluffs up his tail and he has a war cry. I know that a war cry is used in battle to rally the troops. This must mean that Rikki-tikki is brave and powerful, like a soldier.

Skill: Text-Dependent Responses

After finding Rikki-tikki, the English family brought him into their home and took care of him.

③ First Read

During your first reading of each selection, you should just try to get a general idea of the content and message of the reading. Don't worry if there are parts you don't understand or words that are unfamiliar to you. You'll have an opportunity later to dive deeper into the text.

④ Think Questions

These questions will ask you to start thinking critically about the text, asking specific questions about its purpose, and making connections to your prior knowledge and reading experiences. To answer these questions, you should go back to the text and draw upon specific evidence to support your responses. You will also begin to explore some of the more challenging vocabulary words in the selection.

⑤ Skills

Each Skill includes two parts: Checklist and Your Turn. In the Checklist, you will learn the process for analyzing the text. The model student annotations in the text provide examples of how you might make your own notes following the instructions in the Checklist. In the Your Turn, you will use those same instructions to practice the skill.

③ First Read

Read "Rikki-Tikki-Tavi." After you read, complete the Think Questions below.

④ **THINK QUESTIONS**

1. How did Rikki-tikki come to live with the English family? Cite specific evidence from the text to support your answer.

2. What do the descriptions of Nag and the dialogue in paragraphs 23–24 suggest about Nag's character? Cite specific evidence from the text to support your answer.

3. Describe in two to three sentences how Rikki-tikki saves the family from snakes.

4. Find the word **cultivated** in paragraph 18 of "Rikki-Tikki-Tavi." Use context clues in the surrounding sentences, as well as the sentence in which the word appears, to determine the word's meaning. Write your definition here and identify clues that helped you figure out the word's meaning.

5. Use context clues to determine the meaning of **sensible** as it is used in paragraph 79 of "Rikki-Tikki-Tavi." Write your definition of *sensible* here and identify clues that helped you figure out the meaning. Then check the meaning in the dictionary.

⑤ Skill: Character

Use the Checklist to analyze Character in "Rikki-Tikki-Tavi." Refer to the sample student annotations about Character in the text.

••• CHECKLIST FOR CHARACTER

In order to determine how particular elements of a story or drama interact, note the following:

- ✓ the characters in the story, including the protagonist and antagonist
- ✓ the settings and how they shape the characters or plot
- ✓ plot events and how they affect the characters
- ✓ key events or series of episodes in the plot, especially events that cause characters to react, respond, or change in some way
- ✓ characters' responses as the plot reaches a climax and moves toward a resolution of the problem facing the protagonist
- ✓ the resolution of the conflict in the plot and the ways that affects each character

To analyze how particular elements of a story or drama interact, consider the following questions:

- ✓ How do the characters' responses change or develop from the beginning to the end of the story?
- ✓ How does the setting shape the characters and plot in the story?
- ✓ How do the events in the plot affect the characters? How do they develop as a result of the conflict, climax, and resolution?
- ✓ Do the characters' problems reach a resolution? How?

⟳ YOUR TURN

1. How does the mother's love for her son affect her actions in paragraph 37?
   - ○ A. It prompts her to keep her son away from Rikki-tikki.
   - ○ B. It causes a disagreement between her and her husband.
   - ○ C. It makes her show affection towards Rikki-tikki.
   - ○ D. It makes Rikki-tikki feel nervous staying with the family.

2. What does the dialogue in paragraph 40 suggest about Chuchundra?
   - ○ A. He is afraid.
   - ○ B. He is easily fooled.
   - ○ C. He is optimistic.
   - ○ D. He loves Rikki-tikki.

3. Which paragraph shows that Teddy looks to Rikki-tikki for protection?
   - ○ A. 37
   - ○ B. 38
   - ○ C. 39
   - ○ D. 40

Close Read

6

Reread "Rikki-Tikki-Tavi." As you reread, complete the Skills Focus questions below. Then use your answers and annotations from the questions to help you complete the Write activity.

SKILLS FOCUS

1. Identify details that reveal Nag's character when he is first introduced in the story. Explain what inferences you can make about Nag and what makes him a threat.

2. Identify details that reveal Rikki-tikki's character traits as a fighter. Explain how those character traits help Rikki-tikki defeat the snakes.

3. Find examples of Nag and Nagaina's actions and dialogue. How do their words and behaviors create conflict in the plot?

4. Identify details that help you compare and contrast Rikki-tikki and Darzee. Explain what you can infer about Rikki-tikki and Darzee from these details.

5. Analyze details that show how Rikki-tikki beats the snakes. Explain Rikki-tikki's approach to conflict.

WRITE

7

LITERARY ANALYSIS: In this classic story of good vs. evil, Nag and Nagaina are portrayed as the villains. Consider the role and behaviors of the typical villain. Then think about Nag and Nagaina's behaviors, including how they impact the plot and interact with other characters. Do you think that Nag and Nagaina are truly evil, or have they been unfairly cast as villains? Choose a side, and write a brief response explaining your position and analysis. Use several pieces of textual evidence to support your points.

Reading & Writing Companion 21

8

Ready for Marcos

FICTION

Introduction

Twelve-year-old Monica Alvarez has a happy life. She is a star on the track team and has many good friends. But everything changes when her parents bring Marcos, her new baby brother, home from the hospital. Her parents want her to have more responsibilities. Monica wonders what it will mean to be a big sister. Is she ready? Is she willing?

VOCABULARY

8

vivacious
energetic and happy; lively

justify
to support with good reasons

covertly
done in secret

subtle
barely noticeable

Close Read & Skills Focus

6

After you have completed the First Read, you will be asked to go back and read the text more closely and critically. Before you begin your Close Read, you should read through the Skills Focus to get an idea of the concepts you will want to focus on during your second reading. You should work through the Skills Focus by making annotations, highlighting important concepts, and writing notes or questions in the "Notes" column. Depending on instructions from your teacher, you may need to respond online or use a separate piece of paper to start expanding on your thoughts and ideas.

Write

7

Your study of each selection will end with a writing assignment. For this assignment, you should use your notes, annotations, personal ideas, and answers to both the Think and Skills Focus questions. Be sure to read the prompt carefully and address each part of it in your writing.

English Language Learner

8

The English Language Learner texts focus on improving language proficiency. You will practice learning strategies and skills in individual and group activities to become better readers, writers, and speakers.

Extended Writing Project and Grammar

This is your opportunity to use genre characteristics and craft to compose meaningful, longer written works exploring the theme of each unit. You will draw information from your readings, research, and own life experiences to complete the assignment.

1 Writing Project

After you have read all of the unit text selections, you will move on to a writing project. Each project will guide you through the process of writing your essay. Student models will provide guidance and help you organize your thoughts. One unit ends with an **Extended Oral Project,** which will give you an opportunity to develop your oral language and communication skills.

2 Writing Process Steps

There are four steps in the writing process: Plan, Draft, Revise, and Edit and Publish. During each step, you will form and shape your writing project, and each lesson's peer review will give you the chance to receive feedback from your peers and teacher.

3 Writing Skills

Each Skill lesson focuses on a specific strategy or technique that you will use during your writing project. Each lesson presents a process for applying the skill to your own work and gives you the opportunity to practice it to improve your writing.

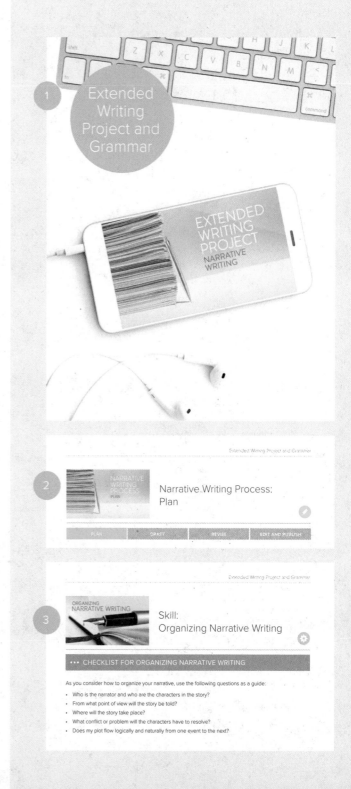

studysync®

ASSIGNMENTS   BINDER   LIBRARY

Conflicts and Clashes

UNIT 1

Conflicts and Clashes

When do differences become conflicts?

Genre Focus: FICTION

Texts

 Paired Readings

Extended Writing Project and Grammar

English Language Learner Resources

Unit 1: Conflicts and Clashes
When do differences become conflicts?

LANGSTON HUGHES

A leader of the Harlem Renaissance, Langston Hughes (1902–1967) was born in Joplin, Missouri, and raised by his grandmother until he was sixteen. Then he moved to Lincoln, Illinois, with his mother and her husband and began to write. He eventually moved to New York City, attended Columbia University, and worked various jobs, including one on a freight ship that sailed down the coast of Africa. Hughes was first published in 1921, with "The Negro Speaks of Rivers" in the pages of *The Crisis*. He'd go on to write eleven plays and numerous works of prose and poetry.

RUDYARD KIPLING

Joseph Rudyard Kipling (1865–1936) was the first English-language writer to be awarded the Nobel Prize for Literature. Born in Bombay, India, Kipling wrote *The Jungle Book* in addition to many short stories and poems, including "Gunga Din" and "The White Man's Burden." While regarded by Henry James as a "complete man of genius," George Orwell and others have since sharply criticized Kipling's views and positions on matters of race and colonialism.

NAOMI SHIHAB NYE

A self-professed "wandering poet," Naomi Shihab Nye (b. 1952) was born to a Palestinian father and an American mother in St. Louis, Missouri; as she was growing up, she also spent time in Jerusalem and San Antonio. She has written or edited over thirty volumes of poetry, including her work *You & Yours*, a best seller. As one juror wrote before Nye won the NSK Neustadt Prize for Children's Literature, "Naomi's incandescent humanity and voice can change the world, or someone's world, by taking a position not one word less beautiful than an exquisite poem."

GARY PAULSEN

Born in Minneapolis, Minnesota, while his father served in the army overseas, Gary Paulsen (b. 1939) didn't meet his father until the age of seven. At age 16, Paulsen fled a home riven by alcoholism to work on a beet farm in North Dakota. Author of *Hatchet*, *Dogsong*, and *Winterdance*, Paulsen has written several coming-of-age stories that focus on the outdoors and the importance of nature. Paulsen has competed in the Iditarod Trail Sled Dog Race and is also an avid sailor. He has a home in Alaska.

ROD SERLING

Rod Serling (1924–1975), may be best known for hosting the television classic anthology series *The Twilight Zone*. But Serling also wrote more than half of the show's 151 episodes, in addition to writing several movies including *The Planet of the Apes*. Serling served in World War II, during which he fought in the Pacific and was awarded the Purple Heart. His wartime experience informed his activism against the Vietnam War later in life.

GARY SOTO

Growing up in California's San Joaquin Valley, Gary Soto (b. 1952) chopped beets and picked grapes in the fields outside his hometown of Fresno to help his family make ends meet. Born to Mexican American parents, Gary lost his father when he was just five years old. He worked and went to college, eventually earning his MFA from the University of California, Irvine. He has published many works of both prose and poetry, including "Oranges," the most anthologized poem in contemporary literature. He lives in Northern California.

JERRY SPINELLI

Jerry Spinelli (b. 1941) has written over thirty books but may be best known for writing *Stargirl*. The story's nonconformist theme resonated so strongly that loyal fans have created their very own "Stargirl Societies" in honor of the title character because she embraces difference as a strength. A film adaptation of the book, produced by Disney, is forthcoming. Spinelli attended Gettysburg College and began writing during his off-time while working on a department store magazine. He lives in Pennsylvania.

NOELLE STEVENSON

Noelle Stevenson (b. 1991) created the eponymous star of her groundbreaking fantasy comic *Nimona* as part of an assignment while still in college. Stevenson worked on the webcomic during her junior year at the Maryland Institute College of Art and turned it into her senior thesis. A literary agent signed her after seeing *Nimona* online, and in 2015, HarperCollins published her work as a graphic novel. Stevenson is also the creator, executive producer, and showrunner of an animated series, "She-Ra and the Princesses of Power." She lives in Los Angeles.

OSCAR CASARES

Brownsville is both the hometown of Oscar Casares (b. 1964) and the title of his debut collection. Brownsville was published by Little, Brown in 2003, just after Casares finished his MFA at the University of Iowa Writers' Workshop. Asked how he became a writer, Casares once said, "I grew up around uncles who were storytellers and so I kind of continued the tradition with family and friends. Then one day I tried to write some of these stories and ended up with completely new ones." He teaches at the University of Texas, his alma mater.

SHARON G. FLAKE

Sharon G. Flake (b. 1955) wrote her bestselling debut novel, *The Skin I'm In*, while working in public relations for a university press. Born in Philadelphia, she earned her Bachelor of Arts degree in English at the University of Pittsburgh where she also minored in Political Science and wrote for the *Pitt News*. After graduation, she took a job at an area youth shelter. During that time, she began work on her bestseller, which also won many awards, including the Coretta Scott King/John Steptoe Award for New Talent. She lives in Pittsburgh.

YOSHIKO UCHIDA

During her senior year at University of California, Berkeley, Yoshiko Uchida (1921–1992) and her family were imprisoned in internment camps for three years in the American West. These events inspired her volume of memoirs, *Desert Exile: The Uprooting of a Japanese American Family*, published in 1982. Her nephew, writer Michiko Kakutani, said that she wrote "with the hope that through knowledge of the past, [our nation] will never allow another group of people in America to be sent into a desert exile ever again." Uchida authored twenty-seven books. She was born in Alameda, California.

Rikki-Tikki-Tavi

FICTION
Rudyard Kipling
1894

Introduction

"Rikki-Tikki-Tavi" is one of the most famous tales from *The Jungle Book*, a collection of short stories published in 1894 by English author Rudyard Kipling (1865–1936). The stories in *The Jungle Book* feature animal characters with anthropomorphic traits and are intended to be read as fables, each illustrating a moral lesson. In this story, Rikki-tikki-tavi is a courageous young mongoose adopted as a pet by a British family living in 19th-century colonial India.

"Rikki-tikki held on with his eyes shut, for now he was quite sure he was dead."

NOTES

1   This is the story of the great war that Rikki-tikki-tavi fought single-handed, through the bath-rooms of the big bungalow in Segowlee cantonment. Darzee, the Tailorbird, helped him, and Chuchundra, the musk-rat, who never comes out into the middle of the floor, but always creeps round by the wall, gave him advice, but Rikki-tikki did the real fighting.

2   He was a mongoose, rather like a little cat in his fur and his tail, but quite like a weasel in his head and his habits. His eyes and the end of his restless nose were pink. He could scratch himself anywhere he pleased with any leg, front or back, that he chose to use. He could fluff up his tail till it looked like a bottle brush, and his war cry as he scuttled through the long grass was: "Rikk-tikk-tikki-tikki-tchk!"

3   One day, a high summer flood washed him out of the burrow where he lived with his father and mother, and carried him, kicking and clucking, down a roadside ditch. He found a little wisp of grass floating there, and clung to it till he lost his senses. When he revived, he was lying in the hot sun on the middle of a garden path, very draggled indeed, and a small boy was saying, "Here's a dead mongoose. Let's have a funeral."

4   "No," said his mother, "let's take him in and dry him. Perhaps he isn't really dead."

5   They took him into the house, and a big man picked him up between his finger and thumb and said he was not dead but half choked. So they wrapped him in cotton wool, and warmed him over a little fire, and he opened his eyes and sneezed.

6   "Now," said the big man (he was an Englishman who had just moved into the bungalow), "don't frighten him, and we'll see what he'll do."

7   It is the hardest thing in the world to frighten a mongoose, because he is eaten up from nose to tail with curiosity. The motto of all the mongoose family is "Run and find out," and Rikki-tikki was a true mongoose. He looked at the cotton wool, decided that it was not good to eat, ran all round the table, sat up and put his fur in order, scratched himself, and jumped on the small boy's shoulder.

Skill:
Textual Evidence

It says that he fluffs up his tail and he has a war cry. I know that a war cry is used in battle to rally the troops. This must mean that Rikki-tikki is brave and powerful, like a soldier.

Skill:
Text-Dependent Responses

After finding Rikki-tikki, the English family brought him into their home and took care of him.

NOTES

8 "Don't be frightened, Teddy," said his father. "That's his way of making friends."

9 "Ouch! He's tickling under my chin," said Teddy.

10 Rikki-tikki looked down between the boy's collar and neck, snuffed at his ear, and climbed down to the floor, where he sat rubbing his nose.

11 "Good gracious," said Teddy's mother, "and that's a wild creature! I suppose he's so tame because we've been kind to him."

12 "All mongooses are like that," said her husband. "If Teddy doesn't pick him up by the tail, or try to put him in a cage, he'll run in and out of the house all day long. Let's give him something to eat."

13 They gave him a little piece of raw meat. Rikki-tikki liked it **immensely**, and when it was finished he went out into the veranda and sat in the sunshine and fluffed up his fur to make it dry to the roots. Then he felt better.

14 "There are more things to find out about in this house," he said to himself, "than all my family could find out in all their lives. I shall certainly stay and find out."

15 He spent all that day roaming over the house. He nearly drowned himself in the bath-tubs, put his nose into the ink on a writing table, and burned it on the end of the big man's cigar, for he climbed up in the big man's lap to see how writing was done. At nightfall he ran into Teddy's nursery to watch how kerosene lamps were lighted, and when Teddy went to bed Rikki-tikki climbed up too. But he was a restless companion, because he had to get up and attend to every noise all through the night, and find out what made it. Teddy's mother and father came in, the last thing, to look at their boy, and Rikki-tikki was awake on the pillow. "I don't like that," said Teddy's mother. "He may bite the child." "He'll do no such thing," said the father. "Teddy's safer with that little beast than if he had a bloodhound to watch him. If a snake came into the nursery now—"

16 But Teddy's mother wouldn't think of anything so awful.

17 Early in the morning Rikki-tikki came to early breakfast in the veranda riding on Teddy's shoulder, and they gave him banana and some boiled egg. He sat on all their laps one after the other, because every well-brought-up mongoose always hopes to be a house mongoose some day and have rooms to run about in; and Rikki-tikki's mother (she used to live in the general's house at Segowlee) had carefully told Rikki what to do if ever he came across white men.

18 Then Rikki-tikki went out into the garden to see what was to be seen. It was a large garden, only half **cultivated**, with bushes, as big as summer-houses, of Marshal Niel roses, lime and orange trees, clumps of bamboos, and thickets of high grass. Rikki-tikki licked his lips. "This is a splendid hunting-ground," he said, and his tail grew bottle-brushy at the thought of it, and he scuttled up

and down the garden, snuffing here and there till he heard very sorrowful voices in a thorn-bush.

19   It was Darzee, the Tailorbird, and his wife. They had made a beautiful nest by pulling two big leaves together and stitching them up the edges with fibers, and had filled the hollow with cotton and downy fluff. The nest swayed to and fro, as they sat on the rim and cried.

20   "What is the matter?" asked Rikki-tikki.

21   "We are very miserable," said Darzee. "One of our babies fell out of the nest yesterday and Nag ate him."

22   "H'm!" said Rikki-tikki, "that is very sad—but I am a stranger here. Who is Nag?"

23   Darzee and his wife only cowered down in the nest without answering, for from the thick grass at the foot of the bush there came a low hiss—a horrid cold sound that made Rikki-tikki jump back two clear feet. Then inch by inch out of the grass rose up the head and spread hood of Nag, the big black cobra, and he was five feet long from tongue to tail. When he had lifted one-third of himself clear of the ground, he stayed balancing to and fro exactly as a dandelion tuft balances in the wind, and he looked at Rikki-tikki with the wicked snake's eyes that never change their expression, whatever the snake may be thinking of.

24   "Who is Nag?" said he. "I am Nag. The great God Brahm[1] put his mark upon all our people, when the first cobra spread his hood to keep the sun off Brahm as he slept. Look, and be afraid!"

25   He spread out his hood more than ever, and Rikki-tikki saw the spectacle-mark on the back of it that looks exactly like the eye part of a hook-and-eye fastening. He was afraid for the minute, but it is impossible for a mongoose to stay frightened for any length of time, and though Rikki-tikki had never met a live cobra before, his mother had fed him on dead ones, and he knew that all a grown mongoose's business in life was to fight and eat snakes. Nag knew that too and, at the bottom of his cold heart, he was afraid.

26   "Well," said Rikki-tikki, and his tail began to fluff up again, "marks or no marks, do you think it is right for you to eat fledglings out of a nest?"

27   Nag was thinking to himself, and watching the least little movement in the grass behind Rikki-tikki. He knew that mongooses in the garden meant death sooner or later for him and his family, but he wanted to get Rikki-tikki off his guard. So he dropped his head a little, and put it on one side.

28   "Let us talk," he said. "You eat eggs. Why should not I eat birds?"

---

1. **Brahm** in Hindu tradition, one of the gods of creation. (Another spelling for this is *Brahma*.)

Skill:
Character

Rikki-tikki is ready to fight a cobra to protect the birds he just met. He's loyal and protective. I think Rikki-tikki's loyalty will lead to danger or success in the plot.

NOTES

29 "Behind you! Look behind you!" sang Darzee.

30 Rikki-tikki knew better than to waste time in staring. He jumped up in the air as high as he could go, and just under him whizzed by the head of Nagaina, Nag's wicked wife. She had crept up behind him as he was talking, to make an end of him. He heard her savage hiss as the stroke missed. He came down almost across her back, and if he had been an old mongoose he would have known that then was the time to break her back with one bite; but he was afraid of the terrible lashing return stroke of the cobra. He bit, indeed, but did not bite long enough, and he jumped clear of the whisking tail, leaving Nagaina torn and angry.

31 "Wicked, wicked Darzee!" said Nag, lashing up as high as he could reach toward the nest in the thorn-bush. But Darzee had built it out of reach of snakes, and it only swayed to and fro.

32 Rikki-tikki felt his eyes growing red and hot (when a mongoose's eyes grow red, he is angry), and he sat back on his tail and hind legs like a little kangaroo, and looked all round him, and chattered with rage. But Nag and Nagaina had disappeared into the grass. When a snake misses its stroke, it never says anything or gives any sign of what it means to do next. Rikki-tikki did not care to follow them, for he did not feel sure that he could manage two snakes at once. So he trotted off to the gravel path near the house, and sat down to think. It was a serious matter for him.

33 If you read the old books of natural history, you will find they say that when the mongoose fights the snake and happens to get bitten, he runs off and eats some herb that cures him. That is not true. The victory is only a matter of quickness of eye and quickness of foot—snake's blow against mongoose's jump—and as no eye can follow the motion of a snake's head when it strikes, this makes things much more wonderful than any magic herb. Rikki-tikki knew he was a young mongoose, and it made him all the more pleased to think that he had managed to escape a blow from behind. It gave him confidence in himself, and when Teddy came running down the path, Rikki-tikki was ready to be petted.

34 But just as Teddy was stooping, something wriggled a little in the dust, and a tiny voice said: "Be careful. I am Death!" It was Karait, the dusty brown snakeling that lies for choice on the dusty earth; and his bite is as dangerous as the cobra's. But he is so small that nobody thinks of him, and so he does the more harm to people.

35 Rikki-tikki's eyes grew red again, and he danced up to Karait with the peculiar rocking, swaying motion that he had inherited from his family. It looks very funny, but it is so perfectly balanced a gait that you can fly off from it at any angle you please, and in dealing with snakes this is an advantage. If Rikki-tikki had only known, he was doing a much more dangerous thing than fighting Nag, for Karait is so small, and can turn so quickly, that unless Rikki bit him close to the back of the head, he would get the return stroke in his eye or his lip. But Rikki did not know. His eyes were all red, and he rocked back and forth, looking for a good place to hold. Karait struck out. Rikki jumped sideways and tried to run in, but the wicked little dusty gray head lashed within a fraction of his shoulder, and he had to jump over the body, and the head followed his heels close.

36 Teddy shouted to the house: "Oh, look here! Our mongoose is killing a snake." And Rikki-tikki heard a scream from Teddy's mother. His father ran out with a stick, but by the time he came up, Karait had lunged out once too far, and Rikki-tikki had sprung, jumped on the snake's back, dropped his head far between his forelegs, bitten as high up the back as he could get hold, and rolled away. That bite paralyzed Karait, and Rikki-tikki was just going to eat him up from the tail, after the custom of his family at dinner, when he remembered that a full meal makes a slow mongoose, and if he wanted all his strength and quickness ready, he must keep himself thin.

37 He went away for a dust bath under the castor-oil bushes, while Teddy's father beat the dead Karait. "What is the use of that?" thought Rikki-tikki. "I have settled it all;" and then Teddy's mother picked him up from the dust and hugged him, crying that he had saved Teddy from death, and Teddy's father said that he was a **providence**, and Teddy looked on with big scared eyes. Rikki-tikki was rather amused at all the fuss, which, of course, he did not understand. Teddy's mother might just as well have petted Teddy for playing in the dust. Rikki was thoroughly enjoying himself.

38 That night at dinner, walking to and fro among the wine-glasses on the table, he might have stuffed himself three times over with nice things. But he remembered Nag and Nagaina, and though it was very pleasant to be patted and petted by Teddy's mother, and to sit on Teddy's shoulder, his eyes would get red from time to time, and he would go off into his long war cry of "Rikk-tikk-tikki-tikki-tchk!"

39 Teddy carried him off to bed, and insisted on Rikki-tikki sleeping under his chin. Rikki-tikki was too well bred to bite or scratch, but as soon as Teddy was asleep he went off for his nightly walk round the house, and in the dark he ran up against Chuchundra, the musk-rat, creeping around by the wall. Chuchundra is a broken-hearted little beast. He whimpers and cheeps all the night, trying to make up his mind to run into the middle of the room. But he never gets there.

NOTES

40 "Don't kill me," said Chuchundra, almost weeping. "Rikki-tikki, don't kill me!"

41 "Do you think a snake-killer kills muskrats?" said Rikki-tikki scornfully.

42 "Those who kill snakes get killed by snakes," said Chuchundra, more sorrowfully than ever. "And how am I to be sure that Nag won't mistake me for you some dark night?"

43 "There's not the least danger," said Rikki-tikki. "But Nag is in the garden, and I know you don't go there."

44 "My cousin Chua, the rat, told me—" said Chuchundra, and then he stopped.

45 "Told you what?"

46 "H'sh! Nag is everywhere, Rikki-tikki. You should have talked to Chua in the garden."

47 "I didn't—so you must tell me. Quick, Chuchundra, or I'll bite you!"

48 Chuchundra sat down and cried till the tears rolled off his whiskers. "I am a very poor man," he sobbed. "I never had spirit enough to run out into the middle of the room. H'sh! I mustn't tell you anything. Can't you hear, Rikki-tikki?"

49 Rikki-tikki listened. The house was as still as still, but he thought he could just catch the faintest scratch-scratch in the world—a noise as faint as that of a wasp walking on a window-pane—the dry scratch of a snake's scales on brick-work.

50 "That's Nag or Nagaina," he said to himself, "and he is crawling into the bath-room sluice[2]. You're right, Chuchundra; I should have talked to Chua."

51 He stole off to Teddy's bath-room, but there was nothing there, and then to Teddy's mother's bathroom. At the bottom of the smooth plaster wall there was a brick pulled out to make a sluice for the bath water, and as Rikki-tikki stole in by the masonry curb where the bath is put, he heard Nag and Nagaina whispering together outside in the moonlight.

52 "When the house is emptied of people," said Nagaina to her husband, "he will have to go away, and then the garden will be our own again. Go in quietly, and remember that the big man who killed Karait is the first one to bite. Then come out and tell me, and we will hunt for Rikki-tikki together."

53 "But are you sure that there is anything to be gained by killing the people?" said Nag.

54 "Everything. When there were no people in the bungalow, did we have any mongoose in the garden? So long as the bungalow is empty, we are king and

---

2. **sluice** a channel for the flow of water, regulated at its head by a gate

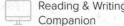

queen of the garden; and remember that as soon as our eggs in the melon bed hatch (as they may tomorrow), our children will need room and quiet."

55 "I had not thought of that," said Nag. "I will go, but there is no need that we should hunt for Rikki-tikki afterward. I will kill the big man and his wife, and the child if I can, and come away quietly. Then the bungalow will be empty, and Rikki-tikki will go."

56 Rikki-tikki tingled all over with rage and hatred at this, and then Nag's head came through the sluice, and his five feet of cold body followed it. Angry as he was, Rikki-tikki was very frightened as he saw the size of the big cobra. Nag coiled himself up, raised his head, and looked into the bathroom in the dark, and Rikki could see his eyes glitter.

57 "Now, if I kill him here, Nagaina will know; and if I fight him on the open floor, the odds are in his favor. What am I to do?" said Rikki-tikki-tavi.

58 Nag waved to and fro, and then Rikki-tikki heard him drinking from the biggest water-jar that was used to fill the bath. "That is good," said the snake. "Now, when Karait was killed, the big man had a stick. He may have that stick still, but when he comes in to bathe in the morning he will not have a stick. I shall wait here till he comes. Nagaina—do you hear me?—I shall wait here in the cool till daytime."

59 There was no answer from outside, so Rikki-tikki knew Nagaina had gone away. Nag coiled himself down, coil by coil, round the bulge at the bottom of the water jar, and Rikki-tikki stayed still as death. After an hour he began to move, muscle by muscle, toward the jar. Nag was asleep, and Rikki-tikki looked at his big back, wondering which would be the best place for a good hold. "If I don't break his back at the first jump," said Rikki, "he can still fight. And if he fights—O Rikki!" He looked at the thickness of the neck below the hood, but that was too much for him; and a bite near the tail would only make Nag savage.

60 "It must be the head," he said at last; "the head above the hood. And, when I am once there, I must not let go."

61 Then he jumped. The head was lying a little clear of the water jar, under the curve of it; and, as his teeth met, Rikki braced his back against the bulge of the red earthenware to hold down the head. This gave him just one second's purchase, and he made the most of it. Then he was battered to and fro as a rat is shaken by a dog—to and fro on the floor, up and down, and around in great circles, but his eyes were red and he held on as the body cart-whipped over the floor, upsetting the tin dipper and the soap dish and the flesh brush, and banged against the tin side of the bath. As he held he closed his jaws tighter and tighter, for he made sure he would be banged to death, and, for the honor of his family, he preferred to be found with his teeth locked. He was

dizzy, aching, and felt shaken to pieces when something went off like a thunderclap just behind him. A hot wind knocked him senseless and red fire singed his fur. The big man had been wakened by the noise, and had fired both barrels of a shotgun into Nag just behind the hood.

62 Rikki-tikki held on with his eyes shut, for now he was quite sure he was dead. But the head did not move, and the big man picked him up and said, "It's the mongoose again, Alice. The little chap has saved our lives now."

63 Then Teddy's mother came in with a very white face, and saw what was left of Nag, and Rikki-tikki dragged himself to Teddy's bedroom and spent half the rest of the night shaking himself tenderly to find out whether he really was broken into forty pieces, as he fancied.

64 When morning came he was very stiff, but well pleased with his doings. "Now I have Nagaina to settle with, and she will be worse than five Nags, and there's no knowing when the eggs she spoke of will hatch. Goodness! I must go and see Darzee," he said.

65 Without waiting for breakfast, Rikki-tikki ran to the thornbush where Darzee was singing a song of triumph at the top of his voice. The news of Nag's death was all over the garden, for the sweeper had thrown the body on the rubbish[3]-heap.

66 "Oh, you stupid tuft of feathers!" said Rikki-tikki angrily. "Is this the time to sing?"

67 "Nag is dead—is dead—is dead!" sang Darzee. "The valiant Rikki-tikki caught him by the head and held fast. The big man brought the bang-stick, and Nag fell in two pieces! He will never eat my babies again."

68 "All that's true enough. But where's Nagaina?" said Rikki-tikki, looking carefully round him.

69 "Nagaina came to the bathroom sluice and called for Nag," Darzee went on, "and Nag came out on the end of a stick—the sweeper picked him up on the end of a stick and threw him upon the rubbish heap. Let us sing about the great, the red-eyed Rikki-tikki!" And Darzee filled his throat and sang.

70 "If I could get up to your nest, I'd roll your babies out!" said Rikki-tikki. "You don't know when to do the right thing at the right time. You're safe enough in your nest there, but it's war for me down here. Stop singing a minute, Darzee."

71 "For the great, the beautiful Rikki-tikki's sake I will stop," said Darzee. "What is it, O Killer of the terrible Nag?"

3. **rubbish** waste or trash

72 "Where is Nagaina, for the third time?"

73 "On the rubbish heap by the stables, mourning for Nag. Great is Rikki-tikki with the white teeth."

74 "Bother my white teeth! Have you ever heard where she keeps her eggs?"

75 "In the melon bed, on the end nearest the wall, where the sun strikes nearly all day. She hid them there weeks ago."

76 "And you never thought it worth while to tell me? The end nearest the wall, you said?"

77 "Rikki-tikki, you are not going to eat her eggs?"

78 "Not eat exactly; no. Darzee, if you have a grain of sense you will fly off to the stables and pretend that your wing is broken, and let Nagaina chase you away to this bush. I must get to the melon-bed, and if I went there now she'd see me."

79 Darzee was a feather-brained little fellow who could never hold more than one idea at a time in his head. And just because he knew that Nagaina's children were born in eggs like his own, he didn't think at first that it was fair to kill them. But his wife was a **sensible** bird, and she knew that cobra's eggs meant young cobras later on. So she flew off from the nest, and left Darzee to keep the babies warm, and continue his song about the death of Nag. Darzee was very like a man in some ways.

80 She fluttered in front of Nagaina by the rubbish heap and cried out, "Oh, my wing is broken! The boy in the house threw a stone at me and broke it." Then she fluttered more desperately than ever.

81 Nagaina lifted up her head and hissed, "You warned Rikki-tikki when I would have killed him. Indeed and truly, you've chosen a bad place to be lame in." And she moved toward Darzee's wife, slipping along over the dust.

82 "The boy broke it with a stone!" shrieked Darzee's wife.

83 "Well! It may be some **consolation** to you when you're dead to know that I shall settle accounts with the boy. My husband lies on the rubbish heap this morning, but before night the boy in the house will lie very still. What is the use of running away? I am sure to catch you. Little fool, look at me!"

84 Darzee's wife knew better than to do that, for a bird who looks at a snake's eyes gets so frightened that she cannot move. Darzee's wife fluttered on, piping sorrowfully, and never leaving the ground, and Nagaina quickened her pace.

85 Rikki-tikki heard them going up the path from the stables, and he raced for the end of the melon patch near the wall. There, in the warm litter above the

melons, very cunningly hidden, he found twenty-five eggs, about the size of a bantam's eggs, but with whitish skin instead of shell.

86 "I was not a day too soon," he said, for he could see the baby cobras curled up inside the skin, and he knew that the minute they were hatched they could each kill a man or a mongoose. He bit off the tops of the eggs as fast as he could, taking care to crush the young cobras, and turned over the litter from time to time to see whether he had missed any. At last there were only three eggs left, and Rikki-tikki began to chuckle to himself, when he heard Darzee's wife screaming:

87 "Rikki-tikki, I led Nagaina toward the house, and she has gone into the veranda, and—oh, come quickly—she means killing!"

88 Rikki-tikki smashed two eggs, and tumbled backward down the melon-bed with the third egg in his mouth, and scuttled to the veranda as hard as he could put foot to the ground. Teddy and his mother and father were there at early breakfast, but Rikki-tikki saw that they were not eating anything. They sat stone-still, and their faces were white. Nagaina was coiled up on the matting by Teddy's chair, within easy striking distance of Teddy's bare leg, and she was swaying to and fro, singing a song of triumph.

89 "Son of the big man that killed Nag," she hissed, "stay still. I am not ready yet. Wait a little. Keep very still, all you three! If you move I strike, and if you do not move I strike. Oh, foolish people, who killed my Nag!"

90 Teddy's eyes were fixed on his father, and all his father could do was to whisper, "Sit still, Teddy. You mustn't move. Teddy, keep still."

91 Then Rikki-tikki came up and cried, "Turn round, Nagaina. Turn and fight!"

92 "All in good time," said she, without moving her eyes. "I will settle my account with you presently. Look at your friends, Rikki-tikki. They are still and white. They are afraid. They dare not move, and if you come a step nearer I strike."

93 "Look at your eggs," said Rikki-tikki, "in the melon bed near the wall. Go and look, Nagaina!"

94 The big snake turned half around, and saw the egg on the veranda. "Ah-h! Give it to me," she said.

95 Rikki-tikki put his paws one on each side of the egg, and his eyes were blood-red. "What price for a snake's egg? For a young cobra? For a young king cobra? For the last—the very last of the brood? The ants are eating all the others down by the melon bed."

96 Nagaina spun clear round, forgetting everything for the sake of the one egg. Rikki-tikki saw Teddy's father shoot out a big hand, catch Teddy by the

Copyright © BookheadEd Learning, LLC

NOTES

shoulder, and drag him across the little table with the tea-cups, safe and out of reach of Nagaina.

97 "Tricked! Tricked! Tricked! Rikk-tck-tck!" chuckled Rikki-tikki. "The boy is safe, and it was I—I—I that caught Nag by the hood last night in the bathroom." Then he began to jump up and down, all four feet together, his head close to the floor. "He threw me to and fro, but he could not shake me off. He was dead before the big man blew him in two. I did it! Rikki-tikki-tck-tck! Come then, Nagaina. Come and fight with me. You shall not be a widow long."

98 Nagaina saw that she had lost her chance of killing Teddy, and the egg lay between Rikki-tikki's paws. "Give me the egg, Rikki-tikki. Give me the last of my eggs, and I will go away and never come back," she said, lowering her hood.

99 "Yes, you will go away, and you will never come back. For you will go to the rubbish heap with Nag. Fight, widow! The big man has gone for his gun! Fight!"

100 Rikki-tikki was bounding all round Nagaina, keeping just out of reach of her stroke, his little eyes like hot coals. Nagaina gathered herself together and flung out at him. Rikki-tikki jumped up and backward. Again and again and again she struck, and each time her head came with a whack on the matting of the veranda and she gathered herself together like a watch spring. Then Rikki-tikki danced in a circle to get behind her, and Nagaina spun round to keep her head to his head, so that the rustle of her tail on the matting sounded like dry leaves blown along by the wind.

101 He had forgotten the egg. It still lay on the veranda, and Nagaina came nearer and nearer to it, till at last, while Rikki-tikki was drawing breath, she caught it in her mouth, turned to the veranda steps, and flew like an arrow down the path, with Rikki-tikki behind her. When the cobra runs for her life, she goes like a whip-lash flicked across a horse's neck.

102 Rikki-tikki knew that he must catch her, or all the trouble would begin again. She headed straight for the long grass by the thorn-bush, and as he was running Rikki-tikki heard Darzee still singing his foolish little song of triumph. But Darzee's wife was wiser. She flew off her nest as Nagaina came along, and flapped her wings about Nagaina's head. If Darzee had helped they might have turned her, but Nagaina only lowered her hood and went on. Still, the instant's delay brought Rikki-tikki up to her, and as she plunged into the rat-hole where she and Nag used to live, his little white teeth were clenched on her tail, and he went down with her—and very few mongooses, however wise and old they may be, care to follow a cobra into its hole. It was dark in the hole; and Rikki-tikki never knew when it might open out and give Nagaina room to turn and strike at him. He held on savagely, and stuck out his feet to act as brakes on the dark slope of the hot, moist earth.

Please note that excerpts and passages in the StudySync® library and this workbook are intended as touchstones to generate interest in an author's work. The excerpts and passages do not substitute for the reading of entire texts, and StudySync® strongly recommends that students seek out and purchase the whole literary or informational work in order to experience it as the author intended. Links to online resellers are available in our digital library. In addition, complete works may be ordered through an authorized reseller by filling out and returning to StudySync® the order form enclosed in this workbook.

Reading & Writing Companion

11

103   Then the grass by the mouth of the hole stopped waving, and Darzee said, "It is all over with Rikki-tikki! We must sing his death song. Valiant Rikki-tikki is dead! For Nagaina will surely kill him underground."

104   So he sang a very mournful song that he made up on the spur of the minute, and just as he got to the most touching part, the grass quivered again, and Rikki-tikki, covered with dirt, dragged himself out of the hole leg by leg, licking his whiskers. Darzee stopped with a little shout. Rikki-tikki shook some of the dust out of his fur and sneezed. "It is all over," he said. "The widow will never come out again." And the red ants that live between the grass stems heard him, and began to troop down one after another to see if he had spoken the truth. Rikki-tikki curled himself up in the grass and slept where he was—slept and slept till it was late in the afternoon, for he had done a hard day's work.

105   "Now," he said, when he awoke, "I will go back to the house. Tell the Coppersmith, Darzee, and he will tell the garden that Nagaina is dead."

106   The Coppersmith is a bird who makes a noise exactly like the beating of a little hammer on a copper pot; and the reason he is always making it is because he is the town crier to every Indian garden, and tells all the news to everybody who cares to listen. As Rikki-tikki went up the path, he heard his "attention" notes like a tiny dinner gong, and then the steady "Ding-dong-tock! Nag is dead—dong! Nagaina is dead! Ding-dong-tock!" That set all the birds in the garden singing, and the frogs croaking, for Nag and Nagaina used to eat frogs as well as little birds.

107   When Rikki got to the house, Teddy and Teddy's mother (she looked very white still, for she had been fainting) and Teddy's father came out and almost cried over him; and that night he ate all that was given him till he could eat no more, and went to bed on Teddy's shoulder, where Teddy's mother saw him when she came to look late at night.

108   "He saved our lives and Teddy's life," she said to her husband. "Just think, he saved all our lives."

109   Rikki-tikki woke up with a jump, for the mongooses are light sleepers.

110   "Oh, it's you," said he. "What are you bothering for? All the cobras are dead. And if they weren't, I'm here."

111   Rikki-tikki had a right to be proud of himself. But he did not grow too proud, and he kept that garden as a mongoose should keep it, with tooth and jump and spring and bite, till never a cobra dared show its head inside the walls.

Copyright © BookheadEd Learning, LLC

Skill:
Text-Dependent Responses

Use the Checklist to analyze Text-Dependent Responses in "Rikki-Tikki-Tavi." Refer to the sample student annotations about Text-Dependent Responses in the text.

••• CHECKLIST FOR TEXT-DEPENDENT RESPONSES

In order to cite several pieces of textual evidence to support an analysis, consider the following:

✓ details from the text to make an inference or draw a conclusion. Inferences are logical guesses about information in a text that is not directly, or explicitly, stated by the author.

- Read carefully and consider why an author gives particular details and information.
- Think about what you already know, and use your own knowledge and experiences to help you figure out what the author does not state directly.
- Cite textual evidence, or the specific words, phrases, sentences, or paragraphs that led you to make an inference.

✓ details that you can use to support your ideas and opinions about a text

✓ explicit evidence of a character's feelings or motivations, or the reasons behind a historical event in a nonfiction text

- Explicit evidence is stated directly in the text and must be cited accurately to support a text-dependent answer or analysis.

To cite several pieces of textual evidence to support an analysis, consider the following questions:

✓ What types of textual evidence can I use to support an analysis of a text?

✓ What explicit evidence can I use to support my analysis?

✓ If I infer things in the text that the author does not state directly, what evidence from the text, along with my own experiences and knowledge, can I use to support my analysis?

✓ Have I used several pieces of textual evidence to support my analysis?

Please note that excerpts and passages in the StudySync® library and this workbook are intended as touchstones to generate interest in an author's work. The excerpts and passages do not substitute for the reading of entire texts, and StudySync® strongly recommends that students seek out and purchase the whole literary or informational work in order to experience it as the author intended. Links to online resellers are available in our digital library. In addition, complete works may be ordered through an authorized reseller by filling out and returning to StudySync® the order form enclosed in this workbook.

Reading & Writing Companion   13

Skill:
Text-Dependent Responses

Read the second Think question from the First Read lesson for "Rikki-Tikki-Tavi" and the writer's responses below. Then, complete the chart by deciding which evidence from the text best supports each response.

↻ YOUR TURN

	Textual Evidence Options
A	Then inch by inch out of the grass rose up the head and spread hood of Nag, the big black cobra, and he was five feet long from tongue to tail.
B	Darzee and his wife only cowered down in the nest without answering, for from the thick grass at the foot of the bush there came a low hiss—a horrid cold sound that made Rikki-tikki jump back two clear feet.
C	"I am Nag. The great God Brahm put his mark upon all our people, when the first cobra spread his hood to keep the sun off Brahm as he slept. Look, and be afraid!"

Response	Textual Evidence
The other animals in the garden are afraid of Nag.	
Nag uses his size to intimidate.	
Nag's own words show how scary he is.	

First Read

Read "Rikki-Tikki-Tavi." After you read, complete the Think Questions below.

☁ THINK QUESTIONS

1. How did Rikki-tikki come to live with the English family? Cite specific evidence from the text to support your answer.

2. What do the descriptions of Nag and the dialogue in paragraphs 23–24 suggest about Nag's character? Cite specific evidence from the text to support your answer.

3. Describe in two to three sentences how Rikki-tikki saves the family from snakes.

4. Find the word **cultivated** in paragraph 18 of "Rikki-Tikki-Tavi." Use context clues in the surrounding sentences, as well as the sentence in which the word appears, to determine the word's meaning. Write your definition here and identify clues that helped you figure out the word's meaning.

5. Use context clues to determine the meaning of **sensible** as it is used in paragraph 79 of "Rikki-Tikki-Tavi." Write your definition of *sensible* here and identify clues that helped you figure out the meaning. Then check the meaning in the dictionary.

Please note that excerpts and passages in the StudySync® library and this workbook are intended as touchstones to generate interest in an author's work. The excerpts and passages do not substitute for the reading of entire texts, and StudySync® strongly recommends that students seek out and purchase the whole literary or informational work in order to experience it as the author intended. Links to online resellers are available in our digital library. In addition, complete works may be ordered through an authorized reseller by filling out and returning to StudySync® the order form enclosed in this workbook.

Reading & Writing Companion   15

Skill:
Textual Evidence

Use the Checklist to analyze Textual Evidence in "Rikki-Tikki-Tavi." Refer to the sample student annotations about Textual Evidence in the text.

••• CHECKLIST FOR TEXTUAL EVIDENCE

In order to support an analysis by citing textual evidence that is explicitly stated in the text, do the following:

✓ Read the text closely and critically.

✓ Identify what the text says explicitly.

✓ Find the most relevant textual evidence that supports your analysis.

✓ Consider why an author explicitly states specific details and information.

✓ Cite the specific words, phrases, sentences, paragraphs, or images from the text that support your analysis.

In order to interpret implicit meanings in a text by making inferences, do the following:

✓ Combine information directly stated in the text with your own knowledge, experiences, and observations.

✓ Cite the specific words, phrases, sentences, paragraphs, or images from the text that support this inference.

In order to cite textual evidence to support an analysis of what the text says explicitly as well as inferences drawn from the text, consider the following questions:

✓ Have I read the text closely and critically?

✓ What inferences am I making about the text? What textual evidence am I using to support these inferences?

✓ Am I quoting the evidence from the text correctly?

✓ Does my textual evidence logically relate to my analysis?

✓ Have I cited several pieces of textual evidence?

 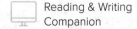

Skill:
Textual Evidence

Complete the chart on the following page by matching the correct background knowledge and implicit meaning with each explicit meaning.

⟳ YOUR TURN

	Background Knowledge and Implicit Meaning Options
A	I know that snakes stand up straight when they are feeling threatened. They do this to scare other animals or people.
B	Rikki-tikki scuttling reminds me of little kids going outside to play. They get so excited when they see a new park or playground. They run up and down and around.
C	Teddy and his mother and father must be scared and nervous. That's why they aren't eating.
D	Here, the author is suggesting that Rikki-tikki is brave and powerful like a hero.
E	Your face turns white when you are scared or nervous.
F	I can infer that Rikki-tikki is very excited about the idea of hunting in the garden.
G	This reminds me of a battle of heroes vs. villains from a movie or comic book.
H	It seems like the cobra might feel threatened or frightened by Rikki-tikki. He's probably sitting up tall in order to protect himself and scare away the mongoose.

Please note that excerpts and passages in the StudySync® library and this workbook are intended as touchstones to generate interest in an author's work. The excerpts and passages do not substitute for the reading of entire texts, and StudySync® strongly recommends that students seek out and purchase the whole literary or informational work in order to experience it as the author intended. Links to online resellers are available in our digital library. In addition, complete works may be ordered through an authorized reseller by filling out and returning to StudySync® the order form enclosed in this workbook.

Reading & Writing
Companion

17

Explicit Evidence	Background Knowledge	Implicit Meaning
Rikki-tikki licked his lips. "This is a splendid hunting-ground," he said, and his tail grew bottle-brushy at the thought of it, and he scuttled up and down the garden, snuffing here and there till he heard very sorrowful voices in a thorn-bush.		
When he had lifted one-third of himself clear of the ground, he stayed balancing to and fro exactly as a dandelion tuft balances in the wind, and he looked at Rikki-tikki with the wicked snake's eyes that never change their expression, whatever the snake may be thinking of.		
Rikki-tikki's eyes grew red again, and he danced up to Karait with the peculiar rocking, swaying motion that he had inherited from his family.		
Teddy and his mother and father were there at early breakfast, but Rikki-tikki saw that they were not eating anything. They sat stone-still, and their faces were white.		

Skill:
Character

Use the Checklist to analyze Character in "Rikki-Tikki-Tavi." Refer to the sample student annotations about Character in the text.

••• CHECKLIST FOR CHARACTER

In order to determine how particular elements of a story or drama interact, note the following:

- ✓ the characters in the story, including the protagonist and antagonist

- ✓ the settings and how they shape the characters or plot

- ✓ plot events and how they affect the characters

- ✓ key events or series of episodes in the plot, especially events that cause characters to react, respond, or change in some way

- ✓ characters' responses as the plot reaches a climax and moves toward a resolution of the problem facing the protagonist

- ✓ the resolution of the conflict in the plot and the ways that affects each character

To analyze how particular elements of a story or drama interact, consider the following questions:

- ✓ How do the characters' responses change or develop from the beginning to the end of the story?

- ✓ How does the setting shape the characters and plot in the story?

- ✓ How do the events in the plot affect the characters? How do they develop as a result of the conflict, climax, and resolution?

- ✓ Do the characters' problems reach a resolution? How?

- ✓ How does the resolution affect the characters?

Skill:
Character

Reread paragraphs 37–42 of "Rikki-Tikki-Tavi." Then, using the Checklist on the previous page, answer the multiple-choice questions below.

⟳ YOUR TURN

1. How does the mother's love for her son affect her actions in paragraph 37?

   ○ A. It prompts her to keep her son away from Rikki-tikki.
   ○ B. It causes a disagreement between her and her husband.
   ○ C. It makes her show affection towards Rikki-tikki.
   ○ D. It makes Rikki-tikki feel nervous staying with the family.

2. What does the dialogue in paragraph 40 suggest about Chuchundra?

   ○ A. He is afraid.
   ○ B. He is easily fooled.
   ○ C. He is optimistic.
   ○ D. He loves Rikki-tikki.

3. Which paragraph shows that Teddy looks to Rikki-tikki for protection?

   ○ A. 37
   ○ B. 38
   ○ C. 39
   ○ D. 40

Close Read

Reread "Rikki-Tikki-Tavi." As you reread, complete the Skills Focus questions below. Then use your answers and annotations from the questions to help you complete the Write activity.

◎ SKILLS FOCUS

1. Identify details that reveal Nag's character when he is first introduced in the story. Explain what inferences you can make about Nag and what makes him a threat.

2. Identify details that reveal Rikki-tikki's character traits as a fighter. Explain how those character traits help Rikki-tikki defeat the snakes.

3. Find examples of Nag and Nagaina's actions and dialogue. How do their words and behaviors create conflict in the plot?

4. Identify details that help you compare and contrast Rikki-tikki and Darzee. Explain what you can infer about Rikki-tikki and Darzee from these details.

5. Analyze details that show how Rikki-tikki beats the snakes. Explain Rikki-tikki's approach to conflict.

✏ WRITE

LITERARY ANALYSIS: In this classic story of good vs. evil, Nag and Nagaina are portrayed as the villains. Consider the role and behaviors of the typical villain. Then think about Nag and Nagaina's behaviors, including how they impact the plot and interact with other characters. Do you think that Nag and Nagaina are truly evil, or have they been unfairly cast as villains? Choose a side, and write a brief response explaining your position and analysis. Use several pieces of textual evidence to support your points.

Please note that excerpts and passages in the StudySync® library and this workbook are intended as touchstones to generate interest in an author's work. The excerpts and passages do not substitute for the reading of entire texts, and StudySync® strongly recommends that students seek out and purchase the whole literary or informational work in order to experience it as the author intended. Links to online resellers are available in our digital library. In addition, complete works may be ordered through an authorized reseller by filling out and returning to StudySync® the order form enclosed in this workbook.

Reading & Writing Companion   21

The Wise Old Woman

FICTION
Yoshiko Uchida
1965

Introduction

"The Wise Old Woman" is a traditional Japanese folktale retold by Yoshiko Uchida (1921–1992), a Japanese American author who grew up in California during the Great Depression. As a child, Uchida's parents taught her to appreciate the customs and folktales of their native land, and as a result, Japanese culture is prevalent in Uchida's writing. Through her writing, Uchida expressed the hope that "all children, in whatever country they may live, have the same love of fun and a good story."

"On and on he climbed, not wanting to stop and leave her behind."

1 Many long years ago, there lived an **arrogant** and cruel young lord who ruled over a small village in the western hills of Japan.

2 "I have no use for old people in my village," he said haughtily. "They are neither useful nor able to work for a living. I therefore **decree** that anyone over seventy-one must be **banished** from the village and left in the mountains to die."

3 "What a dreadful decree! What a cruel and unreasonable lord we have," the people of the village murmured. But the lord fearfully punished anyone who disobeyed him, and so villagers who turned seventy-one were tearfully carried into the mountains, never to return.

4 Gradually there were fewer and fewer old people in the village and soon they disappeared altogether. Then the young lord was pleased.

5 "What a fine village of young, healthy, and hard-working people I have," he bragged. "Soon it will be the finest village in all of Japan."

6 Now, there lived in this village a kind young farmer and his aged mother. They were poor, but the farmer was good to his mother, and the two of them lived happily together. However, as the years went by, the mother grew older, and before long she reached the terrible age of seventy-one.

7 "If only I could somehow **deceive** the cruel lord," the farmer thought. But there were records in the village books and everyone knew that his mother had turned seventy-one.

8 Each day the son put off telling his mother that he must take her into the mountains to die, but the people of the village began to talk. The farmer knew that if he did not take his mother away soon, the lord would send his soldiers and throw them both into a dark dungeon to die a terrible death.

9 "Mother—" he would begin, as he tried to tell her what he must do, but he could not go on.

10 Then one day the mother herself spoke of the lord's dreaded decree. "Well, my son," she said, "the time has come for you to take me to the mountains.

Skill:
Summarizing

- **Who?** the young lord
- **What?** banishes all of the old people to the mountains
- **Where?** the village
- **When?** once the villagers are over the age of seventy-one
- **Why?** He doesn't believe old people are useful or can work.
- **How?** using his power as the ruler of the village

We must hurry before the lord sends his soldiers for you." And she did not seem worried at all that she must go to the mountains to die.

11   "Forgive me, dear mother, for what I must do," the farmer said sadly, and the next morning he lifted his mother to his shoulders and set off on the steep path toward the mountains. Up and up he climbed, until the trees clustered close and the path was gone. There was no longer even the sound of birds, and they heard only the soft wail of the wind in the trees. The son walked slowly, for he could not bear to think of leaving his old mother in the mountains. On and on he climbed, not wanting to stop and leave her behind. Soon, he heard his mother breaking off small twigs from the trees that they passed.

12   "Mother, what are you doing?" he asked.

13   "Do not worry, my son," she answered gently. "I am just marking the way so you will not get lost returning to the village."

14   The son stopped. "Even now you are thinking of me?" he asked, wonderingly.

15   The mother nodded. "Of course, my son," she replied. "You will always be in my thoughts. How could it be otherwise?"

16   At that, the young farmer could bear it no longer. "Mother, I cannot leave you in the mountains to die all alone," he said. "We are going home and no matter what the lord does to punish me, I will never desert you again."

17   So they waited until the sun had set and a lone star crept into the silent sky. Then, in the dark shadows of night, the farmer carried his mother down the hill and they returned quietly to their little house. The farmer dug a deep hole in the floor of his kitchen and made a small room where he could hide his mother. From that day, she spent all her time in the secret room and the farmer carried meals to her there. The rest of the time, he was careful to work in the fields and act as though he lived alone. In this way, for almost two years he kept his mother safely hidden and no one in the village knew that she was there.

18   Then one day there was a terrible **commotion** among the villagers, for Lord Higa of the town beyond the hills threatened to conquer their village and make it his own.

19   "Only one thing can spare you," Lord Higa announced. "Bring me a box containing one thousand ropes of ash and I will spare your village."

20   The cruel young lord quickly gathered together all the wise men of his village. "You are men of wisdom," he said. "Surely you can tell me how to meet Lord Higa's demands so our village can be spared."

21   But the wise men shook their heads. "It is impossible to make even one rope of ash, sire," they answered. "How can we ever make one thousand?"

NOTES

22 "Fools!" the lord cried angrily. "What good is your wisdom if you cannot help me now?"

23 And he posted a notice in the village square offering a great reward of gold to any villager who could help him save their village.

24 But all the people in the village whispered, "Surely, it is an impossible thing, for ash crumbles at the touch of the finger. How could anyone ever make a rope of ash?" They shook their heads and sighed, "Alas, alas, we must be conquered by yet another cruel lord."

25 The young farmer, too, supposed that this must be, and he wondered what would happen to his mother if a new lord even more terrible than their own came to rule over them.

26 When his mother saw the troubled look on his face, she asked, "Why are you so worried, my son?"

27 So the farmer told her of the impossible demand made by Lord Higa if the village was to be spared, but his mother did not seem troubled at all. Instead she laughed softly and said, "Why, that is not such an impossible task. All one has to do is soak ordinary rope in salt water and dry it well. When it is burned, it will hold its shape and there is your rope of ash! Tell the villagers to hurry and find one thousand pieces of rope."

28 The farmer shook his head in amazement. "Mother, you are wonderfully wise," he said, and he rushed to tell the young lord what he must do.

29 "You are wiser than all the wise men of the village," the lord said when he heard the farmer's solution, and he rewarded him with many pieces of gold. The thousand ropes of ash were quickly made and the village was spared.

30 In a few days, however, there was another great commotion in the village as Lord Higa sent another threat. This time he sent a log with a small hole that curved and bent seven times through its length, and he demanded that a single piece of silk thread be threaded through the hole. "If you cannot perform this task," the lord threatened, "I shall come to conquer your village."

31 The young lord hurried once more to his wise men, but they all shook their heads in bewilderment. "A needle cannot bend its way through such curves," they moaned. "Again we are faced with an impossible demand."

32 "And again you are stupid fools!" the lord said, stamping his foot impatiently. He then posted a second notice in the village square asking the villagers for their help.

33 Once more the young farmer hurried with the problem to his mother in her secret room.

Skill:
Theme

The farmer and the people in the village thought Lord Higa's task was impossible. The mother laughed at the task because she knew it was not impossible. She gave great advice!

This dialogue makes me think the theme might be old people are wise.

Please note that excerpts and passages in the StudySync® library and this workbook are intended as touchstones to generate interest in an author's work. The excerpts and passages do not substitute for the reading of entire texts, and StudySync® strongly recommends that students seek out and purchase the whole literary or informational work in order to experience it as the author intended. Links to online resellers are available in our digital library. In addition, complete works may be ordered through an authorized reseller by filling out and returning to StudySync® the order form enclosed in this workbook.

Reading & Writing Companion   **25**

34   "Why, that is not so difficult," his mother said with a quick smile. "Put some sugar at one end of the hole. Then tie an ant to a piece of silk thread and put it in at the other end. He will weave his way in and out of the curves to get to the sugar and he will take the silk thread with him."

35   "Mother, you are remarkable!" the son cried, and he hurried off to the lord with the solution to the second problem.

36   Once more the lord **commended** the young farmer and rewarded him with many pieces of gold. "You are a brilliant man and you have saved our village again," he said gratefully.

37   But the lord's troubles were not over even then, for a few days later Lord Higa sent still another demand. "This time you will undoubtedly fail and then I shall conquer your village," he threatened. "Bring me a drum that sounds without being beaten."

38   "But that is not possible," sighed the people of the village. "How can anyone make a drum sound without beating it?"

39   This time the wise men held their heads in their hands and moaned, "It is hopeless. It is hopeless. This time Lord Higa will conquer us all."

40   The young farmer hurried home breathlessly. "Mother, Mother, we must solve another terrible problem or Lord Higa will conquer our village!" And he quickly told his mother about the impossible drum.

41   His mother, however, smiled and answered, "Why, this is the easiest of them all. Make a drum with sides of paper and put a bumblebee inside. As it tries to escape, it will buzz and beat itself against the paper and you will have a drum that sounds without being beaten."

42   The young farmer was amazed at his mother's wisdom. "You are far wiser than any of the wise men of the village," he said, and he hurried to tell the young lord how to meet Lord Higa's third demand.

43   When the lord heard the answer, he was greatly impressed. "Surely a young man like you cannot be wiser than all my wise men," he said. "Tell me honestly, who has helped you solve all these difficult problems?"

44   The young farmer could not lie. "My lord," he began slowly, "for the past two years I have broken the law of the land. I have kept my aged mother hidden beneath the floor of my house, and it is she who solved each of your problems and saved the village from Lord Higa."

45   He trembled as he spoke, for he feared the lord's displeasure and rage. Surely now the soldiers would be summoned to throw him into the dark dungeon. But when he glanced fearfully at the lord, he saw that the young

ruler was not angry at all. Instead, he was silent and thoughtful, for at last he realized how much wisdom and knowledge old people possess.

46 "I have been very wrong," he said finally. "And I must ask the forgiveness of your mother and of all my people. Never again will I demand that the old people of our village be sent to the mountains to die. Rather, they will be treated with the respect and honor they deserve and share with us the wisdom of their years."

47 And so it was. From that day, the villagers were no longer forced to abandon their parents in the mountains, and the village became once more a happy, cheerful place in which to live. The terrible Lord Higa stopped sending his impossible demands and no longer threatened to conquer them, for he too was impressed.

48 "Even in such a small village there is much wisdom," he declared, "and its people should be allowed to live in peace."

49 And that is exactly what the farmer and his mother and all the people of the village did for all the years thereafter.

Please note that excerpts and passages in the StudySync® library and this workbook are intended as touchstones to generate interest in an author's work. The excerpts and passages do not substitute for the reading of entire texts, and StudySync® strongly recommends that students seek out and purchase the whole literary or informational work in order to experience it as the author intended. Links to online resellers are available in our digital library. In addition, complete works may be ordered through an authorized reseller by filling out and returning to StudySync® the order form enclosed in this workbook.

Reading & Writing
Companion

27

First Read

Read "The Wise Old Woman." After you read, complete the Think Questions below.

☁ THINK QUESTIONS

1. Why did the young lord issue a decree against elderly people? What did the decree say? Cite specific evidence from the second paragraph.

2. Write two to three sentences describing how the farmer's mother saves the village from Lord Higa's threats. Be sure to use evidence from the text in your response.

3. How does the young lord change at the end of the story? What causes this change? Use evidence from the text to support your answer.

4. Use context clues to determine the meaning of **commended** as it is used in paragraph 36 of "The Wise Old Woman." Write your definition here and identify clues that helped you figure out the meaning. Then check the meaning in a dictionary.

5. Find the word **banished** in paragraph 2 of "The Wise Old Woman." Use context clues in the surrounding sentences, as well as the sentence in which the word appears, to determine the word's meaning. Write your definition here and identify clues that helped you figure out its meaning.

Skill:
Summarizing

Use the Checklist to analyze Summarizing in "The Wise Old Woman." Refer to the sample student annotations about Summarizing in the text.

••• CHECKLIST FOR SUMMARIZING

In order to provide an objective summary of a text, note the following:

- ✓ answers to the basic questions *who*, *what*, *where*, *when*, *why*, and *how*

- ✓ when summarizing literature, note the setting, characters, and major events in the plot, including the problem the characters face and how it is solved

- ✓ stay objective, and do not add your own personal thoughts, judgments, or opinions to the summary

To provide an objective summary of a text, consider the following questions:

- ✓ What are the answers to basic *who*, *what*, *where*, *when*, *why*, and *how* questions?

- ✓ Is my summary objective, or have I added my own thoughts, judgments, and personal opinions?

Please note that excerpts and passages in the StudySync® library and this workbook are intended as touchstones to generate interest in an author's work. The excerpts and passages do not substitute for the reading of entire texts, and StudySync® strongly recommends that students seek out and purchase the whole literary or informational work in order to experience it as the author intended. Links to online resellers are available in our digital library. In addition, complete works may be ordered through an authorized reseller by filling out and returning to StudySync® the order form enclosed in this workbook.

Reading & Writing Companion   29

Skill:
Summarizing

Reread paragraphs 6–11 of "The Wise Old Woman." Then, complete the chart by matching the important details with each category to objectively summarize what happened in the text.

↻ YOUR TURN

	Important Detail Options
A	The farmer kept putting off telling his mother it was time to go to the mountains to die.
B	years after the decree
C	the young farmer and the aged mother
D	a village in Japan
E	with sadness
F	The farmer cared for his mother and did not want her to die.

Who	What	Where	When	Why	How

Reading & Writing Companion

Skill:
Theme

Use the Checklist to analyze Theme in "The Wise Old Woman." Refer to the sample student annotations about Theme in the text.

••• CHECKLIST FOR THEME

In order to identify a theme in a text, note the following:

- ✓ the topic of the text

- ✓ whether or not the theme is stated directly in the text

- ✓ details in the text that help to reveal theme

  - • a narrator's or speaker's tone

  - • title and chapter headings

  - • details about the setting

  - • characters' thoughts, actions, and dialogue

  - • the central conflict in the story's plot

  - • the resolution of the conflict

To determine a theme of a text and analyze its development over the course of the text, consider the following questions:

- ✓ What is a theme of the text?

- ✓ When did you become aware of that theme? For instance, did the story's conclusion reveal the theme?

- ✓ How does the theme develop over the course of the text?

Please note that excerpts and passages in the StudySync® library and this workbook are intended as touchstones to generate interest in an author's work. The excerpts and passages do not substitute for the reading of entire texts, and StudySync® strongly recommends that students seek out and purchase the whole literary or informational work in order to experience it as the author intended. Links to online resellers are available in our digital library. In addition, complete works may be ordered through an authorized reseller by filling out and returning to StudySync® the order form enclosed in this workbook.

Reading & Writing
Companion

31

Skill:
Theme

Reread paragraphs 40–46 of "The Wise Old Woman." Then, using the Checklist on the previous page, answer the multiple-choice questions below.

⟳ YOUR TURN

1. The change the young lord undergoes in paragraph 45 suggests a theme about which topic?

   ○ A. Hope
   ○ B. Change
   ○ C. Humility
   ○ D. Fear

2. Identify the theme that best matches the young lord's change in paragraph 46.

   ○ A. Being a good ruler means being willing to accept when you are wrong and change your behavior.
   ○ B. Being a good ruler means being able to get people to comply with your wishes and demands.
   ○ C. People will do good work only when they are afraid.
   ○ D. Love is a stronger motivator to get work done than fear.

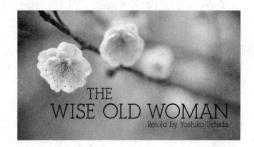

Close Read

Reread "The Wise Old Woman." As you reread, complete the Skills Focus questions below. Then use your answers and annotations from the questions to help you complete the Write activity.

◎ SKILLS FOCUS

1. Reread the beginning of the story, including scenes that describe how the young farmer hides and cares for his mother. Highlight and annotate important details that you would include in a summary. What topics or themes are suggested by these details?

2. Identify scenes that reveal the character traits of the farmer's mother. Explain how her character traits influence the events in the story.

3. Identify evidence that shows how the farmer's mother helped the village avoid conflict. How do her actions contribute to the development of the theme?

✏ WRITE

LITERARY ANALYSIS: Provide a brief objective summary of the story, including only the most important details from the beginning, middle, and end. Then think about how the farmer's mother relies on her son. Think about how the village and the young lord rely on the farmer's mother. What theme is developed through these relationships and the story's resolution? Use several pieces of textual evidence to support your analysis.

Woodsong

INFORMATIONAL TEXT
Gary Paulsen
1990

Introduction

I n his memoir, *Woodsong*, the esteemed outdoorsman, former beaver trapper, and three-time Newbery Honor author Gary Paulsen (b. 1939) tells the story of his interconnected life with nature. From employment-requisite dog sledding in Minnesota, to the thousand-mile race from Settler's Bay to Nome, Alaska, Paulsen's tales usually come down to the bare-bone realities of survival—be it putting food on his family's table or avoiding being dinner for something else. In this excerpt from the first chapter, Paulsen learns a valuable lesson from the wild and often brutal laws of the forest.

"In all my time in the woods, in the wondrous dance of it, I have many times seen predators fail."

from Chapter One

1 I lived in innocence for a long time. I believed in the fairy-tale version of the forest until I was close to forty years old.

2 **Gulled** by Disney and others, I believed Bambi always got out of the fire. Nothing ever really got hurt. Though I hunted and killed it was always somehow clean and removed from reality. I killed yet thought that every story had a happy ending.

3 Until a December morning . . .

4 I was running a dog team around the side of a large lake, just starting out on my trapline[1]. It was early winter and the ice on the lake wasn't thick enough to support the sled and team or I would have gone across the middle. There was a rough trail around the edge of the lake and I was running a fresh eight-dog team so the small loop, which added five or so miles, presented no great difficulty.

5 It was a grandly beautiful winter morning. The temperature was perhaps ten below, with a bright sun that shone through ice crystals in the air so that everything seemed to sparkle. The dogs were working evenly, the gangline[2] up through the middle of them thrumming with the rhythm it has when they are working in perfect **tandem**. We skirted the lake, which lay below and to the right. To the left and rising higher were willows and brush, which made something like a wall next to the trail.

6 The dogs were still running at a lope, though we had come over seven miles, and I was full of them; my life was full of them. We were, as it happens sometimes, dancing with winter. I could not help smiling, just smiling idiotically at the grandness of it. Part of the chant of an ancient Navajo prayer rolled through my mind:

7 *Beauty above me*
Beauty below me
Beauty before me. . .

Skill:
Connotation
and Denotation

This is an important description of the setting. The dictionary definition of fairy tale is "a magical story." This creates a positive emotion because fairy tales are usually happy. The author had a good feeling about the forest.

---

1. **trapline** a route along which traps are set for wild animals or other game
2. **gangline** the central line in front of a sled to which each individual animal is attached

NOTES

Skill:
Connotation
and Denotation

The dictionary definition of stink *is "an unpleasant smell," which has negative connotations. Using this phrase rather than saying the doe "smelled" of fear emphasizes just how terrified the deer is as she runs from the wolves.*

8   That is how I felt then and frequently still feel when I am running dogs. I was in and of beauty and at that **precise** moment a doe, a white-tailed deer, exploded out of some willows on the left side of the team, heading down the bank toward the lake.

9   The snow alongside the trail was about two feet deep and powdery and it followed her in a white shower that covered everything. She literally flew over the lead dog who was a big, white, wolfy-looking male named Dollar. He was so surprised that he dropped, ducked, for part of an instant, then rose—almost like a rock skipping on the trail—and continued running. We were moving so fast and the deer was moving so fast that within a second or two we were several yards past where it happened and yet everything seemed suspended in slow motion.

10   Above all, in the deer, was the stink of fear. Even in that split part of a second, it could be smelled. It could be seen. The doe's eyes were so wide they seemed to come out of her head. Her mouth was jacked open and her tongue hung out to the side. Her jaw and neck were covered with spit, and she stunk of fear.

11   Dogs smell fear at once but I have not always been able to, even when I was afraid. There is something coppery about it, a metallic smell mixed with the smell of urine and feces, when something, when somebody, is afraid. No, not just afraid but ripped with fear, and it was on the doe.

12   The smell excited the dogs and they began to run faster, although continuing down the trail; I turned to look back from the sled and saw why the doe was frightened.

13   Wolves.

14   They bounded over the trail after the doe even as I watched. These were not the large timber wolves but the smaller northern brush wolves, perhaps weighing forty or fifty pounds each, about as large as most of my team. I think they are called northern coyotes.

15   Except that they act as wolves. They pack and have pack social structures like timber wolves, and hunt in packs like timber wolves.

16   And they were hunting the doe.

17   There were seven of them and not one looked down the trail to see me as they jumped across the sled tracks after the deer. They were so **intent** on her, and the smell of her, that I might as well not have existed.

18   And they were gaining on her.

NOTES

19   I stood on the brakes to stop the sled and set the snow-hook to hold the dogs and turned. The dogs immediately swung down off the trail toward the lake, trying to get at the wolves and deer. The snowhook came loose and we began to slide down the lake bank. I jerked the hook from the snow and hooked it on a small poplar that held us.

20   The doe, in horror now, and knowing what was coming, left the bank of the lake and bounded out onto the bad ice. Her tail was fully erect, a white flash as she tried to reach out and get speed, but the ice was too thin.

21   Too thin for all the weight of her on the small, pointed hooves and she went through and down in a huge spray of shattered ice and water.

22   She was up instantly, clambering and working to get back up on top of the ice next to the hole. Through sheer effort in her panic she made it.

23   But it slowed her too much.

24   In those few moments of going through the ice and getting out she lost her lead on the wolves and they were on her.

25   On her.

26   In all my time in the woods, in the wondrous dance of it, I have many times seen predators fail. As a matter of fact, they usually fail. I once saw a beaver come out of a hole on the ice near his lodge in the middle of winter and stand off four wolves. He **sustained** one small bite on his tail and **inflicted** terrible damage with his teeth on the wolves, killing one and wounding the other three. I have seen rabbits outwit foxes and watched red squirrels tease martens and get away with it, but this time it was not to be.

Excerpted from *Woodsong* by Gary Paulsen, published by Simon & Schuster.

Skill: Author's Purpose and Point of View

The author describes his time in the woods as a "wondrous dance." He has seen rabbits outwit foxes. This may be why he thought nothing ever got hurt. But "this time it was not to be." The death of the doe changes the author's point of view.

Please note that excerpts and passages in the StudySync® library and this workbook are intended as touchstones to generate interest in an author's work. The excerpts and passages do not substitute for the reading of entire texts, and StudySync® strongly recommends that students seek out and purchase the whole literary or informational work in order to experience it as the author intended. Links to online resellers are available in our digital library. In addition, complete works may be ordered through an authorized reseller by filling out and returning to StudySync® the order form enclosed in this workbook.

Reading & Writing Companion   37

First Read

Read *Woodsong*. After you read, complete the Think Questions below.

☁ THINK QUESTIONS

1. What does the reader learn about the ice in paragraph 4? How does this information prepare the reader for what happens later in the story? Cite textual evidence in your response.

2. Paulsen uses sensory details—words that appeal to the senses of sight, sound, smell, and taste—to describe the feeling of fear. How does Paulsen describe fear and the reaction of his sled dogs to fear? Refer to the text in your answer.

3. In the final paragraph, Paulsen shares an example of another animal battle. What is that example? How is it different from the story of the wolves and the doe?

4. Find the word **tandem** in paragraph 5 of *Woodsong*. Use context clues in the surrounding sentences, as well as the sentence in which the word appears, to determine the word's meaning. Write your definition here and identify clues that helped you figure out its meaning.

5. Use context clues to determine the meaning of **inflicted** as it is used in last paragraph of *Woodsong*. Write your definition here and identify clues that helped you figure out the meaning. Then check the meaning in a dictionary.

Skill: Connotation and Denotation

Use the Checklist to analyze Connotation and Denotation in *Woodsong*. Refer to the sample student annotations about Connotation and Denotation in the text.

Copyright © BookheadEd Learning, LLC

••• CHECKLIST FOR CONNOTATION AND DENOTATION

In order to identify the connotative meanings of words, use the following steps:

- ✓ First, note unfamiliar words and phrases, key words used to describe important events and ideas, or words that inspire an emotional reaction.

- ✓ Next, determine and note the denotative meaning of words by consulting reference materials such as a dictionary, a glossary, or a thesaurus.

To better understand the meanings of words and phrases as they are used in the text, including connotative meanings, use the following questions:

- ✓ What is the genre or subject of the text? How does that affect the possible meaning of a word or phrase?

- ✓ Does the word create positive, negative, or neutral emotion?

- ✓ What synonyms or alternative phrasing help you describe the connotative meaning of the word?

To analyze the impact of word choice on the meaning of a text, use the following questions as a guide:

- ✓ What is the meaning of the word or phrase? What is the connotation as well as the denotation?

- ✓ If I substitute a synonym based on denotation, is the meaning the same? How does the synonym change the meaning of the text?

Skill: Connotation and Denotation

Reread paragraphs 10–13 of *Woodsong*. Then, using the Checklist on the previous page, answer the multiple-choice questions below.

⟳ YOUR TURN

1. This question has two parts. First, answer Part A. Then, answer Part B.

   Part A: Which answer best describes the connotation of the word *jacked* as it is used in the first paragraph?

   ○ A. open
   ○ B. terrified
   ○ C. strong
   ○ D. surprised

   Part B: Which line from the passage supports your answer in Part A?

   ○ A. The smell excited the dogs and they began to run faster, although continuing down the trail.
   ○ B. Dogs smell fear at once but I have not always been able to, even when I was afraid.
   ○ C. Above all, in the deer, was the stink of fear. Even in that split part of a second, it could be smelled. It could be seen.
   ○ D. Her jaw and neck were covered with spit, and she stunk of fear.

Skill: Author's Purpose and Point of View

Use the Checklist to analyze Author's Purpose and Point of View in *Woodsong*. Refer to the sample student annotations about Author's Purpose and Point of View in the text.

••• CHECKLIST FOR AUTHOR'S PURPOSE AND POINT OF VIEW

In order to identify author's purpose and point of view, note the following:

- ✓ facts, statistics, and graphic aids, as these indicate that an author is writing to inform.

- ✓ descriptive or sensory details and emotional language that may indicate that an author is writing to describe and dramatize events.

- ✓ descriptions that present a complicated process in plain language may indicate that an author is writing to explain.

- ✓ emotional language with a call to action may indicate the author is trying to persuade readers or stress an opinion.

- ✓ the language the author uses can also be a clue to the author's point of view on a subject or topic.

To determine the author's purpose and point of view in a text, consider the following questions:

- ✓ How does the author convey, or communicate, information in the text?

- ✓ Does the author use figurative or emotional language? How does it affect the purpose and point of view?

- ✓ Are charts, graphs, maps and other graphic aids included in the text? For what purpose?

Skill: Author's Purpose and Point of View

Reread paragraphs 5–8 of *Woodsong*. Then, using the Checklist on the previous page, answer the multiple-choice questions below.

⟳ YOUR TURN

1. The author's purpose in using many descriptive and sensory details is to —

   ○ A. describe the scene that morning.

   ○ B. persuade the reader that the outdoors should be enjoyed.

   ○ C. entertain the reader with a scene from nature.

   ○ D. criticize commonly held beliefs about nature.

2. Based on the author's descriptions in paragraphs 5–8, the reader can conclude that he primarily wants to express a feeling of —

   ○ A. kinship with the Navajo.

   ○ B. fatigue from leading the dog sled.

   ○ C. anxiety about danger out in the woods.

   ○ D. appreciation for the beauty of nature.

3. Based on the details in the excerpt, the reader can infer that the author's overall purpose in writing this piece is to show that

   ○ A. When you spend time in nature, you can feel the frightening power of the wilderness.

   ○ B. You should not travel or work alone in nature, unless you have a pack of animals with you.

   ○ C. In certain moments you can feel surrounded by beauty in nature, but there is also danger in the natural world.

   ○ D. Reflecting on Native American literature and customs can enhance your appreciation of nature.

WOODSONG

Close Read

Reread *Woodsong*. As you reread, complete the Skills Focus questions below. Then use your answers and annotations from the questions to help you complete the Write activity.

◎ SKILLS FOCUS

1. Identify details and language used to describe the doe and the wolves. Explain how these details reflect the author's purpose or point of view.

2. Reread paragraphs 5–8. Identify words with specific emotional connotations. Explain why you think the author chose those words.

3. Reread the last paragraph. Identify details that suggest how the author's point of view has changed. Explain how being an outside observer of a conflict between animals affects the author personally.

✏ WRITE

LITERARY ANALYSIS: In this excerpt from his memoir, Gary Paulsen describes wolves attacking and dominating a doe in the forest. Why did Paulsen write about this experience? How did the experience change him? Use textual evidence to answer these questions. In your response, explain how Paulsen uses words with strong connotative meanings and other descriptive details to convey his purpose and point of view.

Please note that excerpts and passages in the StudySync® library and this workbook are intended as touchstones to generate interest in an author's work. The excerpts and passages do not substitute for the reading of entire texts, and StudySync® strongly recommends that students seek out and purchase the whole literary or informational work in order to experience it as the author intended. Links to online resellers are available in our digital library. In addition, complete works may be ordered through an authorized reseller by filling out and returning to StudySync® the order form enclosed in this workbook.

Reading & Writing Companion   **43**

Nimona

FICTION
Noelle Stevenson
2015

Introduction

Comic artist and illustrator Noelle Stevenson (b. 1991) was a National Book Award finalist for her critically acclaimed and groundbreaking graphic novel *Nimona*, an irreverent take on the traditional medieval fantasy narrative. Nimona is the brazen young sidekick to mad scientist and super villain Lord Ballister Blackheart. In this chapter, Nimona and her boss brainstorm ideas on how to best rid themselves of Blackheart's archnemesis, local hero Sir Gold— Ain. Nimona was

"You can't just go around murdering people. There are RULES, Nimona."

Skill:
Textual Evidence

Blackheart says, "If anyone is going to kill him … it's going to be me." The color fades and I see a young Blackheart in a flashback. I can infer that Sir Goldenloin and Blackheart must have a complicated past.

NOTES

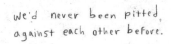

Please note that excerpts and passages in the StudySync® library and this workbook are intended as touchstones to generate interest in an author's work. The excerpts and passages do not substitute for the reading of entire texts, and StudySync® strongly recommends that students seek out and purchase the whole literary or informational work in order to experience it as the author intended. Links to online resellers are available in our digital library. In addition, complete works may be ordered through an authorized reseller by filling out and returning to StudySync® the order form enclosed in this workbook.

Reading & Writing
Companion

47

Text copyright ©2017 by Noelle Stevenson. Used by permission of HarperCollins Publishers.

First Read

Read *Nimona*. After you read, complete the Think Questions below.

 THINK QUESTIONS

1. What are three differences between Blackheart's and Nimona's plans to attack the city? Support your answer using details from the text.

2. Using details from the text, summarize the feud between Blackheart and Sir Goldenloin.

3. How is Nimona's definition of what it means to be a villain different from Blackheart's definition? Support your answer using details from the text.

4. Find the word **emphasis** in panel 6 on page 45 of *Nimona*. Use context clues in the surrounding sentences, as well as the sentence in which the word appears, to determine the word's meaning. Write your definition here and identify clues that helped you figure out its meaning.

5. Use context clues to determine the meaning of **pitted** as it is used in panel 21 on page 47 of *Nimona*. Write your definition here and identify clues that helped you figure out its meaning. Then check the meaning in a dictionary.

Please note that excerpts and passages in the StudySync® library and this workbook are intended as touchstones to generate interest in an author's work. The excerpts and passages do not substitute for the reading of entire texts, and StudySync® strongly recommends that students seek out and purchase the whole literary or informational work in order to experience it as the author intended. Links to online resellers are available in our digital library. In addition, complete works may be ordered through an authorized reseller by filling out and returning to StudySync® the order form enclosed in this workbook.

Reading & Writing Companion   **49**

Skill:
Textual Evidence

Use the Checklist to analyze Textual Evidence in *Nimona*. Refer to the sample student annotations about Textual Evidence in the text.

••• CHECKLIST FOR TEXTUAL EVIDENCE

In order to support an inference by citing evidence that is explicitly stated in the text, do the following:

- ✓ read the text closely and critically

- ✓ identify what the text says explicitly

- ✓ find the most relevant textual evidence that supports your analysis

- ✓ consider why an author explicitly states specific details and information

- ✓ cite the specific words, phrases, sentences, paragraphs, or images from the text that support your analysis

In order to interpret implicit meanings in a text by making inferences, do the following:

- ✓ combine information directly stated in the text with your own knowledge, experiences, and observations

- ✓ cite the specific words, phrases, sentences, paragraphs, or images from the text that support this inference

In order to cite textual evidence to support an analysis of what the text says explicitly as well as inferences drawn from the text, consider the following questions:

- ✓ Have I read the text closely and critically?

- ✓ What inferences am I making about the text? What textual evidence am I using to support these inferences?

- ✓ Am I quoting the evidence from the text correctly?

- ✓ Does my textual evidence logically relate to my analysis?

- ✓ Have I cited several pieces of textual evidence?

 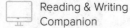

Skill:
Textual Evidence

Complete the chart below by matching the correct background knowledge and implicit meaning with each explicit meaning.

🔄 YOUR TURN

	Background Knowledge and Implicit Meaning Options
A	I know that to get into a special school like the Hero Institution, you have to be one of the best for your age.
B	I know that knights wear armor.
C	A change in Sir Goldenloin's feelings toward Blackheart occurred when they had to compete against each other.
D	Blackheart and Sir Goldenloin appeared to be equally the best.
E	I know that sometimes when friends compete, their friendship can change.
F	Both Blackheart and Sir Goldenloin were young, brave knights.

Explicit Evidence	Background Knowledge	Implicit Meaning
Blackheart and Sir Goldenloin were "heroes in training." They both wear armor in the image.		
Blackheart and Sir Goldenloin were "the two most promising heroes the Institution had ever seen." They are standing next to each other in the image.		
Blackheart and Sir Goldenloin were friends "until the day of the joust." Sir Goldenloin's arm is down while Blackheart's arm is on Goldenloin's back in the image.		

Please note that excerpts and passages in the StudySync® library and this workbook are intended as touchstones to generate interest in an author's work. The excerpts and passages do not substitute for the reading of entire texts, and StudySync® strongly recommends that students seek out and purchase the whole literary or informational work in order to experience it as the author intended. Links to online resellers are available in our digital library. In addition, complete works may be ordered through an authorized reseller by filling out and returning to StudySync® the order form enclosed in this workbook.

Reading & Writing Companion

51

Close Read

Reread *Nimona*. As you reread, complete the Skills Focus questions below. Then use your answers and annotations from the questions to help you complete the Write activity.

◎ SKILLS FOCUS

1. How would you describe Nimona? Cite the specific words, phrases, sentences, or images from the text to support your analysis and inferences.

2. Identify parts in the flashback that help you empathize with Blackheart. Explain what the flashback makes you think and feel about Blackheart.

3. Identify details that you can use to compare and contrast the characters of Nimona and Blackheart. Explain how the two characters are different and similar. Consider how each character responds to plot events.

4. Explain the difference in how Sir Blackheart and Nimona approach conflict. Cite textual evidence to support your response.

✏ WRITE

DEBATE PLAN: Imagine that you are either Nimona or Blackheart. As Nimona, you want to convince Blackheart to adopt your changes to his evil plan. As Blackheart, you want to ensure that Nimona follows your rules of battle. Choose the persona of either Nimona or Blackheart and prepare points for a debate to convince the other character to fight according to your style. Use several pieces of textual evidence to support your argument and any counter-arguments. Be sure to consider what the text says explicitly and your own inferences about the characters.

Stargirl

FICTION
Jerry Spinelli
2000

Introduction

Stargirl is an homage to individuality and self-confidence by Jerry Spinelli (b. 1941), an American author of award-winning children's and young adult fiction. The novel and its sequel, *Love, Stargirl*, have inspired many students to start their own "Stargirl Societies" in schools around the country. When Stargirl first shows up at Mica Area High School, narrator Leo and the other students don't know what to make of her. She acts and dresses differently from everyone else. She doesn't try to fit in; instead, she stands out. Stargirl's antics have everyone convinced

"How long do you think somebody who's *really* like that is going to last around here?"

from Chapter 2

1   I had to admit, the more I saw of her, the easier it was to believe she was a plant, a joke, anything but real. On that second day she wore bright-red baggy shorts with a bib and shoulder straps—overall shorts. Her sandy hair was pulled back into twin plaited pigtails, each tied with a bright-red ribbon. A rouge smudge applied each cheek, and she had even dabbed some oversized freckles on her face. She looked like Heidi. Or Bo Peep.

2   At lunch she was alone again at her table. As before, when she finished eating, she took up her ukulele. But this time she didn't play. She got up and started walking among the tables. She stared at us. She stared at one face, then another and another. The kind of bold, I'm looking at you stare you almost never get from people, especially strangers. She appeared to be looking for someone, and the whole lunchroom had become very uncomfortable.

3   As she approached our table, I thought: *What if she's looking for me?* The thought terrified me. So I turned from her. I looked at Kevin. I watched him grin goofily up at her. He wiggled his fingers at her and whispered, "Hi, Stargirl." I didn't hear an answer. I was **intensely** aware of her passing behind my chair.

4   She stopped two tables away. She was smiling at a pudding-bodied senior named Alan Ferko. The lunchroom was dead silent. She started strumming the uke. And singing. It was "Happy Birthday." When she came to his name she didn't just sing his first name, but his full name:

5   "Happy Birthday, dear Alan Fer-kooooh"

6   Alan Ferko's face turned red as Bo Peep's pigtail ribbons. There was a flurry of whistles and hoots, more for Alan Ferko's sake, I think, than hers. As Stargirl marched out, I could see Hillari Kimble across the lunchroom rising from her seat, pointing, saying something I could not hear.

7   "I'll tell you one thing," Kevin said as we joined the mob in the hallways, "she better be fake."

Copyright © BookheadEd Learning, LLC

8   I asked him what he meant.

9   "I mean if she's real, she's in big trouble. How long do you think somebody who's *really* like that is going to last around here?"

10 Good question.

11 Mica Area High School—MAHS—was not exactly a hotbed of **nonconformity.** There were individual **variants** here and there, of course, but within pretty narrow limits we all wore the same clothes, talked the same way, ate the same food, listened to the same music. Even our dorks and nerds had a MAHS stamp on them. If we happened to somehow distinguish ourselves, we quickly snapped back into place, like rubber bands.

12 Kevin was right. It was unthinkable that Stargirl could survive—or at least survive unchanged—among us. But it was also clear that Hillari Kimble was at least half right: this person calling herself Stargirl may or may not have been a faculty plant for school spirit, but whatever she was, she was not real.

13 She couldn't be.

14 Several times in those early weeks of September, she showed up in something outrageous. A 1920s flapper dress. An Indian buckskin. A kimono. One day she wore a denim miniskirt with green stockings, and crawling up one leg was a parade of enamel ladybug and butterfly pins. "Normal" for her were long, floor-brushing pioneer dresses and skirts.

15 Every few days in the lunchroom she serenaded someone new with "Happy Birthday." I was glad my birthday was in the summer.

16 In the hallways, she said hello to perfect strangers. The seniors couldn't believe it. They had never seen a tenth-grader so bold.

17 In class she was always flapping her hand in the air, asking questions, though the question often had nothing to do with the subject. One day she asked a question about trolls—in U.S. History class.

18 She made a song about isosceles triangles. She sang it to her Plane Geometry class. It was called "Three Sides Have I, But Only Two are Equal."

19 She joined the cross-country team. Our house meets were held on the Mica Country Club golf course. Red flags showed the runners the way to go. In her first meet, out in the middle of the course, she turned left when everyone else turned right. They waited for her at the finish line. She never showed up. She was dismissed from the team.

20 One day a girl screamed in the hallway. She had seen a tiny brown face pop up from Stargirl's sunflower canvas bag. It was her pet rat. It rode to school in the bag every day.

NOTES

NOTES

21 One morning we had a rare rainfall. It came during her gym class. The teacher told everyone to come in. On the way to the next class they looked out the windows. Stargirl was still outside. In the rain. Dancing.

22 We wanted to **define** her, to wrap her up as we did each other, but we could not seem to get past "weird" and "strange" and "goofy." Her ways knocked us off balance. A single word seemed to hover in the cloudless sky over the school:

23 HUH?

24 Everything she did seemed to echo Hillari Kimble: She's not real... She's not real...

25 And each night in bed I thought of her as the moon came through my window. I could have lowered my shade to make it darker and easier to sleep, but I never did. In that moonlit hour, I **acquired** a sense of the otherness of things. I liked the feeling the moonlight gave me, as if it wasn't the opposite of day, but its underside, its private side, when the fabulous purred on my snow-white sheet like some dark cat come in from the desert.

26 It was during one of these nightmoon times that it came to me that Hillari Kimble was wrong. Stargirl *was* real.

Excerpted from *Stargirl* by Jerry Spinelli, published by Ember Publishing.

✏️ WRITE

PERSONAL RESPONSE: Leo states, "If we happened to somehow distinguish ourselves, we quickly snapped back into place, like rubber bands." Explain what Leo means by this observation. How does it apply to him and his classmates? Is it important for individuals to restrict themselves so they can fit in, or should they try to distinguish themselves from others? Make a case for the importance of either conformity or individuality, using Leo's observations of Stargirl.

Seventh Grade

FICTION
Gary Soto
1995

Introduction

Gary Soto (b. 1952) is a Mexican American author born in Fresno, California, at the heart of California's San Joaquin Valley, where Mr. Soto worked as a young man in the area's agricultural fields. It was there he began to reflect on the kinds of stories he wanted to tell. Much of Soto's fiction and poetry focuses on Chicano men and women of all ages, wrapped up in everyday life—and the small moments that reveal the largest truths. This humorous short story, "Seventh Grade," follows young Victor Rodriguez on his first day back at school. As he huddles with his friend Michael about how to impress their female classmates, Victor is struck by his affection for Teresa, leading to both embarrassment and possibility.

"She smiled sweetly and gathered her books. Her next class was French, same as Victor's."

NOTES

Skill:
Setting

The story is set in school at the beginning of the year. Students are back in one place after months of being apart. Seventh-graders do all kinds of things to impress their peers on the first day. Victor takes French class to be close to his crush. I bet this setting is going to lead to some excitement or problems for him.

1   On the first day of school, Victor stood in line half an hour before he came to a wobbly card table. He was handed a packet of papers and a computer card on which he listed his one elective, French. He already spoke Spanish and English, but he thought some day he might travel to France, where it was cool; not like Fresno, where summer days reached 110 degrees in the shade. There were rivers in France, and huge churches, and fair-skinned people everywhere, the way there were brown people all around Victor.

2   Besides, Teresa, a girl he had liked since they were in catechism classes[1] at Saint Theresa's, was taking French, too. With any luck they would be in the same class. Teresa is going to be my girl this year, he promised himself as he left the gym full of students in their new fall clothes. She was cute. And good in math, too, Victor thought as he walked down the hall to his homeroom. He ran into his friend, Michael Torres, by the water fountain that never turned off.

3   They shook hands, *raza*[2]-style, and jerked their heads at one another in a *saludo de vato*[3]. "How come you're making a face?" asked Victor.

4   "I ain't making a face, *ese*. This is my face." Michael said his face had changed during the summer. He had read a GQ magazine that his older brother had borrowed from the Book Mobile and noticed that the male models all had the same look on their faces. They would stand, one arm around a beautiful woman, and **scowl**. They would sit at the pool, their rippled stomachs dark with shadow, and *scowl*. They would sit at dinner tables, cool drinks in their hands, and *scowl*.

5   "I think it works," Michael said. He scowled and let his upper lip quiver. His teeth showed along with the ferocity of his soul. "Belinda Reyes walked by a while ago and looked at me," he said.

6   Victor didn't say anything, though he thought his friend looked pretty strange. They talked about recent movies, baseball, their parents, and the horrors of

---

1. **catechism classes** classes that serve as an introduction to the core principles of the Christian religion
2. **raza** (Spanish) a term referring to peoples of Hispanic descent
3. **saludo de vato** (Spanish) an informal greeting (similar to "What's up?")

picking grapes in order to buy their fall clothes. Picking grapes was like living in Siberia, except hot and more boring.

7   "What classes are you taking?" Michael said, scowling.

8   "French. How 'bout you?"

9   "Spanish. I ain't so good at it, even if I'm Mexican."

10 "I'm not either, but I'm better at it than math, that's for sure."

11 A tinny, three-beat bell propelled students to their homerooms. The two friends socked each other in the arm and went their ways, Victor thinking, man, that's weird. Michael thinks making a face makes him handsome.

12 On the way to his homeroom, Victor tried a scowl. He felt foolish, until out of the corner of his eye he saw a girl looking at him. Umm, he thought, maybe it does work. He scowled with greater **conviction.**

13 In the homeroom, roll was taken, emergency cards were passed out, and they were given a bulletin to take home to their parents. The principal, Mr. Belton, spoke over the crackling loudspeaker, welcoming the students to a new year, new experiences, and new friendships. The students squirmed in their chairs and ignored him, they were **anxious** to go to first period. Victor sat calmly, thinking of Teresa, who sat two rows away, reading a paperback novel. This would be his lucky year. She was in his homeroom, and would probably be in his English and math classes. And, of course, French.

14 The bell rang for first period, and the students herded noisily through the door. Only Teresa lingered, talking with the homeroom teacher.

15 "So you think I should talk to Mrs. Gaines?" she asked the teacher. "She would know about ballet?"

16 "She would be a good bet," the teacher said. Then added, "Or the gym teacher, Mrs. Garza."

17 Victor lingered, keeping his head down and staring at his desk. He wanted to leave when she did so he could bump into her and say something clever.

18 He watched her on the sly. As she turned to leave, he stood up and hurried to the door, where he managed to catch her eye. She smiled and said, "Hi, Victor."

19 He smiled back and said, "Yeah, that's me." His brown face blushed. Why hadn't he said, "Hi, Teresa," or "How was your summer?" or something nice?

20 As Teresa walked down the hall, Victor walked the other way, looking back, admiring how gracefully she walked, one foot in front of the other. So much

Please note that excerpts and passages in the StudySync® library and this workbook are intended as touchstones to generate interest in an author's work. The excerpts and passages do not substitute for the reading of entire texts, and StudySync® strongly recommends that students seek out and purchase the whole literary or informational work in order to experience it as the author intended. Links to online resellers are available in our digital library. In addition, complete works may be ordered through an authorized reseller by filling out and returning to StudySync® the order form enclosed in this workbook.

Reading & Writing Companion   **59**

for being in the same class, he thought. As he trudged to English, he practiced scowling.

21 In English they reviewed the parts of speech. Mr. Lucas, a portly man, waddled down the aisle, asking, "What is a noun?"

22 "A person, place, or thing," said the class in **unison.**

23 "Yes, now somebody give me an example of a person—you, Victor Rodriguez."

24 "Teresa," Victor said **automatically.** Some of the girls giggled. They knew he had a crush on Teresa. He felt himself blushing again.

25 "Correct," Mr. Lucas said. "Now provide me with a place."

26 Mr. Lucas called on a freckled kid who answered, "Teresa's house with a kitchen full of big brothers."

27 After English, Victor had math, his weakest subject. He sat in the back by the window, hoping that he would not be called on. Victor understood most of the problems, but some of the stuff looked like the teacher made it up as she went along. It was confusing, like the inside of a watch.

28 After math he had a fifteen-minute break, then social studies, and finally lunch. He bought a tuna casserole with buttered rolls, some fruit cocktail, and milk. He sat with Michael, who practiced scowling between bites.

29 Girls walked by and looked at him, "See what I mean, Vic?" Michael scowled. "They love it."

30 "Yeah, I guess so."

31 They ate slowly, Victor scanning the horizon for a glimpse of Teresa. He didn't see her. She must have brought lunch, he thought, and is eating outside. Victor scraped his plate and left Michael, who was busy scowling at a girl two tables away.

32 The small, triangle-shaped campus bustled with students talking about their new classes. Everyone was in a sunny mood. Victor hurried to the bag lunch area, where he sat down and opened his math book. He moved his lips as if he were reading, but his mind was somewhere else. He raised his eyes slowly and looked around. No Teresa.

33 He lowered his eyes, pretending to study, then looked slowly to the left. No Teresa. He turned a page in the book and stared at some math problems that scared him because he knew he would have to do them eventually. He looked at the right. Still no sign of her. He stretched out lazily in an attempt to disguise his snooping.

Copyright © BookheadEd Learning, LLC

NOTES

34 Then he saw her. She was sitting with a girlfriend under a plum tree. Victor moved to a table near her and daydreamed about taking her to a movie. When the bell sounded, Teresa looked up, and their eyes met. She smiled sweetly and gathered her books. Her next class was French, same as Victor's.

35 They were among the last students to arrive in class, so all the good desks in the back had already been taken. Victor was forced to sit near the front, a few desks away from Teresa, while Mr. Bueller wrote French words on the chalkboard. The bell rang, and Mr. Bueller wiped his hands, turned to the class, and said, "*Bonjour*.[4]"

36 "*Bonjour*," braved a few students.

37 "*Bonjour*," Victor whispered. He wondered if Teresa heard him.

38 Mr. Bueller said that if the students studied hard, at the end of the year they could go to France and be understood by the populace.

39 One kid raised his hand and asked, "What's 'populace'?"

40 "The people, the people of France."

41 Mr. Bueller asked if anyone knew French. Victor raised his hand, wanting to impress Teresa. The teacher beamed and said, "*Très bien. Parlez-vous français?*[5]"

42 Victor didn't know what to say. The teacher wet his lips and asked something else in French. The room grew silent. Victor felt all eyes staring at him. He tried to bluff his way out by making noises that sounded French.

43 "La me vave me con le grandma," he said uncertainly.

44 Mr. Bueller, wrinkling his face in curiosity, asked him to speak up.

45 Great rosebushes of red bloomed on Victor's cheeks. A river of nervous sweat ran down his palms. He felt awful. Teresa sat a few desks away, no doubt thinking he was a fool. Without looking at Mr. Bueller, Victor mumbled, 'Frenchie oh wewe gee in September."

46 Mr. Bueller asked Victor to repeat what he said.

47 "Frenchie oh wewe gee in September," Victor repeated.

48 Mr. Bueller understood that the boy didn't know French and turned away. He walked to the blackboard and pointed to the words on the board with his steel-edged ruler.

49 "*Le bateau*," he sang.

50 "*Le bateau*," the students repeated.

---

4. **bonjour** (French) hello
5. **Très bien. Parlez-vous français?** (French) Very good. Do you speak French?

51   *"Le bateau est sur l'eau,"* he sang.

52   *"Le bateau est sur l'eau."*

53   Victor was too weak from failure to join the class. He stared at the board and wished he had taken Spanish, not French. Better yet, he wished he could start his life over. He had never been so embarrassed. He bit his thumb until he tore off a sliver of skin.

54   The bell sounded for fifth period, and Victor shot out of the room, avoiding the stares of the other kids, but had to return for his math book. He looked sheepishly at the teacher, who was erasing the board, then widened his eyes in terror at Teresa who stood in front of him. "I didn't know you knew French," she said. "That was good."

55   Mr. Bueller looked at Victor, and Victor looked back. Oh please, don't say anything, Victor pleaded with his eyes. I'll wash your car, mow your lawn, walk your dog—anything! I'll be your best student, and I'll clean your erasers after school.

56   Mr. Bueller shuffled through the papers on his desk. He smiled and hummed as he sat down to work. He remembered his college years when he dated a girlfriend in borrowed cars. She thought he was rich because each time he picked her up he had a different car. It was fun until he had spent all his money on her and had to write home to his parents because he was broke.

57   Victor couldn't stand to look at Teresa. He was sweaty with shame. "Yeah, well, I picked up a few things from movies and books and stuff like that." They left the class together. Teresa asked him if he would help her with her French.

58   "Sure, anytime," Victor said.

59   "I won't be bothering you, will I?"

60   "Oh no, I like being bothered."

61   *"Bonjour."* Teresa said, leaving him outside her next class. She smiled and pushed wisps of hair from her face.

62   "Yeah, right, *bonjour,*" Victor said. He turned and headed to his class. The rosebuds of shame on his face became bouquets of love. Teresa is a great girl, he thought. And Mr. Bueller is a good guy.

63   He raced to metal shop. After metal shop there was biology, and after biology a long sprint to the public library, where he checked out three French textbooks.

64   He was going to like seventh grade.

First Read

Read "Seventh Grade." After you read, complete the Think Questions below.

☁ THINK QUESTIONS

1. What decision does Victor make on the first day of seventh grade, and why does he make it? Cite textual evidence from the selection to support your answer.

2. Why does Michael believe that "scowling" will impress his female classmates? How does Victor react to his friend's idea? Cite textual evidence in your response.

3. Why does Victor pretend that he already knows how to speak French? Does he succeed in achieving his goal? Why or why not? Cite textual evidence from the selection to support your answer.

4. Find the word **anxious** in paragraph 13 of "Seventh Grade." Use context clues in the surrounding sentences, as well as the sentence in which the word appears, to determine the word's meaning. Write your definition here, and identify clues that helped you figure out its meaning.

5. Use context clues to determine the meaning of **automatically** as it is used in paragraph 24 in "Seventh Grade." Write your definition here, and identify clues that helped you figure out the meaning. Then check the meaning in a dictionary.

Skill:
Setting

Use the Checklist to analyze Setting in "Seventh Grade." Refer to the sample student annotations about Setting in the text.

••• CHECKLIST FOR SETTING

In order to identify how particular elements of a story or drama interact, note the following:

✓ the setting of the story

✓ note the characters in the text and the problems they face

✓ how the events of the plot unfold, and how that affects the setting and characters

✓ how the setting shapes the characters and plot

To analyze how particular elements of a story or drama interact, consider the following questions as a guide:

✓ What is the setting(s) of the story?

✓ How does the setting affect the characters and plot?

✓ How does the setting contribute to or help solve the conflict?

✓ How do the characters' decisions affect the plot and setting(s)?

Skill:
Setting

Reread paragraphs 13–19 of "Seventh Grade." Then, using the Checklist on the previous page, answer the multiple-choice questions below.

⟳ YOUR TURN

1. The description of Victor's homeroom in paragraph 13 suggests that —

   ○ A. the school year will be difficult for the students.
   ○ B. the school year will take a dangerous turn.
   ○ C. the school year will be similar to the previous year.
   ○ D. the school year will bring new opportunities for Victor.

2. How does the setting affect Victor's plan to have a conversation with Teresa in paragraph 17?

   ○ A. Their shared class gives Victor an idea of what to say to Teresa.
   ○ B. Like Teresa, Victor is interested in taking ballet.
   ○ C. Their teacher's presence makes Victor feel self-conscious.
   ○ D. Victor knows exactly what he wants to say to Teresa.

3. What does Victor's reaction to his conversation with Teresa, in paragraph 19, reveal about his character?

   ○ A. Victor should have scowled at Teresa instead of trying to talk to her.
   ○ B. Victor realizes he should have been more kind and honest with Teresa.
   ○ C. Victor should have waited until French class to talk to Teresa.
   ○ D. Victor thinks he will never be able to impress Teresa.

Please note that excerpts and passages in the StudySync® library and this workbook are intended as touchstones to generate interest in an author's work. The excerpts and passages do not substitute for the reading of entire texts, and StudySync® strongly recommends that students seek out and purchase the whole literary or informational work in order to experience it as the author intended. Links to online resellers are available in our digital library. In addition, complete works may be ordered through an authorized reseller by filling out and returning to StudySync® the order form enclosed in this workbook.

Reading & Writing Companion   65

Skill:
Compare and Contrast

Use the Checklist to analyze Compare and Contrast in "Seventh Grade."

••• CHECKLIST FOR COMPARE AND CONTRAST

In order to compare and contrast texts within and across different forms and genres, do the following:

✓ first, choose two or more texts with similar subjects or topic

✓ next, identify the qualities or characteristics of each form or genre

✓ then highlight and annotate each text looking for

- ways in which the texts are similar and different

- how each author approaches the topic or subject

- the words and actions of characters or individuals or important events

- textual evidence that reveals each text's theme or central message

To compare and contrast texts within and across different forms or genres, consider the following questions:

✓ In what ways do the texts I have chosen have similar subjects or topics?

✓ What are the qualities or characteristics of each form or genre?

✓ How are the texts similar and different?

✓ How does each author approach the topic or subject?

✓ Have I looked at the words and actions of characters or individuals? What are the important events that occur in each text?

✓ What is the theme or central message of each text?

COMPARE AND CONTRAST

sync•skills

Skill:
Compare and Contrast

Reread paragraphs 7 and 8 and 11 and 12 of "Seventh Grade" and paragraphs 4 and 5 and 7–9 of *Stargirl*. Then, using the Checklist on the previous page, complete the chart below to compare and contrast the passages.

↻ YOUR TURN

	Observation Options
A	Victor copies Michael's scowling to see if it can make him appear more handsome.
B	Stargirl sings "Happy Birthday" to Alan Ferko in the cafeteria.
C	Michael scowls to make himself look handsome.
D	Kevin says Stargirl's strange behavior will cause problems for her in school.
E	Other characters notice and have reactions to the unusual behavior.
F	Characters demonstrate unusual behavior.

"Seventh Grade"	Both	*Stargirl*

Please note that excerpts and passages in the StudySync® library and this workbook are intended as touchstones to generate interest in an author's work. The excerpts and passages do not substitute for the reading of entire texts, and StudySync® strongly recommends that students seek out and purchase the whole literary or informational work in order to experience it as the author intended. Links to online resellers are available in our digital library. In addition, complete works may be ordered through an authorized reseller by filling out and returning to StudySync® the order form enclosed in this workbook.

Reading & Writing
Companion

67

Close Read

Reread "Seventh Grade." As you reread, complete the Skills Focus questions below. Then use your answers and annotations from the questions to help you complete the Write activity.

Copyright © BookheadEd Learning, LLC

◎ SKILLS FOCUS

1. Identify details that show how Victor reveals himself during English class. Explain why you think he is not behaving in a more cautious and guarded manner.

2. Identify evidence that describes how Victor feels during French class. How do his peers and the setting affect him?

3. What lesson is learned in this text about being a young person in school?

4. Both *Stargirl* and "Seventh Grade" deal with potentially embarrassing situations in a school setting. Identify one of those situations in "Seventh Grade." Explain the cause and the outcome of the situation. Then describe how it compares and contrasts with the content in *Stargirl*.

5. Identify textual evidence that shows how Victor is able to avoid a conflict with Mr. Bueller in front of Teresa. Describe how Mr. Bueller is similar to Victor.

✎ WRITE

COMPARE AND CONTRAST: *Stargirl* takes place in high school, while "Seventh Grade" is set in middle school. Write a short response in which you choose two characters, one from each work of fiction, and compare and contrast how the school setting creates conflict for the characters. Use evidence from each text to support your analysis.

The Monsters Are Due on Maple Street

DRAMA
Rod Serling
1960

Introduction

Rod Serling (1924–1975), creator of the science fiction television series *The Twilight Zone,* was one of the most popular writers in television history. One of his best-known scripts, "The Monsters Are Due on Maple Street" is about the reaction of a group of neighbors to a mysterious shadow that passes over their suburban street. After homes lose power and car batteries go dead, a neighborhood boy suggests that alien invaders in human form are responsible for the strange events. As power flickers back on here and there, neighbors become increasingly alarmed, turning their suspicions against one another.

"... maybe one family isn't what we think they are."

**Skill:
Plot**

This event must be the inciting incident. Goodman's car is the only one in the neighborhood that works, which causes a crowd to approach him. Goodman is upset and starts to defend himself. The power outage has turned this typical town into a tense mob.

Steve seems to be joking about monsters, but then things get serious. He suggests that Goodman and his family are different or hiding something. It seems like more conflict is about to start!

from Act I

1 GOODMAN. Wait a minute now. You keep your distance—all of you. So I've got a car that starts by itself—well, that's a freak thing, I admit it. But does that make me some kind of a criminal or something? I don't know why the car works—it just does!

2 [*This stops the crowd momentarily and now* GOODMAN, *still backing away, goes toward his front porch. He goes up the steps and then stops to stand facing the mob.*

3 *We see a long shot of* STEVE *as he comes through the crowd.*]

4 STEVE. [*Quietly.*] We're all on a monster kick, Les. Seems that the general impression holds that maybe one family isn't what we think they are. Monsters from outer space or something. Different than us. Fifth columnists[1] from the vast beyond. [*He chuckles.*] You know anybody that might fit that description around here on Maple Street?

5 GOODMAN. What is this, a gag or something? This a practical joke or something?

6 [*We see a close-up of the porch light as it suddenly goes out. There's a murmur from the group.*]

7 GOODMAN. Now I suppose that's supposed to incriminate me! The light goes on and off. That really does it, doesn't it? [*He look around the faces of the people.*] I just don't understand this— [*He wets his lips, looking from face to face.*] Look, you all know me. We've lived here five years. Right in this house. We're no different from any of the rest of you! We're no different at all. Really . . . this whole thing is just . . . just weird—

---

1. **Fifth columnists** a term commonly used in the 20th century for any secretive group of operators attempting to undermine a larger group from within

8 WOMAN. Well, if that's the case, Les Goodman, explain why— [*She stops suddenly, clamping her mouth shut.*]

9 GOODMAN. [*Softly.*] Explain what?

10 STEVE. [*Interjecting*] Look, let's forget this—

11 CHARLIE. [*Overlapping him.*] Go ahead, let her talk. What about it? Explain what?

12 WOMAN. [*A little **reluctantly**.*] Well . . . sometimes I go to bed late at night. A couple of times . . . a couple of times I'd come out on the porch and I'd see Mr. Goodman here in the wee hours of the morning standing out in front of his house . . . looking up at the sky. [*She looks around the circle of faces.*] That's right, looking up at the sky as if . . . as if he were waiting for something. [*A pause.*] As if he were looking for something.

13 [*There's a murmur of reaction from the crowd again.*

14 *We cut suddenly to a group shot. As* GOODMAN *starts toward them, they back away frightened.*]

15 GOODMAN. You know really . . . this is for laughs. You know what I'm guilty of? [*He laughs.*] I'm guilty of **insomnia.** Now what's the penalty for insomnia? [*At this point the laugh, the humor, leaves his voice.*] Did you hear what I said? I said it was insomnia. [*A pause as he looks around, then shouts.*] I said it was insomnia! You fools. You scared, frightened rabbits, you. You're sick people, do you know that? You're sick people—all of you! And you don't even know what you're starting because let me tell you . . . let me tell you—this thing you're starting—that should frighten you. As God is my witness . . . you're letting something begin here that's a nightmare!

from Act II

16 CHARLIE'S VOICE. [*Shrill, from across the street.*] You best watch who you're seen with, Steve! Until we get this all straightened out, you ain't exactly above suspicion yourself.

17 STEVE. [*Whirling around toward him.*] Or you, Charlie. Or any of us, it seems. From age eight on up.

18 WOMAN. What I'd like to know is—what are we gonna do? Just stand around here all night?

Please note that excerpts and passages in the StudySync® library and this workbook are intended as touchstones to generate interest in an author's work. The excerpts and passages do not substitute for the reading of entire texts, and StudySync® strongly recommends that students seek out and purchase the whole literary or informational work in order to experience it as the author intended. Links to online resellers are available in our digital library. In addition, complete works may be ordered through an authorized reseller by filling out and returning to StudySync® the order form enclosed in this workbook.

Reading & Writing Companion 71

Skill: Dramatic Elements and Structure

Steve is yelling at the other characters. The conflict is getting worse and the suspense is building.

There's a lot of quick back-and-forth dialogue here. It feels hostile. I think this whole story is about to end in tragedy.

Skill: Plot

Steve is getting frustrated and suggests getting rid of suspects with a firing squad! Then, Don accuses Steve of doing things in his basement. The neighbors are turning on one another because they are scared. This story is moving so quickly!

19   CHARLIE. There's nothin' else we can do! [*He turns back looking toward* STEVE *and* GOODMAN *again.*] One of 'em'll tip their hand[2]. They got to.

20   STEVE [*Raising his voice.*] There's something you can do, Charlie. You could go home and keep your mouth shut. You could quit strutting around like a self-appointed hanging judge and just climb into bed and forget it.

21   CHARLIE. You sound real **anxious** to have that happen, Steve. I think we better keep our eye on you too!

22   DON. [*As if he were taking the bit in his teeth, takes a hesitant step to the front.*] I think everything might as well come out now. [*He turns toward* STEVE.] Your wife's done plenty of talking, Steve, about how odd you are!

23   CHARLIE. [*Picking this up, his eyes widening.*] Go ahead, tell us what she's said. [*We see a long shot of* STEVE *as he walks toward them from across the street.*]

24   STEVE. Go ahead, what's my wife said? Let's get it all out. Let's pick out every **idiosyncrasy** of every man, woman, and child on the street. And then we might as well set up some kind of kangaroo court[3]. How about a firing squad[4] at dawn, Charlie, so we can get rid of all the suspects? Narrow them down. Make it easier for you.

25   DON. There's no need gettin' so upset, Steve. It's just that . . . well . . . Myra's talked about how there's been plenty of nights you spent hours down in your basement workin' on some kind of radio or something. Well, none of us have ever seen that radio—

26   [*By this time* STEVE *has reached the group. He stands there defiantly close to them.*]

27   CHARLIE. Go ahead, Steve. What kind of "radio set" you workin' on? I never seen it. Neither has anyone else. Who you talk to on that radio set? And who talks to you?

28   STEVE. I'm surprised at you, Charlie. How come you're so **dense** all of a sudden? [*A pause.*] Who do I talk to? I talk to monsters from outer space. I talk to three-headed green men who fly over here in what look like meteors.

29   [STEVE'S *wife steps down from the porch, bites her lip, calls out.*]

2. **tip their hand** an expression in cards or poker for unintentionally revealing one's secrets or intentions
3. **kangaroo court** a term for an unofficial or mob-like court that operates outside of basic judicial principles
4. **firing squad** a method of execution in which a person is shot repeatedly from close range

30 MRS. BRAND. Steve! Steve, please. [*Then looking around, frightened, she walks toward the group.*] It's just a ham radio[5] set, that's all. I bought him a book on it myself. It's just a ham radio set. A lot of people have them. I can show it to you. It's right down in the basement.

31 STEVE. [*whirls around toward her*] Show them nothing! If they want to look inside our house—let them get a search warrant.

32 CHARLIE. Look, buddy. You can't afford to—

33 STEVE. [*Interrupting*] Charlie, don't tell me what I can afford! And stop telling me who's dangerous and who isn't and who's safe and who's a menace. [*He turns to the group and shouts.*] And you're with him, too—all of you! You're standing here all set to crucify—all set to find a scapegoat—all desperate to point some kind of finger at a neighbor! Well now look, friends, the only thing that's gonna happen is that we'll eat each other up alive—

34 [*He stops abruptly as CHARLIE suddenly grabs his arm.*]

35 CHARLIE. [*In a hushed voice*] That's not the only thing that can happen to us.

36 [*Cut to a long shot looking down the street. A figure has suddenly materialized in the gloom and in the silence we can hear the clickety-clack of slow, measured footsteps on concrete as the figure walks slowly toward them. One of the women lets out a stifled cry. The young mother grabs her boy as do a couple of others.*]

37 TOMMY. [*Shouting, frightened.*] It's the monster! It's the monster!

38 [*Another woman lets out a wail and the people fall back in a group, staring toward the darkness and the approaching figure.*

39 *We see a medium group shot of the people as they stand in the shadows watching. DON MARTIN joins them, carrying a shotgun. He holds it up.*]

40 DON. We may need this.

41 STEVE. A shotgun? [*He pulls it out of DON'S hand.*] Good Lord—will anybody think a thought around here? Will you people wise up? What good would a shotgun do against—

42 [*Now CHARLIE pulls the gun from STEVE's hand.*]

43 CHARLIE. No more talk, Steve. You're going to talk us into a grave! You'd let whatever's out there walk right over us, wouldn't yuh? Well, some of us won't!

---

5. **ham radio set** an amateur radio setup typically used for broadcasting or receiving messages

44 [*He swings the gun around to point it toward the sidewalk. The dark figure continues to walk toward them.*]

45 *The group stands there, fearful,* **apprehensive**, *mothers clutching children, men standing in front of wives.* CHARLIE *slowly raises the gun. As the figure gets closer and closer he suddenly pulls the trigger. The sound of it explodes in the stillness. There is a long angle shot looking down the figure, who suddenly lets out a small cry, stumbles forward onto his knees and then falls forward on his face.* DON, CHARLIE, *and* STEVE *race forward over to him.* STEVE *is there first and turns the man over. Now the crowd gathers around them.*]

46 STEVE [Slowly looks up] It's Pete Van Horn.

47 DON. [*In a hushed voice.*] Pete Van Horn! He was just gonna go over to the next block to see if the power was on—

48 WOMAN. You killed him, Charlie. You shot him dead!

49 CHARLIE. [*Looks around the circle of faces, his eyes frightened, his face contorted.*] But . . . but I didn't know who he was. I certainly didn't know who he was. He comes walkin' out of the darkness—how am I supposed to know who he was? [*He grabs* STEVE.] Steve—you know why I shot! How was I supposed to know he wasn't a monster or something? [*He grabs* DON *now.*] We're all scared of the same thing, I was just tryin' to . . . trying' to protect my home, that's all! Look, all of you, that's all I was tryin' to do. [*He looks down wildly at the body.*] I didn't know it was somebody we knew! I didn't know—

50 [*There's a sudden hush and then an intake of breath. We see a medium shot of the living room window of* CHARLIE'S *house. The window is not lit, but suddenly the house lights come on behind it.*]

51 WOMAN. [*In a very hushed voice.*] Charlie. . . Charlie. . . the lights just went on in your house. Why did the lights just go on?

52 DON. What about it, Charlie? How come you're the only one with lights now?

53 GOODMAN. That's what I'd like to know.

©1960 by Rod Serling, The Monsters Are Due on Maple Street. Reproduced by permission of Carolyn Serling.

First Read

Read "The Monsters Are Due on Maple Street." After you read, complete the Think Questions below.

1. Why are the Maple Street neighbors suspicious of Les Goodman? Respond with direct evidence or inferences from the text.

2. Why are the Maple Street neighbors suspicious of Steve? Include evidence from the text to support your response.

3. Why does Tommy shout, "It's the monster! It's the monster!"? Support your answer with textual evidence.

4. Use context clues to determine the meaning of **insomnia** as it is used in paragraph 15 of "The Monsters Are Due on Maple Street." Write your definition here and identify clues that helped you figure out the meaning. Then check the meaning in a dictionary.

5. Find the word **dense** in paragraph 28 of "The Monsters Are Due on Maple Street." Use context clues in the surrounding sentences, as well as the sentence in which the word appears, to determine the word's meaning. Write your definition here and identify clues that helped you figure out the meaning.

Please note that excerpts and passages in the StudySync® library and this workbook are intended as touchstones to generate interest in an author's work. The excerpts and passages do not substitute for the reading of entire texts, and StudySync® strongly recommends that students seek out and purchase the whole literary or informational work in order to experience it as the author intended. Links to online resellers are available in our digital library. In addition, complete works may be ordered through an authorized reseller by filling out and returning to StudySync® the order form enclosed in this workbook.

Reading & Writing Companion 75

PLOT

Skill: Plot

Use the Checklist to analyze Plot in "The Monsters Are Due on Maple Street." Refer to the sample student annotations about Plot in the text.

••• CHECKLIST FOR PLOT

In order to identify particular elements of a story or drama, note the following:

- ✓ setting details

- ✓ character details, including their thoughts, actions, and descriptions

- ✓ notable incidents or events in the plot

- ✓ characters or setting details that may have caused an event to occur

- ✓ the central conflict and the characters who are involved

- ✓ dialogue between or among characters

- ✓ instances when setting interferes with a character's motivations

To analyze how particular elements of a story or drama interact, consider the following questions:

- ✓ How do the events of the plot unfold in the story?

- ✓ How do characters respond or change as the plot advances?

- ✓ How does the setting shape the characters or the plot?

- ✓ How does a particular scene in the story contribute to the development of the plot?

PLOT

Skill:
Plot

Reread paragraphs 6–15 of "The Monsters Are Due on Maple Street." Then, using the Checklist on the previous page, answer the multiple-choice questions below.

⟳ YOUR TURN

1. This question has two parts. First, answer Part A. Then, answer Part B.

   Part A: What effect do the woman's words and actions in paragraph 12 have on the plot and conflict?

   ○ A. The woman's words and actions cause Steve to interject.

   ○ B. The woman's words and actions cause the crowd to laugh at Goodman.

   ○ C. The woman's words and actions cause confusion.

   ○ D. The woman's words and actions cause the crowd to fear Goodman.

   Part B: Which piece of evidence best supports your answer to Part A?

   ○ A. *"We cut suddenly to a group shot. As* GOODMAN *starts toward them, they back away frightened."*

   ○ B. "You know really . . . this is for laughs. You know what I'm guilty of? [*He laughs.*]"

   ○ C. "STEVE. [*Interjecting*] Look, let's forget this—"

   ○ D. "[*A little reluctantly.*] Well . . . sometimes I go to bed late at night."

2. How does Goodman's reaction in paragraph 7 advance the conflict of the story?

   ○ A. Goodman feels misunderstood. His body language reflects sadness, which creates tension.

   ○ B. Goodman is upset. His body language reflects fear and anxiousness, which creates tension.

   ○ C. Goodman is telling the crowd that he is not to blame. He does not understand their accusations, which creates tension.

   ○ D. Goodman is laughing and looking at the crowd. His body language reflects fear, which creates tension.

Skill: Dramatic Elements and Structure

Use the Checklist to analyze Dramatic Elements and Structure in "The Monsters Are Due on Maple Street." Refer to the sample student annotations about Dramatic Elements and Structure in the text.

••• CHECKLIST FOR DRAMATIC ELEMENTS AND STRUCTURE

In order to identify the dramatic elements and structure of a drama, note the following:

- ✓ the form of the drama, such as

  - • comedy, or a drama that has a happy ending
  - • tragedy, or a drama that ends in death or sadness

- ✓ how the drama's structure, including its acts and scenes, advances the plot

- ✓ the setting of the play and how it affects the characters and plot

- ✓ the language of the play as spoken by characters

- ✓ the information in stage directions, including lighting, sound, and set, as well as details about characters, including exits and entrances

To analyze how a drama's form or structure contributes to its meaning, consider the following questions:

- ✓ How does the use of dialogue and stage directions reveal aspects of the characters and contribute to the drama's meaning?

- ✓ How is each act or scene structured? How do characters enter and leave, how do they speak to each other, and what happens as a result?

- ✓ How do specific acts or scenes develop the plot or advance the conflict?

- ✓ How does the drama's form contribute to the theme or message?

Skill: Dramatic Elements and Structure

Reread paragraphs 48–53 of "The Monsters Are Due on Maple Street." Then, using the Checklist on the previous page, answer the multiple-choice questions below.

♻ YOUR TURN

1. This question has two parts. First, answer Part A. Then, answer Part B.

    Part A: What does Charlie's dialogue in paragraph 49 suggest about the drama's deeper message or meaning?

    ○ A. It explains why Charlie shot Pete Van Horn.

    ○ B. It suggests a message about the importance of protecting family.

    ○ C. It suggests a message about how people fear the unknown.

    ○ D. It suggests that Charlie is an evil character.

    Part B: Select evidence from paragraph 49 that best supports your answer in Part A.

    ○ A. "How was I supposed to know he wasn't a monster or something? [*He grabs* DON *now.*] We're all scared of the same thing . . ."

    ○ B. "I was just tryin' to . . . trying to protect my home, that's all!"

    ○ C. "[*Looks around the circle of faces, his eyes frightened, his face contorted.*]"

    ○ D. "[*He looks down wildly at the body.*] I didn't know it was somebody we knew! I didn't know—"

2. The stage directions in paragraph 49 show that Charlie feels —

    ○ A. confusion

    ○ B. panic

    ○ C. regret

    ○ D. anger

Close Read

Reread "The Monsters Are Due on Maple Street." As you reread, complete the Skills Focus questions below. Then use your answers and annotations from the questions to help you complete the Write activity.

🎯 SKILLS FOCUS

1. The character Charlie is the most accusatory and paranoid of the neighbors. Identify dialogue and/or stage directions that show this, and explain how his qualities affect the other people in the neighborhood or events in the plot.

2. Steve is portrayed as a more rational character than the other neighbors. Identify dialogue and/or stage directions that support Steve's characterization as a level-headed person, and explain why this makes him the "hero" of the story.

3. Identify textual evidence that shows how the characters scapegoat or blame each other. What does this evidence reveal about the main conflict of the drama?

4. Identify and highlight the turning point and unfortunate resolution. Explain how those events contribute to the overall meaning or theme of the play.

5. Explain what message is suggested about society and conflict. Cite textual evidence to support your response.

✏️ WRITE

LITERARY ANALYSIS: How does Rod Serling use plot and dramatic elements and structure to convey a message about conflict in society? Write a short response in which you answer this question. Specify one message, and explain how plot and dramatic elements and structure help to convey it. Use textual evidence to support your answer.

The Skin I'm In

FICTION
Sharon G. Flake
1998

Introduction

American young adult literature author Sharon G. Flake (b. 1955) tells evocative stories that dig deep into the intersection between race and gender in late 20th- and early 21st-century America. Her first and most widely-known novel, *The Skin I'm In*, tells the story of 13-year old Maleeka Madison, who is mired in all of the trials and tribulations of teenage self-discovery. On top of this, Maleeka faces yet another challenge—finding self-love and self-acceptance in her dark skin and African features in a world that seems to devalue both.

"Everybody starts talking at once, asking her questions. Miss Saunders answers 'em all."

Skill:
Point of View

The narrator uses the pronoun "I," so Maleeka must be the narrator and is telling the story. She's only revealing her thoughts. It must be a limited point of view.

It seems as if Maleeka's face says something funny or bad to the world, because she laughs when she reads the prompt. Maybe Maleeka doesn't like the way she looks.

Chapter 4

1   When the second bell rings, I run to Miss Saunders's class like somebody set my shoes on fire. It don't help none. Soon as I walk in, I know I'm in trouble. Everybody's got their head down and they're writing. Miss Saunders nods for me to take out paper and get to my seat. "What does your face say to the world?" is written on the blackboard. I laugh, only it comes out like a sneeze through my nose.

2   Miss Saunders is collecting papers before I even got three sentences down on my paper. She knows I just slipped in. That don't stop her from asking me to answer the question, though.

3   "My face?" I point to myself.

4   "Maleeka's face says she needs to stay out of the sun," Larry Baker says, covering his face with a book.

5   "Naw, man," Gregory Williams says. "Maleeka's face says, Black is beautiful."

6   Miss Saunders don't say nothing. She just crosses her arms and gets real quiet. She don't care if she done embarrassed me again.

7   "Maleeka?" she says.

8   I don't answer her question or look her way. I eye the ceiling and count the blobs of gum hanging there like pretty-colored snot.

9   "Can anybody else tell me what their face says to the world?" Miss Saunders asks. Her gold bangles[1] jingle while she makes her way around the room. Miss Saunders is as quiet as a tiger sneaking up on its **supper.** It's them Italian leather shoes of hers, I guess.

10   Malcolm Moore raises his hand. Malcolm is fine. He's got long, straight hair. Skin the color of a butterscotch milkshake. Gray, sad eyes. He's half and

---

1. **bangles** bracelets or anklets worn as accessories

half—got a white dad and a black momma. He's lucky. He looks more like his dad than his mom.

11 "My face says I'm all that," Malcolm says, rubbing them six chin hairs he calls a beard. "It says to the homies, I'm the doctor of love. I'm good to ya and good for ya."

12 Everybody laughs. Faith, his girlfriend of the week, throws a pencil across the room. It bounces off the back of his chair, and lands between his big feet. Miss Saunders gives Faith the eye, letting her know to cut it out.

13 When the laughing's done, hands go up. Some folks say funny stuff about their face. Others is real serious. Like John-John. He says his face tells the world he doesn't take no stuff. That people better respect him, or else. I never seen nothing like that in John-John's face. He looks more scared than mean. I guess there ain't no **accounting** for what folks see in their own mirrors.

14 When Miss Saunders asks, "What's my face say?" don't nobody say nothing.

15 "Don't get all closed-mouthed, now," she says. "I hear you whispering in the hall. Laughing at me." She walks the aisles again. She stops by me and sits on my desk. "Faces say more than you think. Even mine. Don't be shy. Say what's on your mind."

16 My hand goes up. I figure she's embarrassed me twice since she's been here this week. Now it's her turn. "Not to hurt your feelings...but...I think it says, you know, you're a freak."

17 "That's cold," Chrystal Johnson says, frowning.

18 Miss Saunders put her hands up to her chin like she's praying. She gets up and walks the room, pacing. We don't say nothing. We just listen to the clock tick. **Shuffle** our papers. Watch for some reaction from Miss Saunders.

19 "Freak," she says. "I saw that too when I was young." Then she explains how she was born with her face like that. How when she was little her parents had the preacher pray over it, the old folks work their roots on it, and her grandmother use some **concoction** to change the color of that **blotch** on her cheek so it matched the rest of her skin. Miss Saunders says none of the stuff she tried on her face worked. So she finally figured she'd better love what God gave her.

20 "Liking myself didn't come overnight," she says, "I took a lot of wrong turns to find out who I really was. You will, too." Everybody starts talking at once, asking her questions. Miss Saunders answers 'em all. Some kids even go up to her face and stare and point. She lets them do it too, like she's proud of her face or something.

Skill:
Point of View

Miss Saunders's actions and dialogue show that she has a lot of self-confidence! I can tell from Maleeka's thoughts that she still has a contrasting view. Maleeka seems surprised that the teacher is proud of her appearance.

21   Then Miss Saunders comes over to my desk and stares down at me. "It takes a long time to accept yourself for who you are. To see the poetry in your walk," she says, shaking her hips like she's doing some African dance. Kids bust out laughing. "To look in the mirror and like what you see, even when it doesn't look like anybody else's idea of beauty."

Excerpted from *The Skin I'm In* by Sharon G. Flake, published by Hyperion Books.

First Read

Read *The Skin I'm In*. After you read, complete the Think Questions below.

1. What is it about Maleeka's appearance that makes Larry Baker say she needs to stay out of the sun? Why is this significant to the conversation Miss Saunders is having with the class?

2. What does John-John say his face says to the world? Why doesn't Maleeka believe him?

3. What is it about Miss Saunders's appearance that the students primarily make fun of? Explain why you believe they make fun of it.

4. Read the following dictionary definition:

   account
   ac•count /əˈkount/

   noun

   1. a detailed record of money paid and received
   2. a particular description or report of something that happened

   verb

   1. to form or make up a part of something
   2. to offer a reason or explanation for something

   Which definition most closely matches the meaning of **accounting** as it is used in paragraph 13? Write the correct definition of *accounting* here and explain how you figured out the correct meaning.

5. Miss Saunders says that her grandmother tried to use a **concoction** on her face. Based on context clues, what do you think the word *concoction* means? Write your best definition of *concoction* here and explain how you figured it out.

Skill:
Point of View

Use the Checklist to analyze Point of View in *The Skin I'm In*. Refer to the sample student annotations about Point of View in the text.

In order to identify different points of view, note the following:

✓ the speaker(s) or narrator(s)

✓ how much the narrator(s) or speaker(s) knows and reveals

✓ how the author develops different points of view, through dialogue or story events

✓ what the narrator(s) or speaker(s) says or does that reveals how they feel about other characters and events

✓ how the point of view of the narrator(s) or speaker(s) contrasts with the points of view of other characters in the narrative

To analyze how an author develops and contrasts different points of view of different characters or narrators in a text, consider the following questions:

✓ Is the narrator or speaker objective, or does he or she mislead the reader? How?

✓ What is the narrator's or the speaker's point of view?

- Is the narrator or speaker "all-knowing," or omniscient?

- Is the narrator or speaker limited to revealing the thoughts and feelings of one character?

- Are there multiple narrators or speakers telling the story?

✓ How does the narrator or speaker reveal his or her thoughts about the events or the other characters in the story or poem? How do the narrator's experiences or cultural background affect his or her thoughts?

✓ How does the author reveal different points of view in the story?

✓ How do these different points of view compare and contrast with one another?

Skill:
Point of View

Reread paragraphs 16–19 of *The Skin I'm In*. Then, using the Checklist on the previous page, answer the multiple-choice questions below.

⟳ YOUR TURN

1. This question has two parts. First, answer Part A. Then, answer Part B.

   Part A: What is Miss Saunders's point of view about loving her appearance?

   ○ A. Miss Saunders used to hate her appearance, but she learned to love it.
   ○ B. Miss Saunders used to love her appearance, but now she hates it.
   ○ C. Miss Saunders hates her appearance because people call her a freak.
   ○ D. Miss Saunders has always loved her appearance and has never tried to change it.

   Part B: Which line from the passage supports your answer in Part A?

   ○ A. I figure she's embarrassed me twice since she's been here this week. Now it's her turn.
   ○ B. Miss Saunders put her hands up to her chin like she's praying.
   ○ C. Then she explains how she was born with her face like that.
   ○ D. So she finally figured she'd better love what God gave her.

2. Which sentence from the story lets you know this is limited point of view?

   ○ A. Then she explains how she was born with her face like that.
   ○ B. "I saw that too when I was young."
   ○ C. My hand goes up. I figure she's embarrassed me twice since she's been here this week.
   ○ D. "That's cold," Chrystal Johnson says, frowning.

Please note that excerpts and passages in the StudySync® library and this workbook are intended as touchstones to generate interest in an author's work. The excerpts and passages do not substitute for the reading of entire texts, and StudySync® strongly recommends that students seek out and purchase the whole literary or informational work in order to experience it as the author intended. Links to online resellers are available in our digital library. In addition, complete works may be ordered through an authorized reseller by filling out and returning to StudySync® the order form enclosed in this workbook.

Reading & Writing Companion   **87**

THE SKIN I'M IN

Close Read

Reread *The Skin I'm In*. As you reread, complete the Skills Focus questions below. Then use your answers and annotations from the questions to help you complete the Write activity.

◎ SKILLS FOCUS

1. How do the first few paragraphs indicate that the narrator is using a limited point of view? Highlight evidence from the text, and make annotations to support your explanation.

2. Identify dialogue and actions that reveal Maleeka's classmates' views on self-love and their own appearances.

3. Identify dialogue and actions that reveal Miss Saunders's point of view on self-acceptance and self-love. Explain why this point of view might be surprising to some of her students.

4. Identify evidence of how Miss Saunders's point of view about her appearance changed over time and what led to that change. What lesson or theme is suggested by Miss Saunders's change?

5. What does Maleeka do, say, or think to reveal her point of view on self-acceptance and self-love? How is Maleeka's point of view in conflict with her classmates' or her teacher's points of view?

✏ WRITE

LITERARY ANALYSIS: In this excerpt of *The Skin I'm In*, Maleeka confronts how she feels about herself while learning about others' views on self-love and self-acceptance. How is Maleeka's point of view different from those of the other students and Miss Saunders? How does the author reveal and contrast these views? Use textual evidence, including character dialogue, actions, and thoughts, to support your response.

Mad

POETRY
Naomi Shihab Nye
2000

Introduction

The author of numerous books and collections of poetry, contemporary Arab American poet Naomi Shihab Nye (b. 1952) explores the landscape of the human spirit through allegory, transformative imagery, and the lens of her unique cultural perspective. In this poem, "Mad," Nye sheds new light on the emotional bonds between mothers and their children.

"It gets cold at night on the moon."

1   I got mad at my mother

2   so I flew to the moon.

3   I could still see our house

4   so little in the distance

5   with its **pointed** roof.

6   My mother stood in the front yard

7   like a pin dot

8   searching for me.

9   She **looked** left and right for me.

10   She looked deep and far.

11   Then I whistled and she **tipped** her head.

12   It gets cold at night on the moon.

13   My mother sent up a silver **thread**

14   for me to slide down on.

15   She knows me so well.

16   She knows I like silver.

TEXT COPYRIGHT ©2000 BY NAOMI SHIHAB NYE. GREENWILLOW BOOKS.
Used by permission of HarperCollins Publishers.

WRITE

PERSONAL RESPONSE: This poem is about making up with a loved one after getting angry. Write about a time you made up with a family member or friend after a disagreement or fight. What in the poem reminds you of your disagreement or fight? Was anything different? Support your response with evidence from the text.

Please note that excerpts and passages in the StudySync® library and this workbook are intended as touchstones to generate interest in an author's work. The excerpts and passages do not substitute for the reading of entire texts, and StudySync® strongly recommends that students seek out and purchase the whole literary or informational work in order to experience it as the author intended. Links to online resellers are available in our digital library. In addition, complete works may be ordered through an authorized reseller by filling out and returning to StudySync® the order form enclosed in this workbook.

Reading & Writing Companion

91

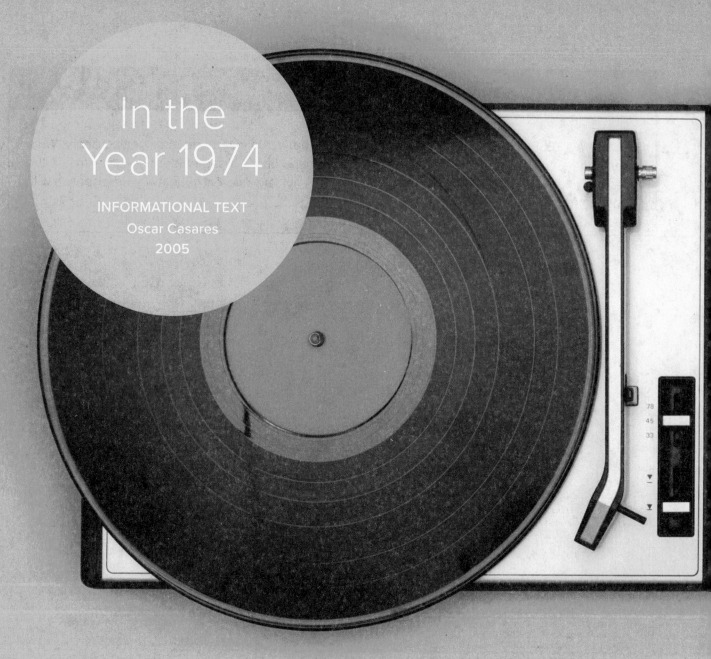

In the Year 1974

INFORMATIONAL TEXT
Oscar Casares
2005

Introduction

study tv

Critically acclaimed author Oscar Casares (b. 1964) is a Texas native who teaches creative writing at the University of Texas at Austin. "In the Year 1974" recalls the summer when ten-year-old Oscar "discovered the world," as he describes it in hindsight. With his aging parents firmly set in their ways, young Oscar is sheltered from the world until he takes a trip to visit his older sister in Austin, where he finds an entirely unfamiliar and exciting world. Upon returning home to Brownsville, he's eager to share a thrilling culinary discovery with his parents—the pepperoni pizza.

"It was as though I'd crossed into another world, one my parents never knew existed."

1   It was only a few months after I turned ten that I discovered the world. Before this time, I had spent most of my life in Brownsville, at the southernmost point of not only Texas but also the continental United States. One of our few excursions from home was driving across the international bridge to Matamoros[1] so I could get what my father considered a "decent" haircut, by which he meant a very short haircut that cost less than a dollar, tip included. The barber would bring out a special cushioned board and lay it across the armrests of the chair. Then I'd climb up and sit still for my haircut, waiting patiently during those times when the barber had to stop and make a *ss-ss-ss* sound at a pretty girl passing in front of his shop. Afterward, my father and I would walk to Plaza Hidalgo, where he could get his boots shined and I could buy a candy from the man standing on the corner with the big glass case. I always went for the calabaza candies, which were made of a rich pumpkin and looked like jewels extracted from deep within the earth.

2   As far south as we were, I knew there was a world beyond Brownsville because my sister and two brothers had left town years earlier. When we drove to Houston to visit my brothers, one of them would take my mother to the mall so she could shop at the big department stores we didn't have at Amigoland Mall. After shopping, we'd go back to my brother's house, eat, rest, maybe eat again, maybe watch TV, and then go to sleep. A couple of days later, we'd get in the car and drive back to Brownsville. My parents weren't interested in seeing Houston. Houston was a big city with a lot of freeways where they were bound to get lost, and did, every time we visited, which was how I ended up seeing more of the city. My parents traveled to Houston to visit family, not to be running around getting lost. They had no interest in the roller coasters at Astroworld or ice-skating at the Galleria or anything else. My father worked as a livestock inspector for the USDA and spent a good part of his day patrolling the Rio Grande on horseback to make sure horses or cattle weren't being crossed into the country. During his rides he had been startled by rattlesnakes, bucked off his horse, and shot at by drug smugglers—he didn't need any more excitement in his life. Besides, it was usually hot in

1. **Matamoros** a Mexican city located right at the U.S. border, in the northeastern state of Tamaulipas

Houston, and he hadn't worked out in the sun the other 51 weeks out of the year so he could drive to another city to sweat on his vacation.

3   I should mention that my parents were older than most parents with a ten-year-old in the house. My mother was 52 and my father was 60. Being older, they had developed certain habits that they weren't going to change. For instance, my father believed in sticking to certain meals. Food fell into three distinct **categories:** Mexican food, which he could eat every day and die a happy man; American food—meals like hamburgers, hot dogs, and fried chicken—which we ate occasionally; and other people's food, which included all the food he refused to eat. Whenever I suggested trying something different, like Chinese food, he'd look at me as if he and my mother might have brought the wrong baby home from the hospital.

4   As I understood it, this was my father's unstated **philosophy:** *We have our food—fajitas, tamales, tacos, enchiladas. It took our people many years to develop these foods. We even have two kinds of tortillas, flour and corn. So tell me why you want to eat other people's food? Leave their food alone. The* chinos *have their own food. They like that white rice. But do you see them eating our rice with those little sticks? No. The Germans, I don't know what they eat, but whatever it is, that's their business. The Italians, they like to add a lot of spices. I tried it one time and it gave me* agruras[2], *and then there I was, burping all night. Your mother had to make me an Alka-Seltzer. And you want me to eat other people's food?*

5   All of which meant that if my father ate carne con papas, I ate carne con papas. If he ate picadillo, I ate picadillo. If he ate taquitos, I ate taquitos. And so on, until 1974, the summer my sister, Sylvia, invited me to stay with her in Austin for two weeks. She and my brother-in-law were in their early twenties, and my nephew was only a year old. One of the first things we did in Austin was walk around the University of Texas, where my sister was a student. Then we rode the elevator all the way up to the top of the UT Tower, and I felt my ears pop for the first time. From the observation deck, I saw tiny people walking around on the street, but I couldn't tell which were the hippies and which were the ones with short hair. Some of my sister's friends wore their hair long, like the hippies I'd seen around town. Rolando had a handlebar mustache and hair down to his shoulders. He was the funniest of my sister's friends, and the smartest. You could ask him any math question, and he'd answer it as though he had a calculator stuck in his head. "What's fifty-six times seventeen?" I'd ask him. And he'd go, "Nine hundred fifty-two." That fast. Rolando came along the night we played putt-putt. He beat all of us because he knew how to hit his ball so it would go under the windmill just right. When we finished playing, he asked me if I wanted a **souvenir.** I said yes, thinking he was going

---

2. **agruras** (Spanish) heartburn

to buy me a T-shirt at the front booth. But instead, he took my putter and tossed it over the fence, into some hedges. Then we all walked out, and Rolando grabbed the putter for me. "There's your souvenir," he said.

6 My last night in town, my sister and brother-in-law asked if I wanted pizza. "Pizza?" I said. I'd never actually tried the food. We drove to a Pizza Inn, and my brother-in-law ordered a pepperoni pizza. The waitress brought plates for everyone, even my baby nephew. I thought of my parents back home and what they might be eating that night. A few minutes later the waitress brought out a steaming pizza and placed it in front of us. None of it seemed real: the triangle shape of my slice, the perfectly round pepperonis, the doughy end crust, the gooey melted cheese. It was as though I'd crossed into another world, one my parents never knew existed. I was still several years away from leaving Brownsville, but in that moment I felt as far from home as I ever would.

7 My mother called the apartment that night.

8 "Guess what we ate?" I said.

9 "What?"

10 "Pizza!"

11 "Pizza?"

12 "Yeah, and when I get home, we're all going to get some."

13 "If that's really what you want, maybe we can try it." She sounded distracted. "Don't hang up," she said. "Somebody wants to talk to you."

14 "Are you having fun?" my father asked.

15 "Yes, sir."

16 "And you been behaving?"

17 "Yes, sir."

18 "That's a good boy." I could hear his stubble brushing against the receiver. "You need to be careful tomorrow, okay?"

19 "I will."

20 "We miss you, *mi'jo.*" He said it softly but clearly.

21 I hesitated for a second. "Okay, see you tomorrow."

22 The next morning my sister made me sit behind the bus driver. She said I wasn't supposed to talk to anyone or get off the bus when it made stops. I told her not to worry, that I had my golf club in case anything happened. The bus pulled out, and my sister and the baby waved good-bye.

NOTES

23 Over the next 350 miles the land changed from hill country to brushland to river valley. I started getting hungry around Corpus Christi and wished that I hadn't eaten my ham and cheese sandwich before the bus left Austin. I wondered if my father would say yes to eating pizza. For a long time I imagined I was in a car on the  other side of the highway, headed north instead of south. After a while, I fell asleep and then woke up just in time to see my hometown: the swaying palm trees; the fat water tower on its skinny legs, a lonely seagull hovering high above the catwalk; the bell tower at Guadalupe Church; the tamale place next to the freeway; the used-car lots, the used-car lots, the used-car lots.

24 I saw my parents standing outside the terminal. My mother was wearing her royal-blue smock from the grocery store where she worked. My father had on the straw cowboy hat that he wore for work every day. He hadn't noticed that one of his pant legs had stuck inside his boot. As soon as the door opened, my mother came up and hugged me. "How was your trip?" she asked. Then my father shook my hand and put his arm around my shoulder. When we got to the car, he put my suitcase in the trunk and told me to sit up front with him. "I hear you want pizza?" he said. I nodded. "You sure?" I nodded again.

25 Most of the lunch crowd had left by the time we got to the Pizza Hut. I slid into a wooden booth, and my parents slid into the other side. My father held on to his hat until the waitress showed him the coat hook on the edge of the booth.

26 "Would you like to see a menu or do you want the **buffet?**" the waitress asked.

27 She looked at my parents, who looked at each other for a second and then looked at me for the answer. But the truth is, I didn't exactly know what she was asking us. The word "buffet" was as foreign to me as the word "pizza" had once been.

28 "No, we just want to order pizza," I told the waitress.

29 My father nodded in approval.

30 "I'm real hungry," I said, "so I want a large pepperoni pizza. My father will eat a medium pepperoni pizza. And bring my mother a small pepperoni pizza."

31 The waitress looked up from her notepad. "You sure you don't want the buffet?" There was that word again.

32 "No, it's okay," I said. "We just want pizza."

33   After she left, we sipped our iced teas and waited for the food. I could tell my father was proud of me for taking charge and ordering our food, the same way he would have.

34   After a while, the waitress came back and set the table. The manager helped her slide another table up against our booth. My father seemed impressed with all the work. The waitress returned a few minutes later and placed a small pepperoni pizza and then a medium one in front of my parents, leaving very little room for their plates and iced teas. My father looked at my mother when he realized how much food we had in front of us. Then the manager set a large pepperoni pizza on the extra table. "Can I get you folks anything else?" he asked.

35   I kept my head down and tried not to make eye contact with my father, which was easy, because he was busy eating more food than I'd ever seen him eat. My mother whispered to him in Spanish about this being a special lunch. To which my father answered, in English, that this would have been more special if we'd gone to a regular restaurant. Then he took a deep breath, exhaled, and continued eating. In the end, the waitress still had to bring out two boxes for the leftovers, and my mother had to dig into her purse to help my father pay for lunch.

36   After this we went back to eating the same foods. As far as I know, my parents have never entered another Italian restaurant. But me, I eat pizza wherever I go—Brooklyn, Chicago, Paris, Mexico City. If some fancy hotel has it on the menu, I know what I'm ordering. If I'm leaving a bar at two in the morning, it's nearly impossible for me to walk past an all-night pizza place. Who knows how many times I've eaten a cold slice while standing next to the refrigerator. Once, I even ordered a pizza in South America. I'd finally saved up enough money to take what I considered my first real vacation. I spent most of my time in Chile, but on New Year's Eve I caught a flight to Ushuaia, Argentina, the city at the southern tip of the continent and the world. To get there we flew over Patagonia, and the massive ice formations looked close enough to touch. Then I spotted the **elusive** straits that Magellan had discovered more than four hundred years earlier. And the land became only more distant and **remote** the farther we traveled into Tierra del Fuego. As we approached the airport in Ushuaia, the plane circled over the Beagle Channel, passing tiny islands of penguin and sea lion colonies along the way. The plane shook **desperately** against the Antarctic wind, and I thought to myself then that this was where wind was invented and here was the origin of the warm breeze we felt so far away in Brownsville. I was traveling alone and that night went out to an Italian restaurant, where I ordered a small mushroom pizza. After dinner I walked to the channel, trying to stay warm while the wind whipped around me and whistled lightly, as if someone were calling me to come closer. I stepped toward the edge of the water and pulled out a bottle of champagne I'd stashed in my jacket. An ocean liner was docked off to the side, and at midnight the crew sounded the ship's horn to mark the new year, 1994. People

were laughing and clapping in the distance. I uncorked the champagne and took my first drink. The Andes were at my back; Antarctica was straight ahead. And the wind never stopped whistling. I stared into the darkness and wondered what else was out there.

©2005 by Oscar Casares, *Texas Monthly*, March 2005. Reproduced by permission of *Texas Monthly*.

✎ WRITE

PERSONAL RESPONSE: Do you think it's important to try new things, even if it means going against the practices of your family? What are the potential benefits and drawbacks? Is conflict likely? Write a short response to this question. Use evidence from the text to support your response.

Thank You, M'am

FICTION
Langston Hughes
1958

Introduction

Langston Hughes (1902–1967) was working as a busboy in Washington, D.C. when he showed some of his poems to famous poet Vachel Lindsay. Lindsay was so impressed that he read the poems that night to an audience. In time, Hughes became one of the first African Americans to make a living as a writer and lecturer, eventually moving back to New York and becoming a leader of the Harlem Renaissance. In Hughes's short story "Thank You, M'am," a teenage boy tries to snatch a woman's purse late one night and is surprised by what happens next.

"You ought to be my son. I would teach you right from wrong."

1 She was a large woman with a large purse that had everything in it but hammer and nails. It had a long strap, and she carried it slung across her shoulder. It was about eleven o'clock at night, and she was walking alone, when a boy ran up behind her and tried to snatch her purse. The strap broke with the single tug the boy gave it from behind. But the boy's weight and the weight of the purse combined caused him to lose his balance so, instead of taking off full blast as he had hoped, the boy fell on his back on the sidewalk, and his legs flew up. The large woman simply turned around and kicked him right square in his blue-jeaned sitter. Then she reached down, picked the boy up by his shirt front, and shook him until his teeth rattled.

2 After that the woman said, "Pick up my pocketbook, boy, and give it here." She still held him. But she bent down enough to permit him to stoop and pick up her purse. Then she said, "Now ain't you ashamed of yourself?"

3 Firmly gripped by his shirt front, the boy said, "Yes'm."

4 The woman said, "What did you want to do it for?"

5 The boy said, "I didn't aim to."

6 She said, "You a lie!"

7 By that time two or three people passed, stopped, turned to look, and some stood watching.

8 "If I turn you loose, will you run?" asked the woman.

9 "Yes'm," said the boy.

10 "Then I won't turn you loose," said the woman. She did not release him.

11 "I'm very sorry, lady, I'm sorry," whispered the boy.

12 "Um-hum! And your face is dirty. I got a great mind to wash your face for you. Ain't you got nobody home to tell you to wash your face?"

13 "No'm," said the boy.

Skill:
Theme

This dialogue makes me aware of a possible theme. She asks the boy flat out if he's ashamed, which hints that the theme is developing: people should feel shame when they do something wrong.

14 "Then it will get washed this evening," said the large woman starting up the street, dragging the frightened boy behind her.

15 He looked as if he were fourteen or fifteen, **frail** and willow-wild, in tennis shoes and blue jeans.

16 The woman said, "You ought to be my son. I would teach you right from wrong. Least I can do right now is to wash your face. Are you hungry?"

17 "No'm," said the being dragged boy. "I just want you to turn me loose."

18 "Was I bothering *you* when I turned that corner?" asked the woman.

19 "No'm."

20 "But you put yourself in **contact** with *me*," said the woman. "If you think that that contact is not going to last awhile, you got another thought coming. When I get through with you, sir, you are going to remember Mrs. Luella Bates Washington Jones."

21 Sweat popped out on the boy's face and he began to struggle. Mrs. Jones stopped, jerked him around in front of her, put a half-nelson[1] about his neck, and continued to drag him up the street. When she got to her door, she dragged the boy inside, down a hall, and into a large kitchenette-**furnished** room at the rear of the house. She switched on the light and left the door open. The boy could hear other roomers laughing and talking in the large house. Some of their doors were open, too, so he knew he and the woman were not alone. The woman still had him by the neck in the middle of her room.

22 She said, "What is your name?"

23 "Roger," answered the boy.

24 "Then, Roger, you go to that sink and wash your face," said the woman, whereupon she turned him loose—at last. Roger looked at the door—looked at the woman—looked at the door—*and went to the sink.*

25 "Let the water run until it gets warm," she said. "Here's a clean towel."

26 "You gonna take me to jail?" asked the boy, bending over the sink.

27 "Not with that face, I would not take you nowhere," said the woman. "Here I am trying to get home to cook me a bite to eat and you snatch my pocketbook! Maybe, you ain't been to your supper either, late as it be. Have you?"

28 "There's nobody home at my house," said the boy.

1. **half-nelson** a wrestling hold of an opponent's neck

NOTES

Skill:
Media

In the filmed version of this part, the camera focuses on Roger's face. He looks embarrassed and sad. Maybe he feels some regret?

In the film, we also see Mrs. Jones get down to Roger's level to talk to him. This angle emphasizes what she's saying: his actions have consequences. Maybe this has to do with the story's meaning. She seems to be really trying to communicate with him.

NOTES

Skill:
Media

The camera focuses on Roger, and he yells, "M'am?" This makes me think he's shocked by Mrs. Jones's statement. Roger doesn't seem so shocked in the written version.

This part is also different from the story. Roger throws the towel on the ground but then picks it up. I think he realizes that the lady has been nice to him, so he should treat her things with respect. This might have something do with the theme.

29 "Then we'll eat," said the woman, "I believe you're hungry—or been hungry—to try to snatch my pocketbook."

30 "I wanted a pair of blue suede shoes," said the boy.

31 "Well, you didn't have to snatch *my* pocketbook to get some suede shoes," said Mrs. Luella Bates Washington Jones. "You could of asked me."

32 "M'am?"

33 The water dripping from his face, the boy looked at her. There was a long pause. A very long pause. After he had dried his face and not knowing what else to do dried it again, the boy turned around, wondering what next. The door was open. He could make a dash for it down the hall. He could run, run, run, run, *run!*

34 The woman was sitting on the day-bed. After a while she said, "I were young once and I wanted things I could not get."

35 There was another long pause. The boy's mouth opened. Then he frowned, but not knowing he frowned.

36 The woman said, "Um-hum! You thought I was going to say *but*, didn't you? You thought I was going to say, *but I didn't snatch people's pocketbooks.* Well, I wasn't going to say that." Pause. Silence. "I have done things, too, which I would not tell you, son—neither tell God, if he didn't already know. So you set down while I fix us something to eat. You might run that comb through your hair so you will look **presentable.**"

37 In another corner of the room behind a screen was a gas plate[2] and an icebox[3]. Mrs. Jones got up and went behind the screen. The woman did not watch the boy to see if he was going to run now, nor did she watch her purse which she left behind her on the day-bed. But the boy took care to sit on the far side of the room where he thought she could easily see him out of the corner of her eye, if she wanted to. He did not trust the woman *not* to trust him. And he did not want to be **mistrusted** now.

38 "Do you need somebody to go to the store," asked the boy, "maybe to get some milk or something?"

39 "Don't believe I do," said the woman, "unless you just want sweet milk yourself. I was going to make cocoa out of this canned milk I got here."

40 "That will be fine," said the boy.

2. **gas plate** a small appliance for cooking
3. **icebox** appliances used to keep food cold prior to the invention of modern refrigerators

41 She heated some lima beans and ham she had in the icebox, made the cocoa, and set the table. The woman did not ask the boy anything about where he lived, or his folks, or anything else that would embarrass him. Instead, as they ate, she told him about her job in a hotel beauty-shop that stayed open late, what the work was like, and how all kinds of women came in and out, blondes, red-heads, and Spanish. Then she cut him a half of her ten-cent cake.

42 "Eat some more, son," she said.

43 When they were finished eating she got up and said, "Now, here, take this ten dollars and buy yourself some blue suede shoes. And next time, do not make the mistake of latching onto *my* pocketbook *nor nobody else's*—because shoes come by devilish like that will burn your feet. I got to get my rest now. But I wish you would behave yourself, son, from here on in."

44 She led him down the hall to the front door and opened it. "Good-night! Behave yourself, boy!" she said, looking out into the street.

45 The boy wanted to say something else other than "Thank you, m'am" to Mrs. Luella Bates Washington Jones, but he couldn't do so as he turned at the barren stoop[4] and looked back at the large woman in the door. He barely managed to say "Thank you" before she shut the door. And he never saw her again.

"Thank You, M'am" from SHORT STORIES by Langston Hughes. Copyright © 1996 by Ramona Bass and Arnold Rampersad. Reprinted by permission of Hill and Wang, a division of Farrar, Straus and Giroux, LLC.

4. **stoop** a porch, entryway steps, or platform at the entrance to a house

First Read

Read "Thank You, M'am." After you read, complete the Think Questions below.

Copyright © BookheadEd Learning, LLC

☁ THINK QUESTIONS

1. How do Roger and Mrs. Luella Bates Washington Jones first meet? What is Mrs. Jones's immediate reaction to this event? Cite specific evidence from the text to support your response.

2. Rather than call the police, what does Mrs. Jones do to Roger? How does Roger initially respond? Cite specific evidence from the text to support your analysis.

3. What reason does Roger give Mrs. Jones for why he tried to snatch her pocketbook? What is one thing Mrs. Jones says in response? How do her words affect him? Cite specific evidence from the text to support your statements.

4. Find the word **contact** in paragraph 20 of "Thank You, M'am." Use context clues in the surrounding sentences, as well as the sentence in which the word appears, to determine the word's meaning. Write your definition here, and identify clues that helped you figure out its meaning.

5. Use context clues to determine the meaning of **presentable** as it is used in paragraph 36 of "Thank You, M'am." Write your definition here, and identify clues that helped you figure out the meaning. Then check the meaning in a dictionary.

Skill:
Media

Use the Checklist to analyze Media in "Thank You, M'am." Refer to the sample student annotations about Media in the text.

••• CHECKLIST FOR MEDIA

In order to determine how to compare and contrast a written story, drama, or poem to its audio, filmed, staged, or multimedia version, do the following:

- ✓ choose a story that has been presented in multiple forms of media, such as a written story and a film adaptation

- ✓ note techniques that are unique to each medium—print, audio, and video:

  - lighting
  - sound
  - color
  - tone and style
  - camera focus and angles
  - word choice
  - structure

- ✓ examine how these techniques may have an effect on the story and its ideas, as well as the reader's, listener's, or viewer's understanding of the work as a whole

- ✓ examine similarities and differences between the written story and its audio or video versions

To compare and contrast a written story, drama, or poem to its audio, filmed, staged, or multimedia version, analyzing the effects of techniques unique to each medium, consider the following questions:

✓ How do different types of media treat story elements?

✓ What techniques are unique to each medium—print, audio, and video?

✓ How does the medium—for example, a film's use of music, sound, and camera angles—affect a person's understanding of the work as a whole?

Skill:
Media

Reread paragraphs 34–36 of "Thank You, M'am." Then, using the Checklist on the previous page, answer the multiple-choice questions below.

↻ YOUR TURN

1. This question has two parts. First, answer Part A. Then, answer Part B.

   Part A: Which of the following details in "Thank You, M'am" is different in the filmed version from the written story?

   ○ A. Mrs. Jones asked Roger to wash his hands to make himself presentable for dinner.

   ○ B. Roger asks Mrs. Jones what kinds of bad things she did when she was his age.

   ○ C. Mrs. Jones admits that she also has done bad things.

   ○ D. Mrs. Jones says, "Everyone has something in common."

   Part B: Which of the following BEST explains the effect of the change detailed in Part A?

   ○ A. The added line suggests a theme that people are connected even though they are different.

   ○ B. The added line helps Roger see that he really should comb his hair.

   ○ C. Mrs. Jones needed to make it clear to Roger that she and his mother have a lot in common.

   ○ D. The added line suggests Roger is related to Mrs. Jones.

2. This question has two parts. First, answer Part A. Then, answer Part B.

   Part A: What film element is added to the scene to enhance the meaning or message?

   ○ A. In the film we see that they're both eating, but in the text, she hasn't made the meal yet.

   ○ B. The film keeps both characters on the screen the whole time.

   ○ C. Mrs. Jones pats Roger on the head as the camera follows her from the couch to the hall.

   ○ D. The camera focuses on Roger's eye roll when Mrs. Jones says everyone has something in common.

Part B: How does the film element added in Part A affect the meaning or message of the story?

○ A. The head pat shows Mrs. Jones relates to Roger and suggests a message about forgiveness.

○ B. The food in the scene emphasizes that food brings people together.

○ C. The scene shows that Roger and Mrs. Jones are connected even though they just met.

○ D. Roger rolling his eyes shows us that he isn't ready to be good yet.

Skill:
Theme

Use the Checklist to analyze Theme in "Thank You, M'am." Refer to the sample student annotations about Theme in the text.

••• CHECKLIST FOR THEME

In order to identify a theme or central idea in a text and analyze its development over the course of the text, note the following:

- ✓ the topic of the text

- ✓ whether or not the theme is stated directly in the text

- ✓ details in the text that help to reveal theme

  - a narrator's or speaker's tone
  - title and chapter headings
  - details about the setting
  - characters' thoughts, actions, and dialogue
  - the central conflict in the story's plot
  - the resolution of the conflict
  - whether or not the theme is stated directly in the text

- ✓ analyze how characters and the problems they face are affected by the setting and what impact this may have on how the theme is developed

To determine a theme or central idea of a text and analyze its development over the course of the text, consider the following questions:

- ✓ What is a theme, or central idea, of the text?

- ✓ When did you become aware of that theme? For instance, did the story's conclusion reveal the theme?

- ✓ How does the theme develop over the course of the text?

Skill:
Theme

Reread paragraphs 8–14 of "Thank You, M'am." Then, using the Checklist on the previous page, answer the multiple-choice questions below.

⟳ YOUR TURN

1. Based on Mrs. Jones's dialogue in paragraphs 12 and 14, the reader can infer that—

   ○ A. Mrs. Jones cares more about appearance than character.
   ○ B. Mrs. Jones is a tough but caring person.
   ○ C. Mrs. Jones plans on taking Roger to the police station after he cleans up.
   ○ D. Mrs. Jones has little sympathy for Roger.

2. Roger's responses in paragraphs 9, 11, and 13 reveal that he—

   ○ A. has no regret for attempting to steal Mrs. Jones's purse.
   ○ B. is planning to kick Mrs. Jones as soon as she lets her guard down.
   ○ C. is clever and wants Mrs. Jones to feel sorry for him so that she lets him go.
   ○ D. shows signs of honesty and likely has a tough life with little guidance from adults.

3. The dialogue in paragraphs 12 through 14 hints that the theme might be—

   ○ A. Sometimes it is important to notice other people's struggles and offer help.
   ○ B. The way you look often reflects the way you feel.
   ○ C. In some cases, the only way to teach a lesson is through fear.
   ○ D. It's important to make a positive first impression.

THANK YOU, M'AM

Close Read

Reread "Thank You, M'am." As you reread, complete the Skills Focus questions below. Then use your answers and annotations from the questions to help you complete the Write activity.

◎ SKILLS FOCUS

1. Identify parts in the story where Mrs. Jones shows concern about Roger's dirty face and hunger. Explain what message the story might be expressing about self-respect.

2. Reread paragraphs 34–36. Identify details that suggest why Mrs. Jones may be helping Roger. Explain what theme, or message about life, is hinted at in these paragraphs.

3. Identify details that may explain why Mrs. Jones gives Roger money to buy blue suede shoes. Explain whether you agree or disagree with her decision and whether you think Roger should have accepted the money.

4. "Mad," "In the Year 1974," and "Thank You, M'am" all deal with clashes between young and old. Identify textual evidence in "Thank You, M'am" that reveals a lesson Mrs. Jones is trying to teach Roger. Explain how that passage compares and contrasts with one of the other pieces.

5. Identify parts in the story where you were surprised by how either Mrs. Jones or Roger responds to the early conflict between the two characters. Explain why the character's actions surprised you and what you expected instead.

✏ WRITE

COMPARE AND CONTRAST: "Thank You, M'am," "In the Year 1974," and "Mad" are about conflicts between young people and older adults. What lessons are learned in each text as a result of these conflicts? Compare and contrast the lesson in "Thank You, M'am" to the lesson in one of the other texts. Remember to support your ideas with evidence from the texts.

Please note that excerpts and passages in the StudySync® library and this workbook are intended as touchstones to generate interest in an author's work. The excerpts and passages do not substitute for the reading of entire texts, and StudySync® strongly recommends that students seek out and purchase the whole literary or informational work in order to experience it as the author intended. Links to online resellers are available in our digital library. In addition, complete works may be ordered through an authorized reseller by filling out and returning to StudySync® the order form enclosed in this workbook.

Reading & Writing Companion   111

Extended Writing Project and Grammar

EXTENDED WRITING PROJECT

NARRATIVE WRITING

Narrative Writing Process: Plan

| PLAN | DRAFT | REVISE | EDIT AND PUBLISH |

Conflict drives stories. Conflict gives characters a purpose and gives readers a reason to care about them. Some conflicts are straightforward: Rikki-tikki-tavi must defeat Nag and Nagaina. Other conflicts are less obvious. In "Seventh Grade," Victor's desire to impress Teresa leads him to lie about being able to speak French. Sources for conflict can seem endless, but determining a conflict early on in your planning can help you figure out your other story elements: character, plot, setting, and theme.

WRITING PROMPT

What conflicts would exist in a world where people can know what others are thinking?

Imagine a world where people can know what others are thinking. What conflicts would cease to exist in that world? What new conflicts would arise? Write a story about a conflict that exists because it's possible to know another person's thoughts. Regardless of the conflict you choose, be sure your narrative includes the following:

- a plot with a beginning, middle, and end
- a clear setting
- characters and dialogue
- a distinct conflict
- a clear theme

Introduction to Narrative Writing

Narrative writing tells a story of experiences or events that have been imagined by a writer or that have happened in real life. Good fiction writing uses effective techniques, relevant descriptive details, and a purposeful structure with a series of events that contain a beginning, middle, and end. The characteristics of fiction writing include:

- setting
- characters
- plot
- theme
- point of view

As you continue with this Extended Writing Project, you'll receive more instruction and practice at crafting each of the characteristics of fiction writing to create your own narrative story.

Before you get started on your own narrative, read this narrative that one student, Jalyn, wrote in response to the writing prompt. As you read the Model, highlight and annotate the features of narrative writing that Jalyn included in her narrative.

NOTES

☰ STUDENT MODEL

The Talent Show

1 Anh Le was good at music, but she was even better at something else. She could hear people's thoughts. She kept it a secret because it was the only way to figure out what went on in people's heads. But sometimes it was more of a curse than a blessing.

2 Like when she quit taking piano lessons, her mother had complained loudly, "How can you waste your natural gift?" *After all that money spent on lessons,* she had thought.

3 But Anh still loved music, and she kept playing every day. When she started middle school, she joined the choir. It became her favorite school activity. She and her friends had fun pretending to be reality-show singers on weekends, using a karaoke machine that belonged to Jennifer's family. Jen's dad was so impressed that he suggested they enter a competition at their local community center. There would be a preliminary round in one month and a final round the following week.

4 The prize was a free ticket to the new amusement park! Anh and her brother had been begging her parents to go since before it opened.

5 "Which song do you think I should sing?" Anh asked. *Which one will make me the winner?* she thought.

6 "I think you should try 'Hero,'" Jennifer said distractedly. She was thinking about riding the spiralling roller coaster.

7 "Yeah, or maybe 'Tonight,'" Valeria added. *How much cotton candy can I eat if I win?*

8 "You two should do a duet," Anh suggested. Their voices went well together. *And my chances to win are probably higher if I do a solo. But then again, they can practice with the karaoke machine.*

9   "We're all going to do great! They'll have to split first place three ways," Jennifer and Valeria said together.

10   Anh realized her friends didn't care about the music as much as she did. They were really just interested in the tickets. She decided that she needed to work hard to beat them.

11   She knew her brother Thao would play the piano for her to practice. She'd just have to make him those peanut butter cookies he'd been thinking about all week. She baked enough to keep him going before the first round of the competition.

12   Soon enough, the big day came. Anh did her warm-up exercises after breakfast in her bedroom. *I'm gonna nail this,* she told herself as she headed downstairs. In the kitchen she heard her brother trying to convince their parents that he couldn't go to the competition. "I feel sick," he said. *I haven't played ANY video games in weeks because of her practicing,* he thought. *I'd rather stay home and do that.* Anh smirked when she realized she'd be on all those rides at the park before Thao. *I'm gonna win. He can sit at home and play video games.*

13   She turned her attention back to the competition. She wanted the right kind of energy to keep the judges awake. She planned to wow them.

14   But when she got to the auditorium, Anh was overwhelmed with nerves. She felt butterflies in her stomach, her mouth was dry, and she could only hear her heart. *What if I forget the words? Or worse, what if I open my mouth and forget how to sing?*

15   . . . *Who are all these newbies?* She heard a competitor thinking. *I'll have no problem taking the trophy home again this year . . .*

16   . . . *We got this!* This time it was Valeria. *Our practice last night came out perfectly . . .*

17   Anh found a quiet area backstage to take some deep breaths. *I know this song,* she thought. *I could actually sing it in my sleep.*

18   When she went onstage, Anh was determined to give it her all. She felt the bright spotlights shining down on her, the crowd got silent, and she could hear the judges tapping their pencils and moving

their papers. She took a deep breath and felt the butterflies in her stomach disappear. As she started to sing, she was able to forget her nervousness and focus on the lyrics. She stood taller and felt even more confident. She didn't miss a single beat! The crowd applauded loudly. Next, the judges weighed in.

19   "I like the emotion you put into it," said one judge dryly. He was an older man in a worn-out suit. *I hope this is over soon . . . I could really go for a steak burrito right now.*

20   Anh managed a half smile and braced herself for the next judge.

21   "You have a nice voice," the young woman said. *This is the last time I do a favor for my sister. If she's going to make us work all day, she needs to pay us!*

22   *. . . She did her best. But we're gonna do even better.* Anh heard Valeria's thoughts drift into her own. She knew she was gonna have to try harder next round. If she made it.

23   After the competition Valeria and Jennifer had already started thinking about choosing their next song. *Should it be a pop song or a classic? How high IS the roller coaster, anyway? I heard a ninth grader already set a record for riding it the most times in one hour . . .*

24   But Anh scored high, and so did Valeria and Jennifer. At the end of the competition they all made it to the second round.

25   The following week, Anh sang with more energy than before, and grinned at her brother from the stage. *I can't wait to see the look on his face when I tell him about all those water slides . . .* she thought as she finished her song.

26   "Another excellent performance. Nice range of emotion," the judge said flatly. He was wearing the same worn suit and thinking about his heartburn.

27   Anh tried hard not to roll her eyes.

28   "You control your voice well," the second judge said. "Lots of nice touches in that song." *At least she was on key this time.*

29   Anh swallowed. *I guess that's a good thing, right?*

30 Anh lined up on the stage with the rest of the contestants at the end of the day, crossing her fingers as she waited to hear her name announced in first place. She wanted to win so badly, and she had practiced so hard for the entire month before the competition! She had been so focused on the music and she remembered how her friends had only really cared about the tickets. She had given it her all!

31 But to her dismay (and the dismay of the previous winner), it was Valeria and Jennifer who took home the trophy. Anh was disappointed to be in second place, but at least she knew her friends would tell her all about the park's rides.

32 *I wish Anh could come with us*, she heard them both think.

Please note that excerpts and passages in the StudySync® library and this workbook are intended as touchstones to generate interest in an author's work. The excerpts and passages do not substitute for the reading of entire texts, and StudySync® strongly recommends that students seek out and purchase the whole literary or informational work in order to experience it as the author intended. Links to online resellers are available in our digital library. In addition, complete works may be ordered through an authorized reseller by filling out and returning to StudySync® the order form enclosed in this workbook.

Reading & Writing Companion   **117**

WRITE

Writers often take notes about story ideas before they sit down to write. Think about what you've learned so far about organizing narrative writing to help you begin prewriting.

- **Genre:** In what sort of genre would you like to write? Most any genre can focus on a conflict. Genres include realistic fiction, science fiction, fantasy, or mystery, to name some examples.

- **Characters:** What types of characters would you like to write about in your narrative?

- **Conflict/Theme:** What conflict will you make your characters deal with? What life lesson will your characters or readers learn from the conflict?

- **Setting:** How might the setting of your story affect the characters and problem?

- **Plot:** What events will lead to the resolution of the conflict while keeping a reader engaged?

- **Point of View:** From which point of view should your story be told, and why?

Response Instructions

Use the questions in the bulleted list to write a one-paragraph summary. Your summary should describe what will happen in your narrative.

Don't worry about including all of the details now. Focus only on the most essential and important elements. You will refer back to this short summary as you continue through the steps of the writing process.

Skill:
Organizing Narrative Writing

••• CHECKLIST FOR ORGANIZING NARRATIVE WRITING

As you consider how to organize your narrative, use the following questions as a guide:

- Who is the narrator and who are the characters in the story?
- From what point of view will the story be told?
- Where will the story take place?
- What conflict or problem will the characters have to resolve?
- Does my plot flow logically and naturally from one event to the next?

Here are some strategies to help you organize your narrative so the event sequence unfolds naturally and logically:

- Introduce the characters and/or a narrator.

  > Characters can be introduced all at once or throughout the narrative.

  > Choose the role each character will play.

  > Choose a point of view.

    o A first-person narrator can be a participant or character in the story.

    o A third-person narrator tells the story as an outside observer.

- Outline the five stages of plot development.

  > Begin with your **exposition**—decide what background information your readers need to know about the characters, setting, and conflict.

  > List the events of the **rising action**—be sure that these events build toward the climax.

  > Describe what will happen during the **climax** of the story—make sure that this is the point of highest interest, conflict, or suspense in your story.

  > List the events of the **falling action**—make sure that these events show what happens to the characters as a result of the climax.

  > Explain the **resolution**—make sure the main conflict is solved or settled.

↻ YOUR TURN

Complete the chart below by placing the student notes and ideas in the correct part of the outline.

	Student Notes and Ideas Options
A	As Karl campaigns, he starts to feel self-conscious. One day, he feels everyone staring at him. Suddenly, he hears what everyone is thinking. He learns that no one really likes him.
B	My main character is Karl. Other characters include his classmates.
C	Karl runs for class president. He is popular, but is self-centered and mean to many less-popular students. Karl doesn't listen to them and thinks they are worthless, but everyone is scared to confront him about this.
D	Karl stops hearing everyone's thoughts. But now he understands people better and listens to them.
E	Karl loses a close race for class president. He is relieved.
F	The story will be told by an outside narrator, or third-person point of view.
G	At the final debate, Karl addresses the whole student crowd. He apologizes for being mean and says he will change.

Part of the Outline	Student Notes and Ideas
Characters	
Narrator	
Exposition	
Rising Action	
Climax	
Falling Action	
Resolution	

♻ YOUR TURN

Plan your narrative story by completing the outline. You may refer to the checklist section as you write.

Part of the Outline	Notes and Ideas
Characters	
Narrator	
Exposition	
Rising Action	
Climax	
Falling Action	
Resolution	

Please note that excerpts and passages in the StudySync® library and this workbook are intended as touchstones to generate interest in an author's work. The excerpts and passages do not substitute for the reading of entire texts, and StudySync® strongly recommends that students seek out and purchase the whole literary or informational work in order to experience it as the author intended. Links to online resellers are available in our digital library. In addition, complete works may be ordered through an authorized reseller by filling out and returning to StudySync® the order form enclosed in this workbook.

Reading & Writing Companion 121

NARRATIVE
WRITING
PROCESS
DRAFT

Narrative Writing Process: Draft

| PLAN | DRAFT | REVISE | EDIT AND PUBLISH |

You have already made progress toward writing your short story. Now it is time to draft your narrative.

✎ WRITE

Use your plan and other responses in your Binder to draft your narrative. You may also have new ideas as you begin drafting. Feel free to explore those new ideas as you have them. You can also ask yourself these questions:

- Have I included specifics about my setting, characters, plot, theme, and point of view?

- Have I made my conflict clear to the reader?

- Does the sequence of events in my story make sense?

Before you submit your draft, read it over carefully. You want to be sure that you've responded to all aspects of the prompt.

Here is Jalyn's short story draft. As you read, identify details that Jalyn includes in her exposition. Because this is a draft, there are some errors that Jalyn will revise as she works toward her final version.

≡ STUDENT MODEL: FIRST DRAFT

NOTES

~~Anh Le was good at music but she knew what people thought. she didn't tell anyone that though.~~

~~Anh started taking piano lessons when she was seven. She quit and her mom got mad.~~

Anh Le was good at music, but she was even better at something else. She could hear people's thoughts. She kept it a secret because it was the only way to figure out what went on in people's heads. But sometimes it was more of a curse than a blessing.

Like when she quit taking piano lessons, her mother had complained loudly, "How can you waste your natural gift?" *After all that money spent on lessons,* she had thought.

But anh still loved music. When she started middle school she joined the choir. It became her favorite school activity. She and her friends had fun pretending to be reality-show singers on weekends, using a karaoke machine that belonged to Jennifer's family. Jen's dad was so impresed that he suggested they enter a local competition. There would be a prelimenary round in one month and a final round the following week.

The friends looked online, found a competition at a nearby community center. The competition was open to kids.

~~"Which song do you think I should sing" Anh asked. She wanted to win.~~

~~"I think you should try 'Hero,'" Jennifer said distractedly.~~

~~So did Valeria. "Whatever." In her head she thought, "How much cotton candy can I eat if I win?"~~

~~Anh thinks they should sing a duet because their voices were good together. She was thinking about how she might have a better~~

Skill: Story Beginnings

Jalyn writes an exciting opening to better engage and orient the reader. She wants to grab the reader's attention with Anh's unique talent. She also wants to give the reader more context.

Please note that excerpts and passages in the StudySync® library and this workbook are intended as touchstones to generate interest in an author's work. The excerpts and passages do not substitute for the reading of entire texts, and StudySync® strongly recommends that students seek out and purchase the whole literary or informational work in order to experience it as the author intended. Links to online resellers are available in our digital library. In addition, complete works may be ordered through an authorized reseller by filling out and returning to StudySync® the order form enclosed in this workbook.

Reading & Writing Companion   123

Skill: Narrative Techniques

Jalyn first decides to write new dialogue to further develop the experiences, events, and characters. She adds dialogue to increase conflict and lead readers from one plot event to the next. She includes dialogue tags so readers can understand which characters are speaking.

~~chance to win with a solo. Then she remembered the karaoke machine. She decided she needed to work hard to beat them.~~

~~"We're all going to do great! They'll have to split first place three ways," they said together.~~

~~Anh realizd her friends didn't care about the music as much as she did. They were really just interested in the tickets. She decided that she needed to work hard to beat them.~~

"Which song do you think I should sing?" Anh asked. *Which one will make me the winner?* she thought.

"I think you should try 'Hero,'" Jennifer said distractedly. She was thinking about riding the spiralling roller coaster.

"Yeah, or maybe 'Tonight,'" Valeria added. *How much cotton candy can I eat if I win?*

"You two should do a duet," Anh suggested. Their voices went well together. *And my chances to win are probably higher if I do a solo. But then again, they can practice with the karaoke machine.*

"We're all going to do great! They'll have to split first place three ways," Jennifer and Valeria said together.

Anh realized her friends didn't care about the music as much as she did. They were really just interested in the tickets. She decided that she needed to work hard to beat them.

She knew her brother Thao would play the piano for her to practice. She'd just have to make him those Peanut Butter cookies he'd been thinking about all week. She baked enough, to keep him going before the first round of the competition.

~~Soon enough, the big day came. Anh did her warm-up excersises after breakfast. she told herself she was gonna win. When she headed downstairs she heard her brother trying to convince their parents that he couldn't go to the competition. "I feel sick," he said. I haven't played ANY video games in weeks because of her practicing, he thought. He wanted to stay home for that instead. Anh was happy~~

~~when she realized she'd be on all those rides at the park before Thao. I'm gonna win. He can sit at home and play video games.~~

Soon enough, the big day came. Anh did her warm-up exercises after breakfast in her bedroom. *I'm gonna nail this*, she told herself as she headed downstairs. In the kitchen she heard her brother trying to convince their parents that he couldn't go to the competition. "I feel sick," he said. *I haven't played ANY video games in weeks because of her practicing,* he thought. *I'd rather stay home and do that.* Anh smirked when she realized she'd be on all those rides at the park before Thao. *I'm gonna win. He can sit at home and play video games.*

She turned her attention back to the competition. She wanted the right kind of energy to keep the judges awake. She planned to do a good job.

But when she got to the auditorium, Anh was overwhelmed with nerves. What if I forget the words? Or worse, what if I open my mouth and forget how to sing?

The other competitores and their parents were all thinking nervously. Who are all these newbys? She heard a competitor thinking. I'll have no problem taking the trophy home again this year . . .

. . . We got this! This time it was valeria. Our practice last night came out perfectly . . .

Anh found a quiet area backstage to take some deep breaths. I know this song, she thought. I could actually sing it in my sleep.

~~Anh was able to forget her nervousness and focus on the lyrics when she started to sing. As she walked out on stage, she was determined to give it her all. The crowd clapped, and then it was time for the two judges to talk.~~

~~"I like the emotion you put into it," said the first judge. Anh heard his thoughts, "i hope this is over soon. I'm hungry. I want a steak burrito. There needs to be some dancing to go with all this singing.~~

 Skill:
Transitions

Jalyn decides to use transition words to signal shifts in the setting as Anh moves around her house. Phrases like "in her bedroom" and "as she headed downstairs" help the reader visualize Anh and signal shifts in the setting as the plot flows.

Please note that excerpts and passages in the StudySync® library and this workbook are intended as touchstones to generate interest in an author's work. The excerpts and passages do not substitute for the reading of entire texts, and StudySync® strongly recommends that students seek out and purchase the whole literary or informational work in order to experience it as the author intended. Links to online resellers are available in our digital library. In addition, complete works may be ordered through an authorized reseller by filling out and returning to StudySync® the order form enclosed in this workbook.

Reading & Writing Companion 125

Skill:
Descriptive
Details

Jalyn adds more descriptive details and precise language to her draft. Descriptive details such as "an older man in a worn-out suit" help readers imagine what Anh sees. Adding "The crowd applauded loudly" conveys the exact volume level of the audience.

~~The other judge, a young woman who looked like a singer herself, said, "You have a nice voice." However she really thought, "Too bad it's a little off-key.~~

As she started to sing, she was able to forget her nervousness and focus on the lyrics. She stood taller and felt even more confident. She didn't miss a single beat! The crowd applauded loudly. Next, the judges weighed in.

"I like the emotion you put into it," said one judge dryly. He was an older man in a worn-out suit. *I hope this is over soon . . . I could really go for a steak burrito right now.*

Anh managed a half smile and braced herself for the next judge.

"You have a nice voice," the young woman said. *This is the last time I do a favor for my sister. If she's going to make us work all day, she needs to pay us!*

. . . She did her best. But we're gonna do even better. Anh heard valeria's thoughts. She knew she was gonna have to try harder next round. If she made it.

Valeria and Jennifer had already started thinking about choosing their next song. *Should it be a Pop song or a Classic? How high IS the roller coaster, anyway? I heard a ninth grader already set a record for riding it the most times in one hour . . .*

But Anh scored high, and so did Valeria and Jennifer. They all scored high enough to made it to the second round so they could come back next week.

The following week, Anh was singing with more energy than before, and grinned at her brother from the stage. *I can't wait to see the look on his face when I tell him about all those water slides . . .*

"Another excellent performance. Nice range of emotion," the Judge said flatly. *He was wearing that suit and thinking about his heartburn.*

Anh tried hard not to roll her eyes.

"You control your voice well," the second Judge said. "Lots of nice touches in that song." She was thinking that maybe Anh was a little less off-key this time. Definitely less off-key than the boy before her.

Anh swallowed. I guess that's a good thin, right?

~~Anh lined up on the stage with the rest of the contestants at the end of the day and she was crossing her fingers as she waited to hear her name announced in first place so she could be the winner and get the tickets. She had practiced so hard! But to her dismay (and the dismay of the previous winner) it was Valeria and Jennifer who took home the Trophy. Anh was disappointed to be in second place, but at least she knew her friends would tell her all about the park's rides.~~

~~She heard them both think. and they weren't even being fake about it. They were thinking positive thoughts because they meant it.~~

Anh lined up on the stage with the rest of the contestants at the end of the day, crossing her fingers as she waited to hear her name announced in first place. She wanted to win so badly, and she had practiced so hard for the entire month before the competition! She had been so focused on the music and she remembered how her friends had only really cared about the tickets. She had given it her all!

But to her dismay (and the dismay of the previous winner), it was Valeria and Jennifer who took home the trophy. Anh was disappointed to be in second place, but at least she knew her friends would tell her all about the park's rides.

I wish Anh could come with us, she heard them both think.

Anh smiled. I'm glad that my secret talent shows me who my real freinds are.

She watched them gigling and posing for the photographer. She knew she could convince her mom to get her a ticket to the park— she'd just heard her thinking about buying Anh a day pass. And her brother was even going to let her win a few video games.

Skill:
Conclusions

To make her draft stronger, Jalyn decides to do three things. First, she includes more character thoughts and feelings. Second, she works in important details to help summarize the main events. Third, she adds a line to reveal why the story matters.

NOTES

. . . Although she'd probably have won if she kept up the piano! She heard her mother think. Anh started to laugh and, walked towards her family who were waiting for her backstage.

"What's so funny?" her brother asked, surprised at her laughter.

"Nothing, punching his shoulder lightly. She was gonna enjoy it when he let her win because he didn't know that she could read his mind because of her secret talent.

Skill:
Story Beginnings

••• CHECKLIST FOR STORY BEGINNINGS

Before you write the beginning of your narrative, ask yourself the following questions:

- What information does my reader need to know at the beginning of the story about the narrator, main character, setting, and the character's conflict?

- What will happen to my character in the story?

- Who is the narrator of my story?

There are many ways you can engage and orient your reader. Here are some strategies to help you establish a context, show the point of view, and introduce the narrator and/or characters:

- Action

  > Instead of beginning with a description of a character, have the character "doing something" that will reveal his or her personality.

  > Opening a story with an immediate conflict can help grab a reader's attention.

- Description

  > Use engaging or interesting description to establish the character, setting, or conflict.

- Dialogue

  > Dialogue can immediately establish the point of view in a story.

    o first person: narrator is a character in the story

    o third person: narrator is outside the story

- A character's internal thoughts can provide information that only the reader knows.

Please note that excerpts and passages in the StudySync® library and this workbook are intended as touchstones to generate interest in an author's work. The excerpts and passages do not substitute for the reading of entire texts, and StudySync® strongly recommends that students seek out and purchase the whole literary or informational work in order to experience it as the author intended. Links to online resellers are available in our digital library. In addition, complete works may be ordered through an authorized reseller by filling out and returning to StudySync® the order form enclosed in this workbook.

Reading & Writing Companion   **129**

YOUR TURN

Read the beginning of each story below. Then, complete the chart by writing the story beginning strategy that correctly matches each paragraph.

Strategy Options		
Action	Description	Dialogue

Story Beginning	Strategy
He was a mongoose, rather like a little cat in his fur and his tail, but quite like a weasel in his head and his habits. His eyes and the end of his restless nose were pink. He could scratch himself anywhere he pleased with any leg, front or back, that he chose to use. "Rikki-Tikki-Tavi"	
"I have no use for old people in my village," he said haughtily. "They are neither useful nor able to work for a living. I therefore decree that anyone over seventy-one must be banished from the village and left in the mountains to die." "The Wise Old Woman"	
It was about eleven o'clock at night, and she was walking alone, when a boy ran up behind her and tried to snatch her purse. "Thank You, M'am"	

✎ WRITE

Use the questions and techniques in the checklist section to revise the beginning of your narrative.

Skill:
Descriptive Details

••• CHECKLIST FOR DESCRIPTIVE DETAILS

First, reread the draft of your narrative and identify the following:

- where descriptive details are needed to convey experiences and events
- vague, general, or overused words and phrases
- places where you want to tell how something looks, sounds, feels, smells, or tastes, such as:

    > experiences

    > events

    > action

Use precise words and phrases, relevant descriptive details, and sensory language to capture the action and convey experiences and events, using the following questions as a guide:

- What experiences and events do I want to convey in my writing?
- Have I included relevant and descriptive details?
- Where can I add descriptive details to describe the characters and the events of the plot?
- How can I use sensory language, or words that describe sights, sounds, feelings, smells, or tastes, to help my reader create a picture of the action, experiences, and events?
- What can I refine or revise in my word choice to make sure that the reader can picture what is taking place?

Please note that excerpts and passages in the StudySync® library and this workbook are intended as touchstones to generate interest in an author's work. The excerpts and passages do not substitute for the reading of entire texts, and StudySync® strongly recommends that students seek out and purchase the whole literary or informational work in order to experience it as the author intended. Links to online resellers are available in our digital library. In addition, complete works may be ordered through an authorized reseller by filling out and returning to StudySync® the order form enclosed in this workbook.

Reading & Writing
Companion

131

YOUR TURN

Choose the best answer to each question.

1. Jalyn would like to add a descriptive sound detail to this sentence from a previous draft. Which sentence BEST adds sound detail to her sentence?

> She watched her friends posing for the photographer.

○ A. She watched her friends posing and giggling for the photographer as the camera snapped and clicked.

○ B. She watched her friends posing for the photographer, the bland dryness of her mouth reminding her of the song she had just worked so hard to sing.

○ C. Inhaling the celebratory scent of flowers given to her by her parents still was not enough to make Anh feel like a winner as she watched her friends posing for the photographer.

○ D. She watched her friends posing for the photographer, their trophy shining and sparkling under the lights above the stage.

2. Jalyn would like to add some detail. Which sentence could BEST follow and provide support for the underlined sentence in the paragraph below?

> Anh turned her attention back to the competition. She wanted the right kind of energy to keep the judges awake. <u>She planned to wow them.</u>

○ A. She breathed in the scent of popcorn that someone in the front row was loudly chewing.

○ B. She heard one judge turn the page of his notebook as he prepared to jot down notes for each performer.

○ C. The judges would hear the smooth sound of her voice and have no choice but to announce her the winner.

○ D. She felt the bright lights on her face as sweat began to form on the palms of her hands.

⟳ YOUR TURN

Complete the chart by writing a descriptive detail that appeals to each sense for your narrative.

Sense	Descriptive Detail
Sight	
Smell	
Touch	
Taste	
Sound	

Skill:
Narrative Techniques

••• CHECKLIST FOR NARRATIVE TECHNIQUES

As you begin to develop the techniques you will use in your narrative, ask yourself the following questions:

- Which characters are talking? How am I organizing the dialogue?

- How quickly or slowly do I want the plot to move? Why?

- Which literary devices can be added to strengthen the characters or plot? How can I better engage the reader?

There are many techniques you can use in a narrative. Here are some methods that can help you write dialogue, pacing, and description to develop experiences, events, and/or characters:

- Use dialogue between characters to explain events or move the action forward.

  > Set all spoken dialogue off in quotation marks, using name tags as needed.

  > Italicize internal thoughts, using identifying name tags as needed.

- Include description to engage the reader and help him or her visualize the characters, setting, and other elements in the narrative.

  > Include only those descriptions relevant to the reader's understanding of the element being described.

  > Consider using literary devices or figurative language such as imagery, metaphors, similes, personification, or idioms.

- Use pacing effectively to convey a sense of urgency or calm in a narrative.

  > To speed up the pace, try using limited description, short paragraphs, brief dialogue, and simpler sentences.

  > To slow down the pace, try using detailed description, longer paragraphs, and more complex sentence structures.

- Use any combination of the above narrative techniques to develop experiences, events, and/or characters.

↻ YOUR TURN

Read each excerpt below. Then, complete the chart by writing the narrative technique that correctly matches each paragraph.

Narrative Technique Options		
Dialogue	Pacing	Description

Excerpt	Excerpt Narrative Technique
"I mean if she's real, she's in big trouble. How long do you think somebody who's really like that is going to last around here?" *Stargirl*	
Then Rikki-tikki went out into the garden to see what was to be seen. It was a large garden, only half cultivated, with bushes, as big as summer-houses, of Marshal Niel roses, lime and orange trees, clumps of bamboos, and thickets of high grass. Rikki-tikki licked his lips. "This is a splendid hunting-ground," he said, and his tail grew bottle-brushy at the thought of it, and he scuttled up and down the garden, snuffing here and there till he heard very sorrowful voices in a thorn-bush. "Rikki-Tikki-Tavi"	
Sweat popped out on the boy's face and he began to struggle. Mrs. Jones stopped, jerked him around in front of her, put a half-nelson about his neck, and continued to drag him up the street. When she got to her door, she dragged the boy inside, down a hall, and into a large kitchenette-furnished room at the rear of the house. She switched on the light and left the door open. The boy could hear other roomers laughing and talking in the large house. "Thank You, M'am"	

Please note that excerpts and passages in the StudySync® library and this workbook are intended as touchstones to generate interest in an author's work. The excerpts and passages do not substitute for the reading of entire texts, and StudySync® strongly recommends that students seek out and purchase the whole literary or informational work in order to experience it as the author intended. Links to online resellers are available in our digital library. In addition, complete works may be ordered through an authorized reseller by filling out and returning to StudySync® the order form enclosed in this workbook.

Reading & Writing Companion **135**

YOUR TURN

Complete the chart below by rewriting part of your narrative using each narrative technique.

Narrative Technique	Rewrite
Dialogue	
Pacing	
Description	

Skill:
Transitions

••• CHECKLIST FOR TRANSITIONS

Before you revise your current draft to include transitions, think about:

- the order of events, including the rising action, climax, falling action, and resolution
- moments where the time or setting changes

Next, reread your current draft and note areas in your narrative where:

- the order of events is unclear or illogical
- changes in time or setting are confusing or unclear. Look for:

  > sudden jumps in time and setting

  > missing or illogical plot events

  > places where you could add more context to help the reader understand where and when plot events are happening

Revise your draft to use a variety of transition words, phrases, and clauses to convey sequence and signal shifts from one time frame or setting to another, using the following questions as a guide:

- Does my exposition provide necessary background information?
- Do the events of the rising action, climax, falling action, and resolution flow naturally and logically?
- Did I include a variety of transition words, phrases, and clauses that show sequence and signal setting and time changes?
- Transitions such as "that night" or "on the first sunny day" can indicate changes in time periods.
- Phrases or clauses such as "a week later, Bob boarded a train to Iowa" can indicate shifts in setting and time.

YOUR TURN

Choose the best answer to each question.

1. Jalyn would like to add some transition words signaling that Anh lined up after the competition. Which transition phrase BEST shows the sequence of events in this passage?

> Anh lined up on the stage with the rest of the contestants.

- ○ A. At the end of the competition, Anh lined up on the stage with the rest of the contestants.
- ○ B. Before Anh lined up on the stage with the rest of the contestants, she went backstage.
- ○ C. In the community center, Anh lined up on the stage with the rest of the contestants.
- ○ D. Anh lined up on the stage, in front of the curtain, with the rest of the contestants.

2. Which passage from the Model below shows a strong transition in time period?

- ○ A. But when she got to the auditorium, Anh was overwhelmed with nerves. *What if I forget the words? Or worse, what if I open my mouth and forget how to sing?*
- ○ B. The following week, Anh sang with more energy than before, and grinned at her brother from the stage. *I can't wait to see the look on his face when I tell him about all those water slides . . .* she thought as she finished her song.
- ○ C. Jen's dad was so impressed that he suggested they enter a competition at their local community center. There would be a preliminary round in one month and a final round the following week.
- ○ D. When she went onstage, Anh was determined to give it her all. She felt the bright spotlights shining down on her, the crowd got silent, and she could hear the judges tapping their pencils and moving their papers.

↻ YOUR TURN

Complete the chart by revising a section of your narrative to include a shift in setting or time.

Transition In	Revision
Time	
Setting	
Time	
Setting	

Skill:
Conclusions

••• CHECKLIST FOR CONCLUSIONS

Before you write your conclusion, ask yourself the following questions:

- Which important details from my story should I summarize or remind readers of in my conclusion?

- What other thoughts and feelings could the characters share with readers in the conclusion?

- Should I express why the narrative matters through character reflections or dialogue?

Below are two strategies to help you provide a conclusion that follows from and reflects on the narrated experiences or events:

- Peer discussion

  > After you have written your introduction and body paragraphs, talk with a partner about possible endings for your narrative, writing notes about your discussion.

  > Review your notes and think about how you want to end your story.

  > Briefly summarize the events in the narrative through the narrator or one of the characters.

  > Describe how the narrator feels about the events he or she experienced.

  > Reveal to readers why the narrative matters through character reflections or dialogue.

  > Write your conclusion.

- Freewriting

  > Freewrite for ten minutes about what you might include in your conclusion. Don't worry about grammar, punctuation, or having fully formed ideas. The point of freewriting is to discover ideas.

  > Review your notes and think about how you want to end your story.

  > Briefly summarize the events in the narrative through the narrator or one of the characters.

  > Describe how the narrator feels about the events he or she experienced.

  > Reveal to readers why the narrative matters through character reflections or dialogue.

  > Write your conclusion.

 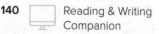

↻ YOUR TURN

Read the excerpts below. Then, complete the chart by matching the correct strategy with each excerpt.

Strategy Options	
A	character or narrator's thoughts and feelings
B	important details to help summarize the story
C	reflections or dialogue to reveal why the narrative matters

Excerpt from *Stargirl*'s Conclusion	Strategy
We wanted to define her, to wrap her up as we did each other, but we could not seem to get past "weird" and "strange" and "goofy." Her ways knocked us off balance. A single word seemed to hover in the cloudless sky over the school: HUH? Everything she did seemed to echo Hillari Kimble: She's not real . . . She's not real . . .	
In that moonlit hour, I acquired a sense of the otherness of things. I liked the feeling the moonlight gave me, as if it wasn't the opposite of day, but its underside, its private side, when the fabulous purred on my snow-white sheet like some dark cat come in from the desert.	
It was during one of these nightmoon times that it came to me that Hillari Kimble was wrong. Stargirl *was* real.	

✎ WRITE

Use the questions in the checklist section to help you freewrite on the graphic organizer or on a piece of paper. Then revise the conclusion of your narrative.

Narrative Writing Process: Revise

PLAN	DRAFT	REVISE	EDIT AND PUBLISH

You have written a draft of your narrative. You have also received input from your peers about how to improve it. Now you are going to revise your draft.

← REVISION GUIDE

Examine your draft to find areas for revision. Keep in mind your purpose and audience as you revise for clarity, development, organization, and style. Use the guide below to help you review:

Review	Revise	Example
Clarity		
Identify places where some narrative techniques would improve your story. First, annotate any places where it is unclear who is speaking. Then, label each piece of dialogue so you know who is speaking.	Use the character's name to show who is speaking. Add description about the speaker.	"You control your voice well," ~~he said~~. the second judge said. "Lots of nice touches in that song." *At least she was on key this time.*
Development		
Identify places where descriptive details are needed to describe important characters and the events of the plot. First, annotate places where vague or overused words are used. Then, annotate where you want to tell how something looks, sounds, feels, smells, or tastes.	Focus on a single event and add descriptive details, such as sensory details or precise action words.	But when she got to the auditorium, Anh was overwhelmed with nerves. She felt butterflies in her stomach, her mouth was dry, and she could only hear her heart. *What if I forget the words? Or worse, what if I open my mouth and forget how to sing?*

Review	Revise	Example
Organization		
Identify places where transitions would improve your story. First, reread and then retell your story. Then, annotate where there is a sudden jump in time and setting.	Rewrite the events in the correct sequence. Use transition words to signal changes in time or setting. Delete any events that are not essential to the story.	When she went onstage, Anh was determined to give it her all. She felt the bright spotlights shining down on her, the crowd got silent, and she could hear the judges tapping their pencils and moving their papers. She took a deep breath and felt the butterflies in her stomach disappear. As she started to sing, she was able to forget her nervousness and focus on the lyrics. ~~As she walked out on stage, she was determined to give it her all.~~ She stood taller and felt even more confident. She didn't miss a single beat! The crowd applauded loudly. Next, the judges weighed in.
Style: Word Choice		
Identify every form of the verb *to be* (*am, is, are, was, were, be, being, been*).	Select sentences to rewrite using action verbs.	Anh ~~was happy~~ smirked when she realized she'd be on all those rides at the park before Thao.
Style: Sentence Variety		
Think about a key event where you want your reader to feel a specific emotion. Long sentences can draw out a moment and make a reader think; short sentences can show urgent actions or danger.	Rewrite a key event making your sentences longer or shorter to achieve the emotion you want your reader to feel.	But Anh scored high, and so did Valeria and Jennifer. ~~They all scored high enough to make it to the second round so they could come back next week.~~ At the end of the competition they all made it to the second round.

✏ WRITE

Use the guide above, as well as your peer reviews, to help you evaluate your narrative to determine areas that should be revised.

Grammar: Basic Spelling Rules I

Spelling *ie* and *ei*

Spelling Conventions	Correct Spelling	Incorrect Spelling
Usually, when *i* and *e* appear together in one syllable, the *i* comes before the *e*.	siege wield fiend	seige weild feind
When *i* and *e* appear after a *c,* the *e* usually comes before the *i.*	conceive receiver	concieve reciever
However, there are exceptions to these patterns.	weird neither protein neighbor	wierd niether protien nieghbor

Suffixes and the Silent *e*

Spelling Conventions	Base Words	Correct Spelling	Incorrect Spelling
When adding a suffix that begins with a consonant to a word that ends with a silent **e**, keep the **e**.	amuse scene	amusement scenery	amusment scenry
When adding a suffix that begins with a vowel to a word that ends with a silent **e**, usually drop the **e**.	agile humane	agility humanity	agilety humanety

Reading & Writing Companion

⟳ YOUR TURN

1. How should the spelling error in this sentence be corrected?

> The Yukon region attracted the subspecies of humanity that would risk the harsh, unyeilding winters and seize any chance to strike it rich.

○ A. Change **subspecies** to **subspeceis**.

○ B. Change **unyeilding** to **unyielding**.

○ C. Change **seize** to **sieze**.

○ D. No change needs to be made to this sentence.

2. How should the spelling error in this sentence be corrected?

> César Chávez helped outlaw dangerous pesticides and end job discrimination, but his greatest achievement was bringing diverse people together to become activeists in a common cause.

○ A. Change **discrimination** to **discriminateion**.

○ B. Change **achievement** to **acheivement**.

○ C. Change **activeists** to **activists**.

○ D. No change needs to be made to this sentence.

3. How should the spelling error in this sentence be corrected?

> In the story "The Lottery," the most suspensful question is who will be chosen, but the most ominous element is the degree of acceptance by the villagers of this regular event.

○ A. Change **suspensful** to **suspenseful**.

○ B. Change **ominous** to **omenous**.

○ C. Change **acceptance** to **acceptence**.

○ D. No change needs to be made to this sentence.

Grammar:
Main and Subordinate Clauses

Main Clause

A clause is a group of words that includes both a subject and a verb (predicate). A clause may be a sentence by itself or part of a sentence.

A **main clause** is also called an independent clause because it expresses a complete thought and can stand alone as a sentence. Every sentence must have at least one main clause, and every main clause must have a subject and a verb. A main clause may be punctuated as a sentence.

Incorrect Main Clause	Correct Main Clause
won the meet	**Harrison won** the meet.
They cold hands	**They had** cold hands.

Subordinate Clause

Like a main clause, a **subordinate clause** must have a subject and a verb, but a subordinate clause does not express a complete thought and cannot stand alone as a sentence. A subordinate clause is also called a dependent clause, because it depends on a main clause to make sense.

Usually, a subordinating conjunction (such as *although, because, unless,* or *since*) introduces a subordinate clause, but the clause may also begin with a relative pronoun (*who, whose, whom, which, that,* or *what*) or adverb (*when, where,* or *why*).

Sentences can have a combination of clauses, but at least one must be a main clause. Two or more main clauses are commonly joined using a comma followed by a conjunction.

Clause	Sentence
Main Clause Subordinate Clause	**A good alternative is the roadside restaurant** where men gather for breakfast before going to work or going hunting.
	A good alternative is the roadside restaurant **where men gather for breakfast before going to work or going hunting**. *Travels with Charley*

⟳ YOUR TURN

1. How should this sentence be revised?

> Rice dishes are easy to prepare they are popular in restaurants.

- ○ A. Insert a comma after the word *prepare*.
- ○ B. Remove the word *they*.
- ○ C. Insert a comma and the conjunction *and* after the word *prepare*.
- ○ D. The sentence does not need revision.

2. How should this sentence be revised?

> Alligators and crocodiles live in tropical regions because are cold-blooded.

- ○ A. Remove the word *in*.
- ○ B. Insert the word *they* after the conjunction *because*.
- ○ C. Replace the word *are* with the word *they*.
- ○ D. The sentence does not need revision.

3. How should this sentence be revised?

> Although many dinosaurs were calm plant-eaters, movies often portray dinosaurs as aggressive, horrifying carnivores.

- ○ A. Remove the word *Although*.
- ○ B. Insert the conjunction *but* after the first comma.
- ○ C. Insert the conjunction *and* after the second comma.
- ○ D. The sentence does not need revision.

4. How should this sentence be revised?

> Ancient people drew pictures on cave walls they wanted to record major events in their lives or because they needed to express their feelings.

- ○ A. Insert the word *when* after the word *walls*.
- ○ B. Remove the infinitive *to record*.
- ○ C. Change the conjunction *or* to the conjunction *and*.
- ○ D. The sentence does not need revision.

Grammar: Simple and Compound Sentences

A simple sentence has one complete subject and one complete predicate. The subject, the predicate, or both may be compound.

Simple Sentence
The ANTS were spending a fine winter's day drying grain collected in the summertime. *Aesop's Fables*

A compound sentence has two or more main clauses (simple sentences).
These main clauses are joined with a comma followed by a coordinating conjunction such as *or, and,* or *but*. They can also be joined by a semicolon (;).

Compound Sentence	Coordinating Conjunction
Father was away on a trading expedition as usual, but our cook, Mandy, was there. *Ella Enchanted*	but

Compound Sentence	Coordinating Conjunction
You can tell he's real happy to have the bird-thing back, and his face isn't quite so fierce. *Freak the Mighty*	and

↻ YOUR TURN

1. How can this sentence be changed into a simple sentence?

> Paramecium are very small a microscope is needed to examine them.

- ○ A. Insert a comma after **small**.
- ○ B. Insert a semicolon after **small**.
- ○ C. Remove the clause **a microscope is needed to examine them**.
- ○ D. No change needs to be made to this sentence.

2. How can this sentence be changed into a simple sentence?

> Liam had a solo in last year's concert, and he hopes to have one this year, too.

- ○ A. Remove the first comma, conjunction, and clause **he hopes to have one this year, too**.
- ○ B. Replace the first comma and conjunction with a semicolon.
- ○ C. Remove **in last year's concert**.
- ○ D. No change needs to be made to this sentence.

3. How can this sentence be changed into a compound sentence?

> Should I take the bus to school, or should I walk?

- ○ A. Change **or** to **but**.
- ○ B. Add **to school** after **walk**.
- ○ C. Change the comma to a semicolon.
- ○ D. No change needs to be made to this sentence.

4. How can this sentence be changed into a compound sentence?

> The storm blew down a tree on our street, there was no other damage.

- ○ A. Add the conjunction **but** after the comma.
- ○ B. Delete the comma and clause **there was no other damage**.
- ○ C. Remove the comma.
- ○ D. No change needs to be made to this sentence.

Narrative Writing Process: Edit and Publish

PLAN	DRAFT	REVISE	EDIT AND PUBLISH

You have revised your narrative based on your peer feedback and your own examination.

Now, it is time to edit your narrative. When you revised, you focused on the content of your narrative. You probably looked at your story's beginning, descriptive details, and narrative techniques. When you edit, you focus on the mechanics of your story, paying close attention to things like grammar and punctuation.

Use the checklist below to guide you as you edit:

☐ Have I followed spelling rules for words that use the suffix -ed?

☐ Have I checked for spelling mistakes in words that add a prefix?

☐ Have I checked that all sentences have a main clause?

☐ Do I have any sentence fragments or run-on sentences?

☐ Have I spelled everything correctly?

Notice some edits Jalyn has made:

- followed spelling rules for words that use the suffix -ed

- followed spelling rules for words that are commonly misspelled

- used a comma and a coordinating conjunction to connect two main clauses

- connected a subordinate clause to a main clause to create a complete sentence

But Anh still loved music, and she kept playing every day. When she started middle ~~schoo.l she~~ school, she joined the choir. It became her favorite school activity. She and her friends had fun pretending to be reality-show singers on ~~weekends using~~ weekends, using a karaoke machine that belonged to Jennifer's family. Jen's dad was so ~~impresed~~ impressed that he suggested they enter a competition at their local community center. There would be a ~~prelimenary~~ preliminary round in one month and a final round the following week.

WRITE

Use the questions on the previous page, as well as your peer reviews, to help you evaluate your narrative to determine areas that need editing. Then edit your narrative to correct those errors.

Once you have made all your corrections, you are ready to publish your work. You can distribute your writing to family and friends, hang it on a bulletin board, or post it on your blog. If you publish online, share the link with your family, friends, and classmates.

Ready for Marcos

FICTION

Introduction

Twelve-year-old Monica Alvarez has a happy life. She is a star on the track team and has many good friends. But everything changes when her parents bring Marcos, her new baby brother, home from the hospital. Her parents want her to have more responsibilities. Monica wonders what it will mean to be a big sister. Is she ready? Is she willing?

VOCABULARY

vivacious
energetic and happy; lively

justify
to support with good reasons

covertly
done in secret

subtle
barely noticeable

pursue
to try to do or achieve something

turmoil
a state of confusion, nervousness, or anxiety

☰ READ

NOTES

1 Three days ago, her parents brought him home from the hospital. From the time her mom and dad walked through the door with their sleeping bundle, everything was different. Her parents drifted through the day as if in a fog. They used to be energetic and **vivacious**, but now they seemed fatigued all the time.

2 On Marcos's fourth day home, Monica woke up and heard her parents talking quietly. She **covertly** walked to the door. "Monica is a big sister now," her dad said. "I think it's time for her to have more responsibilities around the house."

3 Her mom agreed. "We can talk to her at dinner," she added.

4 Monica turned and walked quietly back to her room. She closed the door behind her. *More responsibilities?* she thought to herself.

5   She spent much of the afternoon thinking about how the new baby would change her life. This year she was the fastest seventh grader on the track team. With more responsibilities, could she still **pursue** her dream of making the eighth-grade team? And what about time for her friends?

6   As dinner time grew closer, Monica began to fear the talk with her parents. She heard them cooking in the kitchen, so she ducked into his room where he was sleeping in his crib. Her new little brother—Marcos.

7   Monica looked at Marcos. She wondered how someone so small could **justify** such trouble. Then she looked closely at him. He was so small. She touched his soft cheek. *He's so cute*, Monica thought. Marcos opened his tiny eyes and looked up at her. As she looked at him, Monica felt a **subtle** change. Before she had felt in **turmoil**, but now she felt something new. She was a big sister. She knew how to tie her shoes and ride a bike. Marcos would need someone to show him how to do everything.

8   Later, Monica sat down to dinner. She felt her courage rise. "Mom, Dad, I have something to say," she began. "I'm a big sister now, and I should help more around the house." Her parents looked at each other. "I've done laundry lots of times," Monica explained, "and now I can do it for you and Marcos, too. Plus, I can help with dinner after track practice."

9   Her mom smiled. She said, "You're going to be the best big sister ever!"

First Read

Read the story. After you read, answer the Think Questions below.

☁ THINK QUESTIONS

1. Who is Marcos? How is he related to Monica?

   Marcos is _____.

   He is Monica's _____.

2. Why is Monica worried about making the track team?

   Monica worries that _____.

3. What does Monica promise to do to help her parents?

   Monica promises to _____.

4. Use context to confirm the meaning of the word *turmoil* as it is used in "Ready for Marcos." Write your definition of *turmoil* here.

   Turmoil means _____.

   A context clue is _____.

5. What is another way to say that someone *pursued* his or her dream?

   Someone _____.

Skill:
Analyzing Expressions

★ DEFINE

When you read, you may find English expressions that you do not know. An **expression** is a group of words that communicates an idea. Three types of expressions are idioms, sayings, and figurative language. They can be difficult to understand because the meanings of the words are different from their **literal**, or usual, meanings.

An **idiom** is an expression that is commonly known among a group of people. For example: "It's raining cats and dogs" means it is raining heavily. **Sayings** are short expressions that contain advice or wisdom. For instance: "Don't count your chickens before they hatch" means do not plan on something good happening before it happens. **Figurative** language is when you describe something by comparing it with something else, either directly (using the words *like* or *as*) or indirectly. For example, "I'm as hungry as a horse" means I'm very hungry. None of the expressions are about actual animals.

••• CHECKLIST FOR ANALYZING EXPRESSIONS

To determine the meaning of an expression, remember the following:

✓ If you find a confusing group of words, it may be an expression. The meaning of words in expressions may not be their literal meaning.

- Ask yourself: Is this confusing because the words are new? Or because the words do not make sense together?

✓ Determining the overall meaning may require that you use one or more of the following:

- context clues
- a dictionary or other resource
- teacher or peer support

✓ Highlight important information before and after the expression to look for clues.

YOUR TURN

Read the following excerpt from "Ready for Marcos." Then, complete the multiple-choice questions below.

---

from **"Ready for Marcos"**

Three days ago, her parents brought him home from the hospital. From the time her mom and dad walked through the door with their sleeping bundle, everything was different. Her parents drifted through the day as if in a fog. They used to be energetic and vivacious, but now they seemed fatigued all the time.

On Marcos's fourth day home, Monica woke up and heard her parents talking quietly. She covertly walked to the door. "Monica is a big sister now," her dad said. "I think it's time for her to have more responsibilities around the house."

---

1. What does "in a fog" in paragraph 1 mean?

    ○ A. The weather is bad.

    ○ B. The parents can't see.

    ○ C. The parents are upset.

    ○ D. The parents feel tired.

2. Which context clue helped you determine the meaning of the expression?

    ○ A. "They seemed fatigued all the time."

    ○ B. "Monica woke up and heard her parents talking quietly."

    ○ C. "Monica is a big sister now."

    ○ D. "She covertly walked to the door."

Please note that excerpts and passages in the StudySync® library and this workbook are intended as touchstones to generate interest in an author's work. The excerpts and passages do not substitute for the reading of entire texts, and StudySync® strongly recommends that students seek out and purchase the whole literary or informational work in order to experience it as the author intended. Links to online resellers are available in our digital library. In addition, complete works may be ordered through an authorized reseller by filling out and returning to StudySync® the order form enclosed in this workbook.

Reading & Writing Companion   **157**

Skill:
Conveying Ideas

Copyright © BookheadEd Learning, LLC

 DEFINE

Conveying ideas means communicating a **message** to another person. When speaking, you might not know what word to use to convey your ideas. When you do not know the exact English word, you can try different strategies. For example, you can ask for help from classmates or your teacher. You may use gestures and physical movements to act out the word. You can also try using **synonyms** or **defining** and describing the meaning you are trying to express.

••• **CHECKLIST FOR CONVEYING IDEAS**

To convey ideas for words you do not know when speaking, use the following learning strategies:

✓ Request help.

✓ Use gestures or physical movements.

✓ Use a synonym for the word.

✓ Describe what the word means using other words.

✓ Give an example of the word you want to use.

↻ YOUR TURN

Read the following excerpt from the story. Then imagine that someone is trying to convey the idea of Marcos *sleeping*. Find the correct example for each strategy to complete the chart below.

from **"Ready for Marcos"**
As dinner time grew closer, Monica began to fear the talk with her parents. She heard them cooking in the kitchen, so she ducked into his room where he was sleeping in his crib. Her new little brother—Marcos.

	Examples
A	The person explains that the word means "to rest."
B	The person closes their eyes and puts their head against the desk.
C	The person says, "This is when you close your eyes for a few minutes when you're tired, or when you lie in bed at night."
D	The person uses the similar word *napping*.

Strategies	Examples
Use gestures or physical movements.	
Use a synonym for the word.	
Describe what the word means using other words.	
Give examples of the word you want to use.	

Close Read

✏ WRITE

PERSONAL NARRATIVE: In "Ready for Marcos," Monica experiences a major change in her life. Tell about a big change in your own life. Tell why this was a big change for you. Describe how your life is now, using specific details. Pay attention to spelling patterns as you write.

Use the checklist below to guide you as you write.

☐ What is an event that has changed your life the most?

☐ What are some facts or details that you can give that show this was a big change?

☐ How is your life now?

Use the sentence frames to organize and write your personal narrative.

My life changed in a big way when _____.

It was important because _____.

I used to _____.

Now I _____.

Now my life is _____.

A World Away

Introduction

As Rajeet Basak was about to begin seventh grade in Mumbai, India, his family moved to Chicago, Illinois, for his father's work. Rajeet had to learn to live in a new place. At the end of his first school year, he is interviewed by a reporter for the school newspaper about his experiences in his first year in Chicago. Rajeet explains that some things about the two places are different and some things are the same. What does Rajeet find strange? What does Rajeet think about life in Chicago?

VOCABULARY

adjustment
a small, helpful change

announce
to tell people about something important

positive
good, happy, satisfied

bulky
heavy, hard to move

interview
a formal meeting in which a person answers questions

thermometer
instrument that measures heat and cold

NOTES

≡ READ

1 A World Away

2 by Karen Dennison

3 This year Lakeside Middle School welcomed Rajeet Basak from Mumbai, India. His first year in Chicago was full of **adjustments**, but Rajeet is happy. His experience has been **positive**.

4 In an **interview**, Rajeet explained how he learned about his family's move. "I came home for dinner," Rajeet said. "During dinner, my father **announced** that we'd be moving to Chicago in a few weeks. I was in shock. I couldn't eat."

5 Rajeet did not know how different life would be. In Chicago he was lonely and sad at first. But then October came. Rajeet could think of nothing but the cold. He did not know how soon the long winter would begin.

6   Rajeet said, "We knew it was colder here than in Mumbai. So my mom and I went shopping for a winter coat. It felt heavy and **bulky**. It was hard to move in, but I was glad to have it!"

7   One day Rajeet looked at the **thermometer**. He could not believe the reading was so low. And he could not believe that he saw snow falling. "I didn't know what was happening," Rajeet remembered. "I'd read about snow, but I had never seen it. It was beautiful, but it was freezing cold when I touched it with bare hands. Now I wear gloves lined with wool."

8   The weather was a big shock to Rajeet. His first weeks were lonely. However, Rajeet has new friends. He met them through his interest in sports. "Some sports are the same. Others are not. My friends and I still play soccer. In India, soccer is called "football." Here, there's another sport called football. It is unlike anything I've ever seen! We watch it on TV."

9   Rajeet added that school in Chicago is somewhat different. "In Mumbai, we had bigger classes, but I like it here. I've tried to be respectful to my teachers as we were in Mumbai and as my friends are here."

10 Rajeet also likes American food. "It's less spicy, and there's more meat. But my mom still makes the same things we ate in Mumbai. It's not hard to find Indian spices, and I love a dish of chicken curry."

11 Rajeet has adapted to life here and learns more every day. Next year he hopes to join the soccer team and hopes for a milder winter.

Please note that excerpts and passages in the StudySync® library and this workbook are intended as touchstones to generate interest in an author's work. The excerpts and passages do not substitute for the reading of entire texts, and StudySync® strongly recommends that students seek out and purchase the whole literary or informational work in order to experience it as the author intended. Links to online resellers are available in our digital library. In addition, complete works may be ordered through an authorized reseller by filling out and returning to StudySync® the order form enclosed in this workbook.

Reading & Writing Companion   163

First Read

Read the story. After you read, answer the Think Questions below.

☁ **THINK QUESTIONS**

1. Where did Rajeet live before his family moved?

    Rajeet lived in _____.

2. Why was life in Chicago difficult at first for Rajeet?

    Life in Chicago was difficult because _____.

3. What hopes does Rajeet have for next year?

    Rajeet hopes _____.

4. Use context to confirm the meaning of the word *bulky* as it is used in "A World Away." Write your definition of *bulky* here.

    Bulky means _____.

    A context clue is _____.

5. What is another way to say that an experience is *positive*?

    An experience is _____.

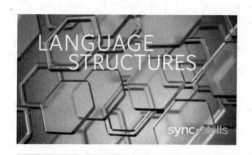

Skill:
Language Structures

★ DEFINE

In every language, there are rules that tell how to **structure** sentences. These rules define the correct order of words. In the English language, for example, a **basic** structure for sentences is subject, verb, and object. Some sentences have more **complicated** structures.

You will encounter both basic and complicated **language structures** in the classroom materials you read. Being familiar with language structures will help you better understand the text.

••• CHECKLIST FOR LANGUAGE STRUCTURES

To improve your comprehension of language structures, do the following:

✓ Monitor your understanding.

- Ask yourself: Why do I not understand this sentence? Is it because I do not understand some of the words? Or is it because I do not understand the way the words are ordered in the sentence?

✓ Break down the sentence into its parts.

- In English, most sentences share the same pattern: subject + verb + object.

  > The subject names who or what is doing the action.

  > The verb names the action or state of being.

  > The object answers questions such as Who?, What?, Where?, and When?

- Ask yourself: What is the action? Who or what is doing the action? What details do the other words provide?

✓ Confirm your understanding with a peer or teacher.

Please note that excerpts and passages in the StudySync® library and this workbook are intended as touchstones to generate interest in an author's work. The excerpts and passages do not substitute for the reading of entire texts, and StudySync® strongly recommends that students seek out and purchase the whole literary or informational work in order to experience it as the author intended. Links to online resellers are available in our digital library. In addition, complete works may be ordered through an authorized reseller by filling out and returning to StudySync® the order form enclosed in this workbook.

Reading & Writing Companion **165**

YOUR TURN

Read the following excerpt from the text. Then, complete the chart by writing the words and phrases into the "Subject," "Verb," and "Object" columns. The first row has been done as an example.

---

from "A World Away"

The weather was a big shock to Rajeet. His first weeks were lonely. However, Rajeet has new friends. He met them through his interest in sports. "Some sports are the same. Others are not. My friends and I still play soccer. In India, soccer is called "football." Here, there's another sport called football. It is unlike anything I've ever seen! We watch it on TV."

Sentence	Subject	Verb	Object
The weather was a big shock to Rajeet.	The weather	was	a big shock to Rajeet
However, Rajeet has new friends.			
Some sports are the same.			
My friends and I still play soccer.			
We watch it on TV.			

Skill: Retelling and Summarizing

★ DEFINE

You can retell and summarize a text after reading to show your understanding. **Retelling** is telling a story again in your own words. **Summarizing** is giving a short explanation of the most important ideas in a text.

Keep your retelling or summary **concise**. Only include important information and keywords from the text. By summarizing and retelling a text, you can improve your comprehension of the text's ideas.

••• CHECKLIST FOR RETELLING AND SUMMARIZING

In order to retell a story or summarize text, note the following:

✓ Identify the main events of the story.

- Ask yourself: What happens in this text? What are the main events that happen at the beginning, the middle, and the end of the text?

✓ Identify the main ideas in a text.

- Ask yourself: What are the most important ideas in the text?

✓ Determine the answers to the six *Wh-* questions.

- Ask yourself: After reading this text, can I answer Who?, What?, Where?, When?, Why?, and How? questions.

↻ YOUR TURN

Read the following excerpt from "A World Away." Then, write each event in the beginning, middle, or end of the chart to retell what happened in the story.

---

from "A World Away"

In an interview, Rajeet explained how he learned about his family's move. "I came home for dinner," Rajeet said. "During dinner, my father announced that we'd be moving to Chicago in a few weeks. I was in shock. I couldn't eat."

Event Options		
Rajeet is in shock and can't eat.	Rajeet came home for dinner	Rajeet's father says they are moving.

Beginning	
Middle	
End	

Close Read

✏ WRITE

ARGUMENTATIVE: For Rajeet, life in Chicago is very different from his life in Mumbai. Did Rajeet adapt to his new life in Chicago? Support your response with events and evidence from the text. Make connections to your own experiences. Pay attention to subject-verb agreement as you write.

Use the checklist below to guide you as you write.

☐ What was Rajeet's life like before?

☐ What is Rajeet's life like now?

☐ What changes did Rajeet make in Chicago?

☐ What changes have you made to adapt to new things in your life?

Use the sentence frames to organize and write your argument.

In Mumbai, there were _____.

In Chicago, the weather is _____.

At first, Rajeet is _____.

Then he makes new _____.

This reminds me of when I _____.

It was different because _____.

I adapted by _____.

Please note that excerpts and passages in the StudySync® library and this workbook are intended as touchstones to generate interest in an author's work. The excerpts and passages do not substitute for the reading of entire texts, and StudySync® strongly recommends that students seek out and purchase the whole literary or informational work in order to experience it as the author intended. Links to online resellers are available in our digital library. In addition, complete works may be ordered through an authorized reseller by filling out and returning to StudySync® the order form enclosed in this workbook.

Reading & Writing Companion   **169**

studysync®

ASSIGNMENTS   BINDER   LIBRARY

Highs and Lows

UNIT 2

Highs and Lows

What do we learn from love and loss?

Genre Focus: POETRY

Texts

 Paired Readings

Extended Writing Project and Grammar

English Language Learner Resources

Please note that excerpts and passages in the StudySync® library and this workbook are intended as touchstones to generate interest in an author's work. The excerpts and passages do not substitute for the reading of entire texts, and StudySync® strongly recommends that students seek out and purchase the whole literary or informational work in order to experience it as the author intended. Links to online resellers are available in our digital library. In addition, complete works may be ordered through an authorized reseller by filling out and returning to StudySync® the order form enclosed in this workbook.

Reading & Writing Companion   **173**

Unit 2: Highs and Lows
What do we learn from love and loss?

CHARLES DICKENS

Novelist, journalist, and critic Charles Dickens (1812–1870) was born in Portsmouth, England. At the age of twelve, his father was sent to debtors' prison, and Dickens left school to work ten-hour days in a factory. These experiences informed his later work, including *Oliver Twist, A Christmas Carol, David Copperfield,* and *Great Expectations.* In total, he wrote fifteen novels, five novellas, hundreds of short stories, and he edited a journal published weekly for twenty years.

ALBERT MARRIN

Albert Marrin (b. 1936) is a graduate of City College of New York and Yeshiva University, where he is a professor of history. His career as an author began while teaching in the East Bronx when he used "storytime" to engage students and tell tales like "Custer's Last Stand." His first book, *War and the Christian Conscience: From Augustine to Martin Luther King, Jr.,* was written for an adult audience, but, missing "storytime," he went on to write three dozen young adult books, beginning in 1982 with his first, *Overlord: D-Day* and the *Invasion of Europe.*

ALFRED NOYES

Alfred Noyes (1880–1958) was born in Wolverhampton, England, and attended Exeter College, Oxford, but did not finish his degree; he missed his finals in 1903 to meet with a publisher for his first volume of poetry, *The Loom of Years,* which received favorable reviews from W. B. Yeats. Over the next five years, he published five books of poetry, as well as two of his most famous poems, "The Highwayman" and "Drake." He went on to write novels as well as literary criticism, a trilogy of poems called *The Torch-Bearers,* and to teach at Princeton University.

EDGAR ALLAN POE

Edgar Allan Poe (1809–1849) was born in Boston, Massachusetts. He was orphaned after his mother Elizabeth died, and he was taken in by John and Frances Allan of Richmond, Virginia. Poe went on to attend the University of Virginia, but left after a year because of problems coming up with his tuition. He then enlisted in the army and attended West Point until he intentionally got himself court-martialed, at which point he focused on writing. At thirty-five, he broke through when his poem "The Raven" was published to instant success. He died five years later in Baltimore.

SUSAN POWER

A member of the Standing Rock Tribe of the Dakotas, Susan Power (b. 1961) was born in Chicago, Illinois. She received degrees from Harvard/Radcliffe University and Harvard Law School. She decided to end her law career and become a writer after having a vision while recovering from an appendectomy. She saw a Dakota Sioux woman standing in her hospital room, who would go on to be a main character in her first novel, *The Grass Dancer,* which won the PEN/Hemingway Award for a First Novel in 1995.

TERESA PALOMO ACOSTA

Born in McGregor, Texas, Teresa Palomo Acosta (b. 1949) is a poet, historian, author, and activist, whose work sheds light on the underrepresented narratives and histories of Mexican American communities in Texas. Both of Acosta's parents were descendants of Mexican migrant workers who settled in Central Texas in the 1930s, and much of her work draws inspiration from this heritage. With Ruthe Winegarten, she co-authored *Las Tejanas: 300 Years of History* about the often-overlooked contributions of Mexican American women to Texas history. Acosta has lived and worked in Austin, Texas, since the late 1970s.

EDWARD BLOOR

Edward Bloor (b. 1950), author of *Tangerine*, was born in Trenton, New Jersey. Bloor worked as high school English teacher before becoming an editor for a major publishing house. During his time there, he wrote several books. On his transition from editor to writer, Bloor said, "My teaching job led to a job in educational publishing, where I was actually required to sit and read young adult novels all day long. So I decided to try it myself." He lives in Winter Garden, Florida.

MARCELA FUENTES

Marcela Fuentes grew up in South Texas, graduated from the University of Texas at Austin, and attended the Iowa Writers' Workshop. She's been published in the *Indiana Review, Bodega Magazine, Blackbird, Stoneslide Corrective, Juked,* and *Vestal Review.* She currently teaches at Texas A&M University as an assistant professor of creative writing and Latinx literature.

ARACELIS GIRMAY

Aracelis Girmay (b. 1977) was born and raised in Orange County, California, attended Connecticut College, and earned her MFA from New York University. She is the author of *Teeth and Kingdom Animalia,* in addition to a collage-based book, *changing, changing.* Girmay's work covers the territory between memory and loss, and what it means to be a citizen in the 21st century. Her poem "Noche de Lluvia, San Salvador" was featured as part of the New York City subway's Poetry in Motion program. She teaches at Hampshire College and Drew University in New Jersey.

WING TEK LUM

Wing Tek Lum (b. 1946) was born in Honolulu, Hawaii. At Brown University, he studied engineering and became an editor of the school's literary journal. He helped organize against the Vietnam War, and was arrested at the Pentagon for protesting. From there, he went to Union Theological Seminary, graduated with a Master of Divinity, and eventually became a social worker. He is the author of two books of poetry, *Expounding the Doubtful Points* and *The Nanjing Massacre: Poems.* He lives in Hawaii.

ALEX SHULTZ

Alex Shultz has written for *Grantland, SLAM, Los Angeles Magazine,* and the *Los Angeles Times.* Raised in Plano, Texas, Shultz studied print and digital journalism at the University of Southern California, where he began writing at the *Daily Trojan* before becoming a sports editor. He lives in Brooklyn, New York, and works as a freelance journalist.

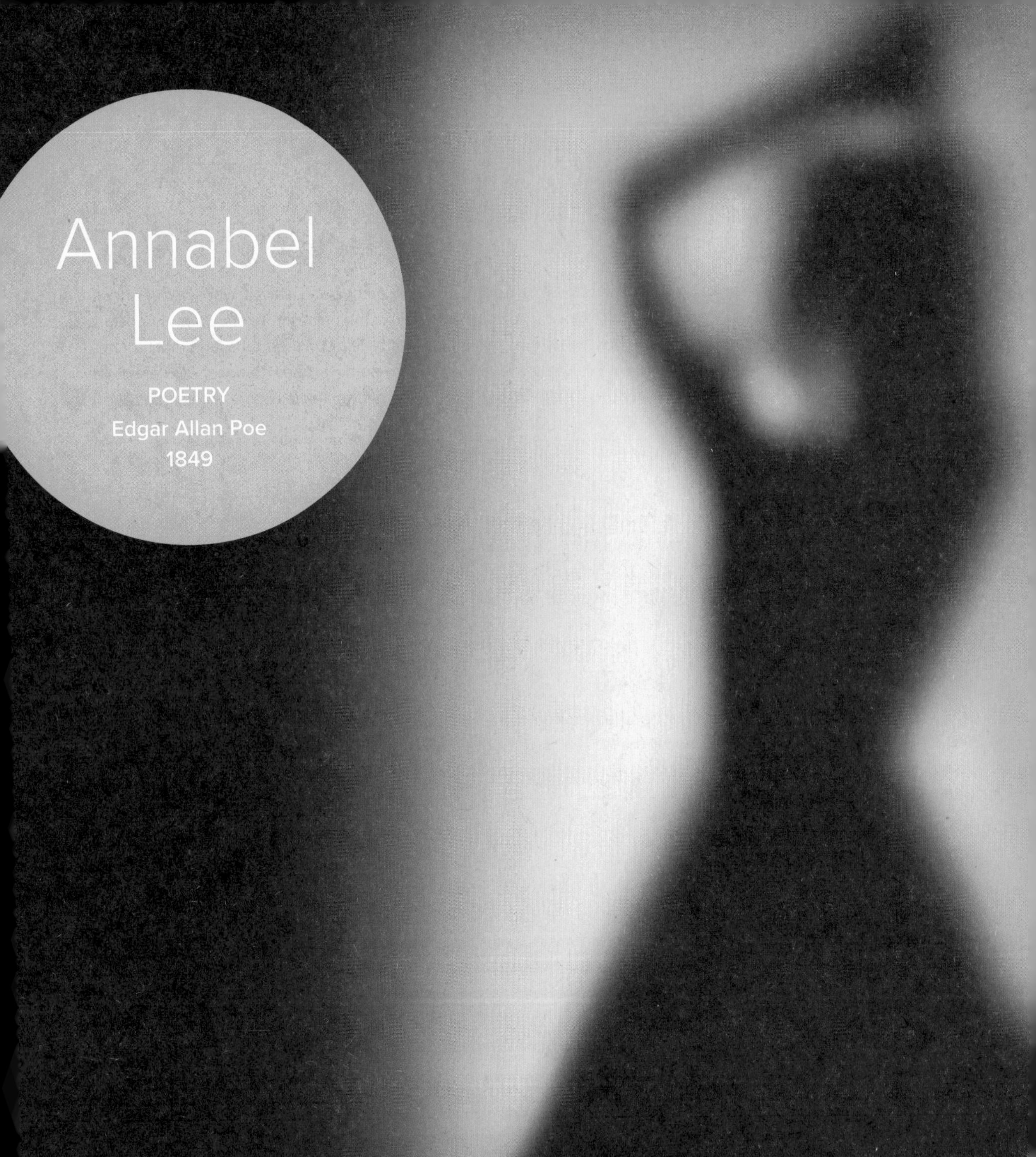

Annabel Lee

POETRY

Edgar Allan Poe

1849

ntroduction

studysync tv

Edgar Allan Poe's (1809–1849) last complete poem, "Annabel Lee," follows a familiar Poe storyline—the death of a beautiful woman. Poe lost many women close to him over the course of his life, and there has been much speculation and debate about who served as the inspiration for the heroine of this poem. Most people believe that Poe wrote the poem about his late wife, Virginia Clemm, who

First Read

Read "Annabel Lee." After you read, complete the Think Questions below.

☁ THINK QUESTIONS

1. What is the relationship between the speaker of the poem and Annabel Lee? Cite textual evidence from the poem to support your answer.

2. What happens to Annabel Lee? Cite textual evidence from the poem to support your answer.

3. Write two to three sentences describing how the speaker is affected by his relationship with Annabel Lee. Cite evidence from the text to support your answer.

4. Find the word **coveted** in line 12 of "Annabel Lee." Use context clues in the surrounding lines, as well as the line in which the word appears, to determine the word's meaning. Write your definition here and identify clues that helped you figure out the meaning.

5. Use context clues to determine the meaning of **dissever** as it is used in line 32 of "Annabel Lee." Write your definition here and identify clues that helped you figure out the meaning. Then check the meaning in a dictionary.

Skill:
Poetic Elements and Structure

Use the Checklist to analyze Poetic Elements and Structure in "Annabel Lee." Refer to the sample student annotations about Poetic Elements and Structure in the text.

••• CHECKLIST FOR POETIC ELEMENTS AND STRUCTURE

In order to identify sound elements chosen by the poet, note the following:

- ✓ the rhyme, rhythm, and meter, if present

- ✓ lines and stanzas in the poem that suggest its meaning

- ✓ other sound elements, such as:

  - alliteration: the repetition of initial consonant sounds, as with the *s* sound in "Cindy sweeps the sand"

  - consonance: the repetition of consonant sounds in the middle and ends of words, as with the *t* sound in "little bats in the attic"

  - assonance: the repetition of vowel sounds in words, as with the long *e* sound in "dreams of bees and sheep"

- ✓ lines or whole stanzas can be arranged to have a specific effect on the reader

To analyze the impact of rhymes and other repetitions of sounds on a specific verse or stanza of a poem, consider the following questions:

- ✓ What sound elements are present in specific stanzas of the poem?

- ✓ What is the effect of different sound elements on the stanza or verse?

- ✓ How do the sound elements emphasize important ideas or the poem's meaning?

Copyright © BookheadEd Learning, LLC

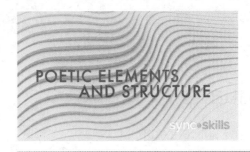

Skill:
Poetic Elements and Structure

Reread lines 34–41 of "Annabel Lee." Then, using the Checklist on the previous page, answer the multiple-choice questions below.

⟳ YOUR TURN

1. What is unusual about the rhymes in lines 34, 36, and 38?

   ○ A. Each line has a word within it that rhymes with its last word.
   ○ B. The lines rhyme with one another.
   ○ C. The rhyming words in these lines all have different vowel sounds.
   ○ D. The rhyming words all end with the sound of the letter *s*.

2. What is the impact of the rhyme scheme in lines 34, 36, and 38 on the stanza?

   ○ A. The rhyme scheme creates a dreamy and light feeling.
   ○ B. The rhyme scheme creates a harsh and angry feeling.
   ○ C. The rhyme scheme has no effect at all.
   ○ D. The rhyme scheme creates an uneasy feeling.

Please note that excerpts and passages in the StudySync® library and this workbook are intended as touchstones to generate interest in an author's work. The excerpts and passages do not substitute for the reading of entire texts, and StudySync® strongly recommends that students seek out and purchase the whole literary or informational work in order to experience it as the author intended. Links to online resellers are available in our digital library. In addition, complete works may be ordered through an authorized reseller by filling out and returning to StudySync® the order form enclosed in this workbook.

Reading & Writing
Companion

181

Skill:
Figurative Language

Use the Checklist to analyze Figurative Language in "Annabel Lee." Refer to the sample student annotations about Figurative Language in the text.

••• CHECKLIST FOR FIGURATIVE LANGUAGE

To identify figures of speech and figurative language in a text, note the following:

✓ words that mean one thing literally and suggest something else

✓ similes, such as "strong as an ox" or metaphors, such as "her eyes were stars"

✓ personification, such as "the daisies danced in the wind"

✓ allusions, or indirect references, to people, texts, events, or ideas, such as

- biblical allusions, such as describing a beautiful place as "The Garden of Eden"
- mythological allusions, such as describing a strong character as "Herculean"
- literary allusions, such as calling someone who likes romance "a real Romeo"

In order to interpret the meaning of a figure of speech in context, ask the following questions:

✓ Does any of the descriptive language in the text compare two seemingly unlike things?

✓ Do any descriptions include "like" or "as," indicating a simile?

✓ Is there a direct comparison that suggests a metaphor?

✓ Is a human quality used to describe an animal, object, force of nature, or idea?

✓ What literary, biblical, or mythological allusions do you recognize?

✓ How does this figure of speech change your understanding of the thing or person being described?

To analyze the impact of figurative language on a text's meaning, use these questions as a guide:

✓ Where does figurative language appear in the text? What does it mean?

✓ Why does the author use figurative language rather than literal language?

Skill:
Figurative Language

Reread lines 27–33 of "Annabel Lee." Then, using the Checklist on the previous page, answer the multiple-choice questions below.

↻ YOUR TURN

1. What is the biblical allusion in this stanza?

   ○ A. our love was stronger by far
   ○ B. Of those who were older than we / Of many far wiser
   ○ C. neither the angels in Heaven above / Nor the demons down under the sea
   ○ D. dissever my soul from the soul / Of the beautiful Annabel Lee

2. What is the effect of the allusion in this stanza?

   ○ A. It suggests that death is confusing and upsetting because both good and evil biblical creatures are against Annabel Lee and the speaker in the poem.
   ○ B. It supports the central idea that the forces of good will always support true love because the angels helped Annabel Lee and the narrator in the poem.
   ○ C. It builds a suspenseful tone by implying a fight between good and evil.
   ○ D. It makes the sound of the poem mirror the dying heartbeat of Annabel Lee.

Skill:
Media

Use the Checklist to analyze Media in "Annabel Lee." Refer to the sample student annotations about Media in the text.

••• CHECKLIST FOR MEDIA

In order to determine how to compare and contrast a written story, drama, or poem to its audio, filmed, staged, or multimedia version, do the following:

- ✓ choose a story that has been presented in multiple forms of media, such as a written story and a film adaptation

- ✓ note techniques that are unique to each medium—print, audio, and video:

  - sound
  - music
  - tone and style
  - word choice
  - structure

- ✓ examine how these techniques may have an effect on the story and its ideas, as well as the reader's, listener's, or viewer's understanding of the work as a whole

- ✓ examine similarities and differences between the written story and its audio or video versions

To compare and contrast a written story, drama, or poem to its audio, filmed, staged, or multimedia version, analyzing the effects of techniques unique to each medium, consider the following questions:

- ✓ How do different types of media treat story elements?

- ✓ What techniques are unique to each medium—print, audio, and video?

- ✓ How does the medium—for example, a film's use of music, sound, and camera angles—affect a person's understanding of the work as a whole?

Skill:
Media

Reread lines 17–26 of "Annabel Lee" and then view this same scene in the video. Then, using the Checklist on the previous page, answer the multiple-choice questions below.

↻ YOUR TURN

1. This question has two parts. First, answer Part A. Then, answer Part B.

   Part A: What sound element helps support the tone of the poem?

   - ○ A. The sound effects of birds
   - ○ B. The music gets louder.
   - ○ C. The gate clangs on the sepulchre.
   - ○ D. The music turns happy.

   Part B: What effect does the sound element in Part A have on the poem?

   - ○ A. It helps build tension.
   - ○ B. It makes it easier to picture what is happening.
   - ○ C. It helps make the poem feel romantic.
   - ○ D. It helps me understand what happened to Annabel Lee.

Close Read

Reread "Annabel Lee." As you reread, complete the Skills Focus questions below. Then use your answers and annotations from the questions to help you complete the Write activity.

 SKILLS FOCUS

1. Identify details that show how the speaker feels about Annabel Lee before and after her death.

2. Identify the rhyme and rhythm in the fifth stanza of the poem. Explain how these poetic elements emphasize the speaker's feelings.

3. The speaker makes several biblical allusions to both angels and demons. What might this suggest about the speaker's feelings or the meaning of the poem?

4. How did the multimedia version use sound elements to emphasize the speaker's feelings or meaning of the poem? Identify and explain one or two examples.

5. Reread the last stanza. Identify details that show how the speaker feels now that his deepest relationship has been lost.

✏ **WRITE**

LITERARY ANALYSIS: How did Poe use rhyme, rhythm, and allusions to help the reader understand how the speaker feels about Annabel Lee? How did the multimedia version use sound to emphasize these same feelings? Write a short response to this question. Remember to use specific examples from the poem and the multimedia version to support your response.

My Mother Pieced Quilts

POETRY
Teresa Palomo Acosta
1976

Introduction

Teresa Palomo Acosta (b. 1949) is a Tejana author, activist, and historian born in McGregor, Texas. The daughter of working-class parents who came to Texas during the Great Depression, Acosta spent much of her youth in and around cotton fields, listening to her family's stories and watching the women sew. In her poem "My Mother Pieced Quilts," Acosta describes in verse how her mother would stitch various pieces of fabric into beautiful quilts, each one summoning its own family history, its own panorama of love and loss.

"oh mother you plunged me sobbing and laughing into our past"

1   they were just meant as covers
2   in winters
3   as weapons
4   against pounding january winds

5   but it was just that every morning I awoke to these
6   october **ripened** canvases
7   passed my hand across their cloth faces
8   and began to wonder how you pieced
9   all these together
10 these strips of gentle communion cotton and flannel
11 nightgowns
12 wedding organdies
13 dime-store velvets

14 how you shaped patterns square and **oblong** and round
15 positioned
16 balanced
17 then cemented them
18 with your thread
19 a steel needle
20 a thimble

21 how the thread darted in and out
22 galloping along the **frayed** edges, tucking them in
23 as you did us at night
24 oh how you stretched and turned and re-arranged
25 your michigan spring faded curtain pieces
26 my father's santa fe work shirt
27 the summer denims, the tweed of fall

28 in the evening you sat at your canvas
29 —our cracked linoleum[1] floor the drawing board
30 me lounging on your arm
31 and you staking out the plan:
32 whether to put the lilac purple of easter against the

---

1. **linoleum** a smooth, man-made floor covering with the consistency of plastic or rubber

33 red plaid of winter-going-into-spring
34 whether to mix a yellow with blue and white and paint
35 the corpus christi[2] noon when my father held your hand
36 whether to shape a five-point star from the
37 **somber** black silk you wore to grandmother's funeral

38 you were the river current
39 carrying the roaring notes
40 forming them into pictures of a little boy reclining
41 a swallow flying
42 you were the caravan master at the reins
43 driving your thread needle **artillery** across the
44 mosaic cloth bridges
45 delivering yourself in separate testimonies

46 oh mother you **plunged** me sobbing and laughing
47 into our past
48 into the river crossing at five
49 into the spinach fields
50 into the plainview cotton rows
51 into tuberculosis wards[3]
52 into braids and muslin dresses
53 sewn hard and **taut** to withstand the thrashings of
54 twenty-five years

55 stretched out they lay
56 armed/ready/shouting/celebrating

57 knotted with love
58 the quilts sing on

"My Mother Pieced Quilts" by Teresa Palomo Acosta is reprinted with permission from the publisher of *In Other Words* (ed. Roberta Fernández) (©1994 Arte Público Press - University of Houston)

✏ WRITE

POEM: The poem "My Mother Pieced Quilts" is told from the child's point of view. Write a poem in response to the child from the perspective of the mother.

---

2. **Corpus Christi** a city in southern Texas on the Gulf of Mexico
3. **tuberculosis wards** private areas of hospitals for patients with tuberculosis, a contagious infection of the lungs

Museum Indians

INFORMATIONAL TEXT
Susan Power
2002

Introduction

Winner of the 1995 Hemingway Foundation/PEN Award for Best First Fiction, Susan Power (b. 1961) has written novels, short stories, and essays, including *The Grass Dancer, Roofwalker,* and *Sacred Wilderness.* Power is a member of the Standing Rock Tribe of the Dakotas and a descendant of Sioux Chief Mato Nupa (Two Bears). Her autobiographical essay "Museum Indians" follows Power and her Dakota-emigrant mother as they navigate the light-polluted landscape of Chicago and come face-to-face with strange markers of their Dakota

"... I cannot imagine my mother being afraid of anything."

1   A snake coils in my mother's dresser drawer; it is thick and black, glossy as sequins. My mother cut her hair several years ago, before I was born, but she kept one heavy braid. It is the three-foot snake I lift from its nest and handle as if it were alive.

2   "Mom, why did you cut your hair?" I ask. I am a little girl lifting a sleek black river into the light that streams through the kitchen window. Mom turns to me.

3   "It gave me headaches. Now put that away and wash your hands for lunch."

4   "You won't cut my hair, will you?" I'm sure this is a whine.

5   "No, just a little trim now and then to even your ends."

6   I return the dark snake to its nest among my mother's slips, arranging it so that its thin tail hides beneath the wide mouth sheared by scissors. My mother keeps her promise and lets my hair grow long, but I am only half of her; my thin brown braids will reach the middle of my back, and in **maturity** will look like tiny garden snakes.

7   My mother tells me stories every day: while she cleans, while she cooks, on our way to the library, standing in the checkout line at the supermarket. I like to share her stories with other people, and chatter like a monkey when I am able to **command** adult attention.

8   "She left the **reservation** when she was sixteen years old," I tell my audience. Sixteen sounds very old to me, but I always state the number because it seems **integral** to my recitation. "She had never been on a train before, or used a telephone. She left Standing Rock[1] to take a job in Chicago so she could help out the family during the war. She was petrified of all the strange people and new surroundings; she stayed in her seat all the way from McLaughlin, South Dakota, to Chicago, Illinois, and didn't move once."

9   I usually laugh after saying this, because I cannot imagine my mother being afraid of anything. She is so tall, a true Dakota[2] woman; she rises against the sun like a skyscraper, and when I draw her picture in my notebook, she takes

Skill:
Figurative Language

The author compares the braid to a snake with a metaphor. The metaphor helps me visualize the hair. It also helps me understand that the writer or her mother might have a connection with animals or nature.

Skill:
Figurative Language

This simile shows her mother's importance in Power's life by comparing her to a tall city building. I know it's a simile because of the word like.

---

1. **Standing Rock** a Native American Reservation located on the border of North and South Dakota
2. **Dakota** a grouping of several Native American peoples, based on their location

NOTES

Skill:
Figurative
Language

The metaphor of the shadow shows that even though she's small, Power is still connected to her mother.

Skill:
Context Clues

I'm not sure what the phrase "mount the stairs" means. It must be a verb. If stairs are involved, it must mean "to go up or down." I looked it up, and it means to "climb up." This makes sense because I can say "we climb up the stairs."

up the entire page. She talks politics and attends sit-ins, wrestles with the Chicago police and says what's on her mind.

10   I am her small shadow and witness. I am the **timid** daughter who can rage only on paper.

11   We don't have much money, but Mom takes me from one end of the city to the other on foot, on buses. I will grow up believing that Chicago belongs to me, because it was given to me by my mother. Nearly every week we tour the Historical Society, and Mom makes a point of complaining about the statue that depicts an Indian man about to kill a white woman and her children: "This is the only monument to the history of Indians in this area that you have on exhibit. It's a shame because it is completely one-sided. Children who see this will think this is what Indians are all about."

12   My mother lectures the guides and their bosses, until eventually that statue disappears.

13   Some days we haunt the Art Institute, and my mother pauses before a Picasso.

14   "He did this during his blue period," she tells me.

15   I squint at the blue man holding a blue guitar. "Was he very sad?" I ask.

16   "Yes, I think he was." My mother takes my hand and looks away from the painting. I can see a story developing behind her eyes, and I tug on her arm to release the words. She will tell me why Picasso was blue, what his thoughts were as he painted this canvas. She relates anecdotes I will never find in books, never see footnoted in a biography of the master artist. I don't even bother to check these references because I like my mother's version best.

17   When Mom is down, we go to see the mummies at the Field Museum of Natural History. The Egyptian dead sleep in the basement, most of them still shrouded in their wrappings.

18   "These were people like us," my mother whispers. She pulls me into her waist. "They had dreams and intrigues and problems with their teeth. They thought their one particular life was of the **utmost** significance. And now, just look at them." My mother never fails to brighten. "So what's the use of worrying too hard or too long? Might as well be cheerful."

19   Before we leave this place, we always visit my great-grandmother's buckskin[3] dress. We mount the stairs and walk through the museum's main hall—past the dinosaur bones all strung together, and the stuffed elephants lifting their trunks in a mute trumpet.

20   The clothed figures are disconcerting because they have no heads. I think of them as dead Indians. We reach the traditional outfits of the Sioux in the

---

3. **buckskin** the skin of a male deer

Plains Indian section, and there is the dress, as magnificent as I remembered. The yoke is completely beaded—I know the garment must be heavy to wear. My great-grandmother used blue beads as a background for the geometrical design, and I point to the azure expanse.

21 "Was this her blue period?" I ask my mother. She hushes me unexpectedly, she will not play the game. I come to understand that this is a solemn call, and we stand before the glass case as we would before a grave.

22 "I don't know how this got out of the family." Mom murmurs. I feel helpless beside her, wishing I could reach through the glass to disrobe the headless mannequin. My mother belongs in a grand buckskin dress such as this, even though her hair is now too short to braid and has been trained to curl at the edges in a saucy flip.

23 We leave our fingerprints on the glass, two sets of hands at different heights pressing against the barrier. Mom is sad to leave.

24 "I hope she knows we visit her dress," my mother says.

25 There is a little buffalo across the hall, stuffed and staring. Mom doesn't always have the heart to greet him. Some days we slip out of the museum without finding his stall.

26 "You don't belong here," Mom tells him on those rare occasions when she feels she must pay her respects. "We honor you," she continues, "because you are a creature of great **endurance** and great generosity. You provided us with so many things that helped us to survive. It makes me angry to see you like this."

27 Few things can make my mother cry; the buffalo is one of them.

28 "I am just like you," she whispers. "I don't belong here either. We should be in the Dakotas, somewhere a little bit east of the Missouri River. This crazy city is not a fit home for buffalo or Dakotas."

29 I take my mother's hand to hold her in place. I am a city child, nervous around livestock and lonely on the plains.

30 I am afraid of a sky without light pollution—I never knew there could be so many stars. I lead my mother from the museum so she will forget the sense of loss. From the marble steps we can see Lake Shore Drive spill ahead of us, and I sweep my arms to the side as if I were responsible for this view. I introduce my mother to the city she gave me. I call her home.

From *Roofwalker* by Susan Power (Minneapolis: Milkweed Editions, 2002). Copyright © 2002 by Susan Power. Reprinted with permission from Milkweed Editions. milkweed.org

First Read

Read "Museum Indians." After you read, complete the Think Questions below.

THINK QUESTIONS

1. What made the mother scared on the train to Chicago? What does the author think about her mother's fears? Cite specific lines from the text in your answer.

2. Write two to three sentences describing the lesson that the mother takes away from the Egyptian mummies in the history museum. Is this a positive or negative lesson? Explain.

3. Why is the mother so deeply affected by the stuffed buffalo? What is her response to its presence behind glass in a museum? Include evidence from the essay in your answer.

4. Find the word **timid** in paragraph 10 of "Museum Indians." Use context clues in the surrounding sentences, as well as the sentence in which the word appears, to determine the word's meaning. Write your definition here, and identify clues that helped you figure out the meaning.

5. Use context clues to determine the meaning of **endurance** as it is used in paragraph 26 of "Museum Indians." Write your definition here, and identify clues that helped you figure out the meaning. Then check the meaning in a dictionary.

 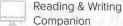

Skill:
Context Clues

Use the Checklist to analyze Context Clues in "Museum Indians." Refer to the sample student annotations about Context Clues in the text.

In order to use context as a clue to infer the meaning of a word or phrase, note the following:

✓ clues about the word's part of speech

✓ clues in the surrounding text about the word's meaning

✓ signal words that cue a type of context clue, such as:

- *for example* or *for instance* to signal an example context clue
- *like, similarly,* or *just as* to signal a comparison clue
- *but*, *however*, or *unlike* to signal a contrast context clue

To determine the meaning of a word or phrase as it is used in a text, consider the following questions:

✓ What is the overall sentence, paragraph, or text about?

✓ How does the word function in the sentence?

✓ What clues can help me determine the word's part of speech?

✓ What text clues can help me figure out the word's definition?

✓ Are there any examples that show what the word means?

✓ What do I think the word means?

To verify the preliminary determination of the meaning of the word or phrase based on context, consider the following questions:

✓ Does the definition I inferred make sense within the context of the sentence?

✓ Which of the dictionary's definitions makes sense within the context of the sentence?

Skill:
Context Clues

Reread paragraph 2 of "Museum Indians." Then, using the Checklist on the previous page as well as the dictionary entry below, answer the multiple-choice questions.

⟳ YOUR TURN

stream \'strēm\
noun
1. a natural body of water flowing on or under the earth
2. a steady flow of a fluid

verb
3. to flow in or as if in a stream
4. to exude a bodily fluid profusely

1. Which definition best matches the way the word *stream* is used in paragraph 2?

   ○ A. a natural body of water flowing on or under the earth
   ○ B. a steady flow of a fluid
   ○ C. to flow in or as if in a stream
   ○ D. to exude a bodily fluid profusely

2. Which word can we use as a context clue to help determine the correct definition of *stream*?

   ○ A. through
   ○ B. window
   ○ C. Mom
   ○ D. sleek

Skill:
Figurative Language

Use the Checklist to analyze Figurative Language in "Museum Indians." Refer to the sample student annotations about Figurative Language in the text.

••• CHECKLIST FOR FIGURATIVE LANGUAGE

To determine the meaning of figures of speech in a text, note the following:

✓ words that mean one thing literally and suggest something else

✓ similes, such as "strong as an ox"

✓ metaphors, such as "her eyes were stars"

✓ allusions, or indirect references, to people, texts, events, or ideas, such as

- describing a setting with the words "the place was a Garden of Eden" (biblical allusion)
- saying of a character whose snooping caused problems, "he opened a Pandora's box" (allusion to mythology)
- calling someone who likes romance "a real Romeo" (allusion to Shakespeare)

In order to interpret the meaning of a figure of speech in context, ask the following questions:

✓ Does any of the descriptive language in the text compare two seemingly unlike things?

✓ Do any descriptions include "like" or "as," indicating a simile?

✓ Is there a direct comparison that suggests a metaphor?

✓ What literary, biblical, or mythological allusions do you recognize?

✓ How does the use of this figure of speech change your understanding of the thing or person being described?

Please note that excerpts and passages in the StudySync® library and this workbook are intended as touchstones to generate interest in an author's work. The excerpts and passages do not substitute for the reading of entire texts, and StudySync® strongly recommends that students seek out and purchase the whole literary or informational work in order to experience it as the author intended. Links to online resellers are available in our digital library. In addition, complete works may be ordered through an authorized reseller by filling out and returning to StudySync® the order form enclosed in this workbook.

Reading & Writing
Companion

197

Skill:
Figurative Language

Reread paragraphs 9–10 of "Museum Indians." Then, using the Checklist on the previous page, answer the multiple-choice questions below.

YOUR TURN

1. This question has two parts. First, answer Part A. Then, answer Part B.

   Part A: The phrase "she rises against the sun like a skyscraper" is an example of a(n)—

   - ○ A. simile
   - ○ B. metaphor
   - ○ C. extended metaphor
   - ○ D. personification

   Part B: Based on the example of figurative language in Part A, the reader can infer that—

   - ○ A. The mother loves her daughter.
   - ○ B. The mother likes to get up early.
   - ○ C. The narrator idolizes her mother.
   - ○ D. The narrator and her mother argue.

Close Read

Reread "Museum Indians." As you reread, complete the Skills Focus questions below. Then use your answers and annotations from the questions to help you complete the Write activity.

⊙ SKILLS FOCUS

1. Identify evidence of the speaker's tone, or attitude, toward her mother in "Museum Indians." Explain how the speaker feels about her mother.

2. In "My Mother Pieced Quilts," the author uses descriptive details, including figurative language, to describe her mother's quilt. Identify details and examples of how the speaker in "Museum Indians" uses figurative language to describe her mother or items in the museum. What is the effect of the figurative language on the meaning or tone of the text?

3. Identify examples of the main idea or message about family in "Museum Indians." Explain what these examples suggest about family or family history.

4. In "My Mother Pieced Quilts," the author's purpose is to explore a family history, including love and loss. The speaker describes in verse how her mother would stitch pieces of fabric into quilts, each one summoning its own family history. Identify details that you can use to compare and contrast the author's purpose in "Museum Indians" with the author's purpose in "My Mother Pieced Quilts."

✎ WRITE

COMPARE AND CONTRAST: Both "My Mother Pieced Quilts" and "Museum Indians" are about love and family history. Compare and contrast the speakers in the two texts and how they interact with their mothers as well as the way they describe their family history. Include examples of figurative language in your analysis. Remember to support your ideas with evidence from the texts.

Please note that excerpts and passages in the StudySync® library and this workbook are intended as touchstones to generate interest in an author's work. The excerpts and passages do not substitute for the reading of entire texts, and StudySync® strongly recommends that students seek out and purchase the whole literary or informational work in order to experience it as the author intended. Links to online resellers are available in our digital library. In addition, complete works may be ordered through an authorized reseller by filling out and returning to StudySync® the order form enclosed in this workbook.

Reading & Writing
Companion

199

The Walking Dance

FICTION
Marcela Fuentes
2017

Introduction

Marcela Fuentes is from South Texas and lives in Iowa City, Iowa, with her husband and son. She has been published in *Indiana Review*, *Storyglossia*, *Blackbird*, and *Vestal Review*. "The Walking Dance" is a short story about Gavin; his wife, Aurora; and their son, Carlos. Gavin has tried for years to fit into his wife's family, and after traveling to Laredo with his in-laws for a family funeral, he may have finally found his place. The story alternates between Gavin and Carlos's perspectives as each learns what it means to find his place within their extended family.

"... Gavin knew he'd made a mistake."

Skill:
Textual
Evidence

1   Gavin and Aurora and their children drove down from Michigan to spend Christmas in San Antonio with Aurora's family. They arrived in San Antonio on a Thursday night, and on Friday morning Aurora's uncle called from Laredo with sad news that Aurora's aunt had passed away.

2   On Sunday morning, Gavin stood in the kitchen with his son, Carlos, Aurora's brother, David, and her father, Frank, and her crazy cousin, Ricky, all of them waiting for Aurora and her mother to finish packing so they could drive to Laredo for Aunt Melchora's funeral.

3   "You guys should just ride with me," David said, gesturing to Gavin and Carlos. Gavin appreciated the invitation because even though he and Aurora made this trip every year, and even though they had been married for ten years, Gavin often still felt like an outsider in Aurora's family, especially among the men.

4   Carlos tugged at Gavin's shirt and said, "Let's go with them, Daddy! Please!" Carlos worshipped his Uncle David and Cousin Ricky. David was strong: he could still airplane eight-year-old Carlos around the room, something Gavin couldn't do anymore—and Cousin Ricky, not to be outdone, knew all the really gross things. Last Christmas he taught Carlos to say the Spanish word for eggs, *huevos*, while burping.

5   A ride with the guys sounded awesome, but Gavin had already promised Aurora he would drive her parents and the kids to Laredo. "We can't, buddy," Gavin told his son, "I promised your mom I'd drive your *abuela*[1] and Grandpa Frank." As soon as he said this, Gavin knew he'd made a mistake.

6   "Oh," Cousin Ricky teased him, "Mrs. Herrera has plans for you?"

7   "Her Highness, Princess Bossy," David said. He always called his sister that. Gavin didn't like it, but he couldn't say anything: it was between Aurora and her brother.

I know that appreciation of something like this means Gavin thinks the invitation might be a turning point in his relationship with the men in Aurora's family. He has had trouble fitting in with the family and is glad for this sign of acceptance.

---

1. *abuela* (Spanish) grandmother

8   "I'm being a man and taking care of my family," Gavin said. He wished Aurora understood that this is what he dealt with when he tried to fit in with the men in her family.

9   "Oh yeah?" David asked, with a sharky grin. "You want an Unknown Taco then, manly-man?"

10   "No, David," Frank, Aurora's father, said sharply. He'd been listening to them from the kitchen doorway. "No Unknown Tacos before the trip."

11   "Oh, come on, Papi," David said. "Gavin's a big boy. Aren't you, Gav?"

12   The Unknown Taco was a rite of passage[2] for men in the Herrera family. It went like this: at some point during the holidays, in front of all the other men, Aurora's father, Frank, asked one of the men if he wanted a taco. If he said yes, Frank made a taco with whatever he found in the kitchen that wasn't poisonous. The man couldn't ask what was in it, and he couldn't spit anything out: he had to finish every bite.

13   And if he said no, he was a total wuss. Forever.

14   All the men had done it. Cousin Ricky, a **massive** man who liked to say his guts were made of cast-iron, had eaten more Unknown Tacos than anyone. He swore his last taco was old coffee grounds, peanut butter, and ketchup. Aurora's brother, David, said the taco Frank gave him once was actually pickle juice and marshmallows sprinkled with eggshells. Even little Carlos had eaten an Unknown Taco. Grandpa Frank went easy on him—birthday cake and stale Halloween candy with hummus[3]—but still.

15   Gavin had been married to Aurora for ten years now, and until this day no one ever asked if he wanted an Unknown Taco. He couldn't say no.

. . .

16   Dad went to the living room, and Carlos stayed in the kitchen to watch Uncle David prepare the Unknown Taco. Uncle David made it super bad—raisins, barbeque sauce, a piece of leftover chicken enchilada, apple vinegar, pancake syrup, and a whole orange peel—and he topped it off with a half can of jalapeños. That was going to wreck his dad for sure. Back home in Michigan, when they went out to dinner his dad always had to get the extra-mild salsa while Carlos, his mom, and even his little sister, Esme, dipped into the hot no problem.

---

2. **rite of passage** an event that marks an important or transitional stage in a person's life, such as birth or transition into adulthood
3. **hummus** a dip or spread made of mashed chickpeas or beans

17 Carlos knew he should tell his dad about the jalapeños, but he worried Uncle David and Cousin Ricky wouldn't let him ride with them if he tattled, and he wanted to ride to Laredo with Uncle David and Cousin Ricky more than anything. They were the most fun people on the planet. Uncle David could do a hundred push-ups with Carlos sitting on his back counting in Spanish. Cousin Ricky was so funny. He was huge. Uncle David always said "Ricky's one chocolate bar from four hundred pounds," but he was still the best dancer in the family. On Christmas Eve, while everyone else was looking at old picture albums, he taught Carlos the Dougie and the South Dallas Swag. Best of all, Uncle David and Ricky didn't care that Carlos was a little kid—they cursed and told Carlos all kinds of stories just like he was one of the men. They made Carlos feel like he was their favorite, not Esme, who usually got all the attention because she was the baby.

18 Uncle David brought the Unknown Taco out and placed it before Dad. "Hold on," Uncle David said, then he pulled a single pink candle from his pocket, and squished it into the taco. "This is a special occasion."

19 Carlos's dad laughed nervously. "Hope you guys took it easy on me," he said.

20 Grandpa Frank stood in the doorway with arms crossed.

21 "You gonna eat your cake or what?" Cousin Ricky asked.

22 Carlos thought about his dad chugging water and his face turning the exact color of a tomato the one time he accidentally dipped into the hot salsa—he knew he should say something.

23 Carlos remained silent though, not about to miss a chance to ride with Uncle David and Cousin Ricky. Poor Dad, but too bad.

• • •

24 Aurora yelled at Gavin through the bathroom door. "It's like you woke up and decided you were gonna do dumb stuff all day!"

25 He groaned from the toilet.

26 "It doesn't even count if David makes the Unknown Taco," Aurora said. "My dad has to make it. Everyone knows that!"

27 When they finally got on the road, Gavin was too sick to drive. He sat in the back with Esme and Frank, while Aurora drove and her mother, Cookie, rode up front. Gavin slit his eyes against the bright winter sunlight, strong even

Skill:
Plot

Uncle David is challenging Gavin to eat the Unknown Taco, a tradition in Aurora's family. This is part of the conflict. Gavin wants to fit into the family.

Gavin responds to this conflict by being nervous. Grandpa Frank is crossing his arms and seems intimidating.

through the tinted windows. The air conditioning blasting directly into his face might have been the only thing keeping him from vomiting.

28   The road south of San Antonio was an empty stretch of barbed wire ranch fences, with mesquite[4] and cactus on either side of the two-lane highway. He was pretending to sleep when he heard Esme say there was a baby dinosaur crossing the highway. "Daddy! Daddy!" she yelled. "Look how small it is! Lookit, lookit, *hurry*!"

29   "Dinosaurs are extinct, honey," Gavin said, his stomach growling like a T-rex.

30   "It's an armadillo," Cookie said. Her name was actually some version of Maria where Cookie is the closest English **approximation** to the nickname, Cuquita. It's a mystery, but there it is. "Be careful, Aurora. There might be more out and I think they're endangered."

31   Aurora didn't answer her mother and she didn't slow down. Cookie the Monster, that's what Aurora called her mother when she acted bossy.

32   "Arrr-mah-di-yoh," Frank said and Esme repeated it with perfect rolling r's. Frank told her armadillos were mammals, not dinosaurs, but she refused to believe him, so Frank handed her his phone to Google it. Gavin and Aurora didn't want their daughter getting addicted to technology and never let Esme use their phones—but Gavin felt too terrible to protest.

33   "Spell it, Grandpa," Esme demanded, her small index finger poised over the touch screen. She couldn't read yet, but she knew her letters in both languages. Gavin listened to Esme and her grandpa spell it together, in Spanish. He didn't understand them very well, but Esme's attempts were bold and clear and her Grandpa Frank praised her every time.

34   She was Grandpa's girl, all right. Frank gave Esme her own set of pet names: *Esme Chula* (She's my pretty girl), *Esme Vida* (She's my life), *Esme Corazón* (She's my heart), and the only one that really annoyed Gavin, *Esme'jita* (She's my daughter). Aurora said it shouldn't bother Gavin, that Frank called all of them a pet name, even him. Which was not really true—Gavin was generic *m'ijo* since he married Aurora. Still, Frank was a better grandparent than Gavin's father, who lived an hour from Gavin and Aurora's house in Michigan but wouldn't come over unless it was someone's birthday and it didn't conflict with his bowling nights.

35   No, Gavin couldn't deny that Frank was a good guy. After all, he had tried to stop Gavin from eating the Unknown Taco. But still, *Esme'jita* bugged Gavin.

4. **mesquite** a type of tree native to the American Southwest that is often spiny and creates thickets

Of course Aurora didn't care: Frank still called her *mis ojos* (my eyes) and she was 36 years old.

36 "You're just jealous," Aurora teased Gavin sometimes, "because he thought of *Esme'jita* first." It was worse than that, though. It was that Gavin knew he wouldn't have thought of anything that good on his own. Only it seemed like he should have.

37 David picked that moment to roar beside them in his pickup truck, honking like a madman. He swerved into the oncoming lane, luckily free of traffic. His candy-apple red truck gleamed. As he pulled it alongside their SUV, Aurora lowered her window and rock'n'roll blared from David's truck.

38 All of a sudden Carlos popped his head and shoulders out of the truck window, with Cousin Ricky's thick forearm locked across his yellow t-shirt. Gavin watched in horror as his son hung out the truck window, shouting a challenge at his mother, "Mommy, you drive like an old lady!"

39 Grandma Cookie screamed, "Ay no! He's going to fall out!"

40 Cousin Ricky yanked Carlos back inside.

41 Aurora rolled the window up, and David's truck sped past them in a haze of black exhaust.

42 "Ricky, you're dead!" Aurora yelled. The SUV lunged after the truck like someone gave it a good kick, and the Unknown Taco leapt into Gavin's chest.

43 Cookie demanded Frank call David, and Frank said something sharp to Aurora in Spanish. Gavin didn't know what, but he knew what her name sounded like when her dad was angry. Aurora kept her foot on the floor and the SUV surged until they were beside David's red truck.

44 "Don't kill the dinosaur, Mommy!" Esme wailed. "Watch out for the dinosaur!" Sure enough, there was another ugly gray armadillo, smack in the middle of the road.

45 Aurora and David both swerved around it, spraying gravel into the ditches along the highway. David honked hard and she honked back, but let off the gas. David pulled ahead, swerved into the right lane, and sped away.

46 "You did it, Mommy," Esme gasped. "You saved the baby dinosaur."

47 "'Course I did, sweetheart," Aurora said. "I'm a professional." She sounded totally calm, as if she hadn't just been scaring them all into fits.

48 There was a fantastic blue horizon in front of Gavin, sweet with high white cloud streaks and David's red truck was already disappearing over the next hill. Gavin couldn't help himself. He vomited.

. . .

49 Coming into Laredo from San Antonio was like approaching a fortress. A military-style checkpoint with armed border patrol agents and German Shepherd police dogs, just to get into the city. Carlos watched from the passenger window of Uncle David's truck while the K-9 patrol sniffed vehicles headed north. Southbound, there were lots of trucks with Minnesota and Wisconsin and even Michigan license plates, all of them piled high with toys and bicycles and skateboards and kitchen appliances and furniture. Sometimes a tarp flapped over it all, other times everything was just tied together with rope. The trucks looked like overflowing shopping carts waiting in line at the checkout.

50 "What's all that?" Carlos asked.

51 "Christmas presents," Uncle David said. "Guys come work in the states and have families in Mexico. So, you know. Daddy's bringing home the bacon."

52 "But like a year's worth of bacon," Ricky added.

53 Carlos could not imagine his dad being away for an entire year, or his dad hauling a big load of gifts across the whole country. Just to visit San Antonio for Christmas, Mom had to give their dog, Chewbacca, knock-out pills and kennel him the whole time, or else Dad complained about bringing him.

54 Yes, Carlos decided, Laredo was definitely a weird city.

55 When they arrived at the funeral home, Carlos noticed a half dozen helicopters parked across the street in a brushy dirt lot behind a barbed wire fence. The compound looked like a circus, with tents and Quonset huts, and men in fatigues, but Uncle David and Ricky didn't find the helicopters unusual. When Carlos pointed them out, Ricky just shrugged and said, "We're on the border." Carlos mulled this over, but it didn't make sense to him. His mom had taken him to Windsor, across the Canadian border from Detroit. There was just a city, then a toll booth, and a cool big tunnel, and then even though they were in Canada, it looked the same.

56 Uncle David and Ricky started to talk about their Aunt Bea. They called her the witch. She was their aunt, which meant she was Carlos's aunt, too. She was supposed to be here at the funeral home, along with at least a hundred other relatives he didn't know.

57   "She's literally a witch?" Carlos asked. His mom was always telling him there's a big difference between literally and figuratively. Literally was the truth; the actual thing. Figuratively was just how you feel, so Carlos asked again, "Like for real a witch?"

58   "She's evil," Uncle David said.

59   "Watch it," Uncle Ricky hissed, looking around.

60   "So it's true?" Carlos persisted.

61   "Don't say that too loud," Uncle David said. "She's crazy."

62   "Yeah," Ricky said. "The last time I saw Aunt Bea was at a family reunion a couple years back. She can't swim, but she was wading into the ocean off of South Padre Island."

63   Uncle David laughed. "Poor Tío just stood there saying, 'C'mon, Beatríz, get in the car already.'"

64   This didn't sound very witchy to Carlos, but it was kind of creepy. Sometimes his mom and dad took Esme and him out to Lake Superior, which was the most water he could imagine in one place. "What if she drowned?" Carlos asked.

65   "Oh Buddy, she wasn't gonna," Uncle David assured him. "She was just being dramatic."

66   "Yeah, no such luck," Ricky said. "*Mírala*, there she is."

67   Ricky pointed with his lips—it looked like a duck-face—toward the steps of the funeral home at an elderly woman wearing a slash of bright red lipstick and a cheetah-print dress: Aunt Bea. "Stay away from her," Ricky told Carlos. "I remember one time we were playing hide and seek, me and David found some *bruja* stuff in the crawl space under the house." Ricky wrinkled his nose. "A rotting watermelon with little ribbons and charms and pins stuck into the rind."

68   "Man, you're scaring him," said Uncle David.

69   "I'm not scared," Carlos countered. He was a little scared, but he had to hear it. Carlos wished his family could move to Texas and live near Mom's family. His family visited from Michigan every Christmas, but it was not enough. The Herreras lived and breathed mysteries. Grandma Cookie was always praying over him with a raw egg in case of the evil eye, and if Carlos ever had a bad

dream, Grandpa Frank sprinkled holy water under the bed to ward off spirits. And when his uncles told these stories, they meant them.

70 "Oh, and that blood," Ricky was saying. "I still think that was chicken blood inside that watermelon. Remember?"

71 "I dunno," said Uncle David, "but she and Tío got in a big fight about it. He started hollering and throwing all her things in the yard. Even the sewing machine."

72 "What nonsense are you telling him?"

73 It was Carlos's Mom, thank goodness. Dad was right behind her. Right away, Carlos could tell his dad was in a bad mood. But still, he was so relieved to see them that he forgot and said, "Hey, Mommy," just like little Esme would.

74 "I better never catch you hanging out of a moving vehicle again," Mom said, hugging him hard. Carlos couldn't see Mom's eyes behind the huge pink sunglasses she was wearing, but she didn't seem too mad, and she never stayed mad for too long anyway. Grandpa Frank said it was because she has a ticklish temper. Even when she got mad, she saw something funny in it. Still, Carlos knew there was no way she would ever let him ride with Uncle David again. He wasn't sorry, though. It had been worth it.

75 Mom was on speaker phone with Grandma Cookie, even though they were in the same parking lot. Grandma said she was taking Esme to the bathroom, and then, still on the phone, Grandma started greeting people inside the funeral home.

76 Mom looked at Carlos. "Hey, you call that lady *Tía* Bea when you say hello. She's your aunt."

77 "Only by marriage," Grandma Cookie said over the phone, then she hung up.

78 "Really?" Dad blurted out.

79 "Stop being such a baby," Mom told him. "She wasn't talking about you."

80 "She said that right in front of me."

81 "No she didn't. Anyway, you barfed in the car."

82 "Whatsamatter, a little sick today, Goldilocks?" Ricky said, patting Dad on the belly like a little baby.

83 Dad ignored Ricky. Mom shook her head.

84 "By the way David, don't let Mom find you, for real. She's so mad at you," Mom said in a bratty tone, just like Esme's when she tattled on Carlos. "See you guys inside."

85 Mom wiggled her fingers at them and strolled off. It was funny when she acted like a sister more than a mom. Carlos had even seen her give Uncle David noogies. That was one of the magic things that happened when they visited Texas.

86 Dad hung his arms over the fence and spit. He looked pale. But he squinted at the helicopters. Carlos was glad someone else noticed them. "Are those Black Hawks?" Dad asked.

87 "They can't be," Ricky said. "Black Hawks would be at a military base. That's not a base."

88 "Actually, yes, they are," said Uncle David. "Those are UH-60s. I should know. Those guys are Border Patrol."

89 "Border Patrol is para-military," Ricky said. "*Para.* That means not really."

90 "What do you know about it?" Uncle David asked. "I'm out there every day."

91 "You've never been in a helicopter in your life," Ricky said.

92 "That's what you think," Uncle David said. "I can't discuss my work."

93 "Whatever," Ricky said.

94 "Man, shut up, you sell air conditioners for a living."

95 They kept bickering and Carlos turned back to look for Tía Bea, who was still on the steps, her pouchy eyes and skin looking fragile, papery, like she was wearing too much powder. Maybe she was just very old. She was spooky. Carlos had no trouble at all imagining her stalking into the Gulf of Mexico, or witch-cursing someone.

96 "Don't stare at her," Uncle David whispered. "She can give the evil eye at twenty paces."

97 She saw them watching her and called across the parking lot in a creaky voice, "Hi, *m'ijos.*"

98 "Hey, Aunt Bea," Uncle David and Ricky shouted, fake-smiling.

• • •

NOTES

99 The chapel service was set for 7 p.m., and Aurora's relatives packed the lobby. Everyone spoke in quiet voices, but there were so many people talking that the air hummed. To Gavin it felt oddly festive. People hugged and laughed. They kissed their hands and pressed them to the giant double photograph on the mantle of the fake fireplace. Half of the picture was a black and white of a young brunette, very nineteen-fifties Elizabeth Taylor, and the other half was a digital color photo of an old woman in a lavender Easter dress, her hair a cropped white nimbus. Aurora had coached Gavin on this. The woman was—had been—Cookie's oldest sister, Melchora.

100 *Melchora, Melchora, rhymes with Aurora.* There was something in the eyes of the black and white girl that he recognized . . . and in the photograph of the old woman there was also an approximation of his wife, which he found disquieting. Gavin looked around. Somewhere in this human traffic jam of a lobby was a widower whom Gavin had never met and whose name he didn't know.

101 He found Esme and Aurora outside the back of the building, on a patio that faced the interstate. Esme wound herself around the railings of the stairs. Grandma Cookie had dressed her in a navy blue herringbone jumper and a new pair of gold shoes, the same color Cookie herself was wearing. All the better to **accentuate** Esme's position as the only granddaughter, Gavin guessed. "Are we ready to go in?" he asked Aurora.

102 Aurora shrugged. It was dark out and she'd taken off her sunglasses. She was backlit by the streetlights and her face was hazy, muted by the shadows, and her eyes were dark. She was older than her aunt had been in the black and white photo, but Gavin could see her in the progression between the photographs, everything mapped out and inevitable, just the eyes looking out at him until they stopped seeing altogether. There was a guy in there with a dead wife, and Gavin didn't even know who he was. Not knowing that guy scared him so much. If something happened to Aurora, he'd be swallowed up by her mammoth family, totally invisible. Barely anyone would know him.

103 Gavin hugged Aurora, and she let him, but gave him a little pinch just so he'd know he was still in the dog house for vomiting in the car. "How's your tummy?" she asked him.

104 "Better," he said. The scary feeling shrank to something small and ridiculous. But it wasn't all the way gone. *Melchora, Melchora, rhymes with Aurora.*

105 It ended up that there wasn't a lot of praying during the chapel service. People came up to the podium beside the casket and told stories about Melchora. A young kid with a ponytail, who everybody called Ponchi, spent the rest of the service Spanish rapping over songs with heavy, thumping bass.

106 "¡Ayla!" Grandpa Frank said. "What is this noise?"

107 "Ponchi lives in Los Angeles," Aurora whispered to Gavin behind her hand. "He's a recording artist."

108 "I like it," said Carlos, grooving in his seat.

109 "Ponchi," said Ricky, rolling his eyes. "Ever since he was a game show contestant on *Univisión* last year, he thinks he's the second coming of Pitbull."

110 "I wrote this one for my grandmother," Ponchi said from beside the casket. "This is '*Abuela Mella*.'"

111 People were shifting, getting out of their seats and soon there were clumps of dancers moving in a slow circle around the room in a **leisurely** *cumbia*. Gavin knew the *cumbia* pretty well, because Aurora was a fan of the late Tejano Queen, Selena. Aurora would holler "That's my jam!" and make Gavin dance around the living room with her. She called it the walking dance. You could be doing anything—cleaning the house, talking on the phone, carrying groceries—and as long as you made the *cumbia* circle, you were doing it right. It was the only dance Gavin was good at because he could walk around doing his own freestyle moves.

112 He watched the line of dancers shift and weave slowly, undulating like a lazy snake among the pews. The relatives were chatting and dancing, then they were weeping and dancing. He didn't know what that Ponchi kid was saying, but it was making some of them smile, some of them hold each other, some of them shake their heads. Cookie and Frank got up, taking Carlos with them. There were so many dancers. Teenage girls in clacky shoes pulled their baby cousins along; in fact, there was Esme, who had slipped off without asking, being swung from spot to spot by two girls. A clutch of burly, tattooed men, one of them with a tiny baby in the beefy crook of an elbow, shuffled along. "Michelangelo," Aurora murmured. "That's the new baby, Michelangelo." He looked like a small, wide-eyed potato. Old men dressed like cowboys. Young men dressed like cowboys, in denim shirts and leather vests; powdered old women, and gyrating young women, all with glittering earrings and shiny hair, danced. Everyone danced. There was the funeral home director, solemn faced and dancing alone, taking his turn around the room. Two boys behind him made faces at his back, but he didn't see them.

113 Cousin Ricky slipped into the groove of dancers, taking the hand of a woman Gavin didn't know. On the dance floor Ricky was mesmerizing, practically a work of art: a giant, hairy mammoth that somehow, even sweating through his Hawaiian shirt, in defiance of all laws of physics and the universe, achieved beauty—that's how deeply he felt the music. He did a slow strut, spun his

NOTES

partner in place, and then again so she revolved around him. Dancers cat-called Ricky and his partner, spurring them on to more twirls.

114   Aurora stood up, dropping her scarf on the pew, and held out her hand to her brother. "C'mon, Davykins," she said. "Dance with me."

115   "Davykins," Gavin snorted, feeling left out. This was the kind of song he could actually dance to. How could she pick David? Everything that had gone wrong today was David's fault! But, no, of course it didn't matter—even if he was thirty years old, David was Aurora's baby brother, and Gavin was just her husband.

116   "¡Vámonos!" David said. He grabbed Gavin's wife by the hand and they hustled into the line. David shook disco fists while Aurora flung her arms out in an exaggerated sprinkler. They shook along the circuit of dancers.

117   "C'mon fool, get up!" Cousin Ricky yelled as he swooped by and lifted Gavin by the blazer. "You're gonna get labeled the non-dancing white guy."

118   "Don't be that guy," Cousin Ricky's dance partner said.

119   Gavin joined them. Being in the mix was **disorienting**, and Gavin shuffled, trying to sway on beat and settling into a pace that wouldn't bump the old lady in front of him and avoided the aggressive spins Cousin Ricky and his partner were doing behind him. It was hard. Gavin couldn't tell if this was the longest song in the history of songs, or more than one song. The tropical beat kept grinding out of the audio mixer: *chuk-chukka-chuk, chuk-chukka-chuk.*

120   Gavin glanced around. The crowd had swallowed Cousin Ricky, and in his place, a short guy with a dirty turkey feather stuck in the hatband of his black Stetson was dancing alone. Suddenly, Carlos intercepted Gavin at the turn near the front of the chapel, where that Ponchi kid was still belting out lyrics.

121   "Daddy," Carlos gasped, with tears in his eyes. "Daddy, that lady is dead! I saw her. She's really dead."

122   "I know, son." He steered Carlos out of the stream of dancers, into an empty pew. "I know, buddy."

123   Gavin didn't know what else to say. Carlos's sobs were hot and damp against his shirt. Across the room, Esme rode on Grandpa Frank's shoulders, squinting with laughter. She had got both hands clamped in Frank's hair, which must have hurt, but Frank kept dancing anyway, one hand holding her steady. Gavin felt dizzy. He couldn't see Aurora anywhere, and everything was

Skill:
Plot

Cousin Ricky is yelling at Gavin for not dancing. This scene shows that Gavin is still struggling to fit in with the family.

Gavin responds by deciding to join even though the place is crowded and he's uncomfortable. He really wants to be part of the family and feel accepted by Aurora's brothers. He's kind of taking a risk here.

closing over him: his son's grief, the never-ending music, all these strangers moving and moving and moving.

124 "What's the matter?" Cookie demanded. She had a special sense: when it came to her grandkids she could smell trouble even in a room full of dancing mourners.

125 "Grandma," Carlos said. "What if you die?"

126 "When I do, you throw me a big party too. I'm putting you in charge. You pick the music."

127 "No! I don't want to be in charge. I want you to be alive!"

128 Carlos shoved his face into her midsection, howling in a way he hadn't since he was younger. Cookie rocked him, clutching him tight and burying her hand in Carlos's wavy hair. She made a noise Gavin could not describe, something like *yooo, yooo, yooo*—soft, wordless crooning, pitched so low Gavin could hear it even through the din.

129 Cookie was a tiny woman, not much bigger than Carlos. She swayed with the effort to hold on to him. She'd been crying, but she was also flushed with the exertion of dancing.

130 That's her sister over there dead, Gavin thought, but she was riding out Carlos's sobs like he was the only thing that mattered in the entire world. Somehow, it was just the three of them together inside the pulsing bass.

131 Gavin didn't know how to talk to his son about death any more than he could dream up sweet nicknames for his daughter. He was not quick-witted like Frank, nor was he cool like David or Ricky. But he could do the walking dance. He remembered what Aurora had told him. "It's a dance you can do carrying a bag of groceries." It was a dance he could do, Gavin decided, even carrying a crying kid.

132 He lifted Carlos out of Cookie's arms. This kiddo was heavy, but Gavin could tough it out for at least one lap around the chapel with his mother-in-law.

133 "Come on," Gavin said, holding a hand out to Cookie. "Let's get back out there."

134 "That's right." Cookie pressed her fist to her eyes, hard. "That's right. Let's go."

Marcela Fuentes is a graduate of the Iowa Writers' Workshop. She's lived all over the United States but most often writes about her home state, Texas.

First Read

Read "The Walking Dance." After you read, complete the Think Questions below.

 THINK QUESTIONS

1. Why does Gavin think it is difficult being around Aurora's family? Cite specific evidence from the text to support your answer.

2. What is Carlos's opinion of his uncle David and Cousin Ricky? How do his opinions affect his decisions and behavior? Cite specific evidence from the text to support your answer.

3. Refer to details in the text to explain why Uncle David and Cousin Ricky call Tía Bea a witch, or *bruja*.

4. Find the word **approximation** in paragraph 30 of "The Walking Dance." Use context clues in the surrounding sentences, as well as the sentence in which the word appears, to determine the word's meaning. Write your definition here and identify clues that helped you figure out the meaning.

5. Use context clues to determine the meaning of **leisurely** as it is used in paragraph 111 of "The Walking Dance." Write your definition here and identify clues that helped you figure out the meaning. Then check the meaning in a dictionary.

PLOT

Skill:
Plot

Use the Checklist to analyze Plot in "The Walking Dance." Refer to the sample student annotations about Plot in the text.

••• CHECKLIST FOR PLOT

In order to identify particular elements of a story or drama, note the following:

- ✓ setting details

- ✓ character details, including their thoughts, actions, and descriptions

- ✓ notable incidents or events in the plot

- ✓ characters or setting details that may have caused an event to occur

- ✓ the central conflict and the characters who are involved

- ✓ dialogue between or among characters

- ✓ instances when setting interferes with a character's motivations

To analyze how particular elements of a story or drama interact, consider the following questions:

- ✓ How do the events of the plot unfold in the story?

- ✓ How do characters respond or change as the plot advances?

- ✓ How does the setting shape the characters or the plot?

- ✓ How does a particular scene in the story contribute to development of the plot?

Please note that excerpts and passages in the StudySync® library and this workbook are intended as touchstones to generate interest in an author's work. The excerpts and passages do not substitute for the reading of entire texts, and StudySync® strongly recommends that students seek out and purchase the whole literary or informational work in order to experience it as the author intended. Links to online resellers are available in our digital library. In addition, complete works may be ordered through an authorized reseller by filling out and returning to StudySync® the order form enclosed in this workbook.

Reading & Writing
Companion

215

PLOT

Skill: Plot

Reread paragraphs 24–27 of "The Walking Dance." Then, using the Checklist on the previous page, answer the multiple-choice questions below.

♻ YOUR TURN

1. How does Aurora's reaction in paragraph 24 relate to the conflict of the story?

   ○ A. It helps to develop the arguing between Aurora and Gavin as the main conflict of the story.

   ○ B. It shows that Gavin's first attempt to fit in with Aurora's family has been unsuccessful.

   ○ C. It builds interest in the story because Aurora is angry that Gavin could not tolerate the Unknown Taco.

   ○ D. It emphasizes that Gavin does not fit in with the family because he makes poor decisions.

2. How is Aurora's statement in paragraph 26 important to the plot?

   ○ A. It suggests that Gavin will never be accepted by Aurora's family.

   ○ B. It foreshadows that Gavin will confront Aurora's brother for tricking him into eating the Unknown Taco.

   ○ C. It reveals that Gavin is still an outsider in Aurora's family because the Unknown Taco he ate didn't count.

   ○ D. It suggests that Aurora and Gavin will continue fighting because Gavin is upset he was tricked by Aurora's brother.

Skill:
Textual Evidence

Use the Checklist to analyze Textual Evidence in "The Walking Dance." Refer to the sample student annotations about Textual Evidence in the text.

••• CHECKLIST FOR TEXTUAL EVIDENCE

In order to support an analysis by citing textual evidence that is explicitly stated in the text, do the following:

- ✓ read the text closely and critically

- ✓ identify what the text says explicitly

- ✓ find the most relevant textual evidence that supports your analysis

- ✓ consider why an author explicitly states specific details and information

- ✓ cite the specific words, phrases, sentences, paragraphs, or images from the text that support your analysis

In order to interpret implicit meanings in a text by making inferences, do the following:

- ✓ combine information directly stated in the text with your own knowledge, experiences, and observations

- ✓ cite the specific words, phrases, sentences, paragraphs, or images from the text that support this inference

In order to cite textual evidence to support an analysis of what the text says explicitly as well as inferences drawn from the text, consider the following questions:

- ✓ Have I read the text closely and critically?

- ✓ What inferences am I making about the text? What textual evidence am I using to support these inferences?

- ✓ Am I quoting the evidence from the text correctly?

- ✓ Does my textual evidence logically relate to my analysis?

- ✓ Have I cited several pieces of textual evidence?

Skill:
Textual Evidence

Reread paragraphs 114–119 of "The Walking Dance." Then, using the Checklist on the previous page, answer the multiple-choice questions below.

⟳ YOUR TURN

1. Which part of the passage provides the clearest evidence that Gavin feels he cannot compete with Aurora's family for her attention?

   ○ A. "C'mon, Davykins," she said. "Dance with me."

   ○ B. But, no, of course it didn't matter—even if he was thirty years old, David was Aurora's baby brother, and Gavin was just her husband.

   ○ C. David shook disco fists while Aurora flung her arms out in an exaggerated sprinkler.

   ○ D. Gavin couldn't tell if this was the longest song in the history of songs, or more than one song.

2. Cousin Ricky's words and actions in paragraph 117 help the reader infer that—

   ○ A. he thinks Gavin is rude and is behaving foolishly.

   ○ B. he wants Gavin to get out on the floor so he can make fun of Gavin.

   ○ C. he wants to include Gavin in the family's activities.

   ○ D. he thinks Gavin does not know how to dance.

3. Which part of the passage provides the best evidence to support the inference that Gavin is uncomfortable on the dance floor?

   ○ A. This was the kind of song he could actually dance to.

   ○ B. "Don't be that guy," Cousin Ricky's dance partner said.

   ○ C. Gavin shuffled, trying to sway on beat and settling into a pace that wouldn't bump the old lady in front of him.

   ○ D. The tropical beat kept grinding out of the audio mixer: *chuk-chukka-chuk, chuk-chukka-chuk.*

 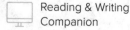 Reading & Writing Companion

Close Read

Reread "The Walking Dance." As you reread, complete the Skills Focus questions below. Then use your answers and annotations from the questions to help you complete the Write activity.

◎ SKILLS FOCUS

1. Identify and highlight notable conflicts or incidents in the plot. Explain why they are important to the plot or how they affect the characters.

2. Identify and highlight the turning point and resolution. Explain how those events impact the characters and contribute to the meaning of the story.

3. Identify and highlight two or three places where a character's actions or dialogue have a direct impact on the plot. Explain how the plot is affected by that character's actions or dialogue.

4. Identify an important message or idea expressed in the story. Highlight examples of this message in the story, and explain how each example demonstrates that idea.

5. Explain what the characters in this story learn from their experiences with love and loss. Highlight examples of characters responding to loss or love, and write a note about how those experiences affect the characters.

✎ WRITE

LITERARY ANALYSIS: How does Marcela Fuentes use plot elements and events such as conflict, turning action, and resolution to convey the theme of this story? Write a short response in which you specify one theme and explain how those plot elements help to convey it. Use several pieces of textual evidence to support your response.

Second Estrangement

POETRY
Aracelis Girmay
2014

Introduction

Aracelis Girmay (b. 1977) has authored three award-winning collections of poetry, including *Kingdom Animalia*, a finalist for the prestigious National Book Critics Circle award. Her poems are often brief and revelatory, commonly exploring themes of the African diaspora in its manifold forms in a voice at once distinct and beautiful. "Second Estrangement" appears in Girmay's book *The Black Maria.*

"Please raise your hand, whomever else of you has been a child, / lost . . ."

Skill:
Poetic Elements
and Structure

1　Please raise your hand,
2　whomever else of you
3　has been a child,
4　lost, in a market
5　or a mall, without
6　knowing it at first, following
7　a stranger, **accidentally**
8　thinking he is yours,
9　your family or parent, even
10　grabbing for his hands,
11　even calling the word
12　you said then for "Father,"
13　only to see the face
14　look strangely down, **utterly**
15　foreign, utterly not the one
16　who loves you, you
17　who are a bird suddenly
18　**stunned** by the glass **partitions**
19　of rooms.
20　　　　　　　　　How far
21　the world you knew, & tall,
22　& filled, finally, with strangers.

The speaker tries to get me to remember how it feels to be a child by asking me to raise my hand. It feels like I'm a kid being talked to.

It's open verse because there's no rhyme or rhythm. The lines are also short and break apart the sentence. This makes me feel weird, like I don't know what's coming next. For each line, I see myself as a kid trying to catch up with my dad!

First Read

Read "Second Estrangement." After you read, complete the Think Questions below.

 THINK QUESTIONS

1. What are the settings mentioned in the poem? Where else could such a situation occur? Cite evidence from the text in support of your answer.

2. What does the writer mean when the speaker calls out the word she "said then for 'Father'"? Cite evidence from the text in support of your answer.

3. To what action does the speaker compare a bird "stunned by the glass partitions"? Cite evidence from the text in support of your answer.

4. What is the meaning of the word **estrangement** as it is used in the text? Write your best definition here, along with a brief explanation of the context clues that helped you arrive at the definition.

5. Based on context clues, what do you think the word **utterly** means? Write your best definition of *utterly* here and explain how you figured it out.

Skill:
Poetic Elements and Structure

Use the Checklist to analyze Poetic Elements and Structure in "Second Estrangement." Refer to the sample student annotations about Poetic Elements and Structure in the text.

••• CHECKLIST FOR POETIC ELEMENTS AND STRUCTURE

In order to identify poetic elements and structure, note the following:

- ✓ the form and overall structure of the poem
- ✓ the rhyme, rhythm, and meter, if present
- ✓ lines and stanzas in the poem that suggest its meaning
- ✓ ways that the poem's form or structure connects to the poem's meaning

To analyze how a poem's form or structure contributes to its meaning, consider the following questions:

- ✓ What poetic form does the poet use? What is the structure?
- ✓ How do the lines and stanzas and their lengths affect the meaning?
- ✓ How do the form and the structure contribute to the poem's meaning?

Skill:
Poetic Elements and Structure

Reread lines 20–22 of "Second Estrangement." Then, using the Checklist on the previous page, answer the multiple-choice questions below.

♻ YOUR TURN

1. The first line contains only two words, "How far." What is the effect of this two-word line?

   ○ A. This is not an important line.
   ○ B. These words are mirroring the meaning of the poem.
   ○ C. There was not enough room on the previous line.
   ○ D. The poet was not very careful when writing.

2. Lines 20–22 are important because they—

   ○ A. include the punctuation "&," which represents being connected to family.
   ○ B. convey the central idea that this is an important moment in a child's life.
   ○ C. help to establish the regular rhyme scheme and meter of this poem.
   ○ D. show that the child will never find her father again.

Close Read

Reread "Second Estrangement." As you reread, complete the Skills Focus questions below. Then use your answers and annotations from the questions to help you complete the Write activity.

◎ SKILLS FOCUS

1. The author repeats the words *you* and *your* throughout the poem. What effect does this have on the reader? Explain how this influences the message of the poem.

2. Reread lines 4–8. How do the lines' length and structure affect the reader? How do their length and structure help to convey their meaning?

3. Identify details in the last three lines that help to develop the theme in the poem. Explain how these details accomplish this.

4. The author of "Second Estrangement" wrote a series of poems with *estrangement* in the title that focus on separation and loss. How does this poem explore the concept of loss? How does the structure of the poem help contribute to the sense of estrangement?

✏ WRITE

LITERARY ANALYSIS: What do you think is the deeper meaning or message of the poem "Second Estrangement"? How does the poet's use of poetic structure, such as open form and line length, contribute to the poem's deeper meaning? Write a response to this question, using evidence from the poem to support your response.

Please note that excerpts and passages in the StudySync® library and this workbook are intended as touchstones to generate interest in an author's work. The excerpts and passages do not substitute for the reading of entire texts, and StudySync® strongly recommends that students seek out and purchase the whole literary or informational work in order to experience it as the author intended. Links to online resellers are available in our digital library. In addition, complete works may be ordered through an authorized reseller by filling out and returning to StudySync® the order form enclosed in this workbook.

Reading & Writing Companion **225**

No Dream Too High: Simone Biles

INFORMATIONAL TEXT
Alex Shultz
2017

Introduction

B orn in 1997, American gymnast Simone Biles overcame a difficult childhood—from the absence of her biological parents to her diminutive, 4-foot-8 frame—to become the most decorated athlete in the history of her sport. In this profile, author Alex Shultz explores the pressures of great expectations and the many sacrifices Biles, a hero to millions, has made on the road to glory. Shultz's profile also reveals how Biles has battled her own demons and the outrage of certain people who remain hostile to the success of an African American woman in a predominantly white sport.

"'Simone's just in her own league. Whoever gets second place, that's the winner.'"

1   The floor routine[1] was all that stood between Simone Biles and her first all-around world championship. Biles smiled from ear to ear, revealing her braces. She was sixteen years old. She sprinted across the mat, effortlessly completing two somersaults and two twists in one leap, a double-double in gymnastics terms. She danced her way to another corner, tilted her chin up, and launched into something no one had ever seen before this event. Biles soared through the air, flipped twice, and landed on her feet, face-forward. The announcers on NBC described it as "a double layout with a half" twist. The crowd knew it as something else: The Biles, a maneuver so exceptional that it was named after her. It was her first major international competition, and Biles had crushed the rest of the field, largely because of a move she had created.

"THE BILES"

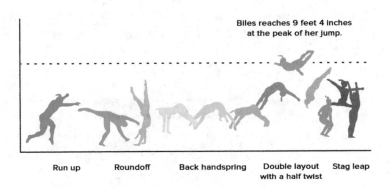

Biles reaches 9 feet 4 inches at the peak of her jump.

| Run up | Roundoff | Back handspring | Double layout with a half twist | Stag leap |

2   The 2013 world championships marked Simone Biles's arrival on the **elite** gymnastics scene. Four years later, her accolades include three all-around world championships, and four gold medals and one bronze at the 2016 Olympics. As Olympics teammate Aly Raisman told the *New Yorker*, "Simone's just in her own league. Whoever gets second place, that's the winner." Biles

---

1. **floor routine** an event in gymnastics competition in which the gymnasts perform various maneuvers on a special spring-loaded floor

Skill: Central or Main Idea

These details suggest the central idea is Biles is an amazing, one-of-a-kind athlete. She's won many awards and is "in her own league."

is a once-in-a-generation athlete with limitless talent and a strong dedication to her sport. She is a gymnast like no other.

Beginnings

3 Were it not for some bad weather, Simone Biles might never have become a gymnast at all. When she was six years old, her daycare redirected an outdoor field trip to a gymnastics studio because of rain. Biles told ESPN that at the time she was a "very crazy, very hyper and energetic" girl capable of mimicking the more difficult moves of some of the older girls at the studio. This attracted the attention of the coaches in attendance. Soon after, she enrolled at Bannon's Gymnastix in Houston.

4 Like anyone starting out at a new sport, Biles struggled with the **fundamentals.** In a profile of Biles for Buzzfeed, Dvora Meyers wrote, "She isn't naturally flexible and couldn't find the right shapes on her leaps and jumps. She also didn't know how to control her immense power, often bounding up and back several feet after landing tumbling passes. And on bars—the most technical event in the women's repertoire[2]—she lacked **finesse."** By the time Biles was 16, though, she was a blossoming star.

5 During the years Biles was developing into an elite athlete, the sport of gymnastics was also changing. In the past, gymnastics was more about finesse than power, and the various competitions within it were graded on a 10-point scale. Many times, the winner of an event would score a perfect 10. That changed in 2006, when the points system split into two: an **execution** score and a difficulty score. The execution score is still out of 10 points and is awarded based on how well a gymnast performs a routine. The difficulty score awards additional points based on the **rigor** of the skills attempted during the routine.

2016 OLYMPICS — WOMEN'S GYMNASTICS ALL-AROUND FINAL — VAULT				
ATHLETE	COUNTRY	DIFFICULTY SCORE (VAULT)	EXECUTION SCORE (VAULT)	FINAL SCORE (VAULT)
Simone Biles	United States	6.300	9.566	15.866
Aly Raisman	United States	6.300	9.333	15.633
Aliya Mustafina	Russia	5.800	9.400	15.200

2. **repertoire** one's collection of skills or things one can do

6   The difficulty score aided Biles because the routines she performs are more challenging than what other gymnasts attempt. For example, prior to her floor routine at the all-around world championships in 2013, she was actually in second place, behind another American competitor, Kyla Ross. Biles's floor program was more difficult than Ross's, though. When Biles finished it with no errors she easily won the title.

7   Part of Biles's natural talent also stems from her height or lack thereof. In some sports, height is an advantage, but gymnasts benefit from being shorter. From 2000–2012, the four all-around gold medal winners at the Olympics were between 5-foot and 5-foot-3. While that might seem short for most athletes, Biles stands at just 4 feet 8 inches. Her height bothered her as a child. As she told *Women's Health*, "it was kind of a struggle being small since everyone would make fun of you," but she's glad she can show others that they can be "short or tall" and become the best.

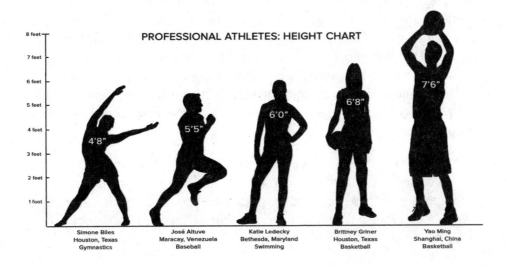

Getting Serious

8   On her way to becoming a world champion, Biles faced tough decisions. In eighth grade, she was training 20 hours a week, far less than other elite gymnasts. If she wanted to be an Olympian, she would have to commit more time to training. For Biles, that meant shifting to homeschooling and taking on more practices. Traveling to competitions would be all business. A *Texas Monthly* story about Biles noted that when they travel "gymnasts are sequestered—they stay in a different hotel from the one in which their families stay—to reduce distractions. If they're allowed out at all, it's for carefully supervised visits to a tourist site or megamall." Still, Biles decided to make the switch. Afterwards, as she told Buzzfeed, "My hours ramped up and we did beam and bars twice a day, which usually I had only done once a day."

9   A few years later, she faced a similar choice when UCLA offered her a full athletic scholarship. To accept the scholarship and attend college with her peers, Biles would have to give up the opportunity for endorsement deals. The NCAA[3] doesn't allow student-athletes to make money off their names while they're in college. Biles once again decided to stick to professional gymnastics. As a professional, she could earn money and continue to face the world's top competition. Explaining her decision to Buzzfeed, Biles said, "I can always still go to college, but the window of opportunity of going professional is very [small] so I had to make a decision."

The Challenges of Fame

10   The first black gymnasts to win any medals during an Olympics competition were Dominique Dawes and Betty Okino in 1992. No black athlete won an individual gold medal at an Olympic gymnastics event until Gabby Douglas in 2012. Douglas, Dawes, and Okino were all subjected to racially-charged criticisms. Since she became a national figure, Biles has had to deal with similar issues. After she won the world championships in 2013, an Italian participant named Carlotta Ferlitto responded with negative comments. She said, "next time we should paint our skin black, so we could win, too." Instead of denouncing Ferlitto's remarks, an Italian spokesperson added, "the current trend in gymnastics . . . is going toward a technique that opens up new chances to athletes of color, well known for power, while penalizing the elegance typical of Eastern Europeans."

11   In October 2016, Biles appeared in a music video for the song "Overnight" with recording artist Jake Miller. In the video, Biles is portrayed as Miller's girlfriend. This led to negative comments about interracial relationships (Miller is white). It also led to outright racism directed at Biles. In response, she tweeted, "everyone forgets that I have feelings."

12   During the 2016 Olympics, Biles also faced intense media scrutiny about her family. She doesn't have a relationship with her biological father, and only occasionally speaks to her biological mother. She was briefly in foster care as a toddler. At age 5, she was adopted by her grandparents, Ron and Nellie Biles, whom she refers to as her parents. She didn't give her upbringing much thought until it became a topic of conversation at the Olympics. Biles told Buzzfeed that the interest in her family is "just kind of thrown at me and it's weird to talk about." Ultimately, she said in an interview with *Us Weekly,* "My parents are my parents, and that's it."

13   Racism and gossip have taken an emotional toll on Biles. Gymnastics can be mentally challenging. Training with tough coaches like Martha Karolyi, who oversees the U.S. women's team, makes it even tougher. According to *Texas*

Skill: Central or Main Idea

The heading makes me think another central idea is that Simone faced challenges throughout her career. The author explains the racial issues she had to deal with in 2013.

The details about Simone becoming a "national figure" and winning a world championship support and develop my first central idea.

---

3. **NCAA** the National Collegiate Athletic Association

Monthly, Biles started working with a sports psychologist named Robert Andrews to help in that area. She was afraid that something was "wrong" with her if she needed to talk to Andrews. He did his best to convince her that wasn't true, and that other top athletes also spoke to him about their anxieties. At first, not much changed. Biles hit a mental wall at the 2013 Secret U.S. Classic. It was her worst performance as a pro. As Buzzfeed describes it, "She fell from the uneven bars, bobbled on the beam, and almost fell off. Next came floor, typically her best piece, where she fell to her knees after a full-twisting double back somersault." Biles's longtime personal coach, Aimee Boorman, removed her from the rest of the competition for her own safety. "She could have done something that could've ended her career right then and there if I let her compete. I could tell that her mind wasn't where it needed to be," Boorman told Buzzfeed.

14 After that competition, Biles **invested** more time with Andrews. She also had some productive heart-to-hearts with Boorman and Karolyi. Her anxieties lessened. Now, she can often be seen laughing during events, while teammates and opponents are understandably more nervous. "I think I was just trying to live up to everyone's expectations that I kind of got lost in competing. I was just so stressed. I didn't know how to deal with a lot of it," Biles told Buzzfeed in the lead-up to the 2016 Olympics.

Not Done Yet

15 Biles is an exceptional athlete. Yet, her commitment to honing that athleticism in the gym and her willingness to make tough choices are what truly set her apart. Along the way, she has gracefully leapt over many hurdles. She has confronted racism and bullying. She has learned to accept the mental challenges that come with competing on the world's biggest stages. Few athletes have been able to stay so **resolute.**

16 Simone Biles isn't done either. She plans to continue participating in domestic and international gymnastics events. She has even hinted at a desire to make another Olympics run at the 2020 games in Tokyo, when she'll be 23. Regardless of whether she competes at the next Olympics, Simone Biles already exemplifies what it means to be an Olympic champion. In a sport where perfect-10 scores no longer exist, she's as close as they come to the perfect gymnast.

ALEX SHULTZ is a freelance writer from Plano, Texas. His work has appeared in Grantland, *Los Angeles Magazine*, the *Los Angeles Times* and *SLAM* magazine.

First Read

Read "No Dream Too High: Simone Biles." After you read, complete the Think Questions below.

☁ THINK QUESTIONS

1. What does the anecdote in the first paragraph mainly tell readers about Simone Biles? Use specific evidence from the text to support your answer.

2. To what particular qualities or skills does the author of the text attribute Simone Biles's success? Similarly, which qualities might prove to be her own worst enemy? Cite examples of both in your response.

3. How has Simone Biles coped with the pressures of fame? Citing evidence from the text, explain how she has dealt with adversity in her life.

4. Based on context clues, what does the word **rigor** mean as it is used in the text? Write your best definition of *rigor* here, along with an explanation of how you inferred its meaning.

5. Read the following dictionary entry:

   invest
   in•vest \in'vest\ *verb*

   1. to spend money with the goal of making a profit
   2. to devote to something
   3. to provide with a particular quality or attribute

   Which definition most closely matches the meaning of **invested** as it is used in paragraph 14? Write the correct definition of *invested* here and explain how you figured it out.

Skill:
Central or Main Idea

Use the Checklist to analyze Central or Main Idea in "No Dream Too High: Simone Biles." Refer to the sample student annotations about Central or Main Idea in the text.

••• CHECKLIST FOR CENTRAL OR MAIN IDEA

In order to identify two or more central ideas in a text, note the following:

- ✓ the central or main idea, or ideas, if explicitly stated

- ✓ when each central idea appears

- ✓ key details in the text that indicate the author's point(s) or message(s)

- ✓ ways that the author uses details to develop a central idea

To determine two or more central ideas in a text and analyze their development over the course of the text, consider the following questions:

- ✓ What main ideas do the paragraphs develop?

- ✓ Where do you see more than one central idea for the text?

- ✓ How does the author use details to develop central ideas?

- ✓ How does the author develop these ideas over the course of the text?

- ✓ How might I objectively summarize the text, including the central ideas?

Please note that excerpts and passages in the StudySync® library and this workbook are intended as touchstones to generate interest in an author's work. The excerpts and passages do not substitute for the reading of entire texts, and StudySync® strongly recommends that students seek out and purchase the whole literary or informational work in order to experience it as the author intended. Links to online resellers are available in our digital library. In addition, complete works may be ordered through an authorized reseller by filling out and returning to StudySync® the order form enclosed in this workbook.

Reading & Writing
Companion

233

Skill:
Central or Main Idea

Reread paragraphs 15–16 of "No Dream Too High: Simone Biles." Then, using the Checklist on the previous page, answer the multiple-choice questions below.

⟳ YOUR TURN

1. This question has two parts. First, answer Part A. Then, answer Part B.

   Part A: What statement best summarizes the two central ideas developed throughout the text?

   ○ A. Simone Biles was a struggling gymnast, and her willingness to work hard made her great.

   ○ B. Simone Biles is a fantastic gymnast, and she would be better if she worked harder.

   ○ C. Simone Biles is a talented and powerful gymnast whose natural gifts set her apart from other athletes in her sport.

   ○ D. Simone Biles is an amazing gymnast, and her ability to work hard and overcome obstacles is what makes her an incredible athlete.

   Part B: Select a sentence that best supports your answer to Part A.

   ○ A. Biles is an exceptional athlete.

   ○ B. Yet, her commitment to honing that athleticism in the gym and her willingness to make tough choices are what truly set her apart.

   ○ C. She has learned to accept the mental challenges that come with competing on the world's biggest stages.

   ○ D. In a sport where perfect-10 scores no longer exist, she's as close as they come to the perfect gymnast.

Close Read

Reread "No Dream Too High: Simone Biles." As you reread, complete the Skills Focus questions below. Then use your answers and annotations from the questions to help you complete the Write activity.

◎ SKILLS FOCUS

1. Find examples of facts, statistics, charts, or graphic aids in paragraphs 1 and 2. What do these examples suggest about the purpose of the paragraphs? What do they suggest about the author's opinion or view of Simone Biles?

2. Identify examples of the many challenges Simone has faced during her young career. What personal sacrifices did she make to achieve success?

3. This article develops two central or main ideas. Highlight evidence of these two central ideas, and explain them in your own words.

4. Identify evidence of how love drove Simone Biles to success and what she had to lose in order to succeed.

✎ WRITE

DEBATE: In this informational text, the author explains that Simone Biles made many sacrifices for the sport she loves. She often had to put gymnastics ahead of everything else. Would you choose a sport and fame over a normal life? What do you think is the better alternative? Prepare points and comments for a debate with your classmates. Use evidence from the text to support your point.

Please note that excerpts and passages in the StudySync® library and this workbook are intended as touchstones to generate interest in an author's work. The excerpts and passages do not substitute for the reading of entire texts, and StudySync® strongly recommends that students seek out and purchase the whole literary or informational work in order to experience it as the author intended. Links to online resellers are available in our digital library. In addition, complete works may be ordered through an authorized reseller by filling out and returning to StudySync® the order form enclosed in this workbook.

Reading & Writing Companion   235

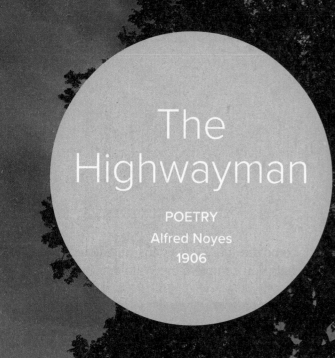

The Highwayman

POETRY
Alfred Noyes
1906

Introduction

In the 18th century, highwaymen menaced England's rural roads. These robbers on horseback held up travelers, demanding that their victims "stand and deliver" their valuables. Yet England's highwaymen inspired sympathetic fascination along with fear. In this poem, Alfred Noyes (1880–1958) draws on the romantic lore of the highwayman to create a tragic scenario of love and sacrifice. Noyes also drew on his own memories of desolate Bagshot Heath in England, where the wind in the trees one wild night gave rise to the poem's opening lines.

"And the highwayman came riding— Riding—riding—"

PART ONE

1 The wind was a **torrent** of darkness among the gusty trees.

2 The moon was a ghostly galleon[1] tossed upon cloudy seas.

3 The road was a ribbon of moonlight over the purple moor[2],

4 And the highwayman came riding—

5   Riding—riding—

6 The highwayman came riding, up to the old inn-door.

In "The Highwayman" by Alfred Noyes, a dashing robber on horseback wins the heart of Bess, whose father is the landlord of an inn.

7 He'd a French cocked-hat[3] on his forehead, a bunch of lace at his chin,

8 A coat of the claret[4] velvet, and breeches of brown doe-skin.

9 They fitted with never a wrinkle. His boots were up to the thigh.

10 And he rode with a jewelled twinkle,

11   His pistol butts a-twinkle,

12 His rapier hilt a-twinkle, under the jewelled sky.

13 Over the cobbles he **clattered** and clashed in the dark inn-yard.

14 He tapped with his whip on the shutters, but all was locked and barred.

15 He whistled a tune to the window, and who should be waiting there

16 But the landlord's black-eyed daughter,

17   Bess, the landlord's daughter,

18 Plaiting a dark red love-knot into her long black hair.

---

1. **galleon** an old, wooden war ship powered by sails
2. **moor** an expanse of boggy, grassy land
3. **French cocked-hat** a hat with a wide, stiff brim that is turned up in places toward the crown of the head
4. **claret** a dark maroon color

Skill:
Media

In both the poem and the video, the yard is dark. In the video, though, the light is shining around Bess. It makes her glow like a star or a diamond. This shows that Bess is the object of desire. Tim and the robber must be madly in love with her!

Skill:
Poetic Elements
and Structure

There is alliteration of the letter "L." "L" has a soft and gentle sound that adds to the romantic feeling of the stanza.

19   And dark in the dark old inn-yard a stable-wicket creaked
20   Where Tim the ostler[5] listened. His face was white and peaked[6].
21   His eyes were hollows of madness, his hair like mouldy hay,
22   But he loved the landlord's daughter,
23   The landlord's red-lipped daughter.
24   Dumb as a dog he listened, and he heard the robber say—

25   "One kiss, my bonny sweetheart, I'm after a prize to-night,
26   But I shall be back with the yellow gold before the morning light;
27   Yet, if they press me sharply, and harry me through the day,
28   Then look for me by moonlight,
29   Watch for me by moonlight,
30   I'll come to thee by moonlight, though hell should bar the way."

31   He rose upright in the stirrups. He scarce could reach her hand,
32   But she loosened her hair in the casement. His face burnt like a brand
33   As the black cascade of perfume came tumbling over his breast;
34   And he kissed its waves in the moonlight,
35   (O, sweet black waves in the moonlight!)
36   Then he tugged at his rein in the moonlight, and galloped away to the west.

---

5. **ostler** a caretaker in charge of horses
6. **peaked** pale and sickly

PART TWO

 NOTES

37 He did not come in the dawning. He did not come at noon;
38 And out of the **tawny** sunset, before the rise of the moon,
39 When the road was a gypsy's ribbon, looping the purple moor,
40 A red-coat troop came marching—
41   Marching—marching—
42 King George's men came marching, up to the old inn-door.

43 They said no word to the landlord. They drank his ale instead.
44 But they gagged his daughter, and bound her, to the foot of her narrow bed.
45 Two of them knelt at her casement, with muskets at their side!
46 There was death at every window;
47   And hell at one dark window;
48 For Bess could see, through her casement, the road that *he* would ride.

49 They had tied her up to attention, with many a sniggering jest.
50 They had bound a musket beside her, with the muzzle beneath her breast!
51 "Now, keep good watch!" and they kissed her. She heard the doomed man say—
52 *Look for me by moonlight;*
53   *Watch for me by moonlight;*
54 *I'll come to thee by moonlight, though hell should bar the way!*

55 She twisted her hands behind her; but all the knots held good!
56 She writhed her hands till her fingers were wet with sweat or blood!
57 They stretched and strained in the darkness, and the hours crawled by like years
58 Till, now, on the stroke of midnight,
59   Cold, on the stroke of midnight,
60 The tip of one finger touched it! The trigger at least was hers!

61 The tip of one finger touched it. She strove no more for the rest.
62 Up, she stood up to attention, with the muzzle beneath her breast.
63 She would not risk their hearing; she would not **strive** again;
64 For the road lay bare in the moonlight;
65   Blank and bare in the moonlight;
66 And the blood of her veins, in the moonlight, throbbed to her love's refrain.

67 *Tlot-tlot; tlot-tlot!* Had they heard it? The horsehoofs ringing clear;
68 *Tlot-tlot; tlot-tlot,* in the distance? Were they deaf that they did not hear?
69 Down the ribbon of moonlight, over the brow of the hill,
70 The highwayman came riding—
71   Riding—riding—
72 The red coats looked to their priming! She stood up, straight and still.

 Skill:
Media

This first part of the scene isn't in the poem at all, but it's kind of implied. The film shows Tim actually telling the redcoats about the highwayman. That's why they know to go to the old inn. It's much clearer what happened! Tim must have been jealous!

 Skill:
Poetic Elements and Structure

The letter "T" is repeated at the end of a lot of words in this passage, which is consonance. The "T" sound sounds kind of like horse hooves and makes the poem feel more urgent as the robber gets closer.

NOTES

73 *Tlot-tlot*, in the frosty silence! *Tlot-tlot*, in the echoing night!
74 Nearer he came and nearer. Her face was like a light.
75 Her eyes grew wide for a moment; she drew one last deep breath,
76 Then her finger moved in the moonlight,
77   Her musket shattered the moonlight,
78 Shattered her breast in the moonlight and warned him—with her death.

79 He turned. He spurred to the west; he did not know who stood
80 Bowed, with her head o'er the musket, drenched with her own blood!
81 Not till the dawn he heard it, and his face grew grey to hear
82 How Bess, the landlord's daughter,
83   The landlord's black-eyed daughter,
84 Had watched for her love in the moonlight, and died in the darkness there.

85 Back, he spurred like a madman, shrieking a curse to the sky,
86 With the white road smoking behind him and his rapier **brandished** high.
87 Blood red were his spurs in the golden noon; wine-red was his velvet coat;
88 When they shot him down on the highway,
89   Down like a dog on the highway,
90 And he lay in his blood on the highway, with a bunch of lace at his throat.

. . .

91 *And still of a winter's night, they say, when the wind is in the trees,*
92 *When the moon is a ghostly galleon tossed upon cloudy seas,*
93 *When the road is a ribbon of moonlight over the purple moor,*
94 *A highwayman comes riding—*
95   *Riding—riding—*
96 *A highwayman comes riding, up to the old inn-door.*

97 *Over the cobbles he clatters and clangs in the dark inn-yard.*
98 *He taps with his whip on the shutters, but all is locked and barred.*
99 *He whistles a tune to the window, and who should be waiting there*
100 *But the landlord's black-eyed daughter,*
101   *Bess, the landlord's daughter,*
102 *Plaiting a dark red love-knot into her long black hair.*

First Read

Read "The Highwayman." After you read, complete the Think Questions below.

 THINK QUESTIONS

1. A love triangle is a situation in which two people love the same third person. What love triangle exists in "The Highwayman"? Cite textual evidence from the selection to support your answer.

2. How do King George's men treat Bess, and why do they treat her that way? Cite textual evidence from the selection to support your answer.

3. How does the highwayman respond when he hears about Bess's death? Cite textual evidence from the selection to support your answer.

4. Find the word **strive** in line 63 of "The Highwayman." Use context clues in the surrounding sentences, as well as the sentence in which the word appears, to determine the word's meaning. Write your definition here and identify clues that helped you figure out the meaning.

5. Use context clues to determine the meaning of **brandish** as it is used in line 86 of "The Highwayman." Write your definition here and identify clues that helped you figure out the meaning. Then check the meaning in a dictionary.

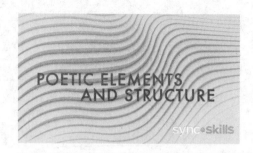

Skill:
Poetic Elements and Structure

Use the Checklist to analyze Poetic Elements and Structure in "The Highwayman." Refer to the sample student annotations about Poetic Elements and Structure in the text.

••• CHECKLIST FOR POETIC ELEMENTS AND STRUCTURE

In order to identify poetic elements and structure, note the following:

✓ the form and overall structure of the poem

✓ the rhyme, rhythm, and meter, if present

✓ lines and stanzas in the poem that suggest its meaning

✓ other sound elements, such as:

- alliteration: the repetition of initial consonant sounds, as with the *s* sound in "Cindy sweeps the sand"

- consonance: the repetition of consonant sounds in the middle and ends of words, as with the *t* sound in "little bats in the attic"

- assonance: the repetition of vowel sounds in words, as with the long *e* sound in "dreams of bees and sheep"

To analyze the impact of rhymes and other repetitions of sounds on a specific verse or stanza of a poem, consider the following questions:

✓ What sound elements are present in specific stanzas of the poem?

✓ What is the effect of different sound elements on the stanza or verse?

Skill:
Poetic Elements and Structure

Reread lines 1–30 from Part One of "The Highwayman." Then, complete the chart on the next page by identifying the effect each sound element has on the verse or stanza.

↻ YOUR TURN

	Letter Bank
A	Repeating the same harsh *C* sound makes the sound of a horse on a road, creating an urgent or excited mood.
B	The repetitions of *K* sounds remind me of how the creak disturbs the silence.
C	The repetition of the *R* sound makes this verse sound like it's flowing, like the ribbon of road and the highwayman's riding.
D	The repeated *G* sound emphasizes the moon and has a gutteral sound that mirrors the stormy imagery.
E	The repeated sound *-inkle* in the description of the highwayman's appearance makes him seem less dangerous because *-inkle* is a funny and whimsical sound.

Text	Sound Element	Effect on Verse or Stanza
The moon was a ghostly galleon tossed upon cloudy seas.	alliteration	
The road was a ribbon of moonlight over the purple moor, And the highwayman came riding— Riding—riding— The highwayman came riding, up to the old inn-door.	consonance	
They fitted with never a wrinkle. His boots were up to the thigh. And he rode with a jewelled twinkle, His pistol butts a-twinkle, His rapier hilt a-twinkle, under the jewelled sky.	rhyme	
Over the cobbles he clattered and clashed in the dark inn-yard.	alliteration	
And dark in the dark old inn-yard a stable-wicket creaked Where Tim the ostler listened. His face was white and peaked.	consonance	

Skill:
Media

Use the Checklist to analyze Media in "The Highwayman." Refer to the sample student annotations about Media in the text.

••• CHECKLIST FOR MEDIA

In order to determine how to compare and contrast a written story, drama, or poem to its audio, filmed, staged, or multimedia version, do the following:

✓ choose a story that has been presented in multiple forms of media, such as a written story and a film adaptation

✓ note techniques that are unique to each medium—print, audio, and video:

- lighting
- sound
- color
- tone and style
- camera focus and angles
- word choice
- structure

✓ examine how these techniques may have an effect on the story and its ideas, as well as the reader's, listener's, or viewer's understanding of the work as a whole

✓ examine similarities and differences between the written story and its audio or video version

To compare and contrast a written story, drama, or poem to its audio, filmed, staged, or multimedia version, analyzing the effects of techniques unique to each medium, consider the following questions:

✓ How do different types of media treat story elements?

✓ What techniques are unique to each medium—print, audio, and video?

✓ How does the medium—for example, a film's use of music, sound, and camera angles—affect a person's understanding of the work as a whole?

Skill:
Media

Reread lines 1–14 of "The Highwayman," and then view this same scene from the video clip of "The Highwayman." Then, using the Checklist on the previous page, answer the multiple-choice questions below and on the next page.

⟳ YOUR TURN

1. This question has two parts. First, answer Part A. Then, answer Part B.

   Part A: Which of the following details in the film version of "The Highwayman" is different from the printed text?

   ○ A. The inn-yard is well lit in the film version.

   ○ B. The highwayman is walking instead of riding in the film.

   ○ C. The stanza describing the highwayman's appearance is missing in the film.

   ○ D. The film version seems light and happy, and the poem seems dark and moody.

   Part B: Which of the following BEST explains why the film version might have presented this detail in Part A in a different way?

   ○ A. The missing stanza described things that wouldn't make sense to modern audiences.

   ○ B. The description of the highwayman's appearance is unnecessary in the film because the viewer can see him.

   ○ C. The clothes described in the poem would have been expensive, and the film couldn't afford to show them.

   ○ D. The filmmakers didn't want to show the weapons described in the missing stanza.

2. Which film element best helps you to understand that the story takes place hundreds of years ago?

    ○ A. The film uses different types of lighting.

    ○ B. The film begins by focusing on objects such as a candle, a tin cup, and a leather boot.

    ○ C. The narrator says that this event takes places hundreds of years ago.

    ○ D. The film does not use film elements to help you understand the time or setting.

3. How does the film use lighting to affect your understanding of the highwayman in the opening scene?

    ○ A. The highwayman is filmed in darker lighting, suggesting he may be unwelcome or dangerous.

    ○ B. The highwayman is filmed in bright lighting, suggesting he may be a hero.

    ○ C. The highwayman is filmed in various lightning, suggesting that he may be a complex character.

    ○ D. The film does not use lighting to help you better understand the highwayman.

Please note that excerpts and passages in the StudySync® library and this workbook are intended as touchstones to generate interest in an author's work. The excerpts and passages do not substitute for the reading of entire texts, and StudySync® strongly recommends that students seek out and purchase the whole literary or informational work in order to experience it as the author intended. Links to online resellers are available in our digital library. In addition, complete works may be ordered through an authorized reseller by filling out and returning to StudySync® the order form enclosed in this workbook.

Reading & Writing Companion   247

Close Read

Reread "The Highwayman." As you reread, complete the Skills Focus questions below. Then use your answers and annotations from the questions to help you complete the Write activity.

◎ SKILLS FOCUS

1. Identify two or three examples of different sound patterns (alliteration, consonance, assonance) in the poem. Explain how these sounds affect the poem's feeling and meaning.

2. Identify two or three examples of rhymes. Explain how they affect the poem's mood.

3. One of the film elements used in the video is lighting. Identify and explain moments where the meaning or tone of the poem is made more clear by the lighting in the film.

4. Identify Bess's final action. Explain what readers can learn about love and loss from the relationship in the poem.

✏ WRITE

LITERARY ANALYSIS: "The Highwayman" is a poem full of different emotions and moods. Identify lines or stanzas in the poem where the mood shifts. How does the poem use sound repetition and other poetic elements to show these changes? How does the film show and enhance these changes in mood? Write a response to answer these questions, analyzing the techniques unique to each medium. Remember to use evidence from the poem and the filmed adaptation.

Flesh and Blood So Cheap:

The Triangle Fire and Its Legacy

INFORMATIONAL TEXT
Albert Marrin
2011

Introduction

The Triangle Shirtwaist Factory fire in 1911 was the most lethal workplace tragedy in American history until the attack on the World Trade Center on September 11, 2001. The Lower Manhattan blaze killed 146 workers, most of them young, female immigrants of Jewish and Italian descent. Author Albert Marrin traces the history of the garment industry, exploring the immigrant experience of the early 1900s, including the sweatshop conditions many new arrivals to America were forced to endure. The Triangle Fire prompted activists to lobby for reforms, resulting in improved safety standards and working conditions.

"Onlookers saw many dreadful sights, none more so than the end of a love affair."

Excerpt from Chapter V

Holocaust

Skill:
Informational
Text Structure

The author is explaining how the fire grew with cause-and-effect structure. Burning fabric caused other pieces to catch on fire. Since the hose was not connected, no water came out, and the fire grew. This is an example of how poor safety standards resulted in tragedy.

1   We will never know for sure what started the Triangle Fire. Most likely, a cutter[1] flicked a hot ash or tossed a live cigarette butt into a scrap bin. Whatever the cause, survivors said the first sign of trouble was smoke pouring from beneath a cutting table.

2   Cutters flung buckets of water at the smoking spot, without effect. Flames shot up, **igniting** the line of hanging paper patterns. "They began to fall on the layers of thin goods underneath them," recalled cutter Max Rothen. "Every time another piece dropped, light scraps of burning fabric began to fly around the room. They came down on the other tables and they fell on the machines. Then the line broke and the whole string of burning patterns fell down." A foreman ran for the hose on the stairway wall. Nothing! No water came. The hose had not been connected to the **standpipe**. Seconds later, the fire leaped out of control.

3   Yet help was already on the way. At exactly 4:45 p.m., someone pulled the eighth-floor fire alarm. In less than two minutes, the horse-drawn vehicles of Engine Company 72 arrived from a firehouse six blocks away. The moment they arrived, the firefighters unloaded their equipment and prepared to swing into action. As they did, the area pumping station raised water pressure in the hydrants near the Asch Building. Other units soon arrived from across the Lower East Side with more equipment.

The Triangle Shirtwaist Factory fire is the deadliest industrial disaster in U.S. history. The factory was located on the eighth, ninth, and tenth floors of the Asch building in New York City.

1. **cutter** a person who works at a table in a clothing factory

4   Meanwhile, workers on the eighth floor rang furiously for the two passenger elevators. Safety experts have always advised against using elevators in a fire. Heat can easily damage their machinery, leaving trapped passengers dangling in space, to burn or **suffocate.** Despite the danger, the operators made several trips, saving scores of workers before heat bent the elevators' tracks and put them out of action.

5   Those who could not board elevators rushed the stairway door. They caused a pileup so that those in front could not open the door. Whenever someone tried to get it open, the crowd pinned her against it. "All the girls were falling on me and they squeezed me to the door," Ida Willensky recalled. "Three times I said to the girls, 'Please, girls, let me open the door. Please!' But they would not listen to me." Finally, cutter Louis Brown barged through the crowd and forced the door open.

6   Workers, shouting, crying, and gasping for air, slowly made their way downstairs. There were no lights in the stairway, so they had to grope their way in darkness. A girl fell; others fell on top of her, blocking the stairs until firefighters arrived moments later. Yet everyone who took the stairway from the eighth floor got out alive, exiting through the Washington Place doors. Those on the ninth floor were not so lucky.

• • •

7   Those who reached the ninth-floor stairway door found it locked. This was not unusual, as employers often locked doors to discourage latecomers and keep out union organizers[2]. "My God, I am lost!" cried Margaret Schwartz as her hair caught fire. Nobody who went to that door survived, nor any who reached the windows.

8   With a wave of fire rolling across the room, workers rushed to the windows, only to meet more fire. Hot air expands. Unless it escapes, pressure will keep building, eventually blowing a hole even in a heavy iron container like a boiler. Heat and pressure blew out the eighth-floor windows. Firefighters call the result "lapping in"—that is sucking flames into open windows above. That is why you see black scorch marks on the wall above the window of a burnt out room.

9   With fire advancing from behind and flames rising before them, people knew they were doomed. Whatever they did meant certain death. By remaining in the room, they chose death by fire or suffocation. Jumping ninety-five feet to the ground meant death on the sidewalk. We cannot know what passed through the minds of those who decided to jump. Yet their thinking, in those

_____

2. **union organizers** people who recruit workers to organize under a union's banner

last moments of life, may have gone like this: If I jump, my family will have a body to identify and bury, but if I stay in this room, there will be nothing left.

10 A girl clung to a window frame until flames from the eighth floor lapped in, burning her face and setting fire to her hair and clothing. She let go. Just then, Frances Perkins reached the scene from her friend's town house on the north side of Washington Square. "Here they come," onlookers shouted as Engine Company 72 reined in their horses. "Don't jump; stay there." Seconds later, Hook and Ladder Company 20 arrived.

11 Firefighters charged into the building, stretching a hose up the stairways as they went. At the sixth-floor landing, they connected it to the standpipe. Reaching the eighth floor, they crawled into the **inferno** on their bellies, under the rising smoke, with their hose. Yet nothing they did could save those at the windows. Photos of the portable towers show streams of water playing on the top three floors. (A modern high-pressure pumper can send water as high as one thousand feet.) Plenty of water got through the windows, but not those with people standing in them. A burst of water under high pressure would have hurled them backward, into the flames.

12 Hoping to catch jumpers before they hit the ground, firefighters held up life nets, sturdy ten-foot-square nets made of rope. It was useless. A person falling from the ninth floor struck with a force equal to eleven thousand pounds. Some jumpers bounced off the nets, dying when they hit the ground; others tore the nets, crashing through to the pavement. "The force was so great it took men off their feet," said Captain Howard Ruch of Engine Company 18. "Trying to hold the nets, the men turned somersaults. The men's hands were bleeding, the nets were torn and some caught fire" from burning clothing. Officers, fearing their men would be struck by falling bodies, ordered the nets removed. The **aerial** ladders failed, too, reaching only to the sixth floor. **Desperate** jumpers tried to grab hold of a rung on the way down, missed, and landed on the sidewalk.

. . .

13 Onlookers saw many dreadful sights, none more so than the end of a love affair. A young man appeared at a window. Gently, he helped a young woman step onto the windowsill, held her away from the building—and let go. He helped another young woman onto the windowsill. "Those of us who were looking saw her put her arms around him and kiss him," Shepherd wrote. "Then he held her out into space and dropped her. But quick as a flash he was on the windowsill himself. . . . He was brave enough to help the girl he loved to a quicker death, after she had given him a goodbye kiss."

. . .

14 By 5:15 p.m., exactly thirty-five minutes after flames burst from beneath a cutting table, firefighters had brought the blaze under control. An hour later, Chief Croker made his inspection. He found that the Asch Building had no damage to its structure. Its walls were in good shape; so were the floors. It had passed the test. It was fireproof.

15 The woodwork, furniture, cotton goods, and people who worked in it were not. Of the 500 Triangle employees who reported for work that day, 146 died. Of these, sixteen men were identified. The rest were women or bodies and body parts listed as "unidentified." The Triangle Fire was New York's worst workplace disaster up to that time. Only the September 11, 2001, terrorist attacks on the twin towers of the World Trade Center took more (about 2,500) lives.

Excerpted from *Flesh and Blood So Cheap: The Triangle Fire and Its Legacy* by Albert Marrin, published by Alfred A. Knopf.

Skill:
Informational
Text Structure

He talks about exact times. This is a sequential text structure. This shows how important time was in this tragedy. So much life was lost in a short time. This is why safety at work is so important.

Please note that excerpts and passages in the StudySync® library and this workbook are intended as touchstones to generate interest in an author's work. The excerpts and passages do not substitute for the reading of entire texts, and StudySync® strongly recommends that students seek out and purchase the whole literary or informational work in order to experience it as the author intended. Links to online resellers are available in our digital library. In addition, complete works may be ordered through an authorized reseller by filling out and returning to StudySync® the order form enclosed in this workbook.

Reading & Writing Companion **253**

First Read

Read *Flesh and Blood So Cheap: The Triangle Fire and Its Legacy*. After you read, complete the Think Questions below.

☁ THINK QUESTIONS

1. What happened at the Triangle Shirtwaist Factory? What caused it? Cite evidence to support your response.

2. Which floor had the most casualties? Why? Be sure to cite evidence from the text in your response.

3. **Mood** is the emotional quality or atmosphere of a story or poem. What is the mood of this text? Support your answer with examples of language from the text.

4. Use context clues to determine the meaning of **standpipe** as it is used in paragraph 2 of *Flesh and Blood So Cheap: The Triangle Fire and Its Legacy*. Write your definition here and identify clues that helped you figure out the meaning.

5. Read the following dictionary entry:

inferno
in•fer•no *noun*

1. a large fire that burns out of control
2. Hell, or a place like it

How does the use of **inferno** in *Flesh and Blood So Cheap: The Triangle Fire and Its Legacy* match both definitions? Explain how you figured out both meanings.

Skill:
Informational Text Structure

Use the Checklist to analyze Informational Text Structure in *Flesh and Blood So Cheap: The Triangle Fire and Its Legacy*. Refer to the sample student annotations about Informational Text Structure in the text.

••• CHECKLIST FOR INFORMATIONAL TEXT STRUCTURE

In order to determine the overall structure of a text, note the following:

- ✓ the topic(s) and how the author organizes information about the topic(s)

- ✓ patterns in a section of text that reveal the text structure, such as:

  - sequences, including the order of events or steps in a process

  - problems and their solutions

  - cause-and-effect relationships

  - comparisons

- ✓ the overall structure of the text and how each section contributes to the development of ideas

To analyze the structure an author uses to organize a text, including how the major sections contribute to the whole and to the development of the ideas, use the following questions as a guide:

- ✓ What organizational pattern does the author use? How does it reveal the text structure used to present information?

- ✓ How does a particular section fit into the overall structure of the text? How does it contribute to the whole and the development of the author's ideas?

- ✓ In what ways does the text structure contribute to the development of ideas in the text?

Skill:
Informational Text Structure

Reread paragraphs 6–7 of *Flesh and Blood So Cheap: The Triangle Fire and Its Legacy.* Then, using the Checklist on the previous page, answer the multiple-choice questions below.

⟳ YOUR TURN

1. This question has two parts. First, answer Part A. Then, answer Part B.

   Part A: Which of the following best describes the structure the author uses to organize the two paragraphs?

   ○ A. sequence

   ○ B. problem-and-solution

   ○ C. cause-and-effect

   ○ D. comparison-and-contrast

   Part B: Which sentence from the excerpt supports your answer to Part A?

   ○ A. "Those on the ninth floor were not so lucky."

   ○ B. "Those who reached the ninth-floor stairway door found it locked."

   ○ C. "There were no lights in the stairway, so they had to grope their way in darkness."

   ○ D. "Workers, shouting, crying, and gasping for air, slowly made their way downstairs."

2. How does the text structure contribute to the development of the author's ideas about workplace safety?

   ○ A. By giving an example of how there were not safety standards throughout the building

   ○ B. By giving a detailed description of how the fire spread on the factory floor

   ○ C. By explaining that the Triangle Shirtwaist Factory fire was a workplace disaster

   ○ D. By focusing on the exact times the events unfolded

Close Read

Reread *Flesh and Blood So Cheap: The Triangle Fire and Its Legacy*. As you reread, complete the Skills Focus questions below. Then use your answers and annotations from the questions to help you complete the Write activity.

◎ SKILLS FOCUS

1. Explain how and why the author uses a cause-and-effect text structure in paragraph 4. Highlight evidence from the text and make annotations to explain your reasoning.

2. In paragraphs 6 and 7, Marrin compares and contrasts what happened to the workers on the eighth and ninth floors. What other text structure does he use in sentences 2–4 of paragraph 6? Highlight the transition word in sentence 2, and make annotations to label the text structure.

3. What text structure does the author use in paragraph 9? How does this organizational structure contribute to the development of ideas? Highlight evidence and make annotations to explain your answer.

4. The tragedy of the Triangle Fire resulted in the loss of many lives. Find evidence from the text that shows reasons why so many workers died so quickly in the fire. In your own words, explain how these deaths could have been prevented.

✎ WRITE

INFORMATIVE: Author Albert Marrin explains how poor working conditions and greedy bosses led to the tragedy at the Triangle Shirtwaist Factory. Identify sections that contribute to the development of this idea. Then analyze the text structures Marrin uses to organize those sections. Support your response with specific examples from the text.

A Christmas Carol

FICTION
Charles Dickens
1843

Introduction

Set in 19th-century London, Charles Dickens's short novel *A Christmas Carol* is considered by many to be one of the most influential works of fiction ever written. In this memorable story, the compassionate Dickens (1812–1870) paints a vivid portrayal of the cold-hearted miser Ebenezer Scrooge, the very embodiment of despair and darkness. Though he will be given a chance to change his ways, in this passage from early in the book, we find Scrooge in his "counting-house" obsessed with ledgers and coins and berating his cheerful nephew on the foolishness

"'Bah!' said Scrooge, 'Humbug!'"

from Stave I: Marley's Ghost

1 Once upon a time—of all the good days in the year, on Christmas Eve—old Scrooge sat busy in his counting-house[1]. It was cold, bleak, biting weather: foggy withal: and he could hear the people in the court outside, go wheezing up and down, beating their hands upon their breasts, and stamping their feet upon the pavement stones to warm them. The city clocks had only just gone three, but it was quite dark already—it had not been light all day—and candles were flaring in the windows of the neighbouring offices, like ruddy smears upon the **palpable** brown air. The fog came pouring in at every chink and keyhole, and was so dense without, that although the court was of the narrowest, the houses opposite were mere phantoms. To see the dingy cloud come drooping down, obscuring everything, one might have thought that Nature lived hard by, and was brewing on a large scale.

2 The door of Scrooge's counting-house was open that he might keep his eye upon his clerk[2], who in a dismal little cell beyond, a sort of tank, was copying letters. Scrooge had a very small fire, but the clerk's fire was so very much smaller that it looked like one coal. But he couldn't replenish it, for Scrooge kept the coal-box[3] in his own room; and so surely as the clerk came in with the shovel, the master predicted that it would be necessary for them to part. Wherefore the clerk put on his white comforter, and tried to warm himself at the candle; in which effort, not being a man of a strong imagination, he failed.

3 "A merry Christmas, uncle! God save you!" cried a cheerful voice. It was the voice of Scrooge's nephew, who came upon him so quickly that this was the first **intimation** he had of his approach.

4 "Bah!" said Scrooge, "Humbug!"

---

1. **counting-house** a building or an office used for keeping books
2. **clerk** a worker who keeps records or books of accounts and finance
3. **coal-box** a box that holds coal before it is used in a fire or furnace

---

5 He had so heated himself with rapid walking in the fog and frost, this nephew of Scrooge's, that he was all in a glow; his face was ruddy and handsome; his eyes sparkled, and his breath smoked again.

6 "Christmas a humbug, uncle!" said Scrooge's nephew. "You don't mean that, I am sure?"

7 "I do," said Scrooge. "Merry Christmas! What right have you to be merry? What reason have you to be merry? You're poor enough."

8 "Come, then," returned the nephew gaily. "What right have you to be dismal? What reason have you to be morose? You're rich enough."

9 Scrooge having no better answer ready on the spur of the moment, said, "Bah!" again; and followed it up with "Humbug."

10 "Don't be cross, uncle!" said the nephew.

11 "What else can I be," returned the uncle, "when I live in such a world of fools as this? Merry Christmas! Out upon merry Christmas! What's Christmas time to you but a time for paying bills without money; a time for finding yourself a year older, but not an hour richer; a time for balancing your books and having every item in 'em through a round dozen of months presented dead against you? If I could work my will," said Scrooge **indignantly,** "every idiot who goes about with 'Merry Christmas' on his lips, should be boiled with his own pudding, and buried with a stake of holly through his heart. He should!"

12 "Uncle!" pleaded the nephew.

13 "Nephew!" returned the uncle sternly, "keep Christmas in your own way, and let me keep it in mine."

14 "Keep it!" repeated Scrooge's nephew. "But you don't keep it."

15 "Let me leave it alone, then," said Scrooge. "Much good may it do you! Much good it has ever done you!"

16 "There are many things from which I might have **derived** good, by which I have not profited, I dare say," returned the nephew. "Christmas among the rest. But I am sure I have always thought of Christmas time, when it has come round—apart from the veneration due to its sacred name and origin, if anything belonging to it can be apart from that—as a good time; a kind, forgiving, charitable, pleasant time; the only time I know of, in the long calendar of the year, when men and women seem by one consent to open their shut-up hearts freely, and to think of people below them as if they really

were fellow-passengers to the grave, and not another race of creatures bound on other journeys. And therefore, uncle, though it has never put a scrap of gold or silver in my pocket, I believe that it has done me good, and will do me good; and I say, God bless it!"

17 The clerk in the Tank involuntarily applauded. Becoming immediately sensible of the **impropriety,** he poked the fire, and extinguished the last frail spark for ever.

18 "Let me hear another sound from you," said Scrooge, "and you'll keep your Christmas by losing your situation! You're quite a powerful speaker, sir," he added, turning to his nephew. "I wonder you don't go into Parliament."

19 "Don't be angry, uncle. Come! Dine with us to-morrow."

20 Scrooge said that he would see him—yes, indeed he did. He went the whole length of the expression, and said that he would see him in that extremity first.

21 "But why?" cried Scrooge's nephew. "Why?"

22 "Why did you get married?" said Scrooge.

23 "Because I fell in love."

24 "Because you fell in love!" growled Scrooge, as if that were the only one thing in the world more ridiculous than a merry Christmas. "Good afternoon!"

25 "Nay, uncle, but you never came to see me before that happened. Why give it as a reason for not coming now?"

26 "Good afternoon," said Scrooge.

27 "I want nothing from you; I ask nothing of you; why cannot we be friends?"

28 "Good afternoon," said Scrooge.

29 "I am sorry, with all my heart, to find you so **resolute.** We have never had any quarrel, to which I have been a party. But I have made the trial in homage[4] to Christmas, and I'll keep my Christmas humour to the last. So A Merry Christmas, uncle!"

30 "Good afternoon!" said Scrooge.

31 "And A Happy New Year!"

4. **homage** an expression of deep respect and admiration; honor

NOTES

32　"Good afternoon!" said Scrooge.

33　His nephew left the room without an angry word, notwithstanding. He stopped at the outer door to bestow the greetings of the season on the clerk, who, cold as he was, was warmer than Scrooge; for he returned them cordially[5].

✏ WRITE

PERSONAL NARRATIVE: The excerpt from *A Christmas Carol* depicts a conflict between an uncle and his nephew during Christmas. Write about a time of conflict during a holiday in your own family. At the end of your narrative, provide a conclusion that follows from and reflects on the experience. Consider how the conflict affected you and your family. What did you learn about love and loss?

---

5. **cordially** politely; in a friendly way

Tangerine

FICTION
Edward Bloor
1997

Introduction

Even though he's legally blind, 12-year-old Paul Fisher can see quite a bit through his bug-eyed, Coke-bottle glasses. His parents don't always do as they say. His beloved sports-star brother, Erik, is a self-absorbed bully. And the town the Fishers have moved to—Lake Windsor Downs, in Tangerine County, Florida—might just be the strangest place on Earth. So strange, in fact, that Paul begins to wonder if it might just be the place for a four-eyed zero to transform himself into a certified hero. In this excerpt from the critically acclaimed young adult novel by Edward Bloor (b. 1950), Paul looks on as his brother's football dreams come crashing down.

"This is the house built on the Erik Fisher Football Dream."

1   The third quarter was as dull as the first two, but Cypress Bay's offense suddenly got it together in the final period. They drove eighty-five yards for a touchdown, most of those yards coming from that big fullback. The kick for the extra point was good, and Cypress Bay led 7–0.

2   Antoine responded with two short runs and then a beautiful forty-yard pass to Terry Donnelly, who was wide open down the left sideline. I could have caught that pass. My grandmother could have caught it, for that matter, but Terry Donnelly dropped it. Antoine had to punt again.

3   That's when I noticed the black clouds rolling in. That whole mess with the visitors' bleachers and Mr. Bridges and the cops had pushed the game past the four o'clock **barrier.** In a matter of minutes we went from sunny skies to *kaboom!* And then down it came, a hard, cold rain. Most of the fans climbed down from the bleachers and ran for their cars. Mom yelled, "Come on, you two!" but Dad said, "No, you go ahead. I'm staying," so I said, "I'm staying, too."

4   Mom was already on the ground. She yelled back, "Fine. Stay. I hope neither of you gets killed." She ran back to the Volvo, leaving us to get soaked. Or worse.

5   The rain turned out to be a blessing for Lake Windsor. The offensive line started pushing Cypress Bay back, letting Antoine move the ball steadily down the field—five yards, six yards, five yards, seven yards. With two minutes to play, the Seagulls were all the way down to the Cypress Bay five-yard line. Antoine faked a run to the right and **lofted** a pass into the left corner of the end zone that some mud-covered Seagull receiver caught for a touchdown. A soggy cheer went up from the few fans left in the bleachers. The score was 7–6, and Erik's big moment had arrived.

6   He came running onto the field in his perfectly clean, mud-free uniform to kick the extra point that would tie the game. Erik had never missed a point. Never. I was expecting to see Arthur Bauer trotting out with him, but number 4 was still standing there on the sideline with the other clean uniforms.

7   The two muddy teams lined up. Erik got into his kicking stance, and Antoine Thomas crouched down in front of him to hold the ball. I said, "Check it out, Dad. Antoine's the holder."

8   "I see," he said grimly. "Erik told me that Arthur would be his holder. I don't think it's such a good idea to throw a surprise like this at your kicker."

9   Dad, and Erik, and I, and everybody else figured that Arthur had taken over Mike Costello's job. But no. There was Antoine, in the crouch, getting ready to spin the laces and set the ball down for Erik.

10 The referee blew his whistle, the clock started to tick, and Lake Windsor's big center snapped the ball. Erik, his head down in total concentration, took two steps forward, like he's rehearsed a million times. His foot started toward the ball in a powerful arc, and then—the most incredible thing happened. Antoine whipped the ball away at the last second, like Lucy does with Charlie Brown. He took off running around the right side and crossed the goal line, untouched, for a two-point conversion. Seagulls led 8–7.

11 At the same moment, Erik, who clearly did not expect Antoine to pull the ball away, kicked at nothing but the air. His left foot went flying off in one direction, his right foot in another. For a split second he was a **parallel** line three feet above the ground. Then he made a perfect banana-peel back-flop landing in the mud. The people around us started laughing, hooting, and cheering, all at the same time. Antoine spiked the ball in the end zone, and all the Lake Windsor players, except Erik, ran over and jumped on him. All the Lake Windsor players on the sideline, except Arthur, started jumping up and down, too.

12 Erik finally got up and walked to the sideline to get his kicking tee. His front was still clean and white, but his back was now filthy. He kicked the ball back to the Cardinals, but they fumbled it away, and that's how it ended. Lake Windsor 8, Cypress Bay 7.

13 When we got back to the car, Mom just said, "From here, it sounded like we won."

14 I wanted to tell her all about Erik's banana-peel back-flop special, but Dad cut in right away. "Yes. We won on a fake kick. They sent Erik out to fake the kick for the extra point. That drew the offense to him, and it cleared the way for Antoine to run it in for two points."

15 Mom thought for a minute. "So Erik did something that helped win the game."

Please note that excerpts and passages in the StudySync® library and this workbook are intended as touchstones to generate interest in an author's work. The excerpts and passages do not substitute for the reading of entire texts, and StudySync® strongly recommends that students seek out and purchase the whole literary or informational work in order to experience it as the author intended. Links to online resellers are available in our digital library. In addition, complete works may be ordered through an authorized reseller by filling out and returning to StudySync® the order form enclosed in this workbook.

Reading & Writing Companion   265

16   "Most definitely," Dad said. "It's not something that shows up in the stats in the newspapers. It's not something people will remember. But it helped win the game."

17   I thought to myself, *Not remember? You've got to be kidding. Erik's flying banana-peel back-flop in the mud is the one thing about this game that everybody* is going to remember.

18   Dad continued talking in this manner throughout dinner, pounding home his theme to Erik—that Erik had contributed big-time to the victory, that Erik had actually made victory possible by being the **decoy.** I don't think Erik was even listening. He was just sitting there, looking down, twisting his varsity ring[1] around and around his finger.

19   After dinner Dad flipped on the TV so we could all watch the local news. The lead story on channel 2 was the revolt of the Cypress Bay fans and their brief takeover of the **condemned** visitors' bleachers.

20   About two-thirds of the way through the broadcast came "The Saturday Sports Roundup." The sports anchorman went through the professional baseball and football stuff, then the college football scores, and then the high school scores. "Lake Windsor 8, Cypress Bay 7."

21   The broadcast ended with a feature called "The Weak in Sports." It was a collection of sports bloopers, and guess who they saved for last.

22   The anchorman said something like, "Finally, a play that looks like it was drawn up by the Three Stooges. Watch closely." And there it was. A ground-level view of the ball being snapped to Antoine, of Erik striding forward confidently, and *Whooo!* Up in the air he flew! It was even more comical than I had remembered. Erik went splashing down into the mud, but he didn't stay there. They rewound the tape so that he popped back up, flopped again, popped back up, and flopped again. Finally, the camera turned toward the end zone to catch Antoine spiking the ball. It zoomed in on his face. Antoine was laughing and pointing his finger at the big center, who was pointing back at him.

23   When the anchorman came back on, he was cracking up. So were all the other news people. The credits started rolling, and they started saying stuff like, "Does that school have a diving team?" and "I hear those mud baths are good for wrinkles."

24   Dad got up and snapped off the TV. The four of us sat there in stony silence.

---

1. **varsity ring** a ring given to a player on a school sports team

25   I was thinking that if I were at somebody else's house, we'd be rolling on the floor and laughing at this. I was thinking that kids all over Florida were rolling on the floor and laughing at this, at Erik Fisher the Flying Placekicker. But this isn't somebody else's house. This is the house built on the Erik Fisher Football Dream.

26   Finally Dad said to Erik, "Hey! All you can do is laugh it off."

27   Mom agreed. "That's right. You just leave it behind you. That's all you can do. You leave it behind you, and it's over with."

28   The four of us got up and went our separate ways—me up to my room.

29   I stared out my window at the back wall. *Forget it, Dad. Forget it, Mom. Erik can't laugh this off. Erik can't leave this humiliation behind him. Someone has to pay for this. I'm not sure why I'm sure. But I am. Someone has to pay for this.*

Excerpted from *Tangerine* by Edward Bloor, published by Houghton Mifflin Harcourt.

✏️ WRITE

PERSONAL RESPONSE: Think about what makes someone a good teammate and why. Are the football players in this excerpt good teammates? Why or why not? Support your answer with examples from the text as well as your own experiences.

My Mother Really Knew

POETRY
Wing Tek Lum
1998

Introduction

The author of multiple collections, Wing Tek Lum (b. 1946) is a contemporary Hawaii-born American poet who uses his poetry as a conduit to explore the human condition. Through the exploration of individual moments and images, he draws lessons both universal and poignant. In the poem presented here, "My Mother Really Knew," Lum's reflection on a single memory illuminates the complex connections between parents and their children.

First Read

Read "My Mother Really Knew." After you read, complete the Think Questions below.

☁ THINK QUESTIONS

1. What is the thing that the speaker's mother knew? How does the author describe it? Cite evidence from the text in your response.

2. Why does the speaker refuse to see his father before going to bed? Be sure to include evidence from the text in your answer.

3. How do the first and last stanzas tell the lesson of the poem? Cite evidence from the text in your response.

4. In line 5, the speaker claims that his father's friends "loved him **nonetheless**." Based on context clues from the first stanza, what do you think the word *nonetheless* means? Write your definition here and identify clues that helped you figure out the meaning.

5. Look at the word *eruption* as it is used in the final stanza. Think of other instances in which you have heard the word *eruption*, as well as related words like *erupt*. Write a definition for *eruption* that includes the various uses.

Please note that excerpts and passages in the StudySync® library and this workbook are intended as touchstones to generate interest in an author's work. The excerpts and passages do not substitute for the reading of entire texts, and StudySync® strongly recommends that students seek out and purchase the whole literary or informational work in order to experience it as the author intended. Links to online resellers are available in our digital library. In addition, complete works may be ordered through an authorized reseller by filling out and returning to StudySync® the order form enclosed in this workbook.

Reading & Writing Companion   271

Skill:
Compare and Contrast

Use the Checklist to analyze Compare and Contrast in "My Mother Really Knew."

••• CHECKLIST FOR COMPARE AND CONTRAST

In order to compare and contrast texts within and across different forms and genres, do the following:

✓ choose two or more texts with similar subjects, topics, settings, or characters

✓ highlight evidence that reveals each text's theme or central message

- • consider what happens as a result of the characters' words and actions
- • note ways in which the texts are similar and different

To compare and contrast texts within and across different forms or genres, consider the following questions:

✓ What are the similarities and differences in the subjects or topics of the texts I have chosen?

✓ Have I looked at the words of each character, as well as what the characters do, to help me determine the theme of each work?

COMPARE AND CONTRAST

sync•skills

Skill:
Compare and Contrast

Reread lines 11–17 of "My Mother Really Knew," paragraph 10 of *Tangerine*, paragraphs 10–12 from *A Christmas Carol*, and the "Common Theme" comparison below. Then, complete the chart by matching the details that support the comparison with the correct text.

♻ YOUR TURN

COMMON THEME: Two people are at odds, and the conflict results in angry feelings and even insults.

Detail Options	
A	One person humiliates another
B	One person refuses to apologize after an argument
C	One person hurts another's feelings

"My Mother Really Knew"	Tangerine	A Christmas Carol

Close Read

Reread "My Mother Really Knew." As you reread, complete the Skills Focus questions below. Then use your answers and annotations from the questions to help you complete the Write activity.

◎ SKILLS FOCUS

1. Highlight examples of figurative language such as imagery or simile in "My Mother Really Knew." Choose one example and explain its meaning. Explain what the figurative language adds to the poem that plain language would not.

2. In *Tangerine*, the mother tries to convince her family to get out of the rain. Identify examples of the mother trying to convince her family in "My Mother Really Knew." Compare the ways in which the two mothers attempt to convince their families.

3. The character Scrooge in *A Christmas Carol* is mean and greedy. Identify a detail that shows which character in "My Mother Really Knew" is most similar to Scrooge. Explain how the characters are similar and different.

4. Identify the lessons that the speaker of "My Mother Really Knew" learns about love from his relationship with his parents and the loss of his father.

✏ WRITE

COMPARE AND CONTRAST: Compare and contrast the conflicts in the family interactions presented in "My Mother Really Knew" and the other two selections—*A Christmas Carol* and *Tangerine*. Remember to use evidence from all three texts to support your analysis.

Extended
Writing
Project and
Grammar

EXTENDED
WRITING
PROJECT
LITERARY ANALYSIS
WRITING

Literary Analysis Writing Process: Plan

PLAN	DRAFT	REVISE	EDIT AND PUBLISH

The authors in this unit all use their writing to explore important relationships. Many of these relationships, like Gavin's in "The Walking Dance," are complicated and difficult. Gavin struggles to feel a sense of belonging in his wife's family. But after attending a funeral service, Gavin finds a connection with them through the experience of love and loss.

WRITING PROMPT

What do we learn from love and loss?

Think about the main characters, narrators, or speakers in the texts from this unit. Choose two or three selections from the unit and write a literary analysis that shows the different types of lessons learned about love and loss. In your analysis, be sure to present an argument in which you explain what lesson each character, narrator, or speaker learns and how love or loss helps them learn this lesson. Be sure your literary analysis includes the following:

- an introduction
- a thesis statement with claims
- coherent body paragraphs
- reasons and evidence
- a conclusion

Writing to Sources

As you gather ideas and information from the texts, or sources, in the unit, be sure to:

- include a claim about each source;
- use evidence from each source; and
- avoid overly relying on one source.

Introduction to Argumentative Writing

An argumentative essay is a form of persuasive writing where the writer makes claim(s) about a topic and then provides evidence—facts, details, examples, and quotations—to convince readers to accept and agree with the writer's claim(s). In order to provide convincing supporting evidence for an argumentative essay, the writer must often do outside research as well as cite the sources of the evidence that is presented. In an essay, a thesis statement usually appears at the end of the introductory paragraph and offers a concise summary of the claim.

A literary analysis is a form of argumentative writing that tries to persuade readers to accept the writer's interpretation of a literary text. Good literary analysis writing builds an argument with claims, convincing reasons, relevant textual evidence, and a clear structure with an introduction with a thesis statement, body paragraphs, and a conclusion. The characteristics of argumentative writing include:

- introduction
- thesis statement
- claims
- textual evidence
- transitions
- formal style
- conclusion

As you continue with this Extended Writing Project, you'll receive more instruction and practice at crafting each of the characteristics of argumentative writing to create your own literary analysis.

Please note that excerpts and passages in the StudySync® library and this workbook are intended as touchstones to generate interest in an author's work. The excerpts and passages do not substitute for the reading of entire texts, and StudySync® strongly recommends that students seek out and purchase the whole literary or informational work in order to experience it as the author intended. Links to online resellers are available in our digital library. In addition, complete works may be ordered through an authorized reseller by filling out and returning to StudySync® the order form enclosed in this workbook.

Reading & Writing Companion   **277**

Before you get started on your own literary analysis, read this literary analysis that one student, Knox, wrote in response to the writing prompt. As you read the Model, highlight and annotate the features of argumentative writing that Knox included in his literary analysis.

NOTES

☰ STUDENT MODEL

Lessons from Love and Loss

1 Relationships have highs and lows. In many cases, relationships are the best thing in life. Other times, relationships are full of conflict. In literature, authors express lessons about love and loss by exploring deep relationships. For example, "My Mother Pieced Quilts" conveys that family and relationships are a combination of both love and loss; a family's history has moments of joy and of pain, but through it all, they are rooted in love. In a similar way, "The Walking Dance" shows that people find their roles in family relationships. "Annabel Lee" reveals that the power of love and loss in relationships can make people unreasonable. The authors of these three texts express in different ways that love and loss teach people about themselves and their relationships.

2 The speaker in "My Mother Pieced Quilts" learns that families move forward together by working together, supporting each other, and loving each other in good times and bad. The speaker watches her mother quilt and writes about "black silk" at "grandmother's/funeral" and the "lilac purple of easter." This shows the pieces of fabric represent both happy and sad memories and all different times and places throughout their family history. The speaker describes the quilts like family members who love and support each other. The quilts are "armed/ready/shouting/celebrating" and "sing on" despite a past of "laughing and sobbing." This shows that the speaker learns loss and tough times are easier when families work together and love each other. The speaker also remembers how these quilts protected her family from the cold, just like families protect each other when times are hard. For example, the speaker talks about how her mother "stretched and turned and re-arranged" fabric to make a quilt. This is just like how parents stretch their resources and make sacrifices to keep their children safe. Overall, it is clear that the speaker learns the importance of loving, supporting, and working with your family.

3   Like the speaker in "My Mother Pieced Quilts," the character Gavin in "The Walking Dance" learns that family relationships take work. Gavin is visiting his wife Aurora's family in San Antonio. Gavin feels like an outsider in the big Herrera family, who tease and ignore him at times. He feels alone at the funeral of Aurora's aunt Melchora. He's only an accessory to Aurora: "If something happened to Aurora, he'd be swallowed up by her mammoth family, totally invisible. Barely anyone would know him." But then grief overcomes Gavin's son Carlos, and he needs his father. Gavin picks up Carlos from his grandmother's arms and joins the ceremonial walking dance with his family. "He lifted Carlos out of Cookie's arms. This kiddo was heavy, but Gavin could tough it out for at least one lap around the chapel with his mother-in-law." They share a moment. Cookie sums it up, "That's right. Let's go." Though his family relationships are not perfect, Gavin learns how to connect with his family members through love and loss.

4   The poem "Annabel Lee" takes a darker turn because Edgar Allan Poe explores the irrational thoughts of a speaker mourning his departed love. The speaker's love for Annabel Lee is so powerful that he believes it makes angels jealous: "The angels, not half so happy in Heaven, / Went envying her and me—." The speaker shows extreme devotion to his relationship, even after the death of Annabel Lee. "And neither the angels in Heaven above / Nor the demons down under the sea / Can ever dissever my soul from the soul / Of the beautiful Annabel Lee." This poetic statement shows that the speaker does not move on from Annabel Lee after losing her. He also holds on to the relationship to make it everlasting. "For the moon never beams, without bringing me dreams / Of the beautiful Annabel Lee." The speaker expresses that deep relationships of love can extend beyond any loss, which includes the profound loss of death. The speaker learns that he cannot move on without Annabel Lee, so his love dominates his thoughts.

5   "My Mother Pieced Quilts," "The Walking Dance," and "Annabel Lee" show how speakers and characters learn about themselves through the challenges of love and loss. The speaker in "My Mother Pieced Quilts" remembers both the highs and lows of her childhood and family history, but through it all is surrounded by love and support. Gavin in "The Walking Dance" learns how to contribute to his family

Copyright © BookheadEd Learning, LLC

through his son's grief. The speaker in "Annabel Lee" learns that his feelings for his lost love overwhelm him. The characters and speakers in these selections focus on their deepest relationships. They make sure they do not fade. This helps the speaker in "My Mother Pieced Quilts" and the character Gavin in "The Walking Dance" stay close with their families. On the other hand, this quality makes it hard for the speaker in "Annabel Lee" to carry on when he loses his love, but he chooses that path. By dealing with love and loss, the characters and speakers learn about their own place in the world.

✏️ WRITE

Writers often take notes before they sit down to write. Think about what you've learned so far about literary analyses to help you begin prewriting.

- Which texts from the unit would you like to write about?

- How do the characters, narrators, or speakers of those texts express their ideas about love and loss?

- What kinds of lessons do the characters, speakers, or narrators learn?

- What kinds of textual evidence might you use to support your ideas?

- What kinds of transitional words and phrases could you use to connect your ideas in a logical way?

Response Instructions

Use the questions in the bulleted list to write a one-paragraph summary. Your summary should identify the two or three texts you want to write about. Explain how the characters, narrators, or speakers of each of those texts learn a lesson.

Don't worry about including all of the details now; focus only on the most essential and important elements. You will refer back to this short paragraph as you continue through the steps of the writing process.

Skill:
Thesis Statement

••• CHECKLIST FOR THESIS STATEMENT

Before you begin writing your thesis statement, ask yourself the following questions:

- What is the prompt asking me to write about?

- What is the topic of my essay? How can I state it clearly for the reader?

- What claim(s) do I want to make about the topic of this essay? Is my opinion clear to my reader?

Here are some methods to introduce and develop your thesis statement clearly:

- Think about the prompt topic.

    > Read the prompt topic closely.

    > Identify keywords or questions in the prompt.

- Select and review your selections to solidify your thesis statement.

    > Select the two or three texts to use.

    > Think about or take notes on the main ideas of each text.

    > Find connections between the main ideas of each text.

- Write a clear statement about the central idea or thesis statement.

    > Let the reader anticipate the body of your essay.

    > Respond completely to the writing prompt.

⟳ YOUR TURN

Complete the chart by matching the student action with the correct step of writing a thesis statement.

	Student Action Options
A	Mike picks the two texts he will use and rereads them, taking notes on the main ideas of each text and how they connect to the topic of his essay. Mike rereads his notes on both the prompt and the text selections. He notices that all of the characters in the different texts persevered through different challenges and were eventually successful.
B	Mike continues to review his notes. Then, he provides a one-sentence summary of his main points: "The characters in these two texts show that challenges and adversity can make you stronger."
C	Mike rereads and highlights keywords in the writing prompt so that he knows what the topic of his essay should be about. He notes that in his essay he will need to analyze how characters react to challenges and adversity in at least two different texts.

Steps to Writing an Effective Thesis Statement	Student Actions
Think about the prompt topic.	
Select and review your selections to solidify your claims.	
Write a clear thesis statement.	

✎ WRITE

Follow the steps in the checklist section to draft a thesis statement for your literary analysis.

Skill: Organizing Argumentative Writing

••• CHECKLIST FOR ORGANIZING ARGUMENTATIVE WRITING

As you consider how to organize your writing for your literary analysis, use the following questions as a guide:

- What is my thesis statement? What claim about each text supports my thesis statement?

- Have I chosen the best organizational structure to present my information logically?

- Can my claims be supported by logical reasoning and relevant evidence?

- Do I have enough evidence to support my thesis statement and claims?

Follow these steps to plan out the organization of your literary analysis, including organizing your reasons and evidence logically:

- Identify and write your thesis statement and claims.

- Choose an organizational structure that will present your claims logically.

- Identify reasons and evidence that support each claim.

- Organize your ideas using an outline or graphic organizer.

↻ YOUR TURN

Read the thesis and claim statements below. Then, complete the chart by matching each statement with its correct place in the outline.

	Thesis Statement and Claim Options
A	In these three works of fiction, the authors use conflict to show readers that people should be valued for the traits that make them unique.
B	The conflict between the cruel lord and the aging mother in "The Wise Old Woman" teaches that elderly people should be valued for their experience and that we all need to rely on each other.
C	After a conflict in the street, it may seem strange that Mrs. Jones invites Roger into her home in "Thank You, Ma'am."
D	In conclusion, through various conflicts, the authors of these three texts were able to show that different traits make us unique and should be valued.
E	There is no one else quite like Stargirl in Jerry Spinelli's novel—other students don't fully understand her, but that's what makes Stargirl special.

Outline	Thesis Statement or Claim
Thesis Statement	
Claim 1: "Wise Old Woman"	
Claim 2: *Stargirl*	
Claim 3: "Thank You, Ma'am"	
Restate Thesis Statement	

↻ YOUR TURN

Complete the chart below by writing your thesis statement and claim for each body paragraph. Repeat your thesis statement for your conclusion.

Outline	Thesis Statement or Claim
Thesis Statement	
Claim 1	
Claim 2	
Claim 3	
Restate Thesis Statement	

Skill: Reasons and Relevant Evidence

As you begin to determine what reasons and relevant evidence will support your claim(s), use the following questions as a guide:

- What is the claim (or claims) that I am making in my argument?
- What textual evidence am I using to support this claim? Is it relevant?
- Am I quoting the source accurately?
- Does my evidence display logical reasoning and relate to the claim I am making?

Use the following steps as a guide to help you determine how you will support your claim(s) with logical reasoning and relevant evidence, using accurate and credible sources:

- Identify the claim(s) you will make in your argument.
- Select evidence from credible sources that will convince others to accept your claim(s).
- Explain the connection between your claim(s) and the evidence and ensure your reasoning is logical, develops naturally from the evidence, and supports your claim.

⟳ YOUR TURN

Read each piece of textual evidence below. Then, complete the chart by deciding which evidence best supports each claim and explain how the evidence supports the claim. The first row has been done for you.

Evidence Options	
A	For example, young viewers learn that those who treat others with pettiness and contempt become rich and famous. In fact, in 2011, one of the stars of *Jersey Shore* was paid more to address Rutgers University students than was Toni Morrison, a Nobel prize–winning author.
B	Today, according to the *Asbury Park Press*, each New Jersey school district spends more than thirty thousand dollars a year devoted to anti-bullying measures.
C	Programs such as *Project Runway*, *The Voice*, and *So You Think You Can Dance* give artists and performers a chance to appear before millions to show their talents.

Claim	Evidence	Explanation
Schools are not doing enough to prevent bullying.	The National Center for Education Statistics reported in 2013 that one of three students is bullied either in school or through social media.	This supports the idea that many students are being bullied and schools are not doing enough.
Most schools are doing their best to stop bullying.		
Reality television is harmful.		
Reality television can be positive.		

↻ YOUR TURN

Complete the chart below by writing a piece of evidence that supports each claim and explain how the evidence supports the claim.

Claim	Evidence	Explanation
Claim for Selection #1		
Claim for Selection #2		
Claim for Selection #3		

Literary Analysis Writing Process: Draft

PLAN	DRAFT	REVISE	EDIT AND PUBLISH

You have already made progress toward writing your literary analysis. Now it is time to draft your literary analysis.

✏ WRITE

Use your plan and other responses in your Binder to draft your literary analysis. You may also have new ideas as you begin drafting. Feel free to explore any new ideas. You can also ask yourself these questions:

- Is my thesis statement clear?
- Is my textual evidence relevant and necessary?
- Does the organizational structure make sense?

Before you submit your draft, read it over carefully. You want to be sure that you've responded to all aspects of the prompt.

Here is Knox's literary analysis. As you read, identify relevant textual evidence that develops his thesis. Because this is a draft, there are some errors that Knox will revise as he works toward his final version.

STUDENT MODEL: FIRST DRAFT

NOTES

Lessons from Love and Loss

~~In literature authors explore lessons about life by exploring relationships. The authors of these three texts showed in different ways that the rewards of deep relationships require effort. The relationships in "My Mother Pieced Quilts," "Walking Dance," and "Annabel Lee" show that people have to work at relationships to maintain and improve them, but no one can make them perfect. These three literary texts show in diverse ways how love and loss teach us that it is important to move forward.~~

Relationships have highs and lows. In many cases, relationships are the best thing in life. Other times, relationships are full of conflict. In literature, authors express lessons about love and loss by exploring deep relationships. For example, "My Mother Pieced Quilts" conveys that family and relationships are a combination of both love and loss; a family's history has moments of joy and of pain, but through it all, they are rooted in love. In a similar way, "The Walking Dance" shows that people find their roles in family relationships. "Annabel Lee" reveals that the power of love and loss in relationships can make people unreasonable. The authors of these three texts express in different ways that love and loss teach people about themselves and their relationships.

The speaker in "My Mother Pieced Quilts" learns that families move forward together and support each other through good times and bad. The speaker watches her mother quilt and writes about "black silk" at "grandmother's/funeral" and the "lilac purple of easter." This shows the pieces of fabric represent both happy and sad memories and all different times and places throughout their family history. The speaker describes the quilts like family members who love and support each other. The quilts are "armed/ready/shouting/celebrating" and "sing on" despite a past of "laughing and sobbing." This shows that the speaker learns loss and tough times are easier when families work together and love each other. This poem shows that even though bad things happened, she still loved her family and had good memories.

 Skill:
Introductions

Knox added several sentences in the beginning of his introductory paragraph to grab his readers' attention. Then, he introduced them to the topic from the prompt, love and loss. Finally, he revised his thesis statement to clarify that the characters in each text learned about themselves and their relationships. He placed his thesis statement last in the introduction.

Copyright © BookheadEd Learning, LLC

NOTES

**Skill:
Transitions**

Knox realizes that he is missing some transitions in this body paragraph. He realizes this paragraph does not logically follow the previous one. He decides to add a stronger topic sentence that introduces his main idea to relate it to the previous paragraph about "My Mother Pieced Quilts." He also decides to add some transitions to better connect his ideas.

~~The short story explores being an outsider to a group. Gavin is visiting his wife Aurora's family in San Antonio. He feels like an outsider in the big Herrera family. Especially at the funeral of Aurora's aunt Melchora. It's as if he's only an accessory to Aurora: "If something happened to Aurora, he'd be swallowed up by her mammoth family, totally invisible. Barely anyone would know him." Grief overcomes Gavin's son Carlos, and he needs his father. Though his family relationships are not perfect, Gavin learns.~~

Like the speaker in "My Mother Pieced Quilts," the character Gavin in "The Walking Dance" learns that family relationships take work. Gavin is visiting his wife Aurora's family in San Antonio. Gavin feels like an outsider in the big Herrera family, who tease and ignore him at times. He feels alone at the funeral of Aurora's aunt Melchora. He's only an accessory to Aurora: "If something happened to Aurora, he'd be swallowed up by her mammoth family, totally invisible. Barely anyone would know him." **But then** grief overcomes Gavin's son Carlos, and he needs his father. Gavin picks up Carlos from his grandmother's arms and joins the ceremonial walking dance with his family. "He lifted Carlos out of Cookie's arms. This kiddo was heavy, but Gavin could tough it out for at least one lap around the chapel with his mother-in-law." They share a moment. Cookie sums it up, "That's right. Let's go." **Though** his family relationships are not perfect, Gavin learns how to connect with his family members through love and loss.

~~The text takes a darker turn and showed how the speaker's focus on a relationship makes him irrational. The thoughts of a speaker mourning his departed love. The speaker's love for Annabel Lee is so powerful that he believes it makes angels jealous. The speaker shows extreme devotion to his relationship even continues after the death of Annabe lee. This poetic statement shows that the speaker does not move on from Annabel Lee after losing her, and he holds onto the relationship to make it everlasting. "For the moon never beams, without bringing me dreams / Of the beautiful Annabel Lee." The speaker expresses that deep relationships of love can extend beyond any loss which includes the profound loss of death. I~~

~~learned that he cannot move on without Annabel Lee, so his love dominates his thoughts.~~

The poem "Annabel Lee" takes a darker turn because Edgar Allan Poe explores the irrational thoughts of a speaker mourning his departed love. The speaker's love for Annabel Lee is so powerful that he believes it makes angels jealous. "The angels, not half so happy in Heaven, / Went envying her and me—." The speaker shows extreme devotion to his relationship, even after the death of Annabel Lee. "And neither the angels in Heaven above / Nor the demons down under the sea / Can ever dissever my soul from the soul / Of the beautiful Annabel Lee." This poetic statement shows that the speaker does not move on from Annabel Lee after losing her. He also holds on to the relationship to make it everlasting. "For the moon never beams, without bringing me dreams / Of the beautiful Annabel Lee." The speaker expresses that deep relationships of love can extend beyond any loss, which includes the profound loss of death. The speaker learns that he cannot move on without Annabel Lee, so his love dominates his thoughts.

~~"My Mother Pieced Quilts," "The Walking Dance," and "Annabel Lee" show that hardships occur even in the strongest relationships. "My Mother Pieced Quilts" shows the upside and downside of family relationships. "Walking Dance" shows how family relationships come together in difficult times. The relationship described in "Annabel Lee" shows the power of love. The speakers and characters do the best they can in these situations and try to move forward. They react to their situations and make their relationships a priority. Otherwise, their relationships would fade away.~~

"My Mother Pieced Quilts," "The Walking Dance," and "Annabel Lee" show how speakers and characters learn about themselves through the challenges of love and loss. The speaker in "My Mother Pieced Quilts" remembers both the highs and lows of her childhood and family history, but through it all is surrounded by love and support. Gavin in "The Walking Dance" learns how to contribute to his family through his son's grief. The speaker in "Annabel Lee" learns that his

Skill:
Style

Knox changes his first sentence to include more academic language (specifying "poem" and the title) and establish an academic tone. He continues to maintain that tone by replacing the first person (I) in the last sentence.

NOTES

Skill:
Conclusions

Knox begins his conclusion by restating his thesis statement a new way. He chose to highlight all three texts and how they taught lessons through love and loss. By repeating his thesis statement one more time, he highlighted the common lesson that all the speakers and characters learned.

feelings for his lost love overwhelm him. The characters and speakers in these selections focus on their deepest relationships. They make sure they do not fade. This helps the speaker in "My Mother Pieced Quilts" and the character Gavin in "The Walking Dance" stay close with their families. On the other hand, this quality makes it hard for the speaker in "Annabel Lee" to carry on when he loses his love, but he chooses that path. By dealing with love and loss, the characters and speakers learn about their own place in the world.

Skill:
Introductions

Before you write your introduction, ask yourself the following questions:

- What is my thesis statement?
- How can I introduce my topic clearly?
- How can I preview my selections?
- How can I "hook" readers' interest?
  - > Start with an attention-grabbing statement.
  - > Begin with an intriguing question.
  - > Use descriptive words to set a scene.

Below are two strategies to help you write a clear and engaging introduction:

- Peer Discussion
  - > Talk about your topic with a partner, explaining what you already know and your ideas about your topic.
  - > Write notes about the ideas you have discussed and any new questions you may have.
  - > Review your notes and think about what will be your thesis statement.
  - > Briefly state your thesis statement.
  - > Write a sentence to introduce the topic.
  - > Write ways you can give readers a "preview" of what they will read in the rest of your essay.
  - > Write a possible "hook."

- Freewriting
  - > Freewrite for ten minutes about your topic. Don't worry about grammar, punctuation, or having fully formed ideas. The point of freewriting is to discover ideas.
  - > Review your notes and think about what will be your thesis statement.
  - > Briefly state your thesis statement.
  - > Write a sentence to introduce the topic.
  - > Write ways you can give readers a "preview" of what they will read in the rest of your essay.
  - > Write a possible "hook."

⟳ YOUR TURN

Read each response from Knox's partner below. Then, match each response to the correct section of the introduction.

	Response Options
A	We all understand love and loss, and authors use our understanding of love and loss to teach us important lessons.
B	Aren't relationships the best and the worst at the same time? They can make you happy and feel loved, but they can also make you feel sad and alone.
C	In all three of these texts, the authors used the speakers to show how love and loss can help us find ourselves.
D	In the poem "Annabel Lee," the speaker loved deeply, but then struggled when they lost the person they loved. In "The Walking Dance," the speaker struggled to find their place in their family; even though they were surrounded by love, it took a loss for them to step up. Finally, in "My Mother Pieced Quilts," the speakers explored how family relationships are made up of many moments of joy and sadness and that the love helps them find themselves and keeps them grounded.

Part of Introduction	Response
Hook	
Introduce topic	
Preview	
Clear thesis statement	

✎ WRITE

Use the steps in the checklist section to revise the introduction of your literary analysis essay.

Skill:
Transitions

••• CHECKLIST FOR TRANSITIONS

Before you revise your current draft to include transitions, think about:

- the key ideas you discuss in your body paragraphs
- how your paragraphs connect together to support your claim(s)
- the relationships among your claim(s), reasons, and evidence

Next, reread your current draft and note areas in your essay where:

- the relationships between your claim(s) and the reasons and evidence are unclear, identifying places where you could add linking words or other transitional devices to make your argument more cohesive. Look for:

  > sudden jumps in your ideas

  > breaks between paragraphs where the ideas in the next paragraph are not logically following from the previous one

Revise your draft to use words, phrases, and clauses to create cohesion and clarify the relationships among claim(s) and reasons, using the following questions as a guide:

- Are there unifying relationships between the claims, reasons, and evidence I present in my argument?
- Have I clarified, or made clear, these relationships?
- What linking words (such as conjunctions), phrases, or clauses could I add to my argument to clarify the relationships between the claims, reasons, and evidence I present?

Please note that excerpts and passages in the StudySync® library and this workbook are intended as touchstones to generate interest in an author's work. The excerpts and passages do not substitute for the reading of entire texts, and StudySync® strongly recommends that students seek out and purchase the whole literary or informational work in order to experience it as the author intended. Links to online resellers are available in our digital library. In addition, complete works may be ordered through an authorized reseller by filling out and returning to StudySync® the order form enclosed in this workbook.

Reading & Writing Companion   **297**

YOUR TURN

Choose the best answer to each question.

1. The following section is from an earlier draft of Knox's essay. Knox has not used the most effective transition in the underlined sentence. Which of the following could he add to the underlined sentence?

> The speaker expresses that deep relationships of love can extend beyond any loss, which includes the profound loss of death. <u>He learns that he cannot move on without Annabel Lee, so his love dominates his thoughts.</u>

   ○ A. For instance,
   ○ B. Equally important,
   ○ C. Finally,
   ○ D. Similarly,

2. The following section is from an earlier draft of Knox's essay. He would like to add a sentence to bring this paragraph to a more effective close. Which sentence could he add after sentence 5 to help achieve this goal?

> (1) In "My Mother Pieced Quilts," the speaker remembers all the different stuff her family did. (2) The speaker remembers how the quilts protected them from the cold and showed her family history. (3) The speaker talks about how her mom sewed all different pieces and parts into the quilt and they protected everyone from the cold. (4) Her mom used all different things for the quilts; she says her mom used pieces that showed "your michigan spring faded curtain pieces / my father's santa fe work shirt / the summer denims, the tweed of fall." (5) She talked about the quilts showing all the family history, good and bad.

   ○ A. Throughout this poem, the speaker realizes that even though her family suffered loss, they were still surrounded by love, and the memories of both were important.
   ○ B. The speaker misses her family, especially her mother.
   ○ C. For example, the speaker would like to remember the good and bad parts of her family history.
   ○ D. I think the speaker is a kind person for remembering her family with love.

↻ YOUR TURN

Complete the chart by writing a transitional sentence below the example that connects ideas with or between paragraphs in your essay.

Purpose	Example and Your Sentence
add information	**In addition,** it is important to remember that female athletes play as many or more games a season than male athletes.
introduce examples	**For example,** the New York Liberty and the Washington Mystics both play 15 more games a season than the New York Knicks and the Washington Wizards.
discuss a contradiction	**Even though** they are working more hours, attending more practices, and playing more games a season, women are being paid less; this may be because there are fewer fans watching and attending their games.
show time sequence	**At this time,** this is changing; female athletes like Hope Solo and Serena Williams are beginning to draw attention to the gender discrepancies in professional sports.
show cause and effect	**As a result,** more people are paying attention to the conditions, pay, and treatment of female athletes.
summarize	**In summary,** I believe it is important that we acknowledge that female professional athletes are working just as hard as their male counterparts and deserve to be recognized for that work.

Skill:
Style

••• CHECKLIST FOR STYLE

First, reread the draft of your argumentative essay and identify the following:

- places where you use slang, contractions, abbreviations, and a conversational tone
- areas where you could use subject-specific or academic language in order to help, persuade, or inform your readers
- moments where you use first person (*I*) or second person (*you*)
- areas where sentence structure lacks variety
- incorrect uses of the conventions of standard English for grammar, spelling, capitalization, and punctuation

Establish and maintain a formal style in your essay, using the following questions as a guide:

- Have I avoided slang in favor of academic language?
- Did I consistently use a third-person point of view, using third-person pronouns (*he, she, they*)?
- Have I varied my sentence structure and the length of my sentences? Apply these specific questions where appropriate:
  - > Where should I make some sentences longer by using conjunctions to connect independent clauses, dependent clauses, and phrases?
  - > Where should I make some sentences shorter by separating any independent clauses?
- Did I follow the conventions of standard English, including:
  - > grammar?
  - > spelling?
  - > capitalization?
  - > punctuation?

↻ YOUR TURN

Complete the chart below by correcting each piece of informal language with the formal language.

Formal/Academic Language Options			
should not	was not	they/she/he (third person)	television
the reader	did not	text	want to

Informal Language	Formal/Academic Language
didn't	
story	
shouldn't	
wanna	
wasn't	
I/me/we (first person)	
you	
TV	

YOUR TURN

Complete the chart by identifying parts of your essay that may need to be rewritten in a more formal style.

Common Informal Language	Rewrite
Contractions	
First Person	
Slang	
Conversational Tone	

Skill:
Conclusions

••• CHECKLIST FOR CONCLUSIONS

Before you write your conclusion, ask yourself the following questions:

- How can I restate the thesis statement in my concluding section? What impression can I make on my reader?

- How can I write my conclusion so that it supports and follows logically from my argument?

- Should I include a call to action?

- How can I conclude with a memorable comment?

Below are two strategies to help you provide a concluding statement or section that follows from and supports the argument presented:

- Peer Discussion

  > After you have written your introduction and body paragraphs, talk with a partner and tell him or her what you want readers to remember, writing notes about your discussion.

  > Review your notes and think about what you wish to express in your conclusion.

  > Rewrite your thesis statement in a different way.

  > Briefly review and explain how your claims about each selection support your thesis.

  > Include a call to action or memorable comment at the end.

  > Write your conclusion.

- Freewriting

  > Freewrite for ten minutes about what you might include in your conclusion. Don't worry about grammar, punctuation, or having fully formed ideas. The point of freewriting is to discover ideas.

  > Review your notes and think about what you wish to express in your conclusion.

  > Rewrite your thesis statement in a different way.

  > Briefly review and explain how your claims about each selection support your thesis.

  > Include a call to action or memorable comment at the end.

  > Write your conclusion.

↻ YOUR TURN

Read each response from Knox's partner below. Then, match each response to the correct section of the conclusion.

	Response Options
A	In the three texts, "Annabel Lee," "The Walking Dance," and "My Mother Pieced Quilts," the characters and speakers show how love and loss taught them lessons about themselves.
B	The authors show us that as human beings, we share these powerful feelings. We also learn so much from them.
C	In both "The Walking Dance" and the poem "Annabel Lee," Gavin and the speaker learn about themselves through the loss of someone dear to them. Gavin learns how important he is to his family and the speaker in "Annabel Lee" learns that he can persevere through the loss of his love. In the poem "My Mother Pieced Quilts," the speaker uses quilts to help her remember a family history that was filled with both love and loss.

Part of Conclusion	Response
Restate thesis statement in a different way	
Review and explain your claims	
Call to action or memorable comment	

✏ WRITE

Use the steps in the checklist section to revise the conclusion of your literary analysis essay.

Literary Analysis Writing Process: Revise

PLAN	DRAFT	REVISE	EDIT AND PUBLISH

You have written a draft of your literary analysis. You have also received input from your peers about how to improve it. Now you are going to revise your draft.

◀◀ REVISION GUIDE

Examine your draft to find areas for revision. Keep in mind your purpose and audience as you revise for clarity, development, organization, and style. Use the guide below to help you review:

Review	Revise	Example
Clarity		
Review your preview statement in your introduction. Identify any sentences where it is not clear which selection you are discussing.	Identify the title, author, speaker or narrator, and names of characters. Provide descriptions so readers understand your statements. Check that these same names and titles are also used throughout body paragraphs and your conclusion.	The poem "Annabel Lee" takes a darker turn and shows how the speaker's focus on the loss of his love makes him irrational.
Development		
Review the development of your claim in the body paragraphs. Identify statements that lack supporting evidence.	Check off each statement that is supported with textual evidence. Add quotations to follow statements that need support.	The speaker's love for Annabel Lee is so powerful that he believes it makes angels jealous: "The angels, not half so happy in Heaven, / Went envying her and me—." The speaker shows extreme devotion to his relationship, so it even continues after the death of Annabel Lee.

Review	Revise	Example
Organization		
Find places where transitions would improve your essay. Review your body paragraphs to identify and annotate any sentences that don't flow in a clear and logical way.	Rewrite the sentences so they appear in a logical sequence, starting with a clear transition or topic sentence. Delete details that are repetitive or not essential to support the thesis.	Like the speaker in "My Mother Pieced Quilts," the character Gavin in "The Walking Dance" learns that family relationships take work.
Style: Word Choice		
Identify sentences that refer to literary concepts. Look for everyday words and phrases that can be replaced with literary terms.	Replace everyday language with literary terms, such as *speaker*, *poem*, and *conflict*.	~~He~~ The speaker learns that he cannot move on without Annabel Lee, so his love dominates his thoughts.
Style: Sentence Variety		
Read your literary analysis aloud. Annotate places where you have too many long or short sentences in a row.	Rewrite sentences by making them longer or shorter for clarity or emphasis.	This poetic statement shows that the speaker does not move on from Annabel Lee after losing her. ~~, and he~~ He holds on to the relationship to make it everlasting.

✏ WRITE

Use the guide above, as well as your peer reviews, to help you evaluate your literary analysis to determine areas that should be revised.

Grammar: Adjective Clauses

A clause is a group of words that has a subject and a predicate. An adjective clause is a subordinate clause that modifies, or describes, a noun or pronoun. It answers the questions *who, what kind*, or *which one*? Many adjective clauses begin with a relative pronoun, including *that, which, who, whom*, or *whose*. Adjective clauses may also begin with *where* or *when*.

Sentence	Noun or Pronoun	Adjective Clause
It was a big change from my **mother who always lets out a screech** if you go near anything... *The Pigman*	mother	who always lets out a screech
His left leg was cut off close by the hip, and under the left shoulder, he carried a **crutch, which he managed with wonderful dexterity,** hopping about upon it like a bird. *Treasure Island*	crutch	which he managed with wonderful dexterity

Please note that excerpts and passages in the StudySync® library and this workbook are intended as touchstones to generate interest in an author's work. The excerpts and passages do not substitute for the reading of entire texts, and StudySync® strongly recommends that students seek out and purchase the whole literary or informational work in order to experience it as the author intended. Links to online resellers are available in our digital library. In addition, complete works may be ordered through an authorized reseller by filling out and returning to StudySync® the order form enclosed in this workbook.

Reading & Writing Companion   **307**

YOUR TURN

1. Choose the revision that uses an adjective clause to modify a noun.

> Christopher drove his mother's car.

- ○ A. Christopher, a young boy, drove his mother's car.
- ○ B. Christopher, who did not have a license, drove his mother's car.
- ○ C. Christopher drove his mother's brand new car.
- ○ D. None of the above

2. Choose the revision that uses an adjective clause to modify a noun.

> Jack's kite looked like a giant caterpillar.

- ○ A. Jack's kite looked like a giant caterpillar that crept across the clouds.
- ○ B. Jack's kite, a box-like contraption, looked like a giant caterpillar.
- ○ C. Jack's kite looked like a giant, creeping caterpillar.
- ○ D. None of the above

3. Choose the revision that uses an adjective clause to modify a noun.

> Umberto forgot his umbrella at the restaurant.

- ○ A. When he got up to leave, Umberto forgot his umbrella at the restaurant.
- ○ B. Umberto, a careful man, forgot his umbrella at the restaurant.
- ○ C. Umberto, who usually never forgets, forgot his umbrella at the restaurant.
- ○ D. None of the above

4. Choose the revision that uses an adjective clause to modify a noun.

> Helen left her nephew in the care of her grandmother.

- ○ A. Helen, who was running late, left her nephew in the care of her grandmother.
- ○ B. Helen left her cute little nephew in the care of her grandmother.
- ○ C. Helen left her nephew in the care of her grandmother because she had no one else to watch him.
- ○ D. None of the above.

Grammar:
Noun Clauses

A clause is a group of words that contains both a subject and a verb. A noun clause is a subordinate clause that acts as a noun in a sentence.

A noun clause usually begins with one of these words: *how, that, what, whatever, when, where, which, whichever, who, whom, whoever, whose,* or *why.*

Noun as Subject	Noun Clause as Subject
The **goalie** should get the MVP award.	**Whoever stopped that last goal attempt** should get the MVP award.

In most sentences containing noun clauses, you can replace the noun clause with a pronoun such as *he* or *it,* and the sentence will still make sense. You can use a noun clause in the same ways you use a noun—as a subject, a direct object, an indirect object, an object of a preposition, and a predicate noun.

Function of Clause	Text
Object of a Preposition	The woman did not ask the boy anything about **where he lived,** his folks, or anything else that would embarrass him. "Thank You, Ma'am"
Direct Object	The woman didn't know **where he lived.**
Subject	**Where he lived** wasn't important to the woman.
Predicate Noun	Quietly listening was **how she found out all she wanted to know.**

YOUR TURN

1. Replace the word in bold with a noun clause.

   > Your athletic skills will be valuable in **hockey**.

   ○ A. football, baseball, or tennis
   ○ B. any preferred sport
   ○ C. whichever sport you choose
   ○ D. No change needs to be made to this sentence.

2. Replace the words in bold with a noun clause.

   > This is **how students select their major**.

   ○ A. the appropriate major
   ○ B. a difficult selection process
   ○ C. about students and their majors
   ○ D. No change needs to be made to this sentence.

3. Replace the words in bold with a noun clause.

   > Choir directors seek **the person with the best voice**.

   ○ A. whoever has the best voice
   ○ B. those with great voices
   ○ C. soloists and chorus members
   ○ D. No change needs to be made to this sentence.

4. Replace the words in bold with a noun clause.

   > **Reaching the next grade level** depends upon your study habits.

   ○ A. Advancement to the next grade level
   ○ B. When you reach the next grade level
   ○ C. Moving forward a grade level
   ○ D. No change needs to be made to this sentence.

Grammar: Complex Sentences

A complex sentence contains at least one main clause and one or more subordinate clauses.

A main clause has a subject and a predicate and can stand alone as a sentence.

A subordinate clause has a subject and a predicate, but it cannot stand alone as a sentence. It depends on the main clause to complete its meaning. A subordinate clause is usually introduced by a subordinating conjunction, such as *when, because, before,* or *after.*

Complex Sentence	Main Clause	Subordinate Clauses
I was reaching for a puzzle part that was just blue sky when a flash of light filled the bay window. *A Long Way from Chicago*	I was reaching for a puzzle part	that was just blue sky when a flash of light filled the bay window.
I don't even have any friends because I had to leave them all behind when we moved here from Watley. *Because of Winn-Dixie*	I don't even have any friends	because I had to leave them all behind when we moved here from Watley.

Please note that excerpts and passages in the StudySync® library and this workbook are intended as touchstones to generate interest in an author's work. The excerpts and passages do not substitute for the reading of entire texts, and StudySync® strongly recommends that students seek out and purchase the whole literary or informational work in order to experience it as the author intended. Links to online resellers are available in our digital library. In addition, complete works may be ordered through an authorized reseller by filling out and returning to StudySync® the order form enclosed in this workbook.

Reading & Writing Companion   **311**

↻ YOUR TURN

1. How could this sentence be changed into a complex sentence?

   > People enjoy this custom, but most do not believe in it.

   ○ A. Replace the comma and **but** with a semicolon.
   ○ B. Remove the comma.
   ○ C. Replace the comma and conjunction **but** with **although**.
   ○ D. No change needs to be made to this sentence.

2. How could this sentence be changed into a simple sentence?

   > Groundhogs eat large amounts of food before they hibernate.

   ○ A. Place **before they hibernate** followed by a comma before **groundhogs**.
   ○ B. Remove **before they hibernate**.
   ○ C. Remove **Groundhogs eat large amounts of food**.
   ○ D. No change needs to be made to this sentence.

3. How could this sentence be changed into a simple sentence?

   > Groundhogs are able to sleep for most of the winter because the food they have eaten turns to fat.

   ○ A. Remove **for most of the winter**.
   ○ B. Remove **because the food they have eaten turns to fat**.
   ○ C. Insert a comma before **because**.
   ○ D. No change needs to be made to this sentence.

4. How could this sentence be changed into a complex sentence?

   > Groundhogs come out of their holes to look for food, and they stop to listen for signs of danger.

   ○ A. Replace the comma and conjunction **and** with a semicolon.
   ○ B. Remove the comma and **and they stop to listen for signs of danger**.
   ○ C. Remove the conjunction **and**, then add the subordinating conjunction *when* before **groundhogs**.
   ○ D. No change needs to be made to this sentence.

Literary Analysis Writing Process: Edit and Publish

PLAN	DRAFT	REVISE	EDIT AND PUBLISH

You have revised your literary analysis based on your peer feedback and your own examination.

Now, it is time to edit your literary analysis. When you revised, you focused on the content of your literary analysis. You probably looked at the thesis statement, reasons and relevant evidence, introduction, and conclusion. When you edit, you should focus on grammar and punctuation.

Use the checklist below to guide you as you edit:

☐ Have I used sentences of varying lengths and structures, including complex and simple sentences?

☐ Have I used noun clauses correctly?

☐ Have I used adjective clauses correctly?

☐ Do I have any sentence fragments or run-on sentences?

☐ Have I spelled everything correctly?

Notice some edits Knox has made:

- Varied sentence length and structure by combining two sentences into one complex sentence.

- Fixed spelling.

- Varied sentence length and structure by creating two sentences out of one.

- Added a comma to use an adjective clause correctly.

Please note that excerpts and passages in the StudySync® library and this workbook are intended as touchstones to generate interest in an author's work. The excerpts and passages do not substitute for the reading of entire texts, and StudySync® strongly recommends that students seek out and purchase the whole literary or informational work in order to experience it as the author intended. Links to online resellers are available in our digital library. In addition, complete works may be ordered through an authorized reseller by filling out and returning to StudySync® the order form enclosed in this workbook.

Reading & Writing Companion   **313**

The poem "Annabel Lee" takes a darker turn ~~and showed how the speaker's focus on a relationship makes him irrational. In this poem,~~ because Edgar Allan Poe explores the irrational thoughts of a speaker mourning his departed love. The speaker's love for Annabel Lee is so powerful that he believes it makes angels jealous: "The angels, not half so happy in Heaven, / Went envying her and me—." The speaker shows extreme devotion to his relationship, even after the death of ~~Annabe lee~~ Annabel Lee. "And neither the angels in Heaven above / Nor the demons down under the sea / Can ever dissever my soul from the soul / Of the beautiful Annabel Lee." This poetic statement shows that the speaker does not move on from Annabel Lee after losing her. ~~; and~~ He also holds on to the relationship to make it everlasting. "For the moon never beams, without bringing me dreams / Of the beautiful Annabel Lee." The speaker expresses that deep relationships of love can extend beyond any ~~loss which~~ loss, which includes the profound loss of death. The speaker learns that he cannot move on without Annabel Lee, so his love dominates his thoughts.

✏ WRITE

Use the questions on the previous page, as well as your peer reviews, to help you evaluate your literary analysis to determine areas that need editing. Then edit your narrative to correct those errors.

Once you have made all your corrections, you are ready to publish your work. You can distribute your writing to family and friends, hang it on a bulletin board, or post it on your blog. If you publish online, share the link with your family, friends, and classmates.

Deep Water

FICTION

Introduction

For best friends Elizabeth and Sophie, swimming is the most important part of their lives. For years, they trained together, working hard to reach their goals. Now, at age 17, they both want the only spot available on a top swim team. How will they prepare for the competition? Who will be good enough to make the team?

V VOCABULARY

enthusiasm

great interest and excitement

inevitably

predictably; unavoidably

performance

process of achieving a goal

propel

to move forward

slot

a position in a group or team

NOTES

☰ READ

1   Elizabeth and Sophie shared everything, especially their **enthusiasm** for swimming. At age 17, their identities began and ended with the word "swimmer." The girls competed with each other, their teammates, and their personal best times.

2   When they first began swimming, Sophie had to struggle to keep up. She worked very hard. She trained long hours to improve her **performance**. Elizabeth was as fierce as a coach. She helped with workouts. The girls spent hours lifting weights. They swam at least eight miles a week. Their competition, focus, and determination increased. Both dreamed of being on Team USA, the swim team that competed internationally.

3   At last, they were to compete in the most important swim meet of their lives. The winner would qualify for Team USA. Only one **slot** was available. Only one girl would make the team. The other competitors would not.

4   It was two weeks before the event. The girls felt a distance growing between them.

5   "We need to talk," Elizabeth declared.

6   "It's about the meet, right?" Sophie said. "We have been working hard and training together. It's not about us anymore. It's about me. It's about you. It's about winning."

7   "You're right," Elizabeth said. "I think it would be better if we train separately."

8   The girls chose different times for training. Although time in the pool **inevitably** overlapped, they swam in widely separated lanes.

9   Elizabeth and Sophie made it to the finals, along with Bethany, another member of their team.

10 The competition began. The girls pushed off the side of the pool. Elizabeth was vaguely aware of Sophie and Bethany. Her focus was on moving through the water as effortlessly as a shark. She **propelled** herself 15 meters before surfacing.

11 Sophie flexed and moved smoothly.

12 In the last lap, each girl pushed herself to reach the other side of the pool. When they surfaced, the roar of the crowd was deafening. The judges wanted to see the video of the finish to determine the true winner. Elizabeth and Sophie looked at each other. They clambered out of the pool and hugged. Then they headed for the locker room. They left before the announcement.

13 "Ladies and gentlemen, the winner of the race and new member of Team USA is..."

Please note that excerpts and passages in the StudySync® library and this workbook are intended as touchstones to generate interest in an author's work. The excerpts and passages do not substitute for the reading of entire texts, and StudySync® strongly recommends that students seek out and purchase the whole literary or informational work in order to experience it as the author intended. Links to online resellers are available in our digital library. In addition, complete works may be ordered through an authorized reseller by filling out and returning to StudySync® the order form enclosed in this workbook.

Reading & Writing Companion   317

First Read

Read the story. After you read, answer the Think Questions below.

☁ THINK QUESTIONS

1. What are the names of the two girls at the beginning of the story? What is their relationship?

   The names of the girls are _____.

   They are _____.

2. What do the two girls spend most of their time doing?

   The girls spend their time _____.

3. How does the girls' relationship change two weeks before the important event?

   The girls' relationship changes _____.

4. Use context to confirm the meaning of the word *slot* as it is used in "Deep Water." Write your definition of *slot* here.

   Slot means _____.

   A context clue is _____.

5. What is another way to say that the plane *propelled* through the air?

   The plane _____.

Skill:
Analyzing Expressions

★ DEFINE

When you read, you may find English expressions that you do not know. An **expression** is a group of words that communicates an idea. Three types of expressions are idioms, sayings, and figurative language. They can be difficult to understand because the meanings of the words are different from their **literal**, or usual, meanings.

An **idiom** is an expression that is commonly known among a group of people. For example: "It's raining cats and dogs" means it is raining heavily. **Sayings** are short expressions that contain advice or wisdom. For instance: "Don't count your chickens before they hatch" means do not plan on something good happening before it happens. **Figurative** language is when you describe something by comparing it with something else, either directly (using the words *like* or *as*) or indirectly. For example, "I'm as hungry as a horse" means I'm very hungry. None of the expressions are about actual animals.

••• CHECKLIST FOR ANALYZING EXPRESSIONS

To determine the meaning of an expression, remember the following:

✓ If you find a confusing group of words, it may be an expression. The meaning of words in expressions may not be their literal meaning.

- Ask yourself: Is this confusing because the words are new? Or because the words do not make sense together?

✓ Determining the overall meaning may require that you use one or more of the following:

- context clues
- a dictionary or other resource
- teacher or peer support

✓ Highlight important information before and after the expression to look for clues.

↻ YOUR TURN

Read paragraphs 10–12 from "Deep Water." Then, complete the multiple-choice questions below.

---

from **"Deep Water"**

The competition began. The girls pushed off the side of the pool. Elizabeth was vaguely aware of Sophie and Bethany. Her focus was on moving through the water as effortlessly as a shark. She propelled herself 15 meters before surfacing.

Sophie flexed and moved smoothly.

In the last lap, each girl pushed herself to reach the other side of the pool. When they surfaced, the roar of the crowd was deafening. The judges wanted to see the video of the finish to determine the true winner. Elizabeth and Sophie looked at each other. They clambered out of the pool and hugged. Then they headed for the locker room. They left before the announcement.

---

1. At the start of paragraph 12, the expression "pushed herself" means:

   ○ A. used her hand to push against her body

   ○ B. stopped someone

   ○ C. pressed against the end of the pool

   ○ D. tried hard

2. Which context clue helped you determine the meaning of "pushed herself"?

   ○ A. "each girl"

   ○ B. "In the last lap"

   ○ C. "When they surfaced"

   ○ D. "moved smoothly"

Skill:
Sharing Information

★ **DEFINE**

Sharing information involves asking for and giving information. The process of sharing information with other students can help all students learn more and better understand a text or a topic. You can share information when you participate in **brief** discussions or **extended** speaking assignments.

●●● **CHECKLIST FOR SHARING INFORMATION**

When you have to speak for an extended period of time, as in a discussion, you ask for and share information. To ask for and share information, you may use the following sentence frames:

✓ To ask for information:

- What do you think about _____?

- Do you agree that _____?

- What is your understanding of _____?

✓ To give information:

- I think _____.

- I agree because _____.

- My understanding is _____.

Please note that excerpts and passages in the StudySync® library and this workbook are intended as touchstones to generate interest in an author's work. The excerpts and passages do not substitute for the reading of entire texts, and StudySync® strongly recommends that students seek out and purchase the whole literary or informational work in order to experience it as the author intended. Links to online resellers are available in our digital library. In addition, complete works may be ordered through an authorized reseller by filling out and returning to StudySync® the order form enclosed in this workbook.

Reading & Writing Companion   **321**

⟳ YOUR TURN

Watch the "Amigo Brothers" StudySyncTV episode ▶. After watching, sort the following statements from the episode into the appropriate columns:

	Statements
A	He is the one to bring up the problem. And he suggests the solution.
B	It's fighting. I thought these guys were all about not doing that.
C	And they go jogging together every morning.
D	Why do it?
E	What's wrong with boxing?
F	So you think Felix is the leader?

Asking for Information	Giving Information

Close Read

WRITE

NARRATIVE: Think about what happens in the story. Finish the final sentence and explain what happens next. Who wins? How do Elizabeth and Sophie react? Pay attention to the *IE* and *EI* spelling rules as you write.

Use the checklist below to guide you as you write.

☐ Who wins the race?

☐ How do Elizabeth and Sophie react?

☐ What happened in the story to lead to the loser's reaction?

Use the sentence frames to organize and write your narrative.

"Ladies and gentlemen, the winner of the race and new member of Team USA is _____

_____ ."

At that moment, Sophie _____

_____

Then Elizabeth _____

_____

In the end, _____

_____

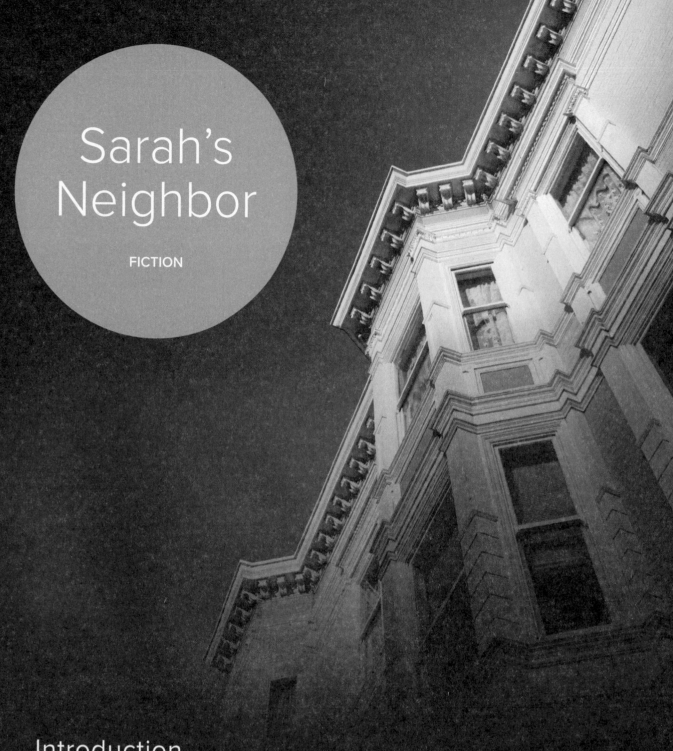

Sarah's Neighbor

FICTION

Introduction

S et in San Francisco shortly after the bombing of Pearl Harbor during World War II, this short story focuses on a preteen girl's struggle to accept her parents' changing attitudes toward their Japanese neighbors, including her best friend, Ayako. As twelve-year-old Sarah watches Ayako through the window, she longs to rekindle their friendship—but she is too scared of her father to disobey.

V VOCABULARY

erupt
to burst suddenly

clasp
to hold tightly

badge
a small pin or patch that gives information about the person wearing it

symbol
an object that represents an idea

accentuate
to call attention to something

vibrate
to shake

authority
power; being the leader

☰ READ

NOTES

1   Sarah looked through the window as she did the dishes. Ayako, her neighbor and former best friend, sat on the swing set outside. She looked as lonely as a ghost. Sarah would have been delighted to drop the silverware and **erupt** through the door to join Ayako. But she knew she couldn't. Her mind flashed to the conversation she had with her parents a few weeks ago, after the Japanese attacked Pearl Harbor.

2   Her father had come home from an arduous shift at the San Francisco police department. People were angry about the bombing. There had been fighting in the streets. They couldn't trust the Japanese anymore—not even Ayako.

NOTES

He pulled out his sergeant's **badge**. He began polishing it as a way of **accentuating** his **authority**. "That girl and her family are the enemy," he'd said.

3   Later, Sarah asked her mother to explain. It didn't make any sense. The bombing of Pearl Harbor was a serious attack. But Ayako hadn't been a part of it. Her mother **clasped** Sarah's hand. "Ayako didn't do anything bad. But she's a **symbol** of the people who did. The sergeant has given you orders. It's best you follow them."

4   Sarah grabbed a plate off the stack and focused on the circular movement of washing. She glued her eyes to the plate to take her mind off Ayako. There would be a harsh penalty if she asked to go play with her friend. Trepidation kept her mouth closed.

5   The next morning, Sarah and her mother made a list of guests for her thirteenth birthday party. Her mother named each child from Sarah's class, and Sarah wrote them down. Then she had an idea. Tightening her grip on the pencil, she urgently sneaked another name into the middle of the list: Ayako's.

6   As she handed the list to her mother, her father came in. He scanned the list over his wife's shoulder. When he got to Ayako's name, he **vibrated** with rage.

7   He faced Sarah and growled. "How many times have I told you that this girl cannot be your friend? I will not have my daughter spending time with someone like her! You will never see this girl again, or I will never see you again. Understand?"

8   Sarah wanted to stand up for herself. She wanted to tell her father that he was wrong, that Ayako is a good person. But all that came out was silence.

First Read

Read the story. After you read, answer the Think Questions below.

☁ THINK QUESTIONS

1. Who is Sarah's neighbor?

   Sarah's neighbor is _____.

2. What event changes Sarah's relationship with her neighbor?

   Sarah's relationship with her neighbor changes _____.

3. What did Sarah do to the list of guests for her birthday party?

   Sarah _____.

4. Use context to confirm the meaning of the word *symbol* as it is used in "Sarah's Neighbor." Write your definition of *symbol* here.

   Symbol means _____.

   A context clue is _____.

5. What is another way to say a mother *clasps* her daughter's hand?

   A mother _____.

Please note that excerpts and passages in the StudySync® library and this workbook are intended as touchstones to generate interest in an author's work. The excerpts and passages do not substitute for the reading of entire texts, and StudySync® strongly recommends that students seek out and purchase the whole literary or informational work in order to experience it as the author intended. Links to online resellers are available in our digital library. In addition, complete works may be ordered through an authorized reseller by filling out and returning to StudySync® the order form enclosed in this workbook.

Reading & Writing
Companion

327

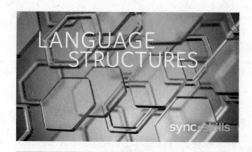

Skill:
Language Structures

★ DEFINE

In every language, there are rules that tell how to **structure** sentences. These rules define the correct order of words. In the English language, for example, a **basic** structure for sentences is subject, verb, and object. Some sentences have more **complicated** structures.

You will encounter both basic and complicated **language structures** in the classroom materials you read. Being familiar with language structures will help you better understand the text.

••• CHECKLIST FOR LANGUAGE STRUCTURES

To improve your comprehension of language structures, do the following:

✓ Monitor your understanding.

- Ask yourself: Why do I not understand this sentence? Is it because I do not understand some of the words? Or is it because I do not understand the way the words are ordered in the sentence?

✓ Break down the sentence into its parts.

- In English, adjectives almost always come before the noun. Example: He had a **big dog.**

  > A **noun** names a person, place, thing, or idea.

  > An **adjective** modifies, or describes, a noun or a pronoun.

  > If there is more than one adjective, they usually appear in the following order separated by a comma: quantity or number, quality or opinion, size, age, shape, color.

    Example: He had a **big, brown dog.**

  > If there is more than one adjective from the same category, include the word *and*.

    Example: He had a **brown and white dog.**

- Ask yourself: What are the nouns in this sentence? What adjectives describe them? In what order are the nouns and adjectives?

✓ Confirm your understanding with a peer or teacher.

↻ YOUR TURN

Read each sentence in the first column. Then, complete the chart by writing the words and phrases into the "Adjective" and "Noun" columns. The first row has been done as an example.

Sentence	Adjective	Noun
Her father had come home from an arduous shift at the San Francisco police department.	arduous	shift
The bombing of Pearl Harbor was a serious attack.		
Sarah grabbed a plate off the stack and focused on the circular movement of washing.		
There would be a harsh penalty if she asked to go play with her friend.		
She wanted to tell her father that he was wrong, that Ayako is a good person.		

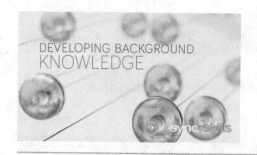

Skill: Developing Background Knowledge

★ DEFINE

Developing background knowledge is the process of gaining information about different topics. By developing your background knowledge, you will be able to better understand a wider variety of texts.

First, preview the text to determine what the text is about. To **preview** the text, read the title, headers, and other text features and look at any images or graphics. As you are previewing, identify anything that is unfamiliar to you and that seems important.

While you are reading, you can look for clues that will help you learn more about any unfamiliar words, phrases, or topics. You can also look up information in another resource to increase your background knowledge.

••• CHECKLIST FOR DEVELOPING BACKGROUND KNOWLEDGE

To develop your background knowledge, do the following:

✓ Preview the text. Read the title, headers, and other features. Look at any images and graphics.

✓ Identify any words, phrases, or topics that you do not know a lot about.

✓ As you are reading, try to find clues in the text that give you information about any unfamiliar words, phrases, or topics.

✓ If necessary, look up information in other sources to learn more about any unfamiliar words, phrases, or topics. You can also ask a peer or teacher for information or support.

✓ Think about how the background knowledge you have gained helps you better understand the text.

⟳ YOUR TURN

Read paragraphs 2–3 from "Sarah's Neighbor." Then, complete the multiple-choice questions below.

---

from "Sarah's Neighbor"

Her father had come home from an arduous shift at the San Francisco police department. People were angry about the bombing. There had been fighting in the streets. They couldn't trust the Japanese anymore—not even Ayako. He pulled out his sergeant's badge. He began polishing it as a way of accentuating his authority. "That girl and her family are the enemy," he'd said.

Later, Sarah asked her mother to explain. It didn't make any sense. The bombing of Pearl Harbor was a serious attack. But Ayako hadn't been a part of it. Her mother clasped Sarah's hand. "Ayako didn't do anything bad. But she's a symbol of the people who did. The sergeant has given you orders. It's best you follow them."

---

1. The details in paragraph 2 show that Americans:

   - ○ A. were upset and mad at the Japanese.
   - ○ B. were scared of the police.
   - ○ C. were tired.
   - ○ D. wanted to fight families that had daughters.

2. Clues that best develop this background knowledge are:

   - ○ A. "arduous shift" and "San Francisco police department"
   - ○ B. "angry at the bombing," "fighting in the streets," and "couldn't trust the Japanese"
   - ○ C. "sergeant's badge," "polishing," and "accentuating his authority"
   - ○ D. "not even Ayako," "That girl and her family," and "the enemy"

3. Sarah's conversation with her mother shows that:

   - ○ A Americans were not affected by World War II.
   - ○ B. Americans believed that Ayako's family caused the attack.
   - ○ C. some people thought the treatment of Japanese-Americans was unfair.
   - ○ D. Americans did not understand what happened at Pearl Harbor.

4. A detail that best develops this background knowledge is:

   - ○ A. "Her mother clasped Sarah's hand."
   - ○ B. "The bombing of Pearl Harbor was a serious attack."
   - ○ C. "'Ayako didn't do anything bad.'"
   - ○ D. "'The sergeant has given you orders.'"

Close Read

✏ WRITE

LITERARY ANALYSIS: How has Sarah's life changed since the bombing of Pearl Harbor? Write a short paragraph in which you explain what her life was like before and what it is like now. Pay attention to matching pronouns and antecedents as you write.

Use the checklist below to guide you as you write.

☐ What was Sarah's life like before the bombing of Pearl Harbor?

☐ What is different about Sarah's life after the bombing of Pearl Harbor?

☐ What are the reasons for the changes in Sarah's life?

☐ How does Sarah feel about the changes in her life?

Use the sentence frames to organize and write your literary analysis.

The bombing of Pearl Harbor was an attack during _____

by the Japanese military against the United States.

Before the bombing of Pearl Harbor, Sarah's best friend was her Japanese-American _____

_____, Ayako.

After Pearl Harbor, Sarah is not _____ to see Ayako.

Sarah's father says that Ayako is an _____ of the country.

Sarah believes that Ayako is a _____.

:::studysync®

ASSIGNMENTS   BINDER   LIBRARY

Chasing the Impossible

UNIT 3

Chasing the Impossible

What makes a dream worth pursuing?

Genre Focus: ARGUMENTATIVE

Texts

 Paired Readings

Extended Writing Project and Grammar

English Language Learner Resources

What makes a dream worth pursuing?

JULIA ALVAREZ

Julia Alvarez (b. 1950) was born in New York City but spent the first ten years of her life living in the Dominican Republic. She attended Connecticut College before transferring to Middlebury College, where she received her bachelor's degree, and then earned a master's degree from Syracuse University. Her first published work was a collection of poetry, *The Homecoming* (1984), which was followed by her first novel, *How the Garcia Girls Lost Their Accents* (1991). She was awarded the National Medal of Arts in 2013 "for her extraordinary storytelling."

GWENDOLYN BROOKS

Pulitzer Prize-winning poet Gwendolyn Brooks (1917–2000) grew up in Chicago, Illinois, published her first poem at thirteen years old, and had written and published seventy-five poems by the age of sixteen. She was the first African American author to win the Pulitzer Prize, awarded for *Annie Allen* in 1950, a collection "devoted to small, carefully cerebrated, terse portraits of the Black urban poor" that chronicled life in the Bronzeville neighborhood of Chicago's South Side.

SAMPSON DAVIS, RAMECK HUNT, AND GEORGE JENKINS

Sampson Davis, Rameck Hunt, and George Jenkins (b. 1973) grew up in Newark, New Jersey, where they bonded over their shared interest in becoming medical professionals. They attended Seton Hall University together for their undergraduate degrees before moving on to medical school. Davis serves as an Emergency Medicine Physician; Hunt is a board-certified internist; Jenkins teaches as an assistant professor of clinical dentistry at Columbia University.

SHARON M. DRAPER

Sharon Mills Draper (b. 1948) was born in Cleveland, Ohio, and graduated from Pepperdine University. As an educator, she has been honored for her work by being invited to The White House on six different occasions. She's been named a National Teacher of the Year and holds three honorary doctorates. Draper is the author of two different *New York Times* Best Sellers, *Copper Sun* and *We Beat the Street*. She lives in Cincinnati.

MOTHER JONES

Mary G. Harris Jones (1837–1930), also known as Mother Jones, was born in Cork City, Ireland. Her family eventually immigrated to Canada, and Jones moved to the United States at the age of twenty-three and became a schoolteacher. In 1867, her husband and four children died during a yellow fever outbreak, and in 1871, she lost her home, shop, and all of her possessions in the Great Chicago Fire. Soon after, she joined the Knights of Labor and began organizing protests and strikes, advocating for children forced to work in Pennsylvania's silk mills.

BARBARA JORDAN

The first African American elected to the Texas Senate, and the first Southern African American woman to be elected to the United States House of Representatives, Barbara Jordan (1936–1996) was also the first woman to deliver a keynote address at a Democratic National Convention. Jordan helped lead impeachment proceedings against then-president Richard Nixon and was awarded the Presidential Medal of Freedom by President Bill Clinton in 1994. She was born in Houston, Texas, and attended Texas Southern University, where she was a national champion debater. She graduated from Boston University School of Law in 1959.

ANN PETRY

Born in Old Saybrook, Connecticut, Ann Petry (1908–1997) authored several books, including her 1946 bestseller *The Street,* which offered commentary on the problems facing African Americans in urban environments. The daughter of a pharmacist, she graduated from the Connecticut College of Pharmacy and worked at her family's drugstore. After getting married, she moved to New York City and began writing short stories for several African American journals, including *The Crisis* and *Opportunity*.

VIRGINIA HAMILTON

Raised in Yellow Springs, Ohio, as the youngest of five children, Virginia Hamilton (1934–2002) authored forty-one books, including *M.C. Higgins, the Great,* which received the National Book Award and the Newbery Medal. She moved to New York City in 1958, where she worked as a receptionist at a museum, as a nightclub singer, and at other odds jobs while she pursued her dream of being a writer. Hamilton's first book, *Zeely* (1967), won multiple awards, and in 1992 she received the Hans Christian Andersen Award for lifetime achievement in children's literature.

JUDITH PINKERTON JOSEPHSON

Judith Pinkerton Josephson is the author of several works, including *Mother Jones: Fierce Fighter for Workers' Rights, Allan Pinkerton: The Original Private Eye,* and *Growing Up in Pioneer America*. She's co-authored three other books and has taught all levels from preschool through junior high, in addition to facilitating seminars for adult writers. When she's not writing, she likes to play the violin, sing, sew, or knit.

DONOVAN LINCOLN

Dr. Don Lincoln (b. 1964) has spent over three decades "studying the most fundamental laws of nature." Lincoln works at Fermilab, the nation's particle physics and accelerator laboratory, where he's served as a senior scientist since 1999. He is also an adjunct professor of physics at the University of Notre Dame, and previously earned his PhD from Rice University in 1994. He is the author of over 1,000 scientific papers, has written magazine and online articles, and has published several books describing particle physics for non-scientists.

We Beat the Street

INFORMATIONAL TEXT
Sharon M. Draper, Sampson Davis,
Rameck Hunt, George Jenkins
2006

Introduction

Growing up in urban Newark, New Jersey, Rameck Hunt, Sampson Davis, and George Jenkins faced many challenges. Yet instead of accepting lives of gangs, drugs and prison, these childhood friends made a pact to overcome these obstacles and become doctors. In the following excerpt from their collective autobiography, *We Beat the Street*, Dr. George Jenkins shares one of his early influences—a teacher who gave him hope for the future.

"There was no doubt as to her power and authority in that classroom."

NOTES

from Chapter 3: Isn't That School in the Ghetto?

1 **GEORGE, AGE 8** "Quit throwin' bottles in the street, man," eight-year-old George Jenkins yelled to his older brother, Garland.

2 "You can't make me," his brother taunted back. He picked up a green wine bottle he found in the gutter and tossed it onto the hard concrete of Muhammad Ali Avenue in Newark, New Jersey. It shattered into dozens of glistening fragments that shimmered in the sunlight.

3 "Suppose a car runs over the glass and gets a flat tire," George asked. Garland was almost ten, and George didn't think he acted his age.

4 "Too bad for them," Garland said as he tossed another bottle. "Hey, now, look at that one—two bounces and a smash!" He cheered as the brown beer bottle exploded and shattered.

5 "Hey, man, I'm outta here. I ain't gonna be late because of you." George glared at his brother before hurrying off in the direction of Louise A. Spencer Elementary School. Garland, he noticed, headed off in the other direction, once again skipping classes for the day.

6 George loved school. Even though it was located in what was described as the "inner city," it was relatively new and neat and clean. His third-grade teacher, Miss Viola Johnson, was a tiny ball of energy with a high-pitched voice and the same honey-colored skin as George's mother. There was no doubt as to her power and **authority** in that classroom. Miss Johnson made every day an adventure, and George hated to miss school, even on days when he was sick.

7 George slid quietly into the room, only a couple of minutes late, and grinned at Miss Johnson, who noticed his tardiness but said nothing.

8 "Today," she began, "we're going to continue talking about the writer named Shakespeare. How long ago did he live?" she asked the class.

9 "Four hundred years ago!" they responded immediately.

NOTES

10 "How many plays did he write?"

11 "Thirty-seven!"

12 George had no idea that Shakespeare was not usually taught in third grade. Miss Johnson simply offered it, and George, as well as the rest of his class, **absorbed** it.

13 "What was so cool about this Shakespeare dude, Miss Johnson?" a boy named Ritchie wanted to know. George wished he just would shut up so Miss Johnson could talk.

14 "Well, for one thing, Shakespeare wore an earring," Miss Johnson offered.

15 "For real? Real gold?" Ritchie seemed to be impressed.

16 "Here's another interesting fact," Miss Johnson said. "In order to seek his **fortune** as an actor and a writer, Shakespeare ran away from home shortly after he got married, leaving his wife and three children to make it without him," Miss Johnson explained.

17 "Sounds like yo' daddy!" Ritchie yelled to the boy sitting next to him. Both of them cracked up with laughter.

18 Every Tuesday she told them all about Shakespeare's time— about kings and castles, as well as about the rats and fleas that lived in the straw that most people used for bedding. "Did you know that during Shakespeare's time almost a third of the people who lived in London died one year from something called the Black Plague?" she asked the class.

19 "Why?" George asked.

20 "There were very few doctors at that time, and they didn't know what we know today about cleanliness and sanitation. Most people just threw their garbage out the window every morning, as well as the contents of their chamber pots. That's what they used at night. Toilets had not been invented yet."

21 "Yuk!" the class responded.

22 The class listened, fascinated and entranced with her stories, which taught them history, literature, math, and science without them even being aware of it. She passed out a children's version of *Hamlet,* full of pictures and explanations, and let them read the play and act out the fight scenes.

23 Every day went quickly in Miss Johnson's class, but she often stayed after school with them to make cookies or build projects. She even took them into New York City sometimes to let them see live plays on Broadway or to hear

 Skill: Connotation and Denotation

Fascinated and entranced have similar definitions. Both mean "to be very interested." The connotations of these words are positive. They make me realize how much George loves school and how amazing his teacher is.

Copyright © Bookhead Ed Learning, LLC

orchestra concerts at Lincoln Center. George loved to listen to the drums and horns and violins as they mixed up together in that huge concert hall.

24 When her students formed the Shakespeare Club, Miss Johnson even helped them get sweaters. They were deep burgundy with the name of the club embroidered on the pocket. George and his classmates wore them proudly to a concert one afternoon.

25 During the intermission,[1] a woman wearing too much perfume and a mink[2] coat, even though it was the middle of spring, walked up to George and said, "What lovely sweaters you and your classmates are wearing."

26 "Thank you, ma'am," George said with a grin, touching the careful embroidery.

27 "What private school do you children attend?" the woman asked.

28 Miss Johnson walked over to the woman and said proudly, "These are students from Louise Spencer Elementary, a public school in the Central Ward."

29 "But they're so well behaved," the woman said with surprise. "Isn't that school in the ghetto?"

30 Miss Johnson gave the woman a look that could have melted that mink coat and led her students away. George looked back at the woman with hurt and confusion. He wished he could have tripped the smelly old lady.

31 On the way back home from this trip, George, always the quiet kid, sat alone on the bus seat. "Mind if I sit next to you, George?" someone asked.

32 He looked up, pulled his long legs out of the aisle, and smiled at her. "Sure, Miss Johnson."

33 "Did that woman upset you?" she asked. George shrugged.

34 "I don't know. She smelled like mothballs."

35 "There will always be people like that, you know," Miss Johnson explained.

36 "Yeah, I know."

37 "And you can either let them hold you back, or you can ignore them and go on and do your thing."

38 "Yeah, I know." George didn't want to admit how much the woman's words had hurt. He changed the subject. "That was a good concert, Miss Johnson. I think it's really cool that you take us to stuff like this."

---

1. **intermission** a short break in the middle of a film, play, or performance
2. **mink** a small carnivorous mammal slaughtered for its fur

39 "Perhaps when you go to college you can learn to write symphonies or plays of your own," she said.

40 "College? I never even thought about it." To George, the idea of college seemed like something foreign and **vague,** like going to China or the moon.

41 "Of course you'll go to college. You're one of the smartest children in my class." Miss Johnson spoke with certainty. "I have high hopes and great expectations for you, George."

42 "Maybe you do, but some kids think it ain't cool to be too smart, you know," George told her.

43 "That's the dumbest thing I ever heard!" Miss Johnson said loudly. The other kids on the bus looked up to see what had upset her.

44 "You don't understand," George said quietly. "It's hard to fit in with your boys if your grades are too good."

45 "Nonsense!" Miss Johnson replied. "You don't really believe that."

46 George grinned at her. "Yeah, I guess you're right. I guess I really don't care what they think of me."

47 "College is cool, George. If you can fit in there, you've got it made."

48 "Doesn't it take a long time?" George asked, chewing on his lip. He felt a combination of excitement and wonder.

49 "It takes four years to complete the first part of college," she explained. "At the end of that time, you'll be four years older whether you go to college or not, so you might as well go and get as much knowledge in your head as you can."

50 George looked out of the bus window and thought about what she had said. As the field-trip bus got closer to his neighborhood in Newark, he looked at the tall, poverty-ridden, high-rise apartments like the one he lived in; the boarded-up and defeated stores; and the trash all over the streets.

51 "I don't know how," he said quietly, helpless in his lack of knowledge.

52 Miss Johnson didn't laugh, however. She just smiled and said, "It's not very hard. Just do your best, keep your nose out of trouble, and one day the doors will open for you."

53 For the first time, George could see a **glimpse** of light, a spark of hope and possibility. College. What a cool idea.

Excerpted from *We Beat the Street* by Sampson Davis, reprinted by Puffin Books.

Skill: Connotation and Denotation

There is a lot of emotion here. Boarded-up means "covered," and defeated means "to lose badly." Both have negative feelings. George describes his neighborhood with these words. He must be upset or confused after his experience at the theater. This phrase also lets me know that George lives in a poor area of town.

First Read

Read *We Beat the Street*. After you read, complete the Think Questions below.

 THINK QUESTIONS

1. Write two or three sentences explaining how George feels about school.

2. Why do the students think Miss Johnson is a good teacher? Cite specific examples from the text.

3. What goal does Miss Johnson inspire George to set for himself? Explain, including evidence from the text in your answer.

4. Read the following dictionary entry:

   absorb

   ab•sorb \ əb'zôrb \ *verb*

   a. to soak up by physical or chemical action
   b. to take in information or knowledge
   c. to reduce the intensity of a sound
   d. to engross or capture someone's attention

   Which definition most closely matches the meaning of **absorbed** as it is used in paragraph 12? Write the correct definition of *absorbed* here and explain how you figured out the correct meaning.

5. Use context clues to determine the meaning of **fortune** as it is used in paragraph 16 of *We Beat the Street*. Write your definition here and identify clues that helped you figure out the meaning.

Skill:
Connotation and Denotation

Use the Checklist to analyze Connotation and Denotation in *We Beat the Street*. Refer to the sample student annotations about Connotation and Denotation in the text.

••• CHECKLIST FOR CONNOTATION AND DENOTATION

In order to identify the connotative meanings of words and phrases, use the following steps:

✓ First, note unfamiliar words and phrases; key words used to describe important individuals, events, and ideas; or words that inspire an emotional reaction.

✓ Next, determine and note the denotative meaning of words by consulting reference materials such as a dictionary, a glossary, or a thesaurus.

To better understand the meanings of words and phrases as they are used in a text, including connotative meanings, use the following questions:

✓ What is the genre or subject of the text? How does that affect the possible meaning of a word or phrase?

✓ Does the word create a positive, negative, or neutral emotion?

✓ What synonyms or alternative phrasing help you describe the connotative meaning of the word?

Skill:
Connotation and Denotation

Reread paragraphs 41–48 of *We Beat the Street*. Then, using the Checklist on the previous page, answer the multiple-choice questions below.

↻ YOUR TURN

1. This question has two parts. First, answer Part A. Then, answer Part B.

   Part A: Which answer best describes the connotation of the word *boys* as it is used in paragraph 44?

   ○ A. young men
   ○ B. friends
   ○ C. brothers
   ○ D. bullies

   Part B: Which line from the passage supports your answer to Part A?

   ○ A. "I have high hopes and great expectations for you, George."
   ○ B. "Nonsense!" Miss Johnson replied. "You don't really believe that."
   ○ C. " . . . some kids think it ain't cool to be too smart, you know."
   ○ D. "You don't understand," George said quietly.

2. This question has two parts. First, answer Part A. Then, answer Part B.

Part A: Which answer best describes the connotation of the phrase *chewing on his lip* as it is used in paragraph 48?

- ○ A. thoughtful
- ○ B. angry
- ○ C. happy
- ○ D. tense

Part B: Which line from the passage supports your answer to Part A?

- ○ A. "I have high hopes and great expectations for you, George."
- ○ B. "Doesn't it take a long time?" George asked
- ○ C. George grinned at her. "Yeah, I guess you're right."
- ○ D. "College is cool, George."

WE BEAT THE STREET

study**sync**®

Close Read

Reread *We Beat the Street*. As you reread, complete the Skills Focus questions below. Then use your answers and annotations from the questions to help you complete the Write activity.

◎ SKILLS FOCUS

1. Identify words or phrases that have positive connotations. Write a note about how those words are used to impact the meaning or your understanding of the text.

2. What main or central ideas are developed about George and Miss Johnson? Highlight evidence from this story that supports the central ideas. Write a note describing how the evidence develops the central idea.

3. Reread paragraphs 22–24 and highlight evidence about his experiences at school. Identify how these experiences influence George.

4. This excerpt from *We Beat the Street* describes the real experiences from the childhood of George Jenkins, who went on to become a doctor. Identify textual evidence that shows Jenkins's purpose in providing this information to readers.

5. The authors of this text explain that, "We hope that our story will add a beacon of hope to young people." Identify a passage from text that you think young people might find hopeful. Then explain why you selected the passage.

✎ WRITE

LITERARY ANALYSIS: In this excerpt from his autobiography, Dr. George Jenkins shares the true story of one of his early influences—a teacher who gave him hope for the future. How did the experiences described in the excerpt affect Jenkins? How does Jenkins's use of words with strong connotations help you better understand the experiences? What impact does his word choice have on readers? Write a response answering these questions using evidence from the text.

The First Americans

ARGUMENTATIVE TEXT
The Grand Council Fire
of American Indians
1927

Introduction

In 1927, Chicago Mayor William Hale Thompson won re-election with the campaign slogan "America First." One of the issues Thompson campaigned on was that American history textbooks had been biased in favor of the British, ignoring the contributions of other immigrant groups, such as the Irish and Germans. Members of the Grand Council Fire of American Indians took issue with Hale's push to revise textbooks to be "100-percent American," writing a public letter to the mayor to demonstrate the ways in which American history had unjustly treated American Indians throughout the years.

"We ask only that our story be told in fairness."

December 1, 1927

To the mayor of Chicago:—

1   You tell all white men "America First." We believe in that. We are the only ones, truly, that are 100 percent. We therefore ask you while you are teaching school children about America First, teach them truth about the First Americans.

2   We do not know if school histories are pro-British, but we do know that they are unjust to the life of our people—the American Indian. They call all white victories, battles, and all Indian victories, massacres. The battle with Custer[1] has been taught to school children as a fearful massacre on our part. We ask that this, as well as other **incidents,** be told fairly. If the Custer battle was a massacre, what was Wounded Knee[2]?

3   History books teach that Indians were murderers—is it murder to fight in self-defense? Indians killed white men because white men took their lands, ruined their hunting grounds, burned their forests, destroyed their buffalo. White men penned our people on **reservations**, then took away the reservations. White men who rise to protect their property are called **patriots**—Indians who do the same are called murderers.

4   White men call Indians **treacherous**—but no mention is made of broken treaties on the part of the white man. White men say that Indians were always fighting. It was only our lack of skill in white man's warfare that led to our defeat. An Indian mother prayed that her boy be a great medicine man[3] rather than a great warrior. It is true that we had our own small battles, but in the main we were peace-loving and home-loving.

5   White men called Indians thieves—and yet we lived in frail skin lodges and needed no locks or iron bars. White men call Indians savages. What is

Skill: Language, Style, and Audience

The authors use the word *murderers* several times in this paragraph. They point out that white men are called patriots when they protect their property while Native Americans are called murderers. The authors are clearly expressing their anger at this unfairness. They demand action.

---

1. **Custer** General George Armstrong Custer (1839–1876) was the leader of U.S. troops killed at the Battle of the Little Bighorn.
2. **Wounded Knee** the massacre of Lakota people that took place at Wounded Knee Creek, South Dakota, on December 29, 1890
3. **medicine man** a ceremonial priest or doctor of Native Americans

Skill:
Summarizing

Who? Grand Council
What? says Indians are
peaceful and civilized
Where? in America
When? now and in
the past

Skill: Language,
Style, and
Audience

In this paragraph, the
authors establish a
more formal and
positive tone. They use
"brilliant oratory" to
formally describe the
elegant speeches made
by their statesmen and
to show their knowledge
as equal of that of
white men. This word
choice shows that the
Native Americans are
proud of their history.

civilization? Its marks are a noble religion and philosophy, original arts, stirring music, rich history and legend. We had these. Then we were not savages, but a civilized race.

6   We made blankets that were beautiful that the white man with all his machinery has never been able to duplicate. We made baskets that were beautiful. We wove in beads and colored quills, designs that were not just decorative motifs, but were the outward **expression** of our very thoughts. We made pottery—pottery that was useful and beautiful as well. Why not make school children acquainted with the beautiful handicrafts in which we were skilled? Put in every school Indian blankets, baskets, pottery.

7   We sang songs that carried in their melodies all the sounds of nature—the running of waters, the sighing of winds, and the calls of the animals. Teach these to your children that they may come to love nature as we love it.

8   We had our statesmen—and their oratory has never been equalled. Teach the children some of these speeches of our people, remarkable for their brilliant oratory. We played games—games that brought good health and sound bodies. Why not put these in your schools? We told stories. Why not teach school children more of the wholesome proverbs and legends of our people? Tell them how we loved all that was beautiful. That we killed game only for food, not for fun. Indians think white men who kill for fun are murderers.

9   Tell your children of the friendly acts of Indians to the white people who first settled here. Tell them of our leaders and heroes and their deeds. Tell them of Indians such as Black Partridge,[4] Shabbona[5] and others who many times saved the people of Chicago at great danger to themselves. Put in your history books the Indian's part in the World War. Tell how the Indian fought for a country of which he was not a citizen, for a flag to which he had no claim, and for a people that have treated him unjustly.

10 The Indian has long been hurt by these unfair books. We ask only that our story be told in fairness. We do not ask you to overlook what we did, but we do ask you to understand it. A true program of America First will give a generous place to the culture and history of the American Indian.

11 We ask this, Chief, to keep sacred the memory of our people.

4. **Black Partridge** an early 19th-century Potawatomi chief who defended settlers at the Battle of Fort Dearborn and signed a treaty with the U.S.
5. **Shabbona** a 19th-century Ottawa/Potawatomi chief who switched sides to the U.S. in the War of 1812

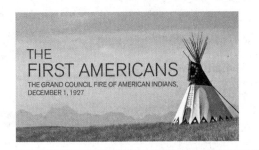

First Read

Read "The First Americans." After you read, complete the Think Questions below.

THINK QUESTIONS

1. According to the letter, what do American history books teach students about Native Americans?

2. According to the letter, what do history books teach students about white men? Cite specific examples mentioned in the letter.

3. What positive examples of Native American culture does the letter discuss?

4. Read the following dictionary entry:

reservation

res•er•va•tion \rez'-ər-vā'-shən\ *noun*
a. public land set aside for special use
b. a guaranteed place at a restaurant or hotel
c. a misgiving or doubt

Which definition most closely matches the meaning of **reservation** as it is used in paragraph 3? Write the correct definition of *reservation* here and explain how you figured out the correct meaning.

5. What is the meaning of the word **expression** as it is used in paragraph 6? Write the definition of *expression* and explain how you figured out the correct meaning.

Please note that excerpts and passages in the StudySync® library and this workbook are intended as touchstones to generate interest in an author's work. The excerpts and passages do not substitute for the reading of entire texts, and StudySync® strongly recommends that students seek out and purchase the whole literary or informational work in order to experience it as the author intended. Links to online resellers are available in our digital library. In addition, complete works may be ordered through an authorized reseller by filling out and returning to StudySync® the order form enclosed in this workbook.

Reading & Writing Companion

351

Skill:
Summarizing

Use the Checklist to analyze Summarizing in "The First Americans." Refer to the sample student annotations about Summarizing in the text.

••• CHECKLIST FOR SUMMARIZING

In order to determine how to write an objective summary of an informational text or other nonfiction texts, note the following:

- ✓ informational text elements, such as individuals, events, or ideas

- ✓ the details that readers must know in order to understand the main idea(s)

- ✓ answers to the basic questions *who, what, where, when, why,* and *how*

- ✓ stay objective, and do not add your own personal thoughts, judgments, or opinions to the summary

To provide an objective summary of an informational text or other nonfiction texts, consider the following questions:

- ✓ Which details develop the main idea(s)?

- ✓ What are the answers to basic *who, what, where, when, why,* and *how* questions?

- ✓ In what order should I put the most important details to make my summary logical?

- ✓ How can I briefly state the most important details in my own words?

- ✓ Is my summary objective, or have I added my own thoughts, judgments, or personal opinions?

Skill:
Summarizing

Reread paragraphs 6–7 of "The First Americans." Then, using the Checklist on the previous page, answer the multiple-choice questions below.

⟳ YOUR TURN

1. Which of the following details from paragraph 6 most clearly supports the main idea of the paragraph?

   ○ A. ". . . white man with all his machinery has never been able to duplicate."

   ○ B. ". . . the outward expression of our very thoughts."

   ○ C. "We made pottery—pottery that was useful and beautiful as well."

   ○ D. "Put in every school Indian blankets, baskets, pottery."

2. What is the best objective summary of paragraph 6?

   ○ A. Native Americans are better than white men at making blankets.

   ○ B. American school children should be given the chance to study the art of Native American handicrafts.

   ○ C. Blankets, pottery, and other arts made by Native Americans are just as good as or better than those made by white artists.

   ○ D. School children in America are taught that white artists make better art than Native American artists.

3. What is the best objective summary of paragraph 7?

   ○ A. The songs sung by Native Americans were absolutely amazing and should be taught in school.

   ○ B. Native American songs reflect the sounds of nature, including the calls of wild animals.

   ○ C. Students can learn to love nature by studying Native American songs, which celebrate nature.

   ○ D. Singing songs about nature is a good way to learn about the natural world.

Please note that excerpts and passages in the StudySync® library and this workbook are intended as touchstones to generate interest in an author's work. The excerpts and passages do not substitute for the reading of entire texts, and StudySync® strongly recommends that students seek out and purchase the whole literary or informational work in order to experience it as the author intended. Links to online resellers are available in our digital library. In addition, complete works may be ordered through an authorized reseller by filling out and returning to StudySync® the order form enclosed in this workbook.

Reading & Writing
Companion

353

LANGUAGE, STYLE, AND AUDIENCE

sync•skills

Skill: Language, Style, and Audience

Use the Checklist to analyze Language, Style, and Audience in "The First Americans." Refer to the sample student annotations about Language, Style, and Audience in the text.

••• CHECKLIST FOR LANGUAGE, STYLE, AND AUDIENCE

In order to determine an author's style, do the following:

✓ identify and define any unfamiliar words or phrases

✓ use context, including the meaning of surrounding words and phrases

✓ note possible reactions to the author's word choice

✓ examine your reaction to the author's word choice and how the author's choice affected your reaction

To analyze the impact of specific word choice on meaning and tone, ask the following questions:

✓ How did your understanding of the language change during your analysis?

✓ What stylistic choices can you identify in the text? How does the style influence your understanding of the language?

✓ How could various audiences interpret this language? What different possible emotional responses can you list?

✓ How does the writer's choice of words impact or create a specific tone in the text?

Skill: Language, Style, and Audience

Reread paragraphs 4–7 of "The First Americans." Then, using the Checklist on the previous page, answer the multiple-choice questions below.

⟳ YOUR TURN

1. In paragraph 4, the use of the word **treacherous** establishes what feeling?

   ○ A. fury
   ○ B. depression
   ○ C. loneliness
   ○ D. elation

2. How does the use of the word **treacherous** contribute to the tone of this part of the letter?

   ○ A. The word *treacherous* shows the sadness the Native American chiefs feel about their own history.
   ○ B. The word *treacherous* shows the dangerous lifestyle of Native Americans and white men.
   ○ C. The word *treacherous* shows the peaceful ways of the Native Americans.
   ○ D. The word *treacherous* shows the anger the Native American chiefs feel about their unfair treatment by white men and the fury they feel about their misrepresentation in history.

3. In paragraph 6, what do the writers mean by "were the outward expression of our very thoughts"?

   ○ A. The angry thoughts the Native Americans have toward the white men
   ○ B. The clothing that Native Americans wear
   ○ C. The beautiful crafts the Native Americans have made from their imagination
   ○ D. The letters Native Americans have written to show their thoughts

4. What is the tone of paragraphs 6 and 7?

   ○ A. formal and proud
   ○ B. sad and lonely
   ○ C. informal and angry
   ○ D. satisfied and thankful

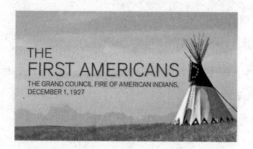

THE
FIRST AMERICANS
THE GRAND COUNCIL FIRE OF AMERICAN INDIANS,
DECEMBER 1, 1927

Close Read

Reread "The First Americans." As you reread, complete the Skills Focus questions below. Then use your answers and annotations from the questions to help you complete the Write activity.

◎ SKILLS FOCUS

1. Identify passages that show the purpose of the letter "The First Americans." Explain what you think motivated the members of the Council to write this letter.

2. Identify examples in the letter of how history books in the 1920s portrayed Native Americans. Summarize how Native Americans were portrayed in textbooks.

3. Identify examples of emotional word choice throughout the letter. Explain the effect of this language on the style of the letter.

4. **Style** is the distinctive use of language to achieve the purpose of the writer. Identify words or phrases that the authors use to create a knowledgeable, formal style. Explain how these formal words or phrases might affect the reader.

5. An ideal version of something is sometimes called a "dream" version. Identify a passage in the text that shows what a "dream" U.S. history textbook would have been for the Grand Council. Explain how the textual evidence supports your ideas.

✎ WRITE

LITERARY ANALYSIS: Objectively summarize the main points of the letter. Then explain how the Grand Council's language and style help to clarify and emphasize the main points. How does their word choice affect the tone or style of the letter? Use evidence from the text to support your analysis.

Harriet Tubman:
Conductor on the Underground Railroad

INFORMATIONAL TEXT
Ann Petry
1955

Introduction

The years prior to the Civil War were especially perilous for once-enslaved people who had escaped, but Harriet Tubman returned again and again to the South to help fugitives gain freedom. Where did her physical and moral courage come from? This excerpt from a biography of Tubman by Ann Petry (1908–1997) describes how six-year-old Harriet learned about life on the plantation and came to understand the bitter truths about slavery.

"There was something free and wild in Harriet . . ."

NOTES

excerpt from Chapter Three: Six Years Old

1 By the time Harriet Ross was six years old, she had **unconsciously absorbed** many kinds of knowledge, almost with the air she breathed. She could not, for example, have said how or at what moment she learned that she was a slave.

Frederick Douglass and Harriet Tubman, two of the best-known African Americans of the Civil War era, were both enslaved in Maryland. Both became leaders in the American abolitionist movement, helping to end slavery in the United States.

2 She knew that her brothers and sisters, her father and mother, and all the other people who lived in the quarter,[1] men, women and children, were slaves.

3 She had been taught to say, "Yes, Missus," "No, Missus," to white women, "Yes, Mas'r," "No, Mas'r," to white men. Or, "Yes, sah," "No, sah."

4 At the same time, someone had taught her where to look for the North Star, the star that stayed **constant,** not rising in the east and setting in the west as the other stars appeared to do; and told her that anyone walking toward the North could use that star as a guide.

5 She knew about fear, too. Sometimes at night, or during the day, she heard the furious galloping of horses, not just one horse, several horses, thud of the hoofbeats along the road, jingle of harness. She saw the grown folks freeze into stillness, not moving, scarcely breathing, while they listened. She could not remember who first told her that those furious hoofbeats meant the patrollers were going past, in pursuit of a runaway. Only the slaves said patterollers,[2] whispering the word.

---

1. **quarter** rooms or lodging
2. **patterollers** gangs of white men who disciplined enslaved people at night

6   Old Rit would say a prayer that the hoofbeats would not stop. If they did, there would be the dreadful sound of screams. Because the runaway slave had been caught, would be whipped, and finally sold to the chain gang.[3]

7   Thus Harriet already shared the uneasiness and the fear of the grownups. But she shared their pleasures, too. She knew moments of pride when the overseer consulted Ben, her father, about the weather. Ben could tell if it was going to rain, when the first frost would come, tell whether there was going to be a long stretch of clear sunny days. Everyone on the plantation admired this skill of Ben's. Even the master, Edward Brodas.

8   The other slaves were in awe of Ben because he could prophesy[4] about the weather. Harriet stood close to him when he studied the sky, licked his forefinger and held it up to determine the direction of the wind, then announced that there would be rain or frost or fair weather.

9   There was something free and wild in Harriet because of Ben. He talked about the arrival of the wild ducks, the thickness of the winter coat of muskrats and of rabbits. He was always talking about the woods, the berries that grew there, the strange haunting cries of some of the birds, the loud sound their wings made when they were disturbed and flew up suddenly. He spoke of the way the owls flew, their feathers so soft that they seemed to glide, soundless, through the air.

10 Ben knew about rivers and creeks and swampy places. He said that the salt water from the Bay reached into the rivers and streams for long distances. You could stick your finger in the river water and lick it and you could taste the salt from the Bay.

11 He had been all the way to the Chesapeake. He had seen storms there. He said the Big Buckwater River, which lay off to the southeast of the plantation, was just a little stream compared to the Choptank, and the Choptank was less than nothing compared to the Bay.

12 All through the plantation, from the Big House to the stables, to the fields, he had a reputation for **absolute** honesty. He had never been known to tell a lie. He was a valued worker and a trusted one.

13 Ben could tell wonderful stories, too. So could her mother, Old Rit, though Rit's were mostly from the Bible. Rit told about Moses and the children of Israel, about how the sea parted so that the children walked across on dry land, about the plague of locusts, about how some of the children were afraid on the long journey to the Promised Land, and so cried out: "It had been better for us to serve the Egyptians, than that we should die in the wilderness."

---

3. **chain gang** a group of men involuntarily chained together for work
4. **prophesy** to have a vision of the future; to predict

14 Old Rit taught Harriet the words of that song that the slaves were forbidden to sing, because of the man named Denmark Vesey, who had urged the other slaves to revolt by telling them about Moses and the children of Israel. Sometimes, in the quarter, Harriet heard snatches of it, sung under the breath, almost whispered: "Go down, Moses . . ." But she learned the words so well that she never forgot them.

15 She was aware of all these things and many other things too. She learned to separate the days of the week. Sunday was a special day. There was no work in the fields. The slaves cooked in the quarter and washed their clothes and sang and told stories.

16 There was another special day, issue day, which occurred at the end of the month. It was the day that food and clothes were issued to the slaves. One of the slaves was sent to the Big House, with a wagon, to bring back the monthly allowance of food. Each slave received eight pounds of pickled pork or its **equivalent** in fish, one bushel of Indian meal (corn meal), one pint of salt.

17 Once a year, on issue day, they received clothing. The men were given two tow-linen shirts, two pairs of trousers, one of tow-linen, the other woolen, and a woolen jacket for winter. The grownups received one pair of yarn stockings and a pair of shoes.

18 The children under eight had neither shoes, stockings, jacket nor trousers. They were issued two tow-linen shirts a year—short, one-piece garments made of a coarse material like burlap, reaching to the knees. These shirts were worn night and day. They were changed once a week. When they were worn out, the children went naked until the next allowance day.

19 Men and women received a coarse blanket apiece. The children kept warm as best they could.

Excerpted from *Harriet Tubman: Conductor on the Underground Railroad* by Ann Petry, published by Amistad Press.

 WRITE

NARRATIVE: Write a story of approximately 300 words about a typical day in Harriet Tubman's life when she was six years old. Generate ideas for your narrative, using these questions: What events might have taken place? What might she have done, heard, seen, and thought about? Base your narrative on details in this passage.

The People Could Fly:
American Black Folktales

FICTION
Virginia Hamilton
1985

Introduction

Virginia Hamilton (1936–2002) was a children's book author who retold African American folklore with humor, magic, and mystery in her collection *The People Could Fly: American Black Folktales*. In this excerpt from the titular folktale, you'll learn about why enslaved West Africans took off their wings and how an old man helped them to fly again.

"They say the people could fly. Say that long ago in Africa, some of the people knew magic."

1 They say the people could fly. Say that long ago in Africa, some of the people knew magic. And they would walk upon the air like climbin' up on a gate. And they flew like blackbirds over the fields. Black, shiny wings flappin' against the blue up there.

2 Then, many of the people were captured for Slavery. The ones that could fly shed their wings. They couldn't take their wings across the water on slave ships. Too crowded, don't you know.

3 The folks were full of **misery,** then. Got sick with the up and down of the sea. So they forgot about flyin' when they could no longer breathe the sweet scent of Africa.

4 Say the people who could fly kept their power, although they shed their wings. They looked the same as the other people from Africa who had been coming over, who had dark skin. Say you couldn't tell anymore one who could fly from one who couldn't.

5 One such who could was an old man, call him Toby. And standin' tall, yet afraid, was a young woman who once had wings. Call her Sarah. Now Sarah carried a babe tied to her back. She **trembled** to be so hard worked and scorned.

6 The slaves **labored** in the fields from sunup to sundown. The owner of the slaves callin' himself their Master. Say he was a hard lump of clay. A hard, glinty coal. A hard rock pile, wouldn't be moved. His Overseer[1] on horseback pointed out the slaves who were slowin' down. So the one called Driver[2] cracked his whip over the slow ones to make them move faster. That whip was a slice-open cut of pain. So they did move faster. Had to.

7 Sarah hoed and chopped the row as the babe on her back slept.

8 Say the child grew hungry. That babe started up **bawling** too loud. Sarah couldn't stop to feed it. Couldn't stop to **soothe** and quiet it down. She let it cry. She didn't want to. She had no heart to **croon** to it.

---

1. **Overseer** a plantation employee in charge of enslaved people
2. **Driver** a deputy of an overseer who kept enslaved people working hard through threats, injury, or intimidation

9   "Keep that thing quiet," called the Overseer. He pointed his finger at the babe. The woman scrunched low. The Driver cracked his whip across the babe anyhow. The babe hollered like any hurt child, and the woman fell to the earth.

10   The old man that was there, Toby, came and helped her to her feet.

11   "I must go soon," she told him.

12   "Soon," he said.

13   Sarah couldn't stand up straight any longer. She was too weak. The sun burned her face. The babe cried and cried, "Pity me, oh, pity me," say it sounded like. Sarah was so sad and starving, she sat down in the row.

14   "Get up, you black cow," called the Overseer. He pointed his hand and the Driver's whip snarled around Sarah's legs. Her sack dress tore into rags. Her legs bled onto the earth. She couldn't get up.

15   Toby was there where there was no one to help her and the babe.

16   "Now, before it's too late," panted Sarah. "Now, Father!"

17   "Yes, Daughter, the time is come," Toby answered. "Go as you know how to go!"

18   He raised his arms, holding them out to her. "*Kum...yali, kum buba tambe*," and more magic words, said so quickly; they sounded like whispers and sighs.

19   The young woman lifted one foot on the air. Then the other. She flew clumsily at first, with the child now held tightly in her arms. Then she felt the magic, the African mystery. Say she rose just as free as a bird. As light as a feather.

20   The Overseer rode after her, hollerin'. Sarah flew over the fences. She flew over the woods. Tall trees could not snag her. Nor could the Overseer. She flew like an eagle now, until she was gone from sight. No one dared speak about it. Couldn't believe it. But it was, because they that was there saw that it was.

Excerpted from *The People Could Fly: American Black Folktales* by Virginia Hamilton, published by Alfred A. Knopf.

First Read

Read "The People Could Fly." After you read, complete the Think Questions below.

 THINK QUESTIONS

1. Why did the people lose their wings? Cite textual evidence from the first two paragraphs to explain your answer.

2. Why does Sarah need to leave the plantation? Use ideas that are directly stated in the text and ideas you have inferred from clues in the selection. Support your inferences with textual evidence.

3. Why is Sarah able to fly without wings at the end of the folktale? Refer to one or more details that are directly stated as well as inferences drawn from the text.

4. Find the word **soothe** in paragraph 8 of "The People Could Fly." Use context clues in the surrounding sentences, as well as the sentence in which the word appears, to determine the word's meaning. Write your definition here and identify clues that helped you figure out the meaning.

5. Use context clues to determine the meaning of the word **labored** as it is used in paragraph 6 of "The People Could Fly." Write your definition and identify clues that helped you figure out the meaning. Then check the meaning in a dictionary.

Skill:
Compare and Contrast

Use the Checklist to analyze Compare and Contrast in "The People Could Fly."

••• CHECKLIST FOR COMPARE AND CONTRAST

In order to compare and contrast texts within and across different forms and genres, do the following:

- ✓ choose two or more texts with similar subjects, topics, settings or characters

- ✓ highlight evidence that reveals each text's theme or central message

  - consider what happens as a result of the characters' words and actions

  - note ways in which the texts are similar and different

To compare and contrast texts within and across different forms or genres, consider the following questions:

- ✓ What are the similarities and differences in the subjects or topics of the texts I have chosen?

- ✓ Have I looked at the words of each character, as well as what the characters do, to help me determine the theme of each work?

Please note that excerpts and passages in the StudySync® library and this workbook are intended as touchstones to generate interest in an author's work. The excerpts and passages do not substitute for the reading of entire texts, and StudySync® strongly recommends that students seek out and purchase the whole literary or informational work in order to experience it as the author intended. Links to online resellers are available in our digital library. In addition, complete works may be ordered through an authorized reseller by filling out and returning to StudySync® the order form enclosed in this workbook.

Reading & Writing Companion   **365**

COMPARE AND CONTRAST
sync skills

Skill:
Compare and Contrast

Reread paragraphs 18–19 of the "The People Could Fly" and paragraph 13 of *Harriet Tubman: Conductor on the Underground Railroad*. Match the observations to the appropriate selection in the chart below.

⟳ YOUR TURN

	Observations
A	Both use figurative language to talk about escaping.
B	Both are about people escaping from oppression.
C	The story about fleeing Israelites represents the enslaved people trying to escape from their oppressors.
D	The enslaved people tell stories about Biblical escapes.
E	Sarah is described as a bird when she escapes.
F	Sarah flies away using magic and help from her friend.

Harriet Tubman	Both	The People Could Fly

Close Read

Reread "The People Could Fly." As you reread, complete the Skills Focus questions below. Then use your answers and annotations from the questions to help you complete the Write activity.

◎ SKILLS FOCUS

1. Both "The People Could Fly" and *Harriet Tubman: Conductor on the Underground Railroad* talk about how secret knowledge empowers enslaved people. Identify evidence where enslaved people have secret knowledge that helps them. Write a note comparing the use of secret knowledge in "The People Could Fly" to the use of secret knowledge in *Harriet Tubman*.

2. Find times in the two stories when enslaved children are afraid. Make annotations to explain how "The People Could Fly" uses the historical facts to show how slavery created a culture of fear.

3. In paragraph 9 of *Harriet Tubman: Conductor on the Underground Railroad*, the author describes Ben's connection to nature by referencing a number of birds—for example, ducks and owls.

Highlight evidence from "The People Could Fly" that refers to birds. Make annotations to explain how the folktale uses bird imagery in comparison to the imagery in *Harriet Tubman*.

4. Find words with connotative meanings that add to the meaning of "The People Could Fly." Write a note to explain how the connotations express the relationship between Toby and Sarah.

5. Both texts focus on the enslavement and mistreatment of enslaved people during the most tragic period in American history. Find details that help you understand how these circumstances led to pursuing dreams in dangerous times, and make notes about how the characters pursue their dreams and what stands in the way.

✏ WRITE

COMPARE AND CONTRAST: *Harriet Tubman: Conductor on the Underground Railroad* and "The People Could Fly" are about similar topics but in different genres. The first is a historical account of slavery in American history. The second is a fictional portrayal of the same topic or theme. How did Virginia Hamilton use historical facts in "The People Could Fly"? What changes does she make and what are the effects? Remember to support your analysis with evidence from the texts.

All Together Now

ARGUMENTATIVE TEXT
Barbara Jordan
1976

Introduction

In 1966, Barbara Jordan (1936–1996) became the first African American woman elected to the Texas State Senate. She later became the first African American woman to represent a southern state in Congress when she was elected to the U.S. House of Representatives in 1972. Jordan worked hard to improve the lives of people in her district, sponsored bills that increased workers' wages, and fought for women's rights. She was considered a gifted public speaker and was selected to give the keynote speech at the 1976 Democratic National Convention in New York. Her highly acclaimed speech is excerpted here.

"For the American idea, though it is shared by all of us, is realized in each one of us."

NOTES

1 Thank you ladies and gentlemen for a very warm reception.

2 It was one hundred and forty-four years ago that members of the Democratic Party first met in convention to select a Presidential candidate. Since that time, Democrats have continued to convene once every four years and draft a party platform[1] and nominate a Presidential candidate. And our

Congresswoman Barbara Jordan was the first African American woman to give the keynote speech at the Democratic National Convention.

meeting this week is a continuation of that tradition. But there is something different about tonight. There is something special about tonight. What is different? What is special?

3 I, Barbara Jordan, am a keynote speaker.[2]

4 A lot of years passed since 1832, and during that time it would have been most unusual for any national political party to ask a Barbara Jordan to deliver a keynote address. But tonight, here I am. And I feel that notwithstanding the past that my presence here is one additional bit of evidence that the American Dream need not forever be **deferred**.

5 Now that I have this grand **distinction**, what in the world am I supposed to say? . . . I could list the many problems which Americans have. I could list the problems which cause people to feel cynical, angry, frustrated: problems which include lack of integrity in government; the feeling that the individual no longer counts; the reality of material and spiritual poverty; the feeling that the grand American experiment is failing or has failed. I could recite these problems, and then I could sit down and offer no solutions. But I don't choose to do that either. The citizens of America expect more. They deserve and they want more than a recital of problems.

Skill: Arguments and Claims

In paragraphs 2 and 3, Jordan claims that her presence is special and different. In paragraph 4, she uses her life and American history as evidence of this. She supports this evidence with reasoning. Jordan explains that the American Dream is a possibility for anyone to achieve. She is the first African American woman to give the keynote speech.

1. **party platform** a document or charter representing the party's official standpoints on major issues
2. **keynote speaker** the headlining speaker at a convention or meeting

Skill: Media

The text is serious here, but Jordan is speaking passionately. I can tell she really cares about America. She emphasizes "all of us" at the end, and she puts a pause between that and "are equal." She wanted to stress the idea that everyone is equal, not just some people.

Skill: Reasons and Evidence

Jordan quotes one of America's founding fathers. I know that "harmony" means "to work together," and "affection" means "love." Jordan uses Jefferson's words to support her claim that people should unify as a nation.

6 We are a people in a quandary about the present. We are a people in search of our future. We are a people in search of a national community. We are a people trying not only to solve the problems of the present, unemployment, inflation,[3] but we are attempting on a larger scale to fulfill the promise of America. We are attempting to fulfill our national purpose, to create and **sustain** a society in which all of us are equal.

. . .

7 And now we must look to the future. Let us heed the voice of the people and recognize their common sense. If we do not, we not only blaspheme our political heritage, we ignore the common ties that bind all Americans. Many fear the future. Many are distrustful of their leaders, and believe that their voices are never heard. Many seek only to satisfy their private wants; to satisfy their private interests. But this is the great danger America faces—that we will cease to be one nation and become instead a collection of interest groups: city against suburb, region against region, individual against individual; each seeking to satisfy private wants. If that happens, who then will speak for America? Who then will speak for the common good?

8 This is the question which must be answered in 1976: Are we to be one people bound together by common spirit, sharing in a common **endeavor;** or will we become a divided nation? For all of its uncertainty, we cannot flee the future. We must not become the "New Puritans" and reject our society. We must address and master the future together. It can be done if we restore the belief that we share a sense of national community, that we share a common national endeavor. It can be done.

9 There is no executive order;[4] there is no law that can require the American people to form a national community. This we must do as individuals, and if we do it as individuals, there is no President of the United States who can veto that decision.

10 As a first step, we must restore our belief in ourselves. We are a generous people, so why can't we be generous with each other? We need to take to heart the words spoken by Thomas Jefferson:

11 "Let us restore to social intercourse that harmony and that affection without which liberty and even life are but dreary things."

12 A nation is formed by the willingness of each of us to share in the responsibility for upholding the common good. A government is invigorated when each one of us is willing to participate in shaping the future of this nation. In this election year, we must define the "common good" and begin again to shape

3. **inflation** an increase in price and a decrease in the value of currency
4. **executive order** an act from the president that has the same impact as law but does not need congressional approval

a common future. Let each person do his or her part. If one citizen is unwilling to participate, all of us are going to suffer. For the American idea, though it is shared by all of us, is realized in each one of us.

13 And now, what are those of us who are elected public officials supposed to do? We call ourselves "public servants" but I'll tell you this: We as public servants must set an example for the rest of the nation. It is hypocritical for the public official to admonish and exhort the people to uphold the common good if we are derelict in upholding the common good. More is required of public officials than slogans and handshakes and press releases. More is required. We must hold ourselves strictly accountable. We must provide the people with a vision of the future.

14 If we promise as public officials, we must deliver. If we as public officials propose, we must produce. If we say to the American people, "It is time for you to be sacrificial"—sacrifice. If the public official says that, we [public officials] must be the first to give. We must be. And again, if we make mistakes, we must be willing to admit them. We have to do that. What we have to do is strike a balance between the idea that government should do everything and the idea, the belief, that government ought to do nothing. Strike a balance.

15 Let there be no **illusions** about the difficulty of forming this kind of a national community. It's tough, difficult, not easy. But a spirit of harmony will survive in America only if each of us remembers that we share a common destiny; if each of us remembers, when self-interest and bitterness seem to prevail, that we share a common destiny.

16 I have confidence that we can form this kind of national community.

• • •

17 I have that confidence.

18 We cannot improve on the system of government handed down to us by the founders of the Republic. There is no way to improve upon that. But what we can do is to find new ways to implement that system and realize our destiny.

19 Now I began this speech by commenting to you on the uniqueness of a Barbara Jordan making a keynote address. Well I am going to close my speech by quoting a Republican President and I ask you that as you listen to these words of Abraham Lincoln, relate them to the concept of a national community in which every last one of us participates:

20 "As I would not be a slave, so I would not be a master. This expresses my idea of Democracy. Whatever differs from this, to the extent of the difference, is no Democracy."

21 Thank you.

First Read

Read "All Together Now." After you read, complete the Think Questions below.

Copyright © BookheadEd Learning, LLC

THINK QUESTIONS

1. According to paragraph 4, Barbara Jordan's presence at the convention is evidence of what symbol?

2. List some of the problems that cause the American "people to feel cynical, angry, frustrated." Cite specific evidence from paragraph 5.

3. According to paragraph 13, who is supposed to set an example for the nation?

4. Find the word **deferred** in paragraph 4 of "All Together Now." Use context clues in the surrounding sentences, as well as the sentence in which the word appears, to determine the word's meaning. Write your definition here and identify clues that helped you figure out the meaning.

5. Use context clues to determine the meaning of **endeavor** as it is used in paragraph 8 of "All Together Now." Write your definition here and identify clues that helped you figure out the meaning. Then check the meaning in a dictionary.

Skill:
Arguments and Claims

Use the Checklist to analyze Arguments and Claims in "All Together Now." Refer to the sample student annotations about Arguments and Claims in the text.

••• CHECKLIST FOR ARGUMENTS AND CLAIMS

In order to trace the argument and specific claims, do the following:

- ✓ identify clues that reveal the author's opinion in the title, introduction, or conclusion

- ✓ note the first and last sentence of each body paragraph for specific claims that help to build the author's argument

- ✓ list the information the author introduces in sequential order

- ✓ use different colors to highlight and distinguish among an author's argument, claims, evidence, or reasons

- ✓ describe the author's argument in your own words

To evaluate the argument and specific claims, consider the following questions:

- ✓ Does the author support each claim with reasoning and evidence?

- ✓ Do the author's claims work together to support his or her overall argument?

- ✓ Which claims are not supported, if any?

Skill:
Arguments and Claims

Reread paragraphs 9–12 of "All Together Now." Then, using the Checklist on the previous page, answer the multiple-choice questions below.

 YOUR TURN

1. Barbara Jordan uses a quotation from Thomas Jefferson as evidence to support her claim that —

   ○ A. there is no law forcing Americans to form a national community.
   ○ B. the President of the United States can veto some decisions.
   ○ C. being kinder to others will help the country as a whole.
   ○ D. freedom is no longer inspiring to Americans.

2. This excerpt of the speech supports Jordan's overall argument by —

   ○ A. showing how much America has progressed in terms of civil rights.
   ○ B. showing the problems caused by divisive politics in America.
   ○ C. showing how willingness to work together will improve the government.
   ○ D. showing that politicians have gotten away with hypocrisy for far too long.

Skill:
Reasons and Evidence

Use the Checklist to analyze Reasons and Evidence in "All Together Now." Refer to the sample student annotations about Reasons and Evidence in the text.

••• CHECKLIST FOR REASONS AND EVIDENCE

In order to identify the reasons and evidence that support an author's claim(s) in an argument, note the following:

- ✓ the argument the author is making

- ✓ the claim or the main idea of the argument

- ✓ the reasons and evidence that support the claim and where they can be found

- ✓ if the evidence the author presents to support the claim is sound, or complete and comprehensive

- ✓ if there is sufficient evidence to support the claim or if more is needed

To assess whether the author's reasoning is sound and the evidence is relevant and sufficient, consider the following questions:

- ✓ What kind of argument is the author making?

- ✓ Is the reasoning, or the thinking behind the claims, sound and valid?

- ✓ Are the reasons and evidence the author presents to support the claim sufficient, or is more evidence needed? Why or why not?

Please note that excerpts and passages in the StudySync® library and this workbook are intended as touchstones to generate interest in an author's work. The excerpts and passages do not substitute for the reading of entire texts, and StudySync® strongly recommends that students seek out and purchase the whole literary or informational work in order to experience it as the author intended. Links to online resellers are available in our digital library. In addition, complete works may be ordered through an authorized reseller by filling out and returning to StudySync® the order form enclosed in this workbook.

Reading & Writing
Companion

375

Skill:
Reasons and Evidence

Reread paragraphs 18–21 of "All Together Now." Then, using the Checklist on the previous page, answer the multiple-choice questions below.

↻ YOUR TURN

1. What type of evidence does Barbara Jordan use in this part of the speech?

   ○ A. the fact that the American system of government cannot be improved
   ○ B. statistics showing how unlikely it is for an African American woman to be asked to give a speech
   ○ C. an example of another national community that succeeds in making progress
   ○ D. a quotation from President Abraham Lincoln

2. Jordan emphasizes that Lincoln was a Republican because —

   ○ A. she is speaking to Democrats and wants to give an example of working with opponents.
   ○ B. she is speaking to Democrats and wants to mock Republicans.
   ○ C. she is speaking to Republicans and wants to insult Democrats.
   ○ D. she is speaking to Republicans and wants to inspire them.

Skill:
Media

Use the Checklist to analyze Media in "All Together Now." Refer to the sample student annotations about Media in the text.

••• CHECKLIST FOR MEDIA

In order to determine how to compare and contrast a text to an audio, video, or multimedia version of the text, note the following:

- ✓ how the same topic can be treated, or presented, in more than one medium, such as audio, video, and multimedia versions of a text

- ✓ how treatments of a topic through different kinds of media can reveal more information about the topic

- ✓ which details are emphasized or absent in each medium, and the reasons behind these choices

- ✓ if similar details about the subject are emphasized, this may make the information seem more important or believable

- ✓ if different details are stressed, a reader or viewer may begin to think about the subject in a new way

To compare and contrast a text to an audio, video, or multimedia version of the text, analyzing each medium's portrayal of the subject, ask the following questions:

- ✓ How are the treatments of the source text similar? How are they different?

- ✓ How does each medium's portrayal affect the presentation of the subject?

- ✓ Why are different media able to emphasize or highlight certain kinds of information better than others?

Skill:
Media

Reread paragraphs 1–4 of "All Together Now" and then listen to the audio version of this portion of the speech. Complete the chart below by matching the correct sound element to the text excerpt and then explain how the sound element affects your understanding.

↻ YOUR TURN

Sound Element	
A	Tone and Emphasis
B	Applause

Text Excerpt	Sound Element	Effect on Understanding
"It was one hundred and forty-four years ago that members of the Democratic Party first met in convention to select a Presidential candidate."	Dramatic Pause	The pauses after "ago" and "first" emphasize how long ago the first convention was. They also suggest that the convention is important and historic.
"I, Barbara Jordan, am a keynote speaker."		
"...one additional bit of evidence that the American Dream need not forever be deferred."		

Close Read

Reread "All Together Now." As you reread, complete the Skills Focus questions below. Then use your answers and annotations from the questions to help you complete the Write activity.

◎ SKILLS FOCUS

1. Identify a claim in the speech that supports Barbara Jordan's main argument. Explain her argument in your own words.

2. Identify and explain a type of evidence that Jordan uses to support her claim. Then give one example of additional evidence that she could add. Explain where in the structure of her argument she could incorporate this evidence.

3. Recall that Barbara Jordan raised her voice and paused when she said, "We are attempting to fulfill our national purpose, to create and sustain a society in which *all of us are equal.*" Highlight this part of the speech and 1 or 2 other lines in which Jordan displays volume, tone, or another audio technique. Write a note explaining how Jordan's delivery impacted or changed your understanding of her argument or claim.

4. Find an example in the speech in which Barbara Jordan talks about the importance of national unity. Explain in your own words why the idea of national unity is worth pursuing.

✎ WRITE

DISCUSSION: Write notes to prepare for a collaborative conversation with a partner or a small group to discuss how to bring students in your community together in a positive way. First, establish a clear position by stating the most significant problem you see within the student community. Then provide reasons and evidence that support your arguments and claims. Finally, work together with your partner or group to reach a consensus about what actions students and staff should take to create a stronger student community.

Please note that excerpts and passages in the StudySync® library and this workbook are intended as touchstones to generate interest in an author's work. The excerpts and passages do not substitute for the reading of entire texts, and StudySync® strongly recommends that students seek out and purchase the whole literary or informational work in order to experience it as the author intended. Links to online resellers are available in our digital library. In addition, complete works may be ordered through an authorized reseller by filling out and returning to StudySync® the order form enclosed in this workbook.

Reading & Writing Companion   379

Mother Jones:
Fierce Fighter for Workers' Rights

INFORMATIONAL TEXT
Judith Pinkerton Josephson
1996

Introduction

Mary Harris Jones (1837–1930), known as Mother Jones, was an American schoolteacher and dressmaker who went on to become a prominent workers' rights activist and community organizer. This excerpt from author Judith Pinkerton Josephson's biography of the fearless crusader describes her groundbreaking demonstrations against unfair child labor practices and her historic 1903 march from Philadelphia to Sagamore Hill, New York, to protest the poor

"What about the little children from whom all song is gone?"

NOTES

from Chapter Nine: The March of the Mill Children[1]

1   "I love children," Mother Jones once told a reporter.

2   In countless shacks and shanties[2] across the country, she had tied the shoes of children, wiped their noses, hugged them while they cried, scrambled to find food for them, fought for their rights. By the turn of the century, almost two million children under the age of sixteen worked in mills, factories, and mines. Images of the child workers Mother Jones had seen stayed with her—the torn, bleeding fingers of the breaker boys,[3] the mill children living on coffee and stale bread.

3   In June 1903, Mother Jones went to Philadelphia, Pennsylvania—the heart of a **vast** textile industry. About one hundred thousand workers from six hundred different mills were on strike there. The strikers wanted their workweek cut from sixty to fifty-five hours, even if it meant lower wages. About a sixth of the strikers were children under sixteen.

4   Nationwide, eighty thousand children worked in the textile industry. In the South, Mother Jones had seen how dangerous their jobs were. Barefooted little girls and boys reached their tiny hands into the **treacherous** machinery to repair snapped threads or crawled underneath the machinery to oil it. At textile union headquarters, Mother Jones met more of these mill children. Their bodies were bone-thin, with hollow chests. Their shoulders were rounded from long hours spent hunched over the workbenches. Even worse, she saw "some with their hands off, some with the thumb missing, some with their fingers off at the knuckles"—victims of mill accidents.

5   Pennsylvania, like many other states, had laws that said children under thirteen could not work. But parents often lied about a child's age. Poor families either put their children to work in the mills or starved. Mill owners looked the other way, because child labor was cheap.

---

1. **Mill Children** children put to work in mills or factories
2. **shanties** small houses improvised from spare building materials and refuse
3. **breaker boys** workers, mostly children, employed to separate impurities from coal by hand after it is mined

6   Mother Jones asked various newspaper publishers why they didn't write about child labor in Pennsylvania. The publishers told her they couldn't, since owners of the mills also owned stock in their newspapers. "Well, I've got stock in these little children," she said, "and I'll arrange a little publicity."

7   Mother Jones, now seventy-three, gathered a large group of mill children and their parents. She led them on a one-mile march from Philadelphia's Independence Square to its courthouse lawn. Mother Jones and a few children climbed up on a platform in front of a huge crowd. She held one boy's arm up high so the crowd could see his mutilated hand. "Philadelphia's mansions were built on the broken bones, the quivering hearts, and drooping heads of these children," she said. She lifted another child in her arms so the crowd could see how thin he was.

8   Mother Jones looked directly at the city officials standing at the open windows across the street. "Some day the workers will take possession of your city hall, and when we do, no child will be sacrificed on the altar of profit." Unmoved, the officials quickly closed their windows.

9   Local newspapers and some New York newspapers covered the event. How, Mother Jones wondered, could she draw national attention to the evils of child labor? Philadelphia's famous Liberty Bell, currently on a national tour and drawing huge crowds, gave her an idea. She and the textile union leaders would stage their own tour. They would march the mill children all the way to the president of the United States—Theodore Roosevelt. Mother Jones wanted the president to get Congress to pass a law that would take children out of the mills, mines, and factories, and put them in school.

10 When Mother Jones asked parents for permission to take their children with her, many hesitated. The march from Philadelphia to Sagamore Hill—the president's seaside mansion on Long Island near New York City—would cover 125 miles. It would be a difficult journey. But finally, the parents agreed. Many decided to come along on the march. Other striking men and women offered their help, too.

11 On July 7, 1903, nearly three hundred men, women, and children—followed by four wagons with supplies—began the long march. Newspapers carried daily reports of the march, calling the group "Mother Jones's Industrial Army," or "Mother Jones's Crusaders." The army was led by a fife-and-drum corps of three children dressed in Revolutionary War uniforms. Mother Jones wore her familiar, lace-fringed black dress. The marchers sang and carried flags, banners, and placards that read "We Want to Go to School!" "We Want Time to Play." **"Prosperity** is Here, Where is Ours?" "55 Hours or Nothing." "We Only Ask for Justice." "More Schools, Less Hospitals."

12 The temperature rose into the nineties. The roads were dusty, the children's shoes full of holes. Many of the young girls returned home. Some of the marchers walked only as far as the outskirts of Philadelphia. For the hundred or

NOTES

so marchers who remained, this trip was an adventure in spite of the heat. They bathed and swam in brooks and rivers. Each of them carried a knapsack with a knife, fork, tin cup, and plate inside. Mother Jones took a huge pot for cooking meals on the way. Mother Jones also took along costumes, makeup, and jewelry so the children could stop in towns along the route and put on plays about the struggle of textile workers. The fife-and-drum corps gave concerts and passed the hat. People listened and donated money. Farmers met the marchers with wagonloads of fruit, vegetables, and clothes. Railroad engineers stopped their trains and gave them free rides. Hotel owners served free meals.

13 On July 10th, marchers camped across the Delaware River from Trenton, New Jersey. They had traveled about forty miles in three days. At first, police told the group they couldn't enter the city. Trenton mill owners didn't want any trouble. But Mother Jones invited the police to stay for lunch. The children gathered around the cooking pot with their tin plates and cups. The policemen smiled, talked kindly to them, and then allowed them to cross the bridge into Trenton. There Mother Jones spoke to a crowd of five thousand people. That night, the policemen's wives took the children into their homes, fed them, and packed them lunches for the next day's march.

14 By now, many of the children were growing weak. More returned home. Some adults on the march grumbled that Mother Jones just wanted people to notice *her*. They complained to reporters that Mother Jones often stayed in hotels while the marchers camped in hot, soggy tents filled with whining mosquitoes. Sometimes Mother Jones did stay in hotels, because she went ahead of the marchers to arrange for lodging and food in upcoming towns and to get publicity for the march.

15 As the remaining marchers pushed on to Princeton, New Jersey, a thunderstorm struck. Mother Jones and her army camped on the grounds of former President Grover Cleveland's estate. The Clevelands were away, and the caretaker let Mother Jones use the big, cool barn for a dormitory.

16 Mother Jones got permission from the mayor of Princeton to speak opposite the campus of Princeton University. Her topic: higher education. She spoke to a large crowd of professors, students, and residents. Pointing to one ten-year-old boy, James Ashworth, she said, "Here's a textbook on economics." The boy's body was stooped from carrying seventy-five-pound bundles of yarn. "He gets three dollars a week and his sister, who is fourteen, gets six dollars. They work in a carpet factory ten hours a day while the children of the rich are getting their higher education." Her piercing glance swept over the students in the crowd.

17 Mother Jones talked about children who could not read or write because they spent ten hours a day in Pennsylvania's silk mills. Those who hired these child workers used "the hands and feet of little children so they might buy automobiles for their wives and police dogs for their daughters to talk French to." She accused the mill owners of taking "babies almost from the cradle."

18 The next night, the marchers slept on the banks of the Delaware River. In every town, Mother Jones drew on what she did best—speaking—to gather support for her cause. One reporter wrote, "Mother Jones makes other speakers sound like tin cans."

19 Battling heat, rain, and swarms of mosquitoes at night, the marchers arrived in Elizabeth. Socialist party members helped house and feed the weary adults and children. The next morning, two businessmen gave Mother Jones her first car ride. She was delighted with this new "contraption."

20 On July 15, Mother Jones wrote a letter to President Roosevelt. She told him how these poor mill children lived, **appealed** to him as a father, and asked him to meet with her and the children. President Roosevelt did not answer Mother Jones's letter. Instead, he assigned secret service[4] officers to watch her. They thought she might be a threat to the president. That made her furious.

21 On July 24, after more than two weeks on the road, the marchers reached New York City. By now, just twenty marchers remained. One of them was Eddie Dunphy, a child whose job was to sit on a high stool eleven hours a day handing thread to another worker. For this he was paid three dollars a week. Mother Jones talked about Eddie and about Gussie Rangnew, a child who packed stockings in a factory. She too worked eleven hours a day for pennies.

22 At one meeting, a crowd of thirty thousand gathered. "We are quietly marching toward the president's home," she told the people. "I believe he can do something for these children, although the press **declares** he cannot."

23 One man wanted the children to have some fun while they were in New York City. Frank Bostick owned the wild animal show at Coney Island, an amusement park and resort. He invited the mill children to spend a day at the park. The children swam in the ocean and played along the beach.

24 When Frank Bostick's wild animal show ended that night, he let Mother Jones speak to the crowd that had attended. To add drama, she had some of the children crawl inside the empty cages. The smells of sawdust and animals hung in the air. But instead of lions and tigers, the cages held children. The children gripped the iron bars and solemnly stared out at the crowd while Mother Jones spoke.

25 "We want President Roosevelt to hear the wail of the children who never have a chance to go to school, but work eleven and twelve hours a day in the textile mills of Pennsylvania," she said, "who weave the carpets that he and you walk upon; and the lace curtains in your windows, and the clothes of the people."

26 She continued, "In Georgia where children work day and night in the cotton mills they have just passed a bill to protect songbirds. What about the little

4. **secret service** independent federal law enforcement

children from whom all song is gone?" After Mother Jones finished speaking, the crowd sat in stunned silence. In the distance, a lone lion roared.

27 The grueling walk had taken almost three weeks. Mother Jones had written the president twice with no answer. On July 29, she took three young boys to Sagamore Hill, where the president was staying. But the secret service stopped them at the mansion's gates. The president would not see them.

28 The group returned to New York City. Discouraged, Mother Jones reported her failure to the newspapers. Most of the marchers decided to return home. She stayed on briefly with the three children. Once more, she wrote President Roosevelt: "The child of today is the man or woman of tomorrow. . . . I have with me three children who have walked one hundred miles. . . . If you decide to see these children, I will bring them before you at any time you may set."

29 The president's secretary replied that the president felt that child labor was a problem for individual states to solve. "He is a brave guy when he wants to take a gun out and fight other grown people," said Mother Jones in disgust, "but when those children went to him, he could not see them."

30 In early August, Mother Jones finally took the last three children home. Soon after, the textile workers gave up and ended their strike. Adults and children went back to work, their working conditions unchanged.

31 Though she had not met with the president, Mother Jones had drawn the attention of the nation to the problem of child labor. She became even more of a national figure. Within a few years, Pennsylvania, New York, New Jersey, and other states did pass tougher child labor laws. The federal government finally passed a child labor law (part of the Fair Labor Standards Act) in 1938—thirty-five years after the march of the mill children.

©1997 by Judith Pinkerton Josephson, MOTHER JONES: FIERCE FIGHTER FOR WORKERS' RIGHTS. Reproduced by permission of Judith Pinkerton Josephson. Watch for the updated e-book of Mother Jones: Fierce Fighter for Workers' Rights as part of the Spotlight Biography Series (eFrog Press) in Spring 2015. Also see www.JudithJosephson.com.

✏ WRITE

PERSONAL RESPONSE: Do you think Mother Jones was an effective leader? Write a brief response to this question. Remember to cite evidence from the text to support your response.

Please note that excerpts and passages in the StudySync® library and this workbook are intended as touchstones to generate interest in an author's work. The excerpts and passages do not substitute for the reading of entire texts, and StudySync® strongly recommends that students seek out and purchase the whole literary or informational work in order to experience it as the author intended. Links to online resellers are available in our digital library. In addition, complete works may be ordered through an authorized reseller by filling out and returning to StudySync® the order form enclosed in this workbook.

Reading & Writing
Companion

385

Speech to the Young: Speech to the Progress-Toward

POETRY
Gwendolyn Brooks
1932

Introduction

Highly regarded and widely admired, Gwendolyn Brooks (1917–2000) was the poet laureate of Illinois and the first African American to win the Pulitzer Prize. In her poem "Speech to the Young: Speech to the Progress-Toward," the speaker gives wise advice to young people about how to live life.

"even if you are not ready for day it cannot always be night."

1 Say to them,
2 say to the down-**keepers**,
3 the sun-**slappers**,
4 the self-**soilers**,
5 the **harmony-hushers**,
6 "even if you are not ready for day
7 it cannot always be night."
8 You will be right.
9 For that is the hard home-run.

10 Live not for battles won.
11 Live not for the-end-of-the-song.
12 Live in the along.

"Speech to the Young: Speech to the Progress-Toward" by Gwendolyn Brooks. Reprinted by Consent of Brooks Permissions.

✎ WRITE

POETRY: Write a poem in response to "Speech to the Young: Speech to the Progress-Toward" about how it feels to achieve the "hard home-run" that Brooks mentions. Use poetic elements and structure as you craft your poem.

Please note that excerpts and passages in the StudySync® library and this workbook are intended as touchstones to generate interest in an author's work. The excerpts and passages do not substitute for the reading of entire texts, and StudySync® strongly recommends that students seek out and purchase the whole literary or informational work in order to experience it as the author intended. Links to online resellers are available in our digital library. In addition, complete works may be ordered through an authorized reseller by filling out and returning to StudySync® the order form enclosed in this workbook.

Introduction

In June of 1903, a textile strike in Philadelphia saw 90,000 workers walk off the job in order to fight for better conditions. Sixteen thousand of these workers were children under the age of 16. News coverage of the strike was scarce, due in large part to the common business interests shared by textile mill owners and news publishers. On July 7, labor leader "Mother" Mary Harris Jones, otherwise known as Mother Jones (1837–1930), announced her plan to march with dozens of children from Philadelphia to Roosevelt's home outside New York City, hoping to draw attention to the harsh conditions experienced by children working in factories. One week into their march, on July 17, 1903, Jones wrote this public letter to President Roosevelt. After receiving no response, Mother Jones wrote to the president once again. She finally received a letter from Roosevelt's secretary, stating that the issue was under the jurisdiction of the states, and that the president would not meet with Mother Jones and her fellow marchers.

"... no child shall die of hunger at the will of any manufacturer in this fair land."

Copyright © BookheadEd Learning, LLC

NOTES

Skill: Language, Style, and Audience

To Theodore Roosevelt
President of the United States
Dear Sir:

1   Being citizens of the United States of America, we, members of the textile industry, take the liberty of addressing this **appeal** to you. As Chief Executive of the United States, you are, in a sense, our father and leader, and as such we look to you for advice and guidance. Perhaps the crime of child slavery has never been forcibly brought to your notice.

Mary Harris "Mother" Jones led a multi-week strike to advocate the end of child labor and harsh factory conditions. Here, child workers pose for a photograph during a strike in Philadelphia, PA, circa 1890.

In the first paragraph, the writer refers to Roosevelt as the "father and leader" of our country and asks for his guidance and advice around the "crime of child slavery." This creates an emotional response for the audience. Although the letter is addressed to President Roosevelt, it was written for the public.

2   Yet, as father of us all, surely the smallest detail must be of interest to you. In Philadelphia, Pa., there are ninety thousand (90,000) textile workers who are on **strike**, asking for a reduction from sixty to fifty-five hours a week. With machinery, Mr. President, we believe that forty-eight hours is sufficient.

3   If the United States Senate had passed the eight-hour bill,[1] this strike might not have occurred. We also ask that the children be taken from the industrial prisons of this nation, and given their right of attending schools, so that in years to come better citizens will be given to this republic.

4   These little children, raked by cruel toil beneath the iron wheels of greed, are starving in this country which you have declared is in the height of **prosperity**—slaughtered, ten hours a day, every day in the week, every week in the month, every month in the year, that our manufacturing aristocracy[2] may live to **exploit** more slaves as the years roll by.

1. **eight-hour bill** the ideal of an eight-hour workday ultimately enshrined in law by the Fair Labor Standards Act of 1938, which established the forty-hour week and overtime for all industries engaged in interstate commerce
2. **manufacturing aristocracy** wealthy factory owners

Skill: Author's Purpose and Point of View

In paragraph 4, Mother Jones brings up the factory owners, saying they "live to exploit" children. These are harsh words and show that her position is the morally correct one.

She also uses a lot of emotional words and addresses Roosevelt directly with the word "you." She is trying to persuade the president and others to protect the children in factories.

5   We ask you, Mr. President, if our commercial[3] greatness has not cost us too much by being built upon the quivering hearts of helpless children? We who know of these sufferings have taken up their cause and are now marching toward you in the hope that your tender heart will counsel with us to abolish this crime.

6   The manufacturers have threatened to starve these children, and we seek to show that no child shall die of hunger at the will of any manufacturer in this fair land. The clergy, whose work this really is, are silent on the crime of ages, and so we appeal to you.

7   It is in the hope that the words of Christ will be more clearly interpreted by you when he said "Suffer little children to come unto me." Our destination is New York City, and after that Oyster Bay.[4] As your children, may we hope to have the pleasure of an audience? We only ask that you advise us as to the best course.

8   In Philadelphia alone thousands of persons will wait upon your answer, while throughout the land, wherever there is organized labor, the people will anxiously await an expression of your **sentiments** toward suffering childhood.

9   On behalf of these people, we beg that you will reply and let us know whether we may expect an audience.

10 The reply should be addressed to "Mother" Jones's Crusaders, en route according to the daily papers.

11 We are very respectfully yours,

"Mother" Jones, Chairman

3. **commercial** related to commerce, trade, and general business activities intended to make profit
4. **Oyster Bay** a municipality of Long Island, New York

First Read

Read "Letter to President Theodore Roosevelt, July 17, 1903." After you read, complete the Think Questions below.

 THINK QUESTIONS

1. What does Mother Jones hope to accomplish with this letter? Explain any specific goals she mentions in the text.

2. What does Mother Jones mean by "industrial prisons" in paragraph 3 of the text? Cite any other places in the letter that help you to make an inference about the meaning of this term. Use evidence to support your understanding of this term's meaning.

3. Why does Mother Jones reach out directly to President Roosevelt? Describe why her previous efforts to stand up for child laborers were unsuccessful.

4. Read the following dictionary entry:

    strike

    strike \ strīk\

    noun

    a. a sudden military attack
    b. a collective refusal to work organized by a group of employees

    verb

    c. to hit someone purposefully and forcefully
    d. (of a disaster, disease or other problem) to occur suddenly and cause harm

    Which definition most closely matches the meaning of **strike** as it is used in paragraph 2? Write the correct definition of *strike* here and explain how you figured out the proper meaning.

5. Based on context clues, what is the meaning of the word **exploit** as it is used in paragraph 4? Write your best definition of *exploit* here, explaining how you figured it out.

 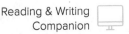

Skill: Language, Style, and Audience

Use the Checklist to analyze Language, Style, and Audience in "Letter to President Theodore Roosevelt, July 17, 1903." Refer to the sample student annotations about Language, Style, and Audience in the text.

••• CHECKLIST FOR LANGUAGE, STYLE, AND AUDIENCE

In order to determine an author's style, do the following:

- ✓ identify and define any unfamiliar words or phrases

- ✓ use context, including the meaning of surrounding words and phrases

- ✓ note possible reactions to the author's word choice

- ✓ examine your reaction to the author's word choice and how the author's word choice affected your reaction

To analyze the impact of specific word choice on meaning and tone, ask the following questions:

- ✓ How did your understanding of the language change during your analysis?

- ✓ What stylistic choices can you identify in the text? How does the style influence your understanding of the language?

- ✓ How could various audiences interpret this language? What different possible emotional responses can you list?

- ✓ How does the writer's choice of words impact or create a specific tone in the text?

Skill: Language, Style, and Audience

Reread paragraphs 2–3 of "Letter to President Theodore Roosevelt, July 17, 1903." Then, using the Checklist on the previous page, answer the multiple-choice questions below.

⟳ YOUR TURN

1. This question has two parts. First, answer Part A. Then, answer Part B.

   Part A: By choosing to use strong, descriptive language in her letter, Mother Jones is—

   ○ A. mocking President Roosevelt for his ineffective leadership.
   ○ B. encouraging readers to write letters to their senators for help.
   ○ C. attempting to make a heartfelt appeal to President Roosevelt.
   ○ D. saying the government and Roosevelt cannot be relied on to reform the textile industry.

   Part B: What evidence from the text BEST supports your response to Part A?

   ○ A. In Philadelphia, Pa., there are ninety thousand (90,000) textile workers who are on strike.
   ○ B. Yet, as father of us all, surely the smallest detail must be of interest to you.
   ○ C. If the United States Senate had passed the eight-hour bill, this strike might not have occurred.
   ○ D. asking for a reduction from sixty to fifty-five hours a week

Please note that excerpts and passages in the StudySync® library and this workbook are intended as touchstones to generate interest in an author's work. The excerpts and passages do not substitute for the reading of entire texts, and StudySync® strongly recommends that students seek out and purchase the whole literary or informational work in order to experience it as the author intended. Links to online resellers are available in our digital library. In addition, complete works may be ordered through an authorized reseller by filling out and returning to StudySync® the order form enclosed in this workbook.

Reading & Writing Companion 393

Skill: Author's Purpose and Point of View

Use the Checklist to analyze Author's Purpose and Point of View in "Letter to President Theodore Roosevelt, July 17, 1903." Refer to the sample student annotations about Author's Purpose and Point of View in the text.

••• CHECKLIST FOR AUTHOR'S PURPOSE AND POINT OF VIEW

In order to identify author's purpose and point of view, note the following:

- ✓ facts, statistics, and graphic aids, as these indicate that the author is writing to inform

- ✓ descriptive or sensory details and emotional language may indicate that the author is writing to describe and dramatize events

- ✓ descriptions that present a complicated process in plain language may indicate that the author is writing to explain

- ✓ emotional language with a call to action may indicate that the author is trying to persuade readers or stress an opinion

- ✓ the language the author uses can also hold clues to the author's point of view on a subject or topic

To determine the author's purpose and point of view in a text, consider the following questions:

- ✓ How does the author convey, or communicate, information in the text?

- ✓ Does the author use figurative or emotional language? How does it affect the purpose and point of view?

- ✓ How does the author distinguish his or her perspective or point of view?

- ✓ Does the author bring up different points of view? How is the author's position or point of view different from opposing points of view?

Skill: Author's Purpose and Point of View

Reread paragraphs 6–9 of "Letter to President Theodore Roosevelt, July 17, 1903." Then, using the Checklist on the previous page, answer the multiple-choice questions below.

🔁 YOUR TURN

1. Which piece of evidence helps to distinguish Mother Jones's position as the position of working people, children, and their families?

   ○ A. "The manufacturers have threatened to starve these children . . ."

   ○ B. "The clergy, whose work this really is, are silent on the crime of ages . . ."

   ○ C. "It is in the hope that the words of Christ will be more clearly interpreted by you . . ."

   ○ D. "On behalf of these people, we beg you will reply . . ."

2. What do words like *suffer* and *hope* suggest about a reason why Mother Jones wrote her letter?

   ○ A. to inform readers about the unfair working condition with facts

   ○ B. to encourage readers to write letters to their senators for help

   ○ C. to persuade readers and stress her opinion by using emotional words

   ○ D. to explain the processes in the textile industry with descriptions

Close Read

LETTER TO PRESIDENT
THEODORE ROOSEVELT,
JULY 17, 1903

Reread "Letter to President Theodore Roosevelt, July 17, 1903." As you reread, complete the Skills Focus questions below. Then use your answers and annotations from the questions to help you complete the Write activity.

◎ SKILLS FOCUS

1. Recall that a claim is a main idea in an argumentative text. Identify one claim the author makes, and rewrite the claim in your own words.

2. Identify evidence that shows the author's purpose in writing this text. Explain what audience the author is writing to and what reasons she has for writing.

3. In the poem "Speech to the Young: Speech to the Progress-Toward," the speaker uses the pronoun *you* in these lines: "even if you are not ready for day / it cannot always be night." In the letter, Mother Jones also uses the pronoun *you* to directly address the intended audience. Identify an example of the pronoun *you* in the letter. Compare and contrast how the pronoun *you* is used in the

letter and the poem. In your response, explain who is being addressed by the pronoun *you* and the message each writer is trying to express.

4. Identify examples of emotional language that Mother Jones used to try to persuade the president to support her cause. How does this language help distinguish Mother Jones's position from others, including the factory owners?

5. Identify evidence that shows Mother Jones's dream for the future. Explain whether you think her dream was worth pursuing.

✏ WRITE

COMPARE AND CONTRAST: Compare and contrast the intended audience and the purpose in the excerpt from *Mother Jones: Fierce Fighter for Workers' Rights*, "Speech to the Young: Speech to the Progress-Toward," and "Letter to President Theodore Roosevelt, July 17, 1903." Why did the authors write these texts? Explain how the audience and the purpose of each text impact its style and language.

Before We Were Free

FICTION
Julia Alvarez
2002

Introduction

Essayist, poet, and novelist Julia Alvarez (b. 1950) has earned commercial and critical success, most notably with the novels *How the Garcia Girls Lost Their Accents*, *In the Time of the Butterflies* and *Yo!* Much of Alvarez's work is inspired by her sudden move from the Dominican Republic to New York in 1960, after her father's role in a failed plot against the dictator Rafael Trujillo led Alvarez's family to flee. *Before We Were Free* takes a page from the author's own childhood, as narrator Anita de la Torre and her older siblings, Lucinda and Mundín, try to get to the bottom of why the military police (SIM) are watching their family's house. The novel is interested in, as Alvarez explains it, "the sons and daughters of those who had been tortured, imprisoned, or murdered—kids like my cousins and my

"We just have to act as if the SIM aren't there and carry on with normal life."

from Chapter 2

1   Lucinda and I wait in her room, listening at the door, tense with **concentration**. When we don't hear noises anymore, Lucinda turns the knob carefully, and we tiptoe out into the hall.

2   The SIM seem to have left. We spot Chucha crossing the patio toward the front of the house, a broom over her shoulder like a rifle. She looks like she's going to shoot the SIM for tracking mud on her clean floors.

3   "Chucha!" We wave to her to come talk to us.

4   "Where's Mami?" I ask, feeling the same mounting panic I felt earlier when Mami left with the SIM. "Is she okay?"

5   "She's on the *teléfono*, calling Don Mundo," Chucha explains.

6   "What about . . . ?" Lucinda wrinkles her nose instead of saying their names.

7   "*Esos animales*," Chucha says, shaking her head. Those animals, the SIM, searched every house in the **compound**, getting more and more destructive when they didn't find what they were looking for, tromping through Chucha's room, turning over her coffin and tearing off the velvet lining. They also stormed through Porfirio's and Ursulina's rooms. "Those two are so terrified," Chucha concludes, "they are packing their things and leaving the house."

8   But the SIM stay. They sit in their black Volkswagens at the top of our drive, blocking our way out.

9   At dinner, Papi says everything will be fine. We just have to act as if the SIM aren't there and carry on with normal life. But I notice that, like the rest of us, he doesn't eat a single bite. And is it really normal that Mami and Papi have us all sleep on mattresses on their bedroom floor with the door locked?

Skill:
Setting

The story is set in a compound of houses. The SIM have invaded "every house in the compound" by "tromping" and storming through rooms. This must be why Chucha is angry at the secret police.

10   We lie in the dark, talking in whispers, Mundín on a mat by himself, Lucinda and I on a larger mattress, and Papi and Mami on theirs they placed right beside ours.

11   "How come you don't just stay up on your bed?" I ask.

12   "Keep your voice down," Mami reminds me.

13   "Okay, okay," I whisper. But I still don't get an answer. "And what about Chucha?" I ask. "She's all by herself at the back of the house."

14   "Don't worry," Mundín says, "I don't think a bullet can get through that coffin!"

15   "Bullets!" I sit right up in bed.

16   "Shhhh!" my whole family reminds me.

17   Those black cars sit there for days and days—sometimes there's only one, sometimes as many as three. Every morning, when Papi leaves for the office, one of the cars starts up its colicky motor and follows him down the hill. In the evening, when he comes home, it comes back with him. I don't know when those SIM ever go to their own houses to eat their suppers and talk with their kids.

18   "Are they really policemen?" I keep asking Mami. It doesn't make any sense. If the SIM are policemen, secret or not, shouldn't we trust them instead of being afraid of them? But all Mami will say is "Shhh!" Meanwhile, we can't go to school because something might happen to us. "Like what?" I ask. Like what Chucha said about people disappearing? Is that what Mami worries will happen to us? "Didn't Papi say we should carry on with normal life?"

19   "Anita, *por favor*," Mami pleads, collapsing in a hall chair. She leans forward and whispers in my ear, "Please, please, you must stop asking questions."

20   "But why?" I whisper back. I can smell her shampoo, which smells like coconuts in her hair.

21   "Because I don't have any answers," she replies.

22   Not that Mami is the only one I try talking to.

23   My brother, Mundín, who's two years older, sometimes explains things to me. But this time when I ask him what's going on, he looks worried and whispers, "Ask Papi." He's biting his nails again, something he stopped doing when he turned fourteen in August.

24   I try asking Papi.

Skill:
Setting

The narrator follows her father to the living room, where he talks to people on the phone. But even here in the living room, he speaks in code. This creates a feeling of danger and suspense. I can see this in the father's reaction.

25 One evening when the phone rings, I follow him into our living room. I hear him say something about some butterflies in a car accident.

26 "Butterflies in a car accident?" I ask, puzzled.

27 He seems startled that I'm in the room. "What are you doing here?" he snaps. I put my hands on my hips. "Honestly, Papi! I live here!" I can't believe he's asking me what I'm doing in our own living room! Of course, he immediately apologizes. "Sorry, *amorcito*, you startled me." His eyes are moist, as if he's holding back tears.

28 "So what about those butterflies, Papi?"

29 "They're not real butterflies," he explains softly. "It's just . . . a nickname for some very special ladies who had an . . . accident last night."

30 "What kind of an accident? And why are they called butterflies anyhow? Don't they have a real name?"

31 Again a shhh.

32 My last **resort** is asking Lucinda. My older sister has been in a vile mood since the SIM cornered us in our own house. Lucinda loves parties and talking on the phone, and she hates being cooped up. She spends most of the time in her room, trying out so many hairstyles that I'm sure that when we finally leave the compound and go to the United States of America, Lucinda will be bald.

33 "Lucinda, por favor, pretty please, tell me what is going on?" I promise her a back rub that she doesn't have to pay me for.

34 Lucinda puts her hairbrush down on her vanity and makes a sign for me to follow her to the patio out back.

35 "We should be okay out here," she whispers, looking over her shoulder.

36 "Why are you whispering?" In fact, everyone has been talking in whispers and low voices this last week, as if the house is full of fussy babies who've finally fallen asleep.

37 Lucinda explains. The SIM have probably hidden microphones in the house and are monitoring our conversations from their VWs.[1]

38 "Why are they treating us like criminals? We haven't done anything wrong."

---

1. **VWs** Volkswagens

NOTES

39   "Shhh!" Lucinda hushes me. For a moment she looks doubtful about continuing to explain things to a little sister who can't keep her voice down. "It's all about T-O-N-I," she says, spelling out our uncle's name in English. "A few months ago, he and his friends were involved in a **plot** to get rid of our dictator."

40   "You mean. . . ." I don't even have to say our leader's name. Lucinda nods solemnly and puts a finger to her lips.

41   Now I'm really confused. I thought we liked El Jefe.[2] His picture hangs in our front entryway with the saying below it: IN THIS HOUSE, TRUJILLO RULES. "But if he's so bad, why does Mrs. Brown hang his picture in our classroom next to George Washington?"

42   "We have to do that. Everyone has to. He's a dictator."

43   I'm not really sure what a dictator does. But this is probably not a good time to ask.

44   It turns out that the SIM discovered the plot and most of our uncle's friends were arrested. As for Tío Toni, nobody knows where he is. "He might be hiding out or they"—Lucinda looks over her shoulder. I know just who she means—"they might have him in custody."

45   "Will they disappear him?"

46   Lucinda seems surprised that I know about such matters. "Let's hope not," she sighs. Tío Toni is a special favorite of hers. At twenty-four, he's not that much older than she, at fifteen, and he is very handsome. All her girlfriends have crushes on him. "Ever since the SIM uncovered that plot, they've been after the family. That's why everyone's left. Tío Carlos and Mamita and Papito —"

47   "Why don't we leave, too, since we're not going to school anyway?"

48   "And **abandon** Tío Toni?" Lucinda shakes her head vigorously. Her pretty auburn hair is up in this hairdo called a chignon, like Princess Grace wears in her magazine wedding pictures. It comes undone and cascades down her back. "What if he comes back? What if he needs our help?" Her voice has risen above her usual whispering.

49   For once in the last few weeks, it's my turn to tell someone else in our house, "SHHHH!"

Excerpted from Before We Were Free *by Julia Alvarez, published by Laurel-Leaf Books.*

---

2. **El Jefe** (Spanish) the chief or boss

First Read

Read *Before We Were Free*. After you read, complete the Think Questions below.

☁ THINK QUESTIONS

1. Why are Lucinda and the narrator listening tensely for noises at the beginning of the excerpt? Explain.

2. How does the narrator's family often respond when the narrator asks questions? Give examples.

3. Why do the narrator and Lucinda whisper about "T-O-N-I"? Explain, citing specific evidence.

4. Read the following dictionary entry:

compound

com•pound \ˈkämˈpoundˌ\

noun

a. a thing that is composed of at least two separate elements
b. a group of buildings or residences in one fenced-in area

verb

c. to put together or form by combining parts
d. to make a problem worse or more intensified

Which definition most closely matches the meaning of **compound** as it is used in paragraph 7? Write the correct definition of *compound* here, and explain how you figured out the correct meaning.

5. Based on context clues, what is the meaning of the word **resort** as it is used in paragraph 32? Write your best definition of *resort* here, explaining how you figured it out.

Skill:
Setting

Use the Checklist to analyze Setting in *Before We Were Free*. Refer to the sample student annotations about Setting in the text.

In order to identify how particular elements of a story interact, note the following:

- ✓ the setting of the story

- ✓ the characters in the text and the problems they face

- ✓ how the events of the plot unfold, and how that affects the setting and characters

- ✓ how the setting shapes the characters and plot

- ✓ cite the specific words, phrases, sentences, paragraphs, or images from the text that support your analysis

To analyze how particular elements of a story interact, consider the following questions as a guide:

- ✓ What is the setting(s) of the story?

- ✓ How does the setting affect the characters and plot?

- ✓ How does the setting contribute to or help solve the conflict?

- ✓ How do the characters' decisions affect the plot and setting(s)?

Skill:
Setting

Reread paragraphs 32–39 from *Before We Were Free*. Then, using the Checklist on the previous page, answer the multiple-choice questions below.

↻ YOUR TURN

1. In this section of the story, the setting changes from —

   ○ A. Lucinda's bedroom to the patio.
   ○ B. a party to Lucinda's bedroom.
   ○ C. the compound to the patio.
   ○ D. the patio to a car.

2. Based on textual evidence, the reader can conclude that Lucinda wants to talk somewhere else because she —

   ○ A. hates being cooped up inside the house.
   ○ B. thinks the SIM will not be able to hear what they say on the patio.
   ○ C. finds it to be cooler outside on the patio.
   ○ D. worries that her parents will be upset if they hear what she says.

3. In paragraph 36, why does the narrator say that it seems "as if the house is full of fussy babies who've finally fallen asleep"?

   ○ A. People in the house are talking in a low voice because they are afraid of being heard by someone else.
   ○ B. People in the house are acting childish because they are tense.
   ○ C. The family members have been having trouble sleeping.
   ○ D. The family is taking care of the children of people who have left.

Close Read

Reread *Before We Were Free*. As you reread, complete the Skills Focus questions below. Then use your answers and annotations from the questions to help you complete the Write activity.

◎ SKILLS FOCUS

1. Identify a detail that shows a change in the setting of the story. Then explain how this change of setting affects character and plot development.

2. Reread paragraph 7. Identify a detail about how some people in the compound are reacting to the secret police (SIM). Explain how this example helps you understand a conflict in the story.

3. Identify an example of language the author uses to create suspense. Explain how this example advances the plot.

4. Reread the dialogue in paragraphs 12–16. How do the characters' words and actions contribute to the mood or feeling of the story? Explain how this mood or feeling is related to the conflict.

5. Identify a detail that supports the idea that staying in the compound is worth it despite the inconveniences and dangers. Explain whether you agree or disagree that the ideal of staying loyal to family members is worth taking risks.

✎ WRITE

LITERARY ANALYSIS: Although Papi says, "Everything will be fine" regarding the secret police (SIM), Alvarez describes a feeling of omnipresent terror in the de la Torre household. Identify and analyze how the setting shows that Papi and the others are afraid and/or have something to fear. Be sure to use textual evidence to support your response.

Machines, not people, should be exploring the stars for now

ARGUMENTATIVE TEXT
Don Lincoln
2017

Introduction

Don Lincoln, Ph.D. (b. 1964) is an American physicist who is best known for research that led to important discoveries within the field of physics. In this text, Lincoln adds to the conversation about robotic versus manned space travel and presents arguments meant to help people consider where the space program ought to direct its attention in the future.

"We have dreamed of a time when humans can travel through space . . . "

NOTES

1   In the last several weeks, two events demanded the attention of space enthusiasts. On March 30, entrepreneur Elon Musk's Space X company successfully reused a previously flown rocket to launch a communication satellite into space. And on April 6, American space **pioneer** John Glenn was laid to rest.

2   In their own way, Musk and Glenn each represent the hopes and dreams of those who delight in the idea of mankind leaving the bounds of Earth and exploring the solar system and, ultimately, the stars.

3   Over the past 50 years, we've seen men first orbit the globe and then walk on the moon. We were gripped by the fictional journeys of the Starship Enterprise, which explored the galaxy, encountering new life and new civilizations. Popcorn in hand, we watched Matt Damon struggle to survive in "The Martian."

Skill: Greek and Latin Affixes and Roots

4   We have dreamed of a time when humans can travel through space as readily as when early mariners[1] unfurled their sails and headed west in search of new lands. But we might not have stopped and asked an important question.

Galactic looks like *galaxy,* so the words could have the same root and a similar meaning. I know the suffix *-ic* forms adjectives. Based on these clues, I think the word *galactic* might describe things in space. I'll check the dictionary to be sure.

5   Should we be doing that?

6   Now, I am not asking whether we should explore the universe. I also dream of the day that we become citizens. The question is whether the initial exploration of space should be done by humans or by robots. I would argue that, for the moment, robotic exploration should have the upper hand.

7   Proponents of the astronaut-preferred camp point, quite rightfully, at the versatility and independence of humans. Fans of human spaceflight are certainly correct when they remind us that humans are highly versatile. People observe the conditions around them and can react to circumstances as needed.

8   However, people are also fragile. They need food, water, and air. They can exist in only a narrow range of temperatures and find **inhospitable** both

---

1. **mariners** people who work as sailors

Skill: Reasons
and Evidence

*Lincoln claims that
manned missions are
expensive. He uses
many examples and
numerical evidence from
past trips to prove this.
He then warns how
expensive a manned trip
to Mars would be.*

*Lincoln's reasoning is
strong and valid.
Spending too much
money is usually a bad
thing. Plus, he points
out that a manned
mission could hurt the
rest of the space
program. Overall, his
reasoning supports the
idea that robots, not
humans, should be
exploring space.*

vacuums and a radioactive environment. While some adventurers might prefer to remain in space forever, many of them expect to land gently back on Earth. All of these considerations are extremely challenging and not important for robotic missions.

9 Engineering spacecraft that satisfies human requirements is also very expensive. The International Space Station cost about $170 billion (all costs given in 2017 dollars), resulting only in a large facility locked in a low earth orbit. The storied Apollo missions included a **mere** six lunar landings, at an inflation-adjusted cost of $120 billion.

10 Possible manned missions to Mars are imagined to cost about $1 trillion, with the outcome being limited exploration of the Red Planet by about 2030 (with some estimates saying 2050). And a mission with that price tag would hamstring[2] the rest of the space program.

11 In contrast, robotic exploration of the solar system is far less costly. The Cassini mission to Saturn cost about $3.2 billion. The Mars Curiosity Rover cost about $2.5 billion. These and other missions have been wildly successful in teaching us about places where literally no one has gone before. Mars missions have explored ancient streams where knee-deep water once flowed and have found organic carbon[3] embedded in surface rocks.

12 In addition, there are methods for exploring the cosmos that don't require actually going to the place under study. The Hubble telescope has perhaps revealed more about the universe than any other scientific instrument, cost about $14 billion, including imaging the first galaxies formed, and played a key role in the discovery that the expansion of the universe is **accelerating**. And the wildly successful planet-hunting Kepler satellite weighs in at under $1 billion.

13 Manned programs can cost tens or hundreds of times more than the robotic missions.

14 But it's not just about the money. There are three important goals we need to achieve from our space program. The first is monitoring our own world, resulting in storm warnings and help in understanding our complex planet, which can best be done by tireless satellites orbiting the Earth. The second is to learn more about our solar system and the more distant universe. On this, the case is also clear: robotic exploration, through either space probes or telescopes, provides a much better yield for much lower money.

---

2. **hamstring** (verb) to foil or prevent an effort from succeeding
3. **organic carbon** carbon found in soil or other natural matter

15 The final goal is that of making humanity a multiplanetary species. By definition, this includes manned spaceflight, but the question is really how we should achieve that objective.

16 Developing human space-faring technology is **crucial**, but first we need to decide where to go. The moon is a dead planet and Mars is not nearly as welcoming as the New World was to the Spanish explorers. In fact, there is no place in our solar system where pioneers can simply drop seeds in the soil and wait for food to pop out of the ground. For that, we need to look at distant stars.

17 And interstellar exploration is also something in which robots will lead the way. Following the identification of a possibly habitable planet by the Kepler satellite or perhaps PLATO, a European Space Agency planet-hunting telescope scheduled to be launched in 2024, the next step would be a survey of the planetary system by an unmanned probe.

18 This might be patterned after billionaire investor Yuri Milner's Breakthrough Starshot, or some other approach. Here, expected advances in artificial intelligence will become crucial. A round-trip radio signal to Proxima Centauri, our nearest stellar neighbor, will take eight years.

19 And if we chose to explore the nearest sun-like star, the signal transit time is more like 24 years. With a multiyear time lag between messages, the interstellar probe will have to be able to execute independent judgment.

20 Only once a habitable planet is identified by these robotic approaches, will it be the time for a manned mission. With a welcoming destination beckoning to them, a team of intrepid men and women will leave the solar system and strike out for a new home. And, at that moment, *homo interstellaris*[4] will come of age.

Skill: Technical Language

Interstellar sounds like a term that is related to space. The previous sentence was about stars, and *inter-* means "between or among," so I think this part means "exploring among the stars." The term makes me think that this is an informative essay, meant to be authoritative.

4. *homo interstellaris* the projected human beings of future space exploration

First Read

Read "Machines, not people, should be exploring the stars for now." After you read, complete the Think Questions below.

1. Why does the author believe that robotic space exploration is better than manned space exploration for now? Provide two pieces of evidence from the text to support your answer.

2. What do humans need to travel in space that robots do not need? Provide examples from the text to support your answer.

3. According to the author, what are the three most important goals of the space program?

4. Use context clues to determine the meaning of **inhospitable** as it is used in paragraph 8 of "Machines, not people, should be exploring the stars for now." Write your definition here and identify clues that helped you figure out the meaning. Then check the meaning in a dictionary.

5. Find the word **mere** in paragraph 9 of "Machines, not people, should be exploring the stars for now." Use context clues in the surrounding sentences, as well as the sentence in which the word appears, to determine the word's meaning. Write your definition here and identify clues that helped you figure out its meaning.

Skill:
Technical Language

Use the Checklist to analyze Technical Language in "Machines, not people, should be exploring the stars for now." Refer to the sample student annotations about Technical Language in the text.

••• CHECKLIST FOR TECHNICAL LANGUAGE

In order to determine the meanings of words and phrases as they are used in a text, note the following:

- ✓ the subject of the book or article

- ✓ any unfamiliar words that you think might be technical terms

- ✓ words that have multiple meanings that change when used with a specific subject

- ✓ the possible contextual meaning of a word, or the definition from a dictionary

To determine the meanings of words and phrases as they are used in a text, including technical meanings, consider the following questions:

- ✓ What is the subject of the informational text?

- ✓ How does the use of technical language help establish the author as an authority on the subject?

- ✓ Are there any technical words that have an impact on the meaning and tone, or quality, of the book or article?

- ✓ Can you identify the contextual meaning of any of the words?

Skill:
Technical Language

Reread paragraphs 13–14 of "Machines, not people, should be exploring the stars for now." Then, using the Checklist on the previous page, answer the multiple-choice questions below.

⟳ YOUR TURN

1. This question has two parts. First, answer Part A. Then, answer Part B.

   Part A: Which sentence below contains multiple technical terms specific to space exploration?

   ○ A. There are three important goals we need to achieve.

   ○ B. The first is monitoring our own world, resulting in storm warnings and help in understanding our complex planet.

   ○ C. But it's not just about the money.

   ○ D. Robotic exploration, through either space probes or telescopes, provides a much better yield for much lower money.

   Part B: What is the effect of the technical terms in Part A?

   ○ A. It helps the tone sounds light and friendly.

   ○ B. It makes the author sound educated and believable.

   ○ C. It makes the author sound like he is trying too hard.

   ○ D. It makes the reader wonder if the author knows what he's talking about.

Skill: Greek and Latin Affixes and Roots

Use the Checklist to analyze Greek and Latin Affixes and Roots in "Machines, not people, should be exploring the stars for now." Refer to the sample student annotations about Greek and Latin Affixes and Roots in the text.

••• CHECKLIST FOR GREEK AND LATIN AFFIXES AND ROOTS

In order to identify Greek and Latin affixes and roots, note the following:

✓ the root

✓ the prefix and/or suffix

To use common, grade-appropriate Greek or Latin affixes and roots as clues to the meaning of a word, use the following questions as a guide:

✓ Can I identify the root of this word? Should I look in a dictionary or other resource?

✓ What is the meaning of the root?

✓ Can I identify the prefix and/or suffix of this word? Should I look in a dictionary or other resource?

✓ What is the meaning of the prefix and/or suffix?

✓ Does this suffix change the word's part of speech?

✓ How do the word parts work together to determine the word's meaning and part of speech?

Skill: Greek and Latin Affixes and Roots

Reread paragraph 12 from "Machines, not people, should be exploring the stars for now." Then, using the Checklist on the previous page as well as the dictionary entries below, answer the multiple-choice questions.

⟳ YOUR TURN

cosmos cos·mos \'koz-məs\ or \kos-mōs\
origin: from the Greek *kosmos* meaning "order, good order, orderly arrangement"

telescope tel·e·scope \'tel-ə-'skōp\
origin: from the Greek *tele-* meaning "far" + *skopos* meaning "watcher"

discovery dis·cov·er·y \dis 'kəv-ə-rē\
origin: from the Latin *dis-* meaning "opposite of" + *cooperire* meaning "to cover up" + *y*, a noun suffix

1. Based on its context and root, what is the most likely meaning of *cosmos*?

   ○ A. an orderly way of doing something
   ○ B. a good guess or approximation
   ○ C. a well-ordered universe
   ○ D. a mysterious and hard-to-reach place

2. Based on its context and root, what is the most likely meaning of *telescope*?

   ○ A. a device that lets you view objects at far distances
   ○ B. a very expensive scientific instrument
   ○ C. an invention that helps you track objects as they move
   ○ D. a gadget that reproduces images in a laboratory

3. Based on its context, suffix, and root, what is the most likely meaning of *discovery*?

   ○ A. in a new or unusual way
   ○ B. the process of hiding something
   ○ C. to become aware of something
   ○ D. the act of finding something

Skill:
Reasons and Evidence

Use the Checklist to analyze Reasons and Evidence in "Machines, not people, should be exploring the stars for now." Refer to the sample student annotations about Reasons and Evidence in the text.

••• CHECKLIST FOR REASONS AND EVIDENCE

In order to identify the reasons and evidence that support an author's claim(s) in an argument, note the following:

- ✓ the argument the author is making

- ✓ the claim or the main idea of the argument

- ✓ the reasons and evidence that support the claim and where they can be found

- ✓ if the evidence the author presents to support the claim is sound, or complete and comprehensive

- ✓ if there is sufficient evidence to support the claim or if more is needed

To assess whether the author's reasoning is sound and the evidence is relevant and sufficient, consider the following questions:

- ✓ What kind of argument is the author making?

- ✓ Is the reasoning, or the thinking behind the claims, sound and valid?

- ✓ Are the reasons and evidence the author presents to support the claim sufficient, or is more evidence needed? Why or why not?

Skill:
Reasons and Evidence

Reread paragraphs 11–12 of "Machines, not people, should be exploring the stars for now." Then, using the Checklist on the previous page, answer the multiple-choice questions below.

🔄 YOUR TURN

1. This question has two parts. First, answer Part A. Then, answer Part B.

   Part A: In paragraph 11, Lincoln claims that robotic space exploration is less expensive than manned space flight. How does he support this claim?

   ○ A. Expert opinions
   ○ B. Quotes
   ○ C. Numerical evidence
   ○ D. Statistics

   Part B: What piece of evidence best supports your answer to Part A?

   ○ A. The Cassini mission to Saturn cost about $3.2 billion. The Mars Curiosity Rover cost about $2.5 billion.

   ○ B. In contrast, robotic exploration of the solar system is far less costly.

   ○ C. Mars missions have explored ancient streams where knee-deep water once flowed and have found organic carbon embedded in surface rocks.

   ○ D. These and other missions have been wildly successful in teaching us about places where literally no one has gone before.

Close Read

Reread "Machines, not people, should be exploring the stars for now." As you reread, complete the Skills Focus questions below. Then use your answers and annotations from the questions to help you complete the Write activity.

◎ SKILLS FOCUS

1. Recall that an author's purpose is his or her reason for writing. Identify a detail that reveals the author's purpose, and explain how he works toward achieving that purpose.

2. Recall that an author uses claims to support his or her argument. Identify two or three claims Don Lincoln uses to support his argument that using robots is the best way to explore space.

3. The text deals with a scientific topic and uses the technical language associated with the field. Identify phrases with technical language, and write a note explaining the impact of that language.

4. Choose one claim that Lincoln uses to support his argument. Explain and assess whether Lincoln's evidence is relevant and sufficient to support the claim.

5. The author and people with an opposing opinion disagree about how to explore space, but they share the same dream. Identify details that tell what that dream is, and explain what makes the dream worth pursuing.

✏ WRITE

INFORMATIVE: Imagine that you are writing a flyer to gain support for America to invest in space technology and exploration. Which points from the article would you include in the flyer to persuade your readers? Write the text for this flyer, using information from the article and, if necessary, research other sources. Use technical language, and include a claim with reasons and evidence to show your audience your stance.

Responses to "Machines, not people, should be exploring the stars for now"

ARGUMENTATIVE TEXT
StudySync
2017

Introduction

n "Machines, not people, should be exploring the stars for now," American physicist Don Lincoln argues that it would be more beneficial to shift our focus to robotic space travel—for now, at least. He takes into consideration both costs and human versus robotic ability to withstand other environments. Although much of space exploration is currently focused on manned space travel, Lincoln concludes that robots should first find habitable planets before manned missions are undertaken. Following are six different reader responses that agree or disagree with the author's points.

"Why should we spend so much to take a risk we do not yet need to take?"

NOTES

Manned Space Exploration Makes Money Too

1   Your concerns about the costs of space exploration are valid. However, you miss an important benefit of these costs, Mr. Lincoln. You did not mention how often space exploration actually creates unexpected value for both the government and businesses. Meeting the challenge of sustaining fragile humans in inhospitable environments requires **innovation**. The Apollo program alone has led to many innovations. They include new athletic shoes, solar panels, heart monitors, pacemakers,[1] and cordless tools. Both the U.S. government and businesses have been able to patent and **generate revenue** from these inventions. These profits may not equal the billions the government must invest in a particular space program, but they are important investments in the country's **economy**.

Isabel Flores
San Jose, CA

A Practical Plan for Space Exploration

2   This plan for future space exploration seems very practical. Space exploration is costly. It makes sense to use a cheaper method for now. Robot missions can determine whether a planet is even worth exploring before committing more resources. Manned programs can cost tens or hundreds of times more than robotic ones. Using robots helps scientists use their resources more wisely. They can

Curiosity is an unmanned rover that was designed to explore Mars as part of NASA's Mars Science Laboratory mission. *Curiosity* was launched from Cape Canaveral on November 26, 2011, and landed on Mars on August 6, 2012.

---

1. **pacemakers** electrical devices placed close to the heart to regulate arrhythmia, or irregular heartbeats

carry out initial explorations of more places, increasing the chances of making an important discovery.

Joon Kim
Ridgefield, NJ

We Should be Brave and Fearless

3   Our country has a long tradition of exploration. The daring achievements of explorers have made the United States a powerful nation. But now America is losing its position at the top. In order to remain a global leader, a nation must be brave, fearless, and willing to take risks. That means America needs to continue to lead the way in space exploration with human astronauts. Men and women traveling into space commands respect and admiration, both nationally and internationally. Are we going to risk our position in the world because we are too cowardly to send humans into space? The only way for our country to advance is to proceed with bravery and fearlessness, and that means sending American men and women, not robots, to explore space.

Nora Jensen
Greenfield, IA

Space Exploration in Perspective

4   I think Mr. Lincoln is correct in **prioritizing** cheaper, unmanned space missions over manned space exploration. This is especially important for government programs like NASA. Limiting the cost of space exploration would allow the U.S. government to invest more money in programs with more urgent need. That money could be used to provide better services to veterans or create more affordable housing. Why should the government invest billions of dollars in a program with no real urgency? Why should we spend so much to take a risk we do not yet need to take? Space exploration is important. But our investment in the future should not be prioritized over addressing the real challenges we face today.

Sylvia Johnson
Washington, D.C.

NOTES

Inspiring Innovation

5 Mr. Lincoln forgets the symbolic importance of manned space programs. They drive innovation not just out of necessity, but also through inspiration. The Apollo missions encouraged many people to seek careers in the sciences. Some became astronauts. Others sought careers in related fields. The ability of humans to make progress in space exploration helps people believe in their own **potential**. Unmanned space exploration does not have the same symbolic effect.

This command capsule, built by North American Rockwell's Space Division for use in human-led space flight, was launched in October 1968 in NASA's first successful Apollo mission. Here, engineers and technicians check the capsule before its departure for Cape Kennedy.

Michael Williams
Houston, TX

Not Worth Dying For

6 Mr. Lincoln rightfully reminds us of the risks involved in sending humans to explore space. Every time we launch a spacecraft with astronauts aboard we put their lives in danger, and too many astronauts have died already. Space exploration is important, but protecting and preserving human life should always be the priority. Unmanned space exploration can complete tasks more efficiently and without the risk of losing human life. It is not only foolish and misguided but downright cruel to keep sending astronauts to their deaths. People in favor of sending humans into space—when we could more safely and effectively send robots instead—have no regard for human life.

Mark Scarborough
Weatherford, TX

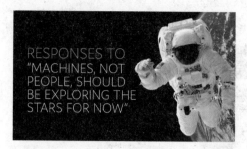

First Read

Read "Responses to 'Machines, not people, should be exploring the stars for now.'" After you read, complete the Think Questions below.

☁ THINK QUESTIONS

1. What is the most important idea of response 2? Provide specific examples from the text to support your answer.

2. Why does the author of response 4 agree that it would be better to use less costly robots in space exploration? What does she say the money saved could be used for instead? Cite two specific examples from the text.

3. What is the main reason Mark Scarborough agrees with Lincoln's article? Use textual evidence to support your answer.

4. Find the word **prioritizing** in response 4. Use context clues in the surrounding sentences, as well as the sentence in which the word appears, to determine the word's meaning. Write your definition here and identify clues that helped you figure out the meaning.

5. Use context clues to determine the meaning of the word **potential** as it is used in response 5. Write your own definition of *potential* and identify clues that helped you figure out the meaning. Then check a dictionary to confirm the definition.

Skill:
Compare and Contrast

Use the Checklist to analyze Compare and Contrast in "Responses to 'Machines, not people, should be exploring the stars for now.'" Refer to the sample student annotations about Compare and Contrast in the text.

••• CHECKLIST FOR COMPARE AND CONTRAST

In order to determine how two or more authors writing about the same topic shape their presentations of key information, use the following steps:

- ✓ First, choose two texts with similar subjects or topics by different authors.

- ✓ Next, identify each author's approach to the subject.

- ✓ After, identify the key information and evidence that each author includes.

- ✓ Then, explain the ways each author shapes his or her presentation of the information in the text.

- ✓ Finally, analyze the similarities and differences in how the authors present:

  - key information

  - evidence

  - their interpretation of facts

To analyze how two or more authors writing about the same topic shape their presentations of key information, consider the following questions:

- ✓ In what ways do the texts I have chosen have similar subjects or topics?

- ✓ How does each author approach the topic or subject?

- ✓ How does each author's presentation of key information differ? How are the presentations the same? How do these similarities and differences change the presentation and interpretation of the facts?

Please note that excerpts and passages in the StudySync® library and this workbook are intended as touchstones to generate interest in an author's work. The excerpts and passages do not substitute for the reading of entire texts, and StudySync® strongly recommends that students seek out and purchase the whole literary or informational work in order to experience it as the author intended. Links to online resellers are available in our digital library. In addition, complete works may be ordered through an authorized reseller by filling out and returning to StudySync® the order form enclosed in this workbook.

Reading & Writing
Companion

423

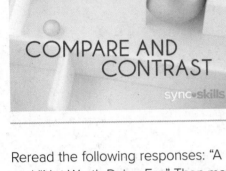

Skill:
Compare and Contrast

Reread the following responses: "A Practical Plan for Space Exploration," "Space Exploration in Perspective," and "Not Worth Dying For." Then match the summary to the appropriate text in the chart below.

↻ YOUR TURN

	Summary
A	Manned space travel is too dangerous, and sending robots helps keep people safe.
B	There are more important things for the government to spend money on than manned space travel.
C	Robotic space exploration is cheaper and more practical.

Common Argument: The bad aspects of manned space travel outweigh the good aspects.

"A Practical Plan for Space Exploration"	"Space Exploration in Perspective"	"Not Worth Dying For"

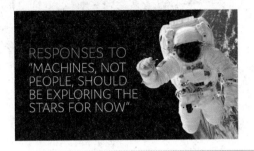

Close Read

Reread "Responses to 'Machines, not people, should be exploring the stars for now.'" As you reread, complete the Skills Focus questions below. Then use your answers and annotations from the questions to help you complete the Write activity.

◎ SKILLS FOCUS

1. Identify different types of evidence in the responses. Write a note explaining whether the evidence provides adequate support for the author's claim.

2. Which of the authors' claims are supported by sufficient evidence and sound reasons? Which are not supported? Highlight claims, and write a note about how the author supports his or her claims.

3. Compare and contrast the different authors' arguments. Identify pertinent examples and supporting evidence the authors use. Write a note explaining how the examples and evidence support their arguments and claims.

4. Choose two responses that you agree with. For each, identify a statement that indicates the author's purpose in writing a response. Then explain how the statement supports the author's purpose.

5. In the fifth response, identify details that show why the dream of human space exploration is worth pursuing. Then explain how these details develop the author's main argument.

✏ WRITE

DISCUSSION: In this informational text, a series of people respond to an argument about how America should invest its money in space exploration. Pretend you are a member of the Congressional budget committee, which helps decide how to spend America's money, and debate the issue with your classmates. Should the government spend money on manned missions to space, or should they focus on robotic missions? Discuss this question with a group of your peers. To prepare for your discussion, use a graphic organizer to write down your ideas about the prompt. Support your ideas with evidence from the text. You may also reference Don Lincoln's original essay. After your discussion, you will write a reflection.

Extended Writing Project and Grammar

EXTENDED WRITING PROJECT
ARGUMENTATIVE WRITING

Argumentative Writing Process: Plan

PLAN	DRAFT	REVISE	EDIT AND PUBLISH

In this unit, you have read and learned about people chasing dreams that seem impossible to them. Sometimes, that dream is a common one, like a college education. In other cases, the dream captures our imaginations and requires major planning to achieve, like space exploration. In all of those cases, the person pursuing that dream knew why it was worth pursuing and worked to gather the information he or she needed to pursue it.

WRITING PROMPT

What are your interests, goals, and dreams? What club, class, or activity would you add to your school to help you achieve these goals or dreams?

Your principal has announced an essay writing contest:

If you had the option of adding a club, a class, or an activity to your school, what would it be and why would it be worth including? Think about why you would like it added to your school's offerings. Why is this club, class, or activity important to the school? How would other students benefit from this addition? Write an argumentative essay to convince your teachers or school leaders to establish this new club, class, or activity. In your essay, present your argument, with clear reasons and relevant evidence. Be sure your essay includes the following:

- an introduction
- a thesis statement with claims
- coherent body paragraphs
- reasons and evidence
- a conclusion

Please note that excerpts and passages in the StudySync® library and this workbook are intended as touchstones to generate interest in an author's work. The excerpts and passages do not substitute for the reading of entire texts, and StudySync® strongly recommends that students seek out and purchase the whole literary or informational work in order to experience it as the author intended. Links to online resellers are available in our digital library. In addition, complete works may be ordered through an authorized reseller by filling out and returning to StudySync® the order form enclosed in this workbook.

Reading & Writing Companion

427

Introduction to Argumentative Writing

An argumentative essay is a form of persuasive writing where the writer makes a claim about a topic and then provides evidence—facts, details, examples, and quotations—to convince readers to accept and agree with the writer's claim. In order to provide convincing supporting evidence for an argumentative essay, the writer must often do outside research as well as cite the sources of the evidence that is presented in the essay.

The characteristics of argumentative writing include:

- introduction
- thesis statement with claims
- reasons and evidence
- transitions
- formal style
- conclusion

As you continue with this Extended Writing Project, you'll receive more instruction and practice in crafting each of the characteristics of argumentative writing to create your own argumentative essay.

Before you get started on your own essay, read this essay that one student, Cameron, wrote in response to the writing prompt. As you read the Model, highlight and annotate the features of argumentative writing that Cameron included in her essay.

≡ STUDENT MODEL

The Case for Makerspace

1   Have you ever built or created something on your own? How amazing would it have been to be able to do that in school! One way to do this is to build a makerspace at North End School. A makerspace is a place where students will be able to use technology to design, experiment, and invent through hands-on practice. Some might argue that we should add more athletic resources or art programs, but a makerspace is one of the only additions to our school that could be used by almost every class: science, math, art, and even English class! Overall, we should add a makerspace to North End School because it's a place to create and do experiments, it will help prepare students for the STEM jobs of the future, and it is a big opportunity for teachers too.

2   Makerspaces are inspiring places where people can learn to create and invent with confidence. Students will learn new skills, boost creativity, and build self-esteem by making things. For example, students can design everything from physics experiments to jewelry. A recent report from the New Media Consortium says, "Schools are turning to makerspaces to facilitate activities that inspire confidence in young learners." Having a makerspace for art or design will help students be confident and well-rounded. This is important because students will be happier and be able to achieve their dreams to be designers, artists, or engineers.

3   A makerspace at our school can help other students at North End pursue interests that can lead to great futures—something we all want. According to the U.S. Bureau of Labor Statistics, jobs in science, technology, engineering, and mathematics (STEM) are increasing by about 1 million from 2012 to 2022. Since the industry is experiencing a growth spurt, the time to act is now. A makerspace would give students an opportunity to learn about new technology with hands-on experience. Our 7th-grade class may have a number of future stars

NOTES

in new technology, but without a makerspace, we might not reach our potential. Imagine feeling like we left this class behind at a critical turning point. We need a makerspace to be ready for the jobs of the future.

4   In addition to preparing students for the future, North End teachers also think a makerspace would benefit the school and students right now. Because a makerspace can be used in many ways, teachers in multiple subjects could use a makerspace for special projects in science, art, and math, and they could also use it for an after-school club. Before last semester ended, interviews were conducted with several teachers at North End. The technology teacher, Mr. Smith, said that a makerspace would "provide students with the opportunity for a powerful experience to enhance their thinking." Ms. Bo, the 7th-grade science teacher, said that "the addition of a makerspace and its equipment would foster creativity, tinkering, and curiosity, which leads to better thinking and better questioning." This clearly shows that teachers think a makerspace would improve the quality of their classes and student thinking.

5   North End School would greatly benefit from a makerspace for three main reasons. Building a makerspace in our school would create a way for students to develop creative skills that would help them in their futures. It would give them a chance to explore new passions and industries. The goal of our studies at school is to help us reach our potential, and research in the fields of STEM and conversations with our own teachers show that the addition of a makerspace to our school would help make our school better.

✏ WRITE

Writers often take notes before they sit down to write. Think about what you've learned so far about argumentative writing to help you begin prewriting.

- What club, class, or activity would you like to add to your school?

- How would this club, class, or activity benefit other students? Why is it worthwhile? List a few reasons.

- Who is your audience and what message do you want to express to your audience?

Response Instructions

Use the questions in the bulleted list to write a one-paragraph summary. Your summary should explain what your essay will be about, including why it will be worthwhile. Don't worry about including all of the details now; focus only on the most essential and important elements in the bulleted list. You will refer back to this short paragraph as you continue through the steps of the writing process.

Please note that excerpts and passages in the StudySync® library and this workbook are intended as touchstones to generate interest in an author's work. The excerpts and passages do not substitute for the reading of entire texts, and StudySync® strongly recommends that students seek out and purchase the whole literary or informational work in order to experience it as the author intended. Links to online resellers are available in our digital library. In addition, complete works may be ordered through an authorized reseller by filling out and returning to StudySync® the order form enclosed in this workbook.

Reading & Writing Companion **431**

Skill:
Thesis Statement

••• CHECKLIST FOR THESIS STATEMENT

Before you begin writing your thesis statement, ask yourself the following questions:

- What is the prompt asking me to write about?

- What is the topic of my essay? How can I state it clearly for the reader?

- What claim(s) do I want to make about the topic of this essay? Is my opinion clear to my reader?

Here are some methods to introduce and develop your claim and topic clearly:

- Think about the topic and central idea of your essay.

  > Is the central idea of an argument stated?

  > Have you identified as many claims as you intend to prove?

- Write a clear statement about the central idea or claim(s). Your thesis statement should:

  > let the reader anticipate the body of your essay

  > respond completely to the prompt

⟳ YOUR TURN

Read the following notes made by Cameron's classmate while he was drafting his thesis statement. Then, complete the chart by writing the corresponding letter for each note in the correct place in the outline.

	Note Options
A	We currently have more students who would like to participate in team sports than the number of teams we have.
B	Establish a pickleball club at North End School.
C	One way to improve North End School is to establish a pickleball club because we currently have more students than teams and pickleball is a growing sport that would be a great addition to school.
D	Pickleball is a growing sport that would be a great addition to student life at our school.

Outline	Note
School Addition:	
Claim 1:	
Claim 2:	
Thesis Statement:	

✎ WRITE

Follow the steps in the checklist section to draft a thesis statement for your argumentative essay.

Skill: Organizing Argumentative Writing

••• CHECKLIST FOR ORGANIZING ARGUMENTATIVE WRITING

As you consider how to organize your writing for your argumentative essay, use the following questions as a guide:

- What is my position on this topic?

- Have I chosen the best organizational structure to present my information logically?

- Can my claim be supported by logical reasoning and relevant evidence?

- Do I have enough evidence to support my claim or thesis?

- How can I organize the reasons and evidence clearly?

- How can I clarify the relationships between my claims and reasons?

Follow these steps to plan out the organization of your argumentative essay, including organizing your reasons and evidence logically:

- Identify and write your thesis.

- Choose an organizational structure that will present your claims logically and clearly.

- Identify reasons and evidence that support each claim.

- Organize your ideas using an outline or graphic organizer.

⟳ YOUR TURN

Imagine a student is just beginning her outline to argue for the addition of a photography studio to her school. Read the statements below. Then, complete the chart by writing the corresponding letter for each statement in the correct place in the outline.

	Statement Options
A	The first reason is that art students would be able to get more practice in the medium of photography.
B	In conclusion, adding a photography studio would improve our school because more students would practice photography, learn about photojournalism, and participate in clubs.
C	A photography studio would be an amazing addition to the art program at North End School because more students would practice photography, learn about photojournalism, and join after-school clubs.
D	The third reason for a photography studio is that it would get more students involved through after-school clubs.
E	Journalism students would be able to learn more about photojournalism.

Outline	Statement
Thesis Statement:	
Claim 1:	
Claim 2:	
Claim 3:	
Repeat Thesis Statement:	

YOUR TURN

Complete the chart below by writing a short summary of what you will focus on in each paragraph of your essay.

Outline	Statement
Thesis Statement:	
Claim 1:	
Claim 2:	
Claim 3:	
Repeat Thesis Statement:	

Skill: Reasons and Relevant Evidence

As you begin to determine what reasons and relevant evidence will support your claim(s), use the following questions as a guide:

*   What is the claim (or claims) that I am making in my argument?

*   What textual evidence am I using to support this claim? Is it relevant?

*   Am I quoting the source accurately?

*   Does my evidence display logical reasoning and relate to the claim I am making?

*   How can I demonstrate my understanding of the topic or source material?

Use the following steps as a guide to help you determine how you will support your claim(s) with logical reasoning and relevant, sufficient evidence, using accurate and credible sources:

*   Identify the claim(s) you will make in your argument.

*   Select sufficient evidence from credible sources that will convince others to accept your claim(s).

*   Explain the connection between your claim(s) and the evidence and ensure your reasoning is logical, develops naturally from the evidence, and supports your claim.

Please note that excerpts and passages in the StudySync® library and this workbook are intended as touchstones to generate interest in an author's work. The excerpts and passages do not substitute for the reading of entire texts, and StudySync® strongly recommends that students seek out and purchase the whole literary or informational work in order to experience it as the author intended. Links to online resellers are available in our digital library. In addition, complete works may be ordered through an authorized reseller by filling out and returning to StudySync® the order form enclosed in this workbook.

Reading & Writing
Companion

437

⟳ YOUR TURN

Read each claim in the chart below. Then, complete the chart by matching the evidence with the claim it best supports and explaining how the evidence sufficiently supports that claim. The first row has been done for you.

Evidence Options	
A	Statistics show that cell phone use while driving causes 1.6 million crashes each year, and nearly one out of every four accidents is caused by texting and driving.
B	Surveys show that 65% of cell phone owners say that their phones have made it a lot easier to stay in touch with the people they care about.
C	Since 1970, the number of fast food restaurants in business has doubled. At the same time, the percentage of the U.S. population suffering from obesity has increased from about 15% to nearly 40% of the population.
D	Less than 5% of adults participate in at least 30 minutes of physical activity every day, and only one in three receive the recommended amount of physical activity each week.

Claim	Evidence	Reasoning
Fast food is contributing to the obesity epidemic.	C	This supports the idea that as the number of fast food restaurants has increased, so has the obesity level.
Americans are also unhealthy because they do not exercise enough.		
Texting while driving is unsafe.		
Cell phones have made positive impacts on our lives.		

Reading & Writing Companion

↻ YOUR TURN

List three claims from your essay. Then, complete the chart by writing a piece of evidence that supports each of your claims and explain how this evidence sufficiently supports the claim.

Claim	Evidence	Reasoning
Claim 1:		
Claim 2:		
Claim 3:		

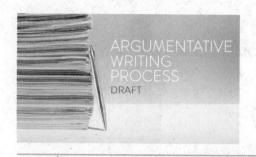

Argumentative Writing Process: Draft

PLAN	DRAFT	REVISE	EDIT AND PUBLISH

You have already made progress toward writing your essay. Now it is time to draft your argumentative essay.

✏ WRITE

Use your plan and other responses in your Binder to draft your essay. You may also have new ideas as you begin drafting. Feel free to explore those new ideas as you have them. You can also ask yourself these questions:

- Have I written my thesis statement clearly?

- Is my textual evidence relevant and necessary?

- Does the organizational structure make sense?

Before you submit your draft, read it over carefully. You want to be sure that you've responded to all aspects of the prompt.

Here is Cameron's essay draft. As you read, identify relevant textual evidence that develops the thesis statement and claims. As Cameron continues to revise and edit her essay, she will find and improve weak spots in her writing, as well as correct any language or punctuation mistakes.

☰ STUDENT MODEL: FIRST DRAFT

The Case for Makerspace

~~I believe our school would benefit from a makerspace. Makerspaces are hubs of activity where people can do many things using a range of technology. We should add a makerspace to North End School because it's a place to create and do experiments, it will help prepare students for jobs in science, and it is a big opportunity for teachers too.~~

Have you ever built or created something on your own? How amazing would it have been to be able to do that in school! One way to do this is to build a makerspace at North End School. A makerspace is a place where students will be able to use technology to design, experiment, and invent through hands-on practice. Some might argue that we should add more athletic resources or art programs, but a makerspace is one of the only additions to our school that could be used by almost every class: science, math, art, and even English class! Overall, we should add a makerspace to North End School because it's a place to create and do experiments, it will help prepare students for the STEM jobs of the future, and it is a big opportunity for teachers too.

~~Makerspaces are a place to create and do experiments. Students will learn new skills, boost creativity, and self-esteem by making things. Students can design everything from physics experiments to jewelry. A recent report from the New Media Consortium says, "Schools are turning to makerspaces to facilitate activities that inspire confidence in young learners." Having a makerspace for art or design will help students be confident and well-rounded. Students will be happier and be able to achieve dreams to be designers, artists, or engineers.~~

Makerspaces are inspiring places where people can learn to create and invent with confidence. Students will learn new skills, boost

Skill:
Introductions

Cameron revised her introductory paragraph. She added a question and a follow-up sentence to hook her reader's attention. Then she acknowledged opposing claims and used them to strengthen her argument.

Please note that excerpts and passages in the StudySync® library and this workbook are intended as touchstones to generate interest in an author's work. The excerpts and passages do not substitute for the reading of entire texts, and StudySync® strongly recommends that students seek out and purchase the whole literary or informational work in order to experience it as the author intended. Links to online resellers are available in our digital library. In addition, complete works may be ordered through an authorized reseller by filling out and returning to StudySync® the order form enclosed in this workbook.

Reading & Writing Companion   441

**Skill:
Transitions**

Cameron decides to add a stronger topic sentence that will help her connect her paragraph to the rest of the essay. She also realizes that there was a sudden jump in her ideas, especially when she began talking about student dreams. She decides to revise the paragraph to create cohesion between it and the rest of her essay.

**Skill:
Style**

Cameron revised this paragraph of her essay so that she established a formal academic tone. She changed instances of the first person (*I* and *we*) to third-person pronouns. Cameron noticed that her tone was very conversational in her draft, so she revised it to be more formal and used her teachers' names and titles to help persuade her readers.

creativity, and build self-esteem by making things. For example, students can design everything from physics experiments to jewelry. A recent report from the New Media Consortium says, "Schools are turning to makerspaces to facilitate activities that inspire confidence in young learners." Having a makerspace for art or design will help students be confident and well-rounded. This is important because students will be happier and be able to achieve their dreams to be designers, artists, or engineers.

A makerspace at our school can help other students at North End follow interests that can lead to great futures—something we all want. According to the U.S. Bureau of Labor Statistics, jobs in science, technology, engineering, and mathematics (STEM) are increasing by about 1 million from 2012 to 2022. Since the industry is experiencing a growth spurt, the time to act is now. A makerspace would give students an opportunity to learn about new technology with hands-on experience. Our 7th-grade class may have a number of future stars in new technology, but without a makerspace, we might not reach our potential. Imagine feeling like we left this class behind at a critical turning point. We need a makerspace to be ready for the jobs of the future.

~~I think that lots of teachers at North End agree with me. As a school community, we should make sure our students get the very best. Mr. Smith and some other teachers all did interviews that they all think it's a great idea. The tech and 7th-grade scince teacher think the makerspace and its equippment would help students and their thinking. I bet we could even use it for an after school club!~~

In addition to preparing students for the future, North End teachers also think a makerspace would benefit the school and students right now. Because a makerspace can be used in many ways, teachers in multiple subjects could use a makerspace for special projects in science, art, and math, and they could also use it for an after-school club. Before last semester ended, interviews were conducted with several teachers at North End. The technology teacher, Mr. Smith, said that a makerspace would "provide students with the opportunity for a powerful experience to enhance their thinking." Ms. Bo, the 7th-grade science teacher, said that "the addition of a makerspace and its equipment would foster creativity, tinkering, and curiosity, which leads to better thinking and better questioning." This clearly shows that teachers think a makerspace would improve the quality of their classes and student thinking.

~~A makerspace is the best addition for our school. It would help students in lots of different ways and make our school better.~~

North End School would greatly benefit from a makerspace for three main reasons. Building a makerspace in our school would create a way for students to develop creative skills that would help them in their futures. It would give them a chance to explore new passions and industries. The goal of our studies at school is to help us reach our potential, and research in the fields of STEM and conversations with our own teachers show that the addition of a makerspace to our school would help make our school better.

Skill:
Conclusions

Cameron made her conclusion stronger by restating her thesis at the beginning of the paragraph and then briefly reviewing the claims and some of the evidence that supported them. She ended with a memorable comment, connecting her argument about a makerspace to the bigger goals of education and how a makerspace would help achieve those goals.

Please note that excerpts and passages in the StudySync® library and this workbook are intended as touchstones to generate interest in an author's work. The excerpts and passages do not substitute for the reading of entire texts, and StudySync® strongly recommends that students seek out and purchase the whole literary or informational work in order to experience it as the author intended. Links to online resellers are available in our digital library. In addition, complete works may be ordered through an authorized reseller by filling out and returning to StudySync® the order form enclosed in this workbook.

Reading & Writing Companion   **443**

Skill:
Introductions

••• CHECKLIST FOR INTRODUCTIONS

Before you write your introduction, ask yourself the following questions:

- How will I "hook" my reader's interest? You might:

  > start with an attention-grabbing statement

  > begin with an intriguing question

- Have I introduced my topic clearly?

- What is my argument and claim(s)? Have I recognized opposing claims that disagree with mine or use a different perspective? How can I use them to strengthen my own?

- Where should I place my thesis statement? You might:

  > put your thesis statement at the end of your introduction to help readers preview your body paragraphs

Below are two strategies to help you introduce your claim and topic clearly in an introduction:

- Peer Discussion

  > Talk about your topic with a partner, explaining what you already know and your ideas about your topic.

  > Write notes about the ideas you have discussed and any new questions you may have.

- Freewriting

  > Freewrite for ten minutes about your topic. Don't worry about grammar, punctuation, or having fully formed ideas. The point of freewriting is to discover ideas.

  > Review your notes and think about what your claim or controlling idea will be.

↻ YOUR TURN

Read the sentences below, taken from the introduction Cameron's friend wrote. Then, complete the chart by placing each sentence in its correct place in the introduction outline.

	Sentence Options
A	Some might argue that our school should focus on adding more academic programs; however, dance can help students who are struggling find an outlet and express themselves positively.
B	One way to improve North End School would be to add a dance club.
C	Don't you think that school should encourage students to follow their dreams and passions?
D	Adding a dance club to North End School would be beneficial for many different kinds of students and is the best thing that we can add to our school.

Introduction Outline	Sentence
Hook	
Introduce the topic & argument	
Recognize opposing claims	
Thesis statement	

✎ WRITE

Use the steps in the checklist section to revise the introduction of your argumentative essay.

Skill:
Transitions

••• CHECKLIST FOR TRANSITIONS

Before you revise your current draft to include transitions, think about:

- the key ideas you discuss in your body paragraphs

- how your paragraphs connect together to support your claim(s)

- the relationships among your claim(s), reasons, and evidence

Next, reread your current draft and note areas in your essay where:

- the relationships between your claim(s) and the reasons and evidence are unclear, identifying places where you could add linking words or other transitional devices to make your argument more cohesive. Look for:

  > sudden jumps in your ideas

  > breaks between paragraphs where the ideas in the next paragraph are not logically following from the previous one

Revise your draft to use words, phrases, and clauses to create cohesion and clarify the relationships among claim(s) and reasons, using the following questions as a guide:

  > Are there unifying relationships between the claims, reasons, and evidence I present in my argument?

  > Have I clarified, or made clear, these relationships?

↻ YOUR TURN

Choose the best answer to each question.

1. Below is a section from a previous draft of Cameron's essay. Cameron has not used an effective transition in the underlined sentence. Which of the following could she add to the underlined sentence?

> This is important because many students have dreams to be designers, artists, and engineers. <u>I have dreams of becoming a shoe designer or an engineer one day.</u>

- ○ A. Similarly,
- ○ B. For example,
- ○ C. Equally important,
- ○ D. However,

2. The following section is from an earlier draft of Cameron's essay. She would like to add a sentence to bring this paragraph to a close more effectively. Which sentence could she add after sentence 4 to achieve this goal?

> (1) A makerspace at our school can help other students at North End pursue interests that can lead to great futures—something we all want. (2) According to the U.S. Bureau of Labor Statistics, jobs in STEM are increasing by about 1 million from 2012 to 2022. (3) The time to act is now. (4) Our 7th-grade class may have a number of future stars in new technology, but without a makerspace, we might not reach our potential.

- ○ A. It would help us grow our art and technology programs.
- ○ B. A survey of students indicated that a makerspace is one of the most popular additions.
- ○ C. In conclusion, by adding one, we may help students here live up to their full potential.
- ○ D. For example, including a makerspace might help more students become interested in science and technology.

⟳ YOUR TURN

Complete the chart by writing a transitional sentence that connects ideas and creates cohesion between paragraphs in your essay.

Purpose	Example	Your Transitional Sentence
add information	**In addition,** it is important to remember athletic programs help students develop social and leadership skills.	
discuss a contradiction	**Even though** another art or music program would be nice, creating more athletic programming for our girls is necessary for things to be equal.	
introduce examples	**For example,** the math and science scores at West Side High School increased by 34% when additional art and music programs were added.	
show time sequence	**At the present time,** there are two teachers who already support this addition.	
summarize	**In summary,** I believe that a new technology club would be the best addition to our school.	

Skill:
Style

First, reread the draft of your argumentative essay and identify the following:

- places where you use slang, contractions, abbreviations, and a conversational tone

- areas where you could use subject-specific or academic language in order to help persuade or inform your readers

- moments where you use the first person (*I*) or second person (*you*)

- areas where your sentence structure lacks variety

- incorrect uses of the conventions of standard English for grammar, spelling, capitalization, and punctuation

Establish and maintain a formal style in your essay, using the following questions as a guide:

- Have I avoided slang in favor of academic language?

- Did I consistently use a third-person point of view, using third-person pronouns (*he, she, they*)?

- Have I varied my sentence structure and the length of my sentences? Ask yourself these specific questions:

  > Where should I make some sentences longer by using conjunctions to connect independent clauses, dependent clauses, and phrases?

  > Where should I make some sentences shorter by separating any independent clauses?

- Did I follow the conventions of standard English, including:

  > grammar?

  > spelling?

  > capitalization?

  > punctuation?

YOUR TURN

Read the sentences showing an informal and formal style below. Then, complete the chart by writing the informal language option that correctly describes each type of informal language that was revised to a formal style.

	Informal Language Options
A	Conversational Tone
B	Contractions
C	First Person
D	Slang

Informal Style	Type of Informal Language	Revised to a Formal Style
They didn't realize how important it was.		They did not realize how important it was.
I think it is important to add a library to our school.		It is important to add a library to North End School.
She quickly got herself together when her mom got there.		She quickly adjusted her behavior when her mom arrived.
Just about everyone thinks that a new band room is the best.		Most of the students surveyed agree that adding a band room would be beneficial.

↻ YOUR TURN

Identify sentences in your essay that are written with informal language. Then, complete the chart by revising the sentences in a more formal style.

Type of Informal Language	Revision
Contractions	
First Person	
Slang	
Conversational Tone	
Abbreviations	

Skill:
Conclusions

Before you write your conclusion, ask yourself the following questions:

- How can I restate the thesis statement in a different way? What impression can I make on my reader?

- How can I write my conclusion so that it supports and follows logically from my argument? Have I left out any important information?

- Should I include a call to action or memorable comment?

Below are two strategies to help you provide a concluding statement or section that follows from and supports the argument presented:

- Peer Discussion

  > After you have written your introduction and body paragraphs, talk with a partner and tell him or her what you want readers to remember, writing notes about your discussion.

  > Review your notes and think about what you wish to express in your conclusion.

- Freewriting

  > Freewrite for ten minutes about what you might include in your conclusion. Don't worry about grammar, punctuation, or having fully formed ideas. The point of freewriting is to discover ideas.

  > Review your notes and think about what you wish to express in your conclusion.

↻ YOUR TURN

Read the sentences below, taken from the conclusion Cameron's friend wrote. Then, complete the chart by placing each sentence in its correct place in the conclusion outline.

	Sentence Options
A	Adding a photography lab to North End School could change the lives of students. This is a powerful opportunity for our school!
B	Creating a photography lab would help North End build a stronger art program and expose students to a new art medium; research shows that strong art programs correlate to stronger academic scores. A photo lab would also improve our school newspaper and inspire students who are interested in advertising and journalism.
C	Adding a photography lab to North End School would be beneficial.

Conclusion Outline	Sentence
Restate thesis in a different way	
Review and explain your claims	
Call to action or memorable comment	

✏ WRITE

Use the steps in the checklist section to revise the conclusion of your argumentative essay.

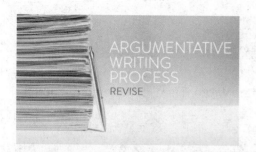

Argumentative Writing Process: Revise

PLAN	DRAFT	REVISE	EDIT AND PUBLISH

You have written a draft of your argumentative essay. You have also received input from your peers about how to improve it. Now you are going to revise your draft.

⬅ REVISION GUIDE

Examine your draft to find areas for revision. Keep in mind your purpose and audience as you revise for clarity, development, organization, and style. Use the guide below to help you review:

Review	Revise	Example
Clarity		
Review your thesis statement in your introduction. Identify any places where it can be clearer or more specific.	Use clear and specific language in your thesis statement to preview what your essay will be about. Think about the research you did and consider using academic or formal language.	Overall, we should add a makerspace to North End School because it's a place to create and do experiments, it will help prepare students for ~~jobs in science~~ the STEM jobs of the future, and it is a big opportunity for teachers too.
Development		
Review the development of your claim in the body paragraphs. Identify statements that lack supporting reasons or evidence.	Check off each claim that is supported by reasons and evidence. Add in additional reasons or evidence to statements that need support.	~~The tech and 7th-grade scince teacher think the makerspace and its equippment would help students and their thinking.~~ The technology teacher, Mr. Smith, said that a makerspace would "provide students with the opportunity for a powerful experience to enhance their thinking."

 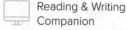

Review	Revise	Example
Organization		
Find places where transitions would improve your essay. Review your body paragraphs to identify and annotate any sentences that don't flow in a clear and logical way.	Rewrite the sentences so they appear in a logical sequence, starting with a clear transition or topic sentence. Delete details that are repetitive or not essential to support the thesis.	~~I think that lots of teachers at North End agree with me. As a school community, we should make sure our students get the very best.~~ In addition to preparing students for the future, North End teachers also think a makerspace would benefit the school and students right now.
Style: Word Choice		
Identify sentences that use informal language. Look for everyday words and phrases that can be replaced with more formal or academic language.	Replace everyday informal language with more formal academic language.	A makerspace at our school can help other students at North End ~~follow~~ pursue interests that can lead to great futures—something we all want.
Style: Sentence Variety		
Read your essay aloud. Annotate places where you have too many long or short sentences in a row.	Rewrite sentences by making them longer or shorter for clarity of emphasis.	Building a makerspace in our school would create a way for students to develop creative skills that would help them in their futures. It would ~~and~~ give them a chance to explore new passions and industries.

✏️ WRITE

Use the guide above, as well as your peer reviews, to help you evaluate your argumentative essay to determine areas that should be revised.

Grammar:
Adverb Clauses

Adverb clauses are subordinate clauses that often modify the verb in the main clause of a complex sentence. The can also modify an adjective or adverb.

Adverb clauses tell *when, where, how, why*, or *under what conditions* the action in the main clause occurs.

Adverb clauses begin with subordinating conjunctions.

Common Subordinating Conjunctions				
after although as because	before if since so that	than though unless until	when whenever where whereas	wherever while

Follow these rules when using adverb clauses:

Rule	Text
Use a comma after an introductory adverb clause.	**If you have ever seen a dragon in a pinch,** you will realize that this was only poetical exaggeration applied to any hobbit, even to Old Took's great-granduncle Bullroarer, who was so huge (for a hobbit) that he could ride a horse. The Hobbit
A comma is usually not necessary before an adverb clause that ends a sentence.	"I saw somebody working on it **when we came up this morning.**" The King of Mazy May

⟳ YOUR TURN

1. How should this sentence be changed?

> Everybody ate dessert after they finished eating the main course.

- ○ A. Insert a comma after the word **dessert**.
- ○ B. Insert a comma after the word **eating**.
- ○ C. Insert a comma after the words **dessert** and **eating**.
- ○ D. No change needs to be made to this sentence.

2. How should this sentence be changed?

> Since it was just painted, do not lean against the wall.

- ○ A. Delete the comma after the word **painted**.
- ○ B. Insert a comma after the word **lean**.
- ○ C. Delete the comma after the word **painted** and insert a comma after the word **since**.
- ○ D. No change needs to be made to this sentence.

3. How should this sentence be changed?

> Whenever I walk to school my cat follows me down the street.

- ○ A. Insert a comma after the word **walk**.
- ○ B. Insert a comma after the word **school**.
- ○ C. Insert a comma after the word **me**.
- ○ D. No change needs to be made to this sentence.

Please note that excerpts and passages in the StudySync® library and this workbook are intended as touchstones to generate interest in an author's work. The excerpts and passages do not substitute for the reading of entire texts, and StudySync® strongly recommends that students seek out and purchase the whole literary or informational work in order to experience it as the author intended. Links to online resellers are available in our digital library. In addition, complete works may be ordered through an authorized reseller by filling out and returning to StudySync® the order form enclosed in this workbook.

Reading & Writing Companion   **457**

Grammar: Compound-Complex Sentences

A compound-complex sentence has two or more main clauses and one or more subordinate clauses. It is a combination of a compound sentence and a complex sentence.

A compound sentence has two main clauses. They can be joined by a semicolon or a comma followed by a coordinating conjunction such as *or, and*, or *but*.

A complex sentence has one main clause and one or more subordinate clauses. The main clause and subordinate clause are usually joined with a subordinating conjunction, such as *when, because, before*, or *after*.

Compound-Complex Sentence
The guards had clubs, and they had carbines, too, which they turned around and used as weapons.
The Other Side of the Sky

Main Clause 1	Main Clause 2	Subordinate Clause
The guards had clubs	they had carbines, too	which they turned around and used as weapons.

Subordinating Conjunction	Coordinating Conjunction
which	and

⟳ YOUR TURN

1. How should this sentence be changed so that it becomes a compound-complex sentence?

> You should drain the grease frequently; too much grease is unhealthy.

- ○ A. Add *when you cook ground beef* after **frequently**.
- ○ B. Replace the semicolon with a comma and the conjunction *and*.
- ○ C. Replace the semicolon with a period and remove **too much grease is unhealthy**.
- ○ D. No change needs to be made to this sentence.

2. How should this sentence be changed so that it becomes a compound-complex sentence?

> We enjoy going to our favorite Mexican restaurant when there is a special deal for groups of six or more, but sometimes we must wait in line for over an hour.

- ○ A. Delete the comma.
- ○ B. Replace the comma and conjunction **but** with a semicolon.
- ○ C. Remove **for over an hour**.
- ○ D. No change needs to be made to this sentence.

3. How should this sentence be changed so that it becomes a compound-complex sentence?

> Whether it is summer or winter, the weather often goes below freezing here.

- ○ A. Replace **whether** with *when*.
- ○ B. Add a semicolon after **here** and add *you will need to buy a warmer coat*.
- ○ C. Remove **whether it is summer or winter**.
- ○ D. No change needs to be made to this sentence.

4. How should this sentence be changed so that it becomes a compound-complex sentence?

> Roses and tulips grow and bloom in the garden.

- ○ A. Add *when it's spring* after **garden**.
- ○ B. Add *when it's spring* before **roses** and add a semicolon after **garden** followed by *I plant them in the fall*.
- ○ C. Add a semicolon after **garden** and then add *I plant them in the fall*.
- ○ D. No change needs to be made to this sentence.

Grammar: Basic Spelling Rules II

Doubled Consonants

Spelling Conventions	Correct Spelling	Incorrect Spelling
Before adding -*ed* or a suffix: When a one-syllable word ends in one consonant following one vowel, double the final consonant.	slap + -*ed* = slapped jog + -*er* = jogger	slaped joger
Double the final consonant if the last syllable of the word is accented and the accent stays there after the suffix is added.	omit + -*ed* = omitted occur + -*ence* = occurrence infer + -*ing* = inferring	omited occurence infering
Before adding -*ly* to a double *l*: When adding -*ly* to a word that ends in *ll*, drop one *l*.	full + -*ly* = fully chill + -*ly* = chilly	fullly chilly

Compound Words

Spelling Conventions	Original Words	Compound Words
When forming compound words, maintain all original spellings.	snow + storm broad + cast	snowstorm broadcast

Spelling -*cede*, -*ceed*, and -*sede*

Spelling Conventions	Correct Spelling	Incorrect Spelling
The only English word ending in -*sede* is *supersede*.	supersede	superceed
Three words end in -*ceed*: *proceed, exceed*, and *succeed*.	proceed exceed succeed	procede exsede succede
All other words ending with the "seed" sound are spelled with -*cede*.	precede recede secede	preceed receed sesede

⟳ YOUR TURN

1. How should the spelling error in this sentence be corrected?

    > The ground was littered on the 5th of July because no one had disposed of their wrapers after the fireworks.

    ○ A. Change **wrapers** to **wrappers and firworks to fireworks**.
    ○ B. Change **wrapers** to **wrappers**.
    ○ C. Change **firworks** to **fireworks**.
    ○ D. No change needs to be made to this sentence.

2. How should the spelling error in this sentence be corrected?

    > This year's ticket sales far excede those for previous years because the community is fully committed to saving the theater program.

    ○ A. Change **excede** to **exceed**.
    ○ B. Change **fully** to **fullly**.
    ○ C. Change **committed** to **commited**.
    ○ D. No change needs to be made to this sentence.

3. How should the spelling error in this sentence be corrected?

    > He finally admitted that the evidence was not compeling enough to make an airtight case.

    ○ A. Change **admitted** to **admited**.
    ○ B. Change **compeling** to **compelling**.
    ○ C. Change **airtight** to **air-tight**.
    ○ D. No change needs to be made to this sentence.

4. How should the spelling error in this sentence be corrected?

    > She often remembered her grandfather's story fondly, and proceeded to share it with her own granddaughters when they were old enough.

    ○ A. Change **grandfather's** to **grand father's**.
    ○ B. Change **proceeded** to **proceded**.
    ○ C. Change **granddaughters** to **grandaughters**.
    ○ D. No change needs to be made to this sentence.

Argumentative Writing Process: Edit and Publish

PLAN	DRAFT	REVISE	EDIT AND PUBLISH

You have revised your argumentative essay based on your peer feedback and your own examination.

Now, it is time to edit your essay. When you revised, you focused on the content of your essay. You probably looked at the thesis statement, reasons and relevant evidence, introduction, and conclusion. When you edit, you should focus on grammar and punctuation.

Use the checklist below to guide you as you edit:

☐ Have I used adverb clauses correctly?

☐ Have I used compound-complex sentences correctly?

☐ Do I have any sentence fragments or run-on sentences?

☐ Have I spelled everything correctly?

Notice some edits Cameron has made:

- Created a compound-complex sentence by adding a subordinate clause and a coordinating conjunction.

- Used an adverb clause to tell when.

- Fixed spelling errors.

In addition to preparing students for the future, North End teachers also think a makerspace would benefit the school and students right now. Because a makerspace can be used in many ways, teachers ~~Teachers~~ in multiple subjects could use a makerspace for special projects in science, art, and math. ~~They~~, and they could also use it for an ~~after school~~ after-school club. Before last semester ended, interviews ~~Interviews~~ were conducted with several teachers at North End. The technology teacher, Mr. Smith, said that a makerspace would "provide students with the opportunity for a powerful experience to enhance their thinking." Ms. Bo, the 7th-grade ~~scince~~ science teacher, said that "the addition of a makerspace and its ~~equippment~~ equipment would foster creativity, tinkering, and curiosity, which leads to better thinking and better questioning." This clearly shows that teachers think a makerspace would improve the quality of their classes and student thinking.

✏ WRITE

Use the questions on the previous page, as well as your peer reviews, to help you evaluate your argumentative essay to determine areas that need editing. Then edit your essay to correct those errors.

Once you have made all your corrections, you are ready to publish your work. You can distribute your writing to family and friends, hang it on a bulletin board, or post it on your blog. If you publish online, share the link with your family, friends, and classmates.

Taking A Stand

INFORMATIONAL TEXT

Introduction

Bullying is a widespread problem, and it can happen anywhere—in school, during activities, or online. This article, "Taking a Stand," details seventh-grader Isabella Petrini's decision to speak out against bullying. Once a bully herself, Petrini started an anti-bullying program at her school. Through it she convinced many others to stop being mean and start trying to understand

VOCABULARY

bullying
using strength or power to get what you want or to make someone feel bad

platform
type of computer hardware or software; operating system

aggressive
prepared and eager to fight or disagree

pledge
written promise

digital
using electronic or computer technology

☰ READ

NOTES

1　Imagine a bad day at school. Maybe you got to class and heard muffled giggling. Maybe you heard buzzing whispers in the hall. Maybe later at home you wept blinding tears.

2　Students often worry about studying and sports at school. But for many students, something is more worrisome: **bullying**. Bullying is "unwanted or **aggressive** behavior." It can happen face to face. Or it can happen through **digital platforms** such as texting and social media.

3　In 2014, almost 30 percent of students said they'd been bullied. Many don't report the bullying. More than 60 percent stay silent. They endure the sickening fear of being bullied. They feel as though no one can help.

4　Bullying has costs. Bullied students are more likely to have health problems like depression and anxiety. They are more likely to struggle in school. Some become bullies themselves.

5   Isabella Petrini knows about bullying. In fifth grade, she was a bully. She and her friends said mean things about others. But in seventh grade, Petrini saw bullying differently. She realized that these comments weren't jokes. They were biting and hurtful. They had the potential to harm others.

6   When Petrini saw the television program *If You Really Knew Me*, she had an idea. On the program, real-life high school students come together and talk about bullying. The goal is to help stop bullying by helping people understand one another.

7   The program turned Petrini into an activist. She wanted to begin an anti-bullying initiative at her school. She and her friends agreed that school could be a better place. People needed to accept one another instead of making stinging insults or passing silent judgment.

8   The girls made a plan. They shared it with the principal. He supported their idea. They organized a school assembly. Petrini showed part of *If You Really Knew Me*. People watched with wide-eyed attention. Students were asked to sign a **pledge** to help stop bullying. The program was popular. Students liked that it was started by students.

9   Petrini and her friends continued their fight. They joined with others in school. Together, they came up with ideas like no-bullying zones. They focused on understanding others and standing up to bullying.

First Read

Read the text. After you read, answer the Think Questions below.

1. What is bullying?

    Bullying is _____.

2. What are two ways bullying can hurt a student?

    Two ways bullying can hurt a student are _____

    _____.

3. What did Petrini and her friends do to take a stand against bullying at their school? Cite evidence from the text to support your answer.

    Petrini and her friends _____

    _____.

4. Use context to confirm the meaning of the word *pledge* as it is used in "Taking a Stand." Write your definition of *pledge* here.

    Pledge means _____.

    A context clue is _____.

5. What is another way to say that some of the students are *aggressive*?

    Some of the students _____.

Please note that excerpts and passages in the StudySync® library and this workbook are intended as touchstones to generate interest in an author's work. The excerpts and passages do not substitute for the reading of entire texts, and StudySync® strongly recommends that students seek out and purchase the whole literary or informational work in order to experience it as the author intended. Links to online resellers are available in our digital library. In addition, complete works may be ordered through an authorized reseller by filling out and returning to StudySync® the order form enclosed in this workbook.

Reading & Writing Companion   **467**

Skill:
Analyzing Expressions

★ DEFINE

When you read, you may find English expressions that you do not know. An **expression** is a group of words that communicates an idea. Three types of expressions are idioms, sayings, and figurative language. They can be difficult to understand because the meanings of the words are different from their **literal**, or usual, meanings.

An **idiom** is an expression that is commonly known among a group of people. For example: "It's raining cats and dogs" means it is raining heavily. **Sayings** are short expressions that contain advice or wisdom. For instance: "Don't count your chickens before they hatch" means do not plan on something good happening before it happens. **Figurative** language is when you describe something by comparing it with something else, either directly (using the words *like* or *as*) or indirectly. For example, "I'm as hungry as a horse" means I'm very hungry. None of the expressions are about actual animals.

••• CHECKLIST FOR ANALYZING EXPRESSIONS

To determine the meaning of an expression, remember the following:

✓ If you find a confusing group of words, it may be an expression. The meaning of words in expressions may not be their literal meaning.

  • Ask yourself: Is this confusing because the words are new? Or because the words do not make sense together?

✓ Determining the overall meaning may require that you use one or more of the following:

  • context clues

  • a dictionary or other resource

  • teacher or peer support

✓ Highlight important information before and after the expression to look for clues.

YOUR TURN

Read the following excerpt from the text. Then, complete the multiple-choice questions below.

---

from **"Taking a Stand"**

The girls made a plan. They shared it with the principal. He supported their idea. They organized a school assembly. Petrini showed part of *If You Really Knew Me*. People watched with wide-eyed attention. Students were asked to sign a pledge to help stop bullying. The program was popular. Students liked that it was started by students.

Petrini and her friends continued their fight. They joined with others in school. Together, they came up with ideas like no-bullying zones. They focused on understanding others and standing up to bullying.

---

1. What does "standing up to" bullying mean in this text?

    ○ A. Petrini and her friends are not sitting in their seats.

    ○ B. Petrini and her friends are trying to stop bullying.

    ○ C. Petrini and her friends are supporting bullying.

    ○ D. Petrini and her friends are walking away from bullying.

2. Which context clue helped you determine the meaning of the expression?

    ○ A. "He supported their idea."

    ○ B. "People watched with wide-eyed attention."

    ○ C. "Students liked that it was started by students."

    ○ D. "Together, they came up with ideas like no-bullying zones."

Please note that excerpts and passages in the StudySync® library and this workbook are intended as touchstones to generate interest in an author's work. The excerpts and passages do not substitute for the reading of entire texts, and StudySync® strongly recommends that students seek out and purchase the whole literary or informational work in order to experience it as the author intended. Links to online resellers are available in our digital library. In addition, complete works may be ordered through an authorized reseller by filling out and returning to StudySync® the order form enclosed in this workbook.

Reading & Writing
Companion

469

Skill:
Main Ideas and Details

★ DEFINE

The **main ideas** are the most important ideas of a paragraph, a section, or an entire text. The **supporting details** are details that describe or explain the main idea.

To **identify** the main idea of a paragraph or a text, you need to decide what the text is mostly about. To **identify** supporting details, you need to decide what information describes or explains the main idea.

••• CHECKLIST FOR MAIN IDEAS AND DETAILS

In order to distinguish between main ideas and supporting details, do the following:

✓ Preview the text. Look at headings, topic sentences, and boldface vocabulary.

- Ask yourself: What is this text about?

✓ Read the text.

- Ask yourself: What are the most important ideas? What details support or explain the most important ideas?

✓ Take notes or use a graphic organizer to distinguish between main ideas and supporting details.

⟳ YOUR TURN

Read paragraphs 5–6 from the text. Then, complete the multiple-choice questions below.

---

from **"Taking a Stand"**

Isabella Petrini knows about bullying. In fifth grade, she was a bully. She and her friends said mean things about others. But in seventh grade, Petrini saw bullying differently. She realized that these comments weren't jokes. They were biting and hurtful. They had the potential to harm others.

When Petrini saw the television program *If You Really Knew Me*, she had an idea. On the program, real-life high school students come together and talk about bullying. The goal is to help stop bullying by helping people understand one another.

---

1. What is the main idea of paragraph 5?

   ○ A. Isabella Petrini is a bully.

   ○ B. Isabella Petrini knows that bullying is harmful.

   ○ C. Bullies' comments are jokes.

   ○ D. Bullies are not harmful to other students until the students are in seventh grade.

2. What is a detail that supports the main idea of paragraph 5?

   ○ A. Petrini's friends in fifth grade were bullies.

   ○ B. Petrini was a bully in fifth grade.

   ○ C. Petrini said mean things in fifth grade.

   ○ D. Petrini realized that her comments could hurt people.

3. What is the main idea of paragraph 6?

   ○ A. The anti-bullying program *If You Really Knew Me* inspired Isabella Petrini.

   ○ B. Isabella Petrini made a TV program to teach students how to stop bullying.

   ○ C. *If You Really Knew Me* is about educating bullies like Isabella Petrini.

   ○ D. Isabella Petrini watched a TV program called *If You Really Knew Me*.

4. What is a detail that supports the main idea of paragraph 6?

   ○ A. She had an idea.

   ○ B. real-life high school students

   ○ C. come together

   ○ D. talk about bullying

Close Read

✏ WRITE

INFORMATIONAL: Write text for a flyer to inform students about bullying in school and why it is a problem. Use information from the selection to support your ideas. Pay attention to the spelling rules for doubling the final consonants and adding prefixes as you write.

Use the checklist below to guide you as you write.

☐ Why is bullying a problem?

☐ What can people do to solve this problem?

☐ What information from the text supports your ideas?

Use the sentence frames to organize and write your informational flyer.

• Bullying is _____

_____.

• As many as 30% of students _____

_____.

• Bullying causes _____

_____.

• We need to stop bullying because _____

_____.

• People can put an end to bullying by _____

_____.

School Lunches:

Who Decides What Students Should Eat?

ARGUMENTATIVE TEXT

Introduction

In these two articles, writers make arguments for and against healthful school lunch programs. One writer argues that healthful school lunch programs benefit students. The other argues that taking away unhealthful options also takes away students' power of choice. After reading their arguments, what will you decide? Should schools determine what students eat for lunch, or should students have the final say?

VOCABULARY

healthful

having qualities that help make someone healthy; good for you

bitter

having a harsh, unpleasant taste

tart

having a sharp or sour taste

soggy

soaked

hearty

filling; satisfying

≡ READ

School Lunches: Who Decides What Students Should Eat?

Point: New Programs Give Healthful Options

1 School lunches have changed in the United States. Many groups advocate for more **healthful** lunches. They work hard to change the kinds of food students eat at school. They want students to eat more healthful foods. They suggest whole grains, fruits, and vegetables.

2 When the new school lunch programs started, many students were reluctant to try the new foods. They did not want to eat crunchy carrots and juicy oranges. They wanted to eat salty chips and sweet cookies. But the protests got quieter. Now, students happily eat the healthful foods. Many schools even have salad bars. Students can make their own salads. They have a lot of options. Students can top crispy lettuce with **tart** tomatoes, **hearty** black beans, or sweet peaches. Now, students embrace healthful foods.

Reading & Writing Companion

3   Healthful school lunches benefit students at lunch. They also benefit students the rest of the day. Research shows that students who eat more healthful lunches eat less sugar and are more physically active. For the good of our students—our most valuable resource—our schools should have healthful lunches.

Counterpoint: New Rules Limit Student Choice

4   Many groups want to change what students eat during school lunch. They want to take away pizza, chips, and soda. Instead, they want students to eat salads, whole wheat pasta, and other healthful foods. They say that these changes will make students healthier and stronger.

5   But these changes cause problems. Many students don't like the more healthful foods. They say these foods don't taste good. After all, nobody wants to eat **bitter**, **soggy** broccoli instead of chicken nuggets! Students throw away a lot of the healthful foods. Then they are hungry by the end of the day. When students are hungry, they are more tired and more distracted in class.

6   Because of the rules, students don't have many choices. They don't have the right to choose what they eat. Some schools have banned the sale of chips, candy, and soda. Students can't even get these foods from school vending machines. Many say that this lack of choice takes away students' rights. Who should have the power to choose which foods are on lunch trays: schools or the students who have to eat those foods?

First Read

Read the text. After you read, answer the Think Questions below.

☁ THINK QUESTIONS

1. What is the goal of more healthful school lunch programs?

   The goal of the more healthful school lunch programs is _____

   _____.

2. According to the text, what are some benefits of more healthful school lunch programs? Cite evidence from the text in your response.

   Some benefits of the programs are _____.

3. Why do some people argue against healthful school lunch programs? Cite evidence from the text in your response.

   Some people argue against the programs _____.

4. Use context to confirm the meaning of the word *soggy* as it is used in "School Lunches: Who Decides What Students Should Eat?" Write your definition of *soggy* here.

   Soggy means _____.

   A context clue is _____.

5. What is another way to say that a meal is *hearty*?

   A meal is _____.

Skill:
Language Structures

★ DEFINE

In every language, there are rules that tell how to **structure** sentences. These rules define the correct order of words. In the English language, for example, a **basic** structure for sentences is subject, verb, and object. Some sentences have more **complicated** structures.

You will encounter both basic and complicated **language structures** in the classroom materials you read. Being familiar with language structures will help you better understand the text.

••• CHECKLIST FOR LANGUAGE STRUCTURES

To improve your comprehension of language structures, do the following:

✓ Monitor your understanding.

- Ask yourself: Why do I not understand this sentence? Is it because I do not understand some of the words? Or is it because I do not understand the way the words are ordered in the sentence?

✓ Pay attention to coordinating conjunctions.

- **Coordinating conjunctions** are used to join words or groups of words that have equal grammatical importance.

  > The coordinating conjunction *and* shows that two or more things are true of a person, object, or event.
  Example: Josefina is a good athlete **and** student.

  > The coordinating conjunction *or* shows a choice between different possibilities.
  Example: Josefina can either do her homework **or** go for a run.

> The coordinating conjunction *but* shows a contrast between people, objects, or events.
> Example: Josefina wants to run **but** should finish her homework first.

✓ Break down the sentence into its parts.

- Ask yourself: What ideas are expressed in this sentence? Are there conjunctions that join ideas or show contrast?

✓ Confirm your understanding with a peer or teacher.

⟳ YOUR TURN

Read each sentence in the first column. Place the letter that identifies the correct coordinating conjunction in the middle column. Place the letter that describes what each conjunction shows in the last column.

Coordinating Conjunction	Shows . . .
A. and	D. a contrast between what will happen
B. but	E. a choice between the options
C. or	F. two things are true about students

Sentence	Coordinating Conjunction	Shows . . .
Students can top crispy lettuce with tart tomatoes, hearty black beans, or sweet peaches.		
These changes will make students healthier, but these changes cause problems.		
Students are more tired and more distracted in class.		

Skill:
Comparing and Contrasting

★ DEFINE

To **compare** is to show how two or more pieces of information or literary elements in a text are similar. To **contrast** is to show how two or more pieces of information or literary elements in a text are different. By comparing and contrasting, you can better understand the **meaning** and the **purpose** of the text you are reading.

••• CHECKLIST FOR COMPARING AND CONTRASTING

In order to compare and contrast, do the following:

✓ Look for information or elements that you can compare and contrast.

   • Ask yourself: How are these two things similar? How are they different?

✓ Look for signal words that indicate a compare-and-contrast relationship.

   • Ask yourself: Are there any words that indicate the writer is trying to compare and contrast two or more things?

✓ Use a graphic organizer, such as a Venn diagram or chart, to compare and contrast information.

YOUR TURN

Read the following excerpts from the text. Then, complete the Compare-and-Contrast chart by writing the letter of the correct example in chart below.

Excerpt 1:

Healthful school lunches benefit students at lunch. They also benefit students the rest of the day. Research shows that students who eat more healthful lunches eat less sugar and are more physically active. For the good of our students—our most valuable resource—our schools should have healthful lunches.

Excerpt 2:

But these changes cause problems. Many students don't like the more healthful foods. They say these foods don't taste good. After all, nobody wants to eat bitter, soggy broccoli instead of chicken nuggets! Students throw away a lot of the healthful foods. Then they are hungry by the end of the day. When students are hungry, they are more tired and more distracted in class.

	Examples
A	If students are hungry, they are tired and distracted.
B	Eating healthy can help students be more physically active.
C	Food can affect how students behave in school.

Healthful Options Are Good	Both	Healthful Options Are Bad

Close Read

✏ WRITE

ARGUMENTATIVE: One author argues that more healthful school lunches benefit students. Another author argues that such programs limit students' choices. Which argument do you agree with? Explain why you agree with the argument. Pay attention to verb tenses as you write.

Use the checklist below to guide you as you write.

☐ Which author do you agree with?

☐ How did that author convince you?

☐ · What personal experience supports your view?

Use the sentence frames to organize and write your argument.

The first author believes that healthful lunches are _____.

The second author thinks that these programs are _____.

I agree with the (first / second) _____ author. I think that _____

_____.

The author's statement that " _____"

was very convincing. Personally, I _____.

studysync®

ASSIGNMENTS   BINDER   LIBRARY

Moment of Truth

UNIT 4

Moment of Truth

How can one event change everything?

Genre Focus: INFORMATIONAL

Texts

Extended Writing Project and Grammar

English Language Learner Resources

How can one event change everything?

LAURIE HALSE ANDERSON

American author Laurie Halse Anderson (b. 1961) was living in Pennsylvania in 1993 when she found herself engrossed in an article in the *Philadelphia Inquirer* about the yellow fever epidemic that had ravaged the city two hundred years earlier. Her book *Fever 1793* (2000) is a fictional work that came out of years of historical research and many drafts. Anderson is currently working on writing an installation of the *Wonder Woman* graphic novels for DC Comics.

DAVID BORNSTEIN

David Bornstein (b. 1974) began his journalism career at the metro desk of *New York Newsday*, and has written three books that focus on the intersection of technology and social innovation. Bornstein has co-authored a column called Fixes with Tina Rosenberg in the *New York Times* since 2010. The column "looks at solutions to social problems and why they work" and has covered broad topics including the successful use of cash as aid for refugees instead of food supplies, as well as how urban spaces can be designed to invite healthier lifestyles.

WILLIAM KAMKWAMBA

William Kamkwamba (b. 1987) was born in Dowa, Malawi, and grew up on his family's farm. His family experienced financial hardship, and Kamkwamba's education was interrupted for five years. At fourteen, he began borrowing books from a library, including an eighth-grade American textbook *Using Energy*—which had a picture of wind turbines on the cover. Inspired, he developed his own wind turbine, and generated power for his family's farm. His story drew wide acclaim and he resumed his education, ultimately graduating from Dartmouth College in 2014.

RANDALL MUNROE

Randall Munroe (b. 1984) grew up the son of an engineer in Easton, Pennsylvania, where he attended the Chesterfield County Mathematics and Science High School at Clover Hill, before graduating from Christopher Newport University with a degree in physics. He went on to work for NASA at the Langley Research Center. When NASA did not renew his employment contract, he moved to Boston to write full time. His webcomic *xkcd* was released in 2005, and reached 70 million hits a month by 2007. He is the author of two books. Munroe lives in Massachusetts.

ERNEST LAWRENCE THAYER

Ernest Lawrence Thayer (1863–1940) began his career as a humor columnist at *The San Francisco Examiner*, where his friend William Randolph Hearst had taken over. Born in Massachusetts, Thayer graduated from Harvard with a degree in philosophy and was an editor of *The Harvard Lampoon*. Thayer is best known for his poem "Casey at the Bat," which he published under his old *Lampoon* pseudonym Phin. Despite the pen name, the poem made him famous, and went on to be performed in public by actors to large crowds. The piece was his last for the paper.

LEO TOLSTOY

Best known as the author of *Anna Karenina* and the epic *War and Peace*, Leo Tolstoy (1828–1910) was an orphan, a college dropout, a gambler, and an artillery officer before he became a writer. He served in the Crimean War, and the horrors he saw there—as well as the witnessing of a public execution in France—helped instill in him a belief in nonviolence and pacifism. A contemporary and friend of Victor Hugo, and a penpal of Mahatma Gandhi, Tolstoy was considered by Virginia Woolf "the greatest of all novelists." He died at the age of eighty-two.

KURT VONNEGUT

The renowned author of *Cat's Cradle* and *The Sirens of Titan*, Kurt Vonnegut (1922–2007) was born in Indianapolis, Indiana, just before the Great Depression. The Depression led his father to sell their home and led his mother to succumb to substance abuse issues. Vonnegut wrote for his high school's student paper, studied chemistry at Cornell University, and later served in the Army during WWII. He was captured during the Battle of the Bulge and was sent to Dresden as a prisoner, an experience which served as the source for *Slaughterhouse-Five*.

VIOLA CANALES

A former field organizer for the United Farm Workers, and a veteran of the United States Army, Viola Canales (b. 1957) grew up in McAllen, Texas. She attended Harvard College for her bachelor's degree and graduated from Harvard Law School. She is the author of a short story collection, *Orange Candy Slices and Other Secret Tales*; a novel, *The Tequila Worm*; and a collection of poetry, *The Little Devil and the Rose: Loteria Poems*. She is currently a professor of law and fiction at Stanford University, where her partner is also a professor.

ERNESTO GALARZA

Born in Mexico, Ernesto Galarza (1905–1984) immigrated to California when he was six years old. As a part of the migrant farm workers' community near Sacramento, at only eight years old he was chosen as a member of "a strike committee in the California wheat fields because he was the only Mexican worker who knew English." Galarza would go on to graduate from Occidental College in Pasadena, earn his Master's degree in history and political science from Stanford University, as well as a Doctorate from Columbia University. He was a poet, labor activist, and professor.

JIM MURPHY

Growing up in an industrial New Jersey town close to New York City, nonfiction author Jim Murphy (b. 1947) spent most of his time outside and not much time reading. This changed when one of Murphy's grade school teachers forbid students to read a particular book; from then on, he read any book he could get his hands on. To this day, his favorite part of the writing process is reading and research, hunting down the surprising details that make the truth stranger than fiction.

PAUL RECER

Paul Recer was a Texas-based journalist. His career spanned several decades and included publications in the *Los Angeles Times, Dallas Times Herald, AP,* and *U.S. News & World Report*. Recer reported on the Apollo and Skylab programs as well as other high-profile aerospace projects. Most notably, Recer covered the 1975 Apollo-Soyuz test project, which was the first joint U.S.-Soviet space flight.

Casey at the Bat

POETRY
Ernest Lawrence Thayer
1888

Introduction

E rnest Thayer (1863–1940) was an American poet who published the poem "Casey at the Bat" in the *San Francisco Examiner* under the pseudonym "Phin." The poem's anonymity and association with DeWolf Hopper, who recited it 10,000 times on the vaudeville stage, led to many false claims about its authorship, and only reluctantly did Thayer eventually step forward to claim the poem as his own. By then, it had become firmly imprinted on the American imagination as the quintessential baseball poem, full of hope, drama, bravado, defeat, and humor. Though some readers may be unfamiliar with at bats and innings, everyone can relate to the final sentiment: "there is no joy in Mudville—mighty Casey has struck out."

"For Casey, mighty Casey, was advancing to the bat."

NOTES

Skill:
Figurative
Language

1 The outlook wasn't brilliant for the Mudville nine that day:
2 The score stood four to two, with but one inning more to play,
3 And then when Cooney died at first, and Barrows did the same,
4 A pall-like silence fell upon the patrons of the game.

5 A straggling few got up to go in deep despair. The rest
6 Clung to the hope which springs eternal in the human breast;
7 They thought, "If only Casey could but get a whack at that—
8 We'd put up even money now, with Casey at the bat."

9 But Flynn **preceded** Casey, as did also Jimmy Blake,
10 And the former was a hoodoo[1], while the latter was a cake;
11 So upon that stricken multitude **grim melancholy** sat,
12 For there seemed but little chance of Casey getting to the bat.

An engraving of a batsman circa 1890

People almost never die in baseball, so died is a metaphor for striking out. According to my dictionary, a pall is a cloth used to cover a coffin, so the description pall-like along with the use of died make this stanza gloomy.

13 But Flynn let drive a single[2], to the wonderment of all,
14 And Blake, the much despisèd, tore the cover off the ball;
15 And when the dust had lifted, and men saw what had occurred,
16 There was Jimmy safe at second and Flynn a-hugging third.

17 Then from five thousand throats and more there rose a lusty yell;
18 It rumbled through the valley, it rattled in the dell;
19 It pounded on the mountain and recoiled upon the flat,
20 For Casey, mighty Casey, was advancing to the bat.

---

1. **hoodoo** someone who brings bad luck
2. **single** in baseball, a single is a base hit in which the batter reaches first base

NOTES

21   There was ease in Casey's manner as he stepped into his place;

22   There was pride in Casey's bearing and a smile lit Casey's face.

23   And when, responding to the cheers, he lightly doffed[3] his hat,

24   No stranger in the crowd could doubt 'twas Casey at the bat.

25   Ten thousand eyes were on him as he rubbed his hands with dirt;

26   Five thousand tongues applauded when he wiped them on his shirt;

27   Then while the writhing pitcher ground the ball into his hip,

28   Defiance flashed in Casey's eye, a sneer curled Casey's lip.

29   And now the leather-covered sphere came hurtling through the air,

30   And Casey stood a-watching it in haughty grandeur there.

31   Close by the sturdy batsman the ball unheeded sped—

32   "That ain't my style," said Casey. "Strike one!" the umpire said.

33   From the benches, black with people, there went up a muffled roar,

34   Like the beating of the storm-waves on a stern and distant shore;

35   "Kill him! Kill the umpire!" shouted someone on the stand;

36   And it's likely they'd have killed him had not Casey raised his hand.

37   With a smile of Christian charity great Casey's **visage** shone;

38   He stilled the rising **tumult;** he bade the game go on;

39   He signaled to the pitcher, and once more the dun[4] sphere flew;

40   But Casey still ignored it and the umpire said, "Strike two!"

41   "Fraud!" cried the maddened thousands, and echo answered "Fraud!"

42   But one scornful look from Casey and the audience was awed.

43   They saw his face grow stern and cold, they saw his muscles strain,

44   And they knew that Casey wouldn't let that ball go by again.

45   The sneer is gone from Casey's lip, his teeth are clenched in hate,

46   He pounds with cruel violence his bat upon the plate;

47   And now the pitcher holds the ball, and now he lets it go,

48   And now the air is shattered by the force of Casey's blow.

49   Oh, somewhere in this favoured land the sun is shining bright,

50   The band is playing somewhere, and somewhere hearts are light;

51   And somewhere men are laughing, and somewhere children shout,

52   But there is no joy in Mudville—mighty Casey has struck out.

---

3. **doffed** took off or lifted slightly, gesturing toward removal without completion

4. **dun** brownish

 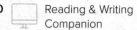

First Read

Read "Casey at the Bat." After you read, complete the Think Questions below.

☁ THINK QUESTIONS

1. How many players bat before Casey in the poem? What are the results of their batting attempts? Cite specific evidence from the poem to support your answer.

2. What is Casey's first line of dialogue? What does his language tell us about him?

3. Describe the setting of the poem. Who is there? What does it sound like? What does it look like? Cite specific evidence from the poem to support your answer.

4. Find the word **visage** in line 37. Use context clues in the surrounding sentences, as well as the sentence in which the word appears, to determine the word's meaning. Write your definition here and identify clues that helped you figure out the meaning.

5. Use context clues to determine the meaning of **melancholy** as it is used in line 11. Write your definition here and identify clues that helped you figure out the meaning. Then check the meaning in a dictionary.

Skill:
Figurative Language

Use the Checklist to analyze Figurative Language in "Casey at the Bat." Refer to the sample student annotations about Figurative Language in the text.

••• CHECKLIST FOR FIGURATIVE LANGUAGE

To determine the meaning of figures of speech in a text, note the following:

✓ words that mean one thing literally and suggest something else

✓ similes, such as "strong as an ox"

✓ metaphors, such as "her eyes were stars"

✓ allusions, or indirect references to people, texts, events, or ideas

✓ personification, such as "the daisies danced in the wind"

✓ other language in the text used in a nonliteral way

In order to interpret the meaning of a figure of speech in context, ask the following questions:

✓ Does any of the descriptive language in the text compare two seemingly unlike things?

✓ Do any descriptions include "like" or "as," indicating a simile?

✓ Is there a direct comparison that suggests a metaphor?

✓ How does the use of this figure of speech change your understanding of the thing or person being described?

In order to analyze the impact of figurative language on the meaning of a text, use the following questions as a guide:

✓ Where does figurative language appear in the text? What does it mean?

✓ Why does the author use figurative language rather than literal language?

Skill:
Figurative Language

Reread lines 9–16 of "Casey at the Bat." Then, using the Checklist on the previous page, answer the multiple-choice questions below.

⟳ YOUR TURN

1. The line "the former was a hoodoo, while the latter was a cake" appears to be using —

   ○ A. similes.
   ○ B. metaphors.
   ○ C. hyperbole.
   ○ D. literal language.

2. In line 14, the dramatic language "tore the cover off the ball" achieves the purpose of telling that Blake —

   ○ A. struck out.
   ○ B. felt angry at Flynn.
   ○ C. threw the ball far.
   ○ D. hit the ball very hard.

Close Read

Reread "Casey at the Bat." As you reread, complete the Skills Focus questions below. Then use your answers and annotations from the questions to help you complete the Write activity.

⊚ SKILLS FOCUS

1. Identify a stanza in which the rhyme scheme builds dramatic tension, and explain how the poet's choices create this effect.

2. Identify an example of figurative language, and explain the effect it has on the poem.

3. Identify a word or phrase that develops the tone or feeling of the last stanza. Explain the connotation of the word or phrase and why it differs from the rest of the poem.

4. Identify the key event in the poem that changes everything. Explain why that moment is important and why it has such a strong effect.

✎ WRITE

LITERARY ANALYSIS: In the poem, Casey is absolutely revered by his fans. How does the poet's use of figurative language reveal the power that Casey has over his fans? Find examples of figurative language in the poem that demonstrate this power.

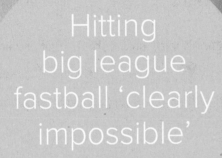

Hitting big league fastball 'clearly impossible'

INFORMATIONAL TEXT
Paul Recer
2000

Introduction

In 1982, former Major League Baseball player Ted Williams called batting "the hardest thing to do in sports." In less than a quarter of a second, a batter must judge the type of oncoming pitch, its speed and location, and whether or not to swing at it. This article and the accompanying video explore why even making contact with a 90-mph pitch—much less hitting it well—is a feat of

"It is a superhuman feat that is 'clearly impossible'. . ."

NOTES

1   A batter facing a 90 mph fastball has less than a quarter second to see the pitch, judge its speed and location, decide what to do, then start to swing.

2   To make contact, the bat must meet the ball within an eighth of an inch of dead center[1] and at **precisely** the right millisecond as the 3-inch spinning sphere whizzes by.

3   It is a superhuman feat that is "clearly impossible," said Robert Adair, a Yale physicist who has studied the science of baseball.

4   Adair reported on his analysis of the art of hitting big league pitching at the American Association for the Advancement of Science meeting this weekend.

5   When big league pitcher Randy Johnson throws a 90 mph fastball, it takes only 400 milliseconds—400 one-thousandths of a second—for the ball to reach the plate, Adair said.

6   It takes about 100 milliseconds for the eye of the batter to see the ball and send the image to the brain. It takes 75 more milliseconds for the brain to **process** the information, and gauge the speed and location of the pitch.

7   During those fractional seconds, the ball already has traveled 14 feet.

8   The batter then must decide, in just 25 milliseconds, whether to swing or to let the ball go by. If the decision is to swing, Adair said the batter's brain then picks a swing pattern—high, low, inside, outside. This takes 100 milliseconds.

9   By the time the batter is ready to start his swing, 225 milliseconds have passed and the ball now is only 25 feet from the plate.

---

1. **dead center** the exact middle point

**Skill:
Media**

Watching the video really helped me understand the ideas explained here. I can imagine the graphics from the video as I read the text. Picturing the graphics helps me keep track of the numbers in the text. If I was just reading this information cold, I think the numbers would all blur together and stop meaning anything.

10 Adair said the swing starts when the brain sends signals to the legs to start the batter's stride forward. It takes 15 milliseconds for the fastest signal to reach the lowest muscle in the leg.

11 The swing itself takes 150 milliseconds, so if the bat is to meet the ball, the swing must begin just 250 milliseconds after the ball left the pitcher's hand.

12 Adair said the swing involves moving a 2-pound bat at more than 80 mph and delivering up to nine horsepower of energy to the ball.

13 During the first 50 milliseconds of the swing, the batter can stop the swing and let the ball pass. But after 100 milliseconds, the bat is moving at 70 percent of its final speed "and the swing can no longer be checked," Adair said. Too much energy is moving forward and there's simply not enough time for the muscles to react.

14 The physicist said the batter not only must gauge where to put the bat, but also precisely time the swing so that baseball and bat arrive at the same place, at the same time.

15 "If the swing by a right-hand batter is seven milliseconds too late, the squarely hit ball will sail foul past first base," he said. "If the swing is early, the ball will be **foul** on the third base side."

16 Adair said that most of the decisions a batter makes about swinging or not comes from information collected by the eye in the first 100 milliseconds of the pitch's flight.

17 In the 1880s, the pitcher's rubber[2] was 50 feet from the plate instead of the current 60 feet, six inches.

18 A Randy Johnson-style pitcher in the 1880s could have delivered the ball to the plate from 50 feet in just 305 milliseconds, Adair said.

19 "The batter might as well just close his eyes and swing after he sees the ball **released**," Adair said.

Copyrighted 2017. Associated Press. 128921:0417PF

2. **rubber** in baseball, the mark on the pitcher's mound from which centerline is established

---

Skill: Technical Language

The writer is using technical language about time, but he is also talking about "signals," which must have a technical meaning here. I know that a signal is something that lets people know what's going to happen, like a turn signal. I think "signal" here must mean "the thing that tells the body what to do."

First Read

Read "Hitting big league fastball 'clearly impossible.'" After you read, complete the Think Questions below.

1. According to the article, what makes hitting a major league baseball seemingly impossible?

2. According to the article, what happens if a right-handed batter swings just milliseconds too early or too late?

3. According to the video, what is the ultimate trait that helps Major Leaguers hit fastballs? Explain what this trait is and how it helps hitters.

4. Read the following dictionary entry:

process
pro·cess \ ˈpräˌses\

noun

1. a particular course of action intended to achieve a result

verb

2. to deal with in a routine way or according to routine procedures
3. to perform mathematical or logical operations on
4. to take in sensory information and respond

Which definition most closely matches the meaning of **process** as it is used in paragraph 6? Write the correct definition of *process* here and explain how you figured out the proper meaning.

5. Read the following dictionary entry:

foul
foul \foul\

verb

1. to pollute or dirty

adjective

2. disgusting to the senses
3. out of the boundaries of play
4. immoral or wicked

Which definition most closely matches the meaning of **foul** as it is used in paragraph 15? Write the correct definition of *foul* here and explain how you figured out the proper meaning.

Skill:
Technical Language

Use the Checklist to analyze Technical Language in "Hitting big league fastball 'clearly impossible.'" Refer to the sample student annotations about Technical Language in the text.

••• CHECKLIST FOR TECHNICAL LANGUAGE

In order to determine the meaning of words and phrases as they are used in a text, note the following:

- ✓ the subject of the book or article

- ✓ any unfamiliar words that you think might be technical terms

- ✓ words that have multiple meanings that change when used with a specific subject

- ✓ the possible contextual meaning of a word, or the definition from a dictionary

To determine the meanings of words and phrases as they are used in a text, including technical meanings, consider the following questions:

- ✓ What is the subject of the informational text?

- ✓ How does the use of technical language help establish the author as an authority on the subject?

- ✓ Are there any technical words that have an impact on the meaning and tone, or quality, of the book or article?

- ✓ Can you identify the contextual meaning of any of the words?

Please note that excerpts and passages in the StudySync® library and this workbook are intended as touchstones to generate interest in an author's work. The excerpts and passages do not substitute for the reading of entire texts, and StudySync® strongly recommends that students seek out and purchase the whole literary or informational work in order to experience it as the author intended. Links to online resellers are available in our digital library. In addition, complete works may be ordered through an authorized reseller by filling out and returning to StudySync® the order form enclosed in this workbook.

Reading & Writing Companion **499**

Skill:
Technical Language

Reread paragraphs 12–15 of "Hitting big league fastball 'clearly impossible.'" Then, using the Checklist on the previous page, answer the multiple-choice questions below.

↻ YOUR TURN

1. This question has two parts. First, answer Part A. Then, answer Part B.

   Part A: What is the effect of the technical terminology in these paragraphs?

   ○ A. It makes the passage difficult to understand because of the complicated vocabulary.

   ○ B. It makes the passage seem authoritative because the language is specific.

   ○ C. It makes the author sound like he does not know what he is talking about because he uses the technical language wrong.

   ○ D. It makes the tone of the passage dark because the technical terms are so serious.

   Part B: Which of the following details BEST supports your response to Part A?

   ○ A. But after 100 milliseconds, the bat is moving at 70 percent of its final speed "and the swing can no longer be checked," Adair said.

   ○ B. Adair said the swing involves moving a 2-pound bat . . . .

   ○ C. Too much energy is moving forward and there's simply not enough time for the muscles to react.

   ○ D. The physicist said the batter not only must gauge where to put the bat, but also precisely time the swing so that baseball and bat arrive at the same place, at the same time.

Skill:
Media

Use the Checklist to analyze Media in "Hitting big league fastball 'clearly impossible.'" Refer to the sample student annotations about Media in the text.

••• CHECKLIST FOR MEDIA

In order to analyze the main ideas and supporting details presented in diverse media formats, note the following:

✓ how the same topic can be treated, or presented, in more than one format or medium

- visually
- quantitatively
- orally

✓ how treatments of a topic through different kinds of media can reveal more information about the topic

✓ which details are emphasized or absent in each medium, and the reasons behind these choices

✓ what the details in each medium have in common, or the main idea in each medium

✓ how the main idea and supporting details help to clarify, or explain, a topic, text, or issue

In order to explain how diverse media formats clarify a topic, text, or issue under study, consider the following questions:

✓ How are the treatments of the source text similar? How are they different?

✓ How do ideas presented in diverse media and formats clarify, or explain, a topic, text, or issue?

✓ How does each medium's portrayal affect the presentation of the subject?

✓ Why are different media able to emphasize or highlight certain kinds of information better than others?

Skill:
Media

Analyze the characteristics of the various media used in the video clip for "Hitting big league fastball 'clearly impossible.'" Then, using the Checklist on the previous page, answer the multiple-choice questions below.

⟳ YOUR TURN

1. The digital graphic at the end of the video clip is included to —

   ○ A. emphasize that batters should not blink or they will miss hitting a ball.
   ○ B. emphasize how little time a batter has to make a decision.
   ○ C. show that a ball travels for 300–400 milliseconds.
   ○ D. show the distance a major league ball travels.

2. Which statement best expresses the purpose of the video clip?

   ○ A. The purpose of the video is to show how tall pitchers have an advantage due to a longer stride.
   ○ B. The purpose of the video is to argue that the distance between the pitcher and the batter should be increased because the ball travels so fast.
   ○ C. The purpose of the video is to show how a major league baseball can be thrown so fast that it travels from the pitcher to the batter in less than half a second.
   ○ D. The purpose of the video is to demonstrate that it is not humanly possible for a batter to hit a ball that travels 90–95 mph.

Close Read

Reread "Hitting big league fastball 'clearly impossible.'" As you reread, complete the Skills Focus questions below. Then use your answers and annotations from the questions to help you complete the Write activity.

◎ SKILLS FOCUS

1. Identify a detail from the first half of "Hitting big league fastball 'clearly impossible'" that is clarified by the video. Explain how the video and the text work together to enhance the idea. Consider both the audio and visual techniques used in the video.

2. An important idea of this article is that hitting a fastball should be impossible. Identify evidence of this idea in the text, and explain how the author supports it with reasoning.

3. This article uses scientific evidence to discuss the difficulty of hitting a fastball. How does the author use technical language to sound like an expert in the subject?

4. Identify one event from the text or video that affects the success of a batter. Explain how this event has an impact on the rest of the batter's experience.

✎ WRITE

INFORMATIVE: Analyze the print and video's portrayal of baseball. How are the video and print similar and different? How do they work together to convey information and enhance the meaning of the selection? How do they help you visualize the difficulty of hitting a major league fastball? Write a response to these questions. Make sure to use evidence from the text and the video to support your response.

The Boy Who Harnessed the Wind:

Creating Currents of Electricity and Hope

INFORMATIONAL TEXT
William Kamkwamba
and Bryan Mealer
2009

Introduction

In 2002, Malawi was a poverty-stricken African nation racked with drought and starvation, and William Kamkwamba (b. 1987) was a 14-year-old boy with a dream of studying science at the country's top boarding school. With his family unable to pay the $80-a-year tuition fee, Kamkwamba seized opportunity where most would see despair. Digging through a junkyard to find scrap parts to build a windmill he read about in a textbook, Kamkwamba created a device that brought water and electricity to his village and bettered not just his own life but also the lives of those around him. In this excerpt, Kamkwamba passes time in the library and finds the

NOTES

"A windmill meant more than just power, it was freedom."

from Chapter Nine

1 After about a month, the school term finally ended and Gilbert was free to hang out. One morning we went to the library to kill some time—we often stayed for hours, just sitting in chairs and reading—but today Mrs. Sikelo was in a rush.

2 "You boys spend hours in here taking my time," she said, "but today I have an appointment. Just find something quickly."

3 "Yes, madame."

4 The reason it took so long was that none of the books were arranged properly. The titles weren't shelved alphabetically, or by subject or author, which meant we had to scan every title to find something we liked. So that day while Gilbert and I looked for a good read, I remembered an English word I'd stumbled across in one of my books.

5 "Gilbert, what's the word *grapes* mean?"

6 "Hmm," he said, "never heard of it. Look it up in the dictionary."

7 The English-Chichewa dictionaries were actually kept on the bottom shelf, but I never really spent much time looking down there. Instead I asked Mrs. Sikelo. So I squatted down to grab one of the dictionaries, and when I did, I noticed a book I'd never seen, pushed into the shelf and slightly concealed. *What is this?* I thought. Pulling it out, I saw it was an American textbook called *Using Energy,* and this book has since changed my life.

8 The cover featured a long row of windmills—though at the time I had no idea what a *windmill* was. All I saw were tall white towers with three blades spinning like a giant fan. They looked like the pinwheel toys Geoffrey and I once made as kids when we were bored. We'd find old water bottles people threw away in the trading center, cut the plastic into blades like a fan, then put a nail through the center attached to a stick. When the wind blew, they would spin. That's it, just a stupid pinwheel.

Skill:
Informational
Text Elements

The author described an important event, when he discovered the textbook that changed his life. The phrase has since seems similar to the signal words as a result, which tells me that this book and the ideas in it about energy greatly influenced the author.

NOTES

9　But the fans on this book were not toys. They were giant beautiful machines that towered into the sky, so powerful that they made the photo itself appear to be in motion. I opened the book and began to read.

10　"Energy is all around you every day," it said. "Sometimes energy needs to be converted to another form before it is useful to us. How can we convert forms of energy? Read on and you'll see."

11　I read on.

12　"Imagine that **hostile** forces have invaded your town, and defeat seems certain. If you needed a hero to 'save the day,' it's unlikely you would go to the nearest university and drag a scientist to the battlefront. Yet, according to legend, it was not a general who saved the Greek city of Syracuse when the Roman fleet attacked it in 214 b.c."

13　It explained how Archimedes[1] used his "Death Ray"—which was really a lot of mirrors—to reflect the sun onto the enemy ships until, one by one, they caught fire and sank. That was an example of how you can use the sun to produce energy.

14　Just like with the sun, windmills could also be used to **generate** power.

15　"People throughout Europe and the Middle East used windmills for pumping water and grinding grain," it said. "When many wind machines are grouped together in wind farms, they can generate as much electricity as a power plant."

16　Suddenly it all snapped together. The blades on these windmills were driven by the wind, much like our toys. In my mind I saw the dynamo, saw myself with the neighbor's bicycle those many nights ago, spinning the pedals so I could listen to the radio, thinking, *What can spin the pedals for me so I can dance?*

17　"The movement energy is provided by the rider," the book had said, explaining the dynamo. *Yes, of course*, I thought, *and the rider is the wind!*

18　The wind would spin the blades of the windmill, rotate the magnets in a dynamo, and create electricity. Attach a wire to the **dynamo** and you could power anything, especially a bulb. All I needed was a windmill, and then I could have lights. No more **kerosene** lamps that burned our eyes and sent us gasping for breath. With a windmill, I could stay awake at night reading instead of going to bed at seven with the rest of Malawi.

---

1. **Archimedes** a famous Greek mathematician, physicist, and inventor who lived from around 287–212 BCE

Skill: Textual Evidence

William describes the benefits the windmill could have for him and his family. He used gas lamps that burned his eyes and lungs. He had to go to bed early because there was no light. I can infer that creating a wind-powered light could make William's life safer, more comfortable, and more productive.

19   But most important, a windmill could also rotate a pump for water and **irrigation**. Having just come out of the hunger—and with famine still affecting many parts of the country—the idea of a water pump now seemed incredibly necessary. If we hooked it up to our shallow well at home, a water pump could allow us to harvest twice a year. While the rest of Malawi went hungry during December and January, we'd be hauling in our second crop of **maize**. It meant no more watering tobacco nursery beds in the *dambo*², which broke your back and wasted time. A windmill and pump could also provide my family with a year-round garden where my mother could grow things like tomatoes, Irish potatoes, cabbage, mustards, and soybeans, both to eat and sell in the market.

20   No more skipping breakfast; no more dropping out of school. With a windmill, we'd finally release ourselves from the troubles of darkness and hunger. In Malawi, the wind was one of the few consistent things given to us by God, blowing in the treetops day and night. A windmill meant more than just power, it was freedom.

21   Standing there looking at this book, I decided I would build my own windmill. I'd never built anything like it before, but I knew if windmills existed on the cover of that book, it meant another person had built them. After looking at it that way, I felt confident I could build one, too.

Excerpted from *The Boy Who Harnessed the Wind: Creating Currents of Electricity and Hope* by William Kamkwamba and Bryan Mealer, published by William Morrow.

2. **dambo** high-altitude wetlands in southern and eastern Africa

NOTES

Skill:
Informational
Text Elements

Here, William talks about how the windmill could really help the village. His ideas and invention could really have an impact. He explains with examples here.

Please note that excerpts and passages in the StudySync® library and this workbook are intended as touchstones to generate interest in an author's work. The excerpts and passages do not substitute for the reading of entire texts, and StudySync® strongly recommends that students seek out and purchase the whole literary or informational work in order to experience it as the author intended. Links to online resellers are available in our digital library. In addition, complete works may be ordered through an authorized reseller by filling out and returning to StudySync® the order form enclosed in this workbook.

Reading & Writing
Companion

507

First Read

Read *The Boy Who Harnessed the Wind: Creating Currents of Electricity and Hope*. After you read, complete the Think Questions below.

☁ THINK QUESTIONS

1. How do you know that the author values education? How does his interest in education help him? Use specific evidence from the text to support your response.

2. What information does this passage give the reader about life in Malawi? Give at least three specific examples from the text.

3. How does the author imagine that a windmill could be used to improve his life in Malawi? Provide two examples from the text.

4. Find the word **generate** as it is used in paragraphs 14 and 15 of *The Boy Who Harnessed the Wind*. Use context clues in the surrounding sentences, as well as the sentence in which the word appears, to determine the word's meaning. Write your definition here and identify clues that helped you figure out the meaning.

5. Use context clues to determine the meaning of the word **irrigation** as it is used in paragraph 19 of *The Boy Who Harnessed the Wind*. Write your definition of *irrigation* here and identify clues that helped you figure out the meaning. Then check the meaning in a dictionary.

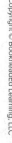

Skill:
Textual Evidence

Use the Checklist to analyze Textual Evidence in *The Boy Who Harnessed the Wind: Creating Currents of Electricity and Hope*. Refer to the sample student annotations about Textual Evidence in the text.

••• CHECKLIST FOR TEXTUAL EVIDENCE

In order to support an analysis by citing textual evidence that is explicitly stated in the text, do the following:

- ✓ read the text closely and critically

- ✓ identify what the text says explicitly

- ✓ find the most relevant textual evidence that supports your analysis

- ✓ consider why an author explicitly states specific details and information

- ✓ cite the specific words, phrases, sentences, paragraphs, or images from the text that support your analysis

In order to interpret implicit meanings in a text by making inferences, do the following:

- ✓ combine information directly stated in the text with your own knowledge, experiences, and observations

- ✓ cite the specific words, phrases, sentences, paragraphs, or images from the text that support this inference

In order to cite textual evidence to support an analysis of what the text says explicitly as well as inferences drawn from the text, consider the following questions:

- ✓ Have I read the text closely and critically?

- ✓ What inferences am I making about the text? What textual evidence am I using to support these inferences?

- ✓ Am I quoting the evidence from the text correctly?

- ✓ Does my textual evidence logically relate to my analysis?

- ✓ Have I cited several pieces of textual evidence?

Skill:
Textual Evidence

Reread paragraphs 16–19 of *The Boy Who Harnessed the Wind: Creating Currents of Electricity and Hope*. Then, using the Checklist on the previous page, answer the multiple-choice questions below.

↻ YOUR TURN

1. What is the most likely reason William was motivated to build the windmill?

   ○ A. He was curious about windmills and how they worked.
   ○ B. He likes to build and create things.
   ○ C. He was bored and didn't have anything else to do in the village.
   ○ D. He realized that a windmill would be the best way to improve life in the village.

2. Select a sentence that suggests a windmill would improve William's family's overall wealth.

   ○ A. "While the rest of Malawi went hungry during December and January, we'd be hauling in our second crop of **maize**."
   ○ B. "It meant no more watering tobacco nursery beds in the dambo, which broke your back and wasted time."
   ○ C. "A windmill and pump could also provide my family with a year-round garden where my mother could grow things like tomatoes, Irish potatoes, cabbage, mustards, and soybeans, both to eat and sell in the market."
   ○ D. "But most important, a windmill could also rotate a pump for water and **irrigation**."

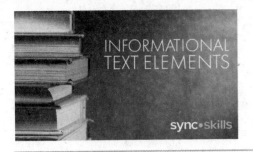

Skill:
Informational Text Elements

Use the Checklist to analyze Informational Text Elements in *The Boy Who Harnessed the Wind: Creating Currents of Electricity and Hope*. Refer to the sample student annotations about Informational Text Elements in the text.

••• CHECKLIST FOR INFORMATIONAL TEXT ELEMENTS

In order to identify the interactions between individuals, events, and ideas in a text, note the following:

- ✓ details in the text that describe or explain important ideas, events, or individuals

- ✓ transition words and phrases that signal interactions between individuals, ideas, or events, such as *because, as a consequence,* or *as a result*

- ✓ an event or sequence of events that influences an individual, a subsequent event, or an idea

- ✓ interactions between ideas and events that play a part in shaping people's thoughts and actions

To analyze the interactions between individuals, events, and ideas in a text, consider the following questions:

- ✓ How are the individuals, ideas, and events in the text related?

- ✓ How do the ideas the author presents affect the individuals in the text?

- ✓ What other features, if any, help readers to analyze the events, ideas, or individuals in the text?

Skill:
Informational Text Elements

Reread paragraphs 16–20 of *The Boy Who Harnessed the Wind: Creating Currents of Electricity and Hope.* Then, using the Checklist on the previous page, answer the multiple-choice questions below.

⟳ YOUR TURN

1. This question has two parts. First, answer Part A. Then, answer Part B.

   Part A: How does the excerpt show how William Kamkwamba's experiences lead to the idea to build a windmill?

   ○ A. by focusing on examples and experiences of how other villages and cities had used windmills

   ○ B. by listing a sequence or series of William's ideas that influenced him and his actions

   ○ C. by giving examples of how the boy and the villagers wanted to keep things the way they were

   ○ D. by explaining how a windmill could improve farming and irrigation in his village

   Part B: What piece of evidence BEST supports your answer in Part A?

   ○ A. "No more skipping breakfast; no more dropping out of school."

   ○ B. "With a windmill, we'd finally release ourselves from the troubles of darkness and hunger."

   ○ C. "Suddenly it all snapped together. The blades on these windmills were driven by the wind much like our toys."

   ○ D. "Having just come out of the hunger—and with famine still affecting many parts of the country—the idea of a water pump now seemed incredibly necessary."

Close Read

Reread *The Boy Who Harnessed the Wind: Creating Currents of Electricity and Hope*. As you reread, complete the Skills Focus questions below. Then use your answers and annotations from the questions to help you complete the Write activity.

◎ SKILLS FOCUS

1. Identify examples that tell about the village in Malawi. Explain how William Kamkwamba's experiences in Malawi influenced his personal goals. Support your answer with explicit evidence from the text as well as your own inferences.

2. Identify several pieces of evidence that explain what message you think the author wants to communicate to his readers. Why do you think Kamkwamba wrote this text?

3. Identify an event in the text that changed William Kamkwamba's life. Explain how the event made a difference for him.

✎ WRITE

INFORMATIVE: The author explains that a windmill was "more than just power." Explain why windmills are so important in Malawi. How would a windmill affect the people of Malawi? Use several pieces of evidence from the text to support your response as well as your own inferences.

An American Plague:

The True and Terrifying Story of the
Yellow Fever Epidemic of 1793

INFORMATIONAL TEXT
Jim Murphy
2003

Introduction

Thought to have originated in Africa, yellow fever spread to the Americas in the 17th and 18th centuries on trading ships. In 1793, the fever struck inhabitants of seaside neighborhoods in Philadelphia with gruesome and heartbreaking results. Author Jim Murphy (b. 1947) takes an unflinching look at this scourge, including the doctors who labored to save the afflicted and discover the causes and cures; the politicians who sought to govern the panicked city; and, last but not least, the victims of the mysterious plague.

"...all was not right in our city."

NOTES

Chapter 2: All Was Not Right

1 "8 or 10 persons buried out of Water St. between Race and Arch Sts.; many sick in our neighborhood, and in ye City generally."
—Elizabeth Drinker, August 21, 1793

2 **Monday, August 19.** It was clear that thirty-three-year-old Catherine LeMaigre was dying, and dying horribly and painfully. Between agonized gasps and groans she muttered that her stomach felt as if it were burning up. Every ten minutes or so her moaning would stop **abruptly** and she would vomit a foul black bile[1].

3 Her husband, Peter, called in two neighborhood doctors to save his young wife. One was Dr. Hugh Hodge, whose own daughter had been carried off by the same fever just days before. Hodge had been an army surgeon during the Revolutionary War, and while stubborn and crusty in his ways, he was a respected physician. The other was Dr. John Foulke, who was a fellow of Philadelphia's prestigious College of Physicians and a member of the Pennsylvania Hospital board.

4 Hodge and Foulke did what they could for their patient. They gave her cool drinks of barley water and apple water to reduce the fever, and red wine with laudanum[2] to help her rest. Her forehead, face, and arms were washed regularly with damp cloths.

5 Nothing worked, and Catherine LeMaigre's condition worsened. Her pulse slowed, her eyes grew bloodshot, her skin took on the pale-yellow color that gave the disease its name. More black vomit came spewing forth. In desperation, the two physicians sent for their esteemed colleague Dr. Benjamin Rush.

---

1. **bile** green fluid produced by the liver to aid digestion
2. **laudanum** an opium-containing solution widely used in the 19th century for pain or as a sleeping aid

NOTES

6 Rush was forty-seven years old and so highly respected that he was often called in by colleagues when they were baffled by a case. His medical training had been extensive, consisting of five years of apprenticeship with the pre-eminent doctor in the United States, John Redman. After this he had gone to Europe to study under the most skilled surgeons and doctors in the western world.

7 He was passionate and outspoken in his beliefs, no matter what the subject. He opposed slavery, felt that alcohol and tobacco should be avoided, urged that the corporal punishment of children be stopped, and thought that the best way to keep a democracy strong was by having universal education. Along with his beliefs went an unimaginable amount of energy. Despite a persistent cough and weak lungs that often left him gasping for air, he worked from early in the morning until late at night—writing letters and papers, visiting patients, rereading the latest medical literature, or attending to any one of a number of institutions and charities he belonged to.

8 Hodge and Foulke told Rush about Catherine LeMaigre's **symptoms** and what they had done to help her. There was nothing much else they could do, Rush said, after the three men left her bedchamber to discuss the case. Rush then noted that in recent days he had seen "an unusual number of bilious fevers, accompanied with symptoms of uncommon malignity." In a grave voice, his seriousness reflected in his intense blue eyes, he added that "all was not right in our city."

9 The two other doctors agreed, and then all three **recounted** the symptoms they had seen. The sickness began with chills, headache, and a painful aching in the back, arms, and legs. A high fever developed, accompanied by constipation. This stage lasted around three days, and then the fever suddenly broke and the patient seemed to recover.

10 But only for a few short hours.

11 The next stage saw the fever shoot up again. The skin and eyeballs turned yellow, as red blood cells were destroyed, causing the bile pigment bilirubin to accumulate in the body; nose, gums, and intestines began bleeding; and the patient vomited stale, black blood. Finally, the pulse grew weak, the tongue turned a dry brown, and the victim became depressed, confused, and **delirious**.

12 Rush noted another sign as well: tiny reddish eruptions on the skin. "They appeared chiefly on the arms, but they sometimes extended to the breast." Physicians called these sores petechiae, which is Latin for skin spots, and Rush observed that they "resembled moscheto bites."

13 Hodge then pointed out that the deaths, including his daughter's, had all happened on or near Water Street. Foulke told of other deaths along the street and said he knew the origin of the fevers: the repulsive smell in the air caused by the rotting coffee on Ball's Wharf.

14 The idea that illness was caused by **microscopic** organisms, such as bacteria and viruses, was not known at the time. Instead, doctors based their medical thinking on the 2,500-year-old Greek humoral theory. This concept stated that good health resulted when body fluids, called humors, were in balance. The humors were phlegm, choler, bile, and blood.

15 Disease arose from an imbalance of these humors—too much of one, not enough of another. Any number of things could cause this condition, such as poor diet, excess drinking, poison, or a dog bite, to name just a few. Even bad news could unsettle the humors and cause illness. So it made sense to Rush, Hodge, and Foulke that the putrid-smelling air could upset people enough to cause an outbreak of violent, fatal fevers.

16 Rush, however, sensed something else. The symptoms he was seeing reminded him of a sickness that had swept through Philadelphia back in 1762, when he was sixteen years old and studying under Dr. Redman. Rush was never shy with his opinions, and standing there in the LeMaigres' parlor, he boldly announced that the disease they now confronted was the dreaded yellow fever.

Excerpted from *An American Plague: The True and Terrifying Story of the Yellow Fever Epidemic of 1793* by Jim Murphy, published by Clarion Books.

✎ WRITE

SUMMARY: Notice that the text says that Dr. Rush "worked from early in the morning until late at night" on a number of tasks, including "writing letters and papers." Physicians often write papers about health-related topics for publication in medical journals. Imagine that you are Dr. Hodge, Dr. Foulke, or Dr. Rush. Summarize for city politicians the health situation in Philadelphia in 1793. What might you say? Write an objective summary introducing the central or main idea and the details that support it, such as facts, definitions, and examples. Be sure not to include your feelings or judgments. Support your writing with textual evidence.

Fever 1793

FICTION
Laurie Halse Anderson
2002

Introduction

Fever 1793 is a novel by Laurie Halse Anderson (b. 1961) that transports readers back to a harrowing episode in the early years of the United States. When a yellow fever epidemic strikes the city of Philadelphia during the sweltering summer of 1793, everything in 14-year-old Matilda Cook's world turns upside down. Forced to leave behind her sick mother and the coffee shop she hoped to run one day, Matilda must figure out how to cope with whatever will come next for her and her grandfather.

"He turned to look back at me anxiously. We were in the center of a dying city."

NOTES

from Chapter Sixteen

September 24, 1793

. . .

1   Grandfather and I were riding along with five fever orphans who were being sent to the orphan house. Grandfather rode at the front with the driver, a relatively clean man with neatly combed hair and a smooth face. He quietly whistled a tune, one of Grandfather's favorites. They would be good company for the journey.

2   I sat on the hardest plank in the back next to a woman named Mrs. Bowles. Two boys huddled together for comfort. They looked like brothers. The other children stared vacantly ahead. One girl looked to be my age. Her neck was dirty and her dress was torn. I wanted to speak to her but couldn't think of what to say. When she saw me looking at her, she turned away.

3   Mrs. Bowles was a straight-backed woman dressed in Quaker[1] gray. She was older than Mother, with kind eyes and laughter lines that curled around the sides of her mouth. As we drove away from the hospital, she picked up the smallest crying child and sat him in her lap. The child's sobs kept time with the rhythm of horse hooves on the road. He wiped his nose on the front of her dress and snuggled closer in her arms.

4   "Mrs. Flagg explained that you have been through a great deal," Mrs. Bowles said gently.

5   "Yes, Ma'am."

6   "These are trying times. They seem to bring out the best and worst in the people around us." We sat in silence, watching as the slate roofs of the houses on the outskirts of the city came into view. Mosquitoes, gnats, and flies

1. **Quaker** a member of the Religious Society of Friends, a Christian religion devoted to peaceful principles

followed the wagon, drawn by the smell of the sweating children and horses. "How old are you, Matilda?"

7   "Fourteen, fifteen in December."

8   "And are you feeling recovered from your illness? Fully recovered?!"

9   I nodded. "My only complaint is that my stomach grumbles all the time."

10 She smiled and shifted the child in her arms. "That is normal enough for someone your age. If I may inquire?" she began delicately.

11 "Yes?"

12 "Have you considered what you might do to help? You have recovered, so you cannot get the fever again. You are young and strong. We have a real need for you."

13 "How can I help anyone? I'm just a girl." As soon as the words were out of my mouth, I wanted to pinch myself. The first time anyone treats me like a woman and I respond like an infant.

14 "You are much more than a girl, let me **assure** you of that. You are older than Susannah there." She inclined her head toward the girl with the dirty neck. "She has lost her family, but we are not taking her in as an orphan. She will help us with the younger children."

15 The child in Mrs. Bowles's lap stirred and whimpered.

16 "Shh. Hush," she whispered to the little one. "I know that you have not received any word from your mother yet. It may be better for you to stay with us. We would keep you fed and warm, and you could provide us with a much-needed extra pair of hands."

17 The wagon had reached the part of the city where new houses and businesses were under construction. Where there should have been an army of carpenters, masons, glaziers, plasterers, and painters, I saw only empty **shells** of buildings, already falling into disrepair after a few weeks of neglect.

18 "Grandfather would not allow it," I said with confidence. "If Mother is still out in the country, then we two shall care for each other. He doesn't know the first thing about shopping at the market or cooking, and I need him to chop wood and, and . . . he will make sure I am well."

19 "It is good you have each other," said Mrs. Bowles in the same **placid** voice. "But you should not leave your house once you arrive. The streets of

Philadelphia are more dangerous than your darkest nightmare. Fever victims lay in the gutters, thieves and wild men lurk on every corner. The markets have little food. You can't wander. If you are determined to return home with your grandfather, then you must stay there until the fever **abates**."

20 Grandfather turned to address us. "We may end up at the Ludingtons' farm after all," he said. "Josiah here tells me there's not much food to be found anywhere, Mattie. I'll write to them again as soon as we arrive home."

21 "Won't do you no good," the driver interrupted. "The post office just closed down. It could take until Christmas before they can deliver letters."

22 Mrs. Bowles patted my arm. "Don't fret, Matilda. If you like, you may choose to take employment at the orphanage. I'm sure the trustees[2] would approve a small **wage** if you helped with the cleaning or minding the children. They have for Susannah. She'll help with the laundry."

23 Susannah didn't look strong enough to wash a teaspoon, much less a tub full of clothing. "What will happen to her when the fever is over?" I whispered.

24 Mrs. Bowles lowered her voice. "She is at a difficult age. She's too old to be treated as a child, but not old enough to be released on her own. Her parents owned a small house. The trustees will sell that and use the money for her dowry. We will hire her out to work as a servant or scullery[3] maid. She's attractive enough. I'm sure she'll find a husband."

25 A fly bit the ear of the child on Mrs. Bowles's lap, and his howl cut off the conversation.

26 Scullery maid, that was one thing I would never be. I imagined Mother's face when she arrived home and found what a splendid job I had done running the coffeehouse. I could just picture it—I would be seeing the last customers out the door when Mother would come up the steps. She would exclaim how clean and well-run the coffeehouse was. Grandfather would point out the fancy dry goods store I was building next door. I would blush, looking quite attractive in my new dress—French, of course. Perhaps I could hire Susannah to do the washing up. That would be a way of helping.

27 I broke off my daydream to take in our surroundings. Grandfather and the driver had stopped swapping stories. He turned to look back at me anxiously. We were in the center of a dying city.

---

2. **trustees** individuals given agency or power over a particular task
3. **scullery** kitchen

NOTES

28 It was night in the middle of the day. Heat from the brick houses filled the street like a bake oven. Clouds shielded the sun, colors were overshot with gray. No one was about; businesses were closed and houses shuttered. I could hear a woman weeping. Some houses were barred against intruders. Yellow rags fluttered from railings and door knockers—pus yellow, fear yellow—to mark the homes of the sick and the dying. I caught sight of a few men walking, but they fled down alleys at the sound of the wagon.

29 "What's that?" I asked, pointing to something on the marble steps of a three-story house.

30 "Don't look, Matilda," said Grandfather. "Turn your head and say a prayer."

31 I looked. It appeared to be a bundle of bed linens that had been cast out of an upper window, but then I saw a leg and an arm.

32 "It's a man. Stop the wagon, we must help him!"

33 "He is past helping, Miss," the driver said as he urged on the horses. "I checked him on the way out to fetch you this morning. He were too far gone to go to the hospital. His family tossed him out so as they wouldn't catch the fever. The death cart will get him soon for burying."

Excerpted from *Fever 1793* by Laurie Halse Anderson, published by Aladdin Paperbacks.

First Read

Read *Fever 1793*. After you read, complete the Think Questions below.

THINK QUESTIONS

1. Based on Mattie's observations of the children on the wagon, what do you think "fever orphans" are? Cite evidence from the text to support your response.

2. What can you infer or guess about Mrs. Bowles, based on the excerpt? Use evidence from the text to support your response.

3. Why isn't Mattie sure whether to accept Mrs. Bowles's offer of work at the orphanage? Explain, pointing to specific lines or passages as support.

4. Find the word **assure** in paragraph 14 of *Fever 1793*. Use context clues in the surrounding sentences, as well as the sentence in which the word appears, to determine the word's meaning. Write your definition here, and identify clues that helped you figure out the meaning.

5. Use context clues to determine the meaning of **abates** as it is used in paragraph 19 of *Fever 1793*. Write your definition here, and identify clues that helped you figure out the meaning. Then check the meaning in a dictionary.

Skill:
Compare and Contrast

Use the Checklist to analyze Compare and Contrast in *Fever 1793*.

In order to determine how two or more authors writing about the same topic shape their presentations of key information, use the following steps:

✓ First, choose two texts with similar subjects or topics by different authors.

✓ Next, identify each author's approach to the subject.

✓ After, identify the key information and evidence that each author includes.

✓ Then, explain the ways each author shapes his or her presentation of the information in the text.

✓ Finally, analyze the similarities and differences in how the authors present:

- historical details the nonfiction text includes that are not included in the fictional account.

- the results of characters' words and actions and how this compares to the cause-and-effect relationships between events in the nonfiction account.

To analyze how two or more authors writing about the same topic shape their presentations of key information, consider the following questions:

✓ What are the characteristics of each genre?

✓ How does the author of fiction portray a time, place, or character in his or her story? How is this similar to and different from a historical account of the same period?

✓ What details does the nonfiction text include that are not included in the fictional narrative? How does this affect the fictional narrative?

Skill:
Compare and Contrast

Reread paragraphs 7 and 8 of *An American Plague* and paragraph 19 of *Fever 1793*. Then, using the Checklist on the previous page, complete the chart below to compare and contrast the passages.

⟲ YOUR TURN

	Observations
A	Explains side effects of the yellow fever using medical terms.
B	Explains that the fever will eventually end or improve.
C	Mrs. Bowles gives advice about how to stay safe during the plague.
D	Describes what fever victims are doing in the streets.
E	Describes what happens as a result of the yellow fever plague.
F	The doctors describe the various stages of the disease.

An American Plague	Both	*Fever 1793*

Close Read

Reread *Fever 1793*. As you reread, complete the Skills Focus questions below. Then use your answers and annotations from the questions to help you complete the Write activity.

◎ SKILLS FOCUS

1. Recall that the central idea in *An American Plague* is that the plague brought devastation to Philadelphia. In the excerpt from *Fever 1793*, identify evidence that supports this central idea. Explain how this evidence helps you better understand the impact of the plague.

2. The plague was an event that affected a large number of people in Philadelphia. Find examples of how the yellow fever outbreak changed everything for the people of Philadelphia in 1793. Write notes about how the fever affected the lives of people from that period.

3. Identify words or phrases with negative emotional connotations. Why might Anderson have used the word or phrase? Write a note explaining the effect or meaning of each word or phrase.

4. The doctors in *An American Plague* are operating without instructions at the onset of the outbreak. In *Fever 1793*, the plague has been going for a while and the characters have a little more information. Find evidence about what the characters in Anderson's novel knew about the disease. Take notes on how their understanding differs from that of the doctors in *An American Plague*.

5. The yellow fever outbreak changes everything for Matilda. For example, instead of following her dream of running a coffeehouse, she must help sick children at an orphanage. Find evidence about how this makes Matilda feel. Write a note about how Matilda reacts to this event and how it changes her life.

✏ WRITE

COMPARE AND CONTRAST: *An American Plague: The True and Terrifying Story of the Yellow Fever Epidemic of 1793* and *Fever 1793* both describe people reacting to a terrifying disease in their community: yellow fever. Compare and contrast people's understanding of the disease in the selections. Then explain how people's understanding of the disease influenced their responses. Use evidence from both texts to support your ideas.

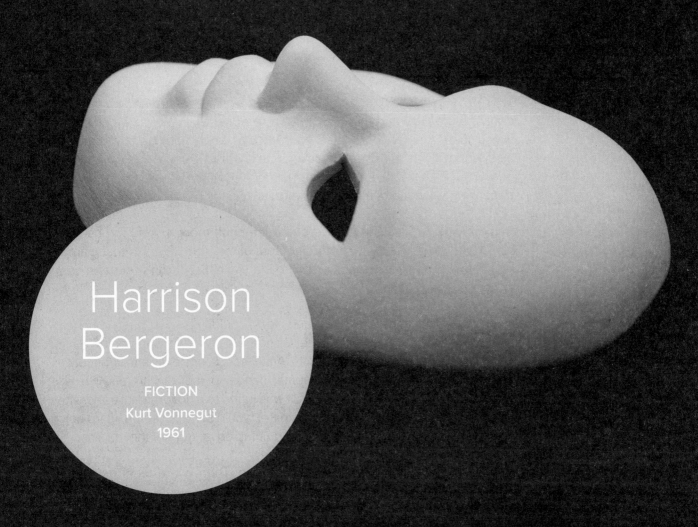

Harrison Bergeron

FICTION
Kurt Vonnegut
1961

Introduction

In "Harrison Bergeron," a widely acclaimed short story by World War II veteran Kurt Vonnegut (1922–2007), the 211th, 212th, and 213th Amendments to the Constitution ensure that all people are equal. No one can be prettier, more athletic, or smarter than anyone else, and order is maintained by the vigilant minions of the Handicapper General. Satirical and alarming, Vonnegut's story considers what happens when a core American value is misinterpreted—and the government controls the very thoughts of its citizens.

"The year was 2081, and everybody was finally equal."

Skill:
Textual Evidence

The first sentence explicitly states the date and the main idea that everybody is equal.

The last sentence describes the Amendments. I know that amendments are laws. The implicit meaning is that the government forces equality on people through laws.

1 THE YEAR WAS 2081, and everybody was finally equal. They weren't only equal before God and the law. They were equal every which way. Nobody was smarter than anybody else. Nobody was better looking than anybody else. Nobody was stronger or quicker than anybody else. All this equality was due to the 211th, 212th, and 213th Amendments to the Constitution, and to the **unceasing** vigilance of agents of the United States Handicapper General[1].

2 Some things about living still weren't quite right, though. April for instance, still drove people crazy by not being springtime. And it was in that clammy month that the H-G men took George and Hazel Bergeron's fourteen-year-old son, Harrison, away.

3 It was tragic, all right, but George and Hazel couldn't think about it very hard. Hazel had a perfectly average intelligence, which meant she couldn't think about anything except in short bursts. And George, while his intelligence was way above normal, had a little mental handicap radio in his ear. He was required by law to wear it at all times. It was tuned to a government transmitter. Every twenty seconds or so, the transmitter would send out some sharp noise to keep people like George from taking unfair advantage of their brains.

4 George and Hazel were watching television. There were tears on Hazel's cheeks, but she'd forgotten for the moment what they were about.

5 On the television screen were ballerinas.

6 A buzzer sounded in George's head. His thoughts fled in panic, like bandits from a burglar alarm.

7 "That was a real pretty dance, that dance they just did," said Hazel.

8 "Huh?" said George.

9 "That dance—it was nice," said Hazel.

---

1. **United States Handicapper General** a parody of the Postmaster General, a ceremonial post as head of the U.S. Post Office

NOTES

10　"Yup," said George. He tried to think a little about the ballerinas. They weren't really very good—no better than anybody else would have been, anyway. They were burdened with sashweights and bags of birdshot, and their faces were masked, so that no one, seeing a free and graceful gesture or a pretty face, would feel like something the cat drug in. George was toying with the vague notion that maybe dancers shouldn't be handicapped. But he didn't get very far with it before another noise in his ear radio scattered his thoughts.

11　George winced. So did two out of the eight ballerinas.

12　Hazel saw him wince. Having no mental handicap herself, she had to ask George what the latest sound had been.

13　"Sounded like somebody hitting a milk bottle with a ball peen hammer[2]," said George.

14　"I'd think it would be real interesting, hearing all the different sounds," said Hazel a little envious. "All the things they think up."

15　"Um," said George.

16　"Only, if I was Handicapper General, you know what I would do?" said Hazel. Hazel, as a matter of fact, bore a strong resemblance to the Handicapper General, a woman named Diana Moon Glampers. "If I was Diana Moon Glampers," said Hazel, "I'd have chimes on Sunday—just chimes. Kind of in honor of religion."

17　"I could think, if it was just chimes," said George.

18　"Well—maybe make 'em real loud," said Hazel. "I think I'd make a good Handicapper General."

19　"Good as anybody else," said George.

20　"Who knows better than I do what normal is?" said Hazel.

21　"Right," said George. He began to think glimmeringly about his abnormal son who was now in jail, about Harrison, but a twenty-one-gun salute in his head stopped that.

22　"Boy!" said Hazel, "that was a doozy, wasn't it?"

---

2. **ball peen hammer** a type of hammer, the head of which is rounded at one end

23 It was such a doozy that George was white and trembling, and tears stood on the rims of his red eyes. Two of the eight ballerinas had collapsed to the studio floor, were holding their temples.

24 "All of a sudden you look so tired," said Hazel. "Why don't you stretch out on the sofa, so's you can rest your handicap bag on the pillows, honeybunch." She was referring to the forty-seven pounds of birdshot in a canvas bag, which was padlocked around George's neck. "Go on and rest the bag for a little while," she said. "I don't care if you're not equal to me for a while."

25 George weighed the bag with his hands. "I don't mind it," he said. "I don't notice it any more. It's just a part of me."

26 "You been so tired lately—kind of wore out," said Hazel. "If there was just some way we could make a little hole in the bottom of the bag, and just take out a few of them lead balls. Just a few."

27 "Two years in prison and two thousand dollars fine for every ball I took out," said George. "I don't call that a bargain."

28 "If you could just take a few out when you came home from work," said Hazel. "I mean—you don't compete with anybody around here. You just sit around."

29 "If I tried to get away with it," said George, "then other people'd get away with it—and pretty soon we'd be right back to the dark ages again, with everybody competing against everybody else. You wouldn't like that, would you?"

30 "I'd hate it," said Hazel.

31 "There you are," said George. "The minute people start cheating on laws, what do you think happens to society?"

32 If Hazel hadn't been able to come up with an answer to this question, George couldn't have supplied one. A siren was going off in his head.

33 "Reckon it'd fall all apart," said Hazel.

34 "What would?" said George blankly.

35 "Society," said Hazel uncertainly. "Wasn't that what you just said?"

36 "Who knows?" said George.

37 The television program was suddenly interrupted for a news bulletin. It wasn't clear at first as to what the bulletin was about, since the announcer, like all announcers, had a serious speech **impediment.** For about half a minute, and

in a state of high excitement, the announcer tried to say, "Ladies and gentlemen."

38 He finally gave up, handed the bulletin to a ballerina to read.

39 "That's all right—" Hazel said of the announcer, "he tried. That's the big thing. He tried to do the best he could with what God gave him. He should get a nice raise for trying so hard."

40 "Ladies and gentlemen," said the ballerina, reading the bulletin. She must have been extraordinarily beautiful, because the mask she wore was hideous. And it was easy to see that she was the strongest and most graceful of all the dancers, for her handicap bags were as big as those worn by two-hundred-pound men.

41 And she had to apologize at once for her voice, which was a very unfair voice for a woman to use. Her voice was a warm, **luminous,** timeless melody. "Excuse me—" she said, and she began again, making her voice absolutely uncompetitive.

42 "Harrison Bergeron, age fourteen," she said in a grackle squawk, "has just escaped from jail, where he was held on suspicion of plotting to overthrow the government. He is a genius and an athlete, is under-handicapped, and should be regarded as extremely dangerous."

43 A police photograph of Harrison Bergeron was flashed on the screen—upside down, then sideways, upside down again, then right side up. The picture showed the full length of Harrison against a background **calibrated** in feet and inches. He was exactly seven feet tall.

44 The rest of Harrison's appearance was Halloween and hardware. Nobody had ever borne heavier handicaps. He had outgrown **hindrances** faster than the H-G men could think them up. Instead of a little ear radio for a mental handicap, he wore a tremendous pair of earphones, and spectacles with thick wavy lenses. The spectacles were intended to make him not only half blind, but to give him whanging headaches besides.

45 Scrap metal was hung all over him. Ordinarily, there was a certain symmetry, a military neatness to the handicaps issued to strong people, but Harrison looked like a walking junkyard. In the race of life, Harrison carried three hundred pounds.

46 And to offset his good looks, the H-G men required that he wear at all times a red rubber ball for a nose, keep his eyebrows shaved off, and cover his even white teeth with black caps at snaggle-tooth random.

Skill:
Word Patterns
and Relationships

I am not sure what the word "hideous" means. Because of the sentence structure and the context of the story, I can tell that "hideous" is an antonym for "beautiful." I think it must mean "very ugly."

NOTES

47   "If you see this boy," said the ballerina, "do not—I repeat, do not—try to reason with him."

48   There was the shriek of a door being torn from its hinges.

49   Screams and barking cries of **consternation** came from the television set. The photograph of Harrison Bergeron on the screen jumped again and again, as though dancing to the tune of an earthquake.

50   George Bergeron correctly identified the earthquake, and well he might have—for many was the time his own home had danced to the same crashing tune. "My God—" said George, "that must be Harrison!"

51   The realization was blasted from his mind instantly by the sound of an automobile collision in his head.

Skill:
Point of View

Harrison does not agree that everyone should be equal, so he takes off all the things meant to keep him down. He says that he is better than everyone else, and he declares that he is the emperor. The other people in the passage keep their handicaps on, and they are all afraid of Harrison.

52   When George could open his eyes again, the photograph of Harrison was gone. A living, breathing Harrison filled the screen.

53   Clanking, clownish, and huge, Harrison stood—in the center of the studio. The knob of the uprooted studio door was still in his hand. Ballerinas, technicians, musicians, and announcers cowered on their knees before him, expecting to die.

54   "I am the Emperor!" cried Harrison. "Do you hear? I am the Emperor! Everybody must do what I say at once!" He stamped his foot and the studio shook.

55   "Even as I stand here—" he bellowed, "crippled, hobbled, sickened—I am a greater ruler than any man who ever lived! Now watch me become what I can become!"

56   Harrison tore the straps of his handicap harness like wet tissue paper, tore straps guaranteed to support five thousand pounds.

57   Harrison's scrap-iron handicaps crashed to the floor.

58   Harrison thrust his thumbs under the bar of the padlock that secured his head harness. The bar snapped like celery. Harrison smashed his headphones and spectacles against the wall.

59   He flung away his rubber-ball nose, revealed a man that would have awed Thor, the god of thunder.

60   "I shall now select my Empress!" he said, looking down on the cowering people. "Let the first woman who dares rise to her feet claim her mate and her throne!"

61 A moment passed, and then a ballerina arose, swaying like a willow.

62 Harrison plucked the mental handicap from her ear, snapped off her physical handicaps with marvelous delicacy. Last of all he removed her mask.

63 She was blindingly beautiful.

64 "Now—" said Harrison, taking her hand, "shall we show the people the meaning of the word dance? Music!" he commanded.

65 The musicians scrambled back into their chairs, and Harrison stripped them of their handicaps, too. "Play your best," he told them, "and I'll make you barons and dukes and earls."

66 The music began. It was normal at first—cheap, silly, false. But Harrison snatched two musicians from their chairs, waved them like batons as he sang the music as he wanted it played. He slammed them back into their chairs.

67 The music began again and was much improved.

68 Harrison and his Empress merely listened to the music for a while—listened gravely, as though synchronizing their heartbeats with it.

69 They shifted their weights to their toes.

Skill:
Word Patterns
and Relationships

70 Harrison placed his big hands on the girl's tiny waist, letting her sense the weightlessness that would soon be hers.

71 And then, in an explosion of joy and grace, into the air they sprang!

72 Not only were the laws of the land abandoned, but the law of gravity and the laws of motion as well.

73 They reeled, whirled, swiveled, flounced, capered, gamboled, and spun.

74 They leaped like deer on the moon.

75 The studio ceiling was thirty feet high, but each leap brought the dancers nearer to it.

76 It became their obvious intention to kiss the ceiling. They kissed it.

77 And then, neutralizing gravity with love and pure will, they remained suspended in air inches below the ceiling, and they kissed each other for a long, long time.

I do not recognize the words "reeled," "flounced," "capered," and "gamboled." These words look like a list, though. They all describe how Harrison and the ballerina spin and jump as they dance. That must mean they are synonyms for "jumped" or "spun."

78   It was then that Diana Moon Clampers, the Handicapper General, came into the studio with a double-barreled ten-gauge shotgun. She fired twice, and the Emperor and the Empress were dead before they hit the floor.

79   Diana Moon Clampers loaded the gun again. She aimed it at the musicians and told them they had ten seconds to get their handicaps back on.

80   It was then that the Bergerons' television tube burned out.

81   Hazel turned to comment about the blackout to George. But George had gone out into the kitchen for a can of beer.

82   George came back in with the beer, paused while a handicap signal shook him up. And then he sat down again. "You been crying?" he said to Hazel.

83   "Yup," she said.

84   "What about?" he said.

85   "I forget," she said. "Something real sad on television."

86   "What was it?" he said.

87   "It's all kind of mixed up in my mind," said Hazel.

88   "Forget sad things," said George.

89   "I always do," said Hazel.

90   "That's my girl," said George. He winced. There was the sound of a riveting gun in his head.

91   "Gee—I could tell that one was a doozy," said Hazel.

92   "You can say that again," said George.

93   "Gee—" said Hazel, "I could tell that one was a doozy."

First Read

Read "Harrison Bergeron." After you read, complete the Think Questions below.

☁ THINK QUESTIONS

1. How does the Handicapper General ensure equality among all people? Explain, citing evidence from the text.

2. Based on the text, what can you infer about George and Hazel's personalities? Cite specific details from the story in your answer.

3. How does the government affect the lives of individual families? Make sure to refer to the text in your answer.

4. The root word *lum*, meaning "light," appears in such words as *luminary* and *illuminate*. With this in mind, along with any relevant context clues, write your best definition of the word **luminous** as it appears in the text.

5. Use context to determine the meaning of the word **consternation** as it is used in the text. Double-check your answer by looking the word up in a dictionary. In your own words, write a definition for *consternation* here.

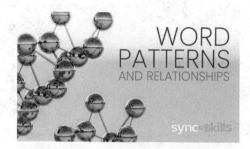

Skill: Word Patterns and Relationships

Use the Checklist to analyze Word Patterns and Relationships in "Harrison Bergeron." Refer to the sample student annotations about Word Patterns and Relationships in the text.

••• CHECKLIST FOR WORD PATTERNS AND RELATIONSHIPS

In order to determine the relationship between particular words to better understand each of the words, note the following:

- ✓ any unfamiliar words in the text

- ✓ the surrounding words and phrases, in order to better understand the meanings or possible relationships between words

- ✓ any analogies that you can use as clues, such as *while apples are smooth, pineapples are abrasive,* in which the contrast between familiar items and the known word *smooth* help to define *abrasive*

- ✓ a synonym or an antonym of the word in the sentence as a clue, such as *Ann was courageous and never timid*, in which the antonym *courageous* helps define *timid*

To use the relationship between particular words to better understand each of the words, consider the following questions:

- ✓ Are these words related to each other in some way? How?

- ✓ What kind of relationship do these words have?

- ✓ Are there any analogies present?

- ✓ Are there any synonyms or antonyms that can help define words?

- ✓ Can any of these words be defined by using analogies or a synonym/antonym word relationship?

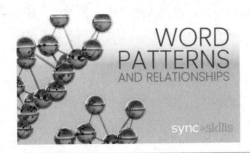

Skill: Word Patterns and Relationships

Reread paragraph 45 of "Harrison Bergeron." Then, using the Checklist on the previous page, answer the multiple-choice questions below.

♻ YOUR TURN

1. This question has two parts. First, answer Part A. Then answer Part B.

Part A: Which of the following best defines the word *symmetry* as used in paragraph 45?

- ○ A. regularity, uniformity
- ○ B. sloppiness, untidiness
- ○ C. randomness, chaos
- ○ D. brilliance, luster

Part B: Which word relationship helps you define the word *symmetry*?

- ○ A. synonym for "walking junkyard"
- ○ B. synonym for "scrap metal"
- ○ C. analogy for "military neatness"
- ○ D. analogy for "strong people"

Skill:
Textual Evidence

Use the Checklist to analyze Textual Evidence in "Harrison Bergeron." Refer to the sample student annotations about Textual Evidence in the text.

••• CHECKLIST FOR TEXTUAL EVIDENCE

In order to support an analysis by citing textual evidence that is explicitly stated in the text, do the following:

✓ read the text closely and critically

✓ identify what the text says explicitly

✓ find the most relevant textual evidence that supports your analysis

✓ consider why an author explicitly states specific details and information

✓ cite the specific words, phrases, sentences, paragraphs, or images from the text that support your analysis

In order to interpret implicit meanings in a text by making inferences, do the following:

✓ combine information directly stated in the text with your own knowledge, experiences, and observations

✓ cite the specific words, phrases, sentences, paragraphs, or images from the text that support this inference

In order to cite textual evidence to support an analysis of what the text says explicitly as well as inferences drawn from the text, consider the following questions:

✓ Have I read the text closely and critically?

✓ What inferences am I making about the text? What textual evidence am I using to support these inferences?

✓ Am I quoting the evidence from the text correctly?

✓ Does my textual evidence logically relate to my analysis?

✓ Have I cited several pieces of textual evidence?

Skill:
Textual Evidence

Reread paragraphs 49–55 of "Harrison Bergeron." Then, using the Checklist on the previous page, answer the multiple-choice questions below.

♻ YOUR TURN

1. Based on explicit details in paragraphs 49 and 52, the reader can infer that George Bergeron is —

   ○ A. in a television studio trying to calm his son, Harrison.
   ○ B. at home watching as his son, Harrison, appears on his television.
   ○ C. at home watching television while an earthquake is shaking his house.
   ○ D. having a nightmare in which his son, Harrison, appears in a photograph.

2. George's explicit thoughts and reactions in paragraphs 50 and 51 imply that —

   ○ A. Harrison Bergeron had violent episodes during his childhood.
   ○ B. Harrison Bergeron inherited his superior intelligence from George.
   ○ C. the government had erased all memories of Harrison from George's brain.
   ○ D. George is afraid of what will happen to his son after this outburst of violence.

3. In paragraph 53 the author describes Harrison as holding the knob to the studio door. This detail implies that —

   ○ A. the studio was built by inept builders.
   ○ B. Harrison is skilled at picking locks.
   ○ C. Harrison has broken the door with his great strength.
   ○ D. Harrison is attempting to fix the door.

Skill:
Point of View

Use the Checklist to analyze Point of View in "Harrison Bergeron." Refer to the sample student annotations about Point of View in the text.

••• CHECKLIST FOR POINT OF VIEW

In order to identify different points of view, note the following:

- ✓ the speaker(s) or narrator(s)

- ✓ how much the narrator(s) or speaker(s) knows and reveals

- ✓ how the author develops different points of view, through dialogue or story events

- ✓ what the narrator(s) or speaker(s) says or does that reveals how he or she feels

- ✓ how the point of view of the narrator(s) or speaker(s) contrasts with the points of view of other characters

To analyze how an author develops and contrasts different points of view of different characters or narrators in a text, consider the following questions:

- ✓ Is the narrator or speaker objective, or does he or she mislead the reader? How?

- ✓ What is the narrator's or the speaker's point of view?

  - • Is the narrator or speaker "all-knowing," or omniscient?
  - • Is the narrator or speaker limited to revealing the thoughts and feelings of one character?

- ✓ How does the narrator or speaker reveal thoughts about the events or the other characters? How do the experiences or cultural background of the narrator affect his or her thoughts?

- ✓ How does the author reveal different points of view in the story?

- ✓ How do these different points of view compare and contrast with one another?

Skill:
Point of View

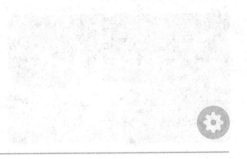

Reread paragraphs 70–79 of "Harrison Bergeron." Then, using the Checklist on the previous page, answer the multiple-choice questions below.

↻ YOUR TURN

1. In paragraphs 70–79, what point of view does the narrator use?

   ○ A. The narrator is omniscient, describing what happened objectively.
   ○ B. The narrator describes the thoughts and feelings of the Handicapper General in a limited point of view.
   ○ C. The narrator describes the thoughts and feelings of Hazel in a limited point of view.
   ○ D. The narrator describes the thoughts and feelings of George in a limited point of view.

2. What is Diana Moon Clampers's point of view on individuality?

   ○ A. She celebrates people's rights to be different and excel in different ways.
   ○ B. She eliminates any differences among people to ensure that everyone is equal.
   ○ C. She removes evidence of individuality, but she is conflicted about the implications.
   ○ D. She wants people to make their own choices about individuality.

3. What excerpt from the passage best supports your answer to question number 2?

   ○ A. They reeled, whirled, swiveled, flounced, capered, gamboled, and spun.
   ○ B. It was then that Diana Moon Clampers, the Handicapper General, came into the studio
   ○ C. They remained suspended in air inches below the ceiling, and they kissed each other for a long, long time.
   ○ D. She aimed it at the musicians and told them they had ten seconds to get their handicaps back on.

Reading & Writing Companion

Close Read

Reread "Harrison Bergeron." As you reread, complete the Skills Focus questions below. Then use your answers and annotations from the questions to help you complete the Write activity.

◎ SKILLS FOCUS

1. The author uses an omniscient narrator to reveal what is going on in the characters' minds. Compare and contrast the characters' points of view in the story and explain how the points of view reveal the conflict in the story.

2. Identify examples of how this government operates and how the rules of the government affect the lives of individuals. Explain what these examples imply about this society.

3. Highlight details at the end of the story that show how George and Hazel react to having seen their son shot and killed on television. Explain whether or not you were surprised by their reaction.

Consider what you know about these characters and describe how their qualities led to this resolution.

4. The story "Harrison Bergeron" has themes of equality and independence. Identify passages in the story that express these themes. Explain what these examples imply about equality and independence.

5. Identify one event when Harrison tries to make a change. What does he sacrifice? Use evidence from the text to prove whether the event resulted in changes to society.

✏ WRITE

LITERARY ANALYSIS: Equality is part of the philosophy of American culture. What statement is Vonnegut making about the idea of equality? Explain how Vonnegut uses point of view and story details to develop and contrast characters and to suggest a message about equality. Support your analysis and any inferences by citing several pieces of textual evidence.

The Last Human Light
(from 'What If?')

INFORMATIONAL TEXT
Randall Munroe
2014

Introduction

A former NASA roboticist, Randall Munroe (b. 1984) founded the lauded web comic *xkcd*, which primarily features stick figures in the throes of mathematical, scientific, philosophical, and romantic dilemmas. "What If?" is the name of Munroe's serial blog of infographic essays proposing scientific solutions to hypothetical questions such as, "If you suddenly began rising steadily at one foot per second, when exactly would you die?" and "What would happen if the moon went away?"

"Most lights wouldn't last long, because the major power grids would go down relatively fast."

NOTES

1   *If every human somehow simply disappeared from the face of the Earth, how long would it be before the last artificial light source would go out?*
    —Alan

2   There would be a lot of contenders for the "last light" title.

3   The superb 2007 book *The World Without Us*, by Alan Weisman, explored in great detail what would happen to Earth's houses, roads, skyscrapers, farms, and animals if humans suddenly vanished. A 2008 TV series called *Life After People* investigated the same premise. However, neither of them answered this particular question.

4   We'll start with the obvious: Most lights wouldn't last long, because the major power grids would go down relatively fast. Fossil fuel plants, which supply the vast majority of the world's electricity, require a steady supply of fuel, and their supply chains do involve humans making decisions.

5   Without people, there would be less demand for power, but our thermostats would still be running. As coal and oil plants started shutting down in the first few hours, other plants would need to take up the slack. This kind of situation

is difficult to handle even with human guidance. The result would be a rapid series of cascade failures, leading to a blackout of all major power grids.

6 However, plenty of electricity comes from sources not tied to the major power grids. Let's take a look at a few of those, and when each one might turn off.

Diesel generators

7 Many remote communities, like those on far-flung islands, get their power from diesel generators. These can continue to operate until they run out of fuel, which in most cases could be anywhere from days to months.

Geothermal plants

8 Generating sections that don't need a human-provided fuel supply would be in better shape. Geothermal plants, which are powered by the Earth's internal heat, can run for some time without human **intervention.**

9 According to the maintenance **manual** for the Svartsengi Island geothermal plant in Iceland, every six months the operators must change the gearbox oil and regrease all electric motors and couplings. Without humans to perform these sorts of maintenance procedures, some plants might run for a few years, but they'd all succumb to corrosion eventually.

Wind turbines

10 People relying on wind power would be in better shape than most. Turbines are designed so that they don't need constant maintenance, for the simple reason that there are a lot of them and they're a pain to climb.

11 Some windmills can run for a long time without human intervention. The Gedser Wind Turbine in Denmark was installed in the late 1950s, and generated power for 11 years without maintenance. Modern turbines are typically rated to run for 30,000 hours (three years) without servicing, and there are no doubt some that would run for decades. One of them would no doubt have at least a status LED[1] in it somewhere.

12 Eventually, most of the wind turbines would be stopped by the same thing that would destroy the geothermal plants: Their gearboxes would seize up.

Hydroelectric dams

13 Generators that **convert** falling water into electricity will keep working for quite a while. The History Channel show *Life After People* spoke with an

---

1. **LED** liquid electronic display

**Skill:
Media**

The boldface headings signal different types of energy sources the writer will discuss and how long they might last. The boldface titles help me keep the different energy sources straight, so I don't confuse a diesel generator with a geothermal plant. The headings are a helpful visual!

**Skill:
Informational
Text Structure**

The author appears to be comparing wind turbines, geothermal plants, and hydroelectric dams. Even with a steady energy source, machines don't last forever. Mechanical failure will cause all three to stop working eventually. This all contributes to his overall point that lights would all stop if humans disappeared.

operator at the Hoover Dam, who said that if everyone walked out, the facility would continue to run on autopilot for several years. The dam would probably succumb to either clogged intakes or the same kind of mechanical failure that would hit the wind turbines and geothermal plants.

Batteries

Skill:
Media

The article is serious and scientific, but the cartoon is funny. The idea of having to buy an infinite number of batteries for an eternal light bulb because they are "not included" is a joke. This helps get across the idea that batteries do not last forever, even when they claim to.

14 Battery-powered lights will all be off in a decade or two. Even without anything using their power, batteries gradually self-**discharge**. Some types last longer than others, but even batteries advertised as having long shelf lives typically hold their charge only for a decade or two.

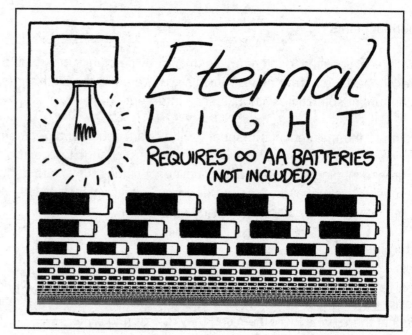

15 There are a few exceptions. In the Clarendon Laboratory at Oxford University sits a battery-powered bell that has been ringing since the year 1840. The bell "rings" so quietly it's almost inaudible, using only a tiny amount of charge with every motion of the clapper. Nobody knows exactly what kind of batteries it uses because nobody wants to take it apart to figure it out.

16 Sadly, there's no light hooked up to it.

Nuclear reactors

17 Nuclear reactors[2] are a little tricky. If they settle into low-power mode, they can continue running almost indefinitely; the energy density of their fuel is just that high. As a certain webcomic put it:

18 Unfortunately, although there's enough fuel, the reactors wouldn't keep running for long. As soon as something went wrong, the core would go into automatic shutdown. This would happen quickly; many things can trigger it, but the most likely culprit would be a loss of external power.

19 It may seem strange that a power plant would require external power to run, but every part of a nuclear reactor's control system is designed so that a failure causes it to rapidly shut down, or "SCRAM[3]." When outside power is lost, either because the outside power plant shuts down or the on-site backup generators run out of fuel, the reactor would SCRAM.

Space probes

20 Out of all human artifacts, our spacecraft might be the longest-lasting. Some of their orbits will last for millions of years, although their electrical power typically won't.

21 Within centuries, our Mars rovers will be buried by dust. By then, many of our satellites will have fallen back to Earth as their orbits decayed. GPS satellites,

---

2. **nuclear reactors** any of several kinds of apparatus that maintain and control a nuclear reaction for the production of energy or artificial elements
3. When Enrico Fermi built the first nuclear reactor, he suspended the control rods from a rope tied to a balcony railing. In case something went wrong, next to the railing was stationed a distinguished physicist with an axe. This led to the probably apocryphal story that SCRAM stands for "Safety Control Rod Axe Man."

in distant orbits, will last longer, but in time, even the most stable orbits will be disrupted by the Moon and Sun.

22 Many spacecraft are powered by solar panels, and others by radioactive decay. The Mars rover *Curiosity*, for example, is powered by the heat from a chunk of plutonium[4] it carries in a container on the end of a stick.

23 *Curiosity* could continue receiving electrical power from the RTG for over a century. Eventually the voltage will drop too low to keep the rover operating, but other parts will probably wear out before that happens.

24 So *Curiosity* looks promising. There's one problem: no lights.

25 *Curiosity has* lights; it uses them to illuminate samples and perform spectroscopy. However, these lights are turned on only when it's taking measurements. With no human instructions, it will have no reason to turn them on.

26 Unless they have humans on board, spacecraft don't need a lot of lights. The *Galileo* probe, which explored Jupiter in the 1990s, had several LEDs in the mechanism of its flight data recorder. Since they emitted infrared rather than visible light, calling them "lights" is a stretch—and in any case, *Galileo* was deliberately crashed into Jupiter in 2003[5].

27 Other satellites carry LEDs. Some GPS satellites use, for example, UV LEDs to control charge buildup in some of their equipment, and they're powered by

4. **plutonium** an isotope of uranium used in weapons and nuclear reactors
5. The purpose of the crash was to safely incinerate the probe so it wouldn't accidentally contaminate the nearby moons, such as the watery Europa, with Earth bacteria.

solar panels; in theory they can keep running as long as the Sun is shining. Unfortunately, most won't even last as long as *Curiosity*, eventually, they'll succumb to space debris **impacts.**

28   But solar panels aren't used in space.

Solar power

29   Emergency call boxes, often found along the side of the road in remote locations, are frequently solar-powered. They usually have lights on them, which provide illumination every night.

30   Like wind turbines, they're hard to service, so they're built to last for a long time. As long as they're kept free of dust and debris, solar panels will generally last as long as the electronics connected to them.

31   A solar panel's wires and circuits will eventually succumb to corrosion, but solar panels in a dry place, with well-built electronics, could easily continue providing power for a century if they're kept free of dust by occasional breezes or rain on the exposed panels.

32 If we follow a strict definition of lighting, solar-powered lights in remote locations could **conceivably** be the last surviving human light source[6].

33 But there's another contender, and it's a weird one.

Cherenkov radiation

34 Radioactivity isn't usually visible.

35 Watch dials used to be coated in radium, which made them glow. However, this glow didn't come from the radioactivity itself. It came from the phosphorescent paint on top of the radium, which glowed when it was irradiated. Over the years, the paint has broken down. Although the watch dials are still radioactive, they no longer glow.

36 Watch dials, however, are not our only radioactive light source.

37 When radioactive particles travel through materials like water or glass, they can emit light through a sort of optical sonic boom. This light is called Cherenkov radiation[7], and it's seen in the distinctive blue glow of nuclear reactor cores.

38 Some of our radioactive waste products, such as cesium-137, are melted and mixed with glass, then cooled into a solid block that can be wrapped in more shielding so they can be safely transported and stored.

---

6. The USSR built some lighthouses powered by radioactive decay, but none are still in operation.

7. **radiation** an effect of nuclear energy, usually in the form of electromagnetic waves of heat or light

39 Cesium-137 has a half-life of thirty years, which means that two centuries later, they'll still be glowing with 1 percent of their original radioactivity. Since the color of the light depends only on the decay energy, and not the amount of radiation, it will fade in brightness over time but keep the same blue color.

40 And thus, we arrive at our answer: Centuries from now, deep in concrete vaults, the light from our most toxic waste will still be shining.

"The Last Human Light" from WHAT IF?: Serious Scientific Answers to Absurd Hypothetical Questions by Randall Munroe. Copyright ©2014 by xkcd Inc. Reprinted by permission of Houghton Mifflin Harcourt Publishing Company. All rights reserved.

Please note that excerpts and passages in the StudySync® library and this workbook are intended as touchstones to generate interest in an author's work. The excerpts and passages do not substitute for the reading of entire texts, and StudySync® strongly recommends that students seek out and purchase the whole literary or informational work in order to experience it as the author intended. Links to online resellers are available in our digital library. In addition, complete works may be ordered through an authorized reseller by filling out and returning to StudySync® the order form enclosed in this workbook.

Reading & Writing
Companion

551

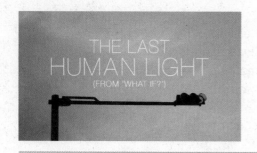

First Read

Read "The Last Human Light." After you read, complete the Think Questions below.

 THINK QUESTIONS

1. Why would the geothermal plants eventually shut down due to corrosion? Cite textual evidence in your response.

2. Why would people relying on wind power be "in better shape than most"? Provide evidence from the text to support your response.

3. Why is the ringing bell in Oxford not exactly relevant to this essay's central question?

4. The word **intervention** in paragraph 8 is derived from the Latin word *venire*, which means "to come," and the Latin *inter-*, which means "between." With this in mind, write your best definition of *intervention* here and explain how its Latin origins relate to the word's meaning.

5. The word **manual** comes from the Latin word *manus*, meaning "hand." Use this information to infer the meaning of *manual* as it is used in paragraph 9.

Skill:
Word Meaning

Use the Checklist to analyze Word Meaning in "The Last Human Light." Refer to the sample student annotations about Word Meaning in the text.

••• CHECKLIST FOR WORD MEANING

In order to find the pronunciation of a word or determine or clarify its precise meaning or its part of speech, do the following:

✓ determine the word's part of speech

✓ consult reference materials, both print and digital, to find the pronunciation of a word or determine or clarify its precise meaning or its part of speech

In order to verify the preliminary determination of the meaning of a word or phrase, do the following:

✓ use context clues to make an inference about the word's meaning

✓ consult a dictionary to verify your preliminary determination of the meaning

✓ be sure to read all of the definitions, and then decide which definition makes sense within the context of the text

To determine a word's precise meaning or part of speech, ask the following questions:

✓ What is the word describing?

✓ How is the word being used in the phrase or sentence?

✓ Have I consulted my reference materials?

Skill:
Word Meaning

Reread paragraph 29 of "The Last Human Light." Then, using the Checklist on the previous page as well as the dictionary entries below, answer the multiple-choice questions.

⟳ YOUR TURN

remote \rə¹ mōt\
adjective

1. situated far from the main centers of population
2. unlikely to occur
3. small in degree

noun

4. a remote control device

Origin: late Middle English (meaning "far apart"): from Latin word *remotus* meaning "removed"

illumination \i-¹lü-mə-¹nā-shən\
noun

1. the act of illuminating or state of being illuminated
2. a light or lighting
3. the intensity of light per unit of area of a surface exposed to light, measured in lumens
4. the act or art of ornamenting a letter, page, or the like with designs

Origin: late Middle English: from Latin *illumino* meaning "light"

1. Which definition best matches the way the word *remote* is used in paragraph 29? Remember to pay attention to the word's part of speech as you make your decision.

   ○ A. Definition 1
   ○ B. Definition 2
   ○ C. Definition 3
   ○ D. Definition 4

2. Which definition best matches the way the word *illumination* is used in paragraph 29?

○ A. Definition 1

○ B. Definition 2

○ C. Definition 3

○ D. Definition 4

Please note that excerpts and passages in the StudySync® library and this workbook are intended as touchstones to generate interest in an author's work. The excerpts and passages do not substitute for the reading of entire texts, and StudySync® strongly recommends that students seek out and purchase the whole literary or informational work in order to experience it as the author intended. Links to online resellers are available in our digital library. In addition, complete works may be ordered through an authorized reseller by filling out and returning to StudySync® the order form enclosed in this workbook.

Reading & Writing
Companion

555

Skill:
Media

Use the Checklist to analyze Media in "The Last Human Light." Refer to the sample student annotations about Media in the text.

••• CHECKLIST FOR MEDIA

In order to determine to identify ideas presented in diverse media and formats, note the following:

✓ how the same topic can be treated, or presented, in more than one format

- visually

- quantitatively

- orally

✓ which details are emphasized or absent in each medium, and the reasons behind these choices

✓ what the details in each medium have in common, or the main idea in each medium

✓ how the main idea and supporting details help to clarify, or explain, a topic, a text, or an issue

In order to determine how to compare and contrast, analyze, or explain ideas presented in diverse media and formats, consider the following:

✓ How are the treatments of the source text similar? How are they different?

✓ How do ideas presented in diverse media and formats clarify, or explain, a topic, a text, or an issue?

✓ How does each medium's portrayal affect the presentation of the subject?

✓ Why are different media able to emphasize or highlight certain kinds of information better than others?

Skill:
Media

Reread paragraphs 17–19 of "The Last Human Light." Then, using the Checklist on the previous page as well as the image below, answer the multiple-choice questions.

↻ YOUR TURN

1. Based on the boldfaced heading in this excerpt, the reader can infer that the section will —

   ○ A. give information about nuclear reactors.
   ○ B. argue that nuclear reactors are the best source of power.
   ○ C. explain why nuclear reactors can be dangerous.
   ○ D. entertain readers with jokes about nuclear reactors.

2. The image in this excerpt develops and clarifies the author's ideas by —

   ○ A. exaggerating the usefulness of nuclear power.
   ○ B. giving information about the different fuel types people use.
   ○ C. comparing the energy density of common fuels.
   ○ D. suggesting that people don't understand nuclear power.

Skill:
Informational Text Structure

Use the Checklist to analyze Informational Text Structure in "The Last Human Light." Refer to the sample student annotations about Informational Text Structure in the text.

••• CHECKLIST FOR INFORMATIONAL TEXT STRUCTURE

In order to determine the overall structure of a text, note the following:

- ✓ the topic(s) and how the author organizes information about the topic(s)

- ✓ patterns in a section of text that reveal the text structure, such as:

  - sequences, including the order of events or steps in a process
  - problems and their solutions
  - cause-and-effect relationships
  - comparisons

- ✓ the overall structure of the text and how each section contributes to the development of ideas

- ✓ headers, charts, or tables that organize topics or categories

To analyze the structure an author uses to organize a text, including how the major sections contribute to the whole and to the development of the ideas, use the following questions as a guide:

- ✓ What organizational pattern does the author use? How does it reveal the text structure used to present information?

- ✓ How does a particular section fit into the overall structure of the text? How does it contribute to the whole and the development of the author's ideas?

- ✓ In what ways does the text structure contribute to the development of ideas in the text?

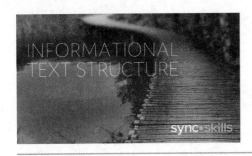

Skill:
Informational Text Structure

Reread paragraphs 14 and 15 of "The Last Human Light." Then, using the Checklist on the previous page, answer the multiple-choice questions below.

⟳ YOUR TURN

1. This question has two parts. First, answer Part A. Then, answer Part B.

   Part A: Which of the following best describes the text structure the author used to organize the two paragraphs?

   - ○ A. sequence
   - ○ B. cause-and-effect
   - ○ C. comparison and contrast
   - ○ D. problem-and-solution

   Part B: How does the text structure identified in Part A contribute to the development of the author's idea that different energy sources have different lifespans?

   - ○ A. By giving a detailed description of exactly how long it would take every type of battery to turn off
   - ○ B. By comparing batteries and other sources of power
   - ○ C. By comparing the lifespan of the battery at Clarendon Laboratory to more typical batteries
   - ○ D. By providing explanations of the mechanical failures that might affect batteries and their lifespans

Close Read

Reread "The Last Human Light." As you reread, complete the Skills Focus questions below. Then use your answers and annotations from the questions to help you complete the Write activity.

◎ SKILLS FOCUS

1. Identify a detail about an energy source that is developed by illustration. Explain how the visual helps you understand the information or author's purpose in the text.

2. Identify an example of cause-and-effect structure in the text. Explain how this structure helps you understand the relationship between important events.

3. Authors may use more than one text structure to organize information. Although "The Last Human Light" often uses cause-and-effect text structure, the subtopics within the article are organized using a different text structure. Identify text features, phrases, or sentences that indicate the text structure used for organizing the subtopics. Then, name the text structure and explain how the highlighted text supports your choice.

4. An argument is an author's overall opinion on a topic. An effective argument is backed by claims and evidence. Highlight a claim from the text. Then explain how it develops the argument of the essay.

5. This article examines how long artificial light would last if humans suddenly disappeared. Choose two or more sources of energy from the article. Then identify and explain what makes them vulnerable or resistant to change.

✏ WRITE

INFORMATIVE: Munroe presents information about multiple topics and categories relating to different power sources. How does the author's organization help readers understand the difficult concepts presented in the text? How do the illustrations and graphic features contribute to your understanding of Munroe's overall argument and the topic? Write a response to these questions. Make sure to support your response with evidence from the text.

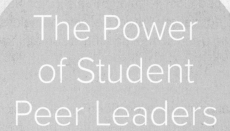

The Power of Student Peer Leaders

INFORMATIONAL TEXT
David Bornstein
2018

Introduction

David Bornstein (b. 1974) is a Canadian journalist and author. He writes for the *New York Times* and is the founder of the Solutions Journalism Network, a non-profit organization. In "The Power of Student Peer Leaders," he profiles PeerForward (formerly College Summit), an initiative that promotes student involvement in school reform movements and education innovation.

"The peer effect is like putting in a high speed computer chip."

1   Moises Urena is a junior at the State University of New York at Albany majoring in human development. He spends much of his spare time mentoring other students and plans to pursue a career in higher education administration.

2   Four years ago, his future was far less clear.

3   He had no plans for college. During his first two years attending high school in New York, he and his mother experienced periods of homelessness, and his home life was full of stress. He skipped class regularly. In his junior year, however, he became serious about his education. "After I became homeless, I realized the only constant in my life had been school and that's something I should stick to," he said.

4   That year, one of Mr. Urena's teachers suggested he take part in a three-day summer workshop run by an organization now called PeerForward, which helps students from low-income backgrounds plan for success after high school. At the workshop, Mr. Urena would not only learn how to navigate the process for applying to college, but would be trained as a peer leader with three other students from his high school and teams from about 30 other schools. They would learn how to guide fellow seniors to apply for college or plan for postsecondary[1] **vocations**.

5   "My teacher told me to try," Mr. Urena said. "I thought, 'Why not?' It actually changed my life."

6   Over the three days, with help from counselors, Mr. Urena selected three schools to apply to; SUNY Albany was his first choice. He wrote a personal essay about how the hardships he'd faced had motivated him to graduate from college. He learned how to apply for financial aid. (Students take note: The Free Application for Federal Student Aid, known as the Fafsa, for the 2019–2020 school year opened on Monday).

7   He also gained confidence from "rap sessions" led by youth **facilitators**. In those sessions, students spoke **candidly** about their fears, insecurities and family pressures, as well as their achievements. "It was the first time I ever

1. **postsecondary** after high school

told people my story of being homeless, growing up with just my mom, struggling not having a father," Mr. Urena said. "I realized that telling my story could help improve the lives of others."

8   He also received a crash course in community organizing: how to build relationships and inspire others through the "public narrative" technique; and how to plan and run a campaign — how to set goals, use data to assess progress, and build **momentum,** for example.

9   Back at school, he and his team members led campaigns for the senior class and school. "It changed the whole atmosphere in the school and created this bonding," Mr. Urena said. That year, according to PeerForward's data, the class's Fafsa completion rate jumped to 65 percent from 24 percent (not all students are eligible for federal aid), and the college application rate increased to 95 percent, up from 69 percent.

10 PeerForward began as an initiative of the organization College Summit, one of the groups selected by President Barack Obama to receive a portion of his Nobel Peace Prize winnings. Over two decades, College Summit had shown it could improve college-entry rates among low-income, minority students; its successes influenced many similarly focused organizations and helped inform education policies. Four years ago, College Summit renamed itself PeerForward and changed its program to focus on youth leadership, the core driver of success in College Summit's work.

11 Last year, PeerForward trained and supported high school seniors in 100 schools. With each four-member peer team of seniors recruiting four juniors and working closely with an adviser (a teacher in their school), PeerForward's 25 employees mobilized 900 people last year. In the schools that PeerForward works with, the ratio of students to college guidance counselors is often 500 to 1 or higher. "If the students aren't doing this, many are not getting college and career counseling at all," said Raquel Figueroa, the Managing Director of **Implementation** for PeerForward.

12 Keith Frome, a co-founder and chief executive of PeerForward, said, "School reform movements and education innovations almost always lack the component of leveraging the power of peer influence." But, he added, "the peer effect is like putting in a high speed computer chip. Anything you want to do with kids, if you leverage peer influence, it will go faster and better."

13 PeerForward asks students to run campaigns to achieve three goals:

• Increase the number of seniors who apply to three or more colleges (this improves the likelihood of enrollment in college).

- Increase the number of seniors who complete the Fafsa before March 1 (earlier completion leads to larger aid packages and better-informed financial decisions).

- Increase the number of students in all grades who have a post-graduation plan of some sort and who can see the connection between college graduation and pursuing a desired career. (Students who make this connection are far more likely to pursue college.)

14   The question, of course, is this: How effective are peer leaders?

15   In a 2017 study in which PeerForward schools were compared with matched counterparts, researchers found an increase to 35 percent, from 28 percent, in completing Fafsa forms on time. Based on average federal aid packages, that translated to an additional 1,400 students in schools using PeerForward's approach who received an estimated $13 million in federal aid. "From a research perspective, it's a very promising model and one that deserves to be rigorously tested," said Lindsay C. Page, assistant professor of education at the University of Pittsburgh, who oversaw the research. For the next study, she wants to do a random assignment of schools.

16   Anecdotally, schools using PeerForward's model, which costs schools $13,500 per year, also report benefits. Eight years ago, the college enrollment rate for Lake Wales High School, in central Florida, was 46 percent. More recently, it has hovered at 80 percent to 85 percent, according to Donna Dunson, the school's principal. "Now kids come into the school believing that they are heading somewhere," she said. "And college doesn't seem so alien for first-generation kids."

17   Ms. Dunson is quick to note that the gains come from many efforts, not just the peer leaders. "But it's critical that students are the ones driving this," she added. "Then they take the ownership. I know that word is overused, but it fits. If you can create the atmosphere and get out of the way, the kids will take it from there. But you have to set the stage for this to happen."

18   Teaching students and educators how to support youth leadership is the core function of PeerForward, Mr. Frome said: "It's about young people and adults partnering in a deep and equitable way. That has to be learned and taught and coached."

19   PeerForward begins its interaction with schools by examining how student leadership resonates with the school's mission. It then invites schools to identify four rising seniors who teachers believe have the qualities to influence their peers.

20   Those students attend a summer workshop. When they return to school in the fall, they recruit four juniors. Early in the year, teams meet with a

PeerForward coach, and their principal and adviser, to discuss how campaign goals should align with school goals. They assign roles including captain, communications manager, social media manager, data manager, secretary, photographer or videographer, and then start planning campaigns.

21 PeerForward provides a web-based scoreboard so that teams can track progress, including in Fafsa and college applications by students. PeerForward has a campaign playbook full of ideas for events and activities, broken down into steps. Throughout the year, coaches meet or call with teams and advisers at least once a month, and teams meet with their advisers at least twice a month. There are training camps in the fall and spring to refresh skills.

22 Students have organized college fairs and job fairs. They bring in school alumni to share college stories. Some have created Fafsa lounges and dances, where the admission ticket is a completed aid form. They have to solve problems and come up with creative incentives[2]. In one school, after parents failed to show up to a Fafsa night, students realized that they needed to provide on-site babysitting. In another school, students persuaded a utility company to offer credits for families that submitted their Fafsa forms by March 1.

23 After PeerForward began working in two Cincinnati public schools three years ago, Laura Mitchell, the district superintendent, established peer leadership collaboratives in her schools. The student collaboratives are focused not just on college access, but on many areas of concern to students including service learning, career counseling, reducing ninth-grade dropout rates, stopping bullying on social media, embedding more attention to the contributions of African-Americans in the curriculum, promoting leadership opportunities for female students, and advancing a culture of respect for women (a program led by male students). "The young people decide on campaigns they want to drive," Ms. Mitchell said. "We help them develop a project plan, give them a budget, and pay a stipend[3] for an adult facilitator."

24 "When you're able to tap into young people's passion, they lean into the experience," she added. "We want them to be partners — to tell us what they want to see in terms of education."

25 "An adult can say to a student, 'You should go to college'," Ruby Noboa, a peer leader at the Urban Assembly School for Applied Math and Science in New York, said. "But if a student says to another student, 'Knowledge is power. We need higher education so we can overcome our oppression,' they're much more likely to listen."

---

2. **incentives** rewards intended to encourage motivation
3 **stipend** a sum of money allotted on a regular basis, usually for some specific purpose

26   When problems arise, it's often because adults have trouble letting students lead, or a principal or adviser is not fully on board. "A big challenge is the belief system," Ms. Figueroa said. "It's not in place in a lot of schools that young people can really effect positive change. When you have an adviser or principal who has that belief system, there will be a lot of challenges."

27   The idea that schools should do more to build youth leadership seems to be gaining traction. "We're getting more and more requests to use this methodology for other things, including college persistence," said Gary Z. Linnen, who went through College Summit's program as a student and is now PeerForward's managing director for program, operations and innovation.

28   "One of the worst lessons that students get from school is that you win by yourself," Mr. Frome said. "In most aspects of life and work, you win and lose together. Students are not taught to think of everyone's success — our grade, our school."

29   Mr. Linnen added, "What's most powerful is when someone sees there's a challenge in their community, and says, 'It's not how do *I* get through this, but how do *we* get through this.'"

30   That was the insight that Mr. Urena said changed his life. "Being in PeerForward made me realize that I was a leader," he said. "I was not in such a happy place before. But I feel very happy now. When I look back on it, the key element for me was finding my passion in helping others and seeing that I can have an impact on others' lives."

✏ WRITE

PERSONAL RESPONSE: Why do you think it's important to have mentors in your life? Write a response in which you answer this question. Use examples from the essay "The Power of Student Peer Leaders" to support your response.

The Three Questions

FICTION
Leo Tolstoy
1885

Introduction

The range of literature by Leo Tolstoy (1828–1910) encompasses the epic sweep of history and romance *(War and Peace)* as well as the compressed gem typified by this parable, "The Three Questions." In an attempt to be the best of all possible rulers, an ambitious king asks three important questions. Unsatisfied with the answers he receives from his courtiers, the king sets out on a

"I have come to you, wise hermit, to ask you to answer three questions. . . ."

1 It once **occurred** to a certain king, that if he always knew the right time to begin everything; if he knew who were the right people to listen to, and whom to avoid; and, above all, if he always knew what was the most important thing to do, he would never fail in anything he might undertake.

2 And this thought having occurred to him, he had it proclaimed throughout his kingdom that he would give a great reward to any one who would teach him what was the right time for every action, and who were the most necessary people, and how he might know what was the most important thing to do.

A 1916 cover illustration by Michael Sevier

3 And learned men came to the King, but they all answered his questions differently.

4 In reply to the first question, some said that to know the right time for every action, one must draw up in advance, a table of days, months and years, and must live strictly according to it. Only thus, said they, could everything be done at its proper time. Others declared that it was impossible to decide beforehand the right time for every action; but that, not letting oneself be **absorbed** in idle pastimes[1], one should always attend to all that was going on, and then do what was most needful. Others, again, said that however attentive the King might be to what was going on, it was impossible for one man to decide correctly the right time for every action, but that he should have a Council of wise men, who would help him to fix the proper time for everything.

5 But then again others said there were some things which could not wait to be laid before a Council, but about which one had at once to decide whether to undertake them or not. But in order to decide that, one must know

---

1. **pastimes** activities that people enjoy doing to pass the time

beforehand what was going to happen. It is only magicians who know that; and, therefore, in order to know the right time for every action, one must consult magicians.

6 Equally various were the answers to the second question. Some said, the people the King most needed were his councillors; others, the priests; others, the doctors; while some said the warriors were the most necessary.

7 To the third question, as to what was the most important occupation: some replied that the most important thing in the world was science. Others said it was skill in warfare; and others, again, that it was religious worship.

8 All the answers being different, the King agreed with none of them, and gave the reward to none. But still wishing to find the right answers to his questions, he decided to consult a hermit, widely **renowned** for his wisdom.

9 The hermit lived in a wood which he never quitted, and he received none but common folk. So the King put on simple clothes, and before reaching the hermit's cell dismounted from his horse, and, leaving his bodyguard behind, went on alone.

10 When the King approached, the hermit was digging the ground in front of his hut. Seeing the King, he greeted him and went on digging. The hermit was frail and weak, and each time he stuck his spade into the ground and turned a little earth, he breathed heavily.

11 The King went up to him and said: "I have come to you, wise hermit, to ask you to answer three questions: How can I learn to do the right thing at the right time? Who are the people I most need, and to whom should I, therefore, pay more attention than to the rest? And, what affairs are the most important, and need my first attention?"

12 The hermit listened to the King, but answered nothing. He just spat on his hand and **recommenced** digging.

13 "You are tired," said the King, "let me take the spade and work awhile for you."

14 "Thanks!" said the hermit, and, giving the spade to the King, he sat down on the ground.

15 When he had dug two beds, the King stopped and repeated his questions. The hermit again gave no answer, but rose, stretched out his hand for the spade, and said:

16 "Now rest awhile—and let me work a bit."

17 But the King did not give him the spade, and continued to dig. One hour passed, and another. The sun began to sink behind the trees, and the King at last stuck the spade into the ground, and said:

18 "I came to you, wise man, for an answer to my questions. If you can give me none, tell me so, and I will return home."

19 "Here comes some one running," said the hermit, "let us see who it is."

20 The King turned round, and saw a bearded man come running out of the wood. The man held his hands pressed against his stomach, and blood was flowing from under them. When he reached the King, he fell fainting on the ground moaning feebly. The King and the hermit unfastened the man's clothing. There was a large wound in his stomach. The King washed it as best he could, and bandaged it with his handkerchief and with a towel the hermit had. But the blood would not stop flowing, and the King again and again removed the bandage soaked with warm blood, and washed and rebandaged the wound. When at last the blood ceased flowing, the man revived and asked for something to drink. The King brought fresh water and gave it to him. Meanwhile the sun had set, and it had become cool. So the King, with the hermit's help, carried the wounded man into the hut and laid him on the bed. Lying on the bed the man closed his eyes and was quiet; but the King was so tired with his walk and with the work he had done, that he crouched down on the threshold, and also fell asleep—so soundly that he slept all through the short summer night. When he awoke in the morning, it was long before he could remember where he was, or who was the strange bearded man lying on the bed and gazing intently at him with shining eyes.

21 "Forgive me!" said the bearded man in a weak voice, when he saw that the King was awake and was looking at him.

22 "I do not know you, and have nothing to forgive you for," said the King.

23 "You do not know me, but I know you. I am that enemy of yours who swore to revenge himself on you, because you executed his brother and seized his property. I knew you had gone alone to see the hermit, and I **resolved** to kill you on your way back. But the day passed and you did not return. So I came out from my ambush to find you, and I came upon your bodyguard, and they recognized me, and wounded me. I escaped from them, but should have bled to death had you not dressed my wound. I wished to kill you, and you have saved my life. Now, if I live, and if you wish it, I will serve you as your most faithful slave, and will bid my sons do the same. Forgive me!"

24 The King was very glad to have made peace with his enemy so easily, and to have gained him for a friend, and he not only forgave him, but said he would send his servants and his own physician to attend him, and promised to restore his property.

25 Having taken leave of the wounded man, the King went out into the porch and looked around for the hermit. Before going away he wished once more to beg an answer to the questions he had put. The hermit was outside, on his knees, sowing seeds in the beds that had been dug the day before.

26 The King approached him, and said:

27 "For the last time, I pray you to answer my questions, wise man."

28 "You have already been answered!" said the hermit, still crouching on his thin legs, and looking up at the King, who stood before him.

29 "How answered? What do you mean?" asked the King.

30 "Do you not see," replied the hermit. "If you had not pitied my weakness yesterday, and had not dug those beds for me, but had gone your way, that man would have attacked you, and you would have repented of not having stayed with me. So the most important time was when you were digging the beds; and I was the most important man; and to do me good was your most important business. Afterwards when that man ran to us, the most important time was when you were attending to him, for if you had not bound up his wounds he would have died without having made peace with you. So he was the most important man, and what you did for him was your most important business. Remember then: there is only one time that is important— Now! It is the most important time because it is the only time when we have any power. The most necessary man is he with whom you are, for no man knows whether he will ever have dealings with any one else: and the most important affair is, to do him good, because for that purpose alone was man sent into this life!"

✏️ WRITE

POETRY: Found poetry is created when a writer takes words and phrases from one text and rearranges them in the form of a poem. Write a found poem to reflect the advice given in "The Three Questions." Remember to use words and phrases from the story.

The Tequila Worm

FICTION
Viola Canales
2005

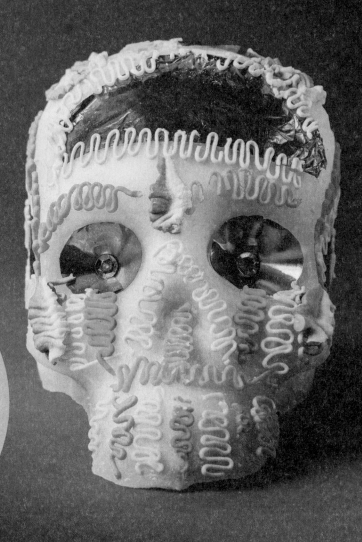

Introduction

A Harvard Law School graduate, a former Army captain, and an award-winning author, Viola Canales (b. 1957) grew up in a Mexican neighborhood of Texas before winning a scholarship to attend a prestigious boarding school far from home. Canales's real-life story is much like that of her fictional character Sofia, the protagonist of *The Tequila Worm*. Facing anti-Mexican sentiment, her mother's skepticism, and homesickness, Sofia breaks free of her barrio to pursue her dream in a strange world that will illuminate the taken-for-granted

"... the last thing I needed was to stand out like a big stupid sign."

"Taco Head"

Skill:
Connotation
and Denotation

1 Mama used to pack two bean tacos for my school lunch day. Every morning she'd get up at five to make a fresh batch of flour masa. She'd roll out and cook one tortilla at a time until she had a big stack of them, nice and hot, and then she'd fill each with beans that she'd fried in bacon grease and flavored with chopped onion in her huge cast-iron skillet.

2 And each morning I would sit at the kitchen table and say, "Mama, can I please have some lunch money too, or a sandwich instead?" But the reply was always the same: "Why, mi'ja[1]? You already have these delicious bean tacos to eat."

3 It wasn't that the tacos weren't good; it was that some kids called all Mexican Americans beaners[2], so the last thing I needed was to stand out like a big stupid sign. All the other kids either bought their lunch at the cafeteria, or took nice, white sandwiches. I started going to the very end of the cafeteria, to turn my back and gobble up my tacos.

4 Then I started eating each taco by first putting it in a bag.

5 It would take me all of five minutes to eat, and then I'd go outside to the playground. I was always the first one there, often the only one for quite a while. But I didn't mind, except on really cold days, when I wished I were still inside.

6 On one cold day, I so **dreaded** going outside that I started eating my second taco rather slowly. "Hey, you!" someone shouted. I turned and found a big girl standing right smack in front of me, her arms crossed over her chest like bullet belts.

7 "What's in the paper bag?" She glared and poked at the bag with her fat finger.

8 I was stunned stupid. She grabbed the bag.

The words *fresh* and *nice* both have good connotations. *Fresh* has a dictionary definition of "being recently made." It has connotations of being healthy and homemade, which makes me think that the tacos are supposed to be delicious. All the positive connotations help me picture how much work Sofia's mom puts into her lunch.

---

1. **mi'ja** (Spanish) contraction of *mi hija*: "my daughter"
2. **beaners** derogatory term for Mexicans

9 "Taco head! Taco head!" She yelled. In seconds, I was surrounded by kids chanting "Taco head! Taco head!"

10 I wanted the ground to open up and **swallow** me whole. Not only was I found out, but the girl had caused my taco to fly open and splatter all over my white sweater.

11 This nightmare went on forever, until Coach Clarke, the girls' PE teacher, blew her whistle and ordered everyone back to their seats.

12 "Sofia," she said, "don't pay attention to them. They're just being mean and silly." She took me to the teachers' lounge and helped me clean up.

13 For two days after that, I went directly to the playground and didn't eat my lunch until I got home after school. And then for two days after that, I ate inside a **stall** in the girls' restroom.

14 The next Monday, Coach Clarke stopped me in the hall. "Sofia, how about we eat lunch together in the cafeteria?"

15 When the lunch bell rang, I found Coach Clarke sitting in the middle of the cafeteria, with students standing all around her. She looked up and waved me over.

16 "Here, Sofia," she said as she pulled out the chair beside her. "Everyone else was begging to sit with me, but I said no, that I was saving this chair for you."

17 I sat down, feeling sick, nervous.

18 "How about we trade?" Coach said. She opened her lunch bag and pulled out a half-sandwich wrapped in plastic. "I'll trade this for one of your tacos."

19 All the kids were staring at us.

20 I **hesitated** and pulled out my lunch. I unwrapped the foil.

21 "Those look good," Coach said, reaching for a taco. "Better than any stupid sandwich I've ever had. See for yourself. Take a bite."

22 I carefully unwrapped the half-sandwich and took a little bite. It was awful, something between sardines and bologna.

23 "Ha! Told you!" Coach Clarke said, laughing. "Here," she said, taking the rest of the sandwich, "you don't have to eat it. Have your taco instead."

24 As I ate one and Coach Clarke ate the other, she kept making all these loud mmmmm sounds. I knew everyone in the cafeteria could hear.

Skill:
Character

Sofia learns that sandwiches are actually gross. Her coach also doesn't think tacos are weird, which will help Sofia see that being different isn't a bad thing. I think that the coach is being nice, and she is going to be the one who helps Sofia be okay with who she is.

25 And the next day we ate lunch together in the middle of the cafeteria. We traded. Again, her half-sandwich was truly awful. Do all sandwiches taste like something between sardines and bologna? I wondered.

26 But this time, as she ate one taco and I the other, she told me stories about herself: how she became a coach because she'd fallen in love with sports at school; how she loved playing soccer most but had also been good at playing field hockey and softball. We laughed when she described the funny skirt she had worn playing field hockey.

27 I told her I liked to play soccer too, with my father and cousins in the street. Then I remembered Clara and her stories, so I told Coach Clarke about Clara and how she told me that I had **inherited** my great-great grandmother's gift for kicking like a mule. I hesitated, then said, "I wish I'd kicked the girl who made fun of me."

28 "Sofia, learn to kick with your head instead."

29 "Like in soccer?"

30 "No, like with your brain. And you know how you can really kick that girl, and really hard?

31 "How?"

32 "By kicking her butt at school, by beating her in English, math, everything— even sports."

33 Coach Clarke and I had lunch together the rest of that week. She asked me for the recipe for the tacos. I had to ask both Papa and Mama for this, since Papa cleaned and cooked the beans before Mama fried them.

34 After that, I wanted to "kick that girl" so bad that I asked Coach Clarke if I could go to the library to study after lunch instead of wasting time on the playground. She arranged it for me. She also told me, "Part of 'kicking that girl' is to eat your tacos proudly, and right in the middle of the cafeteria."

35 That year I kicked that girl in all classes and sports, especially soccer.

36 It wasn't long after my lunches with Coach Clarke that some of the other Mexican American kids started eating their foods out in the open too. And sometimes when I pulled out my lunch, I got offers to trade for sandwiches. But I always ate both my tacos before heading off to the library.

Excerpted from *The Tequila Worm* by Viola Canales, published by Wendy Lamb Books.

First Read

Read *The Tequila Worm*. After you read, complete the Think Questions below.

 THINK QUESTIONS

1. What does Sofia think after taking a bite out of Coach Clarke's sandwich?

2. Why are students gathered around Coach Clarke in the cafeteria?

3. What confusion occurs when Coach Clarke recommends to Sofia that she learn "to kick with her head"?

4. Use context clues to determine the meaning of the word **hesitated** in paragraph 20. Then use a print or an online dictionary to confirm your definition.

5. The Latin word *inhereditare* means "to make an heir." Use this information as well as context clues from the text to determine the meaning of the word **inherited** in paragraph 27. Write your best definition here and explain which context clues helped you reach your answer.

Skill:
Connotation and Denotation

Use the Checklist to analyze Connotation and Denotation in *The Tequila Worm*. Refer to the sample student annotations about Connotation and Denotation in the text.

••• CHECKLIST FOR CONNOTATION AND DENOTATION

In order to identify the connotative meanings of words and phrases, use the following steps:

✓ First, note unfamiliar words and phrases; key words used to describe important individuals, events, and ideas; or words that inspire an emotional reaction.

✓ Next, determine and note the denotative meaning of words by consulting reference materials such as a dictionary, glossary, or thesaurus.

To better understand the meaning of words and phrases as they are used in a text, including connotative, use the following questions:

✓ What is the genre or subject of the text? How does that affect the possible meaning of a word or phrase?

✓ Does the word create a positive, negative, or neutral emotion?

✓ What synonyms or alternative phrasing help you describe the connotative meaning of the word?

Please note that excerpts and passages in the StudySync® library and this workbook are intended as touchstones to generate interest in an author's work. The excerpts and passages do not substitute for the reading of entire texts, and StudySync® strongly recommends that students seek out and purchase the whole literary or informational work in order to experience it as the author intended. Links to online resellers are available in our digital library. In addition, complete works may be ordered through an authorized reseller by filling out and returning to StudySync® the order form enclosed in this workbook.

Reading & Writing
Companion

577

Skill:
Connotation and Denotation

Reread paragraphs 6–9 of *The Tequila Worm*. Then, using the Checklist on the previous page, answer the multiple-choice questions below.

⟳ YOUR TURN

1. Which of the following context clues in paragraph 6 best shows that the denotative meaning of the word *crossed* is "placed crosswise"?

   ○ A. "over her chest like bullet belts"
   ○ B. "standing right smack in front of me"
   ○ C. "someone shouted"
   ○ D. "her arms"

2. Which of the following context clues in paragraph 6 best shows that the word *crossed* has a negative connotation?

   ○ A. "in front of me"
   ○ B. "like bullet belts"
   ○ C. "over her chest"
   ○ D. "her arms"

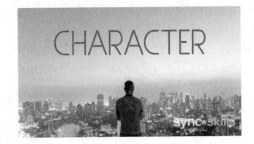

Skill:
Character

Use the Checklist to analyze Character in *The Tequila Worm*. Refer to the sample student annotations about Character in the text.

••• CHECKLIST FOR CHARACTER

In order to determine how particular elements of a story interact, note the following:

- ✓ the characters in the story, including the protagonist and antagonist

- ✓ the settings and how they shape the characters or plot

- ✓ plot events and how they affect the characters

- ✓ key events or series of episodes in the plot, especially events that cause characters to react, respond, or change in some way

- ✓ characters' responses as the plot reaches a climax and moves toward a resolution of the problem facing the protagonist

- ✓ the resolution of the conflict in the plot and the ways that affects each character

To analyze how particular elements of a story interact, consider the following questions:

- ✓ How do the characters' responses change or develop from the beginning to the end of the story?

- ✓ How does the setting shape the characters and plot in the story?

- ✓ How do the events in the plot affect the characters? How do they develop as a result of the conflict, climax, and resolution?

- ✓ Do the characters' problems reach a resolution? How?

- ✓ How does the resolution affect the characters?

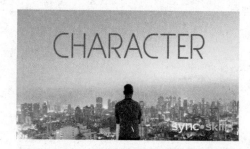

Skill:
Character

Reread paragraphs 6–12 of *The Tequila Worm*. Then, using the Checklist on the previous page, answer the multiple-choice questions below.

⟳ YOUR TURN

1. How does Sofia react to the bullying?

   ○ A. Sofia mocks her bully.

   ○ B. Sofia throws a taco at her.

   ○ C. Sofia doesn't do anything.

   ○ D. Sofia asks for a teacher.

2. What does the dialogue in paragraph 12 suggest about the coach?

   ○ A. It suggests that the coach is kind and helpful.

   ○ B. It suggests that the coach is not great with kids.

   ○ C. It suggests that the coach is angry at the bully.

   ○ D. It suggests that the coach has known Sofia for a long time.

Close Read

Reread *The Tequila Worm*. As you reread, complete the Skills Focus questions below. Then use your answers and annotations from the questions to help you complete the Write activity.

◎ SKILLS FOCUS

1. *The Tequila Worm* is narrated by a teenager named Sofia. Identify her words and phrases that have emotional connotations. Determine the meaning of the words and phrases as they are used in the text. Then explain how the language contributes to the meaning of the story.

2. Identify examples of Coach Clarke's caring behavior in the story, and explain how it influences events.

3. A key theme in "The Three Questions" is that it is important to live in the moment. A main idea of "The Power of Student Peer Leaders" is that teenagers can effectively motivate and positively influence peers. Identify evidence from *The Tequila Worm* that reveals a theme of the text, and explain how that theme compares to the ideas of the other selections.

4. Identify an important event from *The Tequila Worm*, and explain how it changes everything that happens afterwards.

✏ WRITE

DISCUSSION: These three texts relate to the idea of mentorship or role models. Who are mentors in each text? How do they help or change others? Write notes in response to this question to prepare for a group discussion about these three texts.

Barrio Boy

INFORMATIONAL TEXT
Ernesto Galarza
1971

Introduction

Ernesto Galarza (1905–1984) was a Mexican American union leader, activist, professor, and writer who spent most of his life fighting for the rights of farm workers. In *Barrio Boy*, Galarza tells the story of how he immigrated to California and entered the public school system. He explains the challenges he faced as a student, including learning a new language and adjusting to an unfamiliar culture. This excerpt is about Galarza's first day in an American school.

"At Lincoln, making us into Americans did not mean scrubbing away what made us originally foreign."

from Part Four: Life in the Lower Part of Town

1   The two of us walked south on Fifth Street one morning to the corner of Q Street and turned right. Half of the block was occupied by the Lincoln School. It was a three-story wooden building, with two wings that gave it the shape of a double-T connected by a central hall. It was a new building, painted yellow, with a shingled roof that was not like the red tile of the school in Mazatlán. I noticed other differences, none of them very reassuring.

2   We walked up the wide staircase hand in hand and through the door, which closed by itself. A mechanical contraption screwed to the top shut it behind us quietly.

3   Up to this point the adventure of enrolling me in the school had been carefully rehearsed. Mrs. Dodson had told us how to find it and we had circled it several times on our walks. Friends in the *barrio*[1] explained that the director was called a principal, and that it was a lady and not a man. They **assured** us that there was always a person at the school who could speak Spanish.

4   Exactly as we had been told, there was a sign on the door in both Spanish and English: "Principal." We crossed the hall and entered the office of Miss Nettie Hopley.

5   Miss Hopley was at a roll-top desk to one side, sitting in a swivel chair that moved on wheels. There was a sofa against the opposite wall, flanked by two windows and a door that opened on a small balcony. Chairs were set around a table and framed pictures hung on the walls of a man with long white hair and another with a sad face and a black beard.

6   The principal half turned in the swivel chair to look at us over the pinch glasses crossed on the ridge of her nose. To do this she had to duck her head slightly as if she were about to step through a low doorway.

NOTES

Skill:
Central or
Main Idea

The author doesn't explicitly state a central idea here. But these details suggest that one central idea may be that change is hard. Galarza is comparing his old school to his new school. He notices a lot of differences, and he's probably nervous.

---

1. **barrio** Spanish for *neighborhood*

Skill:
Informational
Text Elements

I know that Ernesto was feeling worried and nervous to start at a new school. But when he met Miss Hopley, she was friendly, and he decided that he would like her. She might have an impact on him at Lincoln and his experience in America.

7   What Miss Hopley said to us we did not know but we saw in her eyes a warm welcome and when she took off her glasses and straightened up she smiled wholeheartedly, like Mrs. Dodson. We were, of course, saying nothing, only catching the friendliness of her voice and the sparkle in her eyes while she said words we did not understand. She signaled us to the table. Almost tiptoeing across the office, I maneuvered myself to keep my mother between me and the gringo lady. In a matter of seconds I had to decide whether she was a possible friend or a menace. We sat down.

8   Then Miss Hopley did a **formidable** thing. She stood up. Had she been standing when we entered she would have seemed tall. But rising from her chair she soared. And what she carried up and up with her was a buxom superstructure, firm shoulders, a straight sharp nose, full cheeks slightly molded by a curved line along the nostrils, thin lips that moved like steel springs, and a high forehead topped by hair gathered in a bun. Miss Hopley was not a giant in body but when she **mobilized** it to a standing position she seemed a match for giants. I decided I liked her.

9   She strode to a door in the far corner of the office, opened it and called a name. A boy of about ten years appeared in the doorway. He sat down at one end of the table. He was brown like us, a plump kid with shiny black hair combed straight back, neat, cool, and faintly obnoxious.

10   Miss Hopley joined us with a large book and some papers in her hand. She, too, sat down and the questions and answers began by way of our **interpreter.** My name was Ernesto. My mother's name was Henriqueta. My birth certificate was in San Blas. Here was my last report card from the Escuela Municipal Numero 3 para Varones of Mazatlán, and so forth. Miss Hopley put things down in the book and my mother signed a card.

Skill:
Informational
Text Elements

Ernesto explains how another teacher at Lincoln earned his trust. He seems really at home at school. These moments with his teachers are positive, and he knows that they want to help him become successful.

11   As long as the questions continued, Doña Henriqueta could stay and I was **secure**. Now that they were over, Miss Hopley saw her to the door, dismissed our interpreter and without further ado took me by the hand and strode down the hall to Miss Ryan's first grade.

12   Miss Ryan took me to a seat at the front of the room, into which I shrank—the better to survey her. She was, to skinny, somewhat runty me, of a withering height when she patrolled the class. And when I least expected it, there she was, crouching by my desk, her blond radiant face level with mine, her voice patiently maneuvering me over the awful idiocies of the English language.

13   During the next few weeks Miss Ryan overcame my fears of tall, energetic teachers as she bent over my desk to help me with a word in the pre-primer. Step by step, she loosened me and my classmates from the safe anchorage of the desks for recitations at the blackboard and consultations at her desk.

NOTES

Frequently she burst into happy announcements to the whole class. "Ito can read a sentence," and small Japanese Ito, squint-eyed and shy, slowly read aloud while the class listened in **wonder**: "Come, Skipper, come. Come and run." The Korean, Portuguese, Italian, and Polish first graders had similar moments of glory, no less shining than mine the day I conquered "butterfly," which I had been persistently pronouncing in standard Spanish as boo-ter-flee. "Children," Miss Ryan called for attention. "Ernesto has learned how to pronounce *butterfly*!" And I proved it with a perfect imitation of Miss Ryan. From that celebrated success, I was soon able to match Ito's progress as a sentence reader with "Come, butterfly, come fly with me."

14   Like Ito and several other first graders who did not know English, I received private lessons from Miss Ryan in the closet, a narrow hall off the classroom with a door at each end. Next to one of these doors Miss Ryan placed a large chair for herself and a small one for me. Keeping an eye on the class through the open door she read with me about sheep in the meadow and a frightened chicken going to see the king, coaching me out of my phonetic ruts in words like *pasture, bow-wow-wow, hay,* and *pretty,* which to my Mexican ear and eye had so many unnecessary sounds and letters. She made me watch her lips and then close my eyes as she repeated words I found hard to read. When we came to know each other better, I tried interrupting to tell Miss Ryan how we said it in Spanish. It didn't work. She only said "oh" and went on with *pasture, bow-wow-wow,* and *pretty.* It was as if in that closet we were both discovering together the secrets of the English language and grieving together over the tragedies of Bo-Peep. The main reason I was graduated with honors from the first grade was that I had fallen in love with Miss Ryan. Her radiant, no-nonsense character made us either afraid not to love her or love her so we would not be afraid, I am not sure which. It was not only that we sensed she was with it, but also that she was with us.

15   Like the first grade, the rest of the Lincoln School was a sampling of the lower part of town where many races made their home. My pals in the second grade were Kazushi, whose parents spoke only Japanese; Matti, a skinny Italian boy; and Manuel, a fat Portuguese who would never get into a fight but wrestled you to the ground and just sat on you. Our assortment of nationalities included Koreans, Yugoslavs, Poles, Irish, and home-grown Americans.

16   Miss Hopley and her teachers never let us forget why we were at Lincoln: for those who were alien, to become good Americans; for those who were so born, to accept the rest of us. Off the school grounds we traded the same insults we heard from our elders. On the playground we were sure to be marched up to the principal's office for calling someone a wop, a chink, a

Skill: Central or Main Idea

The details in this section tell me that the kids in this class come from different backgrounds and are immigrants.

But they are all working toward the common goal of learning English. This is another main idea of the text, that the students are united.

NOTES

dago, or a greaser. The school was not so much a melting pot[2] as a griddle where Miss Hopley and her helpers warmed knowledge into us and roasted racial hatreds out of us.

17 At Lincoln, making us into Americans did not mean scrubbing away what made us originally foreign. The teachers called us as our parents did, or as close as they could pronounce our names in Spanish or Japanese. No one was ever scolded or punished for speaking in his native tongue on the playground. Matti told the class about his mother's down quilt, which she had made in Italy with the fine feathers of a thousand geese. Encarnación acted out how boys learned to fish in the Philippines. I astounded the third grade with the story of my travels on a stagecoach[3], which nobody else in the class had seen except in the museum at Sutter's Fort. After a visit to the Crocker Art Gallery and its collection of heroic paintings of the golden age of California, someone showed a silk scroll with a Chinese painting. Miss Hopley herself had a way of expressing wonder over these matters before a class, her eyes wide open until they popped slightly. It was easy for me to feel that becoming a proud American, as she said we should, did not mean feeling ashamed of being a Mexican.

From *Barrio Boy* by Ernesto Galarza. Copyright ©1971 by Ernesto Galarza. Used by permission of University of Notre Dame Press.

---

2. **melting pot** a popular metaphor used in reference to cultural integration in the United States; a "melting pot" is an environment in which people of different ideas, ethnicities, and cultural traits are socially assimilated
3. **stagecoach** a horse-drawn carriage used widely for mail and transport in the 19th century

First Read

Read *Barrio Boy*. After you read, complete the Think Questions below.

☁ THINK QUESTIONS

1. How does Ernesto feel about starting a new school? Cite specific evidence from paragraphs 1–3 in your response.

2. How do Miss Hopley's actions in paragraphs 7 and 8 help Ernesto decide whether the principal is a possible "friend or a menace"?

3. By the end of the text, how does Ernesto feel about being a student at Lincoln? Refer to paragraphs 16–17 in your response.

4. Read the following dictionary entry:

   wonder \'won•der\ *noun*

   1. curiosity
   2. amazement or admiration
   3. doubt

Decide which definition best matches **wonder** as it is used in paragraph 13 of *Barrio Boy*. Write that definition of *wonder* here and indicate which clues found in the text helped you determine the meaning.

5. Which context clues in the passage helped you figure out the meaning of **mobilized**, in paragraph 8? Write your definition of the word *mobilized*. Tell how you figured out the meaning of the word. Then use a print or an online dictionary to confirm the definition.

Please note that excerpts and passages in the StudySync® library and this workbook are intended as touchstones to generate interest in an author's work. The excerpts and passages do not substitute for the reading of entire texts, and StudySync® strongly recommends that students seek out and purchase the whole literary or informational work in order to experience it as the author intended. Links to online resellers are available in our digital library. In addition, complete works may be ordered through an authorized reseller by filling out and returning to StudySync® the order form enclosed in this workbook.

Reading & Writing Companion **587**

Skill:
Central or Main Idea

Use the Checklist to analyze Central or Main Idea in *Barrio Boy*. Refer to the sample student annotations about Central or Main Idea in the text.

••• CHECKLIST FOR CENTRAL OR MAIN IDEA

In order to identify two or more central ideas in a text, note the following:

- ✓ the central or main idea, or ideas, if explicitly stated

- ✓ the topic(s) of the text

- ✓ when the author makes an important point about the topic(s)

- ✓ key details in the text that indicate the author's point(s) or message(s)

- ✓ ways the author uses details to develop a central idea

To determine two or more central ideas in a text and analyze their development over the course of the text, consider the following questions:

- ✓ What main ideas do the paragraphs develop?

- ✓ What important point is the author making about the topic(s)?

- ✓ Where do you see more than one central idea for the text?

- ✓ How does the author use details to develop central ideas?

- ✓ How does the author develop these ideas over the course of the text?

Skill:
Central or Main Idea

Reread paragraphs 14–16 of *Barrio Boy*. Then, using the Checklist on the previous page, answer the multiple-choice questions below.

⟳ YOUR TURN

1. Which statement best conveys the central idea of paragraph 14?

   ○ A. There was room for everyone in Miss Ryan's classroom.
   ○ B. Miss Ryan made her students feel like she was on their side and they were all part of a team together.
   ○ C. Miss Ryan was a transformative teacher who helped Ernesto and many of his classmates.
   ○ D. Miss Ryan gave private lessons to students in the closet.

2. Which statement best conveys the central idea of paragraphs 15–16?

   ○ A. The school was filled with students from all different backgrounds and nationalities.
   ○ B. Outside of school the students were still exposed to discrimination and racism.
   ○ C. Teachers at Lincoln worked hard to teach students to respect others regardless of differences.
   ○ D. Lincoln School was a diverse place, full of many different kinds of people.

Please note that excerpts and passages in the StudySync® library and this workbook are intended as touchstones to generate interest in an author's work. The excerpts and passages do not substitute for the reading of entire texts, and StudySync® strongly recommends that students seek out and purchase the whole literary or informational work in order to experience it as the author intended. Links to online resellers are available in our digital library. In addition, complete works may be ordered through an authorized reseller by filling out and returning to StudySync® the order form enclosed in this workbook.

Reading & Writing Companion   **589**

Skill:
Informational Text Elements

Use the Checklist to analyze Informational Text Elements in *Barrio Boy*. Refer to the sample student annotations about Informational Text Elements in the text.

••• CHECKLIST FOR INFORMATIONAL TEXT ELEMENTS

In order to identify the interactions between individuals, events, and ideas in a text, note the following:

- ✓ details in the text that describe or explain important ideas, events, or individuals

- ✓ transition words and phrases that signal interactions between individuals, ideas, or events such as *because, as a consequence*, or *as a result*

- ✓ an event or sequence of events that influences an individual, a subsequent event, or an idea

- ✓ interactions between ideas and events that play a part in shaping people's thoughts and actions

To analyze the interactions between individuals, events, and ideas in a text, consider the following questions:

- ✓ How are the individuals, ideas, and events in the text related?

- ✓ How do the ideas the author presents affect the individuals in the text?

- ✓ What other features, if any, help readers to analyze the events, ideas, or individuals in the text?

Skill:
Informational Text Elements

Reread paragraphs 15–17 of *Barrio Boy*. Then, using the Checklist on the previous page, answer the multiple-choice questions below.

⟳ YOUR TURN

1. This question has two parts. First, answer Part A. Then, answer Part B.

   Part A: How does the excerpt show that the teachers at Lincoln helped shape Ernesto's ideas about what it meant to be an American?

   ○ A. By showing how the students were from many different backgrounds

   ○ B. By explaining how the teachers taught all the students to accept one another and be proud of their backgrounds and differences

   ○ C. By giving examples of how the teachers taught the students to speak one another's languages

   ○ D. By letting them bring things from home to show their classmates

   Part B: Which of the following details best supports your response to Part A?

   ○ A. "Miss Hopley and her teachers never let us forget why we were at Lincoln: for those who were alien, to become good Americans; for those who were so born, to accept the rest of us."

   ○ B. "The teachers called us as our parents did, or as close as they could pronounce our names in Spanish or Japanese."

   ○ C. "On the playground we were sure to be marched up to the principal's office for calling someone a wop, a chink, a dago, or a greaser."

   ○ D. "Our assortment of nationalities included Koreans, Yugoslavs, Poles, Irish, and home-grown Americans."

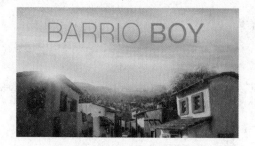

Close Read

Reread *Barrio Boy*. As you reread, complete the Skills Focus questions below. Then use your answers and annotations from the questions to help you complete the Write activity.

◎ SKILLS FOCUS

1. Reread paragraph 17. Write a note about how the teachers and their actions support the idea in the opening sentence: "At Lincoln, making us into Americans did not mean scrubbing away what made us originally foreign." Consider how the teachers' actions impacted the students and the school community.

2. Reread paragraph 8. What does the word *soared* connote about the principal? How does the author's deliberate use of this word and other words in the paragraph help readers to see Miss Hopley through the eyes of a small boy?

3. In paragraph 16, Galarza recollects that the "school was not so much a melting pot as a griddle where Miss Hopley and her helpers warmed knowledge into us and roasted racial

hatreds out of us." What does this metaphor suggest about the school? Explain your answer with additional evidence from the paragraph.

4. Think about how Ernesto changed from the beginning of the selection to the end. How would you describe him early on? How would you describe him at the end? What two central ideas are developed through this change? Use textual evidence to support your answer.

5. Ernesto credits Miss Ryan with "maneuvering . . . [him] over the awful idiocies of the English language." Find and highlight textual evidence in paragraphs 13 and 14 to demonstrate how Miss Ryan accomplishes that mission. Write a sentence explaining how this event impacted Ernesto's experience at the school.

✏ WRITE

INFORMATIVE: Think about what this excerpt from *Barrio Boy* is mostly about. Think about how Ernesto changes from the beginning of the excerpt to the end. What events, individuals, or ideas impacted this change? Then, identify two central or main ideas that are developed over the course of the text. Explain these central or main ideas in your own words. Remember to use textual evidence to support your response.

Extended
Writing
Project and
Grammar

EXTENDED
WRITING
PROJECT
INFORMATIVE
WRITING

Informative Writing Process: Plan

| PLAN | DRAFT | REVISE | EDIT AND PUBLISH |

The texts in this unit feature individuals who achieved great things in life. Ernesto Galarza is a union leader, writer, professor, and activist who was nominated for a Nobel Prize in Literature. Moises Urena is a college student who was able to dramatically change his life trajectory and impact the lives of other students around him. But before they made their impact, there were key events or moments that helped set them on the path to their achievements. Some of those events or moments might have seemed insignificant at the time, but they affected the outcomes of people's lives in important ways.

WRITING PROMPT

How can one key event or moment change everything?

Think carefully about the question above. Then, choose three texts from this unit and explain how one moment or event had a significant impact on a character, an individual, or other events in that text. Identify the moment or event that changed everything and explain how and why it had such an impact. Be sure your informative essay includes the following:

- an introduction
- a thesis statement
- coherent body paragraphs
- supporting details
- a conclusion

Writing to Sources

As you gather ideas and information from the texts in the unit, be sure to:

- use evidence from multiple sources; and
- avoid overly relying on one source.

Introduction to Informative Writing

Informative writing presents a main idea about a topic. Good informative writing develops the main idea with logical thinking and supporting details, including relevant facts, definitions, concrete details, quotations, or other information and examples. Informative writing uses an organized structure with body paragraphs that present key ideas. The characteristics of informative writing include:

- an introduction with a clear thesis statement

- supporting details

- organized body paragraphs with clear transitions

- a formal style

- precise or domain-specific language

- a conclusion that restates the main idea or thesis statement

Text structure refers to the way a writer organizes the information in a nonfiction text. There are several different types of informational text structures. For instance, a writer may:

- describe a process or a series of steps to follow in sequential order

- tell about events in chronological order

- compare and contrast information

- present cause-and-effect relationships

- describe a problem and offer a solution

- define the essential, or most important, qualities of a subject

- classify, or organize, information into categories and subcategories

A writer may use more than one organizational pattern within the same text. In addition, a text structure can be used to organize information about more than one topic.

As you continue with this Extended Writing Project, you'll receive more instruction and practice in crafting each of the characteristics of informative writing to create your own informative essay.

Before you get started on your own informative essay, read this essay that one student, Isaiah, wrote in response to the writing prompt. As you read the Model, highlight and annotate the features of informative writing that Isaiah included in his essay.

NOTES

☰ STUDENT MODEL

One Moment Can Test Our Assumptions

1 Life happens quickly. Sometimes the only thing that separates failure and success is a moment. The changes that take place in a single moment or event can affect everything that happens after it. One moment or event can affect the basic beliefs people hold about themselves and the world around them. Life-changing events are very different for everyone. However, the texts "The Three Questions," "Casey at the Bat," and "The Last Human Light" all show that one moment can change everything by challenging our basic assumptions.

The Three Questions

2 In Leo Tolstoy's short story "The Three Questions," a king assumes that knowing what is most important in life will help him make decisions. He asks a wise hermit, "How can I learn to do the right thing at the right time? Who are the people I most need, and to whom should I, therefore, pay more attention than to the rest? And, what affairs are the most important, and need my first attention?" The hermit, however, does not answer. Instead, a wounded, tired man appears, and the king saves his life. Afterward, the man reveals that he had planned to kill the king and was stabbed by the royal bodyguards. Now, he swears to be loyal to the king forever. The king is grateful for the peaceful ending. Later, the hermit explains how the king's own actions led him to this conclusion. He finally answers the king's questions: "Remember then: there is only one time that is important—Now!" The king originally assumes that what he knows will help him succeed in life. However, he learns that acting in the moment is the only way to live well.

Casey at the Bat

3 In Ernest Lawrence Thayer's classic poem "Casey at the Bat," a single pitch challenges assumptions of success. For example, with

their team losing, the Mudville fans do not hold much hope for victory. However, they change their minds when their star player, Casey, gets to the plate. The fans illustrate this when they say they would "put up even money now, with Casey at the bat." They assume Casey will succeed because he is their hero as well as a fantastic baseball player. The people at the game are ready to bet that Casey will lead the team to victory. Casey, too, is confident. He lets two balls fly by on purpose because he is sure he will hit a home run on the third pitch. But in the end, Casey fails, and the speaker reports, "There is no joy in Mudville—mighty Casey has struck out." Both Casey and his devoted fans assume that the final pitch will lead to the winning hit. In the time it takes for Casey to swing and miss, their assumptions are proven wrong.

The Last Human Light

4   A key moment can also have effects on a much larger scale. We might assume that human-made lights would go out quickly if people disappeared. However, in "The Last Human Light," Randall Munroe predicts that some of our lights could last for centuries. Munroe argues that the sudden disappearance of humans would cause "a rapid series of cascade failures, leading to a blackout of all major power grids." Humans often take lights for granted. We assume that the world would almost immediately go dark if no one were around to look after them. However, Munroe suggests that one kind of human light would stay lit long after humans disappeared. The light that comes from radioactive material, which comes from nuclear or chemical processes, is toxic, meaning it is unwanted and poisonous to living things. Munroe explains that "the light from our most toxic waste will still be shining" centuries from now. Radioactive waste gives off light as it degrades. This process takes a very long time. People assume that human-made lights need our help to continue shining. However, that assumption is not based in fact. Radioactive waste will continue to produce light long after humans' last moment on Earth.

5   Our basic assumptions help us make sense of the world. However, a single moment can put those assumptions to the test. In "The Three Questions," the king learns that his own experience is more valuable than a wise man's advice. The conclusion of "Casey at the Bat" teaches the star player and his fans that they should never take

success for granted. "The Last Human Light" shows that our actions will continue to affect the world long after we're gone. Attitudes in each text are affected by basic assumptions. Assumptions are often built over a lifetime of experience. It only takes a single moment for them to be challenged. Whether the events are large or small in scale, a single moment can change our basic understanding of the world.

✏ WRITE

Writers often take notes about their ideas before they sit down to write an essay. Think about what you've learned so far about organizing informative writing to help you begin prewriting.

- What are your ideas about the effect of an event or moment? What can make a single moment or event important?

- What three informational texts in this unit best reflect your ideas? Why?

- What are the key moments or events in those texts?

- What effect does each moment or event have in the text?

- What textual evidence might you use to support your ideas?

Response Instructions

Use the questions in the bulleted list to write a one-paragraph summary. Your summary should describe what you will discuss in your informative essay like the one on the previous pages.

Don't worry about including all of the details now; focus only on the most essential and important elements. You will refer back to this short summary as you continue through the steps of the writing process.

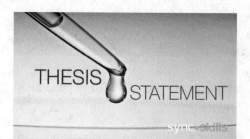

Skill:
Thesis Statement

••• CHECKLIST FOR THESIS STATEMENT

Before you begin writing your thesis statement, ask yourself the following questions:

- What is the prompt asking me to write about?

- What is the topic of my essay? How can I state it clearly for the reader?

- What claim(s) do I want to make about the topic of this essay? Is my opinion clear to my reader?

Here are some methods to introduce your claim and topic clearly:

- Think about the topic and main or central idea of your essay.

  > Is the main idea of your essay clearly stated?

  > Have you identified as many claims as you intend to prove or discuss?

- Write a clear statement about the central idea or claim(s). Your thesis statement should:

  > let the reader anticipate the body of your essay

  > respond completely to the writing prompt

⟳ YOUR TURN

Read the notes Isaiah's classmate has made while drafting his thesis statement. Then, complete the chart below by matching the notes to the correct topic.

	Note Options
A	The king learns that living in the present moment is the most important thing he can do! It saves his life!
B	We learn how the excitement in a crowd can change to shock and disappointment in just one moment.
C	We learn that taking advantage of your time at school and with your teacher can teach you valuable life lessons and skills.
D	"The Three Questions," "Barrio Boy," and "Casey at the Bat" all show how a single moment or event can change how people think or feel.

Topic	Note
"The Three Questions"	
"Barrio Boy"	
"Casey at the Bat"	
Thesis Statement	

✏ WRITE

Follow the steps in the checklist section to draft a thesis statement for your informative essay.

Skill: Organizing Informative Writing

••• CHECKLIST FOR ORGANIZING INFORMATIVE WRITING

As you consider how to organize your writing for your informative essay, use the following questions as a guide:

- What is my topic? How can I summarize the main idea?

- What is the logical order of my ideas, concepts, and information? Do I see a pattern that is similar to a specific text structure?

- Which organizational structure should I use to present my information?

- What organizational structure will create cohesion and aid in comprehension?

- How might using graphics, headings, or some form of multimedia help to present my information?

Here are some strategies to help you organize ideas, concepts, and information and aid comprehension:

- Definition is useful for:

  > defining a difficult idea and providing examples

- Classification is useful for:

  > dividing larger ideas and concepts into subcategories that are easier to understand

- Compare and contrast is useful for:

  > comparing the similarities and differences between two texts, ideas, or concepts

- Cause and effect is useful for:

  > explaining why and how something happened

- Visual elements

  > use headings to organize your essay into groups of information

  > use graphics, such as charts or tables, to visually represent large amounts of information

When you consider which text structure to use, remember to choose one that is appropriate for your writing purpose. For example, if you want to analyze two or more texts, you may select a compare-and-contrast structure to explain the similarities and differences between the texts.

↻ YOUR TURN

Read the thesis statements below. Then, complete the chart by writing the organizational structure that would best convey the ideas of each one.

Organizational Text Structure Options				
chronological	categories and subcategories	problem and solution	cause and effect	sequential

Thesis Statement	Organizational Text Structure
In recent years, bears have had more frequent and more dangerous interactions with people. To keep everyone safe, the bears' habitat should be better preserved.	
There has been a series of important events that have raised the popularity of soccer in the United States.	
You can make delicious homemade kimchi in a few simple steps.	
The growing success of dollar stores can be explained by changes in the ways Americans shop.	
There are a number of free events happening this weekend that will appeal to music lovers, theater buffs, foodies, and more.	

⟳ YOUR TURN

Complete the chart below by writing a short summary of what you will focus on in each paragraph of your informative essay.

Paragraph	Summary
Introduction	
Body Paragraph 1	
Body Paragraph 2	
Body Paragraph 3	
Conclusion	

SUPPORTING DETAILS

sync•skills

Skill:
Supporting Details

••• CHECKLIST FOR SUPPORTING DETAILS

As you look for supporting details to develop your topic, main idea, or thesis statement, ask yourself the following questions:

- What does a reader need to know about the topic in order to understand the main idea?

- What details will support my thesis statement?

- Does this information help to develop and refine my ideas?

- Does this information relate closely to my thesis statement?

- Where can I find better information that will provide stronger support for my point?

Here are some suggestions for how you can develop your topic:

- Review your thesis statement.

- Consider your main idea.

- Note what the reader will need to know in order to understand the topic.

- Be sure to consult credible sources.

- Use different types of supporting details, such as:

  > facts that are specific to your topic and enhance your discussion to establish credibility with your reader and build information

  > definitions to explain difficult concepts or terms

  > concrete details that will add descriptive and detailed material to your topic

  > quotations to directly connect your ideas to your thesis statement

  > examples and other information to support your thesis statement

YOUR TURN

Choose the best answer to each question.

1. Isaiah wants to improve the supporting details of a previous draft of his informative essay. Which quotation can he use to replace the underlined sentence? The quotation he selects should support the idea that the king believed he could gain wisdom through counsel.

> In Leo Tolstoy's short story "The Three Questions," a king assumes that knowing what is most important in life will help him make decisions. <u>He asks many wise men to tell him life's important lessons.</u> This shows that the king assumed wisdom can be learned by talking to people who are considered wise.

○ A. The king promises a reward to anyone "who would teach him what was the right time for every action, and who were the most necessary people, and how he might know what was the most important thing to do."

○ B. The hermit did not answer the king and "just spat on his hand and recommenced digging."

○ C. However, the wisest man was a simple hermit who "lived in a wood which he never quitted, and he received none but common folk."

○ D. When the king asks the hermit for answers, he responds, "You have already been answered!"

2. Isaiah would like to add a supporting detail to a previous draft of his paragraph on "Casey at the Bat." Which quotation could best precede and provide support for his last sentence?

> In "Casey at the Bat," a single pitch challenges the Mudville fans' opinion of their star baseball player. Everyone in Mudville assumes that Casey will get a winning hit. Casey is very confident in himself, too.

○ A. "It pounded on the mountain and recoiled upon the flat, / For Casey, mighty Casey, was advancing to the bat."

○ B. "There was ease in Casey's manner as he stepped into his place; / There was pride in Casey's bearing and a smile lit Casey's face."

○ C. "The sneer is gone from Casey's lip, his teeth are clenched in hate, / He pounds with cruel violence his bat upon the plate."

○ D. "And somewhere men are laughing, and somewhere children shout, / But there is no joy in Mudville—mighty Casey has struck out."

⟳ YOUR TURN

Complete the chart below by identifying a detail from each text you've chosen. Identifying details will help you develop your own thesis.

Texts	Details
Text #1	
Text #2	
Text #3	

Please note that excerpts and passages in the StudySync® library and this workbook are intended as touchstones to generate interest in an author's work. The excerpts and passages do not substitute for the reading of entire texts, and StudySync® strongly recommends that students seek out and purchase the whole literary or informational work in order to experience it as the author intended. Links to online resellers are available in our digital library. In addition, complete works may be ordered through an authorized reseller by filling out and returning to StudySync® the order form enclosed in this workbook.

Reading & Writing Companion 607

Informative Writing Process: Draft

PLAN	DRAFT	REVISE	EDIT AND PUBLISH

You have already made progress toward writing your informative essay. Now it is time to draft your informative essay.

✏ WRITE

Use your plan and other responses in your Binder to draft your essay. You may also have new ideas as you begin drafting. Feel free to explore those new ideas as you have them. You can also ask yourself these questions to ensure that your writing is focused, structured, and coherent:

- Have I included a thesis statement about my ideas on how one moment or event can create change?

- Are my ideas developed and clear to readers, with specific facts, details, and examples?

- Does the organization of my essay make sense? Is it focused, structured, and coherent?

Before you submit your draft, read it over carefully. You want to be sure that you've responded to all aspects of the prompt.

Here is Isaiah's informative essay draft. As he began to write his draft, Isaiah realized that his original thesis statement did not reflect his ideas. He revised his thesis statement to make a better connection between his main ideas. As you read, identify Isaiah's main ideas. As Isaiah continues to revise and edit his essay, he will find and improve weak spots in his writing, as well as correct any language or punctuation mistakes.

≡ STUDENT MODEL: FIRST DRAFT

~~Usually, one moment does not matter that much. Some times a moment changes a lot. The changes that take place in a single moment can affect everything that happens after them. In many stories and essays, one moment greatly affects people's lives. One moment can affect the basic beliefs people hold about themselves and the world around them. The texts "The Three Questions," "Casey at the Bat," and "The Last Human Light" all show that one moment can change every thing by challenging our basic assumptions.~~

Life happens quickly. Sometimes the only thing that separates failure and success is a moment. The changes that take place in a single moment or event can affect everything that happens after it. One moment or event can affect the basic beliefs people hold about themselves and the world around them. Life-changing events are very different for everyone. However, the texts "The Three Questions," "Casey at the Bat," and "The Last Human Light" all show that one moment can change everything by challenging our basic assumptions.

In Leo Tolstoy's short story "The Three Questions," a king assumes that knowing what is most important in life will help him make decisions. He asks a wise hermit, "How can I learn to do the right thing at the right time? Who are the people I most need, and to whom should I, therefore, pay more attention than to the rest? And, what affairs are the most important, and need my first attention?" The hermit, however, do not answer. Instead, a wounded man appears, and the king saves his life. Afterward, the man reveels that he had planed to kill the king and was stabbed by the royal body guards. Now, he swears to be loyal to the king forever. The king is grateful for the peaceful ending. Later, the hermit explains how the king's own actions led him to this conclusion. He finally answers the king's questions: "It is the most important time because it is the only time when we have any power." The king originaly assumes that what he

Skill:
Introductions

Isaiah decided to develop his ideas by writing a stronger opening sentence to hook readers. He also added some details to help preview his ideas about important moments and events. Isaiah decided to keep his thesis statement at the end of his introduction.

knows will help him succede in life. However, he learns that acting in the moment is the only way to live well.

~~In Ernest Lawrence Thayer's classic poem "Casey at the Bat," a single pitch challenges assumptions of success. With their team losing, the Mudville fans does not hold much hope for victory. They change their minds when their star player, Casey, gets to the plate. They assume Casey will succeed. He is their hero. He is a fantastic baseball player. Casey is confident, and the people at the game is ready to bet that Casey will lead the team to victory. She lets two balls fly on purpose because he is sure he will hit a home run on the third pitch. However, Casey fails, and he reports, "there is no joy in Mudville—mighty Casey has struck out." Both Casey and his devoted fans assume that the final pitch would lead to the wining hit. In the time it takes for Casey to swing and miss, their assumptions are proven wrong.~~

In Ernest Lawrence Thayer's classic poem "Casey at the Bat," a single pitch challenges assumptions of success. For example, with their team losing, the Mudville fans do not hold much hope for victory. However, they change their minds when their star player, Casey, gets to the plate. The fans illustrate this when they say they would "put up even money now, with Casey at the bat." They assume Casey will succeed because he is their hero as well as a fantastic baseball player. The people at the game are ready to bet that Casey will lead the team to victory. Casey, too, is confident. He lets two balls fly by on purpose because he is sure he will hit a home run on the third pitch. But in the end, Casey fails, and the speaker reports, "There is no joy in Mudville—mighty Casey has struck out." Both Casey and his devoted fans assume that the final pitch will lead to the winning hit. In the time it takes for Casey to swing and miss, their assumptions are proven wrong.

~~In "Last Human Light," randall munroe predicts that some of our lights could last for centuries. I think he argues that the sudden disappearance of humans would cause the lights to go out quickly. Humans often takes lights for granted. I assumed that the world would almost immediately go dark if no one were around to look after them.~~

Skill: Transitions

Isaiah decided that he should introduce his evidence with transition words like "for example" or "illustrate." He knows that adding these transition words will help make the relationships between ideas in his paragraph clearer and more coherent for readers.

A key moment can also have effects on a much larger scale. We might assume that human-made lights would go out quickly if people disappeared. However, in "The Last Human Light," Randall Munroe predicts that some of our lights could last for centuries. Munroe argues that the sudden disappearance of humans would cause "a rapid series of cascade failures, leading to a blackout of all major power grids." Humans often take lights for granted. We assume that the world would almost immediately go dark if no one were around to look after them.

~~However, I think the author suggests that one kind of human light would stay lit long after humans disappeared. Explains that "the light from our most toxic waste will still be shining" centuries from now. Radioactive waste gives off light as it gets older. These events take a very long time. people assume that human-made lights need our help to continue shining. However, that assumption is not based in fact. Radioactive waste will continue to produce light long after humans' last moment on earth.~~

However, Munroe suggests that one kind of human light would stay lit long after humans disappeared. The light that comes from radioactive material, which comes from nuclear or chemical processes, is toxic, meaning it is unwanted and poisonous to living things. Munroe explains that "the light from our most toxic waste will still be shining" centuries from now. Radioactive waste gives off light as it degrades. This process takes a very long time. People assume that human-made lights need our help to continue shining. However, that assumption is not based in fact. Radioactive waste will continue to produce light long after humans' last moment on Earth.

~~Our basic assumptions help us make sense of the world. However, in "The Three Questions," "Casey at the Bat," and "The Last Human Light," one moment changes every thing by teaching an unexpected lesson. Attitudes in each text is affected by basic assumptions. Assumptions are often built over a life time of experience. It only takes a single moment for them to be challenged. Everyone should try to make assumptions only when absolutely necessary.~~

Our basic assumptions help us make sense of the world. However, a single moment can put those assumptions to the test. In "The Three

NOTES

 Skill:
Style

Isaiah noticed that his tone was conversational, so he revised it to be more formal by eliminating the first-person language, using the author's name, and adding in a direct quote from the text.

 Skill:
Precise Language

By adding one more sentence, Isaiah was able to clearly convey information to his audience using domain-specific language such as "radioactive material" and "nuclear." When he added explanations about the language and topic, he was able to inform his readers about a complicated scientific subject.

Skill:
Conclusions

Isaiah expanded his conclusion to include the main idea from each body paragraph. It now flows logically and helps readers see the connections between all his ideas and the thesis statement.

Questions," the king learns that his own experience is more valuable than a wise man's advice. The conclusion of "Casey at the Bat" teaches the star player and his fans that they should never take success for granted. "The Last Human Light" shows that our actions will continue to affect the world long after we're gone. Attitudes in each text are affected by basic assumptions. Assumptions are often built over a lifetime of experience. It only takes a single moment for them to be challenged. Whether the events are large or small in scale, a single moment can change our basic understanding of the world.

Skill:
Introductions

••• CHECKLIST FOR INTRODUCTIONS

Before you write your introduction, ask yourself the following questions:

- How will you "hook" your reader's interest? You might:
  - > start with an attention-grabbing statement
  - > begin with an intriguing question

- How can I introduce my topic?

- How can I preview my ideas or prepare my reader for what is to follow?

- Where should I place my thesis statement? You might:
  - > put your thesis statement at the end of your introduction to help readers preview your body paragraphs

Below are two strategies to help you introduce your claim and topic clearly in an introduction:

- Peer Discussion
  - > Talk about your topic with a partner, explaining what you already know and your ideas about your topic.
  - > Write notes about the ideas you have discussed and any new questions you may have.
  - > Review your notes and think about how you will craft your introduction.

- Freewriting
  - > Freewrite for ten minutes about your topic. Don't worry about grammar, punctuation, or having fully formed ideas. The point of freewriting is to discover ideas.
  - > Review your notes and think about how you will craft your introduction.

YOUR TURN

Choose the best answer to each question.

1. The following introduction is from a previous draft of Isaiah's essay. Isaiah would like to replace the underlined sentence with a sentence that grabs readers' attention better and better prepares readers for what is to follow. Which of these would be the BEST replacement for the underlined sentence?

> <u>Moments can be really important.</u> A moment might change your life for better or for worse. A moment changes everything in stories, poems, and essays. In these texts, moments change everything by teaching people unexpected lessons.

- ○ A. There have been many important moments in my life.
- ○ B. The word *moment* means "a very small amount of time."
- ○ C. Everyone should understand the importance of moments.
- ○ D. Everything can change in the time it takes to blink your eyes.

2. Reread the final version of Isaiah's introduction. Which part of his introduction is underlined?

> Life happens quickly. Sometimes the only thing that separates failure and success is a moment. The changes that take place in a single moment or event can affect everything that happens after it. One moment or event can affect the basic beliefs people hold about themselves and the world around them. Life-changing events are very different for everyone. <u>However, the texts "The Three Questions," "Casey at the Bat," and "The Last Human Light" all show that one moment can change everything by challenging our basic assumptions.</u>

- ○ A. the "hook"
- ○ B. the topic
- ○ C. the preview of his main ideas
- ○ D. the thesis statement

 WRITE

Use the steps in the checklist to revise the introduction of your informative essay.

Skill:
Transitions

••• CHECKLIST FOR TRANSITIONS

Before you revise your current draft to include transitions, think about:

- the key ideas you discuss in your body paragraphs
- the relationships among ideas and concepts

Next, reread your current draft and note areas in your essay where:

- the organizational structure is not yet apparent
- the relationship between ideas within a paragraph is unclear

Revise your draft to use appropriate transitions to create cohesion and clarify the relationships among ideas and concepts, using the following questions as a guide:

- What kind of transitions should I use to make the organizational structure clear to readers? For example:

  > If you are comparing and contrasting two texts, consider using transitional words like *on the other hand*, *however*, *at the same time*, and *but*.

  > If you are showing cause and effect, consider using transition words like *because* or *as a result*.

- Which transition best connects the ideas within a paragraph? What about ideas across paragraphs? For example:

  > When providing evidence to support an idea, use transitions such as *for example* or *to illustrate*.

  > When transitioning between paragraphs or between examples, use transitions such as *first*, *secondly*, or *in addition to*.

  > When summarizing or bringing ideas together, use transitions such as *overall*, *in conclusion*, or *in the end*.

⟳ YOUR TURN

Choose the best answer to each question.

1. Isaiah is thinking about adding one more piece of evidence to his body paragraph, but he has not used the most effective transition in the underlined sentence. Which of the following could he add to the underlined sentence?

> They assume Casey will succeed because he is their hero as well as a fantastic baseball player. <u>He has helped them win difficult games in the past.</u>

- ○ A. But,
- ○ B. In fact,
- ○ C. Equally important,
- ○ D. However,

2. The following section is from an earlier draft of Isaiah's essay. He wants to add a sentence to bring this paragraph to a close more effectively. Which sentence could he add after sentence 4 to achieve this goal?

> (1) Radioactive waste gives off light as it gets older. (2) These events take a very long time. (3) People assume that human-made lights need our help to continue shining. (4) However, that assumption is not based in fact.

- ○ A. Solar panels are a less dangerous way of continuing to provide light.
- ○ B. Some lights, like those powered by gas, would turn off sooner.
- ○ C. In fact, radioactive waste will continue to produce light long after humans' last moment on Earth.
- ○ D. For example, the lights from radiation fade in brightness but will remain a blue color for centuries.

↻ YOUR TURN

Complete the chart by writing a transitional sentence that creates cohesion and clarifies the relationships between ideas and concepts.

Purpose	Examples of Transitional Words or Phrases	Sentence
Add information	and, in addition, besides, also, equally important, further, likewise, similarly	
Discuss a contradiction	on the other hand, however, rather, on the contrary, at the same time	
Introduce examples	for example, for instance, to illustrate	
Summarize	in conclusion, therefore, in short, as a result	

Skill:
Conclusions

••• CHECKLIST FOR CONCLUSIONS

Before you write your conclusion, ask yourself the following questions:

- How can I rephrase my thesis statement?

- How can I summarize my main idea to show the depth of my knowledge?

- What impression can I make on my reader? Can I close with a memorable comment or statement?

- How can I write my conclusion so that it supports and follows logically from the information I presented?

- Have I left out any important information in my concluding statement that I have presented in my essay?

Below are two strategies to help you craft an effective and relevant conclusion that follows from and supports the information or explanation presented:

- Peer Discussion

  > After you have written your introduction and body paragraphs, talk with a partner and tell him or her what you want readers to remember, writing notes about your discussion.

  > Review your notes and think about what you wish to express in your conclusion.

- Freewriting

  > Freewrite for ten minutes about what you might include in your conclusion. Don't worry about grammar, punctuation, or having fully formed ideas. The point of freewriting is to discover ideas.

  > Review your notes and think about what you wish to express in your conclusion.

⟳ YOUR TURN

Read the pieces of student writing Isaiah's friend has written for his conclusion. Then, complete the chart below by matching each piece of student writing with the correct part of the conclusion.

	Student Writing Options
A	We have all experienced the power of a single moment; it can make or break our days, or even change our lives!
B	In conclusion, key moments or events can change everything.
C	In "The Last Human Light," we saw how in one moment our actions would continue to change the world long after humans are gone. In "Casey at the Bat," it only took one moment for the fans and for Casey to learn that winning is not always a guarantee. In "The Three Questions," the king learns that by staying present in a single moment, he can dramatically change his life.

Part of a Conclusion	Student Writing
Restate thesis in a different way	
Review and explain your main ideas	
Memorable comment	

✏ WRITE

Use the questions in the checklist section to revise the conclusion of your informative essay.

Skill:
Style

••• CHECKLIST FOR STYLE

First, reread the draft of your informative essay and identify the following:

- places where you use slang, contractions, abbreviations, and a conversational tone

- areas where you could use academic language in order to help inform your readers

- moments where you use the first person (*I*) or second person (*you*)

- areas where your sentence structure lacks variety

- incorrect uses of the conventions of standard English for grammar, spelling, capitalization, and punctuation

Establish and maintain a formal style in your essay, using the following questions as a guide:

- Have I avoided slang in favor of academic language?

- Did I consistently use a third-person point of view, using third-person pronouns (*he*, *she*, *they*)?

- Have I varied my sentence structure and the length of my sentences? Ask yourself these specific questions:

  > Where should I make some sentences longer by using conjunctions to connect independent clauses, dependent clauses, and phrases?

  > Where should I make some sentences shorter by separating any independent clauses?

- Did I follow the conventions of standard English, including:

  > grammar?

  > spelling?

  > capitalization?

  > punctuation?

Copyright © BookheadEd Learning, LLC

↻ YOUR TURN

Read each sentence below and see how each one was revised to a more formal style. Then, complete the chart by matching the correct type of informal language to each pair of sentences.

Type of Informal Language Options	
A	Conversational Tone
B	First Person
C	Lack of Capitalization
D	Contractions
E	Abbreviations
F	Slang

Informal Style	Revised to a Formal Style	Type of Informal Language
Many people can't see or understand the importance of these moments.	Many people cannot see or understand the importance of these moments.	
I think a single moment can change everything.	A single moment can change everything.	
When the students at Lincoln School got busted for teasing each other, the teachers took it seriously.	When the students at Lincoln School got caught teasing each other, the teachers took it seriously.	

Informal Style	Revised to a Formal Style	Type of Informal Language
When he wrote "The Three Questions," Leo wanted to show the importance of living in the moment.	In "The Three Questions," Leo Tolstoy wanted to show the importance of living in the moment.	
tolstoy, the author of "the three questions," illustrated the importance of paying attention to those around you.	Tolstoy, the author of "The Three Questions," illustrated the importance of paying attention to those around you.	
In these three texts, ppl will be able to see the power of a single mom.	In these three texts, people will be able to see the power of a single moment.	

↻ YOUR TURN

Identify sentences from your essay that are written using informal language. Then, complete the chart below by rewriting the sentences in a more formal style.

Type of Informal Language	Revision
Contractions	
First Person	
Slang	
Conversational Tone	
Abbreviations	
Lack of Capitalization	

Skill:
Precise Language

••• CHECKLIST FOR PRECISE LANGUAGE

As you consider precise language and domain-specific vocabulary related to a subject or topic, use the following questions as a guide:

* What information am I trying to convey or explain to my audience?
* Are there any key concepts that need to be explained or understood?
* What domain-specific vocabulary is relevant to my topic and explanation?
* Where can I use more precise vocabulary in my explanation?

Here are some suggestions that will help guide you in using precise language and domain-specific vocabulary to inform about or explain a topic:

* Determine the topic or area of study you will be writing about.
* Identify key concepts that need explanation in order to inform readers.
* Research any domain-specific vocabulary that you may need to define.
* Substitute precise, descriptive, and domain-specific language for vague, general, or overused words and phrases.
* Reread your writing to refine and revise if needed.

Please note that excerpts and passages in the StudySync® library and this workbook are intended as touchstones to generate interest in an author's work. The excerpts and passages do not substitute for the reading of entire texts, and StudySync® strongly recommends that students seek out and purchase the whole literary or informational work in order to experience it as the author intended. Links to online resellers are available in our digital library. In addition, complete works may be ordered through an authorized reseller by filling out and returning to StudySync® the order form enclosed in this workbook.

Reading & Writing
Companion

623

YOUR TURN

Read the text excerpts in the chart below. Then, complete the chart by correctly matching the domain and domain-specific vocabulary with each excerpt.

Domain and Domain-Specific Vocabulary Options	
A	Nuclear science
B	The higher education application process
C	Batter, fastball, pitch, swing
D	Phosphorescent, radium, irradiated
E	Counselors, first choice, personal essay, financial aid
F	Influenza, virus, mold, bacteria cultures, bacteria
G	Baseball
H	Medical science

Text Excerpt	Domain	Domain-Specific Vocabulary
"It came from the phosphorescent paint on top of the radium, which glowed when it was irradiated. Over the years, the paint has broken down." "The Last Human Light"		
"A batter facing a 90 mph fastball has less than a quarter second to see the pitch, judge its speed and location, decide what to do, then start to swing." "Hitting big league fastball 'clearly impossible'"		

Text Excerpt	Domain	Domain-Specific Vocabulary
"While researching the influenza virus, Fleming noticed some mold growing on one of his bacteria cultures. He was surprised to find that no bacteria grew anywhere near the mold." "Heroes of Science"		
"Over the three days, with help from counselors, Mr. Urena selected three schools to apply to; SUNY Albany was his first choice. He wrote a personal essay about how the hardships he'd faced had motivated him to graduate from college. He learned how to apply for financial aid." "The Power of Student Peer Leaders"		

↻ YOUR TURN

Identify sentences from your essay that are written without domain-specific vocabulary. Then, complete the chart below by writing the domain and rewriting the sentences using domain-specific vocabulary. The first row has been completed as an example.

Original Sentence	Domain	Revision
The design of the wind fans keeps them running much longer.	Renewable energy	The design of the wind turbines keeps them powered much longer.

Informative Writing Process: Revise

PLAN	DRAFT	REVISE	EDIT AND PUBLISH

You have written a draft of your informative essay. You have also received input from your peers about how to improve it. Now you are going to revise your draft.

◀◀ REVISION GUIDE

Examine your draft to find areas for revision. Keep in mind your purpose and audience as you revise for clarity, development, organization, and style. Use the guide below to help you review:

Review	Revise	Example
Clarity		
Identify the names of selections, authors, and the people you discuss. Annotate any places where it is unclear whom or what you're describing.	When you are quoting from the person who tells a poem, use the word "speaker."	But in the end, Casey fails, and ~~he~~ the speaker reports, "There is no hope in Mudville—mighty Casey has struck out."
Development		
Identify your main ideas. Annotate places where you need to add textual evidence or details to support your ideas.	Make sure to include a quotation or paraphrase to support each of your ideas. Use quotation marks when you are quoting a source directly.	However, they change their minds when their star player, Casey, gets to the plate. The fans illustrate this when they say they would "put up even money now, with Casey at the bat."

Review	Revise	Example
Organization		
Review your body paragraphs. Identify and annotate any sentences that don't flow in a clear and logical way.	Rewrite the sentences so they appear in a clear and logical order, starting with a strong transition or topic sentence. Delete details that are repetitive or not essential to support the thesis statement.	A key moment can also have effects on a much larger scale. We might assume that human-made lights would go out quickly if people disappeared. However, in "The Last Human Light," Randall Munroe predicts that some of our lights could last for centuries.
Style: Word Choice		
Identify weak or repetitive words or phrases that do not clearly express your ideas to the reader.	Replace weak and repetitive words and phrases with more descriptive ones that better convey your ideas.	Radioactive waste gives off light as it ~~ages~~ degrades. This process takes a very long time.
Style: Sentence Variety		
Read your informative essay aloud. Annotate places where you have too many long or short sentences in a row.	Revise short sentences by linking them together. Shorten longer sentences for clarity of emphasis.	They assume Casey will succeed. ~~He~~ because he is their hero. ~~He is~~ as well as a fantastic baseball player.

✏ WRITE

Use the guide above, as well as your peer reviews, to help you evaluate your informative essay to determine areas that should be revised.

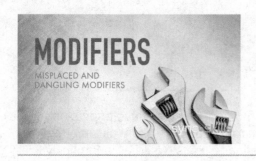

Grammar: Misplaced and Dangling Modifiers

Misplaced Modifiers

Modifiers make the meaning of another word or group of words clearer. A misplaced modifier is a modifier that appears in the wrong position in a sentence. Because of this positioning, it ends up modifying one word when it should modify another.

Modifiers should be placed as close as possible to the word that is being modified.

Type of Modifier	Correct	Incorrect
Adjective	Then Miss Hopley did a **formidable** *thing*. Barrio Boy	Then **formidable** *Miss Hopley* did a thing.
Prepositional Phrase	Caesar staged a *battle* **between two armies**, each with 500 men, 30 cavalrymen, and 20 battle elephants. Gladiator	**Between two armies**, *Caesar* staged a battle, each with 500 men, 30 cavalrymen, and 20 battle elephants.

Dangling Modifiers

Another common modifier error is the **dangling modifier**. This is when the writer includes a modifier but leaves out the thing that is being modified. The modifier is left dangling because it lacks a target.

Correct	Incorrect
With a small squeak of excitement, the *toddler* reached out her tiny hand for the beautifully wrapped gift.	**With a small squeak of excitement**, a tiny *hand* reached out for the beautifully wrapped gift. (Who made a small squeak?)

⟳ YOUR TURN

1. Which revision corrects the error in the sentence?

> Robbing a jewelry store last night, police caught a pair of thieves.

- ○ A. Robbing a jewelry store, police caught a pair of thieves last night.
- ○ B. Police caught a pair of thieves who were robbing a jewelry store last night.
- ○ C. Police who were robbing a jewelry store caught a pair of thieves last night.
- ○ D. No change needs to be made to this sentence.

2. Which revision corrects the error in the sentence?

> Mr. Trevino bought a horse for his daughter named Silver.

- ○ A. As a gift, Mr. Trevino bought a horse for his daughter named Silver.
- ○ B. Named Silver, Mr. Trevino bought a horse for his daughter.
- ○ C. Mr. Trevino bought his daughter a horse named Silver.
- ○ D. No change needs to be made to this sentence.

3. Which revision corrects the error in the sentence?

> As a "C" student, Cal almost passed every history quiz he took.

- ○ A. As a "C" student, Cal passed almost every history quiz he took.
- ○ B. Cal passed almost every history quiz he took as a "C" student.
- ○ C. Cal almost passed every history quiz he took as a "C" student.
- ○ D. No change needs to be made to this sentence.

4. Which revision corrects the error in the sentence?

> After reading that popular mystery novel, Carl believes the new film version will be great.

- ○ A. After reading that popular mystery novel, the new film should be great, according to Carl.
- ○ B. Carl believes the new film version, after reading that popular mystery novel, will be great.
- ○ C. Carl believes the film version will be great after reading that popular mystery novel.
- ○ D. No change needs to be made to this sentence.

Please note that excerpts and passages in the StudySync® library and this workbook are intended as touchstones to generate interest in an author's work. The excerpts and passages do not substitute for the reading of entire texts, and StudySync® strongly recommends that students seek out and purchase the whole literary or informational work in order to experience it as the author intended. Links to online resellers are available in our digital library. In addition, complete works may be ordered through an authorized reseller by filling out and returning to StudySync® the order form enclosed in this workbook.

Reading & Writing Companion   **629**

Grammar: Commas Between Coordinate Adjectives

Writers often use two or more consecutive adjectives to describe a noun. Sometimes you need commas between the adjectives, and sometimes you don't. If two adjectives work together as a unit to modify a noun or pronoun, no comma separates them. If each adjective works on its own and has equal weight in the sentence, then they are **coordinate adjectives**. Coordinate adjectives need a comma to separate them.

Adjectives as a Unit	Coordinate Adjectives
Sasha loves her **warm green** sweater.	Trey enjoys this **challenging, unpredictable** sport.

Use these rules to identify coordinate adjectives.

Rule	Text
If you can switch the order of the adjectives, use a comma.	And then I see her, the blood drained from her face, hands clenched in fists at her sides, walking with **stiff, small** steps up toward the stage. The Hunger Games
If the sentence would sound unnatural with the order of the adjectives switched, do not use a comma.	My pals in the second grade were Kazushi, whose parents spoke only Japanese; Matti, a **skinny Italian** boy; and Manuel, a fat Portuguese who would never get into a fight but wrestled you to the ground and just sat on you. Barrio Boy
If you could insert *and* between the adjectives, use a comma.	"In short, it was an old story, and quite a number of the **earnest, industrious** prospectors had suffered similar losses." The King of Mazy May
If the sentence would sound unnatural with *and* between the adjectives, do not use a comma.	About two miles from Summit was a little mountain, covered with a **dense cedar** brake. The Ransom of Red Chief

⟳ YOUR TURN

1. Which revision corrects the error in this sentence?

> Her little baby brother played with his new wooden blocks.

- ○ A. Her little, baby brother played with his new, wooden blocks.
- ○ B. Her little, baby brother played with his new wooden blocks.
- ○ C. Her little baby brother played with his new, wooden blocks.
- ○ D. No change needs to be made to this sentence.

2. Which revision corrects the error in this sentence?

> My new hiking boots got wet when we sloshed through a swampy wet field.

- ○ A. My new, hiking boots got wet when we sloshed through a swampy wet field.
- ○ B. My new hiking boots got wet when we sloshed through a swampy, wet field.
- ○ C. My new, hiking boots got wet when we sloshed through a swampy, wet field.
- ○ D. No change needs to be made to this sentence.

3. Which revision corrects the error in this sentence?

> Windy cold weather continued for four long days.

- ○ A. Windy, cold weather continued for four long days.
- ○ B. Windy cold weather continued for four, long days.
- ○ C. Windy, cold weather continued for four, long days.
- ○ D. No change needs to be made to this sentence.

4. Which revision corrects the error in this sentence?

> Our school's junior varsity basketball team won the exciting fast-paced game.

- ○ A. Our school's junior, varsity basketball team won the exciting fast-paced game.
- ○ B. Our school's junior varsity basketball team won the exciting, fast-paced game.
- ○ C. Our school's junior, varsity, basketball team won the exciting fast-paced game.
- ○ D. No change needs to be made to this sentence.

Grammar:
Commonly Misspelled Words

By following a few simple steps, you can learn to spell new words—even words that are unfamiliar or difficult. As you write, keep a list of words you have trouble spelling. Then use the steps below to learn to spell those words.

Say it. Look at the word again and say it aloud. Say it again, pronouncing each syllable clearly.

See it. Close your eyes. Picture the word. Visualize it letter by letter.

Write it. Look at the word again and write it two or three times. Then write the word without looking at the printed version.

Check it. Check your spelling. Did you spell it correctly? If not, repeat each step until you can spell it easily.

Here are some words that can sometimes confuse even strong spellers.

Commonly Misspelled Words					
accidentally	alcohol	analyze	beige	canceled	convenient
definite	embarrass	extremely	fried	granddaughter	height
heroes	judgment	laboratory	leisure	niece	pageant
opposite	physician	pronunciation	receipt	recognize	recommend
relative	safely	tomorrow	truly	usually	weird

↻ YOUR TURN

1. How should this sentence be changed?

   > The plot of that new horror movie is extremely weird.

   ○ A. Change **extremely** to **extremly** and **weird** to **wired**.
   ○ B. Change **extremely** to **extreemly and weird** to **weerd**.
   ○ C. Change **weird** to **wierd**.
   ○ D. No change needs to be made to this sentence.

2. How should this sentence be changed?

   > Those we think of as performing brave deeds often become our heros accidently.

   ○ A. Change **accidently** to **accidentilly**.
   ○ B. Change **heros** to **heroes** and **accidently** to **accidentally**.
   ○ C. Change **heros** to **heeroes**.
   ○ D. No change needs to be made to this sentence.

3. How should this sentence be changed?

   > William's physician was able to anylize his blood sample and assure him he was not ill after all.

   ○ A. Change **physician** to **physitian**.
   ○ B. Change **anylize** to **analyze**.
   ○ C. Change **physician** to **physition** and **anylize** to **analize**.
   ○ D. No change needs to be made to this sentence.

4. How should this sentence be changed?

   > I reccomend that you come back tomorow for your receipt.

   ○ A. Change **reccomend** to **recommend** and **tomorow** to **tomorrow**.
   ○ B. Change **reccomend** to **recomend**, **tomorow** to **tommorow**, and **receipt** to **receit**.
   ○ C. Change **receipt** to **receite**.
   ○ D. No change needs to be made to this sentence.

Informative Writing Process:
Edit and Publish

PLAN	DRAFT	REVISE	EDIT AND PUBLISH

You have revised your informative essay based on your peer feedback and your own examination.

Now, it is time to edit your essay. When you revised, you focused on the content of your essay. You probably looked at your story's introduction, transitions, supporting details, style, and conclusion. When you edit, you focus on the mechanics of your essay, paying close attention to things like grammar and punctuation.

Use the checklist below to guide you as you edit:

☐ Have I followed all the rules for using modifiers?

☐ Have I used commas correctly between coordinate adjectives?

☐ Do I have any sentence fragments or run-on sentences?

☐ Have I spelled everything correctly?

Notice some edits Isaiah has made:

- Added a comma between coordinate adjectives.

- Corrected spelling errors.

- Corrected a misplaced modifier.

The hermit, however, does not answer. Instead, a wounded, tired man appears, and the king saves his life. Afterward, the man ~~reveels~~ reveals that he had ~~planed~~ planned to kill the king and was stabbed by the royal ~~body guards royal~~ bodyguards. Now, he swears to be loyal to the king forever. The king is grateful for the peaceful ending. Later, the hermit explains how the king's own actions led him to this conclusion. He finally answers the king's questions: "Remember then: there is only one time that is important—Now!" The king ~~originaly~~ originally assumes that what he knows will help him ~~succede~~ succeed in life. However, he learns that acting in the moment is the only way to live well.

✏ WRITE

Use the questions on the previous page, as well as your peer reviews, to help you evaluate your informative essay to determine areas that need editing. Then edit your essay to correct those errors.

Once you have made all your corrections, you are ready to publish your work. You can distribute your writing to family and friends, hang it on a bulletin board, or post it on your blog. If you publish online, share the link with your family, friends, and classmates.

Please note that excerpts and passages in the StudySync® library and this workbook are intended as touchstones to generate interest in an author's work. The excerpts and passages do not substitute for the reading of entire texts, and StudySync® strongly recommends that students seek out and purchase the whole literary or informational work in order to experience it as the author intended. Links to online resellers are available in our digital library. In addition, complete works may be ordered through an authorized reseller by filling out and returning to StudySync® the order form enclosed in this workbook.

Reading & Writing Companion   **635**

The Belles of the Ballgame

INFORMATIONAL TEXT

Introduction

World War II changed everything about American society, from the workplace to leisure activities. With many of the men fighting overseas, owners feared that major league baseball would be put on hold. The All-American Girls Professional Baseball League stepped up to the plate. The AAGPBL lasted only from 1943 to 1954, but its skilled players and their stories have made the league a lasting part of sports history.

Ⅴ VOCABULARY

distract

to pull attention away

conduct

the way in which a person behaves

pastime

an activity that people enjoy doing to pass the time

attendance

the number of people who go to a place or event

chaperone

an adult who monitors the behavior of young people

☰ READ

NOTES

1   The year was 1942. World War II changed life in the United States. Men were called away to fight. Women took jobs in factories. Spirits were low. Americans looked for an enjoyable activity to **distract** them.

2   Watching a baseball game was an ideal **pastime**. The war effort had thrown a curveball. Many young men were overseas. Minor league baseball had to call a timeout. Philip K. Wrigley, owner of the Chicago Cubs, worried about major league baseball. Wrigley had an idea straight out of left field. Women were reliable pinch hitters in the workplace. Could women also solve baseball's problems?

3   The All-American Girls Professional Baseball League began in 1943. Nearly 300 qualified women tried out. Only 60 were selected. The Racine Belles, Kenosha Comets, South Bend Blue Sox, and Rockford Peaches had fifteen players. Each team had a manager, business manager, and female **chaperone**.

Please note that excerpts and passages in the StudySync® library and this workbook are intended as touchstones to generate interest in an author's work. The excerpts and passages do not substitute for the reading of entire texts, and StudySync® strongly recommends that students seek out and purchase the whole literary or informational work in order to experience it as the author intended. Links to online resellers are available in our digital library. In addition, complete works may be ordered through an authorized reseller by filling out and returning to StudySync® the order form enclosed in this workbook.

Reading & Writing Companion   637

NOTES

4   The players' athletic skills were as strong as the men's. They hit home runs and played through injuries. But they had different requirements. Their uniforms had short skirts. The unofficial motto of the league was "Look like women. Play like men." In addition to their duties on the field, the players had to follow a code of **conduct**. They took classes on how to walk, speak, dress, and apply makeup.

5   Still, women stepped up to the plate. Salaries were high. Young players earned more than their parents did. The fans were welcoming. During the 1943 season, 176,612 fans attended a game. The war ended in 1945. Yet **attendance** rose to 910,000 in 1948. This achievement proved that women's baseball was successful. The owners and players alike hit it out of the park.

6   Some players earned fans of their own. Dorothy "Dottie" Kamenshek was 17 years old when she joined the Rockford Peaches in 1943. During her career, she was chosen for seven all-star teams. She won the batting title two years in a row. She also held the league's record for outs by a fielder. A men's team tried to recruit Kamenshek in 1950, but she did not accept. An injury forced her retirement in 1951.

7   Sadly, attendance fell in the early 1950s. Fans could watch men's major league baseball games on television. Owners failed to go to bat for their players. The league finally struck out after its 1954 season. Still, Kamenshek and the other players are important historic figures. The 1994 film *A League of Their Own* was inspired by Kamenshek and her teammates. *Sports Illustrated* also named Kamenshek one of the 100 greatest female athletes of all time.

First Read

Read the story. After you read, answer the Think Questions below.

☁ THINK QUESTIONS

1. When did the All-American Girls Professional Baseball League begin? What was happening at the time?

   The All-American Girls Professional Baseball League began in _____.

   At the time _____.

2. Write two or three sentences describing the rules the female players had to follow.

   The rules female players had to follow were _____

   _____.

3. Why was Dorothy "Dottie" Kamenshek such a popular player?

   Dottie Kamenshek was a popular player because _____.

4. Use context to confirm the meaning of the word *attendance* as it is used in "The Belles of the Ballgame." Write your definition of *attendance* here.

   Attendance means _____.

   A context clue is _____.

5. What is another way to say that a person's *conduct* is important?

   A person's *conduct* is _____.

Skill:
Analyzing Expressions

 DEFINE

When you read, you may find English expressions that you do not know. An **expression** is a group of words that communicates an idea. Three types of expressions are idioms, sayings, and figurative language. They can be difficult to understand because the meanings of the words are different from their **literal**, or usual, meanings.

An **idiom** is an expression that is commonly known among a group of people. For example: "It's raining cats and dogs" means it is raining heavily. **Sayings** are short expressions that contain advice or wisdom. For instance: "Don't count your chickens before they hatch" means do not plan on something good happening before it happens. **Figurative** language is when you describe something by comparing it with something else, either directly (using the words *like* or *as*) or indirectly. For example, "I'm as hungry as a horse" means I'm very hungry. None of the expressions are about actual animals.

••• CHECKLIST FOR ANALYZING EXPRESSIONS

To determine the meaning of an expression, remember the following:

✓ If you find a confusing group of words, it may be an expression. The meaning of words in expressions may not be their literal meaning.

- Ask yourself: Is this confusing because the words are new? Or because the words do not make sense together?

✓ Determining the overall meaning may require that you use one or more of the following:

- context clues

- a dictionary or other resource

- teacher or peer support

✓ Highlight important information before and after the expression to look for clues.

⟳ YOUR TURN

Read the following excerpt from the text. Match each expression with its meaning in the text. Write the correct answers in the chart below.

---

from **"The Belles of the Ballgame"**

Watching a baseball game was an ideal pastime. The war effort had thrown a curveball. Many young men were overseas. Minor league baseball had to call a timeout. Philip K. Wrigley, owner of the Chicago Cubs, worried about major league baseball. Wrigley had an idea straight out of left field. Women were reliable pinch hitters in the workplace. Could women also solve baseball's problems?

	Meaning in the Text
A	take a break for a period of time
B	replacements
C	cause an unexpected problem
D	strange or unlikely

Expression	Literal Meaning	Meaning in the Text
throw a curveball	throw a ball that suddenly drops or curves to the side	
call a timeout	stop play to discuss a new strategy	
out of left field	coming from a part of the field that is far from the main action	
pinch hitters	players who hit in place of other players	

Please note that excerpts and passages in the StudySync® library and this workbook are intended as touchstones to generate interest in an author's work. The excerpts and passages do not substitute for the reading of entire texts, and StudySync® strongly recommends that students seek out and purchase the whole literary or informational work in order to experience it as the author intended. Links to online resellers are available in our digital library. In addition, complete works may be ordered through an authorized reseller by filling out and returning to StudySync® the order form enclosed in this workbook.

Reading & Writing
Companion

641

Skill:
Supporting Evidence

★ DEFINE

In some informational or argumentative texts, the author may share an opinion. This **opinion** may be the author's **claim** or **thesis**. The author must then provide readers with **evidence** that supports their opinion. Supporting evidence can be details, examples, or facts that agree with the author's claim or thesis.

Looking for supporting evidence can help you confirm your understanding of what you read. Finding and analyzing supporting evidence can also help you form your own opinions about the subject.

••• CHECKLIST FOR SUPPORTING EVIDENCE

In order to find and analyze supporting evidence, do the following:

✓ Identify the topic and the author's claim or thesis.

- Ask yourself: What is this mostly about? What is the author's opinion?

✓ Find details, facts, and examples that support the author's claim or thesis.

- Ask yourself: Is this detail important? How does this detail relate to the thesis or claim?

✓ Analyze the supporting evidence.

- Ask yourself: Is this evidence strong? Do I agree with the evidence?

Copyright © BookheadEd Learning, LLC

⟳ YOUR TURN

Identify the supporting evidence that correctly matches each claim. Write the correct answers in the chart below.

	Supporting Evidence
A	Salaries were high. Young players earned more than their parents did.
B	The 1994 film *A League of Their Own* was inspired by Kamenshek and her teammates. *Sports Illustrated* also named Kamenshek one of the 100 greatest female athletes of all time.
C	During the 1943 season, 176,612 fans attended a game. The war ended in 1945. Yet attendance rose to 910,000 in 1948.

Claim	Supporting Evidence
Women's baseball was successful	
Women stepped up to the plate	
Kamenshek and the other players are important historic figures	

Please note that excerpts and passages in the StudySync® library and this workbook are intended as touchstones to generate interest in an author's work. The excerpts and passages do not substitute for the reading of entire texts, and StudySync® strongly recommends that students seek out and purchase the whole literary or informational work in order to experience it as the author intended. Links to online resellers are available in our digital library. In addition, complete works may be ordered through an authorized reseller by filling out and returning to StudySync® the order form enclosed in this workbook.

Reading & Writing Companion **643**

Close Read

 WRITE

INFORMATIVE: The All-American Girls Professional Baseball League is considered a success even though it ended in 1954. In a short essay, explain why this unique experiment was "successful." Use details and examples from the text to support your ideas. Pay attention to correctly spelling words with suffixes as you write.

Use the checklist below to guide you as you write.

☐ What made the All-American Girls Professional Baseball League a success?

☐ What evidence from the text supports your claim?

☐ What is your conclusion?

Use the sentence frames to organize and write your informational essay.

The All-American Girls Professional Baseball League was a success because _____

_____.

One detail that shows this is _____.

Another detail that supports this claim is _____.

These details prove that _____.

The Future of Wind Energy

INFORMATIONAL TEXT

Introduction

Wind energy is growing more popular in the United States every day. This article explains how wind farms are becoming a part of the American landscape, how wind turbines work, and how one group of researchers may change renewable energy forever.

V VOCABULARY

farm
land that is used for growing crops or raising animals

pivot
to turn around a central location

generate
to bring in existence, to create

renewable
able to be replaced naturally

obvious
easily perceived by the senses or grasped by the mind

NOTES

☰ READ

A New Kind of Farm

1   When you hear the word *farm*, you likely think of crops in neat rows. You may imagine cows in a pasture. Soon, you might imagine something else. Wind farms are growing in number and size.

wind turbines on a wind farm

2 The Roscoe Wind Farm opened in 2009. The farm's 634 turbines **generate** electricity for 230,000 homes. The Texas farm was the world's largest wind farm for less than a year. Today's wind farms are larger and more powerful. A wind farm will open in 2020. The Wind Catcher Energy Connection's 800 turbines will power 800,000 homes. It is clear that wind energy is on the rise. It is less **obvious** how wind turbines work.

How Do Wind Turbines Work?

3 A wind turbine looks like a tall pole with an airplane's propeller. The pole is called the tower. The blades at the top of the tower spin. These blades use the wind to create energy.

4 The wind's natural power turns the blades around a rotor. The rotor then turns a series of shafts, or rounded bars inside the turbine's nacelle. This movement spins the generator, which makes energy. Other parts help create the most energy possible. The yaw drive **pivots** the wind turbine when the wind direction changes. Even though the tower can't move, the yaw drive turns the nacelle so that it is always facing into the wind.

parts of a wind turbine

5 Some parts increase safety. The anemometer measures wind speed. The controller stops the turbine if the wind blows too hard. The blades are more likely to be damaged in high-speed winds. The brake stops the rotor in case of an emergency.

The Future of Wind Turbines

6   Sources of **renewable** energy are becoming more popular. Still, customers look for ways to use more energy at a lower cost. The best way is to build bigger wind turbines.

7   The tower's height affects the amount of energy a turbine can create. Wind speeds increase with height. Taller towers create more energy. The average wind turbine is 70 meters tall, double the size of an average water tower. Many wind turbines are needed to generate power on a large scale. Researchers are working to change large-scale wind energy production.

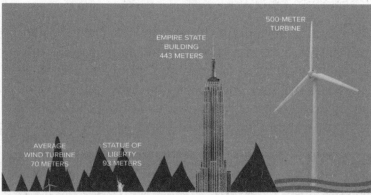

comparing sizes

8   The team plans to make an offshore wind turbine. It will be 500 meters tall. That is taller than the Empire State Building! The plan may not work. If it does, it will change the future.

First Read

Read the text. After you read, answer the Think Questions below.

☁ THINK QUESTIONS

1. What are two changes happening to wind farms?

    Two changes are _____ and

    _____.

2. Write two or three sentences describing how a wind turbine works.

    A wind turbine works by _____

    _____.

3. What do researchers want to build?

    Researchers want to build _____.

4. Use context to confirm the meaning of the word *generate* as it is used in "The Future of Wind Energy." Write your definition of *generate* here.

    Generate means _____.

    A context clue is _____.

5. What is another way to say that an object *pivots*?

    An object _____.

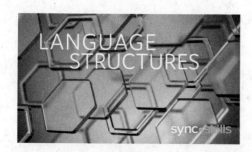

Skill:
Language Structures

Copyright © BookheadEd Learning, LLC

★ DEFINE

In every language, there are rules that tell how to **structure** sentences. These rules define the correct order of words. In the English language, for example, a **basic** structure for sentences is subject, verb, and object. Some sentences have more **complicated** structures.

You will encounter both basic and complicated **language structures** in the classroom materials you read. Being familiar with language structures will help you better understand the text.

••• CHECKLIST FOR LANGUAGE STRUCTURES

To improve your comprehension of language structures, do the following:

✓ Monitor your understanding.

- Ask yourself: Why do I not understand this sentence? Is it because I do not understand some of the words? Or is it because I do not understand the way the words are ordered in the sentence?

✓ Break down the sentence into its parts.

- Pay attention to comparatives and superlatives. The **comparative** form compares things. The **superlative** form compares more than two things.

- Ask yourself: Are there comparatives or superlatives in this sentence? What are they comparing?

✓ Confirm your understanding with a peer or teacher.

YOUR TURN

Write the comparative or superlative adjective in the correct column.

Adjective	Comparative	Superlative
fast		
small		
good		
reliable		
helpful		

Skill:
Visual and Contextual Support

★ DEFINE

Visual support is an image or an object that helps you understand a text. **Contextual support** is a **feature** that helps you understand a text. By using visual and contextual supports, you can develop your vocabulary so you can better understand a variety of texts.

First, preview the text to identify any visual supports. These might include illustrations, graphics, charts, or other objects in a text. Then, identify any contextual supports. Examples of contextual supports are titles, headers, captions, and boldface terms. Write down your **observations**.

Then, write down what those visual and contextual supports tell you about the meaning of the text. Note any new vocabulary that you see in those supports. Ask your peers and your teacher to confirm your understanding of the text.

••• CHECKLIST FOR VISUAL AND CONTEXTUAL SUPPORT

To use visual and contextual support to understand texts, do the following:

- ✓ Preview the text. Read the title, headers, and other features. Look at any images and graphics.

- ✓ Write down the visual and contextual supports in the text.

- ✓ Write down what those supports tell you about the text.

- ✓ Note any new vocabulary that you see in those supports.

- ✓ Create an illustration for the reading and write a descriptive caption.

- ✓ Confirm your observations with your peers and teacher.

⟳ YOUR TURN

Read the following excerpt from the text. Then, complete the multiple choice questions below.

from **"The Future of Wind Energy"**

A New Kind of Farm

When you hear the word *farm*, you likely think of crops in neat rows. You may imagine cows in a pasture. Soon, you might imagine something else. Wind farms are growing in number and size.

wind turbines on a wind farm

1. What is the "new kind of farm" that the heading refers to?

    ○ A. farms with rows of crops

    ○ B. farms with cows in a pasture

    ○ C. wind farms

    ○ D. large farms

2. How can the visual support help students?

    ○ A. It shows students how wind farms work.

    ○ B. It helps students imagine what a wind farm looks like.

    ○ C. It teaches students important vocabulary about wind farms.

    ○ D. It shows students how crops are grown on a farm.

Please note that excerpts and passages in the StudySync® library and this workbook are intended as touchstones to generate interest in an author's work. The excerpts and passages do not substitute for the reading of entire texts, and StudySync® strongly recommends that students seek out and purchase the whole literary or informational work in order to experience it as the author intended. Links to online resellers are available in our digital library. In addition, complete works may be ordered through an authorized reseller by filling out and returning to StudySync® the order form enclosed in this workbook.

Reading & Writing
Companion

653

Close Read

 WRITE

PERSONAL NARRATIVE: Imagine that a wind farm will be constructed in your backyard! Write a paragraph describing how you would feel. Think about what interests you or concerns you about the plan. Recount specific details from the text and its images as you write. Pay attention to using the possessive case correctly as you write.

Use the checklist below to guide you as you write.

☐ What interests you about having a wind farm in your backyard?

☐ What concerns you about having a wind farm in your backyard?

☐ Are you more concerned about or interested in the plan?

☐ What makes you feel this way about wind farms?

Use the sentence frames to organize and write your personal narrative.

I am _____ the plan.

Wind turbines _____. The text says that _____.

Also, a wind farm _____. An image in the text shows _____.

The wind farm would change my life by _____.

I would feel _____.

and _____.

 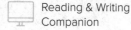

Please note that excerpts and passages in the StudySync® library and this workbook are intended as touchstones to generate interest in an author's work. The excerpts and passages do not substitute for the reading of entire texts, and StudySync® strongly recommends that students seek out and purchase the whole literary or informational work in order to experience it as the author intended. Links to online resellers are available in our digital library. In addition, complete works may be ordered through an authorized reseller by filling out and returning to StudySync® the order form enclosed in this workbook.

:: studysync®

ASSIGNMENTS   BINDER   LIBRARY

Test of Time

UNIT 5

Test of Time

Why do we still read myths and folktales?

> Genre Focus: FICTION—MYTHS & FOLKTALES

Texts

Paired Readings

Extended Writing Project and Grammar

Why do we still read myths and folktales?

AESOP

The ancient Greek author known as Aesop (c. 620–564 BCE) is believed to have been born on the Black Coast near Nesebar in modern-day Bulgaria. Legend has it that he was enslaved by a man named Xanthus, but was eventually freed, before meeting his demise in Delphi on trumped-up charges that saw him thrown off a cliff. Aesop is best known for his fables, stories passed down by oral tradition that he transcribed, intended to teach political, moral, and ethical lessons to young readers.

AIMEE BENDER

Aimee Bender (b. 1969) was born in Southern California, and attended the University of California, San Diego, before earning her MFA at the University of California, Irvine. A former director of the University of Southern California's Ph.D. program in Creative Writing and Literature, she has also taught at UCLA and worked on outreach programs that develop literacy for disadvantaged populations. She is the author of seven books, including *The Particular Sadness of Lemon Cake*, *The Color Master*, and *An Invisible Sign of My Own*. She lives in Los Angeles.

SUZANNE COLLINS

Before penning the *New York Times* best-selling series *The Hunger Games* Trilogy, and seeing her books adapted for the big screen, Suzanne Collins (b. 1962) wrote for the children's television network Nickelodeon. After graduating from Indiana University, she worked as a staff writer for several shows, including *Clarissa Explains It All*, *The Mystery Files of Shelby Woo*, *Little Bear*, and *Oswald*. Not long after, she wrote her first bestselling series, *The Underland Chronicles*. Worldwide, the books she has written have sold over 100 million copies.

ROBERT HAYDEN

When his parents separated, Robert Hayden (1913–1980) was raised from infancy in a foster home filled with anger and violence in the Detroit neighborhood Paradise Valley, where artists like Billie Holiday and Ella Fitzgerald took to the stage. Because of severe nearsightedness, Hayden chose books over sports, kindling a lifetime love. He attended Detroit City College, and went on to the University of Michigan for graduate studies. Hayden may be best known for his works "The Middle Passage" and "Those Winter Sundays." He died in Ann Arbor.

EMMA LAZARUS

Born into a wealthy family, Emma Lazarus (1849–1887) grew up in New York City. Shortly after her father published some of her poetry, she was published by a commercial press and caught the eye of Ralph Waldo Emerson, among others. Over the next ten years, she'd publish another collection of poetry, *Admetus and Other Poems*; a novel, *Alide: An Episode in Goethe's Life*; and a play, *The Spagnoletto*. However, she is best known for her sonnet on the pedestal of the Statue of Liberty, written at the request of fundraisers on behalf of the monument.

JOSEPHINE PRESTON PEABODY

Born in Brooklyn and raised in Massachusetts after the death of her father, Josephine Preston Peabody (1874–1922) grew up in poverty in the home of her maternal grandmother, reading and writing constantly. She had her first poem published at the age of fourteen. After her other poems were published in the *Atlantic Monthly* and *Scribner's Magazine*, a patron funded her schooling, and Peabody enrolled at Radcliffe College. She'd go on to publish collections of poetry, a one-act play, and several other books, while also lecturing at Wellesley.

CHARLOTTE BLAKE ALSTON

Charlotte Blake Alston is a storyteller, singer, and narrator who has performed at the Kennedy Center, Lincoln Center, and abroad from Cape Town, South Africa, to a refugee camp in northern Senegal. Her focus is on African and African American stories, and her solo performances often include accompaniment by traditional instruments, including djembe, kalimba, and the twenty-one-stringed kora. For over two decades she has served as the host for family and school concerts at the Philadelphia Orchestra and at Carnegie Hall.

FARAH AHMEDI

At the age of ten, Afghanistan-born author Farah Ahmedi (b. 1987) was severely injured when she stepped on a landmine. Ahmedi was hospitalized in Germany where she underwent a leg amputation. Upon her return to Afghanistan, Ahmedi's father and sisters were killed in a rocket attack, and her brothers disappeared fleeing the Taliban. She moved to the United States after gaining refugee status, where she won *Good Morning America*'s Story of My Life contest, wrote her memoir, and has become an outspoken humanitarian and advocate for people with disabilities.

JAMES BALDWIN

An educator and administrator for eighteen years, James Baldwin (1841–1925) served as a school superintendent in Indiana before becoming a textbook editor and prolific children's author of more than fifty books. Baldwin's works, of which it is estimated that 26 million copies were sold worldwide, cover topics ranging from Greek mythology to famous American historical figures.

M. R. COX

London native and dedicated folklorist Marian Roalfe Cox (1860–1916) began attending meetings of the British Folklore Society with her mother as a young girl. Described as "pale" and "fragile-looking" in her early years, Cox's diligence was soon apparent. In her twenties, she undertook the project of cataloging and categorizing every version of the "Cinderella" fairy tale told around the world. The resulting anthology, published in 1893, became the definitive text on the subject and expanded our understanding of how stories are passed on across the world.

BARRY STRAUSS

At Cornell University, Barry Strauss (b. 1953) serves as a professor of humanities, history, and the classics. Strauss is a series editor for the Princeton History of the Ancient World series, a military historian, and the author of seven books, including *The Death of Caesar*, *Masters of Command*, and *The Spartacus War*. A former graduate of Cornell University, he received his BA there before moving on to Yale University for his master's and Ph.D. He also currently serves as the director and founder of Cornell's Program on Freedom and Free Societies.

Aesop's Fables

FICTION
Aesop
600 BCE

Introduction

There are facts and fictions surrounding the person known as Aesop. Once an enslaved African who was freed for his wit and intelligence—and reportedly thrown to his death over a precipice by the people of Delphi—Aesop is credited with creating hundreds of fables, though none of his actual writings survive. What can't be disputed is that the short, charming tales of wisdom and folly have left an indelible mark on Western culture. In this selection of seven fables, not all have explicit morals; some you have to figure out.

"Pleasure bought with pains, hurts."

NOTES

The Swollen Fox

1 A VERY HUNGRY FOX, seeing some bread and meat left by shepherds in the hollow of an oak, crept into the hole and made a hearty meal. When he finished, he was so full that he was not able to get out, and began to groan and lament his fate. Another Fox passing by heard his cries, and coming up, inquired the cause of his complaining. On learning what had happened, he said to him, "Ah, you will have to remain there, my friend, until you become such as you were when you crept in, and then you will easily get out."

 Skill:
Theme

Because this is a fable, a lesson will be taught at the end. I think the theme will be related to the lesson. The topic of this fable is about eating. I think the theme might have to do with how eating too much could be a problem.

The Flies and the Honey-Pot

2 A NUMBER of Flies were attracted to a jar of honey which had been overturned in a housekeeper's room, and placing their feet in it, ate greedily. Their feet, however, became so smeared with the honey that they could not use their wings, nor release themselves, and were suffocated. Just as they were expiring, they exclaimed, "O foolish creatures that we are, for the sake of a little pleasure we have destroyed ourselves." Pleasure bought with pains, hurts.

The Hen and the Golden Eggs

3 A COTTAGER[1] and his wife had a Hen that laid a golden egg every day. They supposed that the Hen must contain a great lump of gold in its inside, and in order to get the gold they killed it. Having done so, they found to their surprise that the Hen differed in no respect from their other hens. The foolish pair, thus hoping to become rich all at once, **deprived** themselves of the gain of which they were assured day by day.

 Skill:
Theme

The Fox learns a lesson from another Fox— that he can't get out of the hole until he is hungry again. The Fox's challenge is that he got too big to crawl out! The theme must be that too much of a good thing can lead to trouble.

The Miser

4 A **MISER** sold all that he had and bought a lump of gold, which he buried in a hole in the ground by the side of an old wall and went to look at daily. One of his workmen observed his frequent visits to the spot and decided to watch his movements. He soon discovered the secret of the hidden treasure, and digging down, came to the lump of gold, and stole it. The Miser, on his next visit, found the hole empty and began to tear his hair and to make loud

---

1. **cottager** a person living in a cottage

Copyright © BookheadEd Learning, LLC

lamentations. A neighbor, seeing him overcome with grief and learning the cause, said, "Pray do not grieve so; but go and take a stone, and place it in the hole, and fancy that the gold is still lying there. It will do you quite the same service; for when the gold was there, you had it not, as you did not make the slightest use of it."

The Fox and the Woodcutter

5   A FOX, running before the hounds, came across a Woodcutter felling an oak and begged him to show him a safe hiding-place. The Woodcutter advised him to take shelter in his own hut, so the Fox crept in and hid himself in a corner. The huntsman[2] soon came up with his hounds and inquired of the Woodcutter if he had seen the Fox. He declared that he had not seen him, and yet pointed, all the time he was speaking, to the hut where the Fox lay hidden. The huntsman took no notice of the signs, but believing his word, hastened forward in the chase. As soon as they were well away, the Fox departed without taking any notice of the Woodcutter: whereon he called to him and reproached him, saying, "You ungrateful fellow, you owe your life to me, and yet you leave me without a word of thanks." The Fox replied, "Indeed, I should have thanked you **fervently** if your deeds had been as good as your words, and if your hands had not been traitors to your speech."

The Ants and the Grasshopper

6   THE ANTS were spending a fine winter's day drying grain collected in the summertime. A Grasshopper, **perishing** with famine, passed by and earnestly begged for a little food. The Ants inquired of him, "Why did you not treasure up food during the summer?" He replied, "I had not leisure enough. I passed the days in singing." They then said in **derision:** "If you were foolish enough to sing all the summer, you must dance supperless to bed in the winter."

The Ant and the Grasshopper

The Wolf in Sheep's Clothing

7   ONCE UPON A TIME a Wolf **resolved** to disguise his appearance in order to secure food more easily. Encased in the skin of a sheep, he pastured with the flock deceiving the shepherd by his costume. In the evening he was shut up by the shepherd in the fold; the gate was closed, and the entrance made thoroughly secure. But the shepherd, returning to the fold during the night to obtain meat for the next day, mistakenly caught up the Wolf instead of a sheep, and killed him instantly.

8   Harm seek. Harm find.

---

2. **huntsman** hunter

First Read

Read "Aesop's Fables." After you read, complete the Think Questions below.

☁ THINK QUESTIONS

1. How are the moral lessons in "The Swollen Fox" and "The Flies and the Honey-Pot" alike? Cite textual evidence and explain your answer.

2. How is the Wolf's predicament in "The Wolf in Sheep's Clothing" similar to that of the cottager and his wife in "The Hen and the Golden Eggs"? Cite textual evidence as you compare the two tales.

3. How are the cottager and his wife in "The Hen and the Golden Eggs" similar to the Miser in "The Miser"? What lesson is Aesop teaching in both fables? Cite passages in the text that support your answer.

4. Use context to determine the meaning of the word **deprived** as it is used in the fable "The Hen and the Golden Eggs." Write your definition of *deprived* here and explain what you think it means, based on the word's context clues.

5. The Latin word *fervere* means "to boil." The Latin suffix *-ly*, which means "in what manner," is used in English for many adverbs. Use your knowledge of Latin roots and suffixes to determine the meaning of **fervently** in paragraph 5. Write your definition of *fervently* here, and explain how you figured out its meaning.

Please note that excerpts and passages in the StudySync® library and this workbook are intended as touchstones to generate interest in an author's work. The excerpts and passages do not substitute for the reading of entire texts, and StudySync® strongly recommends that students seek out and purchase the whole literary or informational work in order to experience it as the author intended. Links to online resellers are available in our digital library. In addition, complete works may be ordered through an authorized reseller by filling out and returning to StudySync® the order form enclosed in this workbook.

Reading & Writing Companion **663**

Skill:
Theme

Use the Checklist to analyze Theme in "Aesop's Fables." Refer to the sample student annotations about Theme in the text.

••• CHECKLIST FOR THEME

In order to identify a theme or central idea in a text, note the following:

✓ the subject, topic, or genre of the text

✓ whether or not the theme is stated directly in the text

✓ details in the text that help to reveal theme

- a narrator's or speaker's tone
- title and chapter headings
- details about the setting
- characters' thoughts, actions, and dialogue
- the central conflict in the story's plot
- the resolution of the conflict

To determine a theme or central idea of a text and analyze its development over the course of the text, consider the following questions:

✓ What is a theme or central idea of the text?

✓ When did you become aware of that theme? For instance, did the story's conclusion reveal the theme?

✓ How does the theme develop over the course of the text?

Skill:
Theme

Reread "The Fox and the Woodcutter," paragraph 5 of "Aesop's Fables." Then, using the Checklist on the previous page, answer the multiple-choice questions below.

⟳ YOUR TURN

1. This question has two parts. First, answer Part A. Then, answer Part B.

   Part A: Which of the following statements **best** represents the fable's theme?

   ○ A. Good words are meaningless if you do not act honestly.
   ○ B. Keeping your body in shape is just as important as being smart.
   ○ C. Bad people can get away with crimes if they are smart.
   ○ D. Strangers can be just as helpful as friends when you are in danger.

   Part B: The detail that **best** reveals the theme identified in part A is—

   ○ A. the Woodcutter advises the Fox to take shelter in his own hut.
   ○ B. the huntsman takes no notice of the signs.
   ○ C. the Woodcutter says, "you owe your life to me."
   ○ D. the Fox says, "if your hands had not been traitors to your speech."

Close Read

Reread "Aesop's Fables." As you reread, complete the Skills Focus questions below. Then use your answers and annotations from the questions to help you complete the Write activity.

◎ SKILLS FOCUS

1. Reread "The Flies and the Honey-Pot" and "The Hen and the Golden Eggs." In each fable, identify the lesson and paraphrase it in your own words. Make sure to maintain the meaning and the logical order of the original text. Then explain how the lessons relate to an overall theme about life in general.

2. Identify a theme in one of the last four fables. Explain how this theme is similar to and different from a theme in another fable of your choice.

3. Recall that a miser is someone who hates to spend money. Identify evidence that the Miser has this quality, and explain how this quality influences the events of the fable.

4. The saying that someone is a "wolf in sheep's clothing" comes from the Aesop's fable of that name. Identify evidence of the Wolf's qualities, and explain how those qualities lead to the lesson of the fable.

5. Identify a lesson from one of the fables that is relevant to modern life. Explain an experience you've had that shows the relevance of this lesson.

✎ WRITE

NARRATIVE: Write a fable of your own that demonstrates a clear theme. Use a variety of writing techniques. Make sure to state a lesson at the end of your story as a moral that reflects your chosen theme. In your fable, include animal characters that have human traits.

The Hunger Games

FICTION
Suzanne Collins
2008

Introduction

*T*he *Hunger Games* is a dystopian novel by Suzanne Collins (b. 1962) set in fictional Panem, which is all that remains of post-apocalyptic North America in the not-too-distant future. In punishment for a failed uprising, the government annually requires each of the 12 districts of Panem to choose one boy and one girl to go to the Capitol, where they must participate in a televised battle to the death. At the selection ceremony for District 12, 16-year-old Katniss is horrified by a selection for which she was not prepared.

"The last tribute standing wins."

NOTES

from Chapter 1

1   "You look beautiful," says Prim in a hushed voice.

2   "And nothing like myself," I say. I hug her, because I know these next few hours will be terrible for her. Her first reaping[1]. She's about as safe as you can get, since she's only entered once. I wouldn't let her take out any tesserae[2]. But she's worried about me. That the unthinkable might happen.

3   I protect Prim in every way I can, but I'm powerless against the reaping. The **anguish** I always feel when she's in pain wells up in my chest and threatens to register on my face. I notice her blouse has pulled out of her skirt in the back again and force myself to stay calm. "Tuck your tail in, little duck," I say, smoothing the blouse back in place.

4   Prim giggles and gives me a small "Quack."

5   "Quack yourself," I say with a light laugh. The kind only Prim can draw out of me. "Come on, let's eat," I say and plant a quick kiss on the top of her head.

. . .

6   It's too bad, really, that they hold the reaping in the square—one of the few places in District 12 that can be pleasant. The square's surrounded by shops, and on public market days, especially if there's good weather, it has a holiday feel to it. But today, despite the bright banners hanging on the buildings, there's an air of grimness. The camera crews, perched like buzzards on rooftops, only add to the effect.

7   People file in silently and sign in. The reaping is a good opportunity for the Capitol to keep tabs on the population as well. Twelve- through eighteen-year-olds are herded into roped areas marked off by ages, the oldest in the

---

1. **reaping** the gathering of candidates for the Hunger Games
2. **tesserae** small wood, bone, or stone tablets used as vouchers or tokens that can be offered in exchange for being entered into a drawing to participate in the Hunger Games

front, the young ones, like Prim, toward the back. Family members line up around the perimeter, holding tightly to one another's hands. But there are others, too, who have no one they love at stake, or who no longer care, who slip among the crowd, taking bets on the two kids whose names will be drawn. Odds are given on their ages, whether they're Seam[3] or merchant, if they will break down and weep. Most refuse dealing with the racketeers but carefully, carefully. These same people tend to be informers, and who hasn't broken the law? I could be shot on a daily basis for hunting, but the appetites of those in charge protect me. Not everyone can claim the same.

. . .

8 Just as the town clock strikes two, the mayor steps up to the podium and begins to read. It's the same story every year. He tells of the history of Panem, the country that rose up out of the ashes of a place that was once called North America. He lists the disasters, the droughts, the storms, the fires, the **encroaching** seas that swallowed up so much of the land, the brutal war for what little sustenance remained. The result was Panem, a shining Capitol ringed by thirteen districts, which brought peace and prosperity to its citizens. Then came the Dark Days, the uprising of the districts against the Capitol. Twelve were defeated, the thirteenth obliterated. The Treaty of Treason gave us the new laws to **guarantee** peace and, as our yearly reminder that the Dark Days must never be repeated, it gave us the Hunger Games.

9 The rules of the Hunger Games are simple. In punishment for the uprising, each of the twelve districts must provide one girl and one boy, called tributes, to participate. The twenty-four tributes will be imprisoned in a vast outdoor arena that could hold anything from a burning desert to a frozen wasteland. Over a period of several weeks, the competitors must fight to the death. The last tribute standing wins.

10 Taking the kids from our districts, forcing them to kill one another while we watch—this is the Capitol's way of reminding us how totally we are at their mercy. How little chance we would stand of surviving another rebellion.

. . .

11 It's time for the drawing. Effie Trinket says as she always does, "Ladies first!" and crosses to the glass ball with the girls' names. She reaches in, digs her hand deep into the ball, and pulls out a slip of paper. The crowd draws in a collective breath and then you can hear a pin drop, and I'm feeling nauseous and so desperately hoping that it's not me, that it's not me, that it's not me.

---

3. **Seam** member of the poorest district in Panem

12 Effie Trinket crosses back to the podium, smoothes the slip of paper, and reads out the name in a clear voice. And it's not me.

13 It's Primrose Everdeen.

from Chapter 2

14 There must have been some mistake. This can't be happening. Prim was one slip of paper in thousands! Her chances of being chosen were so **remote** that I'd not even bothered worrying about her. Hadn't I done everything? Taken the tesserae, refused to let her do the same? One slip. One slip in thousands. The odds had been entirely in her favor. But it hadn't mattered.

15 Somewhere far away, I can hear the crowd murmuring unhappily as they always do when a twelve-year-old gets chosen because no one thinks this is fair. And then I see her, the blood drained from her face, hands clenched in fists at her sides, walking with stiff, small steps up toward the stage, passing me, and I see the back of her blouse has become untucked and hangs out over her skirt. It's this detail, the untucked blouse forming a ducktail, that brings me back to myself.

16 "Prim!" The strangled cry comes out of my throat, and my muscles begin to move again. "Prim!" I don't need to shove through the crowd. The other kids make way immediately allowing me a straight path to the stage. I reach her just as she is about to **mount** the steps. With one sweep of my arm, I push her behind me.

17 "I volunteer!" I gasp. "I volunteer as tribute!"

Excerpted from *The Hunger Games* by Suzanne Collins, published by Scholastic Inc.

✏ WRITE

PERSONAL RESPONSE: Were you surprised that Katniss offered to take her sister's place in the reaping? Write a short response explaining your initial reaction to the last scene of the excerpt. Use evidence from the text to support your response.

The Classical Roots of 'The Hunger Games'

INFORMATIONAL TEXT
Barry Strauss
2014

Introduction

Films in *The Hunger Games* series owe their success to more than just the series' leading actress, Jennifer Lawrence, or their exciting blend of action and dystopian political intrigue. As essayist Barry Strauss explains, the story also strikes a more "classical" chord of understanding about human nature. The heroine of *The Hunger Games*, Katniss Everdeen, is a combination of several Greek and Roman goddesses. In *The Hunger Games* author Suzanne Collins's own words, Katniss most closely recalls a female version of the Greek god Theseus, who slayed the Minotaur and saved young Athenians from being sacrificed to a horrific half-man, half-beast.

"Like ancient gladiators, the participants are doomed but idolized."

1   What accounts for the success of "The Hunger Games"? The obvious answer, of course, is the combination of the irresistible Jennifer Lawrence and Hollywood special effects with a **rollicking** good story.

2   But we shouldn't ignore the deeper themes of the tale, which are not only classic but classical, reaching back to Greece and Rome and the very foundations of Western culture.

3   At the heart of the story are three beautiful, heroic young people: Katniss Everdeen and her male romantic interests, Peeta Mellark and Gale Hawthorne. They form a love triangle, but they also represent, from the point of view of the ancients, an aroused citizenry banding together and fighting for freedom against an evil empire.

4   Katniss, played by Ms. Lawrence, is "an updated Theseus," according to the books' author, Suzanne Collins. In Greek myth, Theseus and other young people from Athens were sent as tribute—human sacrificial offerings—to King Minos in Crete. The king turned them over to the Minotaur, a murderous beast who was half-man and half-bull and lived in a maze or labyrinth. The intrepid Theseus killed the Minotaur and saved his countrymen.

5   Like that ancient Greek hero, Katniss defies an oppressive empire and sparks a revolution. But it's an update with a twist. Today's Theseus is female, which calls to mind not only modern girl power but also ancient lore. Her character is inspired by the famous Amazon warriors and Atalanta, the great female runner of Greek myth. Katniss also recalls Artemis, goddess of the hunt—Diana to the Romans—because her preferred weapon is the bow and arrow.

6   Like imperial Rome, the country of "The Hunger Games" is a once-free society now dominated by a **corrupt** and rapacious capital city. A president exercises, in effect, the power of an emperor. He lives in a grand city called the Capitol, and his government feeds off its provinces, much as ancient Rome did. The people of the Capitol radiate a baroque and overripe luxuriousness, like the lords and ladies of imperial Rome, while the provincials are poor and virtuous.

7   This pattern goes back to the great Roman historian Tacitus (ca. 56–117), who drew a contrast between the primitive but free Germans and Britons and the decadent Romans who had lost their republican virtue under the Caesars. Tacitus would have understood why the bad guys in Ms. Collins's Capitol have Latinate first names such as Coriolanus Snow, the coldhearted president, and Caesar Flickerman, the smarmy host of the televised version of the games. Meanwhile, the rebels from the provinces have names that evoke nature ("katniss," for example, is the name of a real, edible plant) or have English or Greek roots—anything but Rome.

8   In "The Hunger Games," the people are kept in line by hunger and entertainment. The privileged folks in the Capitol get both "bread and circuses"—the phrase comes from the Roman satirist Juvenal[1]. The Latin is "panem et circenses," and Panem is the name that Ms. Collins purposefully gives the country where her story is set.

9   The most important entertainers are the participants in the hunger games, a fight to the death, reminiscent of the gladiatorial games of ancient Rome, whose influence Ms. Collins also cites. The games begin with the very Roman ritual of participants entering a stadium on chariots to the wild applause of the crowd. Like ancient gladiators, the participants are doomed but **idolized.**

10   Much as in the myth of Theseus, the participants in the hunger games are offered as tribute to the Capitol, one young man and one young woman from each district of the country. For the lone survivor, the games are a rite of passage. All ancient societies made young people go through such rites. In Athens, new warriors had to survive in the woods, and there is an echo of this in the hunger games, which are set in a jungle.

11   Myths work because their themes are of **abiding** interest, and "The Hunger Games" is no **exception.** We still have rites of passage for young people today. If ours tend to test mental rather than physical **stamina** (college entrance exams are more common than boot camps), they remain daunting and demanding in their own way—which perhaps explains why the life-or-death stakes of "The Hunger Games" strike such a deep chord among our decidedly nonclassical teens.

©2014 by Barry Strauss. Reproduced by permission of Barry Strauss.

---

1. **Juvenal** a Roman poet from the late first and early second century, C.E., who wrote a collection of satirical poems known as the *Satires*

WRITE

PERSONAL RESPONSE: According to the article, what are some of the story elements and themes that create a story that has "abiding interest"? Think about your favorite books, movies, and TV shows. Write a short response that describes how a modern-day book, movie, or TV show that you enjoy reflects at least one traditional story element or theme identified in the article.

The Cruel Tribute

FICTION
James Baldwin
1895

Introduction

James Baldwin (1841–1925) was a self-taught American who served as a superintendent at a school in Indianapolis, Indiana, before becoming a prolific author. He showed particular interest in history and legend, writing more than 30 books, many of which have been published in countries all around the globe. This particular legend is about the King of Crete and the revenge he seeks against the city of Athens, where his son was killed. In response to this incident the King of Crete demands, once every year, a "tribute" from Athens as repayment for the death of his son. Every spring, 14 youths are sent to Crete to be sacrificed—until a young hero puts an end to this slaughter.

"What is the tribute which you require?"

I. THE TREATY.

1   Minos, king of Crete, had made war upon Athens. He had come with a great fleet of ships and an army, and had burned the merchant vessels in the harbor, and had overrun all the country and the coast even to Megara[1], which lies to the west. He had laid waste the fields and gardens round about Athens, had pitched his camp close to the walls, and had sent word to the Athenian rulers that on the morrow[2] he would march into their city with fire and sword and would slay all their young men and would pull down all their houses, even to the Temple of Athena, which stood on the great hill above the town. Then AEgeus, the king of Athens, with the twelve elders who were his helpers, went out to see King Minos and to treat with him.

2   "O mighty king," they said, "what have we done that you should wish thus to destroy us from the earth?"

3   "O cowardly and shameless men," answered King Minos, "why do you ask this foolish question, since you can but know the cause of my wrath? I had an only son, Androgeos by name, and he was dearer to me than the hundred cities of Crete and the thousand islands of the sea over which I rule. Three years ago he came hither to take part in the games which you held in honor of Athena, whose temple you have built on yonder hilltop. You know how he overcame all your young men in the sports, and how your people honored him with song and dance and laurel crown. But when your king, this same AEgeus who stands before me now, saw how everybody ran after him and praised his valor, he was filled with **envy** and laid plans to kill him. Whether he caused armed men to waylay[3] him on the road to Thebes, or whether as some say he sent him against a certain wild bull of your country to be slain by that beast, I know not; but you cannot **deny** that the young man's life was taken from him through the plotting of this AEgeus."

---

1. **Megara** a historic town in West Attica, Greece
2. **on the morrow** tomorrow
3. **waylay** to stop someone and hold them back for conversation or some other distraction

NOTES

4 "But we do deny it—we do deny it!" cried the elders. "For at that very time our king was sojourning[4] at Troezen on the other side of the Saronic Sea, and he knew nothing of the young prince's death. We ourselves managed the city's affairs while he was abroad, and we know whereof we speak. Androgeos was slain, not through the king's orders but by the king's nephews, who hoped to rouse your anger against AEgeus so that you would drive him from Athens and leave the kingdom to one of them."

5 "Will you swear that what you tell me is true?" said Minos.

6 "We will swear it," they said.

7 "Now then," said Minos, "you shall hear my decree. Athens has robbed me of my dearest treasure, a treasure that can never be **restored** to me; so, in return, I **require** from Athens, as tribute, that possession which is the dearest and most precious to her people; and it shall be destroyed cruelly as my son was destroyed."

8 "The condition is hard," said the elders, "but it is just. What is the tribute which you require?"

9 "Has the king a son?" asked Minos.

10 The face of King AEgeus lost all its color and he trembled as he thought of a little child then with its mother at Troezen, on the other side of the Saronic Sea. But the elders knew nothing about that child, and they answered:

11 "Alas, no! he has no son; but he has fifty nephews who are eating up his substance and longing for the time to come when one of them shall be king; and, as we have said, it was they who slew the young prince, Androgeos."

12 "I have naught to do with those fellows," said Minos; "you may deal with them as you like. But you ask what is the tribute that I require, and I will tell you. Every year when the springtime comes and the roses begin to bloom, you shall choose seven of your noblest youths and seven of your fairest maidens, and shall send them to me in a ship which your king shall provide. This is the tribute which you shall pay to me, Minos, king of Crete; and if you fail for a single time, or delay even a day, my soldiers shall tear down your walls and burn your city and put your men to the sword and sell your wives and children as slaves."

13 "We agree to all this, O King," said the elders; "for it is the least of two evils. But tell us now, what shall be the fate of the seven youths and the seven maidens?"

---

4. **sojourning** temporarily visiting somewhere

Skill:
Textual Evidence

The text states that the elders knew nothing about the king's son. This implies that the king keeps secrets from the elders and acts selfishly. Note: the king's refusal to sacrifice his own son is what leads to the cruel tribute.

14   "In Crete," answered Minos, "there is a house called the Labyrinth[5], the like of which you have never seen. In it there are a thousand chambers and winding ways, and whosoever goes even a little way into them can never find his way out again. Into this house the seven youths and the seven maidens shall be thrust, and they shall be left there—"

15   "To perish with hunger?" cried the elders.

16   "To be devoured by a monster whom men call the Minotaur," said Minos.

17   Then King AEgeus and the elders covered their faces and wept and went slowly back into the city to tell their people of the sad and terrible conditions upon which Athens could alone be saved.

18   "It is better that a few should perish than that the whole city should be destroyed," they said.

II. THE TRIBUTE.

19   Years passed by. Every spring when the roses began to bloom seven youths and seven maidens were put on board of a black-sailed ship and sent to Crete to pay the tribute which King Minos required. In every house in Athens there was sorrow and dread, and the people lifted up their hands to Athena on the hilltop and cried out, "How long, O Queen of the Air, how long shall this thing be?"

20   In the meanwhile the little child at Troezen on the other side of the sea had grown to be a man. His name, Theseus, was in everybody's mouth, for he had done great deeds of daring; and at last he had come to Athens to find his father, King AEgeus, who had never heard whether he was alive or dead; and when the youth had made himself known, the king had welcomed him to his home and all the people were glad because so noble a prince had come to dwell among them and, in time, to rule over their city.

21   The springtime came again. The black-sailed ship was rigged for another voyage. The rude Cretan soldiers paraded the streets; and the herald of King Minos stood at the gates and shouted:

22   "Yet three days, O Athenians, and your tribute will be due and must be paid!"

23   Then in every street the doors of the houses were shut and no man went in or out, but every one sat silent with pale cheeks, and wondered whose lot it

---

5. **Labyrinth** In Greek mythology, the Labyrinth was an elaborate building designed by the artist Daedalus for King Minos.

would be to be chosen this year. But the young prince, Theseus, did not understand; for he had not been told about the tribute.

24   "What is the meaning of all this?" he cried. "What right has a Cretan to demand tribute in Athens? and what is this tribute of which he speaks?"

25   Then AEgeus led him aside and with tears told him of the sad war with King Minos, and of the dreadful terms of peace. "Now, say no more," sobbed AEgeus, "it is better that a few should die even thus than that all should be destroyed."

26   "But I will say more," cried Theseus. "Athens shall not pay tribute to Crete. I myself will go with these youths and maidens, and I will slay the monster Minotaur, and defy King Minos himself upon his throne."

27   "Oh, do not be so rash!" said the king; "for no one who is thrust into the den of the Minotaur ever comes out again. Remember that you are the hope of Athens, and do not take this great risk upon yourself."

28   "Say you that I am the hope of Athens?" said Theseus. "Then how can I do otherwise than go?" And he began at once to make himself ready.

29   On the third day all the youths and maidens of the city were brought together in the market place, so that lots[6] might be cast for those who were to be taken. Then two vessels of brass were brought and set before King AEgeus and the herald who had come from Crete. Into one vessel they placed as many balls as there were noble youths in the city, and into the other as many as there were maidens; and all the balls were white save only seven in each vessel, and those were black as ebony.

30   Then every maiden, without looking, reached her hand into one of the vessels and drew forth a ball, and those who took the black balls were borne away to the black ship, which lay in waiting by the shore. The young men also drew lots in like manner, but when six black balls had been drawn Theseus came quickly forward and said:

31   "Hold! Let no more balls be drawn. I will be the seventh youth to pay this tribute. Now let us go aboard the black ship and be off."

32   Then the people, and King AEgeus himself, went down to the shore to take leave of the young men and maidens, whom they had no hope of seeing again; and all but Theseus wept and were brokenhearted.

Skill:
Textual Evidence

Theseus's words imply that he is patriotic and daring. The king's answer implies that he is still being selfish, trying to save his own son. Theseus says he has no choice but to go. The implied meaning is that he is a noble, unselfish hero.

---

6. **lots** objects randomly drawn from a container as part of a decision-making process

Copyright © BookheadEd Learning, LLC

33   "I will come again, father," he said.

34   "I will hope that you may," said the old king. "If when this ship returns, I see a white sail spread above the black one, then I shall know that you are alive and well; but if I see only the black one, it will tell me that you have perished."

35   And now the vessel was loosed from its moorings, the north wind filled the sail, and the seven youths and seven maidens were borne away over the sea, towards the dreadful death which awaited them in far distant Crete.

III. THE PRINCESS.

36   At last the black ship reached the end of its voyage. The young people were set ashore, and a party of soldiers led them through the streets towards the prison, where they were to stay until the morrow. They did not weep nor cry out now, for they had outgrown their fears. But with paler faces and firm-set lips, they walked between the rows of Cretan houses, and looked neither to the right nor to the left. The windows and doors were full of people who were eager to see them.

37   "What a pity that such brave young men should be food for the Minotaur," said some.

38   "Ah, that maidens so beautiful should meet a fate so sad!" said others.

39   And now they passed close by the palace gate, and in it stood King Minos himself, and his daughter Ariadne, the fairest of the women of Crete.

40   "Indeed, those are noble young fellows!" said the king.

41   "Yes, too noble to feed the vile Minotaur," said Ariadne.

42   "The nobler, the better," said the king; "and yet none of them can compare with your lost brother Androgeos."

43   Ariadne said no more; and yet she thought that she had never seen any one who looked so much like a hero as young Theseus. How tall he was, and how handsome! How proud his eye, and how firm his step! Surely there had never been his like in Crete.

44   All through that night Ariadne lay awake and thought of the matchless hero, and grieved that he should be doomed to perish; and then she began to lay plans for setting him free. At the earliest peep of day she arose, and while everybody else was asleep, she ran out of the palace and hurried to the prison. As she was the king's daughter, the jailer opened the door at her bidding and allowed her to go in. There sat the seven youths and the seven

maidens on the ground, but they had not lost hope. She took Theseus aside and whispered to him. She told him of a plan which she had made to save him; and Theseus promised her that, when he had slain the Minotaur, he would carry her away with him to Athens where she should live with him always. Then she gave him a sharp sword, and hid it underneath his cloak, telling him that with it alone could he hope to slay the Minotaur.

45 "And here is a ball of silken thread," she said. "As soon as you go into the Labyrinth where the monster is kept, fasten one end of the thread to the stone doorpost, and then unwind it as you go along. When you have slain the Minotaur, you have only to follow the thread and it will lead you back to the door. In the meanwhile I will see that your ship, is ready to sail, and then I will wait for you at the door of the Labyrinth."

46 Theseus thanked the beautiful princess and promised her again that if he should live to go back to Athens she should go with him and be his wife. Then with a prayer to Athena, Ariadne hastened away.

IV. THE LABYRINTH.

47 As soon as the sun was up the guards came to lead the young prisoners to the Labyrinth. They did not see the sword which Theseus had under his cloak, nor the tiny ball of silk which he held in his closed hand. They led the youths and maidens a long way into the Labyrinth, turning here and there, back and forth, a thousand different times, until it seemed certain that they could never find their way out again. Then the guards, by a secret passage which they alone knew, went out and left them, as they had left many others before, to wander about until they should be found by the terrible Minotaur.

48 "Stay close by me," said Theseus to his companions, "and with the help of Athena who dwells in her temple home in our own fair city, I will save you."

49 Then he drew his sword and stood in the narrow way before them; and they all lifted up their hands and prayed to Athena.

50 For hours they stood there, hearing no sound, and seeing nothing but the smooth, high walls on either side of the passage and the calm blue sky so high above them. Then the maidens sat down upon the ground and covered their faces and sobbed, and said:

51 "Oh, that he would come and put an end to our misery and our lives."

52 At last, late in the day, they heard a **bellowing**, low and faint as though far away. They listened and soon heard it again, a little louder and very fierce and dreadful.

53   "It is he! it is he!" cried Theseus; "and now for the fight!"

54   Then he shouted, so loudly that the walls of the Labyrinth answered back, and the sound was carried upward to the sky and outward to the rocks and cliffs of the mountains. The Minotaur heard him, and his bellowings grew louder and fiercer every moment.

55   "He is coming!" cried Theseus, and he ran forward to meet the beast. The seven maidens shrieked, but tried to stand up bravely and face their fate; and the six young men stood together with firm-set teeth and clinched fists, ready to fight to the last.

56   Soon the Minotaur came into view, rushing down the passage towards Theseus, and roaring most terribly. He was twice as tall as a man, and his head was like that of a bull with huge sharp horns and fiery eyes and a mouth as large as a lion's; but the young men could not see the lower part of his body for the cloud of dust which he raised in running. When he saw Theseus with the sword in his hand coming to meet him, he paused, for no one had ever faced him in that way before. Then he put his head down, and rushed forward, bellowing. But Theseus leaped quickly aside, and made a sharp thrust with his sword as he passed, and hewed off one of the monster's legs above the knee.

Theseus killed the Minotaur, a half-man, half-bull monster that lived in the Labyrinth.

57   The Minotaur fell upon the ground, roaring and groaning and beating wildly about with his horned head and his hoof-like fists; but Theseus **nimbly** ran up to him and thrust the sword into his heart, and was away again before the beast could harm him. A great stream of blood gushed from the wound, and soon the Minotaur turned his face towards the sky and was dead.

58   Then the youths and maidens ran to Theseus and kissed his hands and feet, and thanked him for his great deed; and, as it was already growing dark, Theseus bade[7] them follow him while he wound up the silken thread which was to lead them out of the Labyrinth. Through a thousand rooms and courts and winding ways they went, and at midnight they came to the outer door and saw the city lying in the moonlight before them; and, only a little way off, was the seashore where the black ship was moored which had brought them to Crete. The door was wide open, and beside it stood Ariadne waiting for them.

7. **bade** invited

59 "The wind is fair, the sea is smooth, and the sailors are ready," she whispered; and she took the arm of Theseus, and all went together through the silent streets to the ship.

60 When the morning dawned they were far out to sea, and, looking back from the deck of the little vessel, only the white tops of the Cretan mountains were in sight.

61 Minos, when he arose from sleep, did not know that the youths and maidens had gotten safe out of the Labyrinth. But when Ariadne could not be found, he thought that robbers had carried her away. He sent soldiers out to search for her among the hills and mountains, never dreaming that she was now well on the way towards distant Athens.

62 Many days passed, and at last the searchers returned and said that the princess could nowhere be found. Then the king covered his head and wept, and said:

63 "Now, indeed, I am bereft of all my treasures!"

64 In the meanwhile, King AEgeus of Athens had sat day after day on a rock by the shore, looking and watching if by chance he might see a ship coming from the south. At last the vessel with Theseus and his companions hove in sight, but it still carried only the black sail, for in their joy the young men had forgotten to raise the white one.

65 "Alas! alas! my son has perished!" moaned AEgeus; and he fainted and fell forward into the sea and was drowned. And that sea, from then until now, has been called by his name, the Aegean Sea.

66 Thus Theseus became king of Athens.

Please note that excerpts and passages in the StudySync® library and this workbook are intended as touchstones to generate interest in an author's work. The excerpts and passages do not substitute for the reading of entire texts, and StudySync® strongly recommends that students seek out and purchase the whole literary or informational work in order to experience it as the author intended. Links to online resellers are available in our digital library. In addition, complete works may be ordered through an authorized reseller by filling out and returning to StudySync® the order form enclosed in this workbook.

Reading & Writing Companion   **683**

First Read

Read "The Cruel Tribute." After you read, complete the Think Questions below.

 THINK QUESTIONS

1. Why did AEgeus's nephews kill Androgeos, son of Minos? Briefly describe what they hoped to achieve. Did their plan work as expected? Be sure to cite textual evidence to support your response.

2. Why does Minos demand that fourteen Athenian youths be sent every year as tribute? What kind of tribute would he rather have, but cannot get? Cite textual evidence to support your response.

3. Why does Ariadne decide to help Theseus and the rest of the Athenian tributes? Does she have a specific motive for rescuing this group of tributes, or has she always been against the demands of her father? Be sure to cite textual evidence in your response.

4. Use context clues to determine the meaning of **bellowing** as it is used in paragraph 52 of "The Cruel Tribute." Write your definition here and identify clues that helped you figure out the meaning. Then check the meaning in a dictionary.

5. Find the word **nimbly** in paragraph 57 of "The Cruel Tribute." Use context clues in the surrounding sentences, as well as the sentence in which the word appears, to determine the word's meaning. Write your definition here and identify clues that helped you figure out the meaning.

Skill:
Textual Evidence

Use the Checklist to analyze Textual Evidence in "The Cruel Tribute." Refer to the sample student annotations about Textual Evidence in the text.

••• CHECKLIST FOR TEXTUAL EVIDENCE

In order to support an analysis by citing textual evidence that is explicitly stated in the text, do the following:

- ✓ read the text closely and critically

- ✓ identify what the text says explicitly

- ✓ find the most relevant textual evidence that supports your analysis

- ✓ consider why an author explicitly states specific details and information

- ✓ cite the specific words, phrases, sentences, paragraphs, or images from the text that support your analysis

In order to interpret implicit meanings in a text by making inferences, do the following:

- ✓ combine information directly stated in the text with your own knowledge, experiences, and observations

- ✓ cite the specific words, phrases, sentences, paragraphs, or images from the text that support this inference

In order to cite textual evidence to support an analysis of what the text says explicitly as well as inferences drawn from the text, consider the following questions:

- ✓ Have I read the text closely and critically?

- ✓ What inferences am I making about the text? What textual evidence am I using to support these inferences?

- ✓ Am I quoting the evidence from the text correctly?

- ✓ Does my textual evidence logically relate to my analysis?

- ✓ Have I cited several pieces of textual evidence?

Please note that excerpts and passages in the StudySync® library and this workbook are intended as touchstones to generate interest in an author's work. The excerpts and passages do not substitute for the reading of entire texts, and StudySync® strongly recommends that students seek out and purchase the whole literary or informational work in order to experience it as the author intended. Links to online resellers are available in our digital library. In addition, complete works may be ordered through an authorized reseller by filling out and returning to StudySync® the order form enclosed in this workbook.

Reading & Writing Companion   **685**

Skill:
Textual Evidence

Reread paragraphs 61–66 of "The Cruel Tribute." Then, using the Checklist on the previous page, answer the multiple-choice questions below.

⟳ YOUR TURN

1. Paragraphs 61 to 63 tell what King Minos does when Ariadne cannot be found. Readers can infer from these actions that —

   ○ A. the king is not aware that his daughter helped Theseus and his companions escape.
   ○ B. the king is kept informed of everything that goes on inside the Labyrinth.
   ○ C. the king cares more about his daughter than he once cared about his son.
   ○ D. King Minos realizes that he is being punished for demanding the cruel tribute.

2. Paragraphs 64 and 65 tell what happens to King AEgeus when Theseus comes home. Readers can infer from these events that —

   ○ A. AEgeus knows that he is being punished for his original refusal to sacrifice his own son.
   ○ B. AEgeus recognizes his son as a hero and has faith that he has overcome the Minotaur.
   ○ C. AEgeus dies because he placed so much value on his son.
   ○ D. Theseus would probably have remembered to raise the white sail before reaching the shore.

3. The resolution (the way that the story ends) implies that in the future Athens will —

   ○ A. no longer be threatened by King Minos of Crete.
   ○ B. have royal princes who will become rulers of Crete.
   ○ C. give greater power to the elders and less power to kings.
   ○ D. be ruled by a more courageous and selfless king.

Close Read

Reread "The Cruel Tribute." As you reread, complete the Skills Focus questions below. Then use your answers and annotations from the questions to help you complete the Write activity.

⊚ SKILLS FOCUS

1. Select a character. Identify a detail that shows that character's key qualities. Explain how that character's qualities influence the events of the story.

2. Identify important setting details in the Labyrinth. Explain how the setting of the Labyrinth affects the characters and plot.

3. "The Classical Roots of 'The Hunger Games'" uses Katniss of *The Hunger Games* as an example of a classically heroic figure. Identify heroic traits in Theseus, and explain how his traits reflect themes of what makes a hero.

4. Identify elements of "The Cruel Tribute" that you can recall appearing in *The Hunger Games* or being singled out in "The Classical Roots of 'The Hunger Games.'" Give your opinion as to why these specific elements are of such lasting importance.

✎ WRITE

COMPARE AND CONTRAST: Compare and contrast a character from "The Cruel Tribute" with a character from the excerpt of *The Hunger Games* based on what the texts say implicitly and explicitly about the characters. Remember to use evidence from each text to support your claims.

Please note that excerpts and passages in the StudySync® library and this workbook are intended as touchstones to generate interest in an author's work. The excerpts and passages do not substitute for the reading of entire texts, and StudySync® strongly recommends that students seek out and purchase the whole literary or informational work in order to experience it as the author intended. Links to online resellers are available in our digital library. In addition, complete works may be ordered through an authorized reseller by filling out and returning to StudySync® the order form enclosed in this workbook.

Reading & Writing Companion **687**

The Invisible One
(Algonquin Cinderella)

FICTION
Traditional Algonquin
(collected by Idries Shah)
1979

Introduction

In his expansive collection of folklore, *World Tales*, author and educator Idries Shah (1924–1996) gives credit, in particular, to the work of Marian Roalfe Cox. Late in the 19th century, Cox spent a year gathering more than 300 Cinderella-like tales from traditions and cultures around the world. One of those is the tale presented here, "The Invisible One," which comes from the MicMac Indians of the Eastern Algonquins. It is the story of an invisible man residing in a village who can be seen only by his sister and one other girl, the one who will have the opportunity to marry him. One after another, the girls of the village take a test to try to see the Invisible One. Each of them fails until an unassuming young girl, cast aside by her haughty older sisters, attempts the eye test.

"She would try, she thought, to . . . see the Invisible One."

Copyright © BookheadEd Learning, LLC

1 There was once a large village of the MicMac Indians of the Eastern Algonquins, built beside a lake. At the far end of the **settlement** stood a lodge, and in it lived a being who was always invisible. He had a sister who looked after him, and everyone knew that any girl who could see him might marry him. For that reason there were very few girls who did not try, but it was very long before anyone succeeded.

2 This is the way in which the test of sight was carried out: at evening time, when the Invisible One was due to be returning home, his sister would walk with any girl who might come down to the lakeshore. She, of course, could see her brother, since he was always **visible** to her. As soon as she saw him, she would say to the girls:

3 "Do you see my brother?"

4 "Yes," they would generally reply—though some of them did say, "No."

5 To those who said that they could indeed see him, the sister would say:

6 "Of what is his shoulder strap made?" Some people say that she would enquire:

7 "What is his moose-runner's haul?" or "With what does he draw his sled?"

8 And they would answer:

9 "A strip of rawhide[1]," or "a green **flexible** branch," or something like that.

10 Then she, knowing that they had not told the truth, would say:

11 "Very well, let us return to the wigwam![2]"

12 When they had gone in, she would tell them not to sit in a certain place, because it belonged to the Invisible One. Then, after they had helped to

Skill: Summarizing

Who? the Invisible One, his sister, and the other villagers

What? The sister tests the other girls.

Where? the village

When? in the evening

Why? to help the Invisible One find a wife

How? The girl who can see the Invisible One might marry him.

---

1. **rawhide** stiff, untanned leather
2. **wigwam** a dome-shaped structure made by fastening material over a framework of poles, used by some North American indigenous peoples

Skill:
Plot

I can tell that the sisters are going to be important characters in the story. They treat Oochigeaskw really badly. The conflict between the sisters will be important in the plot.

cook the supper, they would wait with great **curiosity,** to see him eat. They could be sure that he was a real person, for when he took off his moccasins[3] they became visible, and his sister hung them up. But beyond this, they saw nothing of him, not even when they stayed in the place all night, as many of them did.

13   Now there lived in the village an old man who was a widower, and his three daughters. The youngest girl was very small, weak and often ill: and yet her sisters, especially the elder, treated her cruelly. The second daughter was kinder, and sometimes took her side: but the wicked sister would burn her hands and feet with hot cinders, and she was covered with scars from this treatment. She was so marked that people called her *Oochigeaskw*, the Rough-Faced Girl.

14   When her father came home and asked why she had such burns, the bad sister would at once say that it was her own fault, for she had disobeyed orders and gone near the fire and fallen into it.

15   These two elder sisters decided one day to try their luck at seeing the Invisible One. So they dressed themselves in their finest clothes, and tried to look their prettiest. They found the Invisible One's sister and took the usual walk by the water.

16   When he came, and when they were asked if they could see him, they answered, "Of course." And when asked about the shoulder strap or sled cord, they answered: "A piece of rawhide."

17   But of course they were lying like the others, and they got nothing for their pains.

18   The next afternoon, when the father returned home, he brought with him many of the pretty little shells from which wampum[4] was made, and they set to work to string them.

19   That day, poor little Oochigeaskw, who had always gone barefoot, got a pair of her father's moccasins, old ones, and put them into water to soften them so that she could wear them. Then she begged her sisters for a few wampum shells. The elder called her a 'little pest', but the younger one gave her some. Now, with no other clothes than her usual rags, the poor little thing went into the woods and got herself some sheets of birch bark, from which she made a dress, and put marks on it for decoration, in the style of long ago. She made a petticoat and a loose gown, a cap, leggings and a handkerchief. She put on her father's large old moccasins, which were far too big for her, and went

---

3. **moccasin** a soft leather shoe, having the sole turned up on all sides and sewn to the top in a simple gathered seam
4. **wampum** small beads strung together and worn as jewelry or used as money

forth to try her luck. She would try, she thought, to discover whether she could see the Invisible One.

20 She did not begin very well. As she set off, her sisters shouted and hooted, hissed and yelled, and tried to make her stay. And the loafers around the village, seeing the strange little creature, called out "Shame!"

21 The poor little girl in her strange clothes, with her face all scarred, was an awful sight, but she was kindly received by the sister of the Invisible One. And this was, of course, because this noble lady understood far more about things than simply the **mere** outside which all the rest of the world knows. As the brown of the evening sky turned to black, the lady took her down to the lake.

22 "Do you see him?" the Invisible One's sister asked.

23 "I do, indeed—and he is wonderful!" said Oochigeaskw.

24 The sister asked:

25 "And what is his sled string?"

26 The little girl said:

27 "It is the Rainbow."

28 "And, my sister, what is his bow string?"

29 "It is The Spirit's Road—the Milky Way."

30 "So you *have* seen him," said his sister. She took the girl home with her and bathed her. As she did so, all the scars disappeared from her body. Her hair grew again, as it was combed, long, like a blackbird's wing. Her eyes were now like stars: in all the world there was no other such beauty. Then, from her treasures, the lady gave her a wedding garment, and adorned her.

31 Then she told Oochigeaskw to take the *wife's* seat in the wigwam, the one next to where the Invisible One sat, beside the entrance. And when he came in, terrible and beautiful, he smiled and said:

32 "So we are found out!"

33 "Yes," said his sister. And so Oochigeaskw became his wife.

"The Algonquin Cinderella" from WORLD TALES: The Extraordinary Coincidence Of Stories Told In All Times, In All Places by Idries Shah. Copyright ©1979 by Technographia, S.A. and Houghton Mifflin Harcourt Publishing Company. Reprinted by permission of Houghton Mifflin Harcourt Publishing Company. All rights reserved.

Skill:
Plot

The older sisters are so mean and don't want their sister to try to discover if she can see the Invisible One. Some of the villagers are being awful too! This seems like it could be the turning point in the story.

Please note that excerpts and passages in the StudySync® library and this workbook are intended as touchstones to generate interest in an author's work. The excerpts and passages do not substitute for the reading of entire texts, and StudySync® strongly recommends that students seek out and purchase the whole literary or informational work in order to experience it as the author intended. Links to online resellers are available in our digital library. In addition, complete works may be ordered through an authorized reseller by filling out and returning to StudySync® the order form enclosed in this workbook.

Reading & Writing
Companion

691

First Read

Read "The Invisible One." After you read, complete the Think Questions below.

 THINK QUESTIONS

1. How is Oochigeaskw treated by her older sisters? Explain, citing specific details from the text.

2. How does the Invisible One's sister administer the test of sight? What happens to most of the girls who take the test before Oochigeaskw? Explain.

3. What happens to Oochigeaskw after she recognizes the Invisible One? Describe how her life changes after this fateful moment.

4. Which context clues helped you determine the meaning of the word **flexible** as it is used in paragraph 9? Write your own definition of *flexible* and identify which words or phrases helped you understand its meaning.

5. The Greek word *meros* refers to a "part" or "fraction." Using this information, what do you think is the meaning of the word **mere** in paragraph 21? Write your best definition of *mere* and explain how you figured it out.

Skill:
Summarizing

Use the Checklist to analyze Summarizing in "The Invisible One." Refer to the sample student annotations about Summarizing in the text.

••• CHECKLIST FOR SUMMARIZING

In order to determine how to write an objective summary of a text, note the following:

✓ in literature, note the setting, characters, and events in the plot, including the problem the characters face and how it is solved

✓ answers to the basic questions *who, what, where, when, why,* and *how*

✓ stay objective, and do not add your own personal thoughts, judgments, or opinions to the summary

To provide an objective summary of a text, consider the following questions:

✓ What are the answers to basic *who, what, where, when, why,* and *how* questions in literature and works of nonfiction?

✓ In a work of literature, do the details in my summary reflect the development of the theme?

✓ Is my summary objective, or have I added my own thoughts, judgments, and personal opinions?

SUMMARIZING
sync•skills

Skill:
Summarizing

Reread paragraphs 13–19 of "The Invisible One" and the important details below. Then, complete the chart by sorting the important details into the correct category to objectively summarize what happened in the excerpt.

↻ YOUR TURN

	Important Details
A	So that they could marry the Invisible One
B	In the village by the lake
C	A father and his three daughters, the youngest of whom was very weak and treated unkindly
D	One evening and the next day
E	By dressing up in their finest clothes and walking by the water
F	The sisters decided to discover if they could see the Invisible One.

Who	What	Where	When	Why	How

PLOT

Skill:
Plot

Use the Checklist to analyze Plot in "The Invisible One." Refer to the sample student annotations about Plot in the text.

••• CHECKLIST FOR PLOT

In order to identify particular elements of a story or drama, note the following:

✓ setting details

✓ character details, including their thoughts, actions, and descriptions

✓ notable incidents or events in the plot

✓ characters or setting details that may have caused an event to occur

✓ the central conflict and the characters who are involved

✓ dialogue between or among characters

✓ instances when setting interferes with a character's motivations

To analyze how particular elements of a story or drama interact, consider the following questions:

✓ How do the events of the plot unfold in the story?

✓ How do characters respond or change as the plot advances?

✓ How does the setting shape the characters or the plot?

✓ How does a particular scene in the story contribute to the development of the plot?

PLOT

Skill:
Plot

Reread paragraphs 21–33 of "The Invisible One." Then, using the Checklist on the previous page, answer the multiple-choice questions below.

⟳ YOUR TURN

1. This question has two parts. First, answer Part A. Then, answer Part B.

   Part A: Which character action or dialogue leads to the story's resolution?

   ○ A. The moment when the Invisible One's sister takes Oochigeaskw to the lake in the evening

   ○ B. The moment when Oochigeaskw bathes and her hair grows, all her scars disappear, and she is given a wedding garment

   ○ C. The moment when the Invisible One's sister tells Oochigeaskw to take the wife's seat

   ○ D. The moment when Oochigeaskw correctly identifies the Invisible One's sled and bowstring to the sister

   Part B: Which of the following details BEST supports your response to Part A?

   ○ A. The Invisible One's sister asks about the sled bow string to test Oochigeaskw.

   ○ B. When he came into the wigwam, he smiled at her and she became his wife.

   ○ C. After Oochigeaskw answers, the sister says, "So you *have* seen him."

   ○ D. Her scars magically healed, her hair regrew, and her eyes became like stars.

Close Read

Reread "The Invisible One." As you reread, complete the Skills Focus questions below. Then use your answers and annotations from the questions to help you complete the Write activity.

◎ SKILLS FOCUS

1. Identify examples of how the behavior of the Invisible One's sister further develops her character at the beginning of the story.

2. Objectively summarize the beginning, the middle, and the end of the story. Include the most important details.

3. Most of the village girls try their luck at seeing the Invisible One. Identify an event in the text and explain how it encourages Oochigeaskw to try to see the Invisible One.

4. A common theme in folktales is that goodness is rewarded. Identify a moment in "The Invisible One" in which goodness is rewarded, and explain how this theme makes myths and folktales appealing to readers today.

✏ WRITE

NARRATIVE: Write your own version of a Cinderella story using a variety of techniques such as descriptive details and dialogue. Plan out the story to include clear plot events including an inciting incident, a conflict, and a turning point, leading to the resolution of the story.

Please note that excerpts and passages in the StudySync® library and this workbook are intended as touchstones to generate interest in an author's work. The excerpts and passages do not substitute for the reading of entire texts, and StudySync® strongly recommends that students seek out and purchase the whole literary or informational work in order to experience it as the author intended. Links to online resellers are available in our digital library. In addition, complete works may be ordered through an authorized reseller by filling out and returning to StudySync® the order form enclosed in this workbook.

Reading & Writing Companion   697

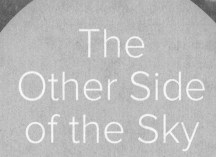

The Other Side of the Sky

INFORMATIONAL TEXT
Farah Ahmedi and Tamim Ansary
2006

Introduction

F arah Ahmedi's memoir *The Other Side of the Sky* is a testament to the power of the human spirit. Missing a leg after stepping on a landmine when she was seven, and with her father and brothers dead from a rocket attack, Ahmedi and her mother decide to flee their home in Kabul in search of a better life. This excerpt from "Escape from Afghanistan" describes their efforts to make it across the border and into Pakistan.

"Night was falling, and we were stranded out there in the open."

from: Escape from Afghanistan

NOTES

1   The gate to Pakistan was closed, and I could see that the Pakistani border guards were letting no one through. People were pushing and shoving and jostling up against that gate, and the guards were driving them back. As we got closer, the crowd thickened, and I could hear the roar and clamor at the gate. The Afghans were yelling something, and the Pakistanis were yelling back. My mother was clutching her side and gasping for breath, trying to keep up. I felt desperate to get through, because the sun was setting, and if we got stuck here, what were we going to do? Where would we stay? There was nothing here, no town, no hotel, no buildings, just the desert.

2   Yet we had no real chance of getting through. Big strong men were running up to the gate in vain. The guards had clubs, and they had carbines, too, which they turned around and used as weapons. Again and again, the crowd surged toward the gate and the guards drove them back with their sticks and clubs, swinging and beating until the crowd **receded**. And after that, for the next few minutes, on our side of the border, people milled about and muttered and stoked their own impatience and worked up their rage, until gradually the crowd gathered strength and surged against that gate again, only to be swept back.

3   We never even got close to the front. We got caught up in the thinning rear end of crowd, and even so, we were part of each wave, pulled forward, driven back. It was hard for me to keep my footing, and my mother was clutching my arm now, just hanging on, just trying to stay close to me, because the worst thing would have been if we had gotten separated. Finally, I saw that it was no use. We were only risking injury. We drifted back, out of the crowd. In the thickening dusk we could hear the dull roar of people still trying to get past the border guards, but we receded into the desert, farther and farther back from the border gate.

4   Night was falling, and we were stranded out there in the open.

· · ·

Skill:
Textual Evidence

The narrator uses the word desperate when she describes trying to get through the gate. This tells me exactly how the narrator and the people around her must have felt in that moment. They were desperate for freedom.

Please note that excerpts and passages in the StudySync® library and this workbook are intended as touchstones to generate interest in an author's work. The excerpts and passages do not substitute for the reading of entire texts, and StudySync® strongly recommends that students seek out and purchase the whole literary or informational work in order to experience it as the author intended. Links to online resellers are available in our digital library. In addition, complete works may be ordered through an authorized reseller by filling out and returning to StudySync® the order form enclosed in this workbook.

Reading & Writing Companion   699

Skill:
Textual Evidence

The guards are taking bribes to let the people through. People are so desperate to leave that they will pay to get out. But the narrator and her mother do not have money to pay, so they must feel even worse. Freedom comes at a high price!

5 On that second day, however, I learned that it was all a question of money. Someone told me about this, and then I watched closely and saw that it was true. Throughout the day, while some of the guards confronted the crowds, a few others lounged over to the side. People approached them quietly. Money changed hands, and the guards then let those people quietly through a small door to the side.

6 Hundreds could have flowed through the main gate had it been opened, but only one or two could get through the side door at a time. The fact that the guards were taking bribes[1] did us no good whatsoever. We did not have the money to pay them. What little we had we would need to get from Peshawar to Quetta. And so the second day passed.

7 At the end of that day we found ourselves camping near a friendly family. We struck up a conversation with them. The woman told us that her husband, Ghulam Ali, had gone to look for another way across the border. He was checking out a goat path that supposedly went over the mountains several miles northeast of the border station. If one could get to Pakistan safely by that route, he would come back for his family. "You can go with us," the woman said.

8 Later that night her husband showed up. "It works," he said. "Smugglers[2] use that path, and they bribe the guards to leave it unguarded. Of course, we don't want to run into any smugglers, either, but if we go late at night, we should be fine."

9 His wife then told him our story, and Ghulam Ali took pity on us. "Yes, of course you can come with us," he said. "But you have had two hard days. You will need some rest before you attempt this mountain crossing. Spend tonight here and sleep well, knowing that you will have nothing to do tomorrow except lounge around, rest, and catch your breath. Tomorrow, do not throw yourself against those border guards again. Let your only work be the gathering of your strength. Then tomorrow night we will all go over the mountain together, with God's grace. I will show you the way. If God wills it, we will follow that smugglers' path to safety. You and your mother are in my care now."

10 So we spent the whole next day there. It was terribly warm and we had no water, but we walked a little way and found a mosque[3] that refugees[4] like us had built over the years, so that people waiting to get across the border would have a place to say their prayers. We got some water to drink at the mosque, and we said *namaz*[5] there too. Somehow we obtained a little bit of bread as well. I can't remember how that turned up, but there it was, and we

---

1. **bribe** an offer of money or another incentive to persuade someone to do something
2. **smugglers** people who transfer items illegally into or out of an area
3. **mosque** a Muslim house of worship
4. **refugees** people forced to flee their own country to escape danger or persecution
5. *namaz* Islamic worship or prayer

ate it. We **sustained** our strength. After sunset we lay down just as if we're going to spend another night. In fact, I did fall asleep for a while. Long after dark—or early the next morning, to be exact, before the sun came up—that man shook us awake. "It's time," he said.

11   We got up and performed our **ablutions** quickly in the darkness, with just sand because that's allowed when you have no access to water. We said our prayers. Then Ghulam Ali began to march into the darkness with his family, and we trudged along silently behind them. After several miles the path began to climb, and my mother began to wheeze. Her asthma was pretty bad at this point, poor thing. No doubt, her anxiety made it worse, but in such circumstances how could she rid herself of anxiety? It was no use knowing that her difficulty was rooted in anxiety, just as it was no use knowing that we could have moved more quickly if we had possessed wings. Life is what it is. The path over that mountain was not actually very long, only a couple of miles. Steep as it was, we could have gotten over in little more than an hour if not for my mother. Because of her, we had to pause every few minutes, so our journey took many hours.

12   I myself hardly felt the exertion. I was walking quite well that day, quite athletically. I had that good **prosthetic** leg from Germany. The foot was a little worn by then, but not enough to slow me down. Thinking back, I'm puzzled, actually. How did I scale that mountain so easily? How did I climb down the other side? These days I find it hard to clamber up two or three flights of stairs, even. I don't know what made me so **supple** and strong that day, but I felt no hardship, no anxiety or fear, just concentration and intensity. Perhaps my mother's problems distracted me from my own. That might account for it. Perhaps desperation gave me energy and made me forget the **rigor** of the climb. Well, whatever the reason, I scrambled up like a goat. The family we were following had a girl only a bit younger than me, and she was moving slowly. Her family used my example to chide her. They kept saying, "Look at that girl. She's missing a leg, and yet she's going faster than you. Why can't you keep up? Hurry now!"

13   That Ghulam Ali was certainly a good man, so patient with us and so compassionate. He had never seen us before, and yet when he met us, he said, "I will help you." That's the thing about life. You never know when and where you will encounter a spot of human decency. I have felt alone in this world at times; I have known long periods of being no one. But then, without warning, a person like Ghulam Ali just turns up and says, "I see you. I am on your side." Strangers have been kind to me when it mattered most. That sustains a person's hope and faith.

Excerpted from *The Other Side of the Sky* by Farah Ahmedi, published by Simon & Schuster.

First Read

Read *The Other Side of the Sky*. After you read, complete the Think Questions below.

☁ THINK QUESTIONS

1. Why were Ahmedi and her mother near the gate to the Pakistani border? Why couldn't they get any nearer to the gate? Cite specific evidence from the text to support your answer.

2. What did Ahmedi learn on the second day about why a few people were being allowed to enter Pakistan? Why didn't this knowledge help her and her mother? Cite specific evidence from the text to support your response.

3. What physical challenges did Ahmedi and her mother face as they crossed the mountain? Why was Ahmedi puzzled by her own physical abilities during the mountain crossing? Cite specific evidence from the text to support your response.

4. Use context clues to determine the meaning of **supple** as it is used in the text. Then write your definition of *supple* here and check a print or online dictionary to confirm your definition.

5. The Latin word *recedere* means "to go back." With this information in mind, write your best definition of **receded** here and explain how you figured out its meaning.

Skill:
Textual Evidence

Use the Checklist to analyze Textual Evidence in *The Other Side of the Sky*. Refer to the sample student annotations about Textual Evidence in the text.

••• CHECKLIST FOR TEXTUAL EVIDENCE

In order to support an analysis by citing textual evidence that is explicitly stated in the text, do the following:

- ✓ read the text closely and critically

- ✓ identify what the text says explicitly

- ✓ find the most relevant textual evidence that supports your analysis

- ✓ consider why an author explicitly states specific details and information

- ✓ cite the specific words, phrases, sentences, paragraphs, or images from the text that support your analysis

In order to interpret implicit meanings in a text by making inferences, do the following:

- ✓ combine information directly stated in the text with your own knowledge, experiences, and observations

- ✓ cite the specific words, phrases, sentences, paragraphs, or images from the text that support this inference

In order to cite textual evidence to support an analysis of what the text says explicitly as well as inferences drawn from the text, consider the following questions:

- ✓ Have I read the text closely and critically?

- ✓ What inferences am I making about the text? What textual evidence am I using to support these inferences?

- ✓ Am I quoting the evidence from the text correctly?

- ✓ Does my textual evidence logically relate to my analysis?

- ✓ Have I cited several pieces of textual evidence?

Skill:
Textual Evidence

Reread paragraphs 10–11 of *The Other Side of the Sky*. Then, using the Checklist on the previous page, answer the multiple-choice questions below.

↻ YOUR TURN

1. Text details in paragraph 10 imply that *namaz* is —

   ○ A. a type of bread.
   ○ B. a type of prayer.
   ○ C. a type of building.
   ○ D. a type of bed.

2. A detail that shows they had to travel in secret is —

   ○ A. they had only a little food and water.
   ○ B. they said prayers before leaving.
   ○ C. they performed ablutions quickly in the darkness.
   ○ D. they used sand instead of water to perform ablutions.

3. You can infer that the group stopped every few minutes because —

   ○ A. they needed to hide from guards.
   ○ B. Ahmedi's mother needed to rest and breathe.
   ○ C. they needed to find the correct path.
   ○ D. Ahmedi needed to rest because of her leg.

Close Read

Reread *The Other Side of the Sky*. As you reread, complete the Skills Focus questions below. Then use your answers and annotations from the questions to help you complete the Write activity.

◎ SKILLS FOCUS

1. Identify evidence of how the author uses a chronological text structure. Explain the effect of this structure and how it helps you to understand the author's feelings.

2. Identify evidence that describes the personal characteristics of Ghulam Ali and his wife. How do these descriptions help you better understand them as individuals?

3. Identify clues that tell about the obstacles and hardships that Farah Ahmedi and her mother had to overcome. Then explain what those clues tell you about how the narrator's personal qualities enabled her to survive.

✏ WRITE

LITERARY ANALYSIS: What ideas related to survival during the most challenging times are implied by this excerpt? Write a brief response answering this question. Remember to use evidence from the text to support your response.

Please note that excerpts and passages in the StudySync® library and this workbook are intended as touchstones to generate interest in an author's work. The excerpts and passages do not substitute for the reading of entire texts, and StudySync® strongly recommends that students seek out and purchase the whole literary or informational work in order to experience it as the author intended. Links to online resellers are available in our digital library. In addition, complete works may be ordered through an authorized reseller by filling out and returning to StudySync® the order form enclosed in this workbook.

Reading & Writing Companion

705

The Story of Anniko

FICTION
Charlotte Blake Alston
2000

Introduction

This adaptation of Molly Melching's French story *Anniko!* is told by storyteller and performer Charlotte Blake Alston. The tale originates from the Wolof language of Senegal, where Melching lived and founded Tostan, a non-profit organization that advocates on behalf of human rights and sustainable development in local communities. Set in a similar village, Anniko's story is one of sudden tragedy and recovery in the welcoming arms of an unexpected community.

"Anniko uttered a silent prayer before she entered that thick forest."

NOTES

1   There was once a little girl named Anniko who lived very happily in a village with her mother, father, sisters, and brothers until—one day—a very sad thing began to happen. A sickness came to her village and swept through like an angry fire. No one was spared—except Anniko.

2   Anniko was grief-stricken and lonely, but she knew she could not remain there. Sadly, she began walking away from her village. She walked and walked until she found herself standing at the edge of a thick, thick forest. There were stories of this forest—stories of those who had entered it but had never returned. There were also stories of a village on the other side of that forest where, just as in Anniko's own home, a stranger would be welcomed in. But she would have to enter that thick forest in order to find the path that would lead her to that village.

3   Anniko uttered a silent prayer before she entered that thick forest. She walked and walked, pushing aside wide leaves and long vines. She grew tired, but she continued on. Well, her prayers were answered that day, and she came to the path that would lead her to the village. She followed that path to the other side of the forest.

4   *What a beautiful country this is*, Anniko thought as she walked. Soon the village came into sight and the villagers all came out to greet her. It was then that Anniko noticed that these villagers had one rather **unique characteristic.** They all had long necks with heads that sat at the tops of their necks. Even their babies had long necks with little heads at the top. Anniko had never seen anything like this before.

5   The villagers were about to greet Anniko, but they couldn't believe their eyes. She had a short neck—much like yours and mine. They had never seen anything like this before and they weren't quite sure what to do or say. One of them asked what a little girl like Anniko would be doing in that forest alone. Anniko began to tell all that had happened to her, her family and her village. Something about Anniko made the Longnecks trust her, so they invited her to stay.

Please note that excerpts and passages in the StudySync® library and this workbook are intended as touchstones to generate interest in an author's work. The excerpts and passages do not substitute for the reading of entire texts, and StudySync® strongly recommends that students seek out and purchase the whole literary or informational work in order to experience it as the author intended. Links to online resellers are available in our digital library. In addition, complete works may be ordered through an authorized reseller by filling out and returning to StudySync® the order form enclosed in this workbook.

Reading & Writing Companion   **707**

6   They were right. Anniko was warm, caring and respectful. She worked, danced and played with the villagers. She **accompanied** the Longnecks to the marketplace and shared in their celebrations and their sorrows. But the thing that was most special about Anniko was that every morning, very early, Anniko would rise and cross the village singing:

Yee si naa leen
Yee si naa leen yen
Yewu nama deyman
Te yee si naa leen itam
Yewu jotnaa
Yee si naa leen
Yee si naa leen yen

which means: *I'm coming to wake you up. I'm up, a new day has begun. I'm coming to wake you also, people.*

7   Singing was very much a part of Anniko's life in her old village but, unbelievable as it might sound, the Longnecks had never heard singing before. They thought this was a wonderful way to be awakened each morning. Soon they would not get up and go about their work until they heard Anniko's sweet song. They loved her even more because of this special gift she brought to them.

8   But in this village—as in all villages in the world—there was one evil, jealous, small-hearted man. He had not liked Anniko from the first day he saw her because she was different. One day he called to her and said, "You do not belong here. You are different from us. You have a—short neck! Differences can only lead to problems in this village. You should take yourself away to avoid bringing trouble here!"

9   The words stung Anniko's heart. Without thinking, she ran off and found herself in the middle of that same thick forest. The rainy season had come so the vines hung longer, the leaves had grown larger, the **foliage** was thicker . . . and Anniko became afraid. She could not even see where she was stepping, so after a while she stopped and rested. Night fell quickly.

10   Early the next morning, all the Longnecks lay in their beds waiting to hear Anniko's sweet song. But there was only silence. One by one, they began to rise from their beds and ask, "Where is Anniko? Have you seen Anniko?" They gathered in the center of the village, and one of the elders said, "I think I know who might know something. Follow me." He led them to the home of that evil, jealous, small-hearted man who told them—almost with pride—how he had spared the village of problems by sending away the different one.

11   The villagers were **furious.** They had to think of a way to help Anniko find her way back. They could not go into the forest because they would become lost themselves. One of Anniko's friends had an idea. She said, "Maybe we can

sing as Anniko has sung to us. Maybe she will hear our voices and that will help her find her way back."

12   Well, not only had the Longnecks never heard singing before Anniko's arrival, they had never tried to sing themselves. They agreed it was important to try. They decided they would sing Anniko's name and tell her they were sad and wanted her back. So they all stood side by side in the center of the village and began to sing for the very first time:

Anniko ni sa wa ni
Anniko ni sa wa ni
Anniko ni sa wa ni
Wo, wo, wo chi ka nay, nay, nay
Wo, wo, wo chi ka nay, nay, nay
Hey, ho bi ci ni
Hey, ho bi ci ni

which means: *Anniko, return quickly. Wo, wo, wo, we are sad without you. Hey, ho, we ask you to return.*

13   They sang and sang, stronger and stronger. Their voices traveled quickly into the forest and reached the place where Anniko sat. When she heard the singing, she knew it was the Longnecks trying to help her find her way home. She followed the sound of the voices to the path that took her into the village once again. The villagers rejoiced when they saw that she was safe with them. They invited her to stay with them as long as she wished.

14   The chief of the village said to Anniko, to the villagers, and to that evil, jealous, small-hearted man: "It is not the length of your neck that is important. It is the goodness of your heart."

From *More Ready-to-Tell Tales from Around the World*, 2005. Used by permission of August House.

✏ WRITE

DISCUSSION: "The Story of Anniko" is a folktale from Senegal. Why do you think it's important to read folktales from different cultures and times? What can you learn from reading folktales in addition to studying history and informational texts about these cultures? Write notes to prepare for a discussion of these questions. Use examples from the text as well as other myths and folktales you have read to support your points.

Please note that excerpts and passages in the StudySync® library and this workbook are intended as touchstones to generate interest in an author's work. The excerpts and passages do not substitute for the reading of entire texts, and StudySync® strongly recommends that students seek out and purchase the whole literary or informational work in order to experience it as the author intended. Links to online resellers are available in our digital library. In addition, complete works may be ordered through an authorized reseller by filling out and returning to StudySync® the order form enclosed in this workbook.

Reading & Writing
Companion

709

Icarus and Daedalus

FICTION
Josephine Preston Peabody
1897

Introduction

In her lifetime, longtime Wellesley professor Josephine Preston Peabody wrote award-winning plays, books of poetry, and also a collection of retellings of Greek mythology. A project perhaps inspired by Nathaniel Hawthorne's *Greek Myths: A Wonder Book for Boys and Girls*, Peabody's *Old Greek Folk Stories Told Anew* added more poetically written tales to those available in the English vernacular, including the miniature tragedy of "Icarus and Daedalus." Daedalus and Icarus, a father and son duo, explore the limits of human ingenuity on their quest for freedom.

"Who could remember to be careful when he was to fly for the first time?"

NOTES

Skill: Setting

1 Among all those mortals who grew so wise that they learned the secrets of the gods, none was more **cunning** than Daedalus.

2 He once built, for King Minos of Crete, a wonderful Labyrinth of winding ways so cunningly tangled up and twisted around that, once inside, you could never find your way out again without a magic clue. But the king's favor veered with the wind, and one day he had his master architect imprisoned in a tower. Daedalus managed to escape from his cell; but it seemed impossible to leave the island, since every ship that came or went was well guarded by order of the king.

3 At length, watching the sea-gulls in the air,—the only creatures that were sure of liberty,—he thought of a plan for himself and his young son Icarus, who was captive with him.

4 Little by little, he gathered a store of feathers great and small. He fastened these together with thread, moulded them in with wax, and so fashioned two great wings like those of a bird. When they were done, Daedalus fitted them to his own shoulders, and after one or two efforts, he found that by waving his arms he could winnow the air and **cleave** it, as a swimmer does the sea. He held himself aloft, wavered this way and that with the wind, and at last, like a great fledgling, he learned to fly.

Daedalus made wings for himself and his son, Icarus.

This story is set in Crete during the rule of King Minos. He was in the story of Theseus and the Minotaur. This was around the same time. I can see that Crete is an island, and that explains why Daedalus couldn't just run away.

5 Without delay, he fell to work on a pair of wings for the boy Icarus, and taught him carefully how to use them, bidding him beware of **rash** adventures among the stars. "Remember," said the father, "never to fly very low or very high, for the fogs about the earth would weigh you down, but the blaze of the sun will surely melt your feathers apart if you go too near."

NOTES

Skill:
Greek and Latin
Affixes and Roots

Captivity looks like captive, so the words could have a similar root and meaning. The suffix -ity makes words into nouns, so I bet this word means something like "imprisonment."

6   For Icarus, these cautions went in at one ear and out by the other. Who could remember to be careful when he was to fly for the first time? Are birds careful? Not they! And not an idea remained in the boy's head but the one joy of escape.

7   The day came, and the fair wind that was to set them free. The father bird put on his wings, and, while the light urged them to be gone, he waited to see that all was well with Icarus, for the two could not fly hand in hand. Up they rose, the boy after his father. The hateful ground of Crete sank beneath them; and the country folk, who caught a glimpse of them when they were high above the tree-tops, took it for a vision of the gods,—Apollo[1], perhaps, with Cupid[2] after him.

8   At first there was a terror in the joy. The wide vacancy of the air dazed them,—a glance downward made their brains reel. But when a great wind filled their wings, and Icarus felt himself sustained, like a halcyon-bird[3] in the hollow of a wave, like a child uplifted by his mother, he forgot everything in the world but joy. He forgot Crete and the other islands that he had passed over: he saw but vaguely that winged thing in the distance before him that was his father Daedalus. He longed for one draught of flight to **quench** the thirst of his captivity: he stretched out his arms to the sky and made towards the highest heavens.

9   Alas for him! Warmer and warmer grew the air. Those arms, that had seemed to uphold him, relaxed. His wings **wavered**, drooped. He fluttered his young hands vainly,—he was falling,—and in that terror he remembered. The heat of the sun had melted the wax from his wings; the feathers were falling, one by one, like snowflakes; and there was none to help.

10   He fell like a leaf tossed down the wind, down, down, with one cry that overtook Daedalus far away. When he returned, and sought high and low for the poor boy, he saw nothing but the bird-like feathers afloat on the water, and he knew that Icarus was drowned.

11   The nearest island he named Icaria, in memory of the child; but he, in heavy grief, went to the temple of Apollo in Sicily, and there hung up his wings as an offering. Never again did he attempt to fly.

---

1. **Apollo** In Greek and Roman mythology, Apollo is the son of Zeus and Leto, and a god of many realms, including music, the sun, poetry, and more.
2. **Cupid** In classical mythology, Cupid is the god of love and attraction.
3. **halcyon-bird** a bird-like figure in Greek mythology with the power to calm the rough ocean waves, symbolizing a sense of peace or tranquility

First Read

Read "Icarus and Daedalus." After you read, complete the Think Questions below.

☁ THINK QUESTIONS

1. What materials were the wings Icarus and Daedalus wore made from? Cite specific evidence from the text to support your answer.

2. What did the country folk who saw the pair flying away from Crete think? Cite specific evidence from the text to support your answer.

3. As Icarus was falling, what did he remember at last? Cite specific evidence from the text to support your answer.

4. Find the word **quench** in paragraph 8 of "Icarus and Daedalus." Use context clues in the surrounding sentences, as well as the sentence in which the word appears, to determine the word's meaning. Write your definition here and identify clues that helped you figure out the meaning.

5. Read the following dictionary entry:

waver
wa•ver \'wāvər\
verb
1. to sway or tremble
2. to become weaker

Which definition most closely matches the meaning of *wavered* in paragraph 9? Write the correct definition of *wavered* here and explain how you figured it out.

Please note that excerpts and passages in the StudySync® library and this workbook are intended as touchstones to generate interest in an author's work. The excerpts and passages do not substitute for the reading of entire texts, and StudySync® strongly recommends that students seek out and purchase the whole literary or informational work in order to experience it as the author intended. Links to online resellers are available in our digital library. In addition, complete works may be ordered through an authorized reseller by filling out and returning to StudySync® the order form enclosed in this workbook.

Reading & Writing Companion 713

Skill: Greek and Latin Affixes and Roots

Use the Checklist to analyze Greek and Latin Affixes and Roots in "Icarus and Daedalus." Refer to the sample student annotations about Greek and Latin Affixes and Roots in the text.

••• CHECKLIST FOR GREEK AND LATIN AFFIXES AND ROOTS

In order to identify Greek and Latin affixes and roots, note the following:

✓ the root

✓ the prefix and/or suffix

To use common, grade-appropriate Greek or Latin affixes and roots as clues to the meaning of a word, use the following questions as a guide:

✓ Can I identify the root of this word? Should I look in a dictionary or other resource?

✓ What is the meaning of the root?

✓ Can I identify the prefix and/or suffix of this word? Should I look in a dictionary or other resource?

✓ What is the meaning of the prefix and/or suffix?

✓ Does this suffix change the word's part of speech?

✓ How do the word parts work together to show the word's meaning and part of speech?

Skill: Greek and Latin Affixes and Roots

Reread paragraph 8 of "Icarus and Daedalus" and the dictionary entries. Then, using the Checklist on the previous page, answer the multiple-choice questions below.

⟳ YOUR TURN

1. **vacancy** va•can•cy \ˈvā-kan-sē\
   Origin: from the Latin *vacare* meaning "to be empty"

   Based on its context and root, what is the most likely meaning of *vacancy*?

   ○ A. vacationing
   ○ B. being empty
   ○ C. empty
   ○ D. emptiness

2. **sustained** sus•tained \sus-ˈtānd\
   Origin: From the Latin *sustinere* meaning "keep up, maintain"

   Based on its context and root, what is the most likely meaning of *sustained*?

   ○ A. held down
   ○ B. held up
   ○ C. held out
   ○ D. extended

3. **vaguely** vague•ly \ˈvāg-lē\
   Origin: from the Latin *vagus* meaning "wandering, uncertain" + the adverbial suffix *-ly*

   Based on its context, suffix, and root, what is the most likely meaning of *vaguely*?

   ○ A. in a wandering way
   ○ B. uncertain
   ○ C. uncertainly
   ○ D. wandering

Skill:
Setting

Use the Checklist to analyze Setting in "Icarus and Daedalus." Refer to the sample student annotations about Setting in the text.

••• CHECKLIST FOR SETTING

In order to identify how particular elements of a story interact, note the following:

- ✓ the setting of the story

- ✓ the characters in the text and the problems they face

- ✓ how the events of the plot unfold, and how that affects the setting and characters

- ✓ how the setting shapes the characters and plot

To analyze how particular elements of a story interact, consider the following questions as a guide:

- ✓ What is the setting(s) of the story?

- ✓ How does the setting affect the characters and plot?

- ✓ How does the plot unfold? How does that affect the setting(s)?

- ✓ How do the characters' decisions affect the plot and setting(s)?

Copyright © BookheadEd Learning, LLC

SETTING

sync

Skill:
Setting

Reread paragraphs 8–11 of "Icarus and Daedalus." Then, using the Checklist on the previous page, answer the multiple-choice questions below.

⟳ YOUR TURN

1. This question has two parts. First, answer Part A. Then, answer Part B.

   Part A: The setting of paragraph 8 affects the characters by —

   ○ A. making the characters feel excited to be home.
   ○ B. making the characters feel terrified from the great height.
   ○ C. making the characters feel bitter for being imprisoned for so long.
   ○ D. making the characters feel shock and joy from the wide-open sky.

   Part B: Which of the following details BEST supports your response to Part A?

   ○ A. At first there was a terror in the joy. The wide vacancy of the air dazed them.
   ○ B. At first there was a terror in the joy . . . he forgot everything in the world but joy.
   ○ C. . . . he forgot everything in the world but joy . . . he saw but vaguely that winged thing in the distance
   ○ D. He longed for one draught of flight to quench the thirst of his captivity.

2. The setting influences the plot of the story by causing —

   ○ A. Icarus's wings to melt.
   ○ B. Daedalus to lose his way.
   ○ C. King Minos to lose sight of them.
   ○ D. Daedalus and Icarus to become exhausted.

Close Read

Reread "Icarus and Daedalus." As you reread, complete the Skills Focus questions below. Then use your answers and annotations from the questions to help you complete the Write activity.

◎ SKILLS FOCUS

1. Identify descriptions of the setting. Explain how these details affect the characters and plot.

2. Consider the characteristics of Daedalus. Find an event in the story and explain how it is a result of Daedalus's traits.

3. Consider the characteristics of Icarus. Find an event in the story and explain how it is a result of Icarus's traits.

4. In both "The Story of Anniko" and "Icarus and Daedalus," characters flee from a dangerous situation to find themselves in another dangerous situation—but with different outcomes. Identify an event from "Icarus and Daedalus" in which the outcome differs from "The Story of Anniko." Then explain a lesson taught by each text.

5. Identify a detail from "Icarus and Daedalus" that expresses the message or theme, and explain how this theme is meaningful to modern readers.

✎ WRITE

COMPARE AND CONTRAST: Write a response comparing and contrasting the settings of "The Story of Anniko" and "Icarus and Daedalus." In your response, explain how the different settings influence characters' actions and plot development. Remember to use evidence from the texts to support your response.

The New Colossus

POETRY
Emma Lazarus
1883

Introduction

Emma Lazarus (1849–1887) was a 19th-century American poet best known for her work "The New Colossus," a poetic tribute to the Statue of Liberty. Originally written for a Liberty fundraiser, the poem lay forgotten for almost 20 years before revived interest led to it being engraved on a brass plaque at the base of the statue in 1903. The title of the poem refers to the Colossus of Rhodes, a towering bronze statue of the sun god Helios that was erected in the ancient Greek city of Rhodes to celebrate a military victory over Cyprus. Almost 100 feet high, the Colossus of Rhodes was one of the tallest statues of its time and is now considered one of the Seven Wonders of the Ancient World.

"Give me your tired, your poor, Your huddled masses yearning to breathe free . . ."

Skill: Figurative Language

The title of the poem is an allusion, or reference, to the Colossus of Rhodes. Referring to ancient Greece adds a sense of importance and grandness. This makes me think both statues are important, even though Lazarus says they are different.

Skill: Poetic Elements and Structure

I know that sonnets are emotional poems that are like songs. Lazarus uses emotional language when talking about immigrants, so the form enhances the emotional effect. It's clear that America gave so much hope to so many people.

1 Not like the **brazen** giant of Greek fame,
2 With conquering limbs astride from land to land;
3 Here at our sea-washed, sunset gates shall stand
4 A mighty woman with a torch, whose flame
5 Is the imprisoned lightning, and her name
6 Mother of **Exiles**. From her beacon-hand
7 Glows world-wide welcome; her mild eyes command
8 The air-bridged harbor that twin cities frame.

9 "Keep, ancient lands, your storied **pomp**!" cries she
10 With silent lips. "Give me your tired, your poor,
11 Your huddled masses yearning to breathe free,
12 The **wretched refuse** of your teeming shore.
13 Send these, the homeless, tempest-tost to me,
14 I lift my lamp beside the golden door!"

Illustration of immigrants arriving in New York City and seeing the Statue of Liberty, 1887

From THE NEW COLOSSUS by Emma Lazarus, Copyright ©2014.

First Read

Read "The New Colossus." After you read, complete the Think Questions below.

☁ THINK QUESTIONS

1. The title of the poem refers to the Colossus of Rhodes—a giant statue of the sun god, Helios—erected in the ancient Greek city of Rhodes to celebrate the city's victory over Cyprus. How do you know from the poem that the "mighty woman with a torch" is also a statue? Cite textual evidence to support your understanding.

2. Who is the "mighty woman with a torch" not like? How is she different? Cite textual evidence to support your answer.

3. To whom is the "mighty woman with a torch" offering a "world-wide welcome"? Cite specific evidence from the poem to support your answer.

4. Find the word **brazen** in the first line of "The New Colossus." Use context clues in the surrounding words, as well as the line in which the word appears, to determine the word's meaning. Write your definition here and identify clues that helped you figure out the meaning.

5. Use context clues to determine the meaning of **exiles** as it is used in line 6 of "The New Colossus." Write your definition here and identify clues that helped you figure out the meaning. Then check the meaning in a dictionary.

Please note that excerpts and passages in the StudySync® library and this workbook are intended as touchstones to generate interest in an author's work. The excerpts and passages do not substitute for the reading of entire texts, and StudySync® strongly recommends that students seek out and purchase the whole literary or informational work in order to experience it as the author intended. Links to online resellers are available in our digital library. In addition, complete works may be ordered through an authorized reseller by filling out and returning to StudySync® the order form enclosed in this workbook.

Reading & Writing
Companion

721

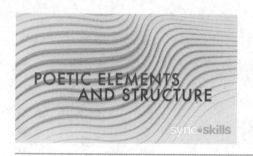

Skill: Poetic Elements and Structure

Use the Checklist to analyze Poetic Elements and Structure in "The New Colossus." Refer to the sample student annotations about Poetic Elements and Structure in the text.

••• CHECKLIST FOR POETIC ELEMENTS AND STRUCTURE

In order to identify poetic elements and structure, note the following:

✓ the form and overall structure of the poem, such as:

- sonnet: a poem with 14 lines broken into two stanzas, with a set rhyme scheme and a set meter

✓ the rhyme, rhythm, and meter, if present

✓ other sound elements, such as:

- alliteration: the repetition of initial consonant sounds, as with the *s* sound in "Cindy sweeps the sand"

✓ lines and stanzas in the poem that suggest its meaning

✓ ways that the poem's form or structure connects to the poem's meaning

To analyze how a poem's form or structure contributes to its meaning, consider the following questions:

✓ What poetic form does the poet use? What is the structure?

✓ How do the lines and stanzas and their lengths affect the meaning?

✓ How do the form and structure contribute to the poem's meaning?

Copyright © BookheadEd Learning, LLC

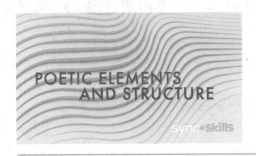

Skill: Poetic Elements and Structure

Reread lines 9–14 of "The New Colossus." Then, using the Checklist on the previous page, answer the multiple-choice questions below.

🔁 YOUR TURN

1. This question has two parts. First, answer Part A. Then, answer Part B.

   Part A: Think about the meaning of the stanza and the effect that the rhyme scheme has on it. What message is expressed in the stanza?

   ○ A. People around the world are in pain.

   ○ B. The statue stands silent.

   ○ C. There is freedom for all in the United States of America.

   ○ D. Many people are huddled in masses.

   Part B: Which set of rhyming lines best supports your answer to Part A?

   ○ A. "'Keep, ancient lands, your storied pomp!' cries she." / "'Send these, the homeless, tempest-tost to me'"

   ○ B. "'Your huddled masses yearning to breathe free,'" / "'Send these, the homeless, tempest-tost to me'"

   ○ C. "'The wretched refuse of your teeming shore.'" / "'Send these, the homeless, tempest-tost to me'"

   ○ D. "With silent lips. 'Give me your tired, your poor,'" / "'The wretched refuse of your teeming shore.'"

Skill:
Figurative Language

Use the Checklist to analyze Figurative Language in "The New Colossus." Refer to the sample student annotations about Figurative Language in the text.

To determine the meanings of figures of speech in a text, note the following:

✓ words that mean one thing literally and suggest something else

✓ similes, such as "strong as an ox"

✓ metaphors, such as "her eyes were stars"

✓ allusions, or indirect references to people, texts, events, or ideas, such as

  • saying of a setting, "the place was a Garden of Eden" (Biblical allusion)

  • saying of a character whose snooping caused problems, "he opened a Pandora's box" (allusion to mythology)

  • calling someone who likes romance "a real Romeo" (allusion to Shakespeare)

✓ other language in the text used in a nonliteral way

In order to interpret the meaning of a figure of speech in context, ask the following questions:

✓ Does any of the descriptive language in the text compare two seemingly unlike things?

✓ Do any descriptions include *like* or *as* to indicate a simile?

✓ Is there a direct comparison that suggests a metaphor?

✓ What literary, Biblical, or mythological allusions do you recognize?

✓ How does the use of this figure of speech change your understanding of the thing or person being described?

In order to analyze the impact of figurative language on the meaning of a text, use the following questions as a guide:

✓ Where does figurative language appear in the text? What does it mean?

✓ Why does the author use figurative language rather than literal language?

Skill:
Figurative Language

Reread lines 9–14 of "The New Colossus." Then, using the Checklist on the previous page, answer the multiple-choice questions below.

↻ YOUR TURN

1. This question has two parts. First, answer Part A. Then, answer Part B.

   Part A: Which of the lines uses figurative language to best convey the message that the United States is a land of opportunity?

   ○ A. "'Keep, ancient lands, your storied pomp!' cries she"

   ○ B. "'I lift my lamp beside the golden door!'"

   ○ C. "'The wretched refuse of your teeming shore.'"

   ○ D. "'Send these, the homeless, tempest-tost to me'"

   Part B: Which of the following best explains how the figure of speech you chose in Part A conveys the message of American opportunity?

   ○ A. The phrase "storied pomp" refers to the riches, which the immigrants may gain by coming to the United States.

   ○ B. The phrase "golden door" conveys the message of American opportunity because it suggests both a precious metal and something opening.

   ○ C. In "wretched refuse" and "teeming shore," Lazarus explains the poverty that motivated many immigrants to come to the United States.

   ○ D. By calling the immigrants "homeless" and "tempest-tost," the poet emphasizes the misery and danger they are leaving behind for new opportunity in the United States.

Close Read

Reread "The New Colossus." As you reread, complete the Skills Focus questions below. Then use your answers and annotations from the questions to help you complete the Write activity.

◎ SKILLS FOCUS

1. "Sea-washed, sunset gates" is a metaphor used in line 3. What might this metaphor mean in the context of the poem? What does it suggest about the poem's deeper meaning or message? How does it affect the poem's tone?

2. Highlight evidence in the last six lines that "The New Colossus" is a sonnet. What is the effect of this structure? Explain your answer using evidence from the text.

3. Emma Lazarus uses an allusion to the Colossus of Rhodes in her poem. What is the effect of this allusion? What is her deeper message about America and its values? Explain your reasoning with evidence from the text.

4. Recall that a tempest is a violent and windy storm. In the poem, it is used in a figurative sense. Highlight its use in line 13. Given the poem's message, how might Lazarus be using "tempest-tost" here?

5. Why do you think we still read this poem about the Statue of Liberty? Why are its themes and message still relevant to people in America today? Explain your answer using evidence from the text.

✏ WRITE

LITERARY ANALYSIS: What does Emma Lazarus want readers to know about the United States? What is the poem's deeper message or theme about America? Use your understanding of figurative language and poetic structure and elements to determine her message.

The Third Elevator

FICTION
Aimee Bender
2009

Introduction

Aimee Bender (b. 1969) is an acclaimed American author known for her distinctive magical realist style. To this end, "The Third Elevator" is a classic Aimee Bender story, bringing together the author's signature wit, melancholy, and whimsy, and setting it in a world of make-believe. In this particular world, there is a rigid order wherein loggers, miners, and royalty are kept separate by three distinct elevators. When two birds of different feathers mate and hatch a mysterious egg, a cloud is released into the air and begins to make inhabitants of the kingdom question just which of the existing boundaries are set in stone.

"One was made of gold, one was made of wood, and the third was made entirely of feathers."

1   The queen took a swan for her pet. The bird was white and large, with a body so puffed out and fluffy it looked just like a small cloud, only with legs, with a beak, and with bright beaded black eyes.

2   "Throw him up in the air," said the queen, "and who knows who we'd fool."

3   But this swan had moods that were heavy. His disposition was not cloud-like at all. He took the world very seriously and sometimes had a hard time because of that. He didn't even like to fly. He preferred swimming instead and, occasionally, would take a dip in the moat, leaving bright white feathers in his trail like the opposite of footprints. To keep her pet company the queen spent much of her day with the swan, and they walked around the castle grounds together. The two were fine companions and the queen respected the swan's sad moods, but she did worry about her pet and wished she could find him a proper mate. She made an effort to introduce him to other, sexy swans, but the queen's swan always arched to the side and refused to interlock his neck with theirs. He was picky. He preferred, in general, to tour the moat.

4   However, on his own time, while the queen was in the castle hearing citizens complain to her crowned head, the swan liked to go visit with the bluebirds who were scattered throughout the royal hedge like huge loud blueberries. The bluebirds were a lively bunch and, on occasion, came out to visit with the royal swan. Once, on a Wednesday, a bluebird runt hopped out, tiny and cobalt[1], and she jumped over to the swan and leapt onto his white lush back.

5   The swan started nervously, but the bluebird insisted that she would not get off the swan's back until they spent the day together. The two strolled around the gardens, discussing flight and seed and feather rot, and the bluebird was very funny and kept the swan laughing his deep trumpeting laugh. It was a beautiful, rich sound, and one that wasn't often heard on the palace grounds. The birds even toured the moat together, the bluebird chattering the whole time. By the end of the day, they were deeply in love.

---

1. **cobalt** a deep blue pigment

Skill: Character

The narrator describes the birds like people. They walk around, have conversations, laugh, and fall in love. I think they'll be important in the story because they are so much like humans. I wonder if their relationship will affect the conflict of the story?

6   So the swan, being highly educated as most royal pets are, went straight to his mistress who was tired and sweaty after listening to complaint after complaint, and wrote a document with fancy ink on thick cream-colored paper declaring that he and the runt bluebird wished to be married. The queen, while having her shoulders massaged, read the note and put down one daintily booted foot.

7   "I don't think so," she said. "You are a royal bird and ought to marry something more—"

8   The bluebird, still nestled like a lapis lazuli[2] necklace on the swan's puffy back, tilted her head.

9   The queen winced. "I mean, you ought to marry something else—" she continued.

10   The swan hung his long white neck and the bluebird flew into the queen's eye. She did not peck it out, but just placed the cold hard cartilage triangle of her beak next to the liquidy white of the queen's tear duct.

11   "Bless you both," said the queen meekly.

* * *

12   The swan said he would not leave his mistress, so the two birds stayed close by, setting up a home just outside the palace grounds where the little bluebird made a nest large enough for the both of them. They were living contentedly in it, getting to know each other, and after a few weeks the runt bluebird laid an unusual egg. It was half the size of her body, and speckled. The **mollified** queen came over and praised its size and shape. The swan paced back and forth.

13   "What will it look like?" he asked the queen. "What if it's moody and depressed like I have been? What if it's a freak bird?"

14   The queen tried to comfort her pet but the swan just paced more. All the citizens of the kingdom were curious, and the egg was the topic of many discussions and debates at the local tavern for weeks. The bluebird chattered and sat in the nest patiently, and the swan brought her seeds and twigs and stroked down her feathers. He told her his worries. She thought they were funny.

15   When the egg finally opened, to the surprise of everyone, it revealed nothing but a cloud, pale blue in color, rising slowly in the air. The queen's mouth dropped open. The bluebird trilled with laughter. The swan, with a proud and

---

2. **lapis lazuli** a blue metamorphic rock, used in jewelry and for decoration

powerful ache in his breast, watched in awe as his child gained altitude, higher and higher, until the cloud lifted up enough to float gently to the next county, the wind hovering beneath it like the sweetest of cradles.

* * *

16   About two miles from the swan's nest was a glass-walled lobby unattached to any building. It stood smack in the center of the kingdom and had for as long as anyone could remember. Inside this lobby were three elevators. One was made of gold, one was made of wood, and the third was made entirely of feathers.

17   The gold elevator would descend ten stories down, down down down, into the middle of the earth. There, it opened its doors to a mineshaft where workers stuck shovels into the walls and picked and pulled until nuggets of gold fell onto their feet. Then they put the gold into the gold elevator. The elevator closed its doors on its own accord when it reached its weight requirement, and a collection agency came and collected the goods once daily. No miners were allowed to get inside the elevator and ride on up to the fresher air of the lobby, the elucidation of sunlight.

18   The elevator made of wood stayed on ground level and had a set of gnarled bark doors at both ends. One set opened to the lobby and the other opened to the muted light of a forest, thick with trees and thickets, flickering with broken lemon-yellow rays. Here, the loggers who were making timber from trees would take their stacks of chopped-up trunks and place them in careful rows inside the wood elevator. The forest was quiet, the ground soft with moss, and the loggers would whistle tunes their mothers had sung to them long ago, when they were as small as the smallest sapling. Now their arms were solid, muscles hard inside skin. They loaded the wood elevator until it was heavy enough, and then its bark doors shut slowly, smelling of resin, and re-opened, on the other side, to the lobby. The loggers returned to chopping and felling and whistling.

19   The feather elevator went forty-five stories high, up on its metal pole, the lightest elevator ever made. Birds eyed its slow **ascent** suspiciously but assumed it was a large rectangular bird, for it smelled like them and even fluttered slightly. But where was the beak? At the forty-fifth floor, the elevator opened its light grayish doors and let the air inside. It could rotate around on its pole there, hoping to catch something in the upper stratosphere. Sometimes curious birds would dart inside its open mouth, sticking old twigs and more feathers inside it, and then the elevator would close up, descend to the lobby, open its doors, and reveal nothing more than scraggle. But once, the elevator descended its forty-five floors, and arrived exactly on time with the other two. At the count of three, from the gold spilled gold, from the wood

tumbled fine logs, and when the feather elevator opened its doors, out drifted one pale blue cloud.

* * *

20   On the other side of the kingdom, touring the moat as usual, the melancholy swan heard word of the caught cloud. He'd never even been to the famous elevators that held up the local economy, operated on their own schedules, and were visited once daily by the gold and timber collectors, but the following afternoon, he waddled over. Unimpressed by the gold and wood, he went directly to the elevator of feathers and stepped inside. He spoke in hushed tones to its walls, whispering to the old shed bones of his friends, persuading it to go high, in the hopes that he would see and catch his own. He felt nervous rising inside the closed box, having never been in such a small space before, but when the doors opened he stood at the edge and trumpeted into the sky for hours, hoping against hope, putting his whole longing into his voice: *Come see me, child, come see me.* Then, just as the sun was starting a long descent, his pale blue offspring came floating by. The swan's heart leapt. Luckily, the wind on this day was just so, and the swan was able to get the cloud back inside the small rectangular elevator with him. The doors shut, and they rode down the forty-five flights together. The swan asked his child polite questions, but the cloud was silent, just floating there in that room of feathers. When they hit ground level, the two did not exit. The swan wasn't entirely sure what to do, what would be a fatherly act, but, following his instinct, he held out his enormous wings and invited the cloud to gather underneath them. There the two huddled, puffy pale feathers against puffy pale atmosphere, until the cloud began to diffuse from the heat, and then the swan ordered the elevator to begin its rise upstairs, which it did, because birds listen to birds, up and up and up. The doors opened to a sky fading to darker blue, and the swan kissed his child and wished it well, promising to return as soon as possible. The cloud floated away from beneath the wings of its father, drifting into the slow-turning black night. The swan decided not to ride the forty-five floors down, and took off out the doors the second before they shut, wingspan as long as a tree trunk, tears in his snapping black bird eyes, the underside of his wing warm and empty.

* * *

21   One of the loggers was a troublesome logger. He kept his axe very sharp and cut everything down except for trees. He felled telephone poles and even got through cement light posts; he chopped down fire hydrants and trellises but he didn't want to cut down the trees because, he said, they were growing. "Why would I do that?" he told everyone else.

Skill:
Character

The narrator tells us right away that the logger is "troublesome." He is skilled, but he doesn't want to cut down trees because they are "growing." This seems to be a pretty clear conflict, because loggers are supposed to cut down trees. His question "Why would I do that?" reveals a really kind personality and shows that his attitude toward trees is totally different from everyone else's.

22   The other loggers found him snobbish. "Just cut the trees," they told him, "come on."

23   But the troublesome logger couldn't. He said every time he put the blade of his axe against the bark of a new tree and prepared to slice in, he felt a clanging in his chest and knew if he cut it down he would have a heart attack at that exact same moment.

24   The other loggers then found him **melodramatic.** "Oh go see the boss," they said. "We don't need all these broken telephone poles and, besides, everyone in the kingdom is angry because they can't call each other up."

25   The logger twitched when he heard that. He didn't like to unconnect people. He'd even tried to help the telephone electrical crew but they just yelled at him to stop messing with the wires, and he felt so **agitated** by their yelling at him that he went and cut down a few more telephone poles about a mile away.

26   The boss logger heard about the troublesome logger and called him into his office the next morning. "Son," he said. "I hear you are unable to cut down trees. You must not be a logger at heart. Your father was a fine logger and his father before him was a fine logger but if you are not a logger at heart then we need to get you out of here."

27   The troublesome logger hung his head. His father had been the finest logger ever known, winning speed awards yearly, filling the elevator so early they often took the day off and went hiking up the trails to look for mountain goats. In fact, when he, the best logger's son, had been old enough to become a logger himself, there was a party to initiate him because his genetic logging legacy was so superior to that of the average man. When he'd cut down his first tree, a small elm, they had popped open a bottle of champagne to mark the spot, cream-colored froth pouring over the stump. The young logger, thirteen at the time, had to sit down because his heart was hurting so badly at the sight of the baby elm on its side, leaves dusting the ground, and he perched on the tiny stump, wet with champagne, while his father made constant toasts and got roaringly drunk.

28   Since then, his father had died in his bed, with loggers surrounding him, holding his hands and looking at him with love. As he closed his eyes for the last time, they all leaned in, like a group of trees, and the wind from the window rustled through their arms. His son sat outside on yet another stump, running his palm over the rings.

29   The young logger looked at the boss and agreed that he was wrong for the job. He said he needed to leave but didn't know where to go.

30 "Well," the boss said, "there's always the mine. They're always looking for good men in the mine."

31 So the logger left the forest of trees he loved and, holding his axe across his chest like a banner, entered the gold elevator and took it ten floors down. The miners were so used to each other they were very surprised to see a new face emerge from the elevator and found the new organization of features disturbing just because it was new.

32 "I'm a former logger," said the logger. "I would like a job here with you. I can dig for gold."

33 The miners jeered at him. "But we don't like loggers," they said.

34 "Please," pleaded the logger.

35 The head miner shrugged and said they always could use extra help. He asked the logger a few questions about **claustrophobia** and then gave him a corner of the cave to work on and told him the best way to get along in the mine was to play poker after dinner and lose. The logger nodded, still clutching his axe. "You won't need that," said the mining boss. The logger clung to it and asked if he could keep it. "I am attached to my axe," he said. The miner handed over a shovel. "Very well," he said. "Just get to work."

36 So the logger began picking apart the wall of the mine. The miners were singing songs—different than the songs the loggers sang—miner songs were in minor keys[3] and tended to be less storytelling-oriented and more repetitive. The logger listened and picked at the wall and hummed along when he thought he'd got the melody down, and then when he hit a chunk of gold in the wall he knocked it out and threw it behind him in the pile.

37 And then felt awful. It was the same feeling he'd had about the tree, a clutching in his chest, at the gold being ripped from the wall and going off into the world to wind up on the wrist of some person somewhere. He doubled over with pain.

38 The miners kept singing.

39 The logger took some deep breaths and then picked up his shovel and began digging at the wall again, with less vigor now, and soon he hit another nugget of gold. He held it, a chip the size of a tooth, and stuck it in his mouth. It fizzed on his tongue. Unable to throw it behind him, he replaced the nugget

---

3. **minor keys** musical scales with note patterns that are sometimes said to produce sadder or more mournful melodies

in the wall and spent some time shoring it back up. Then he picked out a piece of the black wall instead and threw that into the gold pile. He did that for five hours, throwing nuggets of wall into the gold pile, and hiding the nuggets of gold deeper into the wall, and when the boss came around to load up the gold elevator his yell was heard echoing throughout the cave for five minutes after he'd yelled it.

40 "What in the—?" he bellowed.

41 No one answered. The song stopped abruptly in the middle of the counterpoint third round about mountains. Several miners who were eating dinner put down their salami sandwiches nervously. There was not much yelling in the mine due to that echo.

42 The boss toured the miners' faces and when he arrived at the new-miner-former-logger he looked at him and the logger began trembling and stuttering, and the miner just pointed to the elevator and the logger picked up his axe and went back inside. He rode up with the pieces of gold, then walked straight through the wood elevator, and returned to the forest where the trees leaned away from him in the wind.

43 There is no place for me, he thought.

44 He was so agitated he couldn't sleep, so before he went to bed he walked toward a cluster of houses and chopped down two light posts and a mailbox, and curled himself up there on the ground to rest, surrounded by a fanned display of spilled letters.

* * *

45 One of the miners, who regularly filled up the gold elevator and was considered one of the best workers, had watched the logger go up the elevator with curiosity and envy. He hadn't known a person could take that trip.

46 He'd been growing short of breath lately. So, a few hours after the logger had left, the miner told his workmates that he was going to follow that logger and get in the elevator when half the load was full because he had to see the top of the earth again or he was going to die of claustrophobia of the lungs. The miners were a supportive team, because they had to be or they'd all be dead, and so they let him hop inside the gold elevator right before it went up, watching the doors close over his nervous face, cheeks reflecting the piles of metal as if he'd been working for years in sunshine.

47 The doors opened up to that same small lobby, with the two other elevators opening at the same time. Gold spilled onto the ground, and so did the miner.

There were no other humans visible. No sign of that vagabond logger. The miner stepped forward, squinting from the brightness of the glare even though it was early evening—five pm—and the sunlight was cool and lazy. Since he was an honest man, he did not take a nugget of gold but walked out the glass side doors of the lobby, strolling into the surrounding forest. Nearby, he could hear the melodic whistling of the loggers but saw none of them. He breathed in the oxygen thickly, heady from it, and settled himself under a tree. The wood smelled like heaven to the miner, so warm and rich with sun, and he ate some nuts from his pocket and then fell asleep, in oxygenated air, for the first time in over twenty years.

48 The loggers found him as they moved to that part of the forest. It was immediately clear that he wasn't a logger, being that he was covered with tiny black and gold specks from the mine, and so they hauled him, sound asleep, into the elevator with their stacks of wood. He woke up in the lobby again, amidst a pile of timber and lumber.

49 The sun was brighter now and he squinted helplessly at the light. He was hoping to spot the logger from the mine as a guide, but there was no sign of him anywhere. The miner rubbed his eyes. He wasn't sure where to go, so he decided to take the one elevator he hadn't been in up. Up and up and up. He huddled close to the walls. It had been a long time since he'd experienced anything unexpected and he wasn't familiar with this constant rising motion and his heart kept bumping against his throat.

50 When the feather doors opened to sky, the opposite of his life until now, as if he were face to face with the sun, the miner forgot to breathe; he stood there, with the clouds and the birds and the air, speechless. Amen to the firmament, his arms full to the rim of it. Birds—he'd forgotten all about birds!—flew by at face level, wings steady, and the miner laughed out loud at those amazing wingspans. He dazzled his eyes with the brightness of the blue, tears streaming down his cheeks as he clung to those warm feather walls. Who knew there was this kind of ridiculous beauty, just a quarter mile above the mine? He thought of his men, his favorites, fifty-five stories below in darkness, taking chunks out of the earth so that people could decorate their wrists and necks and ankles and fingers.

51 He had to tell them. He had to bring them there, one by one, up to the sky. He wanted them to feel how he felt, to see the birds in such detail, the flash of beaks; he wanted them to breathe in the silver of this gourmet air. After another twenty glorious minutes, and a full rotational view, the elevator went down. The miner hopped out and waited at the gold elevator patiently, and when it opened, full of gold as always, he jumped in it and sank those ten floors. There were his friends, exactly as before, still in the black mining hole, still surrounded by nuggets of gold, a couple of them eating those premade

Please note that excerpts and passages in the StudySync® library and this workbook are intended as touchstones to generate interest in an author's work. The excerpts and passages do not substitute for the reading of entire texts, and StudySync® strongly recommends that students seek out and purchase the whole literary or informational work in order to experience it as the author intended. Links to online resellers are available in our digital library. In addition, complete works may be ordered through an authorized reseller by filling out and returning to StudySync® the order form enclosed in this workbook.

Reading & Writing Companion   735

salami sandwiches bought from the miners' restaurant deeper inside the cave. They looked a little surprised to see their adventurous friend again.

52 "Come with me," said the miner. "You'll never guess how incredible it is. You will never guess what is up there."

53 They all wanted to know before they came. The miner wouldn't tell. All he said was how beautiful it was. He couldn't stop babbling. "Come up," he said, wiping his eyes.

54 No one wanted to.

55 "It's cold up there," said one.

56 "I'm beat," said another miner, curling up in his space on the floor with his gold-dusted pillow and book.

57 "It's incredible," said the adventurous miner. "I must show you. Come with me. Come now."

58 "Tell us," said the other miners. "Then maybe."

59 So the adventurous miner sat down and told of the forest smell of dampness and the crisp air and photosynthesis, and then he told of the feather elevator and the ascent into the sky and the air again, how it was singing air like they'd never breathed before, how the birds' wings were so close he could've touched one with a careful finger and how the feathers would remind them what the word *soft* meant.

60 They listened and nodded but after all that, only one other miner said he felt like going right then. The others had plans to play poker, seven card stud. They said they liked the description and thanked him but explained that they wanted to get a good night's sleep after the game. The miner went and shook them by the shoulders but they still said no, hey, really, thanks anyway. He banged his fist on the rocky wall, which drew blood, but the poker dealer still began shuffling, and the players divvied up the chips, carefully cut from the wall, and after a few more stunned minutes he took the younger fellow with him in the elevator, ten floors up, into the lobby.

61 "You're the only smart one in there," he said, blotting his bloody fist on his pant leg.

62 "I'm real bad at poker," admitted the younger man.

63 Both miners were relieved by the cool night light that was filling the lobby now that the sun was down. The miner wanted to show his friend everything

but he wanted to go to the best part first and so they went straight to the feather elevator and the doors opened and they stepped inside. As soon as their feet were in, the doors shut and it began to rise again, forty-five floors up. The miners held on to each others' shoulders.

64   "I believe I'm afraid of heights," the younger one said.

65   The adventurous miner squeezed the shoulder of his friend. "It's worth it," he said.

66   The elevator smelled of birdseed. The miner put his cheek close to the feathers. The younger miner was starting to hyperventilate from the endless rising and rising, when, finally, the elevator steadied to a stop.

67   "Ready?" said the first.

68   His friend nodded weakly, holding his stomach. The doors opened.

69   The sky was nearly black by now, with stars poking out in tiny white glittering dots. The moon gleamed at half. The adventurous miner had not seen night in those same twenty years. His whole skin bumped up. He felt he should bow but he didn't want to lower his head; he wanted to keep looking and breathing and looking.

70   After a few minutes, he glanced at his younger friend, jittery with the nervousness that comes from sharing something deeply precious. The air was filling him up. He was tempted to try to fly.

71   "Well," he said, unable to keep his voice casual. "So what do you think?"

72   His friend was scratching his head. His breathing had regulated but he looked puzzled.

73   "But it's just like the cave," he said then, pointing to the stars. "Just a whole lot bigger, and it has silver, not gold. I wouldn't want to be a miner here," he said. "It would take such a long long shovel."

74   The adventurous miner was taking so many deep breaths he was starting to get dizzy himself.

75   "It's no cave," he said. "Don't say that."

76   His friend shrugged. "Looks just like the cave to me," he said. "Doesn't feel high at all." He sat at the edge of the box and dangled his legs. The miner crossed his arms. When he spoke, his voice trembled. "I'm showing you the

whole night sky," he said, eyes filling, "and all you have to say for it is that it looks like the cave?"

77   The younger miner didn't look around. The elevator was rotating, very slowly.

78   "See," he said, pointing. "If we got that thing," he said, pointing at the moon which was just coming into their frame of vision, "that would fill up the elevator in one day. Now that would be an easy day."

79   The older miner's head was spinning. He thought quite honestly of pushing the man off the elevator with his foot, kicking him into the air, this man he had spent the last twenty years working with, side by side, gone, in a slim fall.

80   Two swans flew by, bodies lit like opals[4] against the moonlight. The older miner watched their long wings and started to cry.

81   "I've spent my whole life down there," he said.

82   The other man was asleep. When they descended, the miner lugged him out of the feather elevator and stuffed him back in the gold one. The doors shut and down he went. But he himself stayed in the lobby. He slept a long night there on the tiled floor, face pressed to the glass, knees pulled in, a heavy spool unravelling in his chest. He woke only once, in the middle of the night, to notice the swan settled next to him, wings tucked up.

* * *

83   The cloud nestled close to its father. By this point it was confused. It had taken so many trips with the swan down the elevator that it thought it belonged on the ground as well, and spent hours floating one inch above dirt level, **amiable** beside its paternal line.

84   That night it slept beside the man and the bird: buoyant, earthbound.

85   The swan woke up, slightly nervous, because his child was thinning and dissipating and no longer had the robust look of a healthy cloud; his child now looked vague and closer to the curtainy veil of stratus than its usual bouncy alto cumulus self.

86   "Child," he said in the middle of the night, in a low voice so as not to wake the sleeping man next to him with the glowing face, "I think you should go back up and stay there for a while. You belong higher in the atmosphere. I will look at you from down here with such pride and joy," he said.

---

4. **opals** gemstones showing many small points of shifting color against a pale or dark hue

87 The cloud didn't talk but moved one inch closer to the swan's side.

88 The swan repeated himself. The cloud moved closer. The swan stood and took the cloud up with him back to the forty-fifth floor and there they looked out to the world at sunrise, turning lighter and more colorful with each minute, each shade emerging from the darkness, blue first, then green, red last and brightest of all. Applause. The swan asked the cloud to go back out into the air. The cloud didn't move. The swan tried to shove it out, but it is impossible to shove a cloud.

89 Finally they took the elevator back down, forty-five stories. The cloud was spreading into a fog now. The swan picked at the feathers around his breastbone. It was still early morning and the glowing miner was asleep, still glowing. There was a knock on the glass of the lobby and the swan saw his wife, the bluebird. She skipped inside, kissed the vast area of her firstborn, and told her husband she'd laid another egg.

90 The swan blinked, surprised. She said this egg was different—very large and pale green. "What do you think it'll be?" he asked the bluebird nervously, tendrils of cloud swirling on his back. She shrugged her little winged shoulders. "A bird?" she said.

* * *

91 In the morning, all the letters had blown away except one with a return address that read: *King and Queen* on the first line and *Palace* on the second. The logger, still tired and ill, cleared his eyes, and opened the letter. On gold-embossed stationery, it read:

92 *Dear Citizen:*

93 *I am pleased to say you have been selected to be one of the palace courtiers. Please show up at work on Tuesday at eight am sharp and you need not bring anything except this letter, in fact, please don't.*

94 The logger held the letter to his nose. It smelled like flowers and, when he looked closer, he saw that the paper itself was made from hammered-down gardenias, dried into paper stiffness, the smell still caught inside in an olfactory photograph.

95 So the logger showed up on Tuesday at the palace door, which was huge and had no handles, and when he was ushered in he said he was a new courtier and they asked to see the letter and he showed it and then everyone nodded solemnly. "Welcome," said the man with the voice so deep it reverberated in the logger's ribcage. They tried to take away his axe. He

refused. "Sometimes," he explained, "I need to cut things down." They murmured for a while and checked with several levels of authority and then said okay. "But if you get *anywhere* near the king or queen's neck with that," they said, in unison, "we will bomb you to oblivion."

96   The logger nodded, meekly.

97   They sent him to the kitchen to make turtle soup. The kitchen was a huge brassy room with hanging copper pots and pans and piles of white linen tablecloths and a chef with a curling red mustache. The logger was placed at the stove, near a line of sleeping turtles. His job was to pick up each turtle and stick it into a cauldron of boiling water, because the king had requested turtle soup. As might be expected, the logger could not do it. The minute he put the first sleeping turtle in the water and thought he heard a squeak of death so sharp it made his blood curdle into sleet, he fell down, axe and all, and the one turtle boiled and the chef's assistants had to leave their chopping to the chef's annoyance and take the new guy down to the infirmary. There, the nurses were doves and fluttered around, checking his temperature.

98   "I can do no job," the logger said to the air. "I can touch nothing."

99   The doves, eleven in total, nestled into his neck, cooing and soft as breasts, a curved warmth against his carotid artery. He slept like that, and when he woke up he felt much better, renewed, and he sent a prayer up to the dead turtle and his heart seemed to be working steadily, but when he swung his legs out of bed and got ready to go back into the world to find his ever-elusive fate, he discovered that his axe had disappeared.

100   And all the doves were gone. The infirmary was empty. It was perfectly clean and organized and tidy but nothing alive except for him was in it.

101   He busted out the infirmary door into the hallway.

102   "Excuse me?" he said. "Nurse?"

103   The hallway was silent. The carpet was a rich purple and the candles hanging from the walls were dripping elongated beaded tiers of ivory wax.

104   The logger began to panic.

105   He spied a purple-carpeted stairway at the end of the hall and rushed up several flights until he reached a door embossed with gold and he didn't even read the lettering but just charged right on through. These were the chambers of the royal barber, and, inside, the king was sitting on a white chair, covered in a white apron, having his white hair cut.

106   "Have you seen my axe?" cried the logger.

107   The king looked embarrassed. The barber's scissors glinted in the light, encrusted with sapphires. On the floor in the distance the logger spotted a couple of fat rats.

108   "Who is this?" the king asked his nearby courtiers. "You know I don't like to be watched by strangers when my hair is being cut."

109   They had no idea who it was.

110   "I was in the infirmary," said the logger. "Have you seen the doves? I was a courtier for an hour," he said. "But I couldn't cook the turtles for the turtle soup. I need my axe. Where are those doves?"

111   The courtiers, in a group, shrugged. The one with the severe eyebrows looked guiltily at the logger because she knew those doves tended to cause a fair amount of trouble at the infirmary. They were great nurses in daylight but at night seemed to have a problem with kleptomania. She explained this to the logger whose face blanched paler each minute.

112   "Where can I find them?" he said.

113   "They do enjoy riding that feather elevator?" she said.

114   The king, patient up until now because the barber had been cutting some bangs, opened his mouth and ordered the young man out. "Just for that," he bellowed, "I would like MORE turtle soup tonight. Vats and vats of turtle soup!" He was in a bad mood. His wife's good friend the swan had been gone for weeks and she was moody and he couldn't comfort her, and now the barber had just cut one side of his hair too short; the barber'd been distracted by starting to tell his own story of being in the infirmary and getting his fingernail stolen by the doves, so daintily he had not even noticed until he raised his finger up to nibble on the nail and found there was nothing there but skin.

115   "It was very gross," he said now.

116   But no one was listening. The logger was being shoved out by the courtiers through the front door of the palace into the daytime. There, he faced the kingdom for the first time without his axe. He felt small, and odd. He walked, both arms free, all the way to the glass lobby, and stood trembling by the third elevator.

117   There was no button, so he just waited. Everything around him seemed dizzyingly tall. The outside doors of the elevator smelled musty and the feathers were graying.

Please note that excerpts and passages in the StudySync® library and this workbook are intended as touchstones to generate interest in an author's work. The excerpts and passages do not substitute for the reading of entire texts, and StudySync® strongly recommends that students seek out and purchase the whole literary or informational work in order to experience it as the author intended. Links to online resellers are available in our digital library. In addition, complete works may be ordered through an authorized reseller by filling out and returning to StudySync® the order form enclosed in this workbook.

Reading & Writing
Companion

741

118 Within a minute, the doors opened.

119 Inside he found a big white swan and a dirty man from the mine standing solemnly together inside a veil of fog.

* * *

120 Three sets of blinks: logger blink, miner blink, swan blink.

121 Clouds don't blink.

122 "Oh it's you," said the miner at last. "We met in the mine. I was wondering when I'd bump into you up here."

123 The logger nodded. He was staring at the miner who he didn't recognize— the man's face was radiant, trumpets and playing sad marches beneath his skin. He had not seen a single man who looked like that in the mine, and he would've remembered.

124 "I'm looking for my axe," he said. "Seen any doves around here?"

125 The miner didn't respond. Next to him, the swan was trying to pull part of the thinning bluish fog onto its back.

126 "Come on, honey," he said. "Come on."

127 The miner tried to pick up the fog and put it on the swan's back but his hands went straight through, useless. He turned back to the logger.

128 "This elevator appears to be broken," he said. "Are you a repairman?"

129 "No," said the logger.

130 "Can you be a repairman?"

131 "No," said the logger. "All I do is chop things down. I'm the exact opposite of a repairman."

132 "Well, we need to get this cloud back to the sky," said the swan. "It's of **dire** importance. It's too thin to sit on my back anymore so I can't fly it up.

133 "Come on my back," the swan said again, to the fog. "Come on, baby."

134 "That's no cloud," said the logger, and the swan hung his neck in shame.

135 The miner glared. "Can't you see," he said, "that's not very helpful."

136   The logger stepped into the elevator. "You sure you haven't seen any doves?" he asked again.

137   The swan began whispering to the walls of the elevator in bird language, the words mysteriously lengthened and choppy at the same time, and the elevator seemed to creak and listen, but its doors did not shut and nothing moved upward. The cloud was so thin now it filled the whole elevator, filling the air with a blue-whiteness that made it hard to see, like living in the interior of a pearl. Only the swan's black beaded eyes shone through, wet and glassy and wretched with guilt.

138   The three of them stood there, waiting for something to happen. The logger kept flexing his hands. The miner's eyes were closed, remembering.

139   The cloud's vagueness began moving into the lobby itself now.

140   "Shut the lobby doors," ordered the swan, "Hurry! We can't let it get any thinner than the size of the lobby."

141   The miner ran to the glass doors on either end and shut both firmly. Off cue, the bark elevator opened and released a few logs on the ground, like an awkward phrase spoken out of turn at a party by a guest no one is listening to.

142   "I need my axe!" the logger cried out. The agitation was growing in his palms.

143   The swan was weeping openly now, his child the size of the whole lobby.

144   The miner picked up a log and leaned his nose into the wood, breathing in, the smell elemental. "Hey," he said to the logger. "Those doves did come by," he said. "They had an axe, a watch, some gold nuggets, I think a tiny mink coat. Anyway, they flew by, but when they saw the elevator was broken, they left to go somewhere else."

145   The logger's jaw dropped. "You saw the doves?" he said.

146   "This was hours ago," said the miner. "They're long gone."

147   "They had my axe?" said the logger.

148   "And some fur. And gold," said the miner. "And a watch. They're set for a while, those doves."

149   The logger's heart sank like a rock. The swan stepped out of the elevator, neck low and broken as an old daisy stem, and now that all three were out of

it, standing in the lobby, covered in mist and fog, the feather elevator doors closed with a whir, and it began its rise up.

150 "No! Wait!" cried the swan, but it was too late. The feather elevator was already ascending, the box replaced by a pole in their line of vision.

* * *

151 The elevator stayed up for ten hours and the swan would not let the miner or the logger leave the lobby through the side doors because he didn't want his cloud child to dissipate further.

152 "We're stuck here forever," said the swan. "I'm sorry to have to tell you both that, but if you try to leave, I will peck out your eyes."

153 The logger stared at the pole of the feather elevator.

154 The miner wanted to go back to the sky.

155 The logger suggested he take the other elevators out, but the miner didn't want to.

156 "I'm waiting for that," he said, pointing up.

157 The logger didn't know where to go. He could not go back down to the mine where they hated him or to the forest where he was a shame on his father's name. So he sat down. The swan was smoothing down his feathers, one at a time. The fog was still thick enough to make the logger sleepy, so he curled up on the hard tile and closed his eyes.

* * *

158 Come morning, outside the lobby, the bluebird tapped her beak against the glass.

159 "Our egg opened!" she cried out.

160 The swan woke up, chilled from the fog, and pressed his beak against the glass, where it made a triangular smear mark.

161 His eyes were bright and shining, desperate.

162 "Is it alive?" he asked.

163 She nodded, vigorously.

164 "Very," she said through the glass. "It's a lake. A big deep blue one. I floated around on it all evening waiting for you. You should've seen it pour straight out of the shell, for minutes and minutes and minutes, so much water in that one little shell, and then it knew just what to do, how to settle itself."

165 She glimpsed past her husband's great wings.

166 "What are you doing holding our firstborn hostage like that?" she asked.

167 "We had a lake?" he said.

168 She laughed. Her wing feathers were damp. "Let the poor cloud out!" she said. "Poor thing has been cooped up all night! How I love a good cool fog."

169 She hopped over to the lobby door and with some difficulty opened it herself. Within seconds, the fog swooshed out into the air, wrapping around the trunks of trees like cotton, exiting grandly.

170 The swan felt his heart contract then expand, palpitate then release, and with his head and neck a question mark, he left the sleeping miner and the sleeping logger and went to where the nest was. Sure enough, right by the bundle of indented twigs, there was now a small lake with a pretty shore and all sorts of bugs treading the surface. A graceful sapling grew by the side. There was a hint of dampness in the air. The swan stood close to his wife, white feathers melding with her blue ones into a makeshift sky of their own.

171 "Welcome to our family," the swan said meekly. Water lapped over his feet.

* * *

172 After an hour, the logger and miner woke up in the lobby, doors wide open, swan gone, the sunlight bright and shining and hot, the fog cleared. The miner squinted. The feather elevator was back down, its door open also. He went right inside. The doors began closing but he put his foot in the crucial area that stops the close of every elevator and called to the just-waking logger to join him.

173 The logger shook his head.

174 The miner just smiled. "You have something better to do?" he asked.

175 So the logger, bleary from a night of bad dreams, stepped forward, and the two men stood in the elevator. To the miner's purest joy, the doors closed and the elevator rose high, higher, highest, up those forty-five stories.

176 The logger wiped his eyes clean of sleep and said, "I don't know what—"

Please note that excerpts and passages in the StudySync® library and this workbook are intended as touchstones to generate interest in an author's work. The excerpts and passages do not substitute for the reading of entire texts, and StudySync® strongly recommends that students seek out and purchase the whole literary or informational work in order to experience it as the author intended. Links to online resellers are available in our digital library. In addition, complete works may be ordered through an authorized reseller by filling out and returning to StudySync® the order form enclosed in this workbook.

Reading & Writing
Companion

745

177 And the miner said: "This."

178 As if they had heard, the feather elevator doors opened. It was a bright warm spring morning and far below they could see the new sparkling lake that the white swan and blue bluebird swam upon. The forest spread out in a green blanket. The castle glittered in the distance like a wedding cake.

179 "Everything I need," said the miner, sweeping his hand out.

180 The logger's heart was failing. He took a deep breath and looked down. The miner was saying something about the approaching rise of the sun. The logger didn't listen and flung himself out the door of the elevator into the air.

* * *

181 The fall was fast and cold, with blur and clarity both, everything a sheet downward while he saw in detail the flying birds, then the treetops, then the red roofs of houses, then doors, then roots, and he fell like a stone and was certain to die if something of a wind hadn't held and pushed him enough to the right, landing him in the middle of the small newborn lake that was occupied by one swan, one bluebird, and a thousand spinning insects.

182 He fell and struck through, and the water was like glass, but still it broke beneath him and so then he did not have to break.

* * *

183 The miner watched with horror up in his elevator, side by side, gone in a slim fall. He saw the water crash up around the logger's weight, then the swan and bluebird pull the logger from the water, cover him with leaves, and put cloaks of feathers over his brittle body.

184 The bluebird brought him leaf after leaf until he was blanketed. The lake resettled agreeably and returned to mirror. The swan smoothed the logger's forehead, which was heavy with pain, and found the logger to be so agitated that he went to see his old friend the queen. The queen was terribly glad to see her old friend the swan, and they sat in the palace garden while ladybugs flew off the bushes and landed on their faces and backs.

185 "He has nothing to do," said the swan, eating a ladybug. "He feels he has no purpose."

186 The queen took a sip of her turtle tea. "Perhaps," she said, "I can find a job for him," she said. "I'll look into it. And how is your first-born?"

187 The swan hung his head. "I may have chased him off for good," he said.

188   The queen patted the swan's noble skull under those smooth white feathers. She offered her friend a mug of hedge tea. The swan stuck his black beak inside the narrow mouth of the porcelain and drank down the strange dark liquid herbs.

* * *

189   The bluebird called the logger her third child, delivered from the air, from that feather egg cracking open in the sky. "I always wanted three," she told him, nodding.

190   "I want my axe," the logger said, curled up on the ground.

191   The bluebird blinked and brushed his cheek gently with the tip of her wing.

* * *

192   There was now a search party for the missing miner. A couple of men with bags under their eyes and a pasty look were snooping around the lobby looking for him. "He's up there," said the swan, on the way back from his visit with the queen. He pointed with his wing. "Where?" they said, and the swan pointed again, to the small gray box in the sky that was the feather elevator. "Well, we need him downstairs," shouted the men. "No one's as good a worker as he is!"

193   "I won't come down!" yelled the miner, from forty-five stories up. "I will never go back in that mine!"

194   "It's your JOB," called the miners, "we need you! Productivity has plummeted."

195   "Never!" shouted the miner from forty-five stories up. The elevator stood firm in its post above the trees.

196   "It's an order," mumbled the miners.

197   Neither one of them was really breathing in the air or noticing the trees, but one did have a shovel and began chopping at the pole that held up that feather elevator. The shovel was not a sharp blade but he kept hacking away because he was a miner, after all, and used to repetitive movement.

198   Ten minutes away, sitting on the edge of the lake, the sound of chipping metal pricked up the logger's ears. He stumbled to the lobby and found the two miners crouched at the feather elevator pole, chopping away.

199   "You can't do that," he murmured. "You have to leave him there. He's found his calling in the world: air. His calling is air."

Copyright © BookheadEd Learning, LLC

NOTES

200 His voice was meek and tentative, and his legs wobbly, still, from the fall. The other miners ignored him, as he stood there in the lobby, quivering, watching these two men as they chopped, with hideous form, he had to admit, making ineffective dents in the pole. And while he was standing there, right on time, the two other elevators opened and released their goods at the exact same moment. He himself had never seen that before.

201 The metal and timber collectors hadn't arrived yet, and there he was, standing among the two piles.

202 Metal and wood were two ingredients necessary to make the one thing he needed most in the world. He stooped down at the elevator doors, and slowly, with a heavy feeling in his chest, picked up four nuggets of gold and a nice hard oak log. He left the chipping miner jerks and ran with the gold and wood over to the workshop where loggers made their tools. There he spent the whole day, working as fast and neatly as he could, his hand muscles remembering the lessons he had learned as a young boy, fingers flying over the sanding machine, the metal cutter, the blowtorch, the saw, making the best alloy of gold and steel, the best handle of oak and elm, sweating until he'd built a brand new axe, glowing with a golden blade, the handle as smooth as a pebble on the beach. The sun was about to set, and he hoisted it over his shoulder and marched back to the men chopping at the feather elevator.

203 "Stop!" he said loudly.

204 By now, the miners had eaten away at about a fourth of the pole, with messy choppy bites from the shovel. It was starting to affect the balance and the pole swayed just the slightest bit in the breeze.

205 They eyed the glittering axe in the logger's hands. He looked exactly right holding it.

206 "Or what," they said nervously.

207 "Or I'll chop off your heads," said the logger.

208 And he meant it. He didn't really want to chop off any heads, or well, he kind of did, but he kind of didn't, and mostly he wanted to make sure that the adventurous miner would stay put in the sky for as long as he damn well pleased.

209 The other miners put their shovels down.

210 "But we need him in the mine," they whined.

211 "Too bad," said the logger, and the two men stood there for a moment, deciding, and then slunk back down with the gold elevator, shoulders low.

212 The logger was so excited to have an axe again, he went around town and chopped down a mess of stuff, including someone's birdhouse and another person's lamplight. The new blade was even better than his last, this one so sharp from the steel and also so beautiful in the various lights of day—honey gold at sunset, brassy gold at noon, lemon gold at dawn.

213 When he came home that evening, he found the miner shimmying down the elevator pole.

214 "I got hungry," the miner said, once on the ground, gingerly touching the raw insides of his arms.

215 "They want you back," said the logger.

216 The miner shook his head and walked over to the lake where he found the swan and bluebird tucked into each other, floating.

217 "I'm leaving," he said, bowing slightly. "I want to thank you all very much for your tremendous friendship and kindness."

218 The bluebird and the swan swam to the shore, and the miner walked over and gave each a hug: the sweet chirping bluebird, the warm soft feathers of the swan, the stalwart tall logger. Everyone's eyes misted for a minute. Then the miner took off down the lane, a lift in his step, whistling melodic melodies, humming in minor miner keys.

* * *

219 Word got out about the man with the axe made of strong gold, and after a day or so, the king and queen asked the logger if he would please finish the job and chop down that feather elevator, as it had not come down since the other miners had bit at its core and was now a problem with air traffic control. Now that the miner was gone, the logger set to it, and his shoulders and wrists were in bliss, immediately. The act of chopping made him feel so right and the elevator creaked and he knew just the angle to make a quiet fall, a slow— Tim-ber!— over a period of minutes. He ate at that metal pole until it began to creak and sway and at last dipped down, elegant, lying on the ground like a felled column of smoke. Then he removed the feather box from its pole and brought it to the castle, a room of feathers to sit in for those who needed a little special peace and quiet. The queen liked to sit in the feather box very much, as it reminded him of the friend she missed, who smelled exactly like it.

NOTES

220   The other two elevators kept operating on schedule, with an empty space where the third had been. Some birds set up a nest in there.

221   The logger was appointed Earl of Down.

* * *

222   In the evenings, after he'd done his duty chopping down items for the palace, the logger walked to the lake, swinging his golden axe over his shoulder, and spent time with the swan and the bluebird. A few weeks or so after the cutting down of the third elevator, the three friends sat around by the lakeshore, watching the spinning bugs make the smallest circles, missing the miner. It was almost twilight, and the air grew moist with night.

223   "I bet he went to the ocean," said the swan. "He said he wanted to see something big."

224   The logger nodded. He liked to think of that miner, walking and whistling and breathing the air. He took a leaf off the ground and began polishing the gold blade of his axe until it nearly bent under the warmth in his hands.

225   The swan smoothed the feathers in his wings.

226   The bluebird preened herself by the shores of the lake. "Oh look, look," she said, whispering into the water. "Isn't this lovely. Here's your brother now."

227   And from the west, like a long slow breath, the fog was rolling in.

Aimee Bender is the author of the story collections *The Girl in the Flammable Skirt* and *Willful Creatures* and the novels *An Invisible Sign of My Own* and *The Particular Sadness of Lemon Cake.*

First Read

Read "The Third Elevator." After you read, complete the Think Questions below.

☁ THINK QUESTIONS

1. What is "troublesome" about the main logger in the story? Cite specific details to help explain why the logger is seen this way. What is the source of his "troublesome" nature?

2. How does the young miner react when the adventurous miner brings him to the world above ground? Cite evidence from the story illustrating how the young miner feels about the new things he is seeing and experiencing.

3. What is unique about the two eggs that the bluebird hatched? In two to three sentences, use the text to describe what was in the eggs. What might have caused the contents of these eggs to be so different from normal eggs?

4. The other loggers believe that the "troublesome" logger is being **melodramatic**. Based on his behavior, what do you think the word *melodramatic* means? Write your best definition of the word here and explain how you arrived at its meaning.

5. The word **claustrophobia** combines the Latin word *claustrum,* meaning "barrier," and the Greek word *phobos,* meaning "fear." Use this information to determine the meaning of *claustrophobia* in paragraphs 35 and 46. Write your best definition here and explain how you figured it out.

Please note that excerpts and passages in the StudySync® library and this workbook are intended as touchstones to generate interest in an author's work. The excerpts and passages do not substitute for the reading of entire texts, and StudySync® strongly recommends that students seek out and purchase the whole literary or informational work in order to experience it as the author intended. Links to online resellers are available in our digital library. In addition, complete works may be ordered through an authorized reseller by filling out and returning to StudySync® the order form enclosed in this workbook.

Reading & Writing Companion   **751**

Skill:
Character

Use the Checklist to analyze Character in "The Third Elevator." Refer to the sample student annotations about Character in the text.

••• CHECKLIST FOR CHARACTER

In order to determine how particular elements of a story or drama interact, note the following:

✓ the characters in the story, including the protagonist and antagonist

✓ the settings and how they shape the characters or plot

✓ plot events and how they affect the characters

✓ key events or a series of episodes in the plot, especially events that cause characters to react, respond, or change in some way

✓ characters' responses as the plot reaches a climax and moves toward a resolution of the problem facing the protagonist

✓ the resolution of the conflict in the plot and the ways that resolution affects each character

To analyze how particular elements of a story or drama interact, consider the following questions:

✓ How do the characters' responses change or develop from the beginning to the end of the story?

✓ How does the setting shape the characters and plot in the story?

✓ How do the events in the plot affect the characters? How do characters develop as a result of the conflict, climax, and resolution?

✓ Do the characters' problems reach a resolution? How?

✓ How does the resolution affect the characters?

Skill:
Character

Reread paragraphs 45–47 of "The Third Elevator." Then, using the Checklist on the previous page, answer the multiple-choice questions below.

↻ YOUR TURN

1. Based on the description of the miner in paragraph 45, the reader can conclude that —

   - ○ A. the miner is lazy and wants to ride in the elevator.
   - ○ B. the miner is curious to see what is above ground.
   - ○ C. the miner is tired of getting passed over for promotions.
   - ○ D. the miner is very satisfied with his job as a miner.

2. This question has two parts. First, answer Part A. Then, answer Part B.

   Part A: What do the miner's thoughts and actions in paragraph 46 reveal about him?

   - ○ A. He is confident about taking the gold elevator.
   - ○ B. He is frustrated with the other miners on his team.
   - ○ C. He is anxious to breathe fresh air again.
   - ○ D. He is confused about the logger's whereabouts.

   Part B: Which of the following details best supports your response to Part A?

   - ○ A. "One of the miners, who regularly filled up the gold elevator and was considered one of the best workers, had watched the logger go up the elevator with curiosity and envy."
   - ○ B. "He hadn't known a person could take that trip."
   - ○ C. "So, a few hours after the logger had left, the miner told his workmates that he was going to follow that logger and get in the elevator when half the load was full because he had to see the top of the earth again or he was going to die of claustrophobia of the lungs."
   - ○ D. "The miners were a supportive team, because they had to be or they'd all be dead, and so they let him hop inside the gold elevator right before it went up, watching the doors close over his nervous face, cheeks reflecting the piles of metal as if he'd been working for years in sunshine."

Close Read

Reread "The Third Elevator." As you reread, complete the Skills Focus questions below. Then use your answers and annotations from the questions to help you complete the Write activity.

◎ SKILLS FOCUS

1. Identify figurative language that helps develop the swan's personality in the beginning of "The Third Elevator." Explain how that language helps you to understand his behavior with his first child later in the story.

2. Recall that in an omniscient point of view, the narrator reveals thoughts and feelings. In a limited point point of view, a narrator does not refer to thoughts and feelings but describes only what can be heard or seen. Identify evidence of the point of view used to describe the main logger, and explain how this point of view develops the reader's understanding of the story.

3. Identify evidence of the bluebird's behavior in the story, and explain how it influences the other characters.

4. The miner and logger are both looking for a place where they belong. Identify examples of the theme of belonging in the text, and explain what the author has to say about this theme.

5. Myths and folktales often include talking animals that help to express the author's ideas. Identify examples of this element in the story, and explain why this element is still relevant to help express an important idea in the text.

✎ WRITE

LITERARY ANALYSIS: Identify a theme or lesson in this text about family, friendship, or a sense of belonging. How do characters' actions and the author's use of fantasy develop this important idea about real life? Remember to use evidence from the text to support and explain your response.

Perseus

POETRY
Robert Hayden
1966

Introduction

Widely acclaimed for his poetry about the black historical experience, Robert Hayden (1913–1980) was the first African American to serve as Consultant in Poetry to the Library of Congress. Here, Hayden offers a new perspective on the Greek mythical hero Perseus. Gazing down on the severed head of Medusa, the snake-haired Gorgon, Perseus has a moment of self-reflection and acknowledges his powerful and dangerous "thirst . . . to destroy."

"I struck. The shield flashed bare."

Skill:
Connotation
and Denotation

*The description refers
to the snakes on
Medusa's head. The
word serpents means
"snakes," which has a
neutral connotation.
Serpents, however, has
strong negative
connotations—it is
associated with
monsters and evil.*

1 Her sleeping head with its great **gelid** mass
2 of serpents **torpidly** astir[1]
3 burned into the mirroring shield—
4 a **scathing** image **dire**
5 as hated truth the mind accepts at last
6 and **festers** on.
7 I struck. The shield flashed bare.

8 Yet even as I lifted up the head
9 and started from that place
10 of gazing silences and terrored stone,
11 I thirsted to destroy.
12 None could have passed me then—
13 no garland-bearing girl, no priest
14 or staring boy—and lived.

"Perseus." Copyright ©1966 by Robert Hayden, from COLLECTED POEMS
OF ROBERT HAYDEN by Robert Hayden, edited by Frederick Glaysher.
Copyright ©1985 by Emma Hayden. Used by permission of Liveright
Publishing Corporation.

---

1. **astir** moving about, usually excitedly; active

First Read

Read "Perseus." After you read, complete the Think Questions below.

☁ **THINK QUESTIONS**

1. What does line 10 tell you about the setting of Medusa's resting place? Explain, using evidence from the text to support your answer.

2. How is Perseus able to behead the snake-haired Medusa without turning to "terrored stone"? Cite textual evidence to support your answer.

3. After Perseus kills Medusa, what "hated truth" does he acknowledge about himself? Cite textual evidence to support your answer.

4. Use context clues to determine the meaning of **gelid** as it is used in line 1 of "Perseus." Write your definition here, and identify clues that helped you figure out the meaning. Then check the meaning in a dictionary.

5. Find the word **torpidly** in line 2 of "Perseus." Use context clues in the surrounding lines, as well as the stanza in which the word appears, to determine the word's meaning. Write your definition here and identify clues that helped you figure out its meaning.

Please note that excerpts and passages in the StudySync® library and this workbook are intended as touchstones to generate interest in an author's work. The excerpts and passages do not substitute for the reading of entire texts, and StudySync® strongly recommends that students seek out and purchase the whole literary or informational work in order to experience it as the author intended. Links to online resellers are available in our digital library. In addition, complete works may be ordered through an authorized reseller by filling out and returning to StudySync® the order form enclosed in this workbook.

Reading & Writing Companion   **757**

Skill:
Connotation and Denotation

Use the Checklist to analyze Connotation and Denotation in "Perseus." Refer to the sample student annotations about Connotation and Denotation in the text.

••• CHECKLIST FOR CONNOTATION AND DENOTATION

In order to identify the connotative meanings of words and phrases, use the following steps:

✓ first, note unfamiliar words and phrases; key words used to describe important characters, events, and ideas; or words that inspire an emotional reaction

✓ next, determine and note the denotative meaning of words by consulting reference materials such as a dictionary, glossary, or thesaurus

To better understand the meaning of words and phrases as they are used in a text, including connotative meanings, use the following questions:

✓ What is the genre or subject of the text? How does that affect the possible meaning of a word or phrase?

✓ Does the word create a positive, negative, or neutral emotion?

✓ What synonyms or alternative phrasing help you describe the connotative meaning of the word?

To determine the meaning of words and phrases as they are used in a text, including connotative meanings, use the following questions:

✓ What is the meaning of the word or phrase? What is the connotation as well as the denotation?

✓ If I substitute a synonym based on denotation, is the meaning the same? How does it change the meaning of the text?

Skill:
Connotation and Denotation

Reread the second stanza (lines 8–14) of "Perseus." Then, using the Checklist on the previous page, answer the multiple-choice questions below.

⟳ YOUR TURN

1. This question has two parts. First, answer Part A. Then, answer Part B.

   Part A: Which answer best describes the connotation of the word *thirsted*?

   ○ A. hate with the whole heart
   ○ B. be trembling with fear
   ○ C. want badly or crave
   ○ D. want to drink

   Part B: Which textual evidence best supports your answer to Part A?

   ○ A. None could have passed me then . . . and lived.
   ○ B. no garland-bearing girl, no priest / or staring boy
   ○ C. from that place / of gazing silences and terrored stone
   ○ D. Yet even as I lifted up the head / and started from that place

2. This question has two parts. First, answer Part A. Then, answer Part B.

   Part A: In line 13 of "Perseus," how does the phrase "garland-bearing girl" help the reader to understand Perseus's mood?

   ○ A. A "garland-bearing girl" connotes that Perseus would harm someone who is playful.
   ○ B. A "garland-bearing girl" connotes that Perseus would harm someone who is quiet.
   ○ C. A "garland-bearing girl" connotes that Perseus would harm someone who is peaceful and nonthreatening.
   ○ D. A "garland-bearing girl" connotes that Perseus hates flowers.

   Part B: Which lines from the poem best support your answer to Part A?

   ○ A. lines 4 and 5
   ○ B. lines 6 and 7
   ○ C. lines 1 and 2
   ○ D. lines 1–3

Close Read

Reread "Perseus." As you reread, complete the Skills Focus questions below. Then use your answers and annotations from the questions to help you complete the Write activity.

◎ SKILLS FOCUS

1. Use context clues to define the word *mass* as it is used in line 1 of the poem. Analyze why the poet uses this word rather than a synonym. What does this word's connotation suggest about Medusa?

2. What do you notice about the structure of the sentences that make up the first stanza? Explain how this structure impacts the tone of the stanza.

3. Explain the poet's use of the phrase "gazing silences" in line 10. Cite textual evidence by highlighting clues that explain its meaning, and make annotations to explore the connotations of the words.

4. How do the examples Perseus provides in lines 13 and 14 impact the meaning of what he is telling his audience at the end of the poem? How do they fit in with the poem's tone? Highlight and explain specific examples of words and phrases to support your thinking.

5. How are Perseus's experiences relevant to readers today? What lessons can be learned from Perseus's actions? How do they inform us? Support your ideas with textual evidence.

✏ WRITE

LITERARY ANALYSIS: "Perseus" shares with readers the inner struggle of a hero who finds that he is more like his enemy than he realized. How does the author's word choice show Perseus's inner conflict and the poem's meaning? How does the word choice impact the poem's tone? Write a short response answering these questions. Support your writing with specific examples of connotations of words and phrases from the text.

Extended
Writing
Project and
Grammar

EXTENDED
WRITING
PROJECT
RESEARCH WRITING

Research Writing Process: Plan

PLAN	DRAFT	REVISE	EDIT AND PUBLISH

Many of the fables, myths, and folktales that you have read include references to people, places, things, and events from different time periods and cultures. *Aesop's Fables* gives readers insight into ancient values. "The Classical Roots of 'The Hunger Games'" explains how *The Hunger Games* draws inspiration from female Amazon warriors, ancient gladiators, and the Latin language. A reader's curiosity could pull him or her into a variety of topics after reading such rich texts.

WRITING PROMPT

Consider the texts that you've read in this unit. What stories or ideas stood out to you? What topic would you like to know more about?

Identify a research topic and write a report about that topic using an informational text structure. In the process, you will learn how to select a research question, develop a research plan, gather and evaluate source materials, and synthesize and present your research findings. Regardless of which topic you choose, be sure your research paper includes the following:

- an introduction to the research question
- a clear thesis statement that informs the reader
- supporting details from credible sources
- a clear informational text structure
- a conclusion that wraps up your ideas
- a works cited page

Writing to Sources

As you gather ideas and information from the texts in the unit, be sure to:

- use evidence from multiple sources
- avoid overly relying on one source

Introduction to Research Writing

Research writing examines a topic and conveys ideas by citing and analyzing information from credible sources. Good research papers use textual evidence, including facts, statistics, examples, and details from reliable sources, to supply information about a topic and to support the analysis of complex ideas. They also can include relevant print and graphic features as well as multimedia. Research helps writers not only to discover and confirm facts, but also to draw new conclusions about a topic. The characteristics of research writing include:

- an introduction that presents information on your topic with a clear thesis statement
- relevant facts, supporting details, and quotations from credible sources
- analysis of the details to explain how they support the thesis statement
- a clear and logical informational text structure
- a formal style
- a conclusion that wraps up your ideas
- a works cited page

As you continue with this Extended Writing Project, you'll receive more instruction and practice in crafting each of the characteristics of research writing to create your own research paper.

Please note that excerpts and passages in the StudySync® library and this workbook are intended as touchstones to generate interest in an author's work. The excerpts and passages do not substitute for the reading of entire texts, and StudySync® strongly recommends that students seek out and purchase the whole literary or informational work in order to experience it as the author intended. Links to online resellers are available in our digital library. In addition, complete works may be ordered through an authorized reseller by filling out and returning to StudySync® the order form enclosed in this workbook.

Reading & Writing Companion

763

Before you get started on your own research paper, read this research paper that one student, Nicole, wrote in response to the writing prompt. As you read the Model, highlight and annotate the features of research writing that Nicole included in her research paper.

NOTES

≡ STUDENT MODEL

The Storyteller's Legacy

1   Henry Louis Gates, Jr., co-editor of the new anthology *The Annotated African American Folktales*, dedicates the volume to his three-year-old granddaughter. Gates hopes that the collection will help future generations feel as if the stories are as much theirs as they once were his (Siegel). Gates and his co-editor, Maria Tatar, are two links in a very long chain of storytellers who have worked to keep the oral tradition of storytelling alive. These two are not alone. Why is the oral tradition so important to African American culture? Oral tradition is extremely important in African American culture due to its history of preserving culture and legacy in Africa, in early America, and in modern times.

Storytelling Roots in Africa

2   Storytelling began as a way of preserving culture during a time before writing was common. In early Africa, few languages were written; literature was handed down orally. Griots, or storytellers, collected songs and stories as a way of protecting and sharing cultural values and customs. Without written records, these griots had to hold a culture's important information within their brains. Franklin and Moss note, "They kept in their memories the history, law, and traditions of their people and were themselves living dictionaries" (28). As such, storytellers were valuable and honored members of the community.

3   The oral tradition affected every part of Africans' lives. For these early societies, speech was more than a means of communication. It was power. Janice D. Hamlet explains, "The Africans believed in Nommo, which means the generative power of the spoken word. Nommo was believed necessary to actualize life and give man mastery over things" (27). Speaking allowed these Africans to feel in control over their world. This part of the oral tradition would become especially valuable in the years to come, as many Africans were taken against their will and forced into slavery.

Oral Tradition in Early America

4   When the enslaved Africans were brought to America, they lost almost everything. They lost their homes, their friends and families, and, most importantly, their freedom. Yet, there was one thing they were able to bring with them: their oral traditions. Folktales were a way to bond and to preserve African culture in a new and hostile environment: "Told at night, for entertainment as well as instruction, in the traditional African style in which the entire community might be involved in the telling, these stories as performances provided entertainment by which the community could celebrate its identity as a group simply by singing, dancing, and most important, laughing together" (Abrahams 18).

5 Storytelling was an escape from the struggles of their daily lives. Its connection to community values brought comfort. Furthermore, storytelling could provide support through hidden messages. Enslaved people could not express themselves openly; instead, they put their fears, hopes, and support for one another within stories. Such stories often featured animals instead of people. When these stories were overheard, slaveholders did not know what the enslaved people were really talking about. In this way, enslaved people could regain their voices as well as a sense of power (Abrahams 9). The oral tradition had an important practical function, too. An observer might have thought enslaved people were singing "Follow the Drinking Gourd" or "Swing Low, Sweet Chariot" to pass the time, but the lyrics actually concealed coded messages that showed the route to freedom via the Underground Railroad (Hudson 206–207). More than 150 years after the abolition of slavery in the United States, these songs remain an important part of African American culture.

The Oral Tradition Continues Today

6 Today, African American cultural values and customs are shared in many different ways; nevertheless, the lasting effect of the oral tradition is clear. Nommo still plays an active role in African American culture, both in the call-and-response style of African American church services and in hip-hop culture (Hamlet 28). A rap song may seem very different from a traditional folktale, but both share the same heritage.

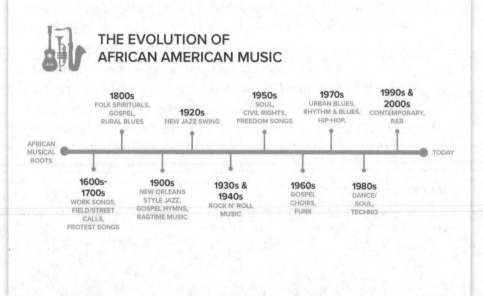

THE EVOLUTION OF
AFRICAN AMERICAN MUSIC

1800s
FOLK SPIRITUALS,
GOSPEL,
RURAL BLUES

1920s
NEW JAZZ SWING

1950s
SOUL,
CIVIL RIGHTS,
FREEDOM SONGS

1970s
URBAN BLUES,
RHYTHM & BLUES,
HIP-HOP,

1990s &
2000s
CONTEMPORARY,
R&B

AFRICAN
MUSICAL
ROOTS

TODAY

1600s-
1700s
WORK SONGS,
FIELD/STREET
CALLS,
PROTEST SONGS

1900s
NEW ORLEANS
STYLE JAZZ,
GOSPEL HYMNS,
RAGTIME MUSIC

1930s &
1940s
ROCK N' ROLL
MUSIC

1960s
GOSPEL
CHOIRS,
FUNK

1980s
DANCE/
SOUL,
TECHNO

7   Storytelling helps us to better understand our past, our present, and our place in the world. Jeff Wallenfeldt says, "It is inevitable, if not essential, that performers take images from the present and wed them to the past, and in that way the past regularly shapes any audience's experience of the present. Storytellers reveal connections between humans—within the world, within a society, within a tribe, within a family" (77). Stories affect us deeply; they form links across generations and across cultures. Every time a story is told, it becomes part of the listener. When enough people hear and share the tale, it becomes a part of our experience. Maybe closeness, not entertainment, is the goal of storytelling: "Perhaps the real reason that we tell stories again and again—and endlessly praise our greatest storytellers—is because humans want to be a part of a shared history" (Delistraty). Differences still separate groups of people in today's society; telling stories helps us focus on what we have in common.

8   In early Africa, griots told stories to help their community remember where they came from. Over hundreds of years, not much has changed. Authors and storytellers as well as editors like Gates and Tatar have retold traditional stories to help today's audiences understand our shared past and to help shape our future. At bedtime, parents can often be found telling their children old stories, not new inventions, because those are the stories their parents once told them. A story may change a bit each time it's told; however, the way stories help us connect with each other remains the same.

Works Cited

Abrahams, Roger, D. *Afro-American Folktales: Stories from Black Traditions in the New World*. Pantheon, 1995.

Delistraty, Cody C. "The Psychological Comforts of Storytelling." *The Atlantic*, 2 Nov. 2014, www.theatlantic.com/health/archive/2014/11/the-psychological-comforts-of-storytelling/381964/.

Franklin, John Hope, and Alfred A. Moss, Jr. *From Slavery to Freedom: A History of African Americans*. Knopf, 2000.

Hamlet, Janice D. "Word! The African American Oral Tradition and Its Rhetorical Impact on American Popular Culture." *Black History Bulletin*, vol. 74, no. 1, 2011, pp. 27–29.

Hudson, J. Blaine. *Encyclopedia of the Underground Railroad*. McFarland, 2006.

Siegel, Robert. "'Annotated African American Folktales' Reclaims Stories Passed Down from Slavery." *All Things Considered*, National Public Radio, 10 Nov. 2017, www.npr.org/2017/11/10/563110377/annotated-african-american-folktales-reclaims-stories-passed-down-from-slavery.

Wallenfeldt, Jeff. *Africa to America: From the Middle Passage Through the 1930s*. Rosen, 2010.

✏️ WRITE

Writers often take notes about ideas before they sit down to write. Think about what you've learned so far about organizing research writing to help you begin prewriting.

- What topic from the unit do you find most interesting? What will you research?

- What do you already know about this topic? What else do you want to learn about the topic?

- Who is your audience and what do you want to inform them about?

- How can you use a question or questions to focus your research?

Response Instructions

Use the questions in the bulleted list to write a one-paragraph research summary. Your summary should describe the topic that you plan to research and discuss what you hope to learn about this topic. Make sure to include at least one question that will guide and focus your research as you write this informative research paper.

Don't worry about including all of the details now; focus only on the most essential and important elements. You will refer back to this short summary as you continue through the steps of the writing process.

Skill:
Planning Research

••• CHECKLIST FOR PLANNING RESEARCH

In order to develop a short research project to answer a question drawing on several sources, do the following:

- Make a list of research tasks.

  > If it is not assigned to you, decide on a major research question.

  > Develop a research plan, a series of steps you can follow to find information to answer your question.

- Search for information.

  > Look for information on your topic, drawing on several sources both online and in books and other reference material.

  > If you don't find the information that you need to answer your major research question, you may need to modify it.

  > Generate additional related, focused questions for further research and investigation.

  > Refocus and revise your research plan as needed.

To develop a short research project to answer a question drawing on several sources, consider the following questions:

- How does the source address ideas, concepts, or other areas related to my research?

- Is my research question too broad or too focused?

- Do I need to change or reconsider my major research question?

- Does information in one source contradict or disprove information in another source? How might I resolve these differences?

YOUR TURN

Read the research questions below. Then, complete the chart by placing each question in the correct category.

	Research Questions
A	What were ancient Romans like?
B	How did smugglers help refugees get across the Afghanistan–Pakistan border in the 1980s?
C	Why do refugees have to flee their home countries?
D	Why did people admire warriors in ancient Rome?
E	What kinds of Cinderella stories are told throughout the world?
F	What issues were causing Afghans to flee their homes and go to Pakistan?
G	Why are the morals in "The Invisible One" and "Adelita" still important today?
H	What values were important to ancient Romans?
I	Did Thailand's Cinderella story, "Kao and the Golden Fish," change how sisters treated each other in the 1990s?

Too Narrow	Appropriate	Too Broad

Please note that excerpts and passages in the StudySync® library and this workbook are intended as touchstones to generate interest in an author's work. The excerpts and passages do not substitute for the reading of entire texts, and StudySync® strongly recommends that students seek out and purchase the whole literary or informational work in order to experience it as the author intended. Links to online resellers are available in our digital library. In addition, complete works may be ordered through an authorized reseller by filling out and returning to StudySync® the order form enclosed in this workbook.

Reading & Writing Companion

771

YOUR TURN

Complete the chart below by brainstorming a list of possible research questions. After you have at least four questions, reread and evaluate each question to determine whether it is too narrow, too broad, or just right. Then build your research plan.

Outline	Research Plan
Possible Research Questions:	
Selected Research Question:	
Step 1:	
Step 2:	
Step 3:	

Skill:
Evaluating Sources

••• CHECKLIST FOR EVALUATING SOURCES

First, reread the sources you gathered and identify the following:

- what kind of source it is, including video, audio, or text, and where the source comes from
- where information seems inaccurate, biased, or outdated
- where information seems irrelevant or incomplete

In order to use advanced searches to gather relevant, credible, and accurate print and digital sources, use the following questions as a guide:

- Is the material up-to-date or based on the most current information?
- Is the material published by a well-established, trustworthy source or expert author?
- Is the material factual, and can it be verified by another source?
- Are there specific terms or phrases in my research question that I can use to adjust my search?
- Can I use "and," "or," or "not" to expand or limit my search?
- Can I use quotation marks to search for exact phrases?

Please note that excerpts and passages in the StudySync® library and this workbook are intended as touchstones to generate interest in an author's work. The excerpts and passages do not substitute for the reading of entire texts, and StudySync® strongly recommends that students seek out and purchase the whole literary or informational work in order to experience it as the author intended. Links to online resellers are available in our digital library. In addition, complete works may be ordered through an authorized reseller by filling out and returning to StudySync® the order form enclosed in this workbook.

Reading & Writing Companion   773

↻ YOUR TURN

Read the factors below. Then, complete the chart by placing them into two categories: those that show a source is credible and reliable and those that do not.

	Factors
A	The article is published on a personal blog of a well-known political satirist.
B	The author has a Ph.D. and works for a university.
C	The article is over 15 years old.
D	The article was just published within the last year using the most recent studies on the topic.
E	The text uses clear facts and strong logic.
F	The author has no last name.

Credible and Reliable	Not Credible and Reliable

YOUR TURN

Complete the chart below by filling in the title and author of a source and answering the questions about it.

Questions	Answers
Source Title and Author:	
Reliable: Is the source material up-to-date or based on the most current information?	
Credible: Is the material published by a well-established source or expert author?	
Accurate: Is the material factual, and can it be verified by another source?	
Should I use this source in my paper?	

Please note that excerpts and passages in the StudySync® library and this workbook are intended as touchstones to generate interest in an author's work. The excerpts and passages do not substitute for the reading of entire texts, and StudySync® strongly recommends that students seek out and purchase the whole literary or informational work in order to experience it as the author intended. Links to online resellers are available in our digital library. In addition, complete works may be ordered through an authorized reseller by filling out and returning to StudySync® the order form enclosed in this workbook.

Reading & Writing
Companion

775

Skill:
Research and Notetaking

••• CHECKLIST FOR RESEARCH AND NOTETAKING

In order to conduct short research projects, drawing on several sources and generating additional related, focused questions for further research and investigation, note the following:

- Think of a question you would like to have answered.

- Look up your topic in an encyclopedia to find general information.

- Find specific, up-to-date information in books and periodicals, on the Internet, and if appropriate, from interviews with experts.

- Use the library's computerized catalog to locate books on your topic, and if you need help finding or using any of these resources, ask a librarian.

- Make sure that each source you use is closely related to your topic.

- Based on your research, create additional focused questions to help you investigate your topic further.

To conduct short research projects, drawing on several sources and generating additional related, focused questions for further research and investigation, consider the following questions:

- Is the information relevant and related to my topic?

- Where could I look to find additional information?

- Is the information I have found current and up-to-date?

- What additional, focused questions could I generate to help me investigate my topic further?

YOUR TURN

Read each bullet point from Nicole's note cards below. Then, complete the chart by placing them into two categories: those that support the oral tradition during slavery and those that support storytelling today.

	Bullet Points
A	Source 4: Storytelling helps us better understand our past, our present, and our place in the world (77).
B	*Additional Question*: How do African American musicians and artists today use storytelling in their songs or raps?
C	Source 3: Folktales were a way to preserve culture. The only belongings that enslaved Africans could bring were their storytelling traditions (4).
D	Source 5: Songs like "Follow the Drinking Gourd" and "Swing Low, Sweet Chariot" contained secret messages to help enslaved people escape (206–207).
E	Source 6: Gates says that storytelling is "like links in a chain," and he wants to make sure the chain continues (Siegel).
F	*Additional Question*: When and where did enslaved Africans tell folktales and sing songs?

The Oral Tradition During Slavery	Storytelling Today

WRITE

Use the steps in the checklist section to identify and gather relevant information from a variety of sources. Write note cards for your sources as well as related questions for further research and investigation. When you have finished, write a brief reflection summarizing some relevant information you researched from at least two sources. End the reflection by writing one or two related questions you still have.

Research Writing Process: Draft

PLAN	DRAFT	REVISE	EDIT AND PUBLISH

You have already made progress toward writing your informative research paper. Now it is time to draft your informative research paper.

✏ WRITE

Use your plan and other responses in your Binder to draft your research paper. You may also have new ideas as you begin drafting. Feel free to explore those new ideas as you have them. You can also ask yourself these questions to ensure that your writing is focused, is organized, and provides evidence and elaboration:

- Have I written a clear thesis statement?
- Am I using a logical informational text structure?
- Have I synthesized information from a variety of sources that will support my thesis statement?

Before you submit your draft, read it over carefully. You want to be sure that you've responded to all aspects of the prompt.

Copyright © BookheadEd Learning, LLC

Here is Nicole's research paper draft. As you read, identify how Nicole used her research question to create a thesis statement and her main ideas and choose the specific facts, details, and examples she uses to develop her ideas.

☰ STUDENT MODEL: FIRST DRAFT

The Storyteller's Legacy

Henry Louis Gates, Jr., dedicates the book *The Annotated African American Folktales* to his three-year-old granddaughter. Gates hopes that the collection will help another generation feel as if the stories are as much theirs as they once were his (Siegel). Gates and his co-editor, Maria Tatar, are two people who have worked to keep the oral tradition of storytelling alive. These two are not alone. Why is the oral tradition so important to African American culture? Oral tradition is important in African American culture due to its history of preserving culture and legacy in Africa, early america, and today.

Storytelling in Africa

~~Storytelling began as a way of preserving culture during a time before writing was common. In early Africa, few languages were written, literature was handed down orally. Griots collected songs and stories as a way of protecting and sharing cultural values and customs. Storytellers were valuable members of the community. The oral tradition effected every part of Africans' lives. Speech was more than a means of communication. It was power. Janice D. Hamlet explains, "The Africans believed in Nommo, which means the generative power of the spoken word. Nommo was believed necessary to actualize life and give man mastery over things" (74). Speaking allowed these Africans to feel in control over their world.~~

Storytelling began as a way of preserving culture during a time before writing was common. In early Africa, few languages were written; literature was handed down orally. Griots, or storytellers, collected songs and stories as a way of protecting and sharing cultural values and customs. Without written records, these griots had to hold a culture's important information within their brains. Franklin and Moss note, "They kept in their memories the history, law, and traditions of their people and were themselves living

Skill:
Critiquing Research

Nicole used her new note cards to add another section to her informative research paper. By reviewing and critiquing her research, Nicole was able to gather more information and include more sources. With this research, Nicole was able to write a more thorough and detailed paper.

Please note that excerpts and passages in the StudySync® library and this workbook are intended as touchstones to generate interest in an author's work. The excerpts and passages do not substitute for the reading of entire texts, and StudySync® strongly recommends that students seek out and purchase the whole literary or informational work in order to experience it as the author intended. Links to online resellers are available in our digital library. In addition, complete works may be ordered through an authorized reseller by filling out and returning to StudySync® the order form enclosed in this workbook.

Reading & Writing Companion   779

dictionaries" (28). As such, storytellers were valuable and honored members of the community.

The oral tradition affected every part of Africans' lives. For these early societies, speech was more than a means of communication. It was power. Janice D. Hamlet explains, "The Africans believed in Nommo, which means the generative power of the spoken word. Nommo was believed necessary to actualize life and give man mastery over things" (27). Speaking allowed these Africans to feel in control over their world. This part of the oral tradition would become especially valuable in the years to come, as many Africans were taken against their will and forced into slavery.

~~Early America~~

~~When the enslaved Africans were brought to America they lost almost everything. Yet, there was one thing they were able to bring with them. Their oral traditions. Folktales were a way to bond and preserve African culture in a new and hostile environment: Told at night, for entertainment as well as instruction, in the traditional African style in which the entire community might be involved in the telling, these stories as performances provided entertainment by which the community could celebrate its identity as a group simply by singing, dancing, and most important, laughing together.~~

Oral Tradition in Early America

When the enslaved Africans were brought to America, they lost almost everything. They lost their homes, their friends and families, and, most importantly, their freedom. Yet, there was one thing they were able to bring with them: their oral traditions. Folktales were a way to bond and to preserve African culture in a new and hostile environment: "Told at night, for entertainment as well as instruction, in the traditional African style in which the entire community might be involved in the telling, these stories as performances provided entertainment by which the community could celebrate its identity as a group simply by singing, dancing, and most important, laughing together" (Abrahams 18).

Thus, storytelling was an escape from the struggles of their daily lives. It's connection to community values brought comfort.

Skill:
Print and Graphic Features

Nicole revised her headings to be more specific and to better preview each section's content. The headers keep her research paper more organized.

Storytelling could provide support through hidden messages. Enslaved people could not express themselves openly, instead, they put they're feelings within stories. Such stories often featured animals instead of people. When these stories were overheard slaveholders did not know what they were really talking about. In this way, enslaved people could regain their voices as well as a sense of power (9). The oral tradition had an important practical function, to. An observer might have thought enslaved people were singing "Follow the Drinking Gourd" or "Swing Low, Sweet Chariot" to pass the time, but the lyrics actually concealed coded messages that showed the route to freedom via the Underground Railroad (Hudson 206–207).

~~Today~~

~~African American cultural and customs are shared in different ways, but oral traditions continue. Nommo is still alive and well in African American culture, both in the call-and-response nature of African American churches and hip hop culture. (Hamlet 28).~~

The Oral Tradition Continues Today

Today, African American cultural values and customs are shared in many different ways; nevertheless, the lasting effect of the oral tradition is clear. Nommo still plays an active role in African American culture, both in the call-and-response style of African American church services and in hip-hop culture (Hamlet 28). A rap song may seem very different from a traditional folktale, but both share the same heritage.

Storytelling helps us to better understand our past, our present, and our place in the world. Jeff Wallenfeldt says, "It is inevitable, if not essential, that performers take images from the present and wed them to the past, and in that way the past regularly shapes any audience's experience of the present. Storytellers reveal connections between humans—within the world, within a society, within a tribe, within a family" (77). Stories effect us a lot, they form links across generations and across cultures. Every time a story is told, it becomes part of the listener. When enough people hear and share the tale it becomes a part of our experiance. Maybe closeness not entertainment is the goal of storytelling: "Perhaps the real reason

Skill:
Paraphrasing

Nicole carefully reread the text to be sure she understood the meaning. Then, she highlighted keywords or phrases in the text that she knew would be important in maintaining the meaning. Nicole rewrote the text in her own words, using the keywords and phrases. By using keywords and phrases when she paraphrased, Nicole was able to maintain the original meaning of the text. As a result, the research paper was a stronger piece of writing and sounded more like Nicole. Most important, she avoided plagiarism.

NOTES

that we tell stories again and again—and endlessly praise our greatest storytellers—is because humans want to be a part of a shared history" (Delistraty). Differences still separate groups of people in today's society, telling stories helps us focus on what we have in comon.

In early Africa, griots told stories. They did this to help their community. The stories helped the community remember where they come from. Over hundreds of years, not much has changed. Authors like Virginia Hamilton and editors like Gates and Tatar have retold traditional stories to help today's audiences understand our shared past and to help shape our future. At bedtime, parents often tell their children old stories not new inventions because those are the stories there parents once told them, a story may change a bit each time its told, however, the way stories help us connect with each other remains the same.

Works Cited:

Abrahams, Roger, D. ~~Afro-American Folktales: Stories from Black Traditions in the New World.~~ 1995.

Delistraty, Cody C. ~~"The Psychological Comforts of Storytelling." The Atlantic, 2 Nov. 2014.~~

Franklin, John Hope, ~~From Slavery to Freedom: A History of African Americans. Knopf. 2000.~~

Abrahams, Roger, D. *Afro-American Folktales: Stories from Black Traditions in the New World.* Pantheon, 1995.

Delistraty, Cody C. "The Psychological Comforts of Storytelling." *The Atlantic*, 2 Nov. 2014, www.theatlantic.com/health/archive/2014/11/the-psychological-comforts-of-storytelling/381964/.

Franklin, John Hope, and Alfred A. Moss, Jr. *From Slavery to Freedom: A History of African Americans.* Knopf, 2000.

Hamlet, Janice D. "Word! The African American Oral Tradition and its Rhetorical Impact on American Popular Culture." *Black History Bulletin*, vol. 74, no. 1, 2011, pp.27–29.

Skill:
Sources and
Citations

Nicole added the publisher to her first citation. She added the website address to the end of the second citation. She also added the second author's name to the third citation. By including all the required information in her citations, Nicole has given proper credit to the sources she used in her research paper. It also lets her readers find these sources on their own.

Hudson, J. Blaine. *Encyclopedia of the Underground Railroad.* McFarland, 2006.

Siegel, Robert. "'Annotated African American Folktales' Reclaims Stories Passed Down From Slavery." *All Things Considered*, National Public Radio, 10 Nov. 2017, www.npr.org/2017/11/10/563110377/annotated-african-american-folktales-reclaims-stories-passed-down-from-slavery

Wallenfeldt, Jeff. *Africa to America: From the Middle Passage Through the 1930s.* Rosen, 2010.

Please note that excerpts and passages in the StudySync® library and this workbook are intended as touchstones to generate interest in an author's work. The excerpts and passages do not substitute for the reading of entire texts, and StudySync® strongly recommends that students seek out and purchase the whole literary or informational work in order to experience it as the author intended. Links to online resellers are available in our digital library. In addition, complete works may be ordered through an authorized reseller by filling out and returning to StudySync® the order form enclosed in this workbook.

Reading & Writing Companion

783

Skill:
Critiquing Research

In order to conduct short research projects to answer a question, drawing on several sources, do the following:

- Generate focused questions that are related to your first question in order to guide additional research as needed.

- Gather relevant, or important, information from different print and digital sources.

- Use search terms effectively when looking for information online, such as using unique terms that are specific to your topic (i.e., "daily life in Jamestown, Virginia" rather than just "Jamestown, Virginia").

- Assess your research for accuracy, credibility, and reliability.

To evaluate and use relevant information while conducting short research projects, consider the following questions:

- Does my research come from multiple print and digital sources?

- Have I used search terms effectively when looking for information online?

- Have I generated additional questions to guide any further research I might want to conduct?

- Are there specific terms or phrases in my research question that I can use to adjust my search?

- Can I use "and," "or," or "not" to expand or limit my search?

- Can I use quotation marks to search for exact phrases?

↻ YOUR TURN

Nicole's friend Sherell shared her research plan with Nicole. In the first column of the chart below, they listed some critiques of Sherell's research. Complete the chart by matching Sherell's next steps to each critique.

Next Steps	
A	Sherell should go to a library and ask the librarian to help her find encyclopedias and nonfiction texts to use in her research paper.
B	Sherell should check that the sources are well known and respected. She should make sure her sources are from experts in their field, university websites, or well-respected publications. When in doubt, she should ask a teacher.
C	After doing some research and taking notes, she should think about additional, focused research questions about her topic that will help her modify her research plan.
D	She should make her search terms more specific by using keywords, phrases, and unique terms with quotation marks and words like "and," "or," and "not."

Critiques	Next Steps
Nicole is unsure about the accuracy, reliability, and credibility of Sherell's sources.	
Sherell did a general online search for information and got over a million results.	
Sherell only has two sources and both of them are online resources.	
Sherell has one general research question, and she is not sure if she will have enough information for a complete informative research paper.	

↻ YOUR TURN

Complete the chart by answering the questions and writing a short summary of what you will do to make changes to your research plan.

Common Questions or Critiques	My Answers and Next Steps
Do you have enough relevant information from a mix of both digital and print sources?	
Did you use search terms effectively when conducting online searches?	
Are your sources and research accurate, reliable, and credible?	
Did you generate additional, focused questions to further and improve your research?	

Skill:
Paraphrasing

In order to paraphrase, note the following:

- Make sure you understand what the author is saying after reading the text carefully.

- Write down words and phrases that are important to include in a paraphrase to maintain the meaning of the text.

- Look up any words or expressions that are unfamiliar.

- Avoid plagiarism by acknowledging all sources for both paraphrased and quoted material.

To paraphrase texts, consider the following questions:

- Do I understand the meaning of the text?

- Does my paraphrase of the text maintain its original meaning? Have I missed any key points or details?

- Have I avoided plagiarism by acknowledging all my sources for both paraphrased and quoted material?

- Have I noted source information, like the title, author's name, and page number?

Please note that excerpts and passages in the StudySync® library and this workbook are intended as touchstones to generate interest in an author's work. The excerpts and passages do not substitute for the reading of entire texts, and StudySync® strongly recommends that students seek out and purchase the whole literary or informational work in order to experience it as the author intended. Links to online resellers are available in our digital library. In addition, complete works may be ordered through an authorized reseller by filling out and returning to StudySync® the order form enclosed in this workbook.

Reading & Writing
Companion

787

YOUR TURN

Read the original text excerpt in the first column of the chart on the following page. In the second column, fill in the keywords from this page that match the text excerpt. Then, in the third column, paraphrase the original text excerpt using the keywords. Remember to cite the author and page number in parentheses. Part of the first row is done for you as an example.

Keywords
cultural traditions
stories
African / African American
songs
storytellers
musical
passed on
again and again
old sayings
proverbs
language
word of mouth
humans want
maintaining
tell stories
shared history
oral tradition
Black church

Original Text Excerpt	Keywords	Paraphrased Text
The oral tradition refers to stories, old sayings, songs, proverbs, and other cultural products that have not been written down or recorded. The forms of oral tradition cultures are kept alive by being passed on by word of mouth from one generation to the next. *Word! The African American Oral Tradition and Its Rhetorical Impact on American Popular Culture*, Janice D. Hamlet, p. 27		To paraphrase: Oral tradition is made up of stories, sayings, and songs or proverbs that have not been written down. These forms of oral tradition are passed down from parents to their children through word of mouth (Hamlet 27).
Perhaps the real reason that we tell stories again and again—and endlessly praise our greatest storytellers—is because humans want to be a part of a shared history. Delistraty, Cody C. "The Psychological Comforts of Storytelling." *The Atlantic*. 2 Nov. 2014. *The Atlantic Online*. Web. April 2019.		
The musical expressions of African Americans and the Black church have been the most significant forces in maintaining and nurturing the surviving African/African American language cultural traditions. *Word! The African American Oral Tradition and Its Rhetorical Impact on American Popular Culture*, Janice D. Hamlet, p. 28		

✏ WRITE

Choose one or two parts of your research paper where information is still in the author's words without quotations or citations or where you can paraphrase the author's words better. Revise those sections using the questions in the checklist.

Skill:
Sources and Citations

In order to cite and gather relevant information from multiple print and digital sources, do the following:

- Select and gather information from a variety of print and digital sources using search terms effectively to narrow your search.

- Check that sources are credible and accurate.

- Quote or paraphrase the data you find and cite it to avoid plagiarism, using parenthetical citations, footnotes, or endnotes to credit sources.

- Be sure that facts, details, and other information support your thesis statement.

- Include all sources in a bibliography, following a standard format such as MLA:

  > Halall, Ahmed. *The Pyramids of Ancient Egypt.* Central Publishing, 2016.

  > For a citation, footnote, or endnote, include the author, title, and page number.

To check that sources are gathered and cited correctly, consider the following questions:

- Did I quote or paraphrase the data I found and cite it to avoid plagiarism?

- Have I relied on one source, instead of looking for different points of view on my topic in other sources?

- Did I include all my sources in my bibliography?

- Are my citations formatted correctly using a standard, accepted format?

⟳ YOUR TURN

Choose the best answer to each question.

1. Below is a section from a previous draft of Nicole's research paper. What change should Nicole make to improve the clarity of her citations?

> Collections of folktales are still being compiled and released, both to honor the past and to help shape the future. "To this very day, folktales are being told, altered, retold, and made. A tale naturally changes as it is told by one person to another."

- ○ A. Add the author's last name in parentheses after the quotation.
- ○ B. Add the page number in parentheses after the quotation.
- ○ C. Add the author's last name and the page number in parentheses after the quotation.
- ○ D. No change needs to be made.

2. Below is a section from a previous draft of Nicole's works cited page. Which revision best corrects her style errors?

> *The People Could Fly*. Hamilton, Virginia, 1985., Knopf.

- ○ A. Hamilton, Virginia. *The People Could Fly*. Knopf.
- ○ B. *The People Could Fly*. Hamilton, Virginia, 1985. Knopf.
- ○ C. Hamilton, Virginia, *The People Could Fly*. 1985, Knopf.
- ○ D. Hamilton, Virginia. *The People Could Fly*. Knopf, 1985.

✎ WRITE

Use the questions in the checklist section to revise your works cited list. Refer to an MLA style guide or the style guide required by your teacher as needed.

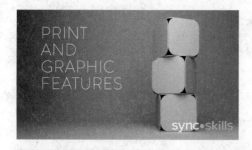

Skill:
Print and Graphic Features

••• CHECKLIST FOR PRINT AND GRAPHIC FEATURES

First, reread your draft and ask yourself the following questions:

- To what extent would including formatting, graphics, or multimedia be effective in achieving my purpose?
- Which formatting, graphics, or multimedia seem most important in conveying information to the reader?
- How is the addition of the formatting, graphics, or multimedia useful to aiding comprehension?

To include formatting, graphics, and multimedia, using the following questions as a guide:

- How can I use formatting to better organize information? Consider adding:

  > titles   > subheadings   > boldface and italicized terms

  > headings   > bullets

- How can I use graphics to better convey information? Consider adding:

  > charts   > timelines   > images with captions

  > graphs   > diagrams

  > tables   > figures and statistics

- How can I use multimedia to add interest and variety? Consider adding a combination of:

  > photographs

  > art

  > audio

  > video

🔁 YOUR TURN

Choose the best answer to each question.

1. Nicole has decided to include a timeline in a draft of a section of her paper titled "Today." Read the section below. How does including a timeline make this section of her paper more effective?

Today

African American cultural and customs are shared in different ways, but oral traditions continue. Nommo still plays an active role in African American culture, both in the call-and-response style of African American church services and in hip-hop culture (Hamlet 28). A rap song may seem very different from a traditional folktale, but both share the same heritage.

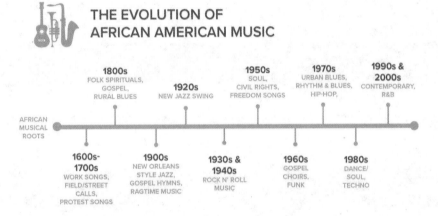

THE EVOLUTION OF AFRICAN AMERICAN MUSIC

AFRICAN MUSICAL ROOTS

1600s–1700s WORK SONGS, FIELD/STREET CALLS, PROTEST SONGS

1800s FOLK SPIRITUALS, GOSPEL, RURAL BLUES

1900s NEW ORLEANS STYLE JAZZ, GOSPEL HYMNS, RAGTIME MUSIC

1920s NEW JAZZ SWING

1930s & 1940s ROCK N' ROLL MUSIC

1950s SOUL, CIVIL RIGHTS, FREEDOM SONGS

1960s GOSPEL CHOIRS, FUNK

1970s URBAN BLUES, RHYTHM & BLUES, HIP-HOP,

1980s DANCE/ SOUL, TECHNO

1990s & 2000s CONTEMPORARY, R&B

Jeff Wallenfeldt says, "It is inevitable, if not essential, that performers take images from the present and wed them to the past, and in that way the past regularly shapes any audience's experience of the present. Storytellers reveal connections between humans—within the world, within a society, within a tribe, within a family" (77). Stories affect us a lot; they form links across generations and across cultures.

- ○ A. The timeline helps readers see the progression of the African American oral tradition, including culture and music.
- ○ B. The timeline helps Nicole organize her information more effectively.
- ○ C. The timeline is an example of multimedia used to add variety and interest to her research paper.
- ○ D. The timeline is a print feature that will highlight a specific section of the text.

2. Nicole wants to revise the header "Today" to better reflect the content of this section from a draft of her paper. Reread the first few sentences of the section and then select the best revision.

Today

African American culture and customs are shared in different ways, but oral traditions continue. Nommo still plays an active role in African American culture, both in the call-and-response style of African American church services and in hip-hop culture (Hamlet 28). A rap song may seem very different from a traditional folktale, but both share the same heritage.

○ A. African American Values and Customs
○ B. The Oral Tradition Continues Today
○ C. Call and Response
○ D. Rap and Folktales

⟳ YOUR TURN

Complete the chart by brainstorming ideas for how you can use print and graphic features to improve your research paper.

Print and Graphic Feature or Multimedia	My Ideas and Changes
How can I use formatting to better organize information?	
How can I use graphics to better convey information?	
How can I use multimedia to add interest and variety?	

Research Writing Process: Revise

PLAN	DRAFT	REVISE	EDIT AND PUBLISH

You have written a draft of your informative research paper. You have also received input from your peers about how to improve it. Now you are going to revise your draft.

← REVISION GUIDE

Examine your draft to find areas for revision. Keep in mind your purpose and audience as you revise for clarity, development, organization, and style. Use the guide below to help you review:

Review	Revise	Example
Clarity		
Label each term that is specific to the topic you've researched. Annotate any places where the meaning of the term is unclear.	Add description to clarify the meaning of any unfamiliar terms.	Griots, or storytellers, collected songs and stories as a way of protecting and sharing cultural values and customs.
Development		
Identify key ideas in your research paper. Annotate places where additional description or information could help develop your ideas.	Make sure you have a strong main idea in each paragraph, and add description or information to develop your ideas.	Nommo is still alive and well in African American culture, both in the call-and-response nature of African American churches and hip hop culture. (Hamlet 28). A rap song may seem very different from a traditional folktale, but both share the same heritage.

Review	Revise	Example
Organization		
Review your body paragraphs. Identify and annotate any sentences that don't flow in a clear and logical way.	Rewrite the sentences so they appear in a clear and logical order, starting with a strong transition or topic sentence. Make sure to include a transition between body paragraphs.	Janice D. Hamlet explains, "The Africans believed in Nommo, which means the generative power of the spoken word. Nommo was believed necessary to actualize life and give man mastery over things" (27). Speaking allowed these Africans to feel in control over their world. This part of the oral tradition would become especially valuable in the years to come, as many Africans were taken against their will and forced into slavery.
Style: Word Choice		
Identify weak or repetitive words or phrases that do not clearly express your ideas to the reader.	Replace weak and repetitive words and phrases with more descriptive ones that better convey your ideas.	Gates and his co-editor, Maria Tatar, are two ~~people~~ links in a very long chain of storytellers who have worked to keep the oral tradition of storytelling alive.
Style: Sentence Variety		
Read your essay aloud. Annotate places where you have too many long or short sentences in a row.	Revise short sentences by linking them together. Shorten longer sentences for clarity of emphasis.	In early Africa, griots told stories. ~~They did this~~ to help their community. ~~The stories helped the community~~ remember where they came from. Over hundreds of years, not much has changed.

✏ WRITE

Use the guide above, as well as your peer reviews, to help you evaluate your informative research paper to determine areas that should be revised.

Grammar:
Participial Phrases

Participial Phrase

A participle is a verb form that acts as an adjective to modify a noun or pronoun. A participle can be present or past. A present participle ends in *-ing*. A past participle usually ends in *-ed* but includes irregular forms as well, such as *chosen* and *sung*.

A participial phrase begins with a present or past participle and includes other words that complete its meaning. Like a participle, a participial phrase acts as an adjective. The phrase can appear before or after the noun or pronoun it modifies. Be sure to place the phrase as close as possible to the modified word in order to make the meaning of the sentence clear..

Correct	Incorrect
Growling furiously, the bear clawed at the bars of its cage.	The bear clawed, growling furiously, at the bars of its cage.
The insects mounted in this frame are part of a much larger collection.	The insects are part of a much larger collection mounted in this frame.

Follow these punctuation rules when using participial phrases:

Rule	Text
Use a comma to set off a participial phrase that begins a sentence.	**Chastened by the experience,** Chang-bo was more careful about what he said outside the family, but his thoughts were running wild. Nothing to Envy: Ordinary Lives in North Korea
Use commas to set off a participial phrase that is not essential to the meaning of the sentence.	The women, **wearing faded house dresses and sweaters,** came shortly after their menfolk. The Lottery
No punctuation is necessary when the phrase is not at the beginning of the sentence and is essential to the meaning of the sentence.	He issued an edict **abolishing gladiatorial combat** in a.d. 323. Gladiator

⟳ YOUR TURN

1. How should this sentence be changed?

   > Life fills a forest springing from every spot.

   - ○ A. Place the phrase **springing from every spot** in the beginning of the sentence, and put a comma after the word **spot**.
   - ○ B. Insert a comma after the word **springing**.
   - ○ C. Insert a comma after the word **Life**.
   - ○ D. No change needs to be made to this sentence.

2. How should this sentence be changed?

   > The radio, tuned to my favorite station, was bothering my mother.

   - ○ A. Delete the comma after the word **radio**.
   - ○ B. Delete the comma after the word **station**.
   - ○ C. Delete both commas after the words **radio** and **station**.
   - ○ D. No change needs to be made to this sentence.

3. How should this sentence be changed?

   > Smoke, billowing from the chimneys, darkened the sky.

   - ○ A. Delete the comma after the word **Smoke**.
   - ○ B. Delete the comma after the word **chimneys**.
   - ○ C. Delete the commas after the word **Smoke** and after the word **chimneys**.
   - ○ D. No change needs to be made to this sentence.

4. How should this sentence be changed?

   > Erik, dreaming of fame sits at the piano.

   - ○ A. Delete the comma after the word **Erik**.
   - ○ B. Insert a comma after the word **fame**.
   - ○ C. Insert a comma after the word **dreaming**.
   - ○ D. No change needs to be made to this sentence.

Grammar: Gerunds and Gerund Phrases

A gerund is a verb form that ends in *-ing* and acts as a noun. A gerund phrase includes the gerund and all the other words that complete its meaning. A gerund phrase is used as a noun phrase in a sentence. That means that a gerund phrase can be the subject of the sentence, the direct object of a verb, and the object of a preposition.

Text	Explanation
Crushing certain plants could add up infinitesimally. A Sound of Thunder	The gerund phrase *crushing certain plants* is the subject of this sentence.
"He started **digging ditches and stuff**, and the next thing you knew, he was sitting by his own swimming pool." Born Worker	The gerund phrase *digging ditches and stuff* is the direct object of the verb *started*. (The word *sitting* is not a gerund. It is part of a verb.)
A year later, he felt guilty for **letting his group down**. A Role to Play	The gerund phrase *letting his group down* is the object of the preposition *for*.

YOUR TURN

1. Which sentence contains a gerund phrase?

   ○ A. Collecting stamps is a fun hobby to have.
   ○ B. Joanne is watching her little brother play.
   ○ C. Are you happy to have a role in the play?
   ○ D. None of the above

2. Which sentence contains a gerund phrase?

   ○ A. Watch where you step!
   ○ B. Coming through the woods, Jack lost his house keys.
   ○ C. Marla enjoys making pizza for the family.
   ○ D. None of the above

3. Which sentence contains a gerund phrase?

   ○ A. Zeke tiptoed into the house softly, scaring the cat.
   ○ B. Jason is going on a visit to his uncle's tree farm.
   ○ C. The red kangaroo hopped quickly through the field.
   ○ D. None of the above

4. Which sentence contains a gerund phrase?

   ○ A. Michael decided to learn how to weave rugs.
   ○ B. You can get into trouble by jumping to conclusions.
   ○ C. The cat was spitting mad.
   ○ D. None of the above

Grammar: Infinitive Phrases

Infinitive Phrases

An infinitive phrase contains an infinitive (such as *to throw*) and other words that complete its meaning. If other words are not present, then the sentence simply contains an infinitive, not an infinitive phrase.

The word *to* is a preposition when it is followed by a noun or pronoun as an object of the preposition. The word *to* used before the base form of a verb is part of the infinitive form of the verb. It is not a preposition.

Infinitive	Infinitive Phrase
Carlos loves **to run**.	Carlos loves **to run marathons**.
Grandma does not want **to cook**.	Grandma does not want **to cook liver and onions tonight**.

Use these guidelines when using infinitive phrases:

Guideline	Text
An infinitive phrase may include a direct object.	Otto shook the ashes out of his pipe and squatted down **to count the rattles**. My Antonia
An infinitive phrase may include an adverb.	If children are aware that their parents can see everything they do, they are more likely **to behave appropriately**. The Dangers of Social Media
An infinitive phrase may include a prepositional phrase.	Encarnación acted out how boys learned **to fish in the Philippines**. Barrio Boy

Infinitive phrases, like infinitives, can function as nouns, adjectives, or adverbs. They often function as nouns and serve as the subject, direct object, or predicate noun in a sentence.

⟳ YOUR TURN

1. How should this sentence be changed to include an infinitive phrase?

> I clambered up the ladder.

- ○ A. Add *to look* after *ladder*.
- ○ B. Add *to the building's roof* after *ladder*.
- ○ C. Add *to see around the building* after *ladder*.
- ○ D. No change needs to be made to this sentence.

2. How should this sentence be changed to include an infinitive phrase?

> To run around the racetrack is exhausting!

- ○ A. Add *to the finish line* after *racetrack*.
- ○ B. Add *after school* after *racetrack*.
- ○ C. Remove *around the racetrack* from the sentence.
- ○ D. No change needs to be made to this sentence.

3. How should this sentence be changed to include an infinitive phrase?

> He wanted to learn.

- ○ A. Add *an eager student,* before *he*.
- ○ B. Add *the rules of badminton* after *learn*.
- ○ C. Remove the word *to*.
- ○ D. No change needs to be made to this sentence.

4. How should this sentence be changed to include an infinitive phrase?

> Dig in a sandbox is one of the most enjoyable experiences of childhood.

- ○ A. Add *to* before *dig*.
- ○ B. Add *to* before *a sandbox*.
- ○ C. Add *furiously* after *dig*.
- ○ D. No change needs to be made to this sentence.

Research Writing Process: Edit and Publish

PLAN	DRAFT	REVISE	EDIT AND PUBLISH

You have revised your research paper based on your peer feedback and your own examination.

Now, it is time to edit your research paper. When you revised, you focused on the content of your research paper. You probably critiqued your sources and reviewed your use of quotations, paraphrasing, and sources. When you edit, you focus on the mechanics of your research paper, paying close attention to things like grammar and punctuation.

Use the checklist below to guide you as you edit:

☐ Have I used a variety of phrases in my writing, including

- participial phrases?

- gerund phrases?

- infinitive phrases?

☐ Do I have any sentence fragments or run-on sentences?

☐ Have I spelled everything correctly?

Notice some edits Nicole has made:

- Changed her phrasing to include a participial phrase.

- Included several infinitive phrases.

- Broke up a run-on sentence into two separate sentences.

In early Africa, griots told stories to help their community remember where they came from. Over hundreds of years, not much has changed. Authors and storytellers as well as editors like Gates and Tatar have retold traditional stories to help today's audiences understand our shared past and to help shape our future. At bedtime, parents ~~often tell~~ can often be found telling their children old stories, not new inventions, because those are the stories their parents once told them~~., a~~ A story may change a bit each time it's told; however, the way stories help us connect with each other remains the same.

✏ WRITE

Use the questions on the previous page, as well as your peer reviews, to help you evaluate your research paper to determine areas that need editing. Then edit your research paper to correct those errors.

Once you have made all your corrections, you are ready to publish your work. You can distribute your writing to family and friends, hang it on a bulletin board, or post it on your blog. If you publish online, share the link with your family, friends, and classmates.

The Legendary Storyteller

INFORMATIONAL TEXT

Introduction

Most readers are likely already familiar with many of Aesop's fables. Parents all over the world have been telling these stories to their children for thousands of years. Despite being possibly the world's best-known storyteller, Aesop remains a mystery. Aesop himself had not been mentioned in writing until a hundred years after his death. The story of his life has been pieced together from numerous, and often conflicting, stories. Some historians question if he ever existed at all.

 VOCABULARY

alias

a name someone uses instead of his or her real name

frame

to falsely make a person look guilty of a crime

counsel

an advisor; someone who gives advice

definitive

absolute and without a doubt

unappreciative

not thankful

NOTES

≡ READ

1 Aesop wrote stories like "The Tortoise and the Hare" and "The Boy Who Cried Wolf." His stories have been told many times in many languages. Phrases like "sour grapes" and "a bird in the hand is worth two in the bush" came from his stories. We know little about Aesop. Aesop never wrote down his tales. We do not know if Aesop made up these stories or just collected them. Some historians think Aesop was not real. These historians think that multiple writers simply took up the **alias** "Aesop." All of our knowledge of Aesop has been passed down in stories, just like his fables.

2 Aesop's most famous fable has a tortoise beat a hare. Many of his stories feature weak and poor heroes. This may be due to how he grew up. Most historians agree that Aesop was born into slavery sometime around 620 B.C.E. We are not sure where Aesop was from. He might have been born on an island near Turkey. He might have been Phrygian. Some historians think he came from Africa. Aesop's stories of animals and tricksters carry on the traditions of African folklore.

3   Aesop was very clever. His intelligence stood out so much that the slaveholder set him free. Aesop traveled and told his stories. He also became involved in politics. He used stories to convince King Croesus of Lydia to lower taxes. Aesop's wisdom impressed King Croesus. He gave Aesop a job as a **counsel** on his court. Aesop also made enemies. King Croesus asked Aesop to give gold to the people of Delphi. There was a mix-up over how much gold each person should receive. The Delphians argued. Aesop decided they were being **unappreciative**. Aesop made up his mind to take the gold back to King Croesus. The angry Delphians decided to **frame** Aesop. The Delphians hid a golden bowl from the Temple of Apollo among Aesop's things. Then the Delphians accused Aesop of stealing the bowl. The Delphians threw Aesop off the nearby cliffs. This was the punishment for thieves in Delphi.

4   Aesop's life was almost as fantastic as his tales themselves. His stories have touched the lives of people all over the world, but historians have not come up with any **definitive** proof that Aesop was a real person. It is fitting that the master storyteller may be a myth himself.

The
Legendary
Storyteller

First Read

Read the text. After you read, answer the Think Questions below.

☁ THINK QUESTIONS

1. What is Aesop most famous for?

   _____

   _____

2. Where did Aesop come from?

   _____

   _____

3. What did the Delphians accuse Aesop of doing?

   _____

   _____

4. Use context to confirm the meaning of the word *frame* as it is used in "The Legendary Storyteller." Write your definition of *frame* here.

   _____

   _____

5. What is another way to say that evidence is *definitive*?

   _____

   _____

Skill:
Language Structures

★ DEFINE

In every language, there are rules that tell how to **structure** sentences. These rules define the correct order of words. In the English language, for example, a **basic** structure for sentences is subject, verb, and object. Some sentences have more **complicated** structures.

You will encounter both basic and complicated **language structures** in the classroom materials you read. Being familiar with language structures will help you better understand the text.

••• CHECKLIST FOR LANGUAGE STRUCTURES

To improve your comprehension of language structures, do the following:

✓ Monitor your understanding.

- Ask yourself: Why do I not understand this sentence? Is it because I do not understand some of the words? Or is it because I do not understand the way the words are ordered in the sentence?

✓ Pay attention to verbs followed by prepositions.

- A **verb** names an action.

  > Example: I **sit** on my chair.

  > This tells the reader what the subject of the sentence is doing (sitting).

- A **preposition** defines the relationship between two or more nouns or verbs in a sentence.

  > Example: I sit **on** my chair.

  > This tells the reader where the subject is doing the action (on a chair).

- Sometimes the preposition comes directly after the verb, but it can also be separated by another word.

  > Example: I **took** it **to** school with me.

- Sometimes the preposition changes the meaning of the verb. This is called a **phrasal verb.**

  > Example: The teacher liked to **call on** the students in the front of the class.

  > The phrasal verb *call on* means "to select someone to share information."

✓ Break down the sentence into its parts.

- Ask yourself: What words make up the verbs in this sentence? Is the verb followed by a preposition? How does this affect the meaning of the sentence?

⟳ YOUR TURN

Notice the verb + preposition pairs in the sentences. Write the letter for each sentence in the correct category.

	Verb + Preposition Pairs
A	His intelligence stood out so much that the slaveholder set him free.
B	Some historians think he came from Africa.
C	Aesop's stories of animals and tricksters carry on the traditions of African folklore.
D	He might have been born on an island near Turkey.

Phrasal Verb	Non-Phrasal Verb

Skill:
Visual and Contextual Support

★ DEFINE

Visual support is an image or an object that helps you understand a text. **Contextual support** is a **feature** that helps you understand a text. By using visual and contextual supports, you can develop your vocabulary so you can better understand a variety of texts.

First, preview the text to identify any visual supports. These might include illustrations, graphics, charts, or other objects in a text. Then, identify any contextual supports. Examples of contextual supports are titles, heads, captions, and boldface terms. Write down your **observations**.

Then, write down what those visual and contextual supports tell you about the meaning of the text. Note any new vocabulary that you see in those supports. Ask your peers and your teacher to confirm your understanding of the text.

••• CHECKLIST FOR VISUAL AND CONTEXTUAL SUPPORT

To use visual and contextual support to understand texts, do the following:

- ✓ Preview the text. Read the title, headers, and other features. Look at any images and graphics.
- ✓ Write down the visual and contextual supports in the text.
- ✓ Write down what those supports tell you about the text.
- ✓ Note any new vocabulary that you see in those supports.
- ✓ Confirm your observations with your peers and teacher.
- ✓ Create an illustration for the reading and write a descriptive caption.

Please note that excerpts and passages in the StudySync® library and this workbook are intended as touchstones to generate interest in an author's work. The excerpts and passages do not substitute for the reading of entire texts, and StudySync® strongly recommends that students seek out and purchase the whole literary or informational work in order to experience it as the author intended. Links to online resellers are available in our digital library. In addition, complete works may be ordered through an authorized reseller by filling out and returning to StudySync® the order form enclosed in this workbook.

Reading & Writing Companion

811

YOUR TURN

Write the letter for each example of Visual and Contextual Supports into the correct columns.

	Support from the Article
A	a map that shows the possible locations of Aesop's birth
B	a caption describing an illustration for "The Tortoise and the Hare"
C	a heading at that says: "Aesop and the Delphians"
D	an illustration of the bowl that the Delphians hid among Aesop's things

Visual	Contextual

Reading & Writing Companion

Close Read

✏️ **WRITE**

INFORMATIVE: How did Aesop's life reflect his fables? Write a short paragraph in which you explain how Aesop's life is similar to his stories. Use details from the text and your background knowledge of fables. Be sure to include appropriate topic vocabulary in your writing. Pay attention to spelling rules as you write.

Use the checklist below to guide you as you write.

☐ What is the main theme in many of Aesop's fables?

☐ What were the major events in Aesop's life?

☐ How is Aesop's life similar to Aesop's fables?

Use the sentence frames to organize and write your informational paragraph.

Many of Aesop's fables are about _____.

The _____ are really _____.

They use their _____ to succeed.

Aesop was a _____.

He used his _____ to _____.

He became _____.

Aesop's life is like his stories. He was an _____,

but he _____.

The Worried Armadillo

FICTION

Introduction

The pressures of school, work, family, and friends can sometimes seem overwhelming. While it's important to care about your responsibilities, too much stress can do more harm than good. In this modern fable, an armadillo learns a lesson about pointless worrying.

V VOCABULARY

mural

an artistic painting on a wall

detergent

a cleaning liquid

commemorate

to honor a memory

kaleidoscope

a toy containing mirrors and colored glass that creates colorful patterns

catastrophe

a disaster

≡ READ

NOTES

1   Once there was an armadillo. Like all armadillos, he had armor protecting his body. Whenever he felt in danger, he could curl up into a ball and nothing could hurt him. His armor was his pride and joy.

2   The armadillo was also an artist. He was known all over the town for his talent, so the mayor asked him to paint a black-and-white **mural** to **commemorate** the town's growth. When he began painting, the armadillo slipped and fell off his ladder. His shell protected him from harm, but paint spattered all over him.

3   The armadillo wailed over this **catastrophe**. Covered in white and black paint, he looked like a soccer ball. He thought that bored children would kick him. A coyote heard his cries of despair. Once she realized he wasn't a soccer ball, she offered him a solution. She had a special **detergent** that could remove stains. She had used it before to clean ink from her fur. The coyote offered to use some of the leftover detergent to fix the armadillo's armor.

4   The coyote filled a tub with water and poured in a liquid from a bottle. The water shifted through a **kaleidoscope** of colors before finally settling on a shade of bright green. The armadillo removed his armor and put it in the tub. The coyote told the armadillo that it would take three days for the detergent to take effect. The armadillo asked if she was pulling his leg. Three days seemed too long to be without his precious armor.

5   With a long face, the armadillo returned to his home. Over the next three days, he was unable to sleep a wink. He'd wonder what would happen if he got into an accident or worse—what would happen if the treatment didn't work? He became unhealthy. He forgot to eat and became rail-thin. When the third day finally came, the armadillo rushed to the coyote's home.

6   The coyote, who never minced words, told the armadillo that he looked terrible. The armadillo explained the sleepless nights and missed meals. Then he asked to see his armor. The coyote retrieved the armor. It was spotless. Excited, the armadillo tried to slide it onto his body, but he had become so thin that the armor fell off. The coyote scolded him for not taking care of himself. She said, "My friend, there's nothing wrong with showing concern, but look at yourself! Worrying didn't fix your problems. It just made things worse."

The Worried Armadillo

First Read

Read the story. After you read, answer the Think Questions below.

☁ THINK QUESTIONS

1. What bad thing happened to the armadillo at the start of the fable?

_____

_____.

2. How does the coyote offer to help the armadillo?

_____

_____.

3. What problem does the armadillo have at the end of the fable?

_____

_____.

4. Use context to confirm the meaning of the word *detergent* as it is used in "The Worried Armadillo." Write your definition of *detergent* here.

_____

_____.

5. What is another way to say that the party was a *catastrophe*?

_____

_____.

Skill:
Analyzing Expressions

 DEFINE

When you read, you may find English expressions that you do not know. An **expression** is a group of words that communicates an idea. Two types of expressions are **idioms** and **sayings**. They can be difficult to understand because the meanings of the words are different from their **literal**, or usual, meanings.

An **idiom** is an expression that is commonly known among a group of people. For example: "It's raining cats and dogs" means it is raining heavily. **Sayings** are short expressions that contain advice or wisdom. For instance: "Don't count your chickens before they hatch" means do not plan on something good happening before it happens. Neither expression is about actual animals.

••• CHECKLIST FOR ANALYZING EXPRESSIONS

To determine the meaning of an expression, remember the following:

✓ If you find a confusing group of words, it may be an expression. The meaning of words in expressions may not be their literal meaning.

- Ask yourself: Is this confusing because the words are new? Or because the words do not make sense together?

✓ Determining the overall meaning may require that you use one or more of the following:

- context clues

- a dictionary or other resource

- teacher or peer support

✓ Highlight important information before and after the expression to look for clues.

⟳ YOUR TURN

Read the following excerpt from paragraph 4 of the story. Then, complete the multiple-choice questions below.

from "The Worried Armadillo"

The coyote filled a tub with water and poured in a liquid from a bottle. The water shifted through a kaleidoscope of colors before finally settling on a shade of bright green. The armadillo removed his armor and put it in the tub. The coyote told the armadillo that it would take three days for the detergent to take effect. The armadillo asked if she was pulling his leg. Three days seemed too long to be without his precious armor.

1. What does "if she was pulling his leg" mean in this story?

    ○ A. if the coyote was holding the armadillo's leg

    ○ B. if the coyote was joking with the armadillo

    ○ C. if the coyote was upset with the armadillo

    ○ D. if the coyote was going to help the armadillo

2. Which context clue helped you determine the meaning of the expression?

    ○ A. "The coyote filled a tub with water and poured in a liquid from a bottle."

    ○ B. "The armadillo removed his armor and put it in the tub."

    ○ C. "three days for the detergent to take effect"

    ○ D. "Three days seemed too long to be without his precious armor."

Skill: Drawing Inferences and Conclusions

★ DEFINE

Making **inferences** means connecting your experiences with what you read. Authors do not always tell readers directly everything that takes place in a story or text. You need to use clues to infer, or make a guess, about what is happening. To make an inference, first find facts, details, and examples in the text. Then think about what you already know. Combine the **text evidence** with your **background knowledge** to draw a **conclusion** about what the author is trying to communicate.

Making inferences and drawing conclusions can help you better understand what you are reading. It may also help you search for and find the author's message in the text.

••• CHECKLIST FOR DRAWING INFERENCES AND CONCLUSIONS

In order to make inferences and draw conclusions, do the following:

✓ Look for information that is missing from the text or that is not directly stated.

- Ask yourself: What is confusing? What is missing?

✓ Think about what you already know about the topic.

- Ask yourself: Have I had a similar experience in my life? Have I learned about this subject in another class?

✓ Combine clues from the text with prior knowledge to make an inference and draw a conclusion.

- Think: I can conclude _____
  because the text says _____
  and I know that _____.

✓ Use text evidence to support your inference and make sure that it is valid.

  Reading & Writing Companion

↻ YOUR TURN

Read the following excerpt from paragraphs 1 and 2 of the story. Then, complete the multiple-choice questions below.

> from "The Worried Armadillo"
>
> Once there was an armadillo. Like all armadillos, he had armor protecting his body. Whenever he felt in danger, he could curl up into a ball and nothing could hurt him. His armor was his pride and joy.
>
> The armadillo was also an artist. He was known all over the town for his talent, so the mayor asked him to paint a black-and-white mural to commemorate the town's growth. When he began painting, the armadillo slipped and fell off his ladder. His shell protected him from harm, but paint spattered all over him.

1. At the beginning of the excerpt, the armadillo:

   ○ A. wants to curl up into a ball.
   ○ B. feels like he is in danger.
   ○ C. loves his armor.
   ○ D. feels like he does not need his armor.

2. A detail that best supports this conclusion is:

   ○ A. "like all armadillos"
   ○ B. "he could curl up"
   ○ C. "nothing could hurt him"
   ○ D. "His armor was his pride and joy."

3. Details at the beginning of paragraph 2 tell that the armadillo is a:

   ○ A. photographer.
   ○ B. friend of the mayor.
   ○ C. very good painter.
   ○ D. historian.

4. A detail that best supports this conclusion is:

   ○ A. "The armadillo was also an artist."
   ○ B. "known all over town for his talent"
   ○ C. "a black-and-white mural"
   ○ D. "the town's growth"

Close Read

✏ WRITE

NARRATIVE: Rewrite the fable so that it teaches a new moral. Use characters, events, and details from the original text. Pay attention to negatives and contractions as you write.

Use the checklist below to guide you as you write.

☐ Which characters are involved?

☐ What is a problem that happens in the fable?

☐ What is the moral that the reader learns?

Use the sentence frames to organize and write your narrative.

Once, there was an armadillo _____.

A coyote heard him crying and _____.

The coyote _____.

But the armadillo _____.

The coyote said, "If you take your armor now, _____

_____."

The coyote said, "Remember that if you are going to do a job well, _____

_____."

UNIT 6

The Power of One

How do we stand out from the crowd?

Genre Focus: DRAMA

Texts

 Paired Readings

Extended Oral Project and Grammar

How do we stand out from a crowd?

MAYA ANGELOU

Maya Angelou (1928–2014) was a poet, essayist, director, and playwright. Her most famous work is *I Know Why the Caged Bird Sings*, an autobiography. She was a member of the Harlem Writers Guild, where she met writer James Baldwin. She was the first black female director in Hollywood, and a Civil Rights activist who worked for Martin Luther King Jr. and Malcolm X. She was awarded the National Medal of the Arts in 2000 by President Bill Clinton, and the Presidential Medal of Freedom in 2011 by President Barack Obama.

LAURA BUSH

Former second-grade teacher and graduate of Southern Methodist University, Laura Lane Welch Bush (b. 1946) was born in Midland, Texas, earned her master's degree in library science from the University of Texas at Austin, and met her husband and future U.S. president George Walker Bush at a backyard barbecue at the home of mutual friends. As First Lady, she established the National Book Festival, was named by the United Nations as an honorary ambassador for the UN's Decade of LIteracy, and in 2002 was honored by the Elie Wiesel Foundation for Humanity.

NIKKI GIOVANNI

Born in Knoxville, Tennessee, poet Nikki Giovanni (b. 1943) graduated from Fisk University with honors in history, and since 1987 has served on the faculty at Virginia Tech, where she is a Distinguished Professor. She is the author of collections of poetry including *Black Feeling, Black Talk / Black Judgement;* and *Re: Creation*. She has received the Langston Hughes Award for Distinguished Contributions to Arts and Letters and the Rosa Parks Women of Courage Award. About her work, Giovanni has said, "Writing is . . . what I do to justify the air I breathe."

LOIS LOWRY

Newbery Medal-winning author Lois Lowry (b. 1937) was born in Honolulu, Hawaii, but relocated often following the path of her father's career in the military, which took her family from Japan to New York, Pennsylvania, California, and Connecticut. Lowry grew up dreaming of becoming a writer, and she found comfort in reading during a childhood of constant relocation. She graduated from the University of Southern Maine with a degree in English literature. Lowry's book *The Giver* has sold over 10 million copies and was adapted into a 2014 film.

KATHRYN SCHULTZ MILLER

Kathryn Schultz Miller is the cofounder of ArtReach Touring Theater, where she has also served as the Artistic Director for over twenty years. Miller is the recipient of a playwriting fellowship from the National Endowment for the Arts and the winner of the 1985 Post-Corbett Award "for literary excellence in playwriting." She is the author of fifty-six published plays, including *Haunted Houses* and *A Thousand Cranes*, which was performed at the Kennedy Center. Fourteen of her plays have been produced at the national level. She lives in Cincinnati.

GREGORY RAMOS

Gregory Ramos studied acting at Playwrights Horizons before earning his MFA in playwriting at UCLA. He has directed, written, and choreographed shows across the country, and served on the faculty of the University of Texas at El Paso, where he founded The Latino Guest Artists Program and the Border Public Theater. At the University of Vermont, he directed the Critical Race and Ethnic Studies Program. He currently teaches and serves as the chair of the school's Department of Theater, and is the board president of the Vermont Shakespeare Festival.

MARGOT LEE SHETTERLY

Long before Margot Lee Shetterly (b. 1969) wrote *Hidden Figures: The Story of the African-American Women Who Helped Win the Space Race*, her father worked as a research scientist at the NASA Langley Research Center. She grew up around other NASA families and later attended the University of Virginia. After pursuing a career in investment banking and launching a magazine in Mexico with her husband, she began research on *Hidden Figures*. The eventual 2016 film adaptation would be nominated for three Oscars and gross $236 million worldwide.

MEKEISHA MADDEN TOBY

Writer, editor, critic, journalist, and podcast producer Mekeisha Madden Toby has worked for the *Los Angeles Times*, *Variety*, CNN, *US Weekly*, espnW, and *Rotten Tomatoes*. Toby graduated with a degree in journalism from Wayne State University in Detroit, Michigan, where she grew up attending Cass Technical High School and working on her school newspaper. She currently hosts her own podcast, *TV Madness with Mekeisha Madden Toby*, which covers the film and television landscape, from Netflix to the big screen. Toby lives in Los Angeles.

BARBARA DEMICK

Barbara Demick began interviewing North Koreans for her future book *Nothing to Envy: Ordinary Lives in North Korea* starting in 2001, when her work for the *Los Angeles Times* brought her to Seoul, South Korea. For her reporting, Demick has won the Overseas Press Club's award, was named a finalist for the National Book Award, and was nominated for the Pulitzer Prize. The Ridgewood, New Jersey, native began her career with the *Philadelphia Inquirer,* when she lived in Sarajevo and worked as a foreign correspondent covering the Bosnian War from 1994–1996.

VELINA HASU HOUSTON

Playwright Velina Hasu Houston (b. 1957) was born in international waters on a military ship en route to the United States from Japan. She grew up in Junction City, Kansas, not far from the base to which her father was assigned, and attended both the University of California at Los Angeles and the University of Southern California. In 1991 she founded USC's Master of Fine Arts in Dramatic Writing program. She currently serves at USC as a Distinguished Professor, the first person of African descent to be named as such, and the Resident Playwright.

The Giver

FICTION
Lois Lowry
1993

Introduction

Lois Lowry (b. 1937) is a two-time Newbery Award winner for her novels *Number the Stars* and *The Giver*. A work of science fiction, *The Giver* focuses on Jonas's community, a place where there is no hunger, disease, or poverty, but also little individual choice. All major decisions are trusted to the Committee of Elders, and at age 12, each community member is assigned a career path by the Committee. In this excerpt, Jonas, who will soon turn 12, expresses his concerns about the future to his parents.

"The Ceremony of Twelve was the last of the Ceremonies. The most important."

NOTES

Excerpt from Chapter 2

1   Jonas shivered. He pictured his father, who must have been a shy and quiet boy, for he was a shy and quiet man, seated with his group, waiting to be called to the stage. The Ceremony of Twelve was the last of the Ceremonies. The most important.

2   "I remember how proud my parents looked—and my sister, too; even though she wanted to be out riding the bicycle publicly, she stopped fidgeting and was very still and attentive when my turn came.

3   "But to be honest, Jonas," his father said, "for me there was not the **element** of suspense that there is with your Ceremony. Because I was already fairly certain of what my Assignment was to be."

4   Jonas was surprised. There was no way, really, to know in advance. It was a secret selection, made by the leaders of the community, the Committee of Elders, who took the responsibility so seriously that there were never even any jokes made about assignments.

5   His mother seemed surprised, too. "How could you have known?" she asked.

6   His father smiled his gentle smile. "Well, it was clear to me—and my parents later confessed that it had been obvious to them, too—what my **aptitude** was. I had always loved the newchildren more than anything. When my friends in my age group were holding bicycle races, or building toy vehicles or bridges with their construction sets, or—"

7   "All the things I do with my friends," Jonas pointed out, and his mother nodded in agreement.

8   "I always participated, of course, because as children we must experience all of those things. And I studied hard in school, just as you do, Jonas. But again and again, during free time, I found myself drawn to the newchildren. I spent almost all of my volunteer hours helping in the Nurturing Center. Of course the Elders knew that, from their observation."

Please note that excerpts and passages in the StudySync® library and this workbook are intended as touchstones to generate interest in an author's work. The excerpts and passages do not substitute for the reading of entire texts, and StudySync® strongly recommends that students seek out and purchase the whole literary or informational work in order to experience it as the author intended. Links to online resellers are available in our digital library. In addition, complete works may be ordered through an authorized reseller by filling out and returning to StudySync® the order form enclosed in this workbook.

Reading & Writing Companion   **829**

9   Jonas nodded. During the past year he had been aware of the increasing level of observation. In school, at recreation time, and during volunteer hours, he had noticed the Elders watching him and the other Elevens. He had seen them taking notes. He knew, too, that the Elders were meeting for long hours with all of the instructors that he and the other Elevens had had during their years of school.

10   "So I expected it, and I was pleased, but not at all surprised, when my Assignment was announced as **Nurturer**," Father explained.

11   "Did everyone applaud, even though they weren't surprised?" Jonas asked.

12   "Oh, of course. They were happy for me, that my Assignment was what I wanted most. I felt very fortunate." His father smiled.

13   "Were any of the Elevens disappointed, your year?" Jonas asked. Unlike his father, he had no idea what his Assignment would be. But he knew that some would disappoint him. Though he respected his father's work, Nurturer would not be his wish. And he didn't **envy** Laborers at all.

14   His father thought. "No, I don't think so. Of course the Elders are so careful in their observations and selections."

15   "I think it's probably the most important job in our community," his mother commented.

16   "My friend Yoshiko was surprised by her selection as Doctor," Father said, "but she was thrilled. And let's see, there was Andrei—I remember that when we were boys he never wanted to do physical things. He spent all the recreation time he could with his construction set, and his volunteer hours were always on building sites. The Elders knew that, of course. Andrei was given the Assignment of Engineer and he was delighted."

17   "Andrei later designed the bridge that crosses the river to the west of town," Jonas's mother said. "It wasn't there when we were children."

18   "There are very rarely disappointments, Jonas. I don't think you need to worry about that," his father reassured him. "And if there are, you know there's an **appeal** process." But they all laughed at that—an appeal went to a committee for study.

19   "I worry a little about Asher's Assignment," Jonas confessed. "Asher's such *fun*. But he doesn't really have any serious interests. He makes a game out of everything."

20   His father chuckled. "You know," he said, "I remember when Asher was a newchild at the Nurturing Center, before he was named. He never cried. He giggled and laughed at everything. All of us on the staff enjoyed nurturing Asher."

21 "The Elders know Asher," his mother said. "They'll find exactly the right Assignment for him. I don't think you need to worry about him. But, Jonas, let me warn you about something that may not have occurred to you. I know I didn't think about it until after my Ceremony of Twelve."

22 "What's that?"

23 "Well, it's the last of the Ceremonies, as you know. After Twelve, age isn't important. Most of us even lose track of how old we are as time passes, though the information is in the Hall of Open Records, and we could go and look it up if we wanted to. What's important is the preparation for adult life, and the training you'll receive in your Assignment."

24 "I know that," Jonas said. "Everyone knows that."

25 "But it means," his mother went on, "that you'll move into a new group. And each of your friends will. You'll no longer be spending your time with your group of Elevens. After the Ceremony of Twelve, you'll be with your Assignment group, with those in training. No more volunteer hours. No more recreation hours. So your friends will no longer be as close."

26 Jonas shook his head. "Asher and I will always be friends," he said firmly. "And there will still be school."

27 "That's true," his father agreed. "But what your mother said is true as well. There will be changes."

28 *"Good* changes, though," his mother pointed out.

Excerpted from *The Giver* by Lois Lowry, published by Houghton Mifflin Harcourt.

✏ WRITE

PERSONAL RESPONSE: What do you think are the positive and negative aspects of living in a society in which each person's future occupation is decided for them? Would you want to live in such a society? Cite evidence from the text to support your response.

Please note that excerpts and passages in the StudySync® library and this workbook are intended as touchstones to generate interest in an author's work. The excerpts and passages do not substitute for the reading of entire texts, and StudySync® strongly recommends that students seek out and purchase the whole literary or informational work in order to experience it as the author intended. Links to online resellers are available in our digital library. In addition, complete works may be ordered through an authorized reseller by filling out and returning to StudySync® the order form enclosed in this workbook.

Reading & Writing Companion

831

Nothing to Envy:
Ordinary Lives in North Korea

INFORMATIONAL TEXT
Barbara Demick
2010

Introduction

n 2006, Barbara Demick won the Joe and Laurie Dine Award for Human Rights Reporting, and was named print journalist of the year by the Los Angeles Press Club. She received these accolades for her groundbreaking insight into the daily lives of North Koreans, who live under a totalitarian regime. In *Nothing to Envy*, Barbara Demick penetrates the shadowy dictatorship in order to share the lives of six ordinary individuals. The following excerpt features two of the main characters: Mrs. Song, a bookkeeper and loyal supporter of Kim Il-sung's regime, and her daughter Oak-hee, who is dangerously inclined to be skeptical. The excerpt begins with Mrs. Song and her husband Chang-bo, an independent thinker, watching television, an activity they proudly share with apartment house neighbors who cannot afford the luxury of TV.

"Spying on one's countrymen is something of a national pastime."

from Chapter Three: The True Believer

1   The program that got Chang-bo in trouble was an **innocuous** business report about a shoe factory producing rubber boots for the rainy season. The camera panned over crisply efficient workers on an assembly line where the boots were being produced by the thousands. The narrator raved about the superb quality of the boots and reeled off the impressive production statistics.

2   "Hah. If there are so many boots, how come my children never got any?" Chang-bo laughed aloud. The words tumbled out of his mouth before he could consider the consequences.

3   Mrs. Song never figured out which neighbor blabbed. Her husband's remark was quickly reported to the head of the *inminban*, the neighborhood watchdogs, who in turn passed on the information to the Ministry for the Protection of State Security. This **ominously** named agency is effectively North Korea's political police. It runs an extensive network of informers. By the accounts of **defectors**, there is at least one informer for every fifty people—more even than East Germany's notorious Stasi, whose files were pried open after German reunification.

4   Spying on one's countrymen is something of a national pastime. There were the young vigilantes from the Socialist Youth League like the one who stopped Mrs. Song for not wearing a badge. They also made sure people weren't violating the dress code by wearing blue jeans or T-shirts with Roman writing—considered a capitalist indulgence—or wearing their hair too long. The party issued regular edicts saying that men shouldn't allow the hair on top of their head to grow longer than five centimeters—though an exemption was granted for balding men, who were permitted seven centimeters. If a violation was severe, the offender could be arrested by the Public Standards Police. There were also *kyuch'aldae*, mobile police units who roamed the streets looking for offenders and had the right to barge into people's houses without notice. They would look for people who used more than their quota of electricity, a light bulb brighter than 40 watts, a hot plate, or a rice cooker. During one of the surprise inspections, one of the neighbors tried to hide their hot plate

under a blanket and ended up setting their apartment on fire. The mobile police often dropped in after midnight to see if there were any overnight guests who might have come to visit without travel permits. It was a serious offense, even if it was just an out-of-town relative, and much worse if the guest happened to be a lover. But it wasn't just the police and the volunteer leagues who did the snooping. Everybody was supposed to be vigilant for subversive behavior and transgressions of the rules. Since the country was too poor and the power supply too unreliable for electronic surveillance, state security relied on human intelligence—snitches[1]. The newspapers would occasionally run feature stories about heroic children who ratted out their parents. To be denounced by a neighbor for bad-mouthing the **regime** was nothing extraordinary.

5   Chang-bo's interrogation lasted three days. The agents yelled and cursed at him, although they never beat him—at least that's what he told his wife. He claimed afterward that his gift with language helped him talk his way out of the bind. He cited the truth in his defense.

6   "I wasn't insulting anybody. I was simply saying that I haven't been able to buy those boots and I'd like to have some for my family," Chang-bo protested indignantly.

7   He made a convincing case. He was a commanding figure with his potbelly and his stern expression. He looked like the epitome of a Workers' Party official. The political police in the end decided not to push the case and released him without charges.

8   When he returned home, he got a tongue-lashing from his wife that was almost harsher than the interrogation. It was the worst fight of their marriage. For Mrs. Song, it was not merely that her husband had been disrespectful of the government; for the first time in her life, she felt the stirrings of fear. Her conduct had always been so impeccable and her **devotion** so genuine that it never occurred to her that she might be vulnerable.

9   "Why did you say such nonsense when there were neighbors in the apartment? Didn't you realize you could have jeopardized everything we have?" she railed at him.

10   In fact, they both realized how lucky they were. If not for Chang-bo's excellent class background and his party membership, he would not have been let off so lightly. It helped, too, that Mrs. Song had at various times been head of the *inminban* in the building and commanded some respect from the state security officers. Chang-bo's offhand remark was precisely the kind of thing

---

1. **snitches** informers

that could result in deportation to a prison camp in the mountains if the offender didn't have a solid position in the community. They had heard of a man who cracked a joke about Kim Jong-il's height and was sent away for life. Mrs. Song personally knew a woman from her factory who was taken away for something she wrote in her diary. At the time, Mrs. Song hadn't felt any pity for the woman. "The traitor probably deserved what she got," she'd said to herself. Now she felt embarrassed for having thought such a thing.

11   The incident seemed to blow over. Chastened by the experience, Chang-bo was more careful about what he said outside the family, but his thoughts were running wild. For many years, Chang-bo had been fighting off the doubts that would periodically creep into his consciousness. Now those doubts were gelling into outright disbelief. As a journalist, Chang-bo had more access to information than ordinary people. At the North Hamgyong Provincial Broadcasting Company, where he worked, he and his colleagues heard uncensored news reports from the foreign media. It was their job to sanitize it for domestic consumption. Anything positive that happened in capitalist countries or especially South Korea, which in 1988 hosted the Summer Olympics, was downplayed. Strikes, disasters, riots, murders—elsewhere— got plenty of coverage.

12   Chang-bo's job was to report business stories. He toured collective farms, shops, and factories with a notebook and tape recorder, interviewing the managers. Back in the newsroom, he would write his stories in fountain pen (there were no typewriters) about how well the economy was doing. He always put a positive spin on the facts, although he tried to keep them at least plausible. By the time they were edited by his superiors in Pyongyang, however, any glimmer of the truth was gone. Chang-bo knew better than anyone that the supposed triumphs of the North Korean economy were **fabrications.** He had good reason to scoff at the report about the rubber boots.

13   He had one trusted friend from the radio station who shared his increasing disdain for the regime. When the two of them got together, Chang-bo would open a bottle of Mrs. Song's *neungju* and, after a few drinks, they would let rip their true feelings.

14   "What a bunch of liars!" Chang-bo would say in an emphatic tone, taking care just the same not to speak loudly enough for the sound to carry through the thin plaster walls between the apartments.

15   "Crooks, all of them."

16   "The son is even worse than the father."

17   Oak-hee eavesdropped on her father and his friend. She nodded quietly in agreement. When her father noticed, he at first tried to shoo her away. Eventually he gave up. Swearing her to secrecy, he took her into his confidence. He told her that Kim Il-sung was not the anti-Japanese resistance fighter he claimed to be so much as a puppet of the Soviet Union. He told her that South Korea was now among the richest countries in Asia; even ordinary working people owned their own cars. Communism, he reported, was proving a failure as an economic system. China and the Soviet Union were now embracing capitalism. Father and daughter would talk for hours, always taking care to keep their voices at a whisper in case a neighbor was snooping around. And, at such times, they always made sure that Mrs. Song, the true believer, was not at home.

Excerpted from Nothing to Envy: Ordinary Lives in North Korea *by Barbara Demick, published by Spiegel & Grau*

 WRITE

PERSONAL RESPONSE: Imagine that you are a journalist and want to write an article explaining to someone why it is so dangerous to speak freely in North Korea. Write an article explaining the challenges concerning people's use of free speech, incorporating examples and information from the text.

A Thousand Cranes

DRAMA
Kathryn Schultz Miller
1990

Introduction

Kathryn Schultz Miller is a playwright and the winner of the 1985 Post-Corbett Award for "literary excellence in playwriting." She served as co-founder and artistic director of ArtReach Touring Theatre based in Cincinnati. Among her produced works are *Island Son*, *The Legend of Sleepy Hollow*, and *Amelia Hart*. *A Thousand Cranes* is based on a true story of a young Japanese girl named Sadako Sasaki who was two years old when the atomic bombs were dropped on Hiroshima and Nagasaki on August 6th and August 9th during the final stages of World War II. At twelve she became ill with "radiation sickness." As she hoped to get better, she attempted to fold a thousand cranes.

"I wished that there will never ever be a bomb like that again."

1   AT RISE: *The playing area is a circle of about 20 feet by 20 feet. Audience is seated on three sides of the playing area. Upstage R of the circle will be a musical or instrument "station" with percussion instruments and recorded music arranged in such a way that at* **appropriate** *times actors may sit comfortably on a stool and contribute music and sound effects to the performance. UL are standing fans of various pastels and varying heights, the tallest being less than 5 feet. To the left and right downstage are two white masks on each side in tube holders about waist high. GRANDMOTHER OBA CHAN will wear a magnificent Japanese mask. ACTORS 1 and 2 will carry white masks when playing the parts of the DOCTORS. SPIRITS will be indicated by red masks on holders but will not actually be worn by actors. SADAKO, KENJI, MOTHER and FATHER will not wear masks. ACTORS 1 and 2 will wear all black. SADAKO wears a* **simple** *western-style school uniform of a skirt and a blouse with a tie.*

2   *The play begins in silence. ACTORS 1 and 2 bow to each other before the music stand. SADAKO watches from behind the music stand. ACTORS 1 and 2 mime lifting a large piece of paper off the floor. In mirrored motions, they carry the paper to DC, carefully place it on the floor and gently smooth it out. They bow again, then turn U. SADAKO crosses down to paper as recorded folding music begins. The mood of the music gentle and pleasant. ACTORS 1 and 2 count with SADAKO as she mimes the folding of a larger-than-life crane.*

3   ALL *(punctuating their words with percussion sounds).* One, two, three, four, five, six, seven, eight, nine . . . *(SADAKO mimes the lifting of the giant bird with both hands. It is very light. She thrusts the bird into flight.)*

4   SADAKO. Ten. *(SADAKO blows as if to launch it. ALL watch it in the sky, from left to right. To AUDIENCE.)* My name is Sadako. I was born in Japan in 1943. My home was called Hiroshima. *(Quiet sound effects come from ACTORS 1 and 2.)* When I was two years old, my mother held me in her arms. She sang a song to me. *(ACTOR 2 sings in a soothing, quiet melody.)* It was a quiet summer morning. Inside our small house my Grandmother was preparing tea. *(SADAKO pauses while ACTOR 2 sings.)* Suddenly there was a tremendous flash of light that cut across the sky! *(A very, very loud startling BOOM noise.*

Skill: Dramatic Elements and Structure

At first, the music is gentle and pleasant. Then when the actors start counting, the stage directions say that there is percussion. This gives the play an urgent tone. The form of this play is probably tragedy.

The music and the percussion all build to Sadako's monologue. I know she has an important story to tell.

SADAKO falls into a kneeling position, covering her head. When all is quiet she stands.) My name is Sadako. This is my story. *(A dramatic rhythm beat, not as loud as before and slowly fading.)*

5   ACTOR 2 *(quietly fading away).* Sixty-seven, sixty-eight, sixty-nine, seventy . . .

6   *(SADAKO and ACTOR 1, now KENJI, have moved U and now KENJI comes bounding on to playing area, out of breath and laughing. He wears a black cap to distinguish himself as KENJI. He begins to count, determining by how many seconds he has won the race with SADAKO. As ACTOR 2's counting fades he picks it up. They say the primary numbers, one and two and three, etc., together.)*

7   ACTOR 2 *(fading).* Seventy . . . seventy-one . . . seventy-two . . .

8   KENJI. One . . . two . . . three . . . four

9   *(SADAKO runs in out of breath and laughing.)*

10   KENJI. Beat you by four seconds.

11   SADAKO. Four? You're lying!

12   KENJI *(laughing).* It was actually four and a half, but I let you have that.

13   SADAKO. Oh! You . . . ! *(Slumping.)* You always win! You should let somebody else win sometime.

14   KENJI. Why, Sadako. You can't mean that I should cheat so that you can win.

15   SADAKO. Oh, it wouldn't be cheating so much as . . . polite.

16   KENJI *(laughing).* And I suppose when you run in the girl's contest next month you'll want the judges to be *polite* and let somebody else win.

17   SADAKO. Well, no.

18   KENJI. I thought so.

19   SADAKO. Oh, Kenji, do you think I have a chance to win?

20   KENJI *(mocking).* You? You win a race against the fastest girls in Hiroshima? You can't win.

21   SADAKO. Why not?

Skill:
Character

I know from the stage directions that this story will be about Sadako. She will probably be the protagonist. I think this is interesting because the play starts with her explaining the bombing of Hiroshima. I wonder if the bomb had any effect on her? She seems happy and loves to race and win. I wonder if the contest will be important in this play. How will it impact Sadako and the plot?

22 KENJI. Because you're a turtle, that's why. A great big lumbering turtle. *(Mimes slow turtle, laughing at his jest.)*

23 SADAKO. I am not a turtle.

24 KENJI. Yes, you are.

25 SADAKO. Am not.

26 KENJI. Are too.

27 SADAKO. Well, if I'm a turtle, then you're a frog!

28 KENJI. A frog?

29 SADAKO. Yes. A great big green one with warts all over it.

30 KENJI. Sadako, you can't possibly mean . . . croak . . . *(Putting her on.)* Well, where on earth could that have come from? Croak!

31 SADAKO. Oh, you.

32 KENJI. Look, Sadako, my hand is turning green . . . croak . . . and it has warts all over it! *(He crouches to a frog position and sticks out his tongue, leaping around, croaking. Uses bill of his cap to indicate the mouth of the croaking frog.)* Croak! Croak!

33 SADAKO *(laughing in spite of herself)*. Now, you stop that. *(She is laughing almost uncontrollably; soon KENJI stops and laughs with her. They stop, leaning on each other, gaining composure.)* Kenji, tell me the truth. Do you think I have *any* chance of winning the races next month?

34 KENJI. Sadako, I will tell you the truth. I believe you will win.

35 SADAKO *(thrilled)*. You really think so? You really, really do?

36 KENJI. Yes. I really, really do.

37 SADAKO. Oh, Kenji! *(She hugs him.)* Wait until I tell my father. He will be so proud of me! *(She starts to go.)*

38 KENJI. Now don't quit practicing!

39 SADAKO. Oh, I won't.

40   KENJI. See you tomorrow?

41   SADAKO. Tomorrow! *(She moves U as if to exit.)*

42   *(KENJI, now ACTOR 1, moves to instrument station and makes music for scene change. SADAKO moves U as ACTOR 2, now MOTHER, moves into the scene. She is counting out candles and putting them on the table. She wears a kimono. ACTOR 1 counts and then fades as MOTHER joins in and finally ends the counting.)*

43   ACTOR 1. One hundred and eighteen, one hundred and nineteen, one hundred and twenty, one hundred and twenty-one, one hundred and twenty-two . . . one hundred and twenty-three . . . *(Again, they speak the primary numbers together.)*

44   MOTHER *(counting candles).* One . . . two . . . three . . . four . . .

45   *(SADAKO comes running in, very excited.)*

46   SADAKO. Mother, Mother! Wait till you hear! I have wonderful news!

47   MOTHER *(not looking up, continues working).* Your shoes, Sadako.

48   SADAKO. Oh. *(She calms down to **remove** her shoes, puts them by the door, then rushes back to MOTHER.)* Wait till I tell you!

49   MOTHER. Sadako, show your respect to your elders.

50   SADAKO. Oh. *(She bows, puts hands together as in prayer and bows her head toward MOTHER.)* Mother, Kenji just told me . . . !

51   MOTHER. Sadako, show your respect to our beloved ancestors. *(Disheartened, SADAKO kneels before an imaginary shrine, hands in prayer and bowing her head. Returns to MOTHER, somewhat **subdued.**)*

52   SADAKO. Mother, I . . .

53   MOTHER. You must wait for your father to tell this earth-shattering news. Now it is time to prepare for dinner.

54   SADAKO. But, Mother . . .

55   MOTHER. Sushi has been prepared, the rice plates have been set. Sadako, you may warm the saki for your father.

Please note that excerpts and passages in the StudySync® library and this workbook are intended as touchstones to generate interest in an author's work. The excerpts and passages do not substitute for the reading of entire texts, and StudySync® strongly recommends that students seek out and purchase the whole literary or informational work in order to experience it as the author intended. Links to online resellers are available in our digital library. In addition, complete works may be ordered through an authorized reseller by filling out and returning to StudySync® the order form enclosed in this workbook.

Reading & Writing Companion   **841**

NOTES

56 SADAKO. Yes, Mother. *(MOTHER straightens candles on the table.)*

57 *(FATHER enters, takes off his shoes.)*

58 SADAKO. Father! *(She runs to him, grabs him in embrace and almost twirls him around.)* Wait till I tell you!

59 FATHER. Well, what is this?

60 MOTHER *(not angry)*. This daughter of yours will not learn **discipline.**

61 FATHER. Your mother is right, Sadako. You must learn moderation in all things.

62 SADAKO. But, Father. I have such wonderful news!

63 FATHER *(warm)*. It seems that everything in your world is wonderful, Sadako. *(Kisses the top of her head.)* You may tell us your news.

64 SADAKO *(looks anxiously at them BOTH)*. Now?

65 FATHER *(laughing)*. Now, Sadako.

66 SADAKO. Kenji says I'm fast enough to win the race next month! Isn't that wonderful? He thinks I can *win!*

67 FATHER *(genuinely impressed)*. You have been practicing very hard.

68 SADAKO. Oh, yes, Father. Kenji and I run every day.

69 FATHER. Kenji is a fast runner, an excellent athlete.

70 SADAKO. Yes, he is, Father. And a good teacher too.

71 MOTHER. Even so, you must use discipline to practice very hard if you really want to win.

72 SADAKO. Oh, I want to win, Mother. I want to win more than anything on earth!

73 FATHER. We are very proud of you, Sadako. *(BOTH parents hug her. MOTHER begins to light candles.)*

74 SADAKO. Mother, why are you lighting candles on the table?

75 MOTHER. Soon it will be Oban, Sadako.

NOTES

76   FATHER. It is the day of the spirits.

77   MOTHER. We light a candle for our ancestors who have died.

78   FATHER. We ask them to return to us and join in our celebration of life.

79   MOTHER *(has lit all but last candle)*. This one is for Oba chan, your Grandmother.

80   SADAKO. I remember her. I was only a baby, but I remember how warm my grandmother's hands were. *(She kneels before the candles. MOTHER and FATHER move away. Their lines now sound like statements in a dream.)*

81   FATHER. Oba chan died in the Thunderbolt.

82   SADAKO. She had a gentle voice.

83   MOTHER. Suddenly there was a great flash of light.

84   SADAKO. Her smile was like sunshine.

85   FATHER. It cut through the sky!

86   SADAKO. Grandmother? Grandmother?

87   MOTHER. The world was filled with blinding light. *(MOTHER and FATHER spin away with arms up in protecting gesture. They twirl to their places behind the music stand where they make percussion sounds.)*

88   SADAKO. Can you hear me, Grandmother?

89   FATHER. It took our friends.

90   SADAKO. Can your spirit really return like they say?

91   MOTHER. It took our home.

92   SADAKO. Are you watching me now? Do you see me when I run?

93   FATHER. It took your Grandmother, Oba chan.

94   *(MOTHER and FATHER now become ACTOR 1 and ACTOR 2. They use a percussion sound that builds and when it stops the silence is startling. They begin to count.)*

95   ACTORS 1 and 2. One hundred and fifty-one . . .

96 SADAKO. One. *(Blows out first candle.)*

97 ACTORS 1 and 2. One hundred and fifty-two . . .

98 SADAKO. Two. *(Blows out second candle.)*

99 ACTORS 1 and 2. One hundred and fifty-three . . .

100 SADAKO. Three. *(Blows out third candle.)*

101 ACTORS 1 and 2. One hundred and fifty-four . . .

102 SADAKO *(before the candle of her GRANDMOTHER, looks up).* Will I win my race, Grandmother? Can you hear me now? *(Turns back to candle.)* Four. *(Blows out candle, stands and looks around.)* Grandmother?

103 *(ACTOR 1 plays a loud dramatic percussion sound that fades. ACTOR 2, using the voice she will use later as GRANDMOTHER, speaks.)*

104 ACTOR 2/GRANDMOTHER *(as she moves slowly, twirling away until she is hidden behind the largest fan).* I hear you, Sadako!

105 *(The loud cymbal[1] sound comes again and fades into a new sound. Now a fast, quick staccato[2] sound is heard from the instrument stand. ACTOR 1 also is KENJI, using only the voice from his location. ACTOR 2 turns U to put on GRANDMOTHER OBA CHAN's mask. SADAKO begins to run in place.)*

106 KENJI *(moving D to replace set piece and back to music stand.)* You little turtle, you'll never win at that speed. *(SADAKO speaks as if he is beside her, running.)*

107 SADAKO *(running).* I am not a turtle!

108 KENJI. Sure you are, that's how fast turtles run, isn't it?

109 SADAKO. Croak, croak, croak! *(They BOTH laugh.)*

110 KENJI. I bet I can make it to the river before you!

111 SADAKO. Bet you can't.

112 KENJI. Bet I can!

---

1. **cymbal** a brass plate that makes a ringing or clashing sound when struck
2. **staccato** (in music) consisting of sharp, separate notes

113 SADAKO. Bet you can't. *(She runs faster in place as percussion sound also speeds up.)*

114 *(ACTOR 2, who now becomes GRANDMOTHER OBA CHAN, turns and raises her arms. Her costume and mask are magnificent. A majestic sound is used by ACTOR 1 to accompany her movement. SADAKO is becoming out of breath. GRANDMOTHER makes a magical gesture toward SADAKO. SADAKO trips and falls.)*

115 KENJI *(still out of scene)*. Sadako, are you alright?

116 SADAKO *(rubbing her hip)*. Oooh . . .

117 KENJI. Here, let me help you up. *(She takes his imaginary hand and stands.)* Are you all right?

118 SADAKO. Yes, I'm fine.

119 KENJI. All right then, let's begin again. *(Again, SADAKO runs very fast to the music. Again, GRANDMOTHER makes her magical gesture. SADAKO falls.)* Sadako?

120 SADAKO. I'm okay. Just a little dizzy, that's all. *(Staccato music begins again very fast, but SADAKO is slowing down.)*

121 KENJI. Discipline, Sadako! *(She speeds up; we can see that she is in pain but she picks up the pace of the run.)*

122 SADAKO. I'm trying, Grandmother. I want to win, Grandmother. I want to fly like the wind!

123 GRANDMOTHER/ACTOR 2. I hear you, Sadako! *(SADAKO moves slowly in a circle, obviously dizzy.)*

124 *(KENJI and GRANDMOTHER become ACTORS 1 and 2. During the following lines, masks on poles will be carried and moved in the air by ACTORS 1 and 2. The masks will be stark white and ghostly. ACTORS 1 and 2 may use many voices and the lines should run into each other to give the impression of many. SADAKO tries to escape the floating faces but they dance around her, bearing down to force her to bed. Recorded music uses a gong sound and heavy beat.)*

125 ACTOR 1. What is the matter with Sadako?

126 ACTOR 2. What is the matter with Sadako?

127 ACTOR 1. Why did she fall?

128 ACTOR 2. Why did she fall?

129 ACTOR 1. What could be wrong?

130 ACTOR 2. What could be wrong?

131 SADAKO. Nothing! I'm just tired, that's all!

132 ACTOR 1. X-ray her chest.

133 ACTOR 2. Examine her blood.

134 ACTOR 1. Put her in a hospital.

135 ACTORS 1 and 2. Hospital, hospital, hospital . . .

136 SADAKO. A hospital? No!

137 ACTOR 1. Put her to bed.

138 ACTOR 2. Put her to bed.

139 SADAKO. But there's nothing wrong with me!

140 ACTOR 1. Why did she fall?

141 ACTOR 2. Why did she fall?

142 ACTOR 1. Take some more tests.

143 ACTOR 2. Take some more tests.

144 ACTOR 1. You'll be just fine.

145 ACTOR 2. Now don't you worry.

146 ACTOR 1. Don't you worry.

147 ACTOR 2. Put her to bed.

148 SADAKO. But I'll miss the race!

149 ACTOR 1. Now don't you worry.

150   ACTOR 2. You'll be just fine.

151   ACTOR 1. Put her to bed.

152   SADAKO. I want to fly like the wind!

153   ACTORS 1 and 2 *(holding white masks above their stands)*. Leukemia[3], leukemia, leukemia, leukemia, leukemia, leukemia . . .

154   SADAKO. Leukemia?

155   *(ACTORS 1 and 2 drop masks into holders with a jarring thud. They become MOTHER and FATHER speaking with faces forward as if speaking to a doctor.)*

156   MOTHER. Leukemia? My little girl? But that's impossible! The atom bomb didn't even do so much as scratch her!

157   FATHER. The atom-bomb sickness? My daughter?

158   SADAKO. But it can't be true, Mother, can it? *(MOTHER and FATHER rush to her seated on the bench.)* I don't have any scars from the bomb. It didn't touch me. It can't be true, can it, Mother?

159   FATHER. There now, dear, they just want to do some more tests.

160   SADAKO. But how can I be sick from the bomb? It killed my grandmother but I wasn't hurt at all.

161   MOTHER *(very gently)*. Sadako, the radiation[4] doesn't always show up right away.

162   SADAKO *(terrified)*. I was only two when the bomb fell.

163   FATHER. It's just a few tests, that's all, sweetheart.

164   MOTHER. You'll be here a few weeks.

165   SADAKO. But the race . . . *(MOTHER and FATHER are fighting back tears.)*

166   MOTHER. We'll be back every day to see you. *(Rushes off to hide tears, to music stand.)*

---

3. **leukemia** a cancer in which the bone marrow and other blood-forming organs produce increased numbers of white blood cells and suppress the production of normal blood cells
4. **radiation** an effect of nuclear reactions, usually in the form of particles or electromagnetic waves

Skill: Dramatic Elements and Structure

The drumming makes things feel urgent again. I wonder if something important is about to happen in the plot.

The actors are all counting with Sadako. This makes me think that her story is bigger than just Sadako. The play must be building up to a larger message for the community or society.

167 FATHER. Get some rest, sweetheart. *(Kisses her. Exits to music stand.)*

168 SADAKO. The race . . .

169 *(ACTOR 1 prepares to become KENJI. Using the instruments to punctuate her lines, ACTOR 2 counts.)*

170 ACTOR 2. Two hundred and thirty-four, two hundred and thirty-five, two hundred and thirty-six, two hundred and thirty-seven . . . *(The counting fades and SADAKO counts. Again, the primary numbers are spoken together by ACTORS 1 and 2 and SADAKO.)*

171 SADAKO. Six, seven, eight, nine, ten . . .

172 *(KENJI enters the scene.)*

173 KENJI. What are you counting?

174 SADAKO *(sees him, delighted)*. Oh, Kenji, I'm so glad you're here! *(They embrace.)*

175 KENJI. What's so interesting out there?

176 SADAKO. I am counting how many trees I can see from my window. This morning I counted the flowers. There were fifty-two. You know, it's only been ten years since the bomb destroyed everything. But look how many trees have grown since then!

177 KENJI. I have a present for you.

178 SADAKO. You do?

179 KENJI. Close your eyes. *(She squinches them very tight. KENJI puts a piece of gold paper on the bed and some scissors.)* Now you can look.

180 SADAKO *(looking at paper)*. What is it?

181 KENJI *(laughs)*. I've figured out a way for you to get well. Watch! *(He slowly folds paper into origami crane. Recorded music used earlier in the mimed folding is heard. He holds the crane in the palm of his hand as if it is very precious and holds it out to SADAKO.)*

182 SADAKO. Kenji, it's beautiful. *(Takes crane.)* But how can this paper crane make me well?

183   KENJI. Don't you remember that old story about the crane? It's supposed to live for a thousand years. If a sick person folds one thousand paper cranes, the gods will grant her wish and make her healthy again. There's your first one.

184   SADAKO *(very touched)*. Oh, Kenji, it's beautiful.

185   KENJI. Make a wish. *(The magical sound of chimes is heard from the music stand. SADAKO holds it out before her, closes her eyes, and her lips move silently. She looks up to KENJI, very moved by his gift.)*

186   SADAKO. Thank you, Kenji. Thank you.

187   KENJI. Don't thank me. You have to fold the rest yourself.

188   SADAKO. I'll start today. *(Looks around.)* But I'll need paper.

189   KENJI *(putting her on)*. Now where in the world could we get some paper? *(Pretends to think, then pulls some out of his satchel.)* Well, what do you know? Look what I have here. *(Hands it to her.)* This ought to keep you busy.

190   SADAKO *(takes the paper, smiles at his fun, becomes serious)*. Kenji?

191   KENJI. Yes?

192   SADAKO *(trying to be strong)*. Who won the race?

193   KENJI *(carefully)*. Oh, I don't remember her name. She wasn't very fast. She was a turtle.

194   SADAKO. But you always said *I* was a turtle.

195   KENJI. Oh, well, I was only teasing when I said that. You're more like that crane there. You run very fast, Sadako, like a bird. Like the wind.

196   SADAKO *(almost ready to cry, bolsters herself)*. So if I'm not a turtle, does that mean you're not a frog?

197   KENJI. What? Me? A frog. Why, that's the silliest thing I ever heard . . . Croak! Oops! There's that sound again. Croak! Uh-oh. It's starting again, Sadako. Look! Croak! I'm turning all green and warty! Croak! Croak! *(He continues to play the frog until SADAKO is laughing helplessly.)*

198   *(A percussion sound bridges the scene into transition. ALL count together. ACTOR 1 brings bough of paper cranes to SADAKO, moves back to music stand. ACTORS 1 and 2 fade away and become MOTHER and FATHER.*

SADAKO continues counting. She is holding a very long rope of colorful paper cranes.)

199   ACTORS 1 and 2 and SADAKO. Four hundred and thirty-two, four hundred and thirty-three, four hundred and thirty-four, four hundred and thirty-five . . .

Skill: Character

Even though Sadako is sick, she is remaining positive and hopeful. I can tell that her energy and attitude are encouraging her parents and making them happy, too! Her friends are still important to her, especially Kenji, and her relationship with him is helping her remain positive and hopeful. Will her positive energy last?

200   SADAKO *(cheerful, counting cranes).* Four hundred and thirty-six, four hundred and thirty-seven, four hundred and thirty-eight!

201   *(She holds them up for MOTHER and FATHER who have just entered.)*

202   SADAKO. See. *(MOTHER and FATHER are very pleased to see her so happy and energetic.)* Kenji taught me! You shouldn't worry about me anymore. Kenji figured out a way for me to get well. Do you remember the story? If a sick person folds a thousand paper cranes then the gods will make her well again. And look. I've already folded four hundred and thirty-eight! *(She holds them up, proud and delighted, full of new vigor.)*

203   MOTHER. Oh, I'm so glad. I thought you would be sad about not being able to run in the races.

204   SADAKO *(trying to hide her sudden sadness).* Oh, that. Oh, I don't think about that old race anymore. Silly old race. What good was it? Kenji said I was better than the girl who ran. He said I run like a bird. It's like I'm flying, he said. Folding cranes is much better than any old race. *(MOTHER and FATHER glance at each other.)* It's kind of like a race anyway, don't you think? If I fold them fast enough I won't have to die. *(SADAKO smiles radiantly at her parents. Her MOTHER gasps and grabs SADAKO, pressing her daughter's head against her breast, and cries. Pause. MOTHER and FATHER move away, leaving SADAKO alone. She is asleep and speaks with her eyes closed.)* Mother? Mother, where are you? Father? Oh, just you wait, Father. I'll make you so proud of me! I'm going to win. I'm going to win! Oh, but Mother! Father? Where are you now? I don't like it here. It's lonely and I don't feel well. It hurts. It HURTS!!

205   *(ACTORS 1 and 2 become DOCTORS and enter the scene.)*

206   ACTOR 1. What's the matter with Sadako?

207   ACTOR 2. What's the matter with Sadako?

208   ACTOR 1. Why did she fall?

209   ACTOR 2. What could be wrong?

210   ACTOR 1. Put her to bed.

211   ACTOR 2. Put her to bed.

212   SADAKO. No, I don't want to stay in bed!

213   ACTOR 1. Now don't you worry.

214   ACTOR 2. You'll be just fine.

215   SADAKO. But it hurts! And I have such bad dreams.

216   ACTORS 1 and 2. Put her to bed. Put her to bed. Put her to bed. Put her to bed. *(They repeat as they move away, their voices fading to a whisper.)*

217   SADAKO. Grandmother? Grandmother? Can you see me? Can you hear me now?

218   *(There is a dramatic percussion sound from ACTOR 1 as ACTOR 2 dons her magnificent GRANDMOTHER mask and enters the scene. She makes a grand entrance with beautiful recorded music and chimes.)*

219   GRANDMOTHER. I hear you, Sadako.

220   SADAKO *(slowly opens her eyes, pause, sees GRANDMOTHER)*. Grandmother! You came back! You returned to earth just like they said.

221   GRANDMOTHER. Yes, I have returned to help you, Sadako.

222   SADAKO. Oh, Grandmother, I hurt so much! It's so cold and lonely here. Can I go home now?

223   GRANDMOTHER *(beckoning)*. I have come to show you something. Come.

224   SADAKO. Oh, I wish I could go with you, Grandmother.

225   GRANDMOTHER. I will take you to the mountains and rivers of our ancestors.

226   SADAKO. Oh, but, Grandmother, how can I go with you? They won't even let me leave my room. They say I have to stay in bed.

227   GRANDMOTHER. You know a way.

228   SADAKO. I do?

229   *(GRANDMOTHER stands stoically as ACTOR 1 brings imagined piece of paper downstage as before. He gently smoothes it on the floor before SADAKO, bows, and moves upstage again.)*

230   SADAKO. Of course. Yes, now I know.

231   *(SADAKO performs the mimed folding of a giant crane. This is a kind of choreographed dance that was used in the introduction. The "folding" is accompanied by specific music used in each folding sequence. GRANDMOTHER moves with SADAKO as she folds in a way that suggests she is directing SADAKO. When the folding is complete, GRANDMOTHER and SADAKO look at each other, then slowly move down to lift the crane together. As they stoop to pick up the crane, a dramatic music with gong sound begins. They carry the crane to bench, SADAKO on left side, GRANDMOTHER on right. They place bench/crane C. GRANDMOTHER stands on bench behind her and ACTOR 1 stands on floor with back to AUDIENCE behind GRANDMOTHER. A whooshing sound is heard as ACTORS contract together to suggest the launching of the bird into flight. ACTOR 1 uses mylar streamers[5] to "flap" elegantly as wings. SADAKO is thrilled. ACTOR 1 counts loud and dramatically, indicating the excitement of the moment. Loud, beautiful, fast-paced music accompanies their glorious flight.)*

232   ACTOR 1. Five hundred and sixty-three, five hundred and sixty-four, five hundred and sixty-five!

233   SADAKO *(thrilled)*. Look, Grandmother, it's just like Kenji said. I fly like the wind! I fly like the wind!

234   ACTOR 1. Five hundred and seventy-one! Five hundred and seventy-two! FIVE HUNDRED AND SEVENTY-THREE!!!

235   SADAKO. I FLY LIKE THE WIND!! *(ACTOR 1 moves before SADAKO and GRANDMOTHER, using the mylar streamers to suggest fires on the ground before them. SADAKO points to streamers.)* Look, Grandmother!

236   GRANDMOTHER. The Yaizu River.

237   SADAKO. But it's burning.

238   GRANDMOTHER. It is All Soul's Day. The day of the spirits.

239   SADAKO. There are hundreds of little boats with candles!

240   GRANDMOTHER. The spirits have visited their loved ones tonight, just as I have visited you. The candles in the river are "farewell fires." Soon the spirits will join us.

---

5. **mylar streamers** flaps of polyester fabric sometimes used in theatre productions

NOTES

241 SADAKO. Join *us?* You mean I'll be able to meet the spirits?

242 GRANDMOTHER. Yes.

243 SADAKO. How wonderful! *(She is very excited, anxiously looking down for a glimpse of the SPIRITS. Pointing.)* There! There! Grandmother, look! *(ACTOR 1 moves around them in a circle holding red masks on poles which seem to "float" around SADAKO and GRANDMOTHER.)*

244 GRANDMOTHER. Those are spirits of a thousand, thousand years.

245 SADAKO *(delighted).* A thousand, thousand years?

246 GRANDMOTHER. Yes. They were once young like you, Sadako.

247 SADAKO. Like me?

248 GRANDMOTHER. Yes.

249 SADAKO *(pointing).* Look! He looks like an *Emperor!* *(ACTOR 1 circles around them, holding a parasol above his head. He moves regally and spins at the sound of gongs, which announce his presence. As he moves away, GRANDMOTHER bows to him.)*

250 GRANDMOTHER. Their valley is deep and their mountains hard to climb. We need not visit there. Our mountain is just ahead.

251 ACTOR 1 *(using streamers as wings again).* Five hundred and ninety-three! Five hundred and ninety-four! Five hundred and ninety-five!

252 GRANDMOTHER *(gesturing to a place before them).* Here is where we will stop.

253 *(ACTOR 1 slows the wings; they mime landing with a whoosh sound as before. ACTOR 1 gently flutters the streamers down to a halt. The music changes from excitement to a quiet, eerie sound of wind instruments. This music will continue through the speeches of the SPIRITS. GRANDMOTHER dismounts the crane, gestures to SADAKO to do the same. SADAKO jumps off the crane, excited with anticipation. ACTOR 1 moves bench. GRANDMOTHER offers SADAKO her arm and leads her around the stage. SADAKO is looking eagerly around. ACTOR 1 puts red mask in holder. He stands behind the waist-high mask among the pastel fans.)*

254 GRANDMOTHER *(gesturing toward mask).* This is the spirit of Mr. Araki. *(ACTOR 1 opens an oriental paper parasol. When he speaks for a SPIRIT he*

Please note that excerpts and passages in the StudySync® library and this workbook are intended as touchstones to generate interest in an author's work. The excerpts and passages do not substitute for the reading of entire texts, and StudySync® strongly recommends that students seek out and purchase the whole literary or informational work in order to experience it as the author intended. Links to online resellers are available in our digital library. In addition, complete works may be ordered through an authorized reseller by filling out and returning to StudySync® the order form enclosed in this workbook.

Reading & Writing Companion **853**

NOTES

will stand behind that mask with the parasol opened above his head. He does not alter his voice to suggest SPIRITs' voices.)

255   ACTOR 1/MR. ARAKI. I was helping to build fire lanes for Hiroshima. The enemy may come soon they said, we must build fire lanes. I was digging with my shovel. I saw the metal grow bright before me. I watched it melt. Everything turned white. Then I was here.

256   *(ACTOR 1 moves parasol in front of his face, closes it as he turns away, leaving the red masks. GRANDMOTHER again offers SADAKO her arm and walks her around the stage as ACTOR 1 places another red mask in its holder. SADAKO is growing confused and a little frightened.)*

257   GRANDMOTHER *(gesturing).* This is the spirit of Mrs. Watanabe.

258   ACTOR 1/MRS. WATANABE *(opens parasol).* I had just prepared a breakfast for my baby boy. I was bending over his basket to pick him up when I felt a tremendous wind blow me across the room. My baby boy has not joined me here. *(Closes parasol as before, leaving the red mask. Again GRANDMOTHER leads SADAKO on her arm, around and up to third red mask.)*

259   GRANDMOTHER *(gesturing).* This is the spirit of Daisuke.

260   ACTOR 1/DAISUKE. I was seven years old when I came here. I had studied my lessons hard for an examination. I was walking to school. I looked up to see a bird fly. Suddenly the sky was on fire. *(Closes parasol, moves to music stand, leaving three red masks placed among the pastel fans.)*

261   SADAKO *(horrified, looking at the masks).* The bomb. They're all talking about the bomb that fell when I was two years old.

262   GRANDMOTHER. The bomb brought me here, Sadako. *(ACTOR 1 begins to count, continues during this conversation.)*

263   ACTOR 1. Six hundred and twenty-eight, six hundred and twenty-nine . . .

264   SADAKO. Yes, I remember.

265   ACTOR 1. Six hundred and thirty-one, six hundred and thirty-two . . .

266   GRANDMOTHER. The bomb has brought you here, Sadako. You must stay with us.

267   SADAKO *(realizing what GRANDMOTHER means, pleading).* But how can that be? I'm twelve years old now. It's been ten years since the bomb fell.

268 GRANDMOTHER. The bomb continues to fall, Sadako. It is falling even now. *(GRANDMOTHER gestures to ACTOR 1, who pauses in his counting. He brings his head up slowly to look directly at SADAKO. Pause. He resumes his counting.)*

269 SADAKO *(panicking)*. But my cranes! I've been folding my cranes as fast as I can!

270 ACTOR 1. Six hundred and thirty-nine . . .

271 SADAKO *(pleading)*. I haven't folded a thousand yet!

272 GRANDMOTHER *(assuring)*. You will have a thousand. You'll see. It is better to leave them for others to finish.

273 SADAKO. Someone will finish them for me? But then how can the cranes grant my wish?

274 GRANDMOTHER *(lovingly)*. What did you wish for, Sadako? *(ACTOR 1 stops counting but continues percussion rhythm during the following line.)*

275 SADAKO. To make you live. To make me better. I wished that there will never ever be a bomb like that again. *(Silence. ACTOR 1 moves dramatically from music stand carrying closed parasol before him as if it is something very precious. He ceremoniously gives it to GRANDMOTHER, bows and returns to his place behind the music stand. GRANDMOTHER moves to SADAKO, holds parasol out to her, nods to encourage her. SADAKO takes the parasol, GRANDMOTHER moves away. ACTOR 1 begins rhythm again. They count together.)*

276 ACTOR 1 and GRANDMOTHER. Six hundred and forty-one, six hundred and forty-two, six hundred and forty-three . . .

277 SADAKO *(solemn)*. Six hundred and forty-four. *(There is the sound of the bomb as she opens the parasol above her head, then brings it down in front of her, like a shield, hiding her face. GRANDMOTHER and ACTOR 1 bow their heads. The bomb sound continues as SADAKO moves to take her place in the fans with the other red masks. Lifts parasol.)* I was two years old and my mother held me in her arms. She sang a song to me. It was a quiet summer morning. Inside our small house my grandmother was preparing tea. Suddenly there was a tremendous flash of light that cut across the sky. *(She moves her parasol to cover her face as before.)*

Please note that excerpts and passages in the StudySync® library and this workbook are intended as touchstones to generate interest in an author's work. The excerpts and passages do not substitute for the reading of entire texts, and StudySync® strongly recommends that students seek out and purchase the whole literary or informational work in order to experience it as the author intended. Links to online resellers are available in our digital library. In addition, complete works may be ordered through an authorized reseller by filling out and returning to StudySync® the order form enclosed in this workbook.

Reading & Writing Companion   855

NOTES

278 *(The bomb sound is quieter this time and slowly fades away. ACTOR 1 becomes KENJI. KENJI enters the scene calling to SADAKO. He uses the bill of his hat as before to make a large mouth for his comical frog. The bill covers his eyes.)*

279 KENJI *(playful)*. Sadako! Oh, Sadako . . . How's the lazy little turtle this morning? You know, I think you're right. I'm becoming more of a frog every day. Why, just this morning I found two warts on my foot. Now what do you make of that? Croak! See, there's that sound again. *(Hopping to her bed.)* You want to see my warts? *(He puts his cap back to see her, laughing. He is stopped when he sees that she is not there.)* Sadako? *(Looks around.)* Sadako? *(He sees rope of cranes, holds it, then sits on the bench. He solemnly removes his hat and bows his head.)*

280 *(From her place at the music stand, ACTOR 2 narrates.)*

281 ACTOR 2. Sadako Sasaki died on October 25, 1955. Her friends and classmates folded three hundred and fifty-six cranes to make a thousand. *(KENJI stands, moves U, mimes getting the large piece of paper as before. He gracefully places it downstage. The folding music begins, KENJI mimes folding movements of giant crane as SADAKO has done. ACTOR 2 begins recorded folding music and moves from the stand to DL.)* Sadako's friends began to dream of building a monument to her and all the children who were killed by the atom bomb. In 1958, the statue was unveiled in the Hiroshima Peace Park. There is Sadako standing on top of a granite mountain. She is holding a golden crane in outstretched arms.

282 KENJI *(as he folds)*. Nine hundred and ninety-seven . . .

283 ACTOR 2. Now every year, children from all over Japan visit her memorial . . .

284 KENJI. Nine hundred and ninety-eight . . .

285 ACTOR 2. And bring thousands of paper cranes to her monument.

286 KENJI. Nine hundred and ninety-nine . . .

287 ACTOR 2. Their wish is engraved on the base of the statue: *(KENJI begins to stand, slowly miming the lifting of the giant crane. He uses both hands as SADAKO did in the beginning. It is very light.)*

288 "This is our cry,
This is our prayer,
Peace in the World."

289 KENJI. One thousand. *(He launches it in the air and blows after it as SADAKO has done before. His outstretched arms follow the path of the bird's flight, turning to a point, indicating the flight across the sky. ACTOR 2 watches the bird with KENJI. From her position U, SADAKO moves her parasol from its shield-like position, holding it above her head. She watches the flight of the bird with KENJI and ACTOR 2. She points up.)*

290 SADAKO *(joyous)*. Look, Grandmother! You were right! *(ALL freeze.)*

THE END

©MCMXC by
KATHRYN SCHULTZ MILLER
Printed in the United States of America
All Rights Reserved
(A THOUSAND CRANES)

Please note that excerpts and passages in the StudySync® library and this workbook are intended as touchstones to generate interest in an author's work. The excerpts and passages do not substitute for the reading of entire texts, and StudySync® strongly recommends that students seek out and purchase the whole literary or informational work in order to experience it as the author intended. Links to online resellers are available in our digital library. In addition, complete works may be ordered through an authorized reseller by filling out and returning to StudySync® the order form enclosed in this workbook.

Reading & Writing
Companion

857

First Read

Read *A Thousand Cranes*. After you read, complete the Think Questions below.

☁ THINK QUESTIONS

1. Briefly explain how Sadako felt upon learning the impact of radiation on her physical health despite the fact that she was "only two when the bomb fell." Use evidence from the text to support your explanation.

2. How does the creation of crane origami contribute to the theme of peace? Be specific and be sure to cite evidence from the story.

3. How might *A Thousand Cranes* be described as a biography? Cite textual evidence to support your answer.

4. The word **discipline** comes from the Latin *disciplina*, which means "instruction, knowledge." With that information in mind, write a definition of *discipline* as it is used in this story. How does your definition compare to or contrast with the Latin definition? Explain, and cite context clues that helped you arrive at your understanding of the word.

5. Use context clues to determine the meaning of the word **subdued.** Write your best definition here, along with words or phrases from the text that were helpful in coming to your conclusion. Finally, check a dictionary to confirm your understanding.

Skill:
Character

Use the Checklist to analyze Character in *A Thousand Cranes*. Refer to the sample student annotations about Character in the text.

In order to determine how particular elements of a story or drama interact, note the following:

✓ the characters in the story, including the protagonist and antagonist

✓ the settings and how they shape the characters or plot

✓ plot events and how they affect the characters

✓ key events or series of episodes in the plot, especially events that cause characters to react, respond, or change in some way

✓ characters' responses as the plot reaches a climax and moves toward a resolution of the problem facing the protagonist

✓ the resolution of the conflict in the plot and the ways that affects each character

To analyze how particular elements of a story or drama interact, consider the following questions:

✓ How do the characters' responses change or develop from the beginning to the end of the story?

✓ How does the setting shape the characters and plot in the story?

✓ How do the events in the plot affect the characters? How do characters develop as a result of the conflict, climax, and resolution?

Please note that excerpts and passages in the StudySync® library and this workbook are intended as touchstones to generate interest in an author's work. The excerpts and passages do not substitute for the reading of entire texts, and StudySync® strongly recommends that students seek out and purchase the whole literary or informational work in order to experience it as the author intended. Links to online resellers are available in our digital library. In addition, complete works may be ordered through an authorized reseller by filling out and returning to StudySync® the order form enclosed in this workbook.

Reading & Writing Companion   859

Skill:
Character

Reread lines 200–204 of *A Thousand Cranes*. Then, using the Checklist on the previous page, answer the multiple-choice questions below.

⟳ YOUR TURN

1. Based on the dialogue and stage directions in lines 200–204, the reader can conclude that —

   ○ A. Sadako is upset and worried about getting better.
   ○ B. Sadako is hopeful that the cranes will help her.
   ○ C. Sadako is bored and tired of being in the hospital.
   ○ D. Her parents are upset by the cranes.

2. This question has two parts. First, answer Part A. Then, answer Part B.

   Part A: What do the dialogue and stage directions in line 204 reveal about Sadako?

   ○ A. that her priorities have changed since she became ill
   ○ B. that she wants only to rest now
   ○ C. that she is still focused on racing when she gets better
   ○ D. that she is frightened of her illness

   Part B: Which of the following details best supports your response to Part A?

   ○ A. "It's kind of like a race anyway, don't you think?"
   ○ B. "Kenji said I was better than the girl who ran."
   ○ C. "Father. I'll make you so proud of me!"
   ○ D. "Folding cranes is much better than any old race."

Skill: Dramatic Elements and Structure

Use the Checklist to analyze Dramatic Elements and Structure in *A Thousand Cranes*. Refer to the sample student annotations about Dramatic Elements and Structure in the text.

••• CHECKLIST FOR DRAMATIC ELEMENTS AND STRUCTURE

In order to identify the dramatic elements and structure of a drama, note the following:

- ✓ the form of the drama, such as comedy or tragedy

- ✓ how the acts and scenes advance the plot

- ✓ the setting of the play and whether or how it changes in each act or scene

- ✓ the language of the play, such as prose or verse, as spoken by characters

- ✓ the use of dramatic devices such as

  - soliloquy or monologue, when a character speaks his or her thoughts aloud directly to the audience while alone on stage

  - asides, when a character shares private thoughts with the audience when other characters are on stage

  - the information in stage directions, including lighting, sound, and set, as well as details about characters, including exits and entrances

To analyze how a drama's form or structure contributes to its meaning, consider the following questions:

- ✓ How does the use of stage directions contribute to the play's meaning or message?

- ✓ How is each act or scene structured? How do characters enter and leave, how do they speak to each other, and what happens as a result?

- ✓ How does the drama's form or structure contribute to the play's meaning or message?

Skill: Dramatic Elements and Structure

Reread lines 270–278 of *A Thousand Cranes*. Then, using the Checklist on the previous page, answer the multiple-choice questions below.

♺ YOUR TURN

1. This question has two parts. First, answer Part A. Then, answer Part B.

   Part A: How do the sound elements in the scene help you identify the form of the play?

   ○ A. The sound elements make the play feel like a spooky tragedy.
   ○ B. The sound elements make the play feel like a comedy.
   ○ C. The sound elements make the play feel like a serious tragedy.
   ○ D. The sound elements do not help the reader identify the form of the play.

   Part B: Which of the following details BEST supports your response to Part A?

   ○ A. GRANDMOTHER *(lovingly)*. What did you wish for, Sadako? *(ACTOR 1 stops counting)*
   ○ B. SADAKO. To make you live. To make me better. I wished that there will never ever be a bomb like that again. *(Silence. ACTOR 1 moves dramatically from music stand)*
   ○ C. *She opens the parasol above her head, then brings it down in front of her, like a shield, hiding her face. GRANDMOTHER and ACTOR 1 bow their heads.*
   ○ D. I was two years old and my mother held me in her arms. She sang a song to me. It was a quiet summer morning.

Close Read

Reread *A Thousand Cranes.* As you reread, complete the Skills Focus questions below. Then use your answers and annotations from the questions to help you complete the Write activity.

SKILLS FOCUS

1. Sadako is a happy and hopeful child. Identify dialogue and/or stage directions that show this, and explain how her qualities affect the other people in the neighborhood.

2. The sound elements of the play contribute to its tone. Identify evidence of the sound elements adding to the tone of the play and explain the effect of the sound elements.

3. The drama *A Thousand Cranes* is a tragedy. It also offers a hopeful and positive message. Identify evidence that supports the play's message or deeper meaning. Explain what society can learn from Sadako's story.

4. Sadako and Jonah in *The Giver* both have complicated relationships with their futures. Compare how the characters are developed in the two stories.

5. *The Giver*, *Nothing to Envy*, and *A Thousand Cranes* all involve characters that stand out in very different ways. Identify how Sadako stands out from the crowd in *A Thousand Cranes* and explain what causes her to stand out.

WRITE

DISCUSSION: *The Giver, Nothing to Envy,* and *A Thousand Cranes* all feature children reacting to their societies. What do these three texts suggest about the relationship between the individual and society? To prepare for your discussion, use the graphic organizer to write down your ideas about the prompt. Support your ideas with evidence from the text. After your discussion, write a reflection.

Please note that excerpts and passages in the StudySync® library and this workbook are intended as touchstones to generate interest in an author's work. The excerpts and passages do not substitute for the reading of entire texts, and StudySync® strongly recommends that students seek out and purchase the whole literary or informational work in order to experience it as the author intended. Links to online resellers are available in our digital library. In addition, complete works may be ordered through an authorized reseller by filling out and returning to StudySync® the order form enclosed in this workbook.

Reading & Writing Companion   **863**

Remarks at the UNESCO Education for All Week Luncheon

INFORMATIONAL TEXT
Laura Bush
2006

Introduction

Soon after her husband George W. Bush was elected president in 2000, Laura Bush (b. 1946) promised to make education a major focus during her time as first lady. In 2006, Mrs. Bush was named an honorary ambassador for the United Nations' Decade of Literacy. Shortly after that, she gave this speech, announcing that she would host the first-ever White House Conference on Global Literacy. The announcement was made at an event celebrating Education for All Week, a multinational event put on by the United Nations Educational, Scientific and Cultural Organization (UNESCO). Mrs. Bush's work in education began as a teacher and a librarian. In this speech, she draws on her experiences as an educator in order to promote the conference's theme of "Every Child Needs a Teacher."

"Literacy and freedom are inseparable."

NOTES

1   Thank you, Secretary Spellings, for the very kind introduction, and for the great work that you're doing for young people.

2   I also want to thank Ambassador[1] Ensenat and the State Department for hosting this event. Learning — whether it's about other cultures and countries, or about ourselves — is at the heart of diplomacy. So I appreciate your bringing us together today to discuss how we can better educate the world's children.

First Lady Laura Bush delivers remarks at an Education for All Luncheon in Washington, D.C.

3   I'd also like to acknowledge UNESCO's Assistant Director General for Education, Peter Smith. Peter, thank you so much for joining us today. And, of course, I want to thank all of Your Excellencies, the very distinguished ambassadors who are here with us. We're joined today by all of the female ambassadors here in Washington, and I knew there was a reason Ambassador Ensenat was looking so sharp. (Laughter.) So thank you, ambassadors. Thank you for coming, and for your commitment to education.

4   We're also joined by a number of people that I've known since my husband was governor, as we've worked on reading issues, first in Texas and then in the United States. Some **experts** in literacy are here with you today. I think maybe everyone has at least one expert on literacy at their table, so I hope you'll get to know them and talk to them.

5   As the Honorary Ambassador of the United Nations Literacy Decade, I'm happy to be with you to mark the beginning of Education for All Week, and to talk about why Every Child Needs a Teacher.

Skill: Reasons and Evidence

The ideas of "Education for All" and "Every Child Needs a Teacher" imply that more teachers are needed because every child deserves a formal education.

---

1. **ambassador** a diplomat acting as an official representative of a country in international relations

Skill: Reasons and Evidence

This paragraph offers a reason to support the claim that more teachers are needed. The reason is that many children around the world are growing up without teachers and without a formal education. Two pieces of evidence support this reason: 100 million children do not have access to school (numerical data), and HIV/AIDS is devastating the teaching population in Africa (a fact).

6   All of us can remember the teachers who made a difference in our lives. Margaret just told us about her Ms. Brown. My favorite was my second grade teacher, Ms. Gnagy. I wanted to grow up and be just like her. And I did, so I became a teacher, and then a librarian. And I was with her last week in Midland, Texas, when I was out there when the George Bush childhood home was dedicated, the home that President George Bush Number 41, as we call him, and President Bush Number 43 and Governor Jeb Bush from Florida all lived in the 1950s. It was a house the Bushes bought in 1951. And while I was there, my second grade teacher, Ms. Gnagy, was there at the luncheon, and George's second grade teacher, Ms. Watson, was there, as well. (Laughter.) So that's so fun to have this long history with teachers that meant so much to us.

7   I know that who we are today, all of us, every one of us in this room, who we are is because of teachers that we had throughout our lives. Many children across the globe, though, are growing up without teachers and without any hope for a formal education. Around the world, more than 100 million children do not have access to schools. The situation is especially serious in Africa, where HIV/AIDS is devastating the teaching population.

8   Training more teachers is vital to UNESCO's goal of making sure every child has access to a basic, quality education by 2015. This is important for every country, but especially for developing countries[2], where limited resources often mean that the neediest children are not educated. We have to make sure that all children — boys and girls, rich and poor — have access to a good education.

9   One of the best ways we can improve educational opportunities for all is by spreading literacy. And one of the most important reasons every child should have a teacher is so that every child can learn to read.

10   There's no such thing as a quality, basic education for a person who cannot read or write. Reading is the bedrock on which the entire mind is built — one book, one essay, one instruction manual at a time. And reading doesn't just allow people to enjoy literary treasures. It allows them to become entrepreneurs[3], or engineers, or lawmakers, or doctors. In villages around the world, mothers who read can then teach their children how to read. Literate mothers can also participate in their economies, and they can earn a living for themselves and their families. So widespread literacy isn't a luxury for healthy societies — it's a basic requirement.

2. **developing countries** typically referring to poorer and/or more agrarian nations that are not caught up to Western standards of industrialization or wealth
3. **entrepreneur** a successful business person who organizes and manages a business

11 Across the globe, more than 800 million people are **illiterate**. Eighty-five percent of them live in just 34 countries, concentrated in regions affected by poverty. And more than two-thirds of the 771 million adults who cannot read a simple book, or write a basic sentence, are women.

12 I've visited many countries around the world, and I've seen how efforts to expand literacy are improving lives, especially for women and girls.

13 Last year, I visited the Women's Teacher Training Institute in Kabul, which was established through a partnership between the government of Afghanistan and USAID. At the Institute, which is also a dorm so that women who come in from the provinces to study have a safe place to live, women are then trained to be teachers. Then they go home and they train more teachers in a cascading effect with an attempt to train about 6,000 teachers in a very short amount of time so that the schools in Afghanistan, as they're being rebuilt, will have teachers.

14 In January, I was in Ghana, at the Accra Teacher Training College. Ghana is participating in the Textbooks and Learning Materials Program. As part of the program, six American universities, minority-serving universities, have partnered with six African countries to produce and **distribute** 15 million primary school textbooks — that would be kindergarten through eighth grade textbooks — for African students. The Textbook program is part of President Bush's African Education Initiative, a $600 million commitment that's already helped to train more than 300,000 teachers in sub-Saharan Africa.

15 And these textbooks, in the Textbook program, will be published in Africa. They'll be written with the help of these U.S. universities, with African educators, so that the books are Africa-centric, they're traditional, they talk about things that children who are studying them know about and live with every day.

16 Then, last month in Pakistan, I met with teachers and students involved in UNESCO and Children Resources International programs that improve teacher training and **promote** family literacy. I talked with Mehnaz Aziz, the Pakistan country director for Children's Resources International. Mehnaz shared with me how over the last three years, CRI has been training teachers in new methodologies. Before, teachers lacked instructional materials, and they used rote memorization and corporal punishment. Now they have money for school buildings, teaching aids and materials, and children can learn through drama and art.

17 Mehnaz also told me that before, parents had little involvement with their children's schools. But now mothers were coming, Mehnaz said. "It's one of the big changes. Reading — the mothers are also learning, reading books, and reading with their children."

18 Teaching people to read and write is about more than just improving literacy skills. Another Pakistani educator, Fakhira Najib, said to me, "The students aren't just learning reading and writing. They're curious now." These are just some of the examples of the difference a commitment to education and literacy is making worldwide. These strides come at such an important time, as we witness a tide of freedom spreading across the globe. This is not a coincidence. Literacy and freedom are inseparable.

19 Literacy is the foundation of personal freedom. Being able to read, and choosing what we read, is how we shape our beliefs, our minds, and our characters. Reading brings self-reliance and independence. For many women and their children, literacy can even mean the difference between life and death. A mother who can read can understand the label on a food container. She knows how to follow the instructions on a bottle of medicine. She's more likely to make wise decisions about her life that will keep her and her children healthy.

20 Literacy is the foundation of economic freedom. Free markets require informed consumers, and that means consumers who can read. Wider literacy also increases economic participation, which leads to more stable and vibrant economies. When we launched the U.N. Literacy Decade in New York, we were joined by a woman from the Philippines, Pampay Usman. Growing up, Pampay didn't have the opportunity to go to school. And although she couldn't read or write, she was able to manage a small market. You can imagine how hard and frustrating her work was, because she couldn't write down the names of her customers, or the goods they bought. She had to remember their faces, and every item they purchased.

21 The day Pampay joined an adult literacy class in her village, her life changed forever. She learned to write her name and address. She learned to read prices on groceries, and her business grew. Pampay is an example of how teaching one woman to read can lead to greater prosperity for herself and for the others who depend upon her.

22 Literacy is also the basis of political freedom. Around the world, more and more countries are embracing democracy and liberty. But for people to participate in a democracy, they have to be educated about their country's laws and traditions, which means they have to be able to read.

23 We saw this last October, when millions of copies of Iraq's draft constitution were printed and distributed to voters. Millions of Iraqis read their proposed charter, and then braved the threat of violence to cast their ballots. They risked their lives for a written document, language that enshrines their rights, and charts their future course for their new democracy.

24   Literacy improves the lives of mothers and children. Literacy boosts economies. And literacy helps people make good, informed decisions about their health.

25   Today, I'm delighted to announce that this September, during the opening of the 61st session of the U.N. General Assembly, we'll convene a Conference on Global Literacy in New York. Working in cooperation with the U.S. Department of Education, the U.S. State Department, the U.S. Agency for International Development, and UNESCO, the United Nations Scientific and Cultural Organization, we'll be looking at literacy programs that work, and connecting countries with the information they need to implement similar programs. The Conference will also encourage leaders from around the world to become involved in literacy in their own countries, and then to learn ways to support UNESCO's goal of Education for All by 2015.

26   This week, as we work to make sure that Every Child Has a Teacher, it's important to remember that we're all teachers. A person who's never stood by a blackboard still teaches by example. By **demonstrating** our commitment to literacy, we can let millions of people know that reading and writing are important.

27   So thank you for having me here today. Thank you for your commitment to education. And I hope I'll see you at the Conference in New York in September. Thank you all very much.

Please note that excerpts and passages in the StudySync® library and this workbook are intended as touchstones to generate interest in an author's work. The excerpts and passages do not substitute for the reading of entire texts, and StudySync® strongly recommends that students seek out and purchase the whole literary or informational work in order to experience it as the author intended. Links to online resellers are available in our digital library. In addition, complete works may be ordered through an authorized reseller by filling out and returning to StudySync® the order form enclosed in this workbook.

Reading & Writing Companion   **869**

REMARKS AT THE **UNESCO EDUCATION FOR ALL WEEK** LUNCHEON

First Read

Read "Remarks at the UNESCO Education for All Week Luncheon." After you read, complete the Think Questions below.

☁ THINK QUESTIONS

1. What skill does Bush see as the foundation of a good education? Cite places in the text where she emphasizes this important skill.

2. What specific types of freedom does Bush say will be promoted by the spread of literacy? Refer to paragraphs 19–22 in your response.

3. Name two nations where Bush is attempting to promote literacy goals. Provide evidence from the text of ways the literacy initiatives she mentions will have a direct impact in these countries.

4. Use context clues to determine the meaning of **illiterate** as it is used in paragraph 11 of "Remarks at the UNESCO Education for All Week Luncheon." Write your definition here and identify clues that helped you figure out its meaning.

5. Keeping in mind that the Latin prefix *dis-* means "apart" and the root *tribuere* means "to give," write your definition of **distribute** here.

Skill:
Reasons and Evidence

Use the Checklist to analyze Reasons and Evidence in "Remarks at the UNESCO Education for All Week Luncheon." Refer to the sample student annotations about Reasons and Evidence in the text.

••• CHECKLIST FOR REASONS AND EVIDENCE

In order to identify the reasons and evidence that support the speaker's claim(s) in an argument, note the following:

- ✓ the argument the speaker is making

- ✓ the claim or the main idea of the argument

- ✓ the reasons and evidence that support the claim and where they can be found

- ✓ if the evidence the author presents to support the claim is sound, or complete and comprehensive

- ✓ if there is sufficient evidence to support the claim or if more is needed

To assess whether the speaker's reasoning is sound and the evidence is relevant and sufficient, consider the following questions:

- ✓ What kind of argument is the speaker making?

- ✓ Is the reasoning, or the thinking behind the claims, sound and valid?

- ✓ Are the reasons and evidence the speaker presents to support the claim sufficient, or is more evidence needed? Why or why not?

Please note that excerpts and passages in the StudySync® library and this workbook are intended as touchstones to generate interest in an author's work. The excerpts and passages do not substitute for the reading of entire texts, and StudySync® strongly recommends that students seek out and purchase the whole literary or informational work in order to experience it as the author intended. Links to online resellers are available in our digital library. In addition, complete works may be ordered through an authorized reseller by filling out and returning to StudySync® the order form enclosed in this workbook.

Reading & Writing Companion   871

Skill:
Reasons and Evidence

Reread paragraphs 20–22 from "Remarks at the UNESCO Education for All Week Luncheon." Then, using the Checklist on the previous page, answer the multiple-choice questions below.

↻ YOUR TURN

1. Mrs. Bush uses the personal story of Pampay Usman as —

   ○ A. the claim, or central idea, of her argument.
   ○ B. a piece of evidence that supports economic freedom as a reason why learning to read is important.
   ○ C. a piece of evidence that supports political freedom as a reason why learning to read is important.
   ○ D. a reason for drawing attention to illiteracy among women.

2. Which general statement does Mrs. Bush imply by the reasons and evidence she presents in her speech?

   ○ A. People who live in democracies should be required by law to learn to read.
   ○ B. People have to learn to read before they will demand democratic governments.
   ○ C. Teaching adults to read and write is just as important as teaching children.
   ○ D. Many women have children and others who are economically dependent on them.

REMARKS AT THE **UNESCO EDUCATION FOR ALL WEEK** LUNCHEON

Close Read

Reread "Remarks at the UNESCO Education for All Week Luncheon." As you reread, complete the Skills Focus questions below. Then use your answers and annotations from the questions to help you complete the Write activity.

◎ SKILLS FOCUS

1. Identify various types of evidence that Mrs. Bush uses. Explain how that evidence helps to support her argument.

2. Mrs. Bush is speaking to a very specific audience in this speech. Identify language that helps create the tone of the speech, and write a note about how that tone is appropriate for the audience.

3. Identify where Bush states a main or central idea in the speech and write a note about how she develops that idea in the following paragraphs.

4. Identify parts of Laura Bush's speech that describe the effects of education on individuals. Explain how personal achievements, especially learning how to read and write, can help a person stand out from the crowd.

✏ WRITE

ARGUMENTATIVE: In "Remarks at the UNESCO Education for All Week Luncheon," Laura Bush argues that literacy is vital for all children. What are Mrs. Bush's main claims? How does she use reasons and evidence to support her argument and claims sufficiently? Be sure to use evidence from the text in your response.

Hidden Figures

INFORMATIONAL TEXT
Margot Lee Shetterly
2016

Introduction

M argot Lee Shetterly's *Hidden Figures* is the story of African American women in the 1940s and '50s who overcame great obstacles in their careers as aeronautical engineers. These women, called "computers" because they calculated numbers, persevered at a time in history when not only were most professions closed to women, but also when racial discrimination was legal. In 2016, their story was brought to the screen with Taraji P. Henson, Octavia Spencer, and Janelle Monáe.

"There was only one way to find out: try it."

from Chapter 9

Specialization

1   Men often came to the laboratory as junior engineers and were allowed to design and conduct their own experiments. Researchers took the men under their wings, teaching them the ropes. Women, on the other hand, had to work much harder to overcome other people's low expectations. A woman who worked in the central computing pool was one step removed from the research, and the engineers' assignments sometimes lacked the context to give the computer much knowledge about the project.

2   The work of most of the women was anonymous. Even a woman who had worked closely with an engineer on a research report rarely saw her name on the final **publication**. The engineers assumed it didn't matter; after all, she was just a woman, and many of the men were blind to the fact that a woman might have the same **ambitions** as a man.

3   Sometimes a computer's work impressed an engineer so much that he invited her to join him working full-time with a wind tunnel group[1]. For the women, this meant an opportunity to get closer to the research, and perhaps specialize in a particular subfield of aeronautics[2]. A computer who could not only process data but also understand how to **interpret** it was more valuable to the team than a pool computer with more general knowledge. Specialization became the key to managing the increasingly complex nature of aeronautical research in the postwar era.

Sonic Boom

4   Many of the Langley engineers shared a dream: they wanted to design an aircraft capable of flying faster than the speed of sound. And the women at

NOTES

Skill: Author's Purpose and Point of View

Shetterly describes how male junior engineers worked versus female employees. These details show that the author's purpose is to inform readers that women had a harder time being directly involved in research. The author's language makes me think she views this treatment as unfair.

---

1. **wind tunnel group** a group of researchers at NASA who design and test new generations of aircraft, both commercial and military, as well as NASA space vehicles, including the Space Shuttle
2. **aeronautics** the theory and practice of navigation through air

NOTES

Langley were no exception. They dreamed of this exciting possibility, which was seeming less far-fetched by the day. To pursue this dream, in 1947, a group of thirteen employees, including two former East Computers, were sent to the Mojave Desert in the western part of the United States to establish a high-speed flight research center. Their mission: to build the fastest airplane in the world, one that could fly faster than the speed of sound.

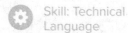

Skill: Technical Language

I have not heard the phrase sonic boom before. This essay is about aeronautical engineering. The author used the term sonic boom to describe how they pierced the sound barrier, so sonic boom might mean "a big sound."

5   The speed of sound is about 760 miles per hour. The exact number varies, depending on temperature, altitude, and humidity. Scientists used to think that flying faster than the speed of sound was impossible! But they were wrong.

6   "Mach 1" is the term for something moving at the speed of sound. When an object is moving this fast, the air molecules in front of the object can't get out of the way quickly enough, so they become compressed and form a shock wave. That shock wave is the noise we hear from the crack of a bullwhip or the firing of a bullet.

7   Scientists weren't sure what would happen to a pilot or his plane if he flew at Mach 1. Some researchers thought that the plane or the pilot would be destroyed by the power of the shock wave. Others disagreed.

8   There was only one way to find out: try it.

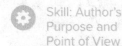

Skill: Author's Purpose and Point of View

The author gives more facts and details about the female computers' role for this project. The author's purpose is to inform about their contributions and importance to the success of NASA's projects. We learn that they worked hard to contribute to the success of research and were promoted for their efforts.

9   On October 14, 1947, pilot Chuck Yeager flew over the Mojave Desert in an NACA-developed experimental research plane called the Bell X-1. And he pierced the sound barrier for the first time in history! The plane caused a loud noise—a sonic boom, just like the shockwave from the bullet and the bullwhip—but the pilot and the plane were safe. The female computers on the ground verified the data **transmitted** from the instruments attached to the X-1 on its record-breaking flight.

10 At the Mojave Desert facility, the computers who helped with this experiment had the chance to do significant work and get credit for it. They were promoted from "computer" to the higher position of "junior engineer," and were named as the authors of research reports, a necessary first step in the career of an engineer. And for a woman, it was an extraordinary achievement. It meant that the whole world would see that she had contributed to a worthy piece of research, and that she was an important member of an engineering team.

11 Dorothy Hoover, another black woman who worked in West Computing, was the first African-American woman to leave the computing pool and get a chance at a research job, working directly for an engineer. She had earned an undergraduate degree in math from Arkansas Agricultural, Mechanical & Normal College and a master's degree in mathematics from Atlanta University, and she taught in three states before coming to Langley in 1943. She was excellent at **abstract** concepts and complex equations. She had been assigned many of the most challenging problems and always submitted flawless work.

NOTES

12 As a talented mathematician with an independent mind, Dorothy Hoover was a perfect addition to any research team. Her visibility with engineers increased with her promotion. She answered the computers' questions and understood complex math so well that she sometimes knew more than many of the engineers in the lab.

The Section Leader

13 Dorothy Vaughan was an excellent leader within the West Area computing pool. In 1947, one of her bosses got sick and was out of the office for a month. The next year, the boss fell ill again. Then, in early 1949, Dorothy's boss began to act strangely at work. She suffered a mental breakdown and was forced to leave her job.

14 This tragic incident left the computing pool without a leader. But the engineers at the laboratory decided to choose Dorothy to be the temporary head of the entire section. This was the first time an African-American woman had been assigned a management role at Langley. At the time, it was unthinkable for a man to report to a woman. Men were always ultimately the people in charge. Women who had an interest in management were limited to heading a section in one of the computing pools or a division with female workers—but they always reported to a man. For Dorothy, the new job was a lot like being at the head of a high school classroom and reporting to a principal, who was usually a man.

15 It would take Dorothy Vaughan two years to earn the full title of "section head." The men she worked for held her in limbo[3]: the laboratory had never had a black supervisor before, and they may have delayed making what seemed like a groundbreaking decision. Dorothy, however, was patient. Her promotion was made official when a memo circulated in January 1951: "Effective this date, Dorothy J. Vaughan, who has been acting head of West Area Computers unit, is hereby appointed head of that unit."

16 Dorothy took on the new responsibilities with confidence. Many of the women in West Computing knew she was the best candidate, and so did many engineers. In time her bosses realized it, too. History would prove them all right: there was no one better qualified for the job than Dorothy Vaughan.

Excerpted from *Hidden Figures* by Margot Lee Shetterly, published by HarperCollins.

---

3. **limbo** a period of waiting for a decision that is uncertain

 Skill: Technical Language

Laboratory is a technical term. The context tells me it is the place where Dorothy Vaughan worked. Before this paragraph, we know she was in a different building from the engineers. Using the word *laboratory* here shows the importance of Dorothy Vaughan's promotion and her contributions to science and math.

First Read

Read *Hidden Figures*. After you read, complete the Think Questions below.

☁ THINK QUESTIONS

1. Why did the engineers working on the project to break the sound barrier have to analyze data from instruments attached to the X-1 aircraft?

2. What kind of educational background did Dorothy Hoover have? Why was that background appropriate for her job?

3. Why did it take Dorothy Vaughan longer than it might have for other engineers to become head of her unit?

4. Use context clues to determine the meaning of **transmit** as it is used in paragraph 9 of *Hidden Figures*. Write your definition here and identify clues that helped you figure out its meaning.

5. Read the following dictionary entry:

   interpret in·ter·pret \in 'tər prət\ *verb*

   1. to translate orally or in sign language the words of a person speaking another language
   2. to explain the meaning of (information, words, or actions)
   3. to reenact in a particular way that conveys one's understanding of a creator's ideas

   Which definition most closely matches the meaning of **interpret** as it is used in paragraph 3? Write the correct definition of *interpret* here and explain how you figured out the correct meaning.

Skill:
Technical Language

Use the Checklist to analyze Technical Language in *Hidden Figures*. Refer to the sample student annotations about Technical Language in the text.

••• CHECKLIST FOR TECHNICAL LANGUAGE

In order to determine the meanings of words and phrases as they are used in a text, note the following:

- ✓ the subject of the book or article

- ✓ any unfamiliar words that you think might be technical terms

- ✓ words that have multiple meanings that change when used with a specific subject

- ✓ the possible contextual meaning of a word, or the definition from a dictionary

To determine the meanings of words and phrases as they are used in a text, including technical meanings, consider the following questions:

- ✓ What is the subject of the informational text?

- ✓ How does the use of technical language help establish the author as an authority on the subject?

- ✓ Are there any technical words that have an impact on the meaning and tone, or quality, of the book or article?

- ✓ Can you identify the contextual meaning of any of the words?

Please note that excerpts and passages in the StudySync® library and this workbook are intended as touchstones to generate interest in an author's work. The excerpts and passages do not substitute for the reading of entire texts, and StudySync® strongly recommends that students seek out and purchase the whole literary or informational work in order to experience it as the author intended. Links to online resellers are available in our digital library. In addition, complete works may be ordered through an authorized reseller by filling out and returning to StudySync® the order form enclosed in this workbook.

Reading & Writing
Companion   879

Skill:
Technical Language

Reread paragraphs 4–5 of *Hidden Figures*. Then, using the Checklist on the previous page, answer the multiple-choice questions below.

⟳ YOUR TURN

1. This question has two parts. First, answer Part A. Then, answer Part B.

   Part A: Which sentence below contains multiple technical terms specific to space exploration?

   ○ A. Their mission: to build the fastest airplane in the world, one that could fly faster than the speed of sound.

   ○ B. The speed of sound is about 760 miles per hour.

   ○ C. The exact number varies, depending on temperature, altitude, and humidity.

   ○ D. Scientists used to think that flying faster than the speed of sound was impossible!

   Part B: What is the effect of the technical terms in Part A?

   ○ A. The technical language used makes the paragraph easier to read.

   ○ B. The technical language used communicates the complexity of the work the women supported.

   ○ C. The technical language used establishes the author as an authority on the subject.

   ○ D. The technical language used helps the author explain why human computers were important.

Skill: Author's Purpose and Point of View

Use the Checklist to analyze Author's Purpose and Point of View in *Hidden Figures*. Refer to the sample student annotations about Author's Purpose and Point of View in the text.

••• CHECKLIST FOR AUTHOR'S PURPOSE AND POINT OF VIEW

In order to identify author's purpose and point of view, note the following:

✓ facts, statistics, and graphic aids, as these indicate that the author is writing to inform.

✓ descriptive or sensory details and emotional language may indicate that the author is writing to describe and dramatize events.

✓ descriptions that present a complicated process in plain language may indicate that the author is writing to explain.

✓ emotional language with a call to action may indicate that the author is trying to persuade readers or stress an opinion.

✓ the language the author uses can also be clues to the author's point of view on a subject or topic.

To determine the author's purpose and point of view in a text, consider the following questions:

✓ How does the author convey, or communicate, information in the text?

✓ Does the author use figurative or emotional language? How does it affect the purpose and point of view?

Skill: Author's Purpose and Point of View

Reread paragraphs 4–8 of *Hidden Figures*. Then, using the Checklist on the previous page, answer the multiple-choice questions below.

↻ YOUR TURN

1. Based on the details in paragraph 4, the reader can conclude that —

   ○ A. the author wants to persuade readers to become aeronautical engineers.

   ○ B. the author wants to inform readers that both men and women shared a dream to build a plane faster than sound.

   ○ C. the author wants to entertain readers with a far-fetched story.

   ○ D. the author wants to inform readers about the role of men in research.

2. The discussion of Mach 1 in paragraphs 6–8 reveals the author's point of view that —

   ○ A. temperature, altitude, and humidity affect the speed of sound.

   ○ B. scientists were foolish to test the boundaries of engineering knowledge.

   ○ C. flying at Mach 1 was an important milestone in engineering research.

   ○ D. Mach 1 is the most dangerous speed to fly an airplane.

Close Read

Reread *Hidden Figures*. As you reread, complete the Skills Focus questions below. Then use your answers and annotations from the questions to help you complete the Write activity.

◎ SKILLS FOCUS

1. Identify details about the author's purpose and point of view in the "Specialization" section of the text. Explain how these details reveal what the author is trying to express.

2. Identify the point of view in "The Section Leader," starting at paragraph 13. Explain why the author may have used this point of view to explain these events.

3. In *Hidden Figures,* the African-American women featured in the text had to overcome many challenges before they were able to engage actively in research with their male colleagues. Using textual evidence, identify an instance of discrimination in *Hidden Figures.*

4. Identify two or three technical terms in the excerpt. Define these words using context clues or a dictionary. Then explain how each word impacts the meaning or tone of the text.

5. The author of *Hidden Figures* tells how Dorothy Vaughan rose to position of "section head"—the first for an African-American woman—and was eventually held in high esteem by her colleagues in the computer pool and the research department. Explain how personal achievements, like these, help a person stand out from the crowd.

✏ WRITE

LITERARY ANALYSIS: What is the author's purpose and point of view in the excerpt from *Hidden Figures*? How does the author's use of technical words impact the excerpt's meaning or tone? Write a response answering these questions using specific examples from the text.

Miami Dancer Follows Dreams While Planning for the Future

INFORMATIONAL TEXT
Mekeisha Madden Toby
2018

Introduction

Journalist and cultural critic Mekeisha Madden Toby profiles Elijah Omary Muhammad, one of the finalists for the prestigious National YoungArts Foundation competition. Muhammad was chosen from a pool of over ten thousand applicants from the visual, literary, design and performing arts disciplines. In this profile, Muhammad outlines his work ethic, his inspiration, and his goals for the future—and performs his eye-catching routine.

"There's a bridge that connects everything and I've found that bridge."

1 The wave of rhythm that slowly takes over eighteen-year-old dancer Elijah Omary Muhammad's body begins as a motion in his right arm, extending to his left arm and then his left leg before he takes a few steps and turns around.

2 This is the intro to the dance routine that helped make Elijah one of the National YoungArts Foundation's 170 finalists from ten different artistic **disciplines**. An estimated 10,000 young performers applied, but Elijah's dedication and **panache** make him unique.

A Different Approach

3 "I do this a little bit differently than most people," says Elijah, who goes by the stage name "IntEnsE" and works tirelessly to live up to his nickname. "When I went to YoungArts, everybody had their own way and style of choreography[1], but I did mine in my living room."

4 "Sometimes, I would put earphones in and just focus on the intricate beats," he says. "I would do the moves over and over again until I could mentally see myself doing it. I used my instincts to figure out what should come next when I looked in the mirror. It's a very strong song so I felt it."

5 The song Elijah chose is called "Mercy" by Jacob Banks, a tune that first gained attention during a tragic scene on the premium cable drama "Power"—but when the Miami Northwestern Senior High School graduate arranged his hip-hop-inspired dance moves using this music, the effect was more dramatic than **melancholy**.

6 Although the routine itself is very serious, Elijah's playful nature shines through via his facial expressions and poked-out tongue. "I learned everything I know watching cartoons," Elijah says. "When I was younger, I'd watch 'Tom and Jerry' and 'Looney Tunes' and watch how they'd move. I would rewind and

1. **choreography** the specific steps and movements that are associated with a dance or other organized movement

Skill:
Media

The article starts off describing the beginning of the dance in detail. But I didn't realize how quick Elijah's moves were. I am glad I got to see the dance myself, or I would have assumed the beginning was slower.

Skill: Informational
Text Elements

This detail shows how Elijah got his unique style of dancing. The article talks about how Elijah's dancing is unusual, and this helps explain that he developed his style not from imitating other dancers but from imitating cartoons.

fast-forward and watch it fast and slow and try and imitate it. That's how I got started by watching their movements and seeing if I could do it," he says. "I didn't even start out dancing. I took what I learned from those cartoons and started doing magic tricks. I made those moves part of my magic act to make people laugh."

Planning for the Future

7   Although he's having fun, dancing is no laughing matter for Elijah, now that he has graduated from high school and is considering how he can **incorporate** dance into his life professionally. He hopes to attend Miami Dade College, and his dream job is in advertising, which would allow him to make commercials for a living.

8   "Everything happens for a reason and everything is connected," Elijah says. "I have a background in technology that I can use to my advantage. I can also pursue advertising. I don't see why my dancing has to stop. I can use my knowledge to teach dance classes online where I advertise and market the classes to students all over the world. There's a bridge that connects everything and I've found that bridge."

Skill: Informational Text Elements

This is a pertinent detail about how Elijah is pursuing more practical things. Another central idea of the article is that Elijah is doing practical things in addition to dancing, and this shows me why he is doing that.

9   There's also his father, who is proud of his Elijah's dancing, but wants him to proceed with caution: "My dad wants me to have a back-up plan," Elijah says. "He says I need to have a degree and to do something I can fall back on if dance doesn't work out. He doesn't want me to give up on my dream, but he wants me to stay grounded."

A Well-rounded Education

10   YoungArts also helps Elijah pursue his dreams, which has been its goal since the National YoungArts Foundation opened its doors in 1981. Ted Arison, the businessman who created Carnival Cruise Lines, founded the nonprofit with his wife, Lin, the two of them believing that the best way to invest in the arts was to identify and nurture young artists such as Elijah.

11   One of the celebrated components of YoungArts is its strong community of 20,000-plus alumni, who encourage a lifetime of opportunity and support. Notable alumni include Kerry Washington, Anna Gunn, and Timothee Chalamet.

12   Although there is a heavy push for S.T.E.M. (science, technology, engineering and math) in schools, including the arts creates a well-rounded education, argues Arne Duncan, the former U.S. Secretary of Education. "As core

Copyright © BookheadEd Learning, LLC

NOTES

academic subjects, the arts and **humanities** equip young persons with the capacities to learn from the past, question the present, and envision new possibilities for the future," he says. "A well-rounded curriculum that embraces the arts and humanities is not a luxury but a necessity in the information age."

13   Aisha Brooks was Elijah's theater teacher at Miami Northwestern Senior High School, and although she has taught for 16 years, she says she will never forget Elijah and how well-rounded, enthusiastic, and confident he is.

14   "Elijah is very committed and creative," Brooks says. "He can do it all. He would choreograph dances and work with the students to create routines for our shows. And because he has a technical mind, he'd mix music for me and the chorus teacher, too. Elijah's not afraid to speak for himself. He was the one who was confident enough to speak up and tell me what he could do. But he also wasn't afraid to ask for help," Brooks adds. "If he could not do a move, he'd ask the dance teacher for help. He's going to go far in life."

15   As for the future, Elijah took classes at a few Miami dance studios, but yearned for more challenging routines—so he started his own dance team. Now he's learning new styles and touring and performing across the country, while also working with AmeriCorps to support himself and save money for college.

16   "Success does not come easily," Elijah says. "You have to work hard. You'll know you're doing what you're destined to do if things don't come easily. If there are constant roadblocks and problems, then you're on the right track."

First Read

Read "Miami Dancer Follows Dreams While Planning for the Future." After you read, complete the Think Questions below.

1. Describe Elijah's process for learning dance moves. Explain, using evidence from the text to support your answer.

2. What is Elijah's "bridge"—and what does it connect? Cite evidence from the text to support your answer.

3. Explain Elijah's father's attitude on his son's passion for dance. How do the visions of father and son overlap and diverge? Cite evidence from the text to support your response.

4. What is the meaning of the word **panache** as it is used in the text? Write your best definition here, along with a brief explanation of the context clues that helped you determine its meaning.

5. Use context clues to determine the meaning of the word **melancholy** as it is used in the text. Write your definition of *melancholy* here, and explain how you figured it out.

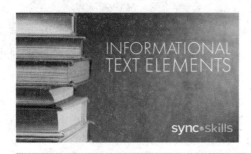

Skill:
Informational Text Elements

Use the Checklist to analyze Informational Text Elements in "Miami Dancer Follows Dreams While Planning for the Future." Refer to the sample student annotations about Informational Text Elements in the text.

••• CHECKLIST FOR INFORMATIONAL TEXT ELEMENTS

In order to identify the interactions between individuals, events, and ideas in a text, note the following:

✓ details in the text that describe or explain important ideas, events, or individuals

✓ transition words and phrases that signal interactions between individuals, ideas, or events, such as *because, as a consequence,* or *as a result*

✓ an event or sequence of events that influences an individual, a subsequent event, or an idea

✓ interactions between ideas and events that play a part in shaping people's thoughts and actions

To analyze the interactions between individuals, events, and ideas in a text, consider the following questions:

✓ How are the individuals, ideas, and events in the text related?

✓ How do the ideas the author presents affect the individuals in the text?

✓ What other features, if any, help readers to analyze the events, ideas, or individuals in the text?

Copyright © BookheadEd Learning, LLC

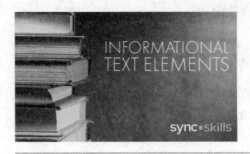

Skill:
Informational Text Elements

Reread paragraphs 13–15 of "Miami Dancer Follows Dreams While Planning for the Future." Then, using the Checklist on the previous page, answer the multiple-choice questions below.

↻ YOUR TURN

1. This question has two parts. First, answer Part A. Then, answer Part B.

   Part A: What type of informational text element is in paragraph 14?

   ○ A. The list of the different things Elijah does for the school is supporting evidence for the claim in the previous paragraph.

   ○ B. The fact that Elijah is creative is a pertinent detail about the main idea of the whole article.

   ○ C. The detail that Elijah is not afraid to speak for himself supports the central idea in the following paragraph.

   ○ D. The evidence that Elijah is taking dance classes supports the idea in paragraph 13.

   Part B: Which of the following details BEST supports your response to Part A?

   ○ A. "but yearned for more challenging routines—so he started his own dance team."

   ○ B. "'Elijah is very committed and creative,' Brooks says."

   ○ C. "she says she will never forget Elijah and how well-rounded, enthusiastic, and confident he is"

   ○ D. "If he could not do a move, he'd ask the dance teacher for help. He's going to go far in life."

Skill:
Media

Use the Checklist to analyze Media in "Miami Dancer Follows Dreams While Planning for the Future." Refer to the sample student annotations about Media in the text.

••• CHECKLIST FOR MEDIA

In order to determine how to identify ideas presented in diverse media and formats, note the following:

- ✓ how the same topic can be treated, or presented, in more than one formats

  - visually
  - quantitatively
  - orally

- ✓ how treatments of a topic through different kinds of sources can reveal more information about the topic

- ✓ which details are emphasized or absent in each medium, and the reasons behind these choices

- ✓ what the details in each medium have in common, or the main idea in each medium

- ✓ how the main idea and supporting details help to clarify, or explain, a topic, text, or issue

In order to determine how to compare and contrast, analyze, or explain ideas presented in diverse media and formats, consider the following:

- ✓ How are the treatments of the source text similar? How are they different?

- ✓ How do ideas presented in diverse media and formats clarify, or explain, a topic, text, or issue?

- ✓ How does each medium's portrayal affect the presentation of the subject?

- ✓ Why are some media able to emphasize or highlight certain kinds of information better than others?

Skill:
Media

Reread paragraphs 5–6 of "Miami Dancer Follows Dreams While Planning for the Future" and watch the video clip. Then, using the Checklist on the previous page, answer the multiple-choice questions below.

⟳ YOUR TURN

1. This question has two parts. First, answer Part A. Then, answer Part B.

   Part A: What can you see about Elijah's dancing in the video that reflects and clarifies what the writer says in the passage?

   ○ A. I can see that Elijah's dancing is classic and graceful.

   ○ B. I can tell from the video that Elijah was inspired by music videos.

   ○ C. The video shows me that Elijah didn't need to practice as much as the other dancers.

   ○ D. I can see how Elijah drew inspiration from things like cartoons.

   Part B: Which of the following details from the video BEST supports your response to Part A?

   ○ A. When Elijah falls down and moves his whole body to the heartbeat noise

   ○ B. The music Elijah chose for his performance

   ○ C. When Elijah spins on his knees

   ○ D. When Elijah moves and dances to the beat of the music

Close Read

Reread "Miami Dancer Follows Dreams While Planning for the Future." As you reread, complete the Skills Focus questions below. Then use your answers and annotations from the questions to help you complete the Write activity.

◎ SKILLS FOCUS

1. The title of this article implies that one of the main ideas is Elijah is a well-rounded student. Identify evidence that supports the idea that Elijah is a well-rounded student. Explain how that evidence relates to the main idea.

2. Elijah works hard to stand out. Identify pertinent examples that show how Elijah excelled through hard work. Explain how the evidence relates to Elijah's hard work.

3. The video that accompanies this article shows the dance that the article talks about. Identify elements from the medium that deepen your understanding of Elijah's dancing. Explain how the video adds to your understanding.

4. The author uses specific vocabulary to let the readers know what kind of person Elijah is. Identify words with emotional or positive connotations that help you understand Elijah. Explain how the connotation affects your understanding of Elijah.

5. Elijah is an outstanding young man in a lot of different ways. Identify evidence about how Elijah stands out from the crowd. Write a note about how the evidence shows Elijah standing out.

✏ WRITE

DEBATE: The article talks about how Elijah likes both STEM topics and the arts. Which do you think is more important? Is it more important to focus on science and technology or the arts and humanities? Prepare points and comments for a debate with your classmates. Use evidence from the text to support your point.

Please note that excerpts and passages in the StudySync® library and this workbook are intended as touchstones to generate interest in an author's work. The excerpts and passages do not substitute for the reading of entire texts, and StudySync® strongly recommends that students seek out and purchase the whole literary or informational work in order to experience it as the author intended. Links to online resellers are available in our digital library. In addition, complete works may be ordered through an authorized reseller by filling out and returning to StudySync® the order form enclosed in this workbook.

Reading & Writing Companion   893

Reality TV and Society

ARGUMENTATIVE TEXT
2014

Introduction

studysync tv

In these two articles, the writers make arguments for and against reality TV shows. One writer discusses the negative impacts of shows like *Jersey Shore* and *Here Comes Honey Boo Boo*, while the other focuses on the positive influence of shows like *American Idol* and *Supernanny.* Both writers present strong arguments and support their claims with evidence. Which of the arguments do you find more convincing?

"Viewers see that people without talent or hard work can become rich and famous."

Reality TV Shows: Harmless entertainment or bad influence?

Point: Stop Rewarding Bad Behavior

1   Television has been an important part of American life for nearly seven decades. But instead of improving with age, programming has degenerated into mindless reality TV. Even though these programs claim to picture real people in real situations, there is actually very little *real* in reality TV. There is, however, a real **influence** on TV viewers, and this influence is often negative, especially on young people. Many people claim that reality TV portrays an accurate and vivid picture of our society. But if what Americans see on reality TV is truly who we are, then we are in big trouble.

2   According to Nielsen, a television ratings company, in 2014 nearly 300 million Americans ages two and up live in homes with televisions. That figure represents more than 90 percent of the population who have access to hundreds of channels and the programs they show. Unfortunately, ratings show that many television viewers are choosing *Here Comes Honey Boo Boo* over political talk shows, broadcasts of national political conventions, or other programming reflecting issues that affect us all.

3   Of course, reality TV has turned many people into instant celebrities. Viewers see that people without talent or hard work can become rich and famous. All they have to do is behave badly in front of the camera. But what message does this send to young people? According to Russ Rankin, who often writes for the arts, young people are not viewing reality TV as mindless entertainment. They look up to the programs' stars and imitate them. They are easily influenced by what they see, and they see that bad behavior is rewarded. Young viewers learn that those who treat others with pettiness and contempt become rich and famous. In fact, in 2011, one of the stars of *Jersey Shore* was paid more to address Rutgers University students than was Toni Morrison, a Nobel prize-winning author.

4   Tom Green is a comedian and actor who benefited from reality TV. Yet he is one of the most vocal voices against the genre. The difference for him, he

Skill: Arguments
and Claims

This paragraph is about the people on reality TV. The Point author claims that reality TV stars convince people that bad behavior will make them famous. He supports this claim with the fact that reality stars get paid a lot. The author reasons that viewers learn that pettiness is rewarded.

NOTES

Skill: Arguments
and Claims

This part also supports
the argument that
reality TV is harmful.
Here, the Point author
claims that the
networks need to take
responsibility for the
effects of reality TV.
The author then uses a
quote from Tom Green
and reasons that
networks should do
more to counteract the
harm caused by reality
TV. They've done similar
work to influence people
before.

says, is that he was not **exploited** and was in charge of his program. As the demand increased for more outrageous and negative programs, Green saw that "the audience became addicted to the cheap thrills." The quality of TV degenerated. He says, "The days of looking up to inventors, artists, and genuinely successful people are gone. Most people assume the behavior they see on TV is acceptable simply because it is on TV in the first place. Our media is shaping culture and training the audience to no longer demand quality programming. I had always presumed that the major corporations that ruled our media were far more responsible than I. Apparently, I was wrong."

5   Television producer Michael Slezak, senior editor of TVLine.com, says that he thinks reality TV shows are so prevalent because "networks love a good reality show since they're less expensive to produce. They don't require drawing in big stars."

6   It seems that no matter how often people are told that what they are watching is far from reality, they still watch. They continue to nurture false expectations that they too could become rich and famous if only they could be selected to participate in reality TV. In a recent survey, 10 percent of British teenagers were motivated by the dream of money and success. They said they would give up a good education to become a reality TV star.

7   It's not really the job of television networks to police the influences of television on culture and society. Yet networks do need to take some responsibility for what they have created with reality TV. As Tom Green says, "The networks should self-regulate by putting power back into the hands of artists and comedians." The media has done a massively good job of influencing society against smoking. They are now working on educating the public about obesity and healthy eating habits. They should be just as concerned about influencing the public about intelligent viewing and showing the best of how people should treat one another.

"These shows inspire young viewers. They see people like them succeeding."

Counterpoint: Reality TV Can Educate and Inspire

8   Which came first: the chicken or the egg? This age-old question can easily be applied to the **controversy** surrounding reality television. Have these shows **corrupted** our society? Or do they reflect the natural changes that have occurred in the way we see our world?

9   Most people who claim that reality TV has had a negative effect on society are mainly referring to shows that focus on celebrities such as *Keeping up with the Kardashians* or on contrived competitions such as *Survivor. Survivor* can be said to build teamwork, but the challenges the contestants face are admittedly not real. And even though the participants are not in any real danger, they are encouraged to create drama to thrill viewers.

10   Other competitive reality TV shows truly showcase talent. Programs such as *Project Runway, American Idol, America's Got Talent,* and *So You Think You Can Dance* give artists and performers the chance to appear before millions of TV viewers. As a result, the careers of many participants have been launched by way of these programs, even though these contestants did not win the competition. One dancer from Texas, for example, has danced professionally in music videos and on TV shows such as *Glee* since appearing on *So You Think You Can Dance*. These shows inspire young viewers. They see people like them succeeding. So they may think, "I can do that." In this way, reality shows encourage young people to reach for the stars.

American Idol judges Lionel Richie, Katy Perry, and Luke Bryan, along with host Ryan Seacrest, search for America's next music sensation.

11 Reality shows that focus on the lives of everyday people may also give people comfort. As the Greek philosopher Aristotle once said of those who attended theater performances, they did so "to be cured, relieved, restored to psychic health." Viewers can identify with people who seem just like them. They see people with problems similar to (or worse than) their own. As a result, they may realize that their own struggles are not as bad as they thought.

12 Reality TV also introduces viewers to lifestyles, cultures, and people different from themselves. The NAACP reported in 2008 that reality programs are the only segment of television that fairly represents nonwhite groups. At least the people viewers see reflect the wide **diversity** of people in our nation.

13 Some reality TV shows actually improve society. For example, shows such as *Hoarders* increase public awareness of a serious mental health problem. Other shows, such as *Supernanny,* give parents and caregivers tips on how to handle children.

14 Blaming reality TV for society's challenges is a convenient way to avoid taking a hard look at ourselves and finding solutions to our problems. Life is messy, and reality TV honestly reveals that truth. Once we realize that we are far from perfect, we can learn to accept others for who they are. Certainly, acceptance of others, with all their faults, is a big step toward creating a better society for everyone.

First Read

Read "Reality TV and Society." After you read, complete the Think Questions below.

☁ THINK QUESTIONS

1. What position does the Point author take in the debate over reality TV? Cite two pieces of evidence from the Point essay to support your answer.

2. The Point author uses the opinion of comedian Tom Green to support the argument. How does Green's opinion help the author explain what has caused the quality of TV to decline? Cite specific evidence from paragraph 4 of the Point essay to support your answer.

3. What position does the Counterpoint author take in the debate over reality TV? Cite two pieces of evidence from paragraphs 12 and 13 to support your response.

4. Read the following dictionary entry:

   cor·rupt /kə'rəpt/

   verb

   1. to cause to be dishonest or immoral in manners or actions
   2. to cause errors or unintentional alterations to occur

   adjective

   1. dishonest for personal gain
   2. evil or immoral
   3. rotten or decaying

   Which definition most closely matches the meaning of **corrupted** in paragraph 8? Write the correct definition of *corrupted* here and explain how you figured it out.

5. Use context clues to determine the meaning of the word **controversy** as it is used in the text. Write your definition of *controversy* here. Then look up the definition in an online or print dictionary to confirm or revise your meaning.

Please note that excerpts and passages in the StudySync® library and this workbook are intended as touchstones to generate interest in an author's work. The excerpts and passages do not substitute for the reading of entire texts, and StudySync® strongly recommends that students seek out and purchase the whole literary or informational work in order to experience it as the author intended. Links to online resellers are available in our digital library. In addition, complete works may be ordered through an authorized reseller by filling out and returning to StudySync® the order form enclosed in this workbook.

Reading & Writing Companion

899

Skill:
Arguments and Claims

Use the Checklist to analyze Arguments and Claims in "Reality TV and Society." Refer to the sample student annotations about Arguments and Claims in the text.

••• CHECKLIST FOR ARGUMENTS AND CLAIMS

In order to trace the argument and specific claims, do the following:

✓ identify clues that reveal the author's opinion in the title, introduction, or conclusion

✓ note the first and last sentence of each body paragraph for specific claims that help to build the author's argument

✓ list the information the author introduces in sequential order

✓ use different colors to highlight and distinguish among an author's argument, claims, evidence, or reasons

✓ describe the author's argument in your own words

To evaluate the argument and specific claims, consider the following questions:

✓ Does the author support each claim with reasoning and evidence?

✓ Do the author's claims work together to support his or her overall argument?

✓ Which claims are not supported, if any?

Skill:
Arguments and Claims

Reread paragraph 11 of the Counterpoint section and analyze the structure of the passage. Then, complete the chart below by identifying the claim in the passage as well as the reasoning behind the claim and the evidence that supports it.

⟳ YOUR TURN

	Answer Bank
A	Viewers who see people like themselves struggling may realize their problems are not so bad.
B	In Ancient Greece, watching people struggle helped people feel better and be "cured" or "restored."
C	Reality TV provides viewers with a sense of comfort and well-being.

Claim	Reason	Evidence

Skill:
Compare and Contrast

Use the Checklist to analyze Compare and Contrast in "Reality TV and Society."

••• CHECKLIST FOR COMPARE AND CONTRAST

In order to determine how two or more authors writing about the same topic shape their presentations of key information, use the following steps:

✓ first, choose two texts with similar subjects or topics by different authors

✓ next, identify each author's approach to the subject

✓ after, identify the key information and evidence each author includes

✓ then, explain the ways each author shapes the presentation of the information in the text

✓ finally, analyze the similarities and differences in how the authors present:

- key information
- evidence
- their interpretation of facts

To analyze how two or more authors writing about the same topic shape their presentations of key information, consider the following questions:

✓ In what ways do the texts I have chosen have similar subjects or topics?

✓ How does each author approach the topic or subject?

✓ How does each author's presentation of key information differ? How are they the same? How do these similarities and differences change the presentation and interpretation of the facts?

Skill:
Compare and Contrast

Reread paragraph 6 of the Point essay and paragraph 10 of the Counterpoint essay from "Reality TV and Society." Then, using the Checklist on the previous page, complete the chart below by sorting the observations to compare and contrast the passages.

⟳ YOUR TURN

	Observations
A	Reality TV gives young people false expectations.
B	Reality TV makes people hope for fame and fortune.
C	Reality TV encourages young people to follow their dreams.
D	Reality TV inspires young people.
E	Reality TV influences young people.
F	Reality TV harms young people.

Point	Both	Counterpoint

Please note that excerpts and passages in the StudySync® library and this workbook are intended as touchstones to generate interest in an author's work. The excerpts and passages do not substitute for the reading of entire texts, and StudySync® strongly recommends that students seek out and purchase the whole literary or informational work in order to experience it as the author intended. Links to online resellers are available in our digital library. In addition, complete works may be ordered through an authorized reseller by filling out and returning to StudySync® the order form enclosed in this workbook.

Reading & Writing Companion   903

Close Read

Reread "Reality TV and Society." As you reread, complete the Skills Focus questions below. Then use your answers and annotations from the questions to help you complete the Write activity.

◎ SKILLS FOCUS

1. Identify details in the conclusion of each section of the article that connect to the section's claim. Explain how the conclusion of each section relates to the claim.

2. Identify reasons and evidence the writer uses to support a claim in the Point section. Explain how the reasons and evidence sufficiently support the claim.

3. Identify reasons and evidence the writer uses to support a claim in the Counterpoint section. Explain how the reasons and evidence sufficiently support the claim.

4. Compare and contrast the different authors' arguments. Identify pertinent examples and supporting evidence the authors use. Write a note explaining how the authors emphasize and explain the examples and evidence that support their arguments or claims.

5. Identify an example of how viewers, contestants, and participants interact with reality TV. Explain how reality TV reflects the human desire to stand out from the crowd.

✏ WRITE

DEBATE: With your classmates, debate whether reality TV is good or bad for society. To prepare for the debate, write your claim and provide three reasons with evidence to support your claim. Use examples from the text as well as from your own experience and research.

The Matsuyama Mirror

DRAMA
Velina Hasu Houston
1994

Introduction

Velina Hasu Houston (b. 1957) was born to an American father and a Japanese mother—in an American household modeled after Japanese traditions. Today, she is a playwright, poet, essayist, and professor. In this excerpt from *The Matsuyama Mirror*, a Japanese man named Otoosan returns to his village of Matsuyama after a journey, bearing gifts for his family. But he also bears the news that his wife has died in a riding accident—news his daughters do not yet know. When he must give them the news about their mother, he tries to comfort their grief with reassurances and gifts. Aiko's gift, in particular, proves to be very useful for connecting to her mother's spirit.

"Are you not curious about your present, Aiko?"

CAST OF CHARACTERS

AIKO
TOORIKO
OKAASAN (also GRAND MISTRESS OF MATSUYAMA)
OTOOSAN
YUKIKO OBASAN
Aiko's Chorus of Dolls: FIRST KOKESHI
                       SECOND KOKESHI
                       THIRD KOKESHI

NOTE

One Kuro-ko (stage assistant in Japanese tradition) is needed. This responsibility can be carried out by any actor in the company.

SETTING

1600s. Matsuyama, Japan; and a magical world.

. . .

1   *(Sounds of horses are heard from off stage. Aiko tries to run out, but is stopped by OTOOSAN who enters covered with snow. He conceals **grimness** with a smile for his children. He carries a satchel[1] filled to **capacity**.)*

2   OTOOSAN: Good daughters. Hello.

3   TOORIKO: *(Bowing low)* Welcome home, Otoosan.

4   AIKO: Welcome, Father.

5   OTOOSAN: Where are you going in such a hurry, Aiko?

6   TOORIKO: Out into the snow to find you!

---

1. **satchel** a bag, typically carried over the shoulder

7   AIKO: Where is Mother?

8   OTOOSAN: It is so cold. Let me sit for a—

9   AIKO: Is she with the horses?

10   TOORIKO: Quiet, Aiko!

11   *(Tooriko helps him off with his coat. He and Tooriko sit around the candle. Incredulous, Aiko puts on her father's coat and prepares to leave.)*

12   OTOOSAN: Take off my coat and sit, Aiko.

13   AIKO: Tell me where she is.

14   OTOOSAN: Sit.

15   *(Otoosan takes the coat off of her and forces her to sit.)*

16   Children, your mother has . . . left us.

17   AIKO: What? No. No.

18   OTOOSAN: . . . there has been . . . an accident.

19   *(The breath knocked out of her, Aiko sits motionlessly. Tooriko is quiet with shock for a moment and then weeps uncontrollably.)*

20   AIKO: *(**Eerie** calmness)* You must tell me what has happened to my mother.

21   OTOOSAN: The snow. An accident with the horses. Her head struck a rock. When they found her, she was already . . .

22   AIKO: How can you sit there like a piece of stone?

23   TOORIKO: Aiko!

24   AIKO: How can you? What are you?

25   OTOOSAN: The bearer of our pain so that you can go on.

26   TOORIKO: Oh, this family. Pull yourself together, Father.

27   OTOOSAN: Your mother drifts in the winds tonight, seeking her next existence. We must keep the sky clear; we must not weep.

Skill:
Word Meaning

I am not sure what the word drifts means, but I can tell it's a verb. Drifts is what the mother or her spirit is doing tonight. There are more verbs that show the family's reaction to the mother's death and her spirit drifting. Otoosan says they must keep the sky clear, and Aiko asks for her mother to come back. I wonder if these will help me understand the meaning of drifts in this line?

NOTES

28   AIKO: Bring her back. *(To the ether)* Come back, Okaasan. Come back! Please, please, come back.

29   OTOOSAN: Enough, gentle Aiko-chan . . . we must go on as usual . . .

30   AIKO: What? How?

31   TOORIKO: Shall we sit around like fools and weep?

32   AIKO: You never loved her like I did.

33   TOORIKO: I am older and I have loved her longer.

34   AIKO: And I love her best.

35   *(Otoosan reaches for the satchel and removes two packages.)*

36   OTOOSAN: Here. Your gifts. Come. Let us be as curious and happy as we always are when I return from my journeys.

37   AIKO: I only want the return of my mother.

38   OTOOSAN: What do you think I brought you, Aiko-chan?

39   AIKO: Who will I ask for help when I am learning new embroidery[2]?

40   TOORIKO: I will help you.

41   AIKO: You do not help. You order.

42   OTOOSAN: We will all help each other.

43   AIKO: Tooriko-san will only help herself and her husband.

44   TOORIKO: What is wrong with that? If you ever grow up, you will bring a husband to live here with you and Otoosan. You will know secrets that will make you selfish sometimes, too.

45   OTOOSAN: Yes, Aiko, I will find you a strong, patient man.

46   TOORIKO: In this case, perhaps a saint is required.

47   OTOOSAN: And Tooriko will always be near. Her husband plans to build their new house just on the other side of the village.

---

2. **embroidery** decorative cloth with designs sewn into it with thread

Skill:
Media

When I was reading it, I thought that this scene was just two sisters bickering. When I listened to the audio version, though, I thought the scene was funny. Tooriko's line could have just been mean, but the actor makes it comedic with her performance.

48   AIKO: It might as well be on the other side of the universe.

49   OTOOSAN: When I am gone, you two sisters will be all that is left of our family. Can you not be **civil** to one another? Come, Aiko-chan. Come sit by me.

50   AIKO: Who will cook tonight, Otoosan?

51   TOORIKO: I will cook.

52   AIKO: You? The taste will kill— Sorry. But you don't know how to cook. You don't.

53   OTOOSAN: Your aunt will come tomorrow to help.

54   AIKO: Aunt Yukiko!

55   OTOOSAN: This is a time to find strength in family. Yukiko Obasan is good and kind.

56   AIKO: And rough as a tree trunk.

57   TOORIKO: But sturdy and lasting.

58   OTOOSAN: Are you not curious about your present, Aiko? Perhaps it will give you a little light in this darkness?

59   AIKO: *(Facetiously)* Oh I am certain.

60   OTOOSAN: Then if I have brought a new doll, must I find another little girl to give it to?

61   AIKO: Otoosan? Could the gods have made a mistake? Can they be persuaded to give back my mother?

62   OTOOSAN: Open your present, dear child.

63   AIKO: How can I behold these gifts at such a time?

64   TOORIKO: Because we need to. If I stare at the tatami[3] all night and cry, then I will not make it to morning.

65   OTOOSAN: Here, Tooriko-san.

66   *(She opens her gift. It is a scarf.)*

---

3. **tatami** a straw mat forming a traditional Japanese floor covering

NOTES

67   TOORIKO: Thank you, Otoosan. I shall save it.

68   OTOOSAN: Do not save it. Wear it. Make yourself look beautiful. Today. Now. And for you, Aiko-chan.

69   *(He takes out a silver, sparkling box. Immediately, the Kuro-ko tinkles wind chimes and Aiko looks around, startled as if she hears something. Aiko holds the box and slowly opens it, scattering sparkling dust. She takes out a large silver and gold lacquered mirror with angel hair hanging in shreds from it. It leaves her in a state of awe. Tooriko is afraid of it.)*

70   AIKO: What is it, Father?

71   OTOOSAN: It is called a "mirror."

72   AIKO: ". . . mirror . . ."

73   TOORIKO: Does it belong in the house?

74   OTOOSAN: It is magic. Look in the glass.

75   AIKO: *(Startled)* There is a girl in the glass!

76   OTOOSAN: *(Laughs)* And who does she look like?

77   *(Aiko dares look again and gasps. Tooriko's curiosity is quelled by fear.)*

78   AIKO: It is Mother, when she was a young girl!

79   *(Tooriko screams in fright and Otoosan silences her with a gentle look.)*

80   OTOOSAN: It seems so, does it not?

81   AIKO: Mother has become a child in this mirror. How can that be so? What have you done? Have you put her in the mirror? Can I get her out?

82   TOORIKO: No! No! We will all be cursed.

83   OTOOSAN: Whenever you miss your mother, look in this mirror and you will find her looking back at you.

84   *(Warm, loving woman's laughter is heard only by Aiko who jumps in surprise and fear.)*

85   TOORIKO: *(Staring at her)* You are possessed.

NOTES

86   AIKO: There is a spirit in the mirror! I can hear her; can you hear—

87   OTOOSAN: No one else in Matsuyama has such a mirror. You will be the talk of the town.

88   TOORIKO: And not just because of this mirror.

89   *(Aiko brandishes the mirror toward her sister who jumps in fright.)*

90   Keep that thing away from me! It is black magic.

91   OTOOSAN: It is healing magic.

92   *(Removes a porcelain doll from his satchel.)*

93   I brought this porcelain doll for your mother.

94   *(He offers it to Tooriko, but she motions for him to offer it to Aiko. He hands it to Aiko. Her **pleasure** gives Tooriko pleasure.)*

95   For you, Aiko-chan.

96   AIKO: Thank you, Otoosan.

97   *(He picks up his things and leaves. Tooriko tries to blow out the candle and Aiko stops her.)*

98   Leave it be.

99   TOORIKO: But it is almost burned away. There is no use for it.

100 AIKO: Let it burn and, when it is gone, I want its scent to linger in my hair and kimono.

101 TOORIKO: Little sister, learn to be practical. As you can see, our parents are not immortal.

102 AIKO: But they are. Mother lives. I saw her in this mirror.

103 TOORIKO: Put that thing away!

104 AIKO: But I really saw her. I did!

105 TOORIKO: Aiko-chan, childhood is a butterfly feeding on the dew of youth. And the dew disappears quickly. You must grow up.

NOTES

106   AIKO: No. Never-never-no.

107   TOORIKO: Oh, how can you behave so when she has died this night? Do you not see that the gods have punished her for riding out into the snow like a soldier?

108   AIKO: She is a soldier, a soldier of the soul, like me! I shall ride, too, and I will return in one piece with Mother at my side.

109   TOORIKO: Dear Aiko . . . Good night.

110   AIKO: The night shall never be good again.

111   *(Tooriko leaves. Aiko stares into the mirror as the Kuro-ko tinkles the wind chimes. Lights crossfade . . .)*

By Velina Hasu Houston, 2015. Published by and performances licensed through YouthPLAYS (https://www.youthplays.com). Reproduced by permission of YouthPLAYS.

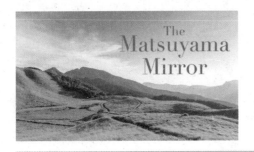

First Read

Read *The Matsuyama Mirror*. After you read, complete the Think Questions below.

☁ THINK QUESTIONS

1. This play takes place in a setting in which nobody has ever seen a mirror before. When Tooriko exclaims that the mirror is "black magic," Otoosan corrects her by saying that it is "healing magic." What does he mean by this? Why would he decide that Aiko needed this magic more than her sister or himself? Cite the text to support your answer.

2. At the end of this scene, Tooriko tries to blow out the candle lighting their home, but Aiko stops her, even though she has no practical need for the candle. What might be the reason for this? Use what you know about Aiko's character to speculate a couple of possibilities.

3. Although the two sisters seem to have a difficult relationship, there are moments in the dialogue and stage directions that hint that each feels a sisterly love for the other. Find them and list them here.

4. Use context clues to determine the meaning of the word **civil** as it is used in the play. Write your definition of *civil* here, along with the parts of the text that helped you arrive at that definition. Then check a dictionary to confirm your understanding.

5. The roots of the noun **capacity** are the Latin word *capiō,* which means "to hold/contain," and the Latin suffix *-itās,* which is used to create the noun form of other words that are adjectives or verbs. Keeping these roots in mind, write a definition of *capacity* as it appears in the text, and explain how your knowledge of its root words helped you arrive at that meaning.

Please note that excerpts and passages in the StudySync® library and this workbook are intended as touchstones to generate interest in an author's work. The excerpts and passages do not substitute for the reading of entire texts, and StudySync® strongly recommends that students seek out and purchase the whole literary or informational work in order to experience it as the author intended. Links to online resellers are available in our digital library. In addition, complete works may be ordered through an authorized reseller by filling out and returning to StudySync® the order form enclosed in this workbook.

Reading & Writing Companion

913

Skill:
Word Meaning

Use the Checklist to analyze Word Meaning in *The Matsuyama Mirror*. Refer to the sample student annotations about Word Meaning in the text.

••• CHECKLIST FOR WORD MEANING

In order to find the pronunciation of a word or determine or clarify its precise meaning or its part of speech, do the following:

- ✓ try to determine the word's part of speech from the context

- ✓ consult reference materials, both print and digital, to find the pronunciation of a word or determine or clarify its precise meaning or its part of speech

- ✓ consult general and specialized reference materials, both print and digital, to find the pronunciation of a word or determine or clarify its precise meaning or its part of speech

In order to verify the preliminary determination of the meaning of a word or phrase, do the following:

- ✓ use context clues to make an inference about the word's meaning

- ✓ consult a dictionary to verify your preliminary determination of the meaning

- ✓ be sure to read all of the definitions, and then decide which definition makes sense within the context of the text

To determine a word's precise meaning or part of speech, ask the following questions:

- ✓ What is the word describing?

- ✓ How is the word being used in the phrase or sentence?

- ✓ Have I consulted my reference materials?

Skill:
Word Meaning

Reread the stage directions and lines 97–101 from *The Matsuyama Mirror* and the dictionary entries below. Use the dictionary entry to determine the meaning, word origin, and part of speech. Then, using the Checklist from the previous page, answer the multiple-choice questions that follow.

↻ YOUR TURN

---

linger \'lin-gər\ *verb*

1: to be slow in parting or in quitting something
2: to remain alive although gradually dying
3: to remain existent although often waning in strength, importance, or influence
4: to be slow to act

Origin: from Middle English *lengeren* "to dwell"

---

1. Which definition best matches the word *linger* as used in line 100? Remember to pay attention to the word's part of speech as you make your decision.

   ○ A. Definition 2
   ○ B. Definition 4
   ○ C. Definition 1
   ○ D. Definition 3

Please note that excerpts and passages in the StudySync® library and this workbook are intended as touchstones to generate interest in an author's work. The excerpts and passages do not substitute for the reading of entire texts, and StudySync® strongly recommends that students seek out and purchase the whole literary or informational work in order to experience it as the author intended. Links to online resellers are available in our digital library. In addition, complete works may be ordered through an authorized reseller by filling out and returning to StudySync® the order form enclosed in this workbook.

Reading & Writing
Companion

915

immortal \(,)i-mor-tel\

adjective

1: exempt from death
2: exempt from oblivion
3: connected with or relating to immortality

noun

4: one exempt from death
5: a person whose fame is lasting

Origin: from Middle English, from Latin *immortalis,* from *in- + mortalis*

2. Which definition best matches the way the word *immortal* is used in line 101? Remember to use the word's part of speech as you make your decision.

   O A. Definition 1
   O B. Definition 4
   O C. Definition 2
   O D. Definition 5

Skill:
Media

Use the Checklist to analyze Media in *The Matsuyama Mirror*. Refer to the sample student annotations about Media in the text.

••• CHECKLIST FOR MEDIA

In order to determine how to compare and contrast a written story, drama, or poem to its audio, filmed, staged, or multimedia version, do the following:

✓ choose a story that has been presented in multiple forms of media, such as a written story and a film adaptation

✓ note techniques that are unique to each medium—print, audio, and video:

- sound
- music
- tone and style
- word choice
- structure

✓ examine how these techniques may have an effect on the story and its ideas, as well as the reader's, listener's, or viewer's understanding of the work as a whole

✓ examine similarities and differences between the written story and its audio or video version

To compare and contrast a written story, drama, or poem to its audio, filmed, staged, or multimedia version, analyzing the effects of techniques unique to each medium, consider the following questions:

✓ How do different types of media treat story elements?

✓ What techniques are unique to each medium—print, audio, and video?

✓ How does the medium—for example, a film's use of music, sound, and camera angles—affect a person's understanding of the work as a whole?

Skill:
Media

Reread lines 50–57 of the play and listen to the audio clip. Use the Checklist on the previous page, to determine the answers to the multiple-choice questions

⟳ YOUR TURN

1. This question has two parts. First, answer Part A. Then, answer Part B.

    Part A: How does the audio version help you understand the character of Aiko in this clip?

    ○ A. I can tell Aiko is stubborn.
    ○ B. I can tell that she loves her aunt.
    ○ C. I can tell that Aiko is funny.
    ○ D. I can tell that Aiko is sad.

    Part B: Which of the following performances from the audio clip BEST supports your response to Part A?

    ○ A. AIKO: Sorry. But you don't know how to cook. You don't.
    ○ B. AIKO: And rough as a tree trunk.
    ○ C. OTOOSAN: This is a time to find strength in family.
    ○ D. AIKO: Aunt Yukiko!

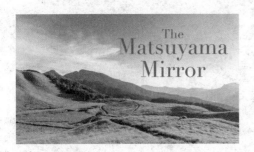

Close Read

Reread *The Matsuyama Mirror*. As you reread, complete the Skills Focus questions below. Then use your answers and annotations from the questions to help you complete the Write activity.

◎ SKILLS FOCUS

1. The characters in this story experience a great loss. How do the plot elements reveal aspects of the characters to the reader?

2. Dramatic elements help set the scene of a play and give the reader information about what they would see and hear at the show. How do the stage directions help you understand the tone of the play?

3. Think back to the audio recording of the play. How did the sound elements affect your understanding of the characters and tone of the play?

4. Aiko does not feel like she fits in with her family. What about Aiko makes her stand out? How does the play support the idea that Aiko is outstanding?

✏ WRITE

LITERARY ANALYSIS: Listening to a performance of a play is a different experience than reading the script. How do the sound elements affect your understanding of the characters? Use specific examples from the text and the audio to show how the audio contributes to your understanding of the characters.

Please note that excerpts and passages in the StudySync® library and this workbook are intended as touchstones to generate interest in an author's work. The excerpts and passages do not substitute for the reading of entire texts, and StudySync® strongly recommends that students seek out and purchase the whole literary or informational work in order to experience it as the author intended. Links to online resellers are available in our digital library. In addition, complete works may be ordered through an authorized reseller by filling out and returning to StudySync® the order form enclosed in this workbook.

Reading & Writing Companion 919

New Directions

INFORMATIONAL TEXT
Maya Angelou
1993

Introduction

Maya Angelou (1928–2014) was an American poet, essayist, and activist best known for her heralded autobiography, *I Know Why the Caged Bird Sings*. "New Directions" is another well-known nonfiction piece by Angelou. In this biographical essay, she recounts the life of her grandmother, Annie Johnson. When Annie's marriage ended in 1903, she realized that she must work in order to support her two small boys. As an African American woman, her choices were limited, yet Annie "cuts a new path" for herself through hard work and resourcefulness. In sharing her grandmother's story, Angelou teaches readers a

"She had indeed stepped from the road which seemed to have been chosen for her . . ."

Copyright © BookheadEd Learning, LLC

NOTES

1   In 1903 the late Mrs. Annie Johnson of Arkansas found herself with two toddling sons, very little money, a slight ability to read and add simple numbers. To this picture add a disastrous marriage and the **burdensome** fact that Mrs. Johnson was a Negro.

2   When she told her husband, Mr. William Johnson, of her dissatisfaction with their marriage, he **conceded** that he too found it to be less than he expected, and had been secretly hoping to leave and study religion. He added that he thought God was calling him not only to preach but to do so in Enid, Oklahoma. He did not tell her that he knew a minister in Enid with whom he could study and who had a friendly, unmarried daughter. They parted amicably, Annie keeping the one-room house and William taking most of the cash to carry himself to Oklahoma.

3   Annie, over six feet tall, big-boned, decided that she would not go to work as a **domestic** and leave her "precious babes" to anyone else's care. There was no possibility of being hired at the town's cotton gin[1] or lumber mill[2], but maybe there was a way to make the two factories work for her. In her words, "I looked up the road I was going and back the way I come, and since I wasn't satisfied, I decided to step off the road and cut me a new path." She told herself that she wasn't a fancy cook but that she could "mix groceries well enough to scare hungry away and from starving a man."

4   She made her plans **meticulously** and in secret. One early evening to see if she was ready, she placed stones in two five-gallon pails and carried them three miles to the cotton gin. She rested a little, and then, discarding some rocks, she walked in the darkness to the saw mill[3] five miles farther along the dirt road. On her way back to her little house and her babies, she dumped the remaining rocks along the path.

---

1. **cotton gin** a machine that separates cotton from seeds
2. **lumber mill** a factory where timber is cut into rough planks
3. **saw mill** a factory in which logs are sawed into lumber

5   That same night she worked into the early hours boiling chicken and frying ham. She made dough and filled the rolled-out pastry with meat. At last she went to sleep.

6   The next morning she left her house carrying the meat pies, lard, an iron brazier, and coals for a fire. Just before lunch she appeared in an empty lot behind the cotton gin. As the dinner noon bell rang, she dropped the savors[4] into boiling fat and the aroma rose and floated over to the workers who spilled out of the gin, covered with white lint, looking like specters[5].

7   Most workers had brought their lunches of pinto beans and biscuits or crackers, onions and cans of sardines, but they were tempted by the hot meat pies which Annie ladled out of the fat. She wrapped them in newspapers, which soaked up the grease, and offered them for sale at a nickel each. Although business was slow, those first days Annie was determined. She balanced her appearances between the two hours of activity.

8   So, on Monday if she offered hot fresh pies at the cotton gin and sold the remaining cooled-down pies at the lumber mill for three cents, then on Tuesday she went first to the lumber mill presenting fresh, just-cooked pies as the lumbermen covered in sawdust emerged from the mill.

9   For the next few years, on balmy spring days, blistering summer noon, and cold, wet, and wintry middays, Annie never disappointed her customers, who could count on seeing the tall, brown-skin woman bent over her brazier, carefully turning the meat pies. When she felt certain that the workers had become dependent on her, she built a stall between the two hives of industry and let the men run to her for their lunchtime provisions.

10   She had indeed stepped from the road which seemed to have been chosen for her and cut herself a brand-new path. In years that stall became a store where customers could buy cheese, meal, syrup, cookies, candy, writing tablets, pickles, canned goods, fresh fruit, soft drinks, coal, oil, and leather soles for worn-out shoes.

11   Each of us has the right and the responsibility to **assess** the roads which lie ahead, and those over which we have traveled, and if the future road looms **ominous** or unpromising, and the roads back uninviting, then we need to gather our resolve and, carrying only the necessary baggage, step off that road into another direction. If the new choice is also unpalatable, without embarrassment, we must be ready to change that as well.

---

4. **savors** flavors or seasonings
5. **specters** ghosts or spirits

WRITE

PERSONAL RESPONSE: What does author Maya Angelou think of her grandmother? Why do you think she tells her grandmother's story? Write a response to these questions. Remember to use evidence from the text to support your response.

Please note that excerpts and passages in the StudySync® library and this workbook are intended as touchstones to generate interest in an author's work. The excerpts and passages do not substitute for the reading of entire texts, and StudySync® strongly recommends that students seek out and purchase the whole literary or informational work in order to experience it as the author intended. Links to online resellers are available in our digital library. In addition, complete works may be ordered through an authorized reseller by filling out and returning to StudySync® the order form enclosed in this workbook.

Reading & Writing Companion **923**

Choices

POETRY
Nikki Giovanni
1978

Introduction

Nikki Giovanni (b. 1943) calls herself a "Black American, a daughter, a mother, a professor of English." She is also the recipient of 25 honorary degrees, as well as an award-winning poet, writer, and activist who gives voice to issues of social justice and identity. Her poem "Choices" speaks to her inner struggle to make the best of any situation, especially when faced with limitations. Rather than quitting or dwelling on her limitations, she "chooses" to act, think, and move in some way—and, in doing so, chooses to pursue her own personal progress.

"it's not the same thing
but it's the best i can do"

1 if i can't do
2 what i want to do
3 then my job is to not
4 do what i don't want
5 to do

6 it's not the same thing
7 but it's the best i can
8 do

9 if i can't have
10 what i want . . . then
11 my job is to want
12 what i've got
13 and be **satisfied**
14 that at least there
15 is something more
16 to want

17 since i can't go
18 where i need
19 to go . . . then i must . . . go
20 where the signs point
21 though always understanding
22 **parallel** movement
23 isn't **lateral**

Skill: Poetic Elements and Structure

The poem is written in open verse, without a fixed rhyme scheme or meter. However, the repetition of the word "do" creates a rhythm and emphasizes action. This contributes to the poem's meaning about making choices.

The repetition of "do" expresses the idea of active choice in the poem. Placing "not" at the end of a line emphasizes this word and expresses the idea of using free will and making choices despite limitations.

NOTES

24 when i can't **express**
25 what i really feel
26 i practice feeling
27 what i can express
28 and none of it is **equal**
29 i know
30 but that's why mankind
31 alone among the mammals
32 learns to cry

"Choices" from COTTON CANDY ON A RAINY DAY by NIKKI GIOVANNI. COPYRIGHT ©1978 BY NIKKI GIOVANNI. Reprinted by permission of HarperCollins Publishers.

CHOICES

First Read

Read "Choices." After you read, complete the Think Questions below.

☁ THINK QUESTIONS

1. According to the first stanza, what is the speaker's "job"?

2. What are the speaker's feelings about satisfaction and wanting? Cite evidence from the third stanza to support your answer.

3. Does the speaker feel free to fully express her feelings? Cite evidence from the final stanza in your response.

4. Read the following dictionary entry:

   parallel par•al•lel \'per ə, lel\
   noun

   1. something that is similar or comparable to something else

   verb

   1. to remain side by side with something in a line

   adjective

   1. side-by-side at a distance that is continuously the same

   Which definition most closely matches the meaning of **parallel** as it is used in line 22? Write the correct definition of *parallel* here and explain how you figured out the proper meaning.

5. Read the following dictionary entry:

   express ex•press \ik'spres\
   verb

   1. to represent using a number or formula
   2. to say or make known

   adjective

   1. happening quickly or at a high speed
   2. stated directly or explicitly

   Which definition most closely matches the meaning of **express** as it is used in line 24? Write the correct definition of *express* here and explain how you figured out the proper meaning.

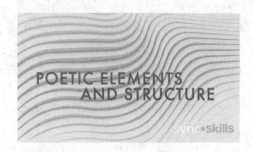

Skill: Poetic Elements and Structure

Use the Checklist to analyze Poetic Elements and Structure in "Choices." Refer to the sample student annotations about Poetic Elements and Structure in the text.

••• CHECKLIST FOR POETIC ELEMENTS AND STRUCTURE

In order to identify poetic elements and structure, note the following:

- ✓ the form and overall structure of the poem

- ✓ the rhyme, rhythm and meter, if present

- ✓ other sound elements, such as:

  - alliteration: the repetition of initial consonant sounds, as with the *s* sound in "Cindy sweeps the sand"

- ✓ lines and stanzas in the poem that suggest its meaning

- ✓ ways that the poem's form or structure connects to the poem's meaning

To analyze how a drama's or poem's form or structure contributes to its meaning, consider the following questions:

- ✓ What poetic form does the poet use? What is the structure?

- ✓ How do the lines and stanzas and their length affect the meaning?

- ✓ How do the form and structure contribute to the poem's meaning?

To analyze the impact of rhymes and other repetitions of sounds on a specific verse or stanza of a poem, consider the following questions:

- ✓ What sound elements are present in specific stanzas of the poem?

- ✓ What is the effect of different sound elements on the stanza or verse?

Copyright © BookheadEd Learning, LLC

Skill: Poetic Elements and Structure

Reread lines 6–8 of "Choices." Then, using the Checklist on the previous page, answer the multiple-choice questions below.

♻ YOUR TURN

1. The third line contains only one word, "do." The reader can conclude that —

   ○ A. this is not an important line.
   ○ B. this word is being emphasized.
   ○ C. there was not enough room on the previous line.
   ○ D. the poet was not very careful when writing.

2. Lines 6–8 are important to the poem because they —

   ○ A. include a lowercase "i" to show that the speaker feels powerless and cannot make a choice.
   ○ B. express the theme that it is important to make choices even when there are limitations.
   ○ C. help to establish the regular rhyme scheme and meter of this poem.
   ○ D. convey the idea that one's best effort is not always good enough.

Please note that excerpts and passages in the StudySync® library and this workbook are intended as touchstones to generate interest in an author's work. The excerpts and passages do not substitute for the reading of entire texts, and StudySync® strongly recommends that students seek out and purchase the whole literary or informational work in order to experience it as the author intended. Links to online resellers are available in our digital library. In addition, complete works may be ordered through an authorized reseller by filling out and returning to StudySync® the order form enclosed in this workbook.

Reading & Writing Companion **929**

Close Read

Reread "Choices." As you reread, complete the Skills Focus questions below. Then use your answers and annotations from the questions to help you complete the Write activity.

◎ SKILLS FOCUS

1. Identify the use of repetition in the third stanza. Explain how these elements impact the meaning of the poem.

2. Identify the use of repetition and spacing in the fourth stanza. Explain how these elements and structures help you to understand what the poet is trying to say.

3. Identify a detail in the fifth stanza that develops the theme of the poem and explain how the detail supports the theme.

4. The speaker faces limitations but continues to value her individuality. How does the poem suggest that we stand out from the crowd?

✏ WRITE

COMPARE AND CONTRAST: In "New Directions," Maya Angelou tells the story of how her grandmother started a career for herself to support her family. It has an important message about overcoming obstacles and creating a new path for yourself. How does Nikki Giovanni use poetic elements and structure to express a similar message or theme? Use evidence from the text to support your answer.

Cuentos de Josefina
(Josephine's Tales)

DRAMA
Gregory Ramos
2016

Introduction

Cuentos de Josefina (Josephine's Tales) is a collection of interconnected plays by Gregory Ramos, narrated by young Josefina and her little brother, Ignacio. The two of them tell stories and folktales that weave together Mexican folklore with modern settings and situations, exploring what it means to leave one land in search of another, and the value in maintaining ties to one's past. The short play excerpted here, "The Tale of the Haunted Squash," is a story of greed and superstition. Read along as Josefina and Ignacio tell the tale of a young couple, Filiberto and Elvira, who disobey an agreement and reap the rewards—but only at a certain cost.

"Maybe I wasn't born under a lucky star after all."

CHARACTERS:

JOSIE, female.
JOSEFINA, female.
YOUNG JOSEFINA, female. Age 15.
IGNACIO, male. Age 11.
FILIBERTO, male.
ELVIRA, female.
LA TÍA, female.
SEÑOR TRUJILLO, male.
EL ESQUELETO, any gender.
NEIGHBOR, any gender.
OLD MAN (RODOLFO), male.
GUESTS 1–4, any gender.
ACTORS 5–8, any gender.

TALE 2: THE TALE OF THE HAUNTED SQUASH

1 YOUNG JOSEFINA: Filiberto and his wife Elvira faced hard times.

2 (*FILIBERTO and ELVIRA enter with meager belongings.*)

3 IGNACIO: There was a drought. And they were forced to leave their *pueblito* (village).

4 YOUNG JOSEFINA: On the train, leaving the village, Filiberto played a high stakes card game.

5 (*Actors assemble for card game.*)

6 IGNACIO: Desperate to improve their situation, he bet the few pesos that he and Elvira had saved.

7 ELVIRA: Filiberto, no!!!

8 YOUNG JOSEFINA: But—he won! And lost! And won! And lost. And finally . . .

9   FILIBERTO: I won the deed to land!

10   *(SEÑOR TRUJILLO and Filiberto sign deed. They shake hands.)*

11   *Gracias* (Thank you), Señor Trujillo.

12   *(Elvira inspects the deed as Señor Trujillo slinks away.)*

13   ELVIRA: (*Suddenly:*) *Mira!* (Look!) There's a **clause** here that says we're forbidden to plant in the west garden. Why?

14   FILIBERTO: Who cares? It's a house and ten acres and it's ours! *Híjole*[1]! My mother always said I was born under a lucky star.

15   YOUNG JOSEFINA: So, Filiberto and Elvira settled into their new house. Elvira made bread in the kitchen and peddled it on the streets, but there was a lot of competition. Filiberto planted tomatoes, carrots and lettuces only in the east garden. They grew, but they were puny and sickly and he tried to sell them.

16   *(Elvira and Filiberto count their earnings at the end of the day.)*

17   ELVIRA: Ten, eleven, twelve *centavos*[2]. That's all?

18   FILIBERTO: I tell you, no one wants my vegetables. They're puny and sickly.

19   ELVIRA: If we could only plant in the west garden. The soil there is so rich.

20   FILIBERTO: We can't.

21   ELVIRA: Why not?

22   FILIBERTO: We signed an agreement.

23   ELVIRA: Who's going to know?

24   FILIBERTO: Elvira!

25   YOUNG JOSEFINA: (*Narrating:*) That next day, Elvira did not make bread to peddle on the streets. Instead, while Filiberto was peddling his puny vegetables in the market, she went into town, bought a bag of *calabaza* (pumpkin) seeds and spent the entire day in the warm sun sowing the seeds in the west garden.

---

1. **Híjole!** an expression used to express surprise
2. **centavos** a monetary unit equal to one hundredth of the basic unit

Skill: Dramatic Elements and Structure

Elvira and Filiberto are talking to each other, but Josefina is talking to the audience. Josefina is telling the audience about the plot so we know what is happening. She lets us know that both characters are having problems. Maybe these problems will be related to the play's lesson?

26 *(Elvira sows seeds. End of day, she's spent.)*

27 FILIBERTO: Elvira, I'm home.

28 *(Elvira cleans up quickly and runs into the house.)*

29 Here's the money from today's sales.

30 ELVIRA: (*Counting*:) Five, ten, fourteen, fifteen *centavos*. That's all?

31 FILIBERTO: How did the bread sales go today?

32 ELVIRA: How do you think? Lousy. If only we could . . .

33 FILIBERTO: No!

34 ELVIRA: But we're barely surviving!

35 FILIBERTO: Maybe I wasn't born under a lucky star after all.

36 *(He starts off, deflated.)*

37 ELVIRA: Filiberto . . .

38 *(Rooster [actor] crows.)*

39 YOUNG JOSEFINA: But . . . the next morning, Filiberto and Elvira discovered something in the west garden.

40 *(Filiberto stands in the west garden surrounded by* calabazas *[pumpkins].)*

41 FILIBERTO: Elvira! *Ven! Mira!* (Come! Look!)

42 ELVIRA: Filiberto, *qué pasó* (what happened)?

43 FILIBERTO: *Mira!*

44 ELVIRA: *Híjole!*

45 FILIBERTO: Beautiful, ripe *calabazas*.

46 ELVIRA: Ripe and beautiful! We can sell them at the *mercado* (market) and make so much money!

47 FILIBERTO: Where did they come from?

48 ELVIRA: What difference does it make? This is just the luck we've been waiting for.

49 FILIBERTO: Wait. We can't sell them.

50 ELVIRA: Can't sell them? *Estás loco*? (Are you crazy?)

51 FILIBERTO: We promised not to plant here.

52 ELVIRA: *Pues* (Well), if you're not selling them, I am. I'm going to load up the wagon with all of these beautiful, ripe *calabazas* and I'm not coming home until every last one is sold. If you want to try and peddle those sickly vegetables from the other garden, be my guest.

53 *(Filiberto looks at his puny vegetables, then at Elvira's beautiful* calabazas.*)*

54 FILIBERTO: Let's cut these and get them on the wagon!

55 ELVIRA: *Andale!* (Go for it!)

56 ACTOR 5: But as Filiberto and Elvira began to cut the *calabazas* from the vines, they made an incredible discovery. The squashes opened up when they touched them and inside—

57 FILIBERTO: Silver!

58 ELVIRA: Gold!

59 ACTOR 8: Every squash they opened **contained** a precious metal. Which of course to them meant—

60 ELVIRA & FILIBERTO: Money!!!

61 FILIBERTO: *(Extracting silver from a* calabaza:*)* Well this beats peddling bread on the streets!

62 ELVIRA: Ooooh. Let's spend it!

63 ACTOR 5: And spend, they did.

64 JOSIE: They didn't use the money to buy a new wagon.

65 JOSEFINA: Or to invest in new vegetable seeds for planting.

66 ACTOR 8: Or to purchase flour for Elvira's bread.

NOTES

Skill: Dramatic Elements and Structure

The short dialogue goes quickly back and forth between Filiberto and Elvira and lets me know this is a tense scene. I can see how stressed the two characters are by their problems.

The stage directions here help me understand what Filiberto is thinking. Since I'm reading and not watching the play, the stage directions let me know what is happening on stage. Filiberto is comparing his options, and the options are really unequal.

Please note that excerpts and passages in the StudySync® library and this workbook are intended as touchstones to generate interest in an author's work. The excerpts and passages do not substitute for the reading of entire texts, and StudySync® strongly recommends that students seek out and purchase the whole literary or informational work in order to experience it as the author intended. Links to online resellers are available in our digital library. In addition, complete works may be ordered through an authorized reseller by filling out and returning to StudySync® the order form enclosed in this workbook.

Reading & Writing Companion   935

67 ACTOR 6: Instead, they bought new clothes, Elvira got some fine jewelry, and with the rest, they threw a party for all the neighbors.

68 *(Party music drops hard. Party with neighbors ensues.)*

69 ELVIRA: *Mira.* We had so much squash I made a delicious squash soup for the guests.

70 *(Party continues. GUESTS eat pumpkin soup and dance. Party dies down. Guests leave.)*

71 JOSIE: After the party, Filiberto and Elvira were cleaning up and . . .

72 *(Elvira pours soup into a container. The soup has turned to blood. She screams.)*

73 FILIBERTO: *Ay, Dios mío!* (Oh, my God!)

74 ELVIRA: What happened to my soup?

75 FILIBERTO: It's turned to blood!

76 ELVIRA: That can't be! There has to be some explanation.

77 FILIBERTO: *Sangre!* Blood! This is a *maldición* (curse)!

78 ELVIRA: *Cálmate!* (Calm down!)

79 FILIBERTO: We weren't supposed to plant in the west garden!

80 ELVIRA: Don't be **superstitious.**

81 FILIBERTO: We are not planting in that garden again. Ever!

82 ELVIRA: But, Filiberto—

83 FILIBERTO: It's a curse!!! *Ayyyy!*

84 *(Filiberto runs off terrified.)*

85 YOUNG JOSEFINA: So they went back to peddling bread and the sickly vegetables from the other garden.

86 ELVIRA: (*Peddling*:) *Pan caliente! Tengo pan caliente!* (Fresh bread! I have fresh bread here!)

87　FILIBERTO: *Zanahorias! Lechugas! Jitomate!* (Carrots! Lettuce! Tomato!)

88　*(Elvira and Filiberto at the end of the day counting their earnings.)*

89　ELVIRA: Ten, eleven, twelve, thirteen *centavos*. That's all!!!?

90　FILIBERTO: (*Sadly*:) That's all.

91　ELVIRA: We don't even have enough to make it through the week. Filiberto . . .

92　FILIBERTO: No.

93　ELVIRA: I'm tired of peddling bread on the streets and going to bed hungry. We're going to starve. Why shouldn't we have a little comfort and luxury?

94　FILIBERTO: But—

95　ELVIRA: Remember when we bought all those new clothes and threw a big party for all the neighbors? That was niiiiice.

96　*(Filiberto regards her skeptically.)*

97　We're planting another crop of *calabazas* and this time we're planting more!

99　FILIBERTO: But, but, but—

99　ELVIRA: You say you aren't lucky? Hah! I say maybe this is the luck you've been waiting for. *Vámanos!* (Let's go!)

100　ACTOR 7: So Elvira and Filiberto sowed another crop in the garden. And yes, they planted even more.

101　ACTOR 6: The very next morning the garden was abundant with big, fat, ripe, healthy *calabazas*.

102　*(Elvira opens a squash and pulls out money.)*

103　ELVIRA: (*Gleefully*:) Ahhhh! I'm going to buy another new wardrobe! And this time we have enough money to **renovate** the house. Hey, we might even buy the land next door and expand!!!

104　JOSEFINA: And that's just what they did. They bought the land next door and built a brand new big house. They bought new furniture and then, because of course they wanted to share their new status with their neighbors, they threw a *fiesta*. A big *fiesta*!

Please note that excerpts and passages in the StudySync® library and this workbook are intended as touchstones to generate interest in an author's work. The excerpts and passages do not substitute for the reading of entire texts, and StudySync® strongly recommends that students seek out and purchase the whole literary or informational work in order to experience it as the author intended. Links to online resellers are available in our digital library. In addition, complete works may be ordered through an authorized reseller by filling out and returning to StudySync® the order form enclosed in this workbook.

Reading & Writing Companion　937

105 *(Party music drops again. Another party ensues. Elvira and Filiberto are greeted by guests as if they were royalty. And they love it.)*

106 YOUNG JOSEFINA: Elvira and Filiberto enjoyed the praise and considerable envy of their neighbors. Everyone drank and laughed and danced the night away. And then, just at the stroke of midnight, the heavens sent a moonbeam directly into the west garden.

107 GUEST 1: Hey everyone. Look! Look at those vines over there in the garden.

108 GUEST 2: Something's happening.

109 GUEST 1: They're growing!

110 GUEST 3: And . . . and they're moving this way!

111 GUEST 1: The vines are going to attack us!

112 GUEST 4: *Ay, Dios!* Everybody run!

113 *(Guests scramble. The music stops.)*

114 YOUNG JOSEFINA: The vines from the west garden had a life of their own. They ran along the ground, over the garden fences, around the patio and up the sides of the house until the whole place was engulfed in squash vines.

115 *(Guests cry out.)*

116 FILIBERTO: It's okay, everyone, just stay calm. There is an explanation for this, it's okay.

117 *(Elvira emerges from the crowd with squash vines growing out of her head.)*

118 ELVIRA: That's right, stay calm, stay calm.

119 *(Everyone freezes. They take in the horrible sight of Elvira.)*

120 GUEST 1: Aaaaaah!!!! Look at her hair!

121 GUEST 2: It's not hair!

122 GUEST 3: Vines are growing out of her skull!

123 GUEST 1: Aaaah! It's horrible.

124 GUEST 2: She's a—a—a monster!

125   GUEST 4: It's a curse!!

126   ELVIRA: Wait! What's wrong? Where is everybody going?

127   *(The guests scream and scramble away. Filiberto stands frozen.)*

128   What's happened?

129   FILIBERTO: You have . . . *enredaderas de calabaza* (pumpkin vines) growing out of your head.

130   ELVIRA: I . . . whaaaah?

131   *(Elvira feels her head.)*

132   Ahhhhhh!!!!!!!!! What's happened?

133   FILIBERTO: It's a *maldición*, I'm telling you! We never should have planted in that garden.

134   ELVIRA: Well, it's too late for that now.

135   FILIBERTO: What are we going to do?

136   ELVIRA: I'm going to tell you what *you're* going to do.

137   FILIBERTO: Me?!!

138   ELVIRA: You are going to find that Señor Trujillo from the card game, and get to the bottom of this.

139   FILIBERTO: Me . . . ?

140   ELVIRA: Do you expect me to do it? I can't go out in public like this. I'm a monster!

141   *(Elvira dissolves into tears.)*

142   FILIBERTO: Don't cry.

143   ELVIRA: I just wanted to have a few nice things for once. Does that make me a bad person?

144   FILIBERTO: Well, maybe we did overdo it a bit.

145   *(More tears from Elvira.)*

NOTES

146   There, there. It's okay. I'll try to get to the bottom of this.

147   ELVIRA: Don't try. Do it!

148   JOSIE: Filiberto went door to door to see if he could locate someone from the Trujillo family.

149   FILIBERTO: Excuse me, do you know where I can find the Trujillos?

150   *(Sound of door shutting. He goes to next house.)*

151   Excuse me, do you know where I can find the Trujillos?

152   *(Sound of door shutting. He goes to next house.)*

153   ACTOR 6: Word had spread about a strange curse that had befallen Filiberto and his wife, and the town wanted nothing to do with them.

154   FILIBERTO: Excuse me, do you know who where I can find—

155   NEIGHBOR: You! We went to your lousy party and now everyone in town is allergic to squash! You're cursed! Get away from my house.

156   *(OLD MAN approaches. He's been following Filiberto.)*

157   OLD MAN: Hey. Psst. Psst. I know who you're looking for.

158   FILIBERTO: You do?

159   OLD MAN: Yes. And I'll tell you where to go under one condition.

160   FILIBERTO: What is it?

161   OLD MAN: Do you accept? Yes or no?

162   FILIBERTO: *(Tentatively:)* Yes.

163   OLD MAN: You must give *her* a message.

164   FILIBERTO: . . . *Bueno* (Okay), I can do that.

165   OLD MAN: Your land was previously owned by the *Tía* (Aunt). Eugenia Trujillo. Go to the house behind the big iron gates on the *Calle Aldama* (Aldama Street).

166   FILIBERTO: You mean . . . the house that everyone says is haunted?

167 OLD MAN: The very one. Do you want to find her or don't you?

168 FILIBERTO: I do. What's the message?

169 OLD MAN: Tell her . . . Rodolfo is still waiting for her.

170 FILIBERTO: Rodolfo is waiting.

171 OLD MAN: (*Correcting him:*) *Still* waiting.

172 FILIBERTO: Rodolfo is *still* waiting for her.

173 YOUNG JOSEFINA: Filiberto left the old man and set off to the stone house behind the big iron gates on the other side of town.

174 (*Filiberto clangs the iron knocker on the gate. Nothing. He clangs it again.*)

175 FILIBERTO: Hello! Is anybody home?

176 YOUNG JOSEFINA: He tried for hours. But no one answered.

177 (*He clangs again and calls out.*)

178 FILIBERTO: Is anybody home?

179 ACTOR 6: He became weary.

180 FILIBERTO: Anybody . . . ?

181 YOUNG JOSEFINA: And when he was ready to give up and walk away, he was reminded of poor Elvira waiting for him at home.

182 (*Memory of Elvira with vines growing out of her head.*)

183 ELVIRA: Don't try. Do it!!!

184 YOUNG JOSEFINA: So with no other options, Filiberto scaled the huge iron gate.

185 (*Filiberto climbs the tall gate and lands on the other side.*)

186 FILIBERTO: Such a magnificent courtyard. And grand fountain. Ooooh. I'm trespassing.

187 LA TÍA: (*Off:*) Who is there?

188 FILIBERTO: Hello . . . Hello . . . My name is Filiberto. I'm sorry to enter your home. I knocked for hours but no one answered.

189 LA TÍA: (*Off.*) That means I don't want visitors, *tonto!*

190 FILIBERTO: I'm sorry, but errrr . . . I have a message for you.

191 LA TÍA: (*Off.*) A message?

192 FILIBERTO: Yes, but first . . . my wife and I live the home on *Calle San Antonio*. I won the land in . . .

193 *(A strange figure enters from the shadows. It's* LA TÍA *[The Aunt]. She is wearing black from head to toe and is covered in a diaphanous black veil.)*

194 LA TÍA: *Ah, si.* (Oh, yes.) My nephew told me you won the land fair and square. Now go, and stay away from us.

195 FILIBERTO: But . . . something strange is happening in the garden.

196 LA TÍA: Something strange?

197 FILIBERTO: Something horrible.

198 LA TÍA: Ah hah. You signed an agreement with the deed to that land.

199 FILIBERTO: Yes, but—

200 LA TÍA: Did you abide by that agreement?

201 FILIBERTO: Well, but my wife. Well . . . no. Not exactly—

202 LA TÍA: And now you've discovered the **consequences.**

203 FILIBERTO: Please. We have to sell the house back to you.

204 LA TÍA: Impossible.

205 FILIBERTO: We weren't told there was a curse. That wasn't fair.

206 LA TÍA: You signed the agreement!

207 FILIBERTO: But something has happened to my wife.

208 LA TÍA: Leave my home. You're trespassing.

209   FILIBERTO: We have nowhere else to turn.

210   LA TÍA: You made your choice and sealed your fate. Now, get out!

211   *(She turns to leave.)*

212   FILIBERTO: Wait, please!

213   *(Filiberto pursues, reaches out and grabs her veil. He unwittingly pulls it off her head, revealing an elaborate spray of squash vines coming out of her skull. She screams.)*

214   LA TÍA: Don't look at me!

215   FILIBERTO: You too!

216   LA TÍA: Leave me alone.

217   FILIBERTO: What causes this? Is it a *maldición?*

218   LA TÍA: Yes! Yes! Yes! What else?

219   FILIBERTO: We have to undo what's been done.

220   LA TÍA: You can't.

221   FILIBERTO: There has to be a way.

222   LA TÍA: You aren't brave enough to face it. No one is. I chose to live my life like this instead.

223   FILIBERTO: But . . . I'll face it. I have to.

224   LA TÍA: *(Sizing him up:)* You? Bah!

225   FILIBERTO: Wha . . . what is it? Tell me, please. I have to help my wife!

226   LA TÍA: Dig into the dirt in the west garden at midnight on a full moon. And if you attempt it, heaven help you.

227   FILIBERTO: Why? What's there?

228   LA TÍA: No one knows. For centuries no one has been brave enough or foolish enough to try.

229   FILIBERTO: I will.

230   LA TÍA: Hmph!

231   FILIBERTO: For my wife, I will be brave!

232   *(He starts to leave. She calls after him.)*

233   LA TÍA: And my message?

234   FILIBERTO: Ah. Your message. The message is—Rodolfo is still waiting for you.

235   LA TÍA: (*A painful memory:*) Rodolfo . . . ?

236   *(La Tía begins to cry. She covers her head with the veil as she runs off sobbing. Filiberto heads home.)*

237   JOSIE: As fate would have it, that very night there was a full moon and by the time Filiberto returned home, it was just about midnight . . .

238   *(Someone hands Filiberto a shovel. He begins digging. Elvira enters.)*

239   ELVIRA: Filiberto, I was so worried about you. What are you doing?

240   FILIBERTO: I found the woman who owned this place.

241   ELVIRA: And? Will she buy it back from us?

242   FILIBERTO: No, but she told me what has to be done.

243   ELVIRA: That's why you're digging?

244   FILIBERTO: There's no telling what kind of evil is beneath this soil. It might be the devil himself. But I'm going to do it and break this curse.

245   ELVIRA: But Filiberto.

246   FILIBERTO: Go back to the house and wait for me. Please. Just go.

247   ELVIRA: Whatever evils there are to face, we'll face them together.

248   *(Someone hands Elvira a shovel. They dig.)*

249   YOUNG JOSEFINA: So together, they dug. Filiberto told Elvira about the old *Tía* and the old man, and he told her about the message from Rodolfo. And they dug all through the night under the full moon. Until—

250   *(Filiberto's shovel hits a hard surface.)*

251 FILIBERTO: Here! I've found something.

252 *(Elvira moves to Filiberto and together they uncover his discovery.)*

253 ELVIRA: What is this?

254 FILIBERTO: It's a huge wooden box, like a . . .

255 FILIBERTO & ELVIRA: *(Recoiling in fear:)* . . . A coffin!

256 ELVIRA: Don't go near it. Maybe it's my fate to live the rest of my life as this horrible thing. Maybe I deserve this for being so greedy.

257 FILIBERTO: We have to free you. And who knows how many generations of people fell into this maldición. It has to stop.

258 *(Filiberto reaches down to open the coffin.)*

259 ELVIRA: Wait! What if this is a trick?

260 FILIBERTO: We have to take that chance.

261 ELVIRA: Wait! What if the old woman is part of all this evil?

262 FILIBERTO: There's no way to know. Stand back!

263 ELVIRA: Filiberto!!!

264 *(Filiberto opens the coffin. They gasp.)*

265 FILIBERTO: *Un esqueleto!* (A skeleton!)

266 ELVIRA: And look! Gold! Silver!

267 FILIBERTO: It's a fortune!

268 ELVIRA: And jewels! Oooh, they're so beautiful!

269 FILIBERTO: Don't touch them!

270 ELVIRA: But they're so shiny and pretty!

271 *(She grabs at the jewels. Music swells as a huge ESQUELETO [skeleton] emerges from the coffin, along with glittering silver and gold pieces. Filiberto and Elvira scream. The skeleton towers over them.)*

NOTES

272 EL ESQUELETO: Who are you?

273 FILIBERTO: We are Filiberto and Elvira. We live here on this land.

274 EL ESQUELETO: And why do you open my coffin?

275 ELVIRA: There's been a *maldición*.

276 EL ESQUELETO: What kind of *maldición?*

277 ELVIRA: What kind? Hellooooo??? Look at me!

278 FILIBERTO: We were told if we find the secret buried in this garden, we could cure the *maldición*.

279 EL ESQUELETO: The *maldición* of this garden is against greed. Now the story is revealed. When I, Juan Ortiz Orizaba, died, my treasure was buried with me to hide it from the greedy Spaniards. But before my wife could dig the treasure out, death took her and I've been stuck here ever since. Look into the coffin.

280 *(Filiberto and Elvira peer into the coffin.)*

281 FILIBERTO: Gold and silver!

282 ELVIRA: And jewels!

283 EL ESQUELETO: The *maldición* ends when there is no more greed on this land or in this house!

284 ELVIRA: No more greed.

285 FILIBERTO: We promise!

286 ELVIRA: Er . . . okay!

287 EL ESQUELETO: Riches are for the purpose of generosity!

288 FILIBERTO: *La generosidad* (generosity)!

289 *(A huge wind kicks up. It swirls around Filiberto and Elvira. El Esqueleto disappears. Suddenly Elvira is back to normal.)*

290 FILIBERTO: Your head!

291 ELVIRA: (*Feeling her head:*) I'm me again!

292 *(They embrace. La Tía enters. She no longer has vines growing out of her skull.)*

293 LA TÍA: You did it. You had the courage to remove the curse.

294 FILIBERTO: *(Reaching to Elvira:)* We did it, together.

295 *(The Old Man enters.)*

296 LA TÍA: Rodolfo.

297 OLD MAN: I heard a great wind and saw a bright light coming from this place of my fondest memories.

298 LA TÍA: You came back.

299 OLD MAN: I told you I would wait for you.

300 LA TÍA: I'm sorry I shunned you, but I couldn't bear for you to look at me, I was so horrible.

301 OLD MAN: And I told you it didn't matter, *mi amor.*

302 (La Tía *and the Old Man embrace.)*

303 FILIBERTO: And now we will share in these riches . . . with others!

304 LA TÍA: What a good idea. We can build a library for the town.

305 ELVIRA: And start an orphanage.

306 FILIBERTO: And a public garden so people can plant vegetables for their families.

307 OLD MAN: There are many uses for these treasures!

308 ELVIRA: *(To audience:)* Filiberto and Elvira found many ways to give to others. They went down in the history of the *pueblo* as great philanthropists.

309 FILIBERTO: *(To audience:)* But neither of them ever went near a squash again.

310 *(Music rises. Actors take a bow, then quickly take their places for the next tale. Young Josefina steps down.)*

Please note that excerpts and passages in the StudySync® library and this workbook are intended as touchstones to generate interest in an author's work. The excerpts and passages do not substitute for the reading of entire texts, and StudySync® strongly recommends that students seek out and purchase the whole literary or informational work in order to experience it as the author intended. Links to online resellers are available in our digital library. In addition, complete works may be ordered through an authorized reseller by filling out and returning to StudySync® the order form enclosed in this workbook.

Reading & Writing Companion   **947**

CUENTOS DE JOSEFINA
(JOSEPHINE'S TALES)

First Read

Read *Cuentos de Josefina.* After you read, complete the Think Questions below.

☁ THINK QUESTIONS

1. Why do you think Filiberto remarks, "Maybe I wasn't born under a lucky star after all"? Explain.

2. Although bad things keep happening to them, Filiberto and Elvira continue to plant crops in the west garden. Why? Explain, citing specific evidence from the text.

3. How do Filiberto and Elvira gain perspective or wisdom from their struggles? Cite textual evidence to support your answer.

4. Read the following dictionary entry:

   contain
   con•tain \ kən'tān \ verb
   1. to carry or hold something within
   2. to control or restrain a feeling
   3. to stop something from spreading further

   Which definition most closely matches the meaning of **contain** as it is used in the text? Write the correct definition of *contain* here and explain how you figured out the correct meaning.

5. Based on context clues in the text, what do you think **consequences** means as it is used in paragraph 202? Write your best definition of *consequences* here, explaining how you arrived at its meaning. Does this word have a positive, negative, or neutral connotation?

Skill: Dramatic Elements and Structure

Use the Checklist to analyze Dramatic Elements and Structure in *Cuentos de Josefina*. Refer to the sample student annotations about Dramatic Elements and Structure in the text.

In order to identify the dramatic elements and structure of a drama, note the following:

- ✓ the form of the drama, such as comedy or tragedy

- ✓ how the acts and scenes advance the plot

- ✓ the setting of the play and whether or how it changes in each act or scene

- ✓ the language of the play, such as prose or verse, as spoken by characters

- ✓ the use of dramatic devices such as

  - soliloquy, when a character speaks his or her thoughts aloud directly to the audience while alone on stage

  - asides, when a character shares private thoughts with the audience when other characters are on stage

  - the information in stage directions, including lighting, sound, and set, as well as details about characters, including exits and entrances

To analyze how a drama's form or structure contributes to its meaning, consider the following questions:

- ✓ How does the use of figurative language contribute to the play's meaning?

- ✓ How is each act or scene structured? How do characters enter and leave, how do they speak to each other, and what happens as a result?

- ✓ How does the form, such as verse, contribute to the theme or message?

Please note that excerpts and passages in the StudySync® library and this workbook are intended as touchstones to generate interest in an author's work. The excerpts and passages do not substitute for the reading of entire texts, and StudySync® strongly recommends that students seek out and purchase the whole literary or informational work in order to experience it as the author intended. Links to online resellers are available in our digital library. In addition, complete works may be ordered through an authorized reseller by filling out and returning to StudySync® the order form enclosed in this workbook.

Reading & Writing Companion   **949**

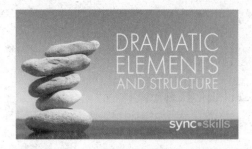

Skill: Dramatic Elements and Structure

Reread paragraphs 178–193 of *Cuentos de Josefina*. Then, using the Checklist on the previous page, answer the multiple-choice questions below.

♻ YOUR TURN

1. This question has two parts. First, answer Part A. Then, answer Part B.

   Part A What is the effect of the stage directions on this scene?

   ○ A. The stage directions help the reader picture what is happening on stage.

   ○ B. The stage directions help the reader understand what the characters are thinking.

   ○ C. The stage directions help the reader figure out what will happen next in the plot.

   ○ D. The stage directions help the reader identify the villain and the hero of the story.

   Part B Which of the following details BEST supports your response to Part A?

   ○ A. He became weary.

   ○ B. (Filiberto climbs the tall gate and lands on the other side.)

   ○ C. I'm sorry to enter your home. I knocked for hours but no one answered.

   ○ D. Filiberto scaled the huge iron gate.

CUENTOS DE JOSEFINA
(JOSEPHINE'S TALES)

Close Read

Reread *Cuentos de Josefina*. As you reread, complete the Skills Focus questions below. Then use your answers and annotations from the questions to help you complete the Write activity.

◎ SKILLS FOCUS

1. Identify evidence of how the playwright uses stage directions or dialogue to portray the characters. Explain what the dramatic elements tell you about the characters and why they choose to act as they do.

2. Identify details that reveal the qualities of the characters and setting in the play. Explain how the characters and setting influence the events of the plot of the play.

3. How do the narrators' asides influence the plot and tone of the play? Explain the dramatic element and how it influences your understanding of the play.

4. Identify examples that state or imply one or more universal themes in the play. Explain how the theme is reflected in the characters' actions and in the development of the plot.

5. Identify evidence of how Filiberto and Elvira stood out from the crowd, in both negative and positive ways. Explain how their desire to stand out from, or blend in with, the crowd drives the plot of the drama.

✏ WRITE

LITERARY ANALYSIS: Folktales have wide and lasting appeal because they teach lessons about universal ideas and experiences common across cultures and time periods. Write a response in which you identify a lesson with a universal appeal. In your response, explain how the author uses dramatic elements and structures, such as dialogue and asides, to help teach a lesson or moral.

Extended
Oral
Project and
Grammar

EXTENDED
ORAL
PROJECT

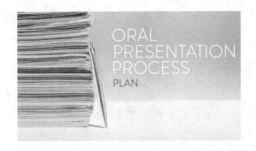

Oral Presentation Process: Plan

PLAN	DRAFT	REVISE	EDIT AND PRESENT

The texts in *The Power of One* unit take a variety of forms. Some of them are intended to be performed on a stage, and some are meant to be read on the page. You have also read, listened to, or watched a long list of powerful stories, plays, and other works throughout the year. We can reflect on which texts or productions best educate, entertain, and inspire audiences. We can also think about and research why these works are important and what message their authors have about individuals and society.

WRITING PROMPT

What literary work, film, or dramatic production would you recommend to your classmates? Why is this work important? How does this work entertain, inspire, or educate?

Prepare an argumentative presentation convincing your classmates to read or see a favorite literary work, film, or dramatic production. Be sure to include a clear position or thesis statement. In your reasoning, explain why this work is important and what made it entertaining, educational, or inspirational. Include evidence from at least three reliable sources. One source should be your recommended work itself and one should include diverse media formats, including video, audio, graphics, and print or digital texts. Research focuses could include the work's deeper message, historical or cultural significance, or genre or information about the author or director.

In your presentation, be sure to employ the following in order to communicate your ideas effectively:

- a clear position or thesis statement
- reasons and evidence that support the position
- reliable and credible sources
- consistent eye contact and clear oral communication
- gestures to emphasize or communicate ideas visually
- multimedia and visual displays
- a works cited page

Introduction to Oral Presentation

Argumentative oral presentations use body language, visual supports, and engaging writing to convince an audience about an issue. Good oral presentations use effective speaking techniques, relevant facts and anecdotes, and a purposeful structure. The characteristics of argumentative oral presentations include:

- a clear position or thesis statement
- reasons and evidence that support the position
- reliable and credible sources
- consistent eye contact and clear oral communication
- gestures to emphasize or communicate ideas visually
- multimedia and visual displays
- a works cited page

These characteristics can be organized into four major categories: context, structure, style and language, and elements of effective communication. As you continue with this Extended Oral Project, you'll receive more instruction and practice in crafting each of the presentation characteristics to create your oral presentation.

Before you get started on your own argumentative oral presentation, read this oral presentation that one student, Theo, wrote in response to the writing prompt. As you read the Model, highlight and annotate the features of argumentative writing that Theo included in his oral presentation.

☰ STUDENT MODEL

Monsters and a Message

By Theo

Introduction:

When you look at this picture of some neighbors, you might think they look concerned. Maybe they are discussing the guy who never cuts his grass. You would never know that chaos is about to break out on Maple Street. If you're like me, when you see a black-and-white TV show, you immediately assume that it is going to be boring and old-fashioned.

Introduction (Continued):

But I think it's worth taking a chance on an episode of *The Twilight Zone* series called "The Monsters Are Due on Maple Street." Even though the episode aired in 1960, it tells an important story.

Position or Thesis Statement:

I recommend "The Monsters Are Due on Maple Street" for three reasons.

- First, it's entertaining to watch because it has elements of science fiction and suspense.

- Second, it comments on important historical and political issues of its time.

- Finally, the episode teaches a valuable lesson about the danger of spreading rumors.

I recommend "The Monsters Are Due on Maple Street" because...

- It is entertaining to watch because it has elements of science fiction and suspense.
- It comments on important historical and political issues of its time.
- The episode teaches a valuable lesson about the danger of spreading rumors.

Reason #1:

The science-fiction elements and suspense in "The Monsters Are Due on Maple Street" keep the audience guessing and on the edge of their seat. Science fiction is a genre that often tells stories about futuristic science and technology, outer space, or aliens. Suspense is a genre that heightens feelings of surprise, excitement, and anxiety. The episode has elements of science fiction and ends in a twist. The viewers have to keep asking themselves whether things are coincidences or evidence of something the neighbors are trying to hide.

Entertaining Science Fiction and
Suspense Elements

Science Fiction
- Often tells stories about futuristic science and technology, outer space, or aliens
- Deals with the impact of actual or imagined science on society or individual people

Suspense
- Gives readers or viewers feelings of surprise, excitement, or anxiety
- Creates tension by putting the characters in a fast-paced and interesting story that ends with a twist

Copyright © BookheadEd Learning, LLC

Reason #1 (Continued):

First, a strange object passes over the town, causing electronics to stop working. Then, Les Goodman's car starts on its own, and people become suspicious, thinking he might be part of an alien invasion. Goodman struggles to explain what is happening to him. He says, "So I've got a car that starts by itself . . . I don't know why the car works—it just does!" Neither the characters nor the viewers know what to believe. Is it aliens? Is it something else? Nobody knows.

Reason #1 (Continued):

"The Monsters Are Due on Maple Street" also grabs your attention through tense and suspenseful action. From the moment the object passes over Maple Street, you begin to feel as though something is not right. Goodman is frightened, too. His dialogue foreshadows the violence to come. He says, "As God is my witness . . . you're letting something begin here that's a nightmare!" Knowing that something bad might happen makes you want to watch every scene closely. The episode's plot is full of surprises that will make your jaw drop and your heart pound in your chest. You never know what is going to happen next.

Reason #2:

Many episodes of *The Twilight Zone*, including "The Monsters Are Due on Maple Street," also addressed important historical and political issues of the time. Rod Serling could educate and inform people on historical or political issues using science fiction.

Commentary on Important Politics and History

"I found that it was all right to have Martians saying things that Democrats and Republicans could never say."
-Rod Serling, creator of *The Twilight Zone*

"Rod Serling: Submitted for Your Approval" (1995)

Reason #2 (Continued):

"The Monsters Are Due on Maple Street" was written in 1960, just years after the Red Scare. The Red Scare was a time in American history when many people were fearful of communist politics. During the Red Scare, many people were spying on neighbors to uncover secret communists. Some people were arrested. "Reds" was a nickname for communists at the time. Serling created "The Monsters Are Due on Maple Street" in response to a rising distrust between some Americans. The actions of the neighbors on Maple Street can be seen as commentary on the paranoia associated with the Red Scare. However, this episode wasn't just entertainment or a history lesson; it's also a life lesson.

Reason #3:

The story also sends a powerful message about gossip. It reminds audiences that spreading unfair rumors can lead to disaster.

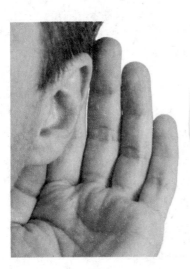
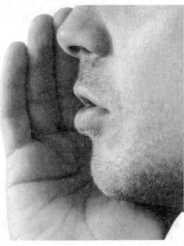

Reason #3 (Continued):

In the episode, enough people spread the rumor that Goodman is dangerous that everyone begins to think it is true. Another neighbor, Steve, tries to convince people to fight back against group pressure. He promises that "the only thing that's gonna happen is that we'll eat each other up alive." Steve has the courage to stand up for Goodman even though everyone is spreading bad rumors about him. Steve does not want to accuse someone who could be innocent.

An Important Lesson About Gossip

"You're standing here all set to crucify—all set to find a scapegoat—all desperate to point some kind of finger at a neighbor! Well now look, friends, the only thing that's gonna happen is that we'll eat each other up alive—"

"The Monsters Are Due on Maple Street" (1960)

Reason #3 (Continued):

Unfortunately, Steve's warning is too late. At the episode's climax, a man named Charlie shoots and kills a shadowy figure that he thinks is a monster. The "monster" turns out to be their neighbor, Pete Van Horn. Afterwards, Charlie is frightened, and he asks, "How was I supposed to know he wasn't a monster or something?" So many people had shared the rumor of a monster that Charlie thought the monster had to be real. If there had not been a terrible rumor, Charlie probably would not have acted so violently.

"How was I supposed to know he wasn't a monster or something? We're all scared of the same thing, I was just tryin' to . . . trying' to protect my home, that's all! Look, all of you, that's all I was tryin' to do."

"The Monsters Are Due on Maple Street" (1960)

NOTES

Conclusion:

"The Monsters Are Due on Maple Street" is much more than an exciting *Twilight Zone* episode. It uses suspense and attention-grabbing science-fiction elements. You will enjoy a gripping story while learning a bit about the political and historical topics of the 1950s and '60s. You also learn a lesson that applies just as well to rumors and gossip as it does to aliens.

Thank You and Works Cited:

Thank you for your time, and I hope you watch Rod Serling's "The Monsters Are Due on Maple Street" soon!

Works Cited

"Joseph McCarthy Begins Hearings Investigating U.S. Army." *History.com*, A&E Television Networks, 13 Nov. 2009, https://www.history.com/this-day-in-history/mccarthy-army-hearings-begin.

NBC News. "The Headline for a Newspaper Reads, 'All 11 Reds Are Convicted.'" *NBC News Archives Xpress*, https://www.nbcnewsarchivesxpress.com/contentdetails/6921.

"Rod Serling: Submitted for Your Approval." *American Masters*, season 10, episode 1, PBS, 29 Nov. 1995.

"The Monsters Are Due on Maple Street." *The Twilight Zone*, season 1, episode 22, CBS, 4 Mar. 1960.

"Top 10 Twilight Zone Episodes." *Time*, 2 Oct. 2009, http://entertainment.time.com/2009/10/02/top-10-twilight-zone-episodes/slide/the-monsters-are-due-on-maple-street-1960/.

✏ **WRITE**

Writers often take notes about arguments before they sit down to write. Think about what you've learned so far about organizing argumentative presentations to help you begin prewriting.

- **Purpose:** What literary work, film, or dramatic production have you enjoyed this year? Why should your classmates watch or read this work?

- **Reasons:** Why is this work important? How does this work entertain, inspire, or educate?

- **Evidence:** What evidence and details from your literary work, film, or dramatic production will you include? What other research might you need to do about the author or director, the genre, or the work's historical or cultural importance?

- **Organization**: How can you organize your presentation so that it is clear and easy to follow?

- **Clear Communication**: Who is your audience? How will you make sure that your audience can hear and understand you?

- **Technology and Visual Aids**: How can you use technology to engage your audience? What images or other visual aids could you use during your presentation?

Response Instructions

Use the questions in the bulleted list to write a one-paragraph summary. Your summary should describe what you will discuss in your oral presentation like the one on the previous pages.

Don't worry about including all of the details now; focus only on the most essential and important elements. You will refer back to this short summary as you continue through the steps of the writing process.

Skill: Evaluating Sources

••• CHECKLIST FOR EVALUATING SOURCES

First, reread the sources you gathered and identify the following:

- what kind of source it is, including video, audio, or text, and where the source comes from

- where information seems inaccurate, biased, or outdated

- where information seems irrelevant or incomplete

In order to use advanced searches to gather relevant, credible, and accurate print and digital sources, use the following questions as a guide:

- Is the material published by a well-established source or expert author?

- Is the material up-to-date or based on the most current information?

- Is the material factual, and can it be verified by another source?

- Are there specific terms or phrases in my research question that I can use to adjust my search?

- Can I use "and," "or," or "not" to expand or limit my search?

- Can I use quotation marks to search for exact phrases?

Please note that excerpts and passages in the StudySync® library and this workbook are intended as touchstones to generate interest in an author's work. The excerpts and passages do not substitute for the reading of entire texts, and StudySync® strongly recommends that students seek out and purchase the whole literary or informational work in order to experience it as the author intended. Links to online resellers are available in our digital library. In addition, complete works may be ordered through an authorized reseller by filling out and returning to StudySync® the order form enclosed in this workbook.

Reading & Writing Companion **963**

⟳ YOUR TURN

Read the factors below. Then, complete the chart by placing them into two categories: those that show a source is credible and reliable and those that do not.

	Factors
A	The video is objective, uses clear facts, and includes several different viewpoints.
B	The author is a reporter for an internationally recognized newspaper.
C	The article states only the author's first name and does not include any expert qualifications.
D	The text relies on loaded language or broad generalizations to persuade readers.
E	The article includes clear arguments and counterarguments that can be verified by other sources.
F	The website is for a personal podcast.

Credible and Reliable	Not Credible or Reliable

YOUR TURN

Complete the chart below by filling in the title and author of a source and answering the questions about it.

Source Title and Author:	
Reliable: Is the source material up-to-date or based on the most current information?	
Credible: Is the material published by a well-established source or expert author?	
Accurate: Is the material factual, and can it be verified by another source?	
Evaluation: Should I use this source in my oral presentation?	

Skill: Organizing an Oral Presentation

••• CHECKLIST FOR ORGANIZING AN ORAL PRESENTATION

In order to present claims and findings using appropriate eye contact, adequate volume, and clear pronunciation, do the following:

- Decide whether your presentation will be delivered to entertain, critique, inform, or persuade.

- Identify your audience in order to create your content.

- Choose a style for your oral presentation, either formal or informal.

- Use pertinent, or relative and appropriate, descriptions, facts, and details.

- Emphasize salient, or relevant and significant, points in a focused, clear manner.

- Include multimedia components and visual displays to clarify claims and findings and emphasize salient, or relevant, points.

- Use appropriate eye contact, adequate volume, and clear pronunciation.

To present claims and findings using appropriate eye contact, adequate volume, and clear pronunciation, consider the following questions:

- Have I decided on the purpose of my presentation and identified my audience?

- Have I chosen a style for my oral presentation, either formal or informal?

- Did I make sure that the descriptions, facts, and details I present are pertinent and support what I have to say?

- Have I emphasized relevant, salient points in a clear, coherent manner?

- Did I include multimedia components and visual displays to clarify claims and emphasize salient points?

- Did I practice using appropriate eye contact, adequate volume, and clear pronunciation?

⟳ YOUR TURN

Read the following quotations from a student's outline of her oral presentation and complete the chart on the next page by matching each with the corresponding component of her oral presentation.

	Quotations
A	My classmates and my teachers.
B	Finally, the most important reason to read it is because even though it is an old story, readers today can still relate to the theme and message about greed.
C	I think everyone should read "The Tale of the Haunted Squash" because it is entertaining, teaches a lesson about greed, and reminds readers to be grateful.
D	I also need to make eye contact with audience members in different parts of the room as I speak.
E	I will use a formal style because this is an academic presentation to my peers and teachers.
F	I will repeat my evaluation, reminding readers that this story will entertain them and teach them a lesson about greed. Then I will include a works cited slide to make sure I properly credit all my sources.
G	This is a funny and entertaining story; readers will laugh at the characters and their mishaps throughout the play.
H	I will include pictures of squash and a garden. I might try to find a video clip of the play or an audio clip of the story being told in the original Spanish.
I	To convince my classmates that they should read "The Tale of the Haunted Squash."
J	Although this story is filled with humor, it also has exciting and dramatic moments that will keep readers on the edge of their seats as they read.

⟳ YOUR TURN

Oral Presentation Component	Quotation from Oral Presentation Outline
Purpose	
Audience	
Style	
Thesis Statement	
Reason 1	
Reason 2	
Reason 3	
Conclusion	
Multimedia	
Oral Presentation Skills	

✏ WRITE

Use the questions in the checklist to outline your oral presentation. Be sure to present your thesis and support for that thesis in a logical order. Your outline should emphasize important points and show how they are connected to one another.

Skill: Considering Audience and Purpose

••• CHECKLIST FOR CONSIDERING AUDIENCE AND PURPOSE

In order to adapt speech to a variety of contexts and tasks, demonstrating a command of formal English when indicated or appropriate, note the following:

- your claims, findings, or salient points as well as pertinent facts, details, or examples

- your purpose, or reason for presenting

- your audience, the people who listen to an oral response or presentation

- your register, including your use of formal or informal English

- your volume and pronunciation of words

- your tone, or your attitude toward your subject matter

- your vocabulary and voice, including words to use for a specific occasion or in a particular context

To better understand how to adapt speech to a variety of contexts and tasks, demonstrating a command of formal English when indicated or appropriate, consider the following questions:

- What are my claims or findings? How can I emphasize my salient points?

- Did I include pertinent facts, details, or examples to support my claims or points in my presentation?

- What is my purpose for my oral response or presentation?

- Who is listening to my oral response or presentation?

- How should I adapt or change my register for my audience and task?

- What volume should I use? Do I know how to pronounce all the words correctly?

- How should I change my voice, tone, or vocabulary?

YOUR TURN

Read each example of student behaviors during a presentation. Then, complete the chart by filling in the strategy that best matches each example.

Strategies			
Vocabulary	Voice	Tone	Register

Example	Strategy
A student speaks loudly and lively to show that she finds the topic of her presentation exciting.	
A student uses words like *electorate* and *house of representatives* to prove her expertise in politics to the audience.	
A student makes jokes to emphasize his friendly personality and the humor in his presentation topic.	
A student uses slang because he is talking to a small group of his friends.	

WRITE

Form a small group with a few of your classmates. Take turns explaining the ideas in your outline to the group. When you finish, write a reflection about your purpose and your interaction with the audience. What was your purpose for speaking? How did your audience affect how you spoke? How did you use register, tone, and voice to accomplish your purpose and reach your audience? What vocabulary words or sentences will you change when writing your draft to better adapt your speech and emphasize your points?

Oral Presentation Process: Draft

| PLAN | DRAFT | REVISE | EDIT AND PRESENT |

You have already made progress toward writing your oral presentation. Now it is time to draft your argumentative oral presentation.

✏ WRITE

Use your plan and other responses in your Binder to draft your oral presentation. You may also have new ideas as you begin drafting. Feel free to explore those new ideas as you have them. You can also ask yourself these questions:

- Have I clearly stated a position about a literary work, film, or production?
- Do I give logical reasons in my critique of the literary work, film, or production?
- Have I organized my ideas using a clear text structure?

Before you submit your draft, read it over carefully. You want to be sure that you've responded to all aspects of the prompt.

Here is Theo's oral presentation draft. As you read, notice how Theo develops his draft to grab the audience's attention.

NOTES

Skill:
Communicating
Ideas

Theo adds important information so his readers will understand whom or what he is discussing.

Skill:
Reasons and
Relevant Evidence

Theo's presentation includes information that is not sufficiently supported by evidence and sound reasoning. He did not provide enough evidence to support his claim. Theo decides to revise his focus on a single claim and add details that help explain his ideas.

☰ STUDENT MODEL: FIRST DRAFT

Monsters and a Message

When you look at this picture of some neighbors, you might think they look concerned, so you would never know that chaos is about to breakout on Maple Street. [slide with neighbors talking and looking]. If you're like me, you see a black-and-white TV show and immediately assume that it is going to be boring and old-fashioned. ~~But I think it's worth taking a chance on "The Monsters Are Due on Maple Street".~~

But I think it's worth taking a chance on an episode of *The Twilight Zone* series called "The Monsters Are Due on Maple Street."

It's entertaining to watch and you can actually learn a lot about history from this episode and learn an important lesson for today. I recommend "The Monsters Are Due on Maple Street" because the episode tells an important story.

The episode is entertaining because the science-fiction and suspense elements. A bunch of weird things happen in the episode. The viewers have to keep asking themselves whether things are coincidences. Goodman is frightened. His dialog foreshadows the violence in the episode. He says, "As God is my witness . . . you're letting something begin here that's a nightmare!" ~~Knowing that something bad might happen makes you want to watch every scene closely. You want to know what is going to happen next!~~

Knowing that something bad might happen makes you want to watch every scene closely. The episode's plot is full of surprises that will make your jaw drop and your heart pound in your chest. You never know what is going to happen next.

Many episodes of *The Twilight Zone* including "The Monsters Are Due on Maple Street" addressed important social and political issues of the time. Rod Serling could educate and inform people on social or political issues using science fiction. He once said, "I found it was all right to have Martians saying things Democrats or Republicans could never say" (PBS American Masters).

[Show slide with quote.]

"I found that it was all right to have Martians saying things that Democrats and Republicans could never say."

–Rod Serling, creator of *The Twilight Zone*

"Rod Serling: Submitted for Your Approval" (1995)

"The Monsters Are Due on Maple Street" was written in 1960, just years before The Red Scare [slide with information about the Red Scare or video]. The Red Scare was a time in American history when people were fearful of communist politics, "Reds" was a nickname for communists during this time. During the Red Scare, many neighbors were spying on neighbors to uncover secret communists. Some people were even arrested. Serling created "The Monsters Are Due on Maple Street" in response to rise in distrust between Americans.

"The Monsters Are Due on Maple Street" reminds audiences that spreading unfair rumors can lead to disaster. In the episode, enough people spread the rumor that Goodman is dangerous that everyone begins to think it is true. A man tries to convince people to fight back against group pressure. It promises that "the only thing that's gonna happen is that we'll eat each other up alive" [slide with this quote]. The man has the courage to stand up for Goodman even though everyone is spreading bad rumors about the man. Steve does not want to hurt someone who is actually innocent. Unfortunately, his warning is too late. At the episode's climax, a man named Charlie shoots and kills a shadowy figure. Charlie thinks the figure is a monster. Charlie eventually figures out the the "monster" is his neighbor, Pete Van Horn. Charlie is frightened, and he asks, "How was I supposed to know he wasn't a monster or something?" Charlie thought the monster had to be real because so many people had shared the rumor of a monster. If there had not been a terrible rumor, Charlie probably would not have acted so violently.

"The Monsters Are Due on Maple Street" is much more than an exciting TV episode. Watching the episode, you question what is real, and you wonder what will happen next. I recommend that everyone watch this episode to enjoy a gripping story and to learn more about the politics of the 1950s and 60s. You will also learn a lesson that applies just as well to rumors and gossip as it does to aliens! [slide with thank you to the audience and my works cited page after]

NOTES

Skill: Sources and Citations

The quotation on Theo's slide credits the speaker, as well as the title of the source in which Theo found the quote. Theo also made sure to include the publication date. Although simply identifying the title of the work would have been enough to connect the quote to the corresponding entry in the works cited list, the additional reference to the date lends credibility to his presentation.

Skill:
Communicating Ideas

••• CHECKLIST FOR COMMUNICATING IDEAS

In order to present claims and findings using appropriate eye contact, adequate volume, and clear pronunciation, note the following:

- When writing your presentation, emphasize salient, or relevant and significant, points.

- Present your claims and findings in a focused, coherent way, making sure that the information you present is organized clearly and easily understandable.

- Use pertinent, or valid and important, facts and details to support and accentuate, or highlight, the main ideas or themes in your presentation.

- Include examples wherever possible to support your main idea.

- Remember to use adequate eye contact.

- Speak at an adequate volume so you can be heard by everyone.

- Use correct pronunciation.

To better understand how to present claims and findings and use appropriate eye contact, adequate volume, and clear pronunciation, consider the following questions:

- Have I used appropriate eye contact when giving my presentation?

- Did I speak at an adequate volume and use correct pronunciation?

- Did I include pertinent facts and details and accentuate the main ideas or themes in my presentation?

- Were my findings presented in a clear and coherent way?

YOUR TURN

Below are several examples of students communicating their ideas. To complete the chart, fill in the strategy that matches each example.

Strategies
Keep your posture
Make eye contact
Speak clearly
Use gestures

Example	Strategy
A student slows down her speech while pronouncing words in a foreign language.	
A student practices how he will stand to make sure he will be comfortable throughout his presentation.	
A student uses her fingers to count along as she presents a list.	
A student looks at a classmate at the front of the classroom before switching to someone sitting in the back.	

Please note that excerpts and passages in the StudySync® library and this workbook are intended as touchstones to generate interest in an author's work. The excerpts and passages do not substitute for the reading of entire texts, and StudySync® strongly recommends that students seek out and purchase the whole literary or informational work in order to experience it as the author intended. Links to online resellers are available in our digital library. In addition, complete works may be ordered through an authorized reseller by filling out and returning to StudySync® the order form enclosed in this workbook.

Reading & Writing Companion **975**

✏ WRITE

Take turns reading your presentation aloud to a partner.

When you are presenting:

- Employ steady eye contact to help keep your listeners' attention.
- Use an appropriate speaking rate, volume, and enunciation to clearly communicate with your listeners.
- Use natural gestures to add meaning and interest as you speak.
- Keep in mind conventions of language, and avoid informal or slang speech.

When you finish, write a reflection about your experience of communicating ideas. How clearly did you speak while giving your presentation? How well did you use eye contact, speaking rate, volume, enunciation, gestures, and conventions of language to communicate your ideas? How can you better communicate your ideas in the future?

Skill: Reasons and Relevant Evidence

••• CHECKLIST FOR REASONS AND RELEVANT EVIDENCE

In order to identify if a speaker's argument and specific claims are sound, note the following:

- the argument the speaker is making

- the claim (or claims) that the speaker is making in his or her argument

- the evidence the speaker is using to support this claim

- the logical reasoning the speaker is using

In order to determine the relevancy and sufficiency of the evidence that a speaker is using to support his or her claim(s), use the following questions as a guide:

- Does the speaker use sufficient evidence to support the claim?

- Does the speaker's evidence clearly and logically support the claim?

- Are the speaker's reasoning and evidence sound?

YOUR TURN

Read the section of Mica's presentation about the article "The Power of Student Peer Leaders" below. Then, complete the chart by identifying the argument and specific claims of the section.

What we read should inspire us and connect directly to our lives. I think that it is important middle school students like us all take the time to read "The Power of Student Peer Leaders." This is a valuable article to read because it will inspire readers with the true story of a fellow student, familiarize them with the college application process, and remind them of the importance of student leadership.

Argument and Claims	
A	This article will inspire readers with the true story of a student and his successful journey.
B	This article will teach readers about the power of student leadership, and how it positively impacts student leaders and other students around them.
C	Everyone should read "The Power of Student Peer Leaders."
D	After reading this, readers will be more familiar with the college application process and better equipped to navigate it in the future.

Argument	
Claim 1	
Claim 2	
Claim 3	

YOUR TURN

Complete the chart below by reading the claim, reasoning, and evidence and then writing in the third column to explain whether the reasoning and evidence are clear and sound. The first one has been completed for you.

Claim	Reasoning and Evidence	Explain
This article will inspire readers with the true story of a student and his successful journey.	Moises was a struggling homeless student in high school. His life changed when he joined a student leadership organization; the organization helped him apply to three colleges and complete the Fasfa. He become a student leader at his school and helped support other students on their journey to college.	The reasoning and evidence are strong because the writer offers many pieces of evidence that clearly and logically support the claim.
After reading this, readers will be more familiar with the college application process and better equipped to navigate it in the future.	The article explains how Moises, who is now a junior in college at the State University of New York at Albany, wrote a personal essay for his college application.	
This article will teach readers about the power of student leadership and how it positively impacts student leaders and other students around them.	After being trained as a peer leader, Moises applied to three colleges and applied for financial aid through Fasfa. He grew his confidence in public speaking. He also worked to create a campaign to increase the college application rate at his school, and it increased to 95% from 69%.	

Skill:
Sources and Citations

••• CHECKLIST FOR SOURCES AND CITATIONS

In your presentation, provide citations for any information that you obtained from an outside source. This includes the following:

- direct quotations
- paraphrased information
- tables, charts, and data
- images
- videos
- audio files

Your citations should be as brief and unobtrusive as possible. Follow these general guidelines:

- The citation should indicate the author's last name and the page number(s) on which the information appears (if the source has numbered pages), enclosed in parentheses.
- If the author is not known, the citation should list the title of the work.

At the end of your presentation, include a slide with your works cited list, following the formatting guidelines of a standard and accepted format. These are the elements and the order in which they should be listed for works cited entries:

- author
- title of source
- publisher
- publication date
- location
- for web sources, the URL

Not all of these elements will apply to each citation, and there are often exceptions. Include only the elements that are relevant for the source. Consult with your teacher as needed.

⟳ YOUR TURN

Complete the chart by listing the elements and examples in the correct order according to the standard formatting style for a works cited list.

	Elements and Examples
A	Confessore, Nick
B	publication
C	author
D	23 Jan. 2019
E	"He Reported on Facebook. Now He Approaches It With Caution."
F	https://www.nytimes.com/2019/01/23/technology/personaltech/facebook-online-privacy.html?rref=collection%2Ftimestopic%2FSocial%20Media&action=click&contentCollection=timestopics&region=stream&module=stream_unit&version=latest&contentPlacement=4&pgtype=collection
G	*The New York Times*
H	URL
I	publication date
J	title of source

Element	Example

WRITE

Use the questions in the checklist section to create or revise your citations and works cited list. Make sure that each slide with researched information briefly identifies the source of the information. When you have completed your citations, compile a list of all your sources and write out your works cited list. Refer to an MLA style guide or the style guide required by your teacher as needed.

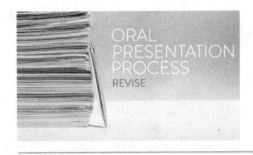

Oral Presentation Process: Revise

| PLAN | DRAFT | REVISE | EDIT AND PRESENT |

You have written a draft of your oral presentation. You have also received input from your peers about how to improve it. Now you are going to revise your draft.

◀◀ REVISION GUIDE

Examine your draft to find areas for revision. Keep in mind your purpose and audience as you revise for clarity, development, organization, and style. Use the guide below to help you review:

Review	Revise	Example
Clarity		
Identify places where more information or details would clarify the points that you present.	Add important information so your readers will understand whom or what you are discussing.	But I think it's worth taking a chance on an episode of *The Twilight Zone* series called "The Monsters Are Due on Maple Street."

Review	Revise	Example
Development		
Identify ideas in your presentation that are not developed with evidence and reasons. Annotate places where your argument lacks support.	Focus on a single claim and add details that help explain your ideas.	Knowing that something bad might happen makes you want to watch every scene closely. The episode's plot is full of surprises that will make your jaw drop and your heart pound in your chest. You never know what is going to happen next.
Organization		
Use transitions when switching between ideas or topics. Annotate places where the topic changes in your oral presentation.	Add short transitions that show the connections between your ideas within and across paragraphs.	Serling created "The Monsters Are Due on Maple Street" in response to a rising distrust between some Americans. The actions of the neighbors on Maple Street can be seen as commentary on the paranoia associated with the Red Scare. However, this episode wasn't just entertainment or a history lesson; it's also a life lesson.
Style: Word Choice		
Identify paragraphs or sentences that repeat the same word.	Replace overly repetitive vocabulary with a synonym.	"The Monsters Are Due on Maple Street" also grabs your attention through its tense and ~~attention-grabbing~~ suspenseful action.

Review	Revise	Example
Style: Sentence Variety		
Look for series of sentences that have similar lengths. Annotate any places where a conjunction or transition could vary the length of sentences you use.	Shorten a section of long sentences or join shorter sentences together.	"The Monsters Are Due on Maple Street" was written in 1960, just years after the Red Scare~~, which was~~. The Red Scare was a time in American history when many people were fearful of communist politics. During the Red Scare, many people were spying on neighbors to uncover secret communists~~, some~~. Some people were arrested. "Reds" was a nickname for communists at the time. Serling created "The Monsters Are Due on Maple Street" in response to a rising distrust between some Americans.

✏ WRITE

Use the guide above, as well as your peer reviews, to help you evaluate your oral presentation to determine areas that should be revised.

Once you have finished revising your draft, you can then focus on determining how you will deliver your presentation, practicing reading it aloud and noting key words or phrases you want to emphasize. You can also create the visual and multimedia components that will accompany the presentation, making sure they are clear and engaging.

Please note that excerpts and passages in the StudySync® library and this workbook are intended as touchstones to generate interest in an author's work. The excerpts and passages do not substitute for the reading of entire texts, and StudySync® strongly recommends that students seek out and purchase the whole literary or informational work in order to experience it as the author intended. Links to online resellers are available in our digital library. In addition, complete works may be ordered through an authorized reseller by filling out and returning to StudySync® the order form enclosed in this workbook.

Reading & Writing Companion

985

Grammar:
Economy of Language

In general, writing should be as brief as possible while still containing all the meaning an author wishes to convey. Any words that do not add to that meaning should be deleted. Writing that contains unnecessary, imprecise, or repetitive words is considered to be wordy. Wordiness is a sign of weak or unedited writing.

A knowledge of economy of language can help an author edit for wordiness. "Economy," in this usage, means "efficient, using the fewest possible words to write a sentence."

Strategy	Edited for Wordiness	Not Yet Edited for Wordiness
Use one or two words to take the place of an awkward or imprecise description.	The **distant** tiger growled loud enough for them to hear.	The tiger, which was very far ahead of them in the distance, growled loud enough for them to hear.
Replace multi-word terms with single-word synonyms.	**Because** food costs are rising, the school board announced that lunch prices will go up **soon**.	Due to the fact that food costs are rising, the school board announced that lunch prices will go up in the not-too-distant future.
Choose specific nouns, verbs, and adjectives instead of awkward or long description.	Omar **assumed** that Sarah **admired** his **leadership** in the study group.	Omar thought, but could not say for sure, that Sarah respected and approved of the way he could guide and direct everyone in the study group.
Eliminate words, phrases, or sentences that repeat information.	Twice a week, Pierre played tennis with Yvette. She was a top player on the school's tennis team.	Twice a week, Pierre played tennis with Yvette. She was a good athlete. She was a member of and top player on the school's tennis team.

⟳ YOUR TURN

1. How should this sentence be edited to reduce wordiness?

> Elena had to drop out of college on account of the fact that her family needed her financial support.

- ○ A. Replace **had to drop** with **had dropped**.
- ○ B. Replace **on account of the fact that** with **because**.
- ○ C. Delete **financial support**.
- ○ D. No change needs to be made to this sentence.

2. How should this sentence be edited to reduce wordiness?

> Not all people believe that a college education should cost something; some people believe it should cost nothing. There are many opinions on the subject.

- ○ A. Delete **There are many opinions on the subject.**
- ○ B. Delete **; some people believe it should cost nothing**.
- ○ C. Delete **; some people believe it should cost nothing. There are many opinions on the subject**.
- ○ D. No change needs to be made to this sentence.

3. How should this sentence be edited to reduce wordiness?

> Donna took me to a theme park and it was a very fascinating place to be.

- ○ A. We went to a theme park and had a fascinating time.
- ○ B. I was taken by Donna to a fascinating theme park.
- ○ C. Donna took me to a fascinating theme park.
- ○ D. No change needs to be made to this sentence.

4. How should this sentence be edited to reduce wordiness?

> Sara Jane often wrote songs for the high school glee club, that being the organization which frequently performed her work, and later wrote the score for a Broadway musical.

- ○ A. Delete **that being the organization which frequently performed her work.**
- ○ B. Delete **that being the organization**.
- ○ C. Delete **that being**.
- ○ D. No change needs to be made to this sentence.

Grammar:
Noun Clauses

A clause is a group of words that contains both a subject and a verb. A noun clause is a subordinate clause that acts as a noun in a sentence.

A noun clause usually begins with one of these words: *how, that, what, whatever, when, where, which, whichever, who, whom, whoever, whose,* or *why.* To identify most noun clauses, locate a clause with one of these words. Then, replace the noun clause with a pronoun such as *she, he, it,* or *they.* The sentence should still make sense.

Locate Noun Clause	Replace with a Pronoun
Do you remember **when we watched the movie**?	Do you remember **it**?

You can use a noun clause in the same ways you use a noun—as a subject, a direct object, an indirect object, an object of a preposition, and a predicate noun.

Function of Clause	Text
Object of a Preposition	Yet networks do need to take some responsibility for **what they have created with reality TV**. Reality TV and Society
Direct Object	Network executives don't understand **what they have created with reality TV**.
Subject	**What they have created** is having a negative impact on TV and society.
Predicate Noun	Reality TV is **what they have created**.

⟳ YOUR TURN

1. Replace the words in bold with a noun clause.

> **The lady at the front desk** will check out your books.

- ○ A. Either the manager or her assistant
- ○ B. The woman with the name tag
- ○ C. Whoever works at the front desk
- ○ D. No change needs to be made to this sentence.

2. Replace the words in bold with a noun clause.

> **The person with the most experience** will likely get the job offer.

- ○ A. The most experienced person
- ○ B. Whoever has the most experience
- ○ C. Experiencing the most
- ○ D. No change needs to be made to this sentence.

3. Replace the words in bold with a noun clause.

> The teacher talked about **how his students worked very hard yesterday**.

- ○ A. working very hard yesterday
- ○ B. the hardworking students
- ○ C. worked the hardest while in his class
- ○ D. No change needs to be made to this sentence.

4. Replace the words in bold with a noun clause.

> During lunch, all of the students ate **the cafeteria's pizza**.

- ○ A. what the cafeteria made that day
- ○ B. delicious cafeteria food
- ○ C. eating the pizza
- ○ D. No change needs to be made to this sentence.

Oral Presentation Process: Edit and Present

PLAN	DRAFT	REVISE	EDIT AND PRESENT

You have revised your oral presentation based on your peer feedback and your own examination. Now, it is time to edit your presentation. When you revised, you focused on the content of your presentation. You probably practiced communicating your ideas and considering your audience and purpose. When you edit, you focus on the mechanics of your presentation, paying close attention to things like grammar and punctuation.

Use the checklist below to guide you as you edit:

☐ Have I used noun clauses correctly?

☐ Have I edited for economy of language?

☐ Have I spelled everything correctly?

☐ Did I include transitions to create cohesion and clarify ideas in my presentation?

☐ Have I added digital media or visuals to enhance my presentation?

Notice some edits Theo has made:

- Edited to include a noun clause

- Edited for economy of language by combining related sentences to create one shorter sentence

- Edited for economy of language by removing wordy descriptions and shortening sentences

- Added transition words.

- Added in a note to include more visuals.

[slide with an image of a mysterious object flying across sky] First, a strange object passes over the town, causing electronics to stop working. Then, Les Goodman's car starts on its own and people become suspicious~~,. The neighbors think Goodman~~ thinking he **might be part of an alien invasion. Goodman struggles to explain** ~~the strange event.~~ what is happening to him. He says, **"So I've got a car that starts by itself . . . I don't know why the car works—it just does!" Neither the characters nor the viewers know what to believe.** ~~As the people of Maple Street get more worried, you want to pick a side: either Les Goodman is innocent or it he is hiding dangerous secrets. However, there are no clear answers in "The Monsters Are Due on Maple Street." Having to decide for yourself makes watching the episode a thrilling experience.~~ Is it aliens? Is it something else? Nobody knows.

✏ WRITE

Use the questions on the previous page, as well as your peer reviews, to help you evaluate your oral presentation to determine areas that need editing. Then edit your presentation to correct those errors. Finally, rehearse your presentation, including both the delivery of your written work and the strategic use of digital media you plan to incorporate.

Once you have made all your corrections and rehearsed with your digital media selections, you are ready to present your work. You may present to your class or to a group of peers. You can record your presentation to share with family and friends or to post on your blog. If you publish online, share the link with your family, friends, and classmates.

The Monsters Backstage

DRAMA

Introduction

" "The Monsters Backstage" is set in the moments before the curtain rises on a high school play. After the lead actor's wig mysteriously goes missing, the characters try to figure out what happened. Tensions rise as the actors' focus turns from the play to their suspicions of each other. Will they find the wig? Is one of the actors responsible for its disappearance? Whether or not they find answers to these questions, the show must go on.

V VOCABULARY

rehearse

to practice a performance

sabotage

to destroy something on purpose

mannequin

a figure that is shaped like a human body and is used for making or displaying clothes

accusation

a statement that claims someone has done something wrong

ridiculous

absurd or unreasonable

☰ READ

NOTES

1   [SCENE: *It is the opening night of a high school play.* EMMA, OLIVIA, TYLER, *and* CHRIS *wear costumes inspired by clothing from the late 1800s. The curtain is down. The actors hear the audience members talking.* EMMA *and* CHRIS *exchange worried glances.* TYLER *plays on his phone. As the scene opens,* OLIVIA *applies lipstick.*]

2   OLIVIA [*smiling in a mirror*]: Oh, that's perfect! [*She puts the makeup away and faces her castmates.*] Can you believe that it is nearly showtime? The time spent **rehearsing** is about to pay off. The curtain will rise soon, so break a leg! I'm confident this play will be a smash!

3   CHRIS: Of course you are. You've starred in plays since second grade. Emma and I are terrified!

4   OLIVIA: You'll be great! Tyler, I recommend that you put down the phone. I need one finishing touch. Emma, can you get my wig? I put it on the **mannequin** after dress rehearsal.

5   EMMA [*walks offstage and returns empty-handed*]: There is nothing on the mannequin's head. Are you sure that's where you left your wig?

6   OLIVIA [*annoyed*]: Yes.

7   EMMA: That's weird. It's not as if we have monsters backstage who take our stuff. Maybe someone accidentally moved it.

8   OLIVIA [*panicking*]: Help me find it!

9   [CHRIS *and* EMMA *walk off stage, whispering to each other.*]

10 TYLER [*rolling his eyes*]: Do you even need the wig?

11 OLIVIA: Don't be **ridiculous**. The wig helps me get into character. I bet you hid it. Is that your idea of a joke, or did you want to **sabotage** the play? You clearly do not want to be here!

12 TYLER [*suddenly angry*]: Now who's being ridiculous? I skipped basketball practice to rehearse for this play! I bet the Stage Fright Twins hid your wig so we can't go on.

13 [CHRIS *and* EMMA *enter, shaking their heads.*]

14 OLIVIA: Did you hide my wig to stop the play? I can't believe it.

15 EMMA [*shocked*]: That's because you shouldn't. If I hid your wig, why was I just looking for it? Use your brain! These wild **accusations** cause trouble. We should work together to find a solution.

16 OLIVIA: Like how you and Chris worked together to find a solution for your stage fright?

17 CHRIS: Or maybe Olivia hid her own wig to get more attention. Is that it?

18 [EMMA, OLIVIA, TYLER, *and* CHRIS *shout at each other. Suddenly, the curtain rises. The actors see the audience and freeze.*]

First Read

Read the play. After you read, answer the Think Questions below.

1. Who are the characters in the play? What are they doing?

_____

_____

2. Write two or three sentences describing the problems that the characters face.

_____

_____

3. Which characters are nervous about the play, and how do you know?

_____

_____

4. Use context to confirm the meaning of the word *sabotage* as it is used in "The Monsters Backstage." Write your definition of *sabotage* here.

_____

_____

5. What is another way to say that an idea is *ridiculous*?

_____

_____

Please note that excerpts and passages in the StudySync® library and this workbook are intended as touchstones to generate interest in an author's work. The excerpts and passages do not substitute for the reading of entire texts, and StudySync® strongly recommends that students seek out and purchase the whole literary or informational work in order to experience it as the author intended. Links to online resellers are available in our digital library. In addition, complete works may be ordered through an authorized reseller by filling out and returning to StudySync® the order form enclosed in this workbook.

Reading & Writing Companion   **995**

ANALYZING
EXPRESSIONS

sync skills

Skill:
Analyzing Expressions

★ DEFINE

When you read, you may find English expressions that you do not know. An **expression** is a group of words that communicates an idea. Three types of expressions are idioms, sayings, and figurative language. They can be difficult to understand because the meanings of the words are different from their **literal**, or usual, meanings.

An **idiom** is an expression that is commonly known among a group of people. For example, "It's raining cats and dogs" means it is raining heavily. **Sayings** are short expressions that contain advice or wisdom. For instance, "Don't count your chickens before they hatch" means do not plan on something good happening before it happens. **Figurative** language is when you describe something by comparing it with something else, either directly (using the words *like* or *as*) or indirectly. For example, "I'm as hungry as a horse" means I'm very hungry. None of the expressions are about actual animals.

••• CHECKLIST FOR ANALYZING EXPRESSIONS

To determine the meaning of an expression, remember the following:

✓ If you find a confusing group of words, it may be an expression. The meaning of words in expressions may not be their literal meaning.

- Ask yourself: Is this confusing because the words are new? Or because the words do not make sense together?

✓ Determining the overall meaning may require that you use one or more of the following:

- context clues

- a dictionary or other resource

- teacher or peer support

✓ Highlight important information before and after the expression to look for clues.

⟳ YOUR TURN

Read the excerpts and the literal meaning of each expression. Write the expression's meaning as it is used in the text into the correct row.

	Meaning in the Text
A	think
B	good luck with a theatrical performance
C	start the performance

#	Excerpt	Literal Meaning	Meaning in the Text
1	OLIVIA [*smiling in a mirror*]: … The time spent rehearsing is about to pay off. The curtain will rise soon, so **break a leg**! I'm confident this play will be a smash!	break a bone in the leg	
2	EMMA [*shocked*]: That's because you shouldn't. If I hid your wig, why was I just looking for it? **Use your brain**! These wild accusations cause trouble. We should work together to find a solution.	use the organ in your head that controls your body's activities	
3	TYLER [*suddenly angry*]: … I bet the Stage Fright Twins hid your wig so we can't **go on**.	continue	

Skill:
Analyzing and Evaluating Text

★ DEFINE

Analyzing and **evaluating** a text means reading carefully to understand the author's **purpose** and **message**. In informational texts, authors may provide information or opinions on a topic. They may be writing to inform or persuade a reader. In fictional texts, the author may be **communicating** a message or lesson through their story. They may write to entertain, or to teach the reader something about life.

Sometimes authors are clear about their message and purpose. When the message or purpose is not stated directly, readers will need to look closer at the text. Readers can use text evidence to make inferences about what the author is trying to communicate. By analyzing and evaluating the text, you can form your own thoughts and opinions about what you read.

••• CHECKLIST FOR ANALYZING AND EVALUATING TEXT

In order to analyze and evaluate a text, do the following:

✓ Look for details that show *why* the author is writing.

- Ask yourself: Is the author trying to inform, persuade, or entertain? What are the main ideas of this text?

✓ Look for details that show *what* the author is trying to say.

- Ask yourself: What is the author's opinion about this topic? Is there a lesson I can learn from this story?

✓ Form your own thoughts and opinions about the text.

- Ask yourself: Do I agree with the author? Does this message apply to my life?

🔄 **YOUR TURN**

Read the following excerpt from the story. Then, complete the multiple-choice questions below.

---

from "The Monsters Backstage"

9   [CHRIS *and* EMMA *walk off stage, whispering to each other.*]

10   TYLER [*rolling his eyes*]: Do you even need the wig?

11   OLIVIA: Don't be ridiculous. The wig helps me get into character. I bet you hid it. Is that your idea of a joke, or did you want to sabotage the play? You clearly do not want to be here!

12   TYLER [*suddenly angry*]: Now who's being ridiculous? I skipped basketball practice to rehearse for this play! I bet the Stage Fright Twins hid your wig so we can't go on.

---

1.   What is the author trying to show in the excerpt?

  ○ A. Tyler hid Olivia's wig so that he could spend more time on his phone.
  ○ B. Two other characters hid Olivia's wig to ruin the play.
  ○ C. Olivia cannot do the play without her wig, and so she is ready to quit.
  ○ D. Despite what Olivia thinks, Tyler wants the play to go on.

2.   What text evidence helped you infer this?

  ○ A. Emma and Chris are whispering to each other.
  ○ B. Tyler asks Olivia if she even needs the wig.
  ○ C. Olivia thinks Tyler hid the wig as a joke.
  ○ D. Tyler skipped basketball practice to rehearse the play.

Please note that excerpts and passages in the StudySync® library and this workbook are intended as touchstones to generate interest in an author's work. The excerpts and passages do not substitute for the reading of entire texts, and StudySync® strongly recommends that students seek out and purchase the whole literary or informational work in order to experience it as the author intended. Links to online resellers are available in our digital library. In addition, complete works may be ordered through an authorized reseller by filling out and returning to StudySync® the order form enclosed in this workbook.   Reading & Writing Companion   999

THE MONSTERS BACKSTAGE

Close Read

 WRITE

NARRATIVE: In this play, a missing wig causes distrust and conflict backstage. Select a character, and describe the events of the story from his or her point of view. How does your character feel? What does he or she think? What message or lesson does he or she learn? Pay attention to irregularly spelled words as you write.

Use the checklist below to guide you as you write.

☐ What does your character do during the play?

☐ What emotions does your character experience during the play?

☐ What does your character think about the other characters and the situation?

☐ What lesson does your character learn?

Use the sentence frames to organize and write your narrative.

My name is _____. Before the play, I _____, and I was _____.

The others needed to _____, so I _____.

Then I _____, but _____.

I was _____. I even _____.

We all started to _____.

I learned a valuable lesson. I learned that it is important to _____.

Peer Pressure vs. Teenagers

ARGUMENTATIVE TEXT

Introduction

Peer pressure is something everyone has to deal with, but it especially affects teenagers. In this text, learn what peer pressure is and what researchers have discovered about this phenomenon that has such a strong hold over the lives of young people.

V VOCABULARY

influence
to affect people

cognitive
involving brain activity

psychologist
a person who studies behavior
and the mind

achieve
to reach a goal

risky
having a danger of loss or
injury

NOTES

≡ READ

1   Nearly everyone has experienced peer pressure. A peer is someone who is the same age as you. Peer pressure is **influence** from peers. People, especially teenagers, behave differently when they experience peer pressure.

2   Peer pressure may cause young people to make bad choices. When teenagers behave badly, is it because they are trying to make their friends think they're cool? Researchers have been attempting to answer this question.

3   **Psychologists** have studied the effects of peer pressure on adolescents. Brett Laursen is a professor of psychology at Florida Atlantic University. Laursen says peer pressure "begins as soon as children start to pay attention to what other children think about them." Peer pressure will become even stronger as young people gain more control over their daily lives. Kevin M. King is a psychology professor at the University of Washington. King explains that students in middle school and high school have increasing freedom to

make choices. As children get older and more aware of other people's opinions, the effects of peer pressure can become more serious.

4   Peer pressure can affect students. In Sweden, researchers studied children who have friends that feel exhausted from school. These children often showed less interest in school themselves. Another study had adolescents play a driving computer game. Then the researchers told the players that they were being watched by peers in another room. The players' driving became more **risky**. The players crashed more frequently. Peer pressure can make driving and other activities more risky. Teenagers may get hurt or make bad decisions.

5   Researchers Dustin Albert, Jason Chein, and Laurence Steinberg have found that the structure of the brain may be why peer pressure affects teenagers more than other age groups. When younger teenagers do something risky and their friends like it, the brain records this "reward." The teenager becomes more likely to repeat the behavior. This makes it more likely something bad will happen to the teenager. As a teenager grows older, the brain's **cognitive** control system matures. Then it is easier for the teen to resist peer pressure.

6   How should teenagers deal with peer pressure? The answer is to make it work to their advantage. Laursen points out that children can do better academically when they study with friends who **achieve** at a higher level. These friends can give a push, in a friendly way, to get the person to work harder.

First Read

Read the text. After you read, answer the Think Questions below.

☁ THINK QUESTIONS

1. What is peer pressure?

_____

_____

2. What are the dangers of peer pressure?

_____

_____

3. Write two or three sentences describing how a teenager who is not doing well in school can deal with peer pressure.

_____

_____

4. Use context to confirm the meaning of the word *psychologist* as it is used in "Peer Pressure vs. Teenagers." Write your definition of *psychologist* here.

_____

_____

5. What is another way to say that an action is *risky*?

_____

_____

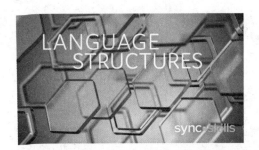

Skill:
Language Structures

★ DEFINE

In every language, there are rules that tell how to **structure** sentences. These rules define the correct order of words. In the English language, for example, a **basic** structure for sentences is subject, verb, and object. Some sentences have more **complicated** structures.

You will encounter both basic and complicated **language structures** in the classroom materials you read. Being familiar with language structures will help you better understand the text.

••• CHECKLIST FOR LANGUAGE STRUCTURES

To improve your comprehension of language structures, do the following:

 Monitor your understanding.

- Ask yourself: Why do I not understand this sentence? Is it because I do not understand some of the words? Or is it because I do not understand the way the words are ordered in the sentence?

✓ Pay attention to **perfect tenses** as you read. There are three perfect tenses in the English language: the present perfect, past perfect, and future perfect.

- **Present perfect tense** can be used to indicate a situation that began at a prior point in time and continues into the present.
    > Combine *have* or *has* with the past participle of the main verb.
    Example: I **have played** basketball for three years.

- **Past perfect tense** can describe an action that happened before another action or event in the past.
    > Combine *had* with the past participle of the main verb.
    Example: I **had learned** how to dribble a ball before I could walk!

- **Future perfect tense** expresses one future action that will begin and end before another future event begins or before a certain time.
    > Use *will have* or *shall have* with the past participle of a verb.
    Example: Before the end of the year, I **will have played** more than 100 games!

✓ Break down the sentence into its parts.

- Ask yourself: What actions are expressed in this sentence? Are they completed or are they ongoing? What words give me clues about when an action is taking place?

✓ Confirm your understanding with a peer or teacher.

Reading & Writing
Companion

YOUR TURN

Notice the perfect tense in each sentence. Write each sentence into the correct column.

Sentences	
A	Before next week, we will have finished this chapter.
B	I walked home after the game had ended.
C	I have finished my homework.
D	The tickets will have sold out by this evening.
E	She has won.
F	I had finished my homework before you called.

Present Perfect	Past Perfect	Future Perfect

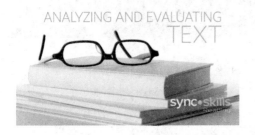

Skill:
Analyzing and Evaluating Text

★ DEFINE

Analyzing and **evaluating** a text means reading carefully to understand the author's **purpose** and **message**. In informational texts, authors may provide information or opinions on a topic. They may be writing to inform or persuade a reader. In fictional texts, the author may be **communicating** a message or lesson through their story. They may write to entertain, or to teach the reader something about life.

Sometimes authors are clear about their message and purpose. When the message or purpose is not stated directly, readers will need to look closer at the text. Readers can use text evidence to make inferences about what the author is trying to communicate. By analyzing and evaluating the text, you can form your own thoughts and opinions about what you read.

••• CHECKLIST FOR ANALYZING AND EVALUATING TEXT

In order to analyze and evaluate a text, do the following:

✓ Look for details that show *why* the author is writing.

- Ask yourself: Is the author trying to inform, persuade, or entertain? What are the main ideas of this text?

✓ Look for details that show *what* the author is trying to say.

- Ask yourself: What is the author's opinion about this topic? Is there a lesson I can learn from this story?

✓ Form your own thoughts and opinions about the text.

- Ask yourself: Do I agree with the author? Does this message apply to my life?

Please note that excerpts and passages in the StudySync® library and this workbook are intended as touchstones to generate interest in an author's work. The excerpts and passages do not substitute for the reading of entire texts, and StudySync® strongly recommends that students seek out and purchase the whole literary or informational work in order to experience it as the author intended. Links to online resellers are available in our digital library. In addition, complete works may be ordered through an authorized reseller by filling out and returning to StudySync® the order form enclosed in this workbook.

Reading & Writing Companion   **1007**

↻ YOUR TURN

Read the following excerpt from the text. Then, complete the multiple-choice questions below.

---

from "Peer Pressure vs. Teenagers"

Researchers Dustin Albert, Jason Chein, and Laurence Steinberg have found that the structure of the brain may be why peer pressure affects teenagers more than other age groups. When younger teenagers do something risky and their friends like it, the brain records this "reward." The teenager becomes more likely to repeat the behavior. This makes it more likely something bad will happen to the teenager. As a teenager grows older, the brain's cognitive control system matures. Then it is easier for the teen to resist peer pressure.

---

1. What is the author's purpose for this text?

   ○ A. to persuade
   ○ B. to entertain
   ○ C. to inform
   ○ D. to provide an opinion

2. What message is the author trying to communicate in this paragraph?

   ○ A. Teenagers need activities to help their brains develop.
   ○ B. Teenagers like to repeat the same behaviors.
   ○ C. As teenagers age, their brains mature.
   ○ D. As teenagers grow older, the structure of their brains mature, and they are able to more easily resist peer pressure.

Close Read

✏ WRITE

ARGUMENTATIVE: At the end of the article, the author suggests that peer pressure can be useful for teens. How can it be useful? Do you agree or disagree? Write a short paragraph that analyzes and evaluates the author's position. Include your own position and ideas, and use details from the text to support your claim. Pay attention to main verbs and helping verbs as you write.

Use the checklist below to guide you as you write.

☐ How does the author say that peer pressure can be useful?

☐ Why do you agree or disagree with the author?

☐ What text details support your opinion?

Use the sentence frames to organize and write your argument.

The author suggests that peer pressure can be useful for teens when _____.

I think the author is _____.

The author's _____ is a _____ idea.

If a student is _____, it can definitely _____.

But _____.

Peer pressure can be _____ for teens.

Please note that excerpts and passages in the StudySync® library and this workbook are intended as touchstones to generate interest in an author's work. The excerpts and passages do not substitute for the reading of entire texts, and StudySync® strongly recommends that students seek out and purchase the whole literary or informational work in order to experience it as the author intended. Links to online resellers are available in our digital library. In addition, complete works may be ordered through an authorized reseller by filling out and returning to StudySync® the order form enclosed in this workbook.

PHOTO/IMAGE CREDITS:

p. 171, iStock.com/PKM1

p. 171, iStock.com/borchee

p. 173, iStock.com/PKM1

p. 173, iStock.com/hanibaram, iStock.com/seb_ra, iStock.com/Martin Barraud

p. 174, Charles Dickens - London Stereoscopic Company/Stringer/Hulton Archive/Getty

p. 174, Albert Marrin - JIM WATSON/Staff/AFP/Getty

p. 174, Alfred Noyes - E. O. Hoppe/Contributor/The LIFE Picture Collection/Getty Images

p. 174, Edgar Allen Poe - Universal History Archive/Contributor/Universal Images Group/Getty Images

p. 174, Susan Power - Raphael GAILLARDE/Contributor/Gamma-Rapho/Getty Images

p. 176, iStock.com/Diane Labombarbe

p. 177, Culture Club/Hulton Archive/Getty Images

p. 179, iStock.com/Diane Labombarbe

p. 180, iStock.com/Andrey_A

p. 181, iStock.com/Andrey_A

p. 182, iStock.com/fotogaby

p. 183, iStock.com/fotogaby

p. 184, iStock.com/Hohenhaus

p. 185, iStock.com/Hohenhaus

p. 186, iStock.com/Diane Labombarbe

p. 187, iStock.com/dmfoss

p. 190, iStock.com/ImagineGolf

p. 194, iStock.com/ImagineGolf

p. 195, iStock.com/donatas1205

p. 196, iStock.com/donatas1206

p. 197, iStock.com/fotogaby

p. 198, iStock.com/fotogaby

p. 199, iStock.com/ImagineGolf

p. 200, iStock.com/Floortje

p. 214, iStock.com/Floortje

p. 215, iStock.com/Gemini-Create

p. 216, iStock.com/Gemini-Create

p. 217, istock.com/urbancow

p. 218, istock.com/urbancow

p. 219, iStock.com/Floortje

p. 220, iStock.com/WLDavies

p. 222, iStock.com/WLDavies

p. 223, iStock.com/Andrey_A

p. 224, iStock.com/Andrey_A

p. 225, iStock.com/WLDavies

p. 226, iStock.com/cmannphoto

p. 227, StudySync

p. 228, StudySync

p. 231, StudySync

p. 232, iStock.com/cmannphoto

p. 233, iStock.com/ThomasVogel

p. 234, iStock.com/ThomasVogel

p. 235, iStock.com/cmannphoto

p. 236, iStock.com/Paul Grecaud

p. 240, Universal History Archive/Univeral Images Group/Getty Images

p. 241, iStock.com/Paul Grecaud

p. 242, iStock.com/Andrey_A

p. 244, iStock.com/Andrey_A

p. 245, iStock.com/Hohenhaus

p. 246, iStock.com/Hohenhaus

p. 248, iStock.com/Paul Grecaud

p. 249, iStock.com/

p. 250, Hulton Archive/Archive Photos/Getty Images

p. 254, iStock.com/

p. 255, iStock.com/Caval

p. 256, iStock.com/Caval

p. 257, iStock.com/

p. 258, iStock.com/Liliboas

p. 263, iStock.com/Anastasiia_Guseva

p. 268, iStock.com/phaitoons

p. 271, iStock.com/phaitoons

p. 272, iStock.com/Martin Barraud

p. 273, iStock.com/Martin Barraud

p. 274, iStock.com/phaitoons

p. 275, iStock.com/Martin Barraud

p. 276, iStock.com/Martin Barraud

p. 282, iStock.com/gopixa

p. 284, iStock.com/fstop123

p. 287, iStock.com/domin_domin

p. 290, iStock.com/Martin Barraud

p. 295, iStock.com/bo1982

p. 297, iStock.com/Jeff_Hu

p. 300, iStock.com/Fodor90

p. 303, iStock.com/stevedangers

p. 305, iStock.com/Martin Barraud

p. 307, iStock/Vimvertigo

p. 309, iStock/Vimvertigo

p. 311, ©iStock.com/wildpixel

p. 313, iStock.com/Martin Barraud

p. 315, iStock.com/stanley45

p. 316, stevecoleimages/iStock

p. 316, PeopleImages/iStock

p. 316, goodynewshoes/iStock

p. 316, abadonian/iStock

p. 316, iStock.com

p. 318, iStock.com/stanley45

p. 319, iStock.com/Ales_Utovko

p. 321, iStock.com/Zoran Kolundzija

p. 323, iStock.com/stanley45

p. 324, iStock.com/halbergman

p. 325, Todor Tsvetkov/iStock

p. 325, kickimages/iStock

p. 325, jtgriffin07/iStock

p. 325, typhoonski/iStock

p. 325, Beboy_ltd/iStock

p. 325, iStock.com

p. 325, choness/iStock

p. 327, iStock.com/halbergman

p. 328, iStock.com/BlackJack3D

p. 330, iStock.com/Mlenny

p. 332, iStock.com/halbergman

p. 483, iStock.com/spooh
p. 483, ©iStock.com/eyewave, ©iStock.com/subjug, ©iStock.com/Ivantsov, iStock.com/borchee, ©iStock.com/seb_ra
p. 485, iStock.com/hanibaram, iStock.com/seb_ra, iStock.com/Martin Barraud
p. 485, iStock.com/spooh
p. 486, Laurie Halse Anderson- David Livingston/Contributor/Getty Images Entertainment
p. 486, David Bornstein - Thos Robinson/Stringer/Getty Images Entertainment
p. 486, William Kamkwamba - Bobby Longoria/Contributor/Getty Images Entertainment
p. 486, Randall Munroe - ZUMA Press, Inc./Alamy Stock Photo
p. 486, Ernest Lawrence Thayer - New York Public Library: A.G. Spalding Baseball Collection
p. 487, Leo Tolstoy - Archive Pics/Alamy Stock Photo
p. 487, Kurt Vonnegut - Ulf Andersen/Contributor/Hulton Archive/Getty
p. 488, iStock.comEHStock
p. 489, iStock/benoitb
p. 491, iStock.com/THEPALMER
p. 492, iStock.com/fotogaby
p. 493, iStock.com/fotogaby
p. 494, iStock.com/THEPALMER
p. 495, iStock.com/Kameleon007
p. 498, iStock.com/Kameleon008
p. 499, iStock/Orla
p. 500, iStock/Orla
p. 501, ©iStock.com/Hohenhaus
p. 502, ©iStock.com/Hohenhaus
p. 503, iStock.com/Kameleon008
p. 504, iStock.com/toddarbini
p. 508, iStock.com/toddarbini
p. 509, iStock.com/urbancow
p. 510, iStock.com/urbancow
p. 511, iStock.com/eskaylim
p. 512, iStock.com/eskaylim
p. 513, iStock.com/toddarbini
p. 514, iStock.com/uanmonino
p. 518, iStock.com/Ron_Thomas
p. 523, iStock.com/Ron_Thomas
p. 524, iStock.com/Martin Barraud
p. 525, iStock.com/Martin Barraud
p. 526, iStock.com/Ron_Thomas
p. 527, iStock.com/photogress
p. 535, iStock.com/photogress
p. 536, ©iStock.com
p. 537, ©iStock.com
p. 538, iStock.com/urbancow
p. 539, iStock.com/urbancow
p. 540, iStock.com/yipengge
p. 541, iStock.com/yipengge
p. 542, iStock.com/photogress
p. 543, iStock.com/RITA
p. 544, Serious Scientific Answers to Absurd Hypothetical Questions by Randall Munroe. Copyright © 2014 by xkcd Inc. Reprinted by permission of Houghton Mifflin Harcourt Publishing Company. All rights reserved.
p. 546, Serious Scientific Answers to Absurd Hypothetical Questions by Randall Munroe. Copyright © 2014 by xkcd Inc. Reprinted by permission of Houghton Mifflin Harcourt Publishing Company. All rights reserved.
p. 547, Serious Scientific Answers to Absurd Hypothetical Questions by Randall Munroe. Copyright © 2014 by xkcd Inc. Reprinted by permission of Houghton Mifflin Harcourt Publishing Company. All rights reserved.
p. 548, Serious Scientific Answers to Absurd Hypothetical Questions by Randall Munroe. Copyright © 2014 by xkcd Inc. Reprinted by permission of Houghton Mifflin Harcourt Publishing Company. All rights reserved.
p. 549, Serious Scientific Answers to Absurd Hypothetical Questions by Randall Munroe. Copyright © 2014 by xkcd Inc. Reprinted by permission of Houghton Mifflin Harcourt Publishing Company. All rights reserved.
p. 550, Serious Scientific Answers to Absurd Hypothetical Questions by Randall Munroe. Copyright © 2014 by xkcd Inc. Reprinted by permission of Houghton Mifflin Harcourt Publishing Company. All rights reserved.

p. 551, Serious Scientific Answers to Absurd Hypothetical Questions by Randall Munroe. Copyright © 2014 by xkcd Inc. Reprinted by permission of Houghton Mifflin Harcourt Publishing Company. All rights reserved.
p. 543, iStock.com/RITA
p. 553, iStock.com/janrysavy
p. 554, iStock.com/janrysavy
p. 556, ©iStock.com/Hohenhaus
p. 557, ©iStock.com/Hohenhaus
p. 557, Serious Scientific Answers to Absurd Hypothetical Questions by Randall Munroe. Copyright © 2014 by xkcd Inc. Reprinted by permission of Houghton Mifflin Harcourt Publishing Company. All rights reserved.
p. 558, iStock.com/Caval
p. 559, iStock.com/Caval
p. 560, iStock.com/RITA
p. 561, iStock.com/kupicoo
p. 567, iStock.com/epicurean
p. 568, Public Domain
p. 572, iStock.com/fergregory
p. 576, iStock.com/fergregory
p. 577, iStock.com/Orla
p. 578, iStock.com/Orla
p. 579, ©iStock.com/deimagine
p. 580, ©iStock.com/deimagine
p. 581, iStock.com/fergregory
p. 582, ©iStock.com/gaiamoments
p. 587, iStock.com/fergregory
p. 588, iStock.com/ThomasVogel
p. 589, iStock.com/ThomasVogel
p. 590, iStock.com/eskaylim
p. 591, iStock.com/eskaylim
p. 592, iStock.com/fergregory
p. 593, iStock.com/hanibaram, iStock.com/seb_ra, iStock.com/Martin Barraud
p. 594, iStock.com/Martin Barraud
p. 600, iStock.com/gopixa
p. 602, iStock.com/ThomasVogel
p. 605, iStock.com/Tevarak
p. 608, iStock.com/Martin Barraud
p. 613, iStock.com/bo1982
p. 615, iStock/Jeff_Hu
p. 618, iStock.com/stevedangers
p. 620, iStock/Fodor90
p. 623, iStock.com/peepo
p. 626, iStock.com/Martin Barraud
p. 628, iStock.com/Mr_Twister
p. 630, iStock.com/wwing
p. 632, iStock.com/efks
p. 634, iStock.com/Martin Barraud
p. 636, iStock.com/Moussa81
p. 637, iStock/DragonImages
p. 637, iStock/LightFieldStudios
p. 637, iStock.com/SbytovaMN
p. 637, iStock.com/monkeybusinessimages
p. 637, iStock.com/Steve Debenport
p. 639, iStock.com/Moussa81
p. 640, ©iStock.com/Ales_Utovko
p. 642, ©iStock.com/BlackJack3D
p. 644, iStock.com/Moussa81
p. 645, iStock.com/pedrosala
p. 645, iStock.com/James Pintar
p. 645, iStock.com/mustafagull
p. 645, iStock.com/CHKnox
p. 645, iStock.com/arashenkovAnton
p. 645, iStock.com/shakzu
p. 645, iStock.com/thebroker
p. 647, iStock.com/thebroker
p. 648, StudySync
p. 649, iStock.com/pedrosala
p. 650, iStock.com/BlackJack3D
p. 652, iStock.com/AlexandrBognat
p. 653, iStock.com/thebroker
p. 654, iStock.com/pedrosala

p. 823, iStock.com/OgnjenO
p. 823, ©iStock.com/eyewave, ©iStock.com/subjug, ©iStock.com/Ivantsov, iStock.com/borchee, ©iStock.com/seb_ra
p. 823, republica/iStock.com
p. 825, iStock.com/hanibaram, iStock.com/seb_ra, iStock.com/Martin Barraud
p. 825, iStock.com/OgnjenO
p. 826, Maya Angelou - Deborah Feingold/Contributor/Getty Corbis Entertainment
p. 826, Laura Bush - MCT/Contributor/Tribune News Service/Getty
p. 826, Nikki Giovanni - Mireya Acierto/Contributor/WireImage/Getty Images
p. 826, Lois Lowry - Jim Spellman/Contributor/WireImage/Getty Images
p. 826, Kathryn Schultz Miller - Used by permission of Kathryn Schultz Miller
p. 827, Gregory Ramos - Used by permission of Gregory Ramos
p. 827, Margot Lee Shetterly - Jason LaVeris/Contributor/FilmMagic/Getty
p. 827, Mekeisha Madden Toby - Photos courtesy of Mekeisha Madden Toby
p. 828, ©iStock.com/Paolo Cipriani
p. 832, iStock.com/chaoss
p. 837, iStock.com/mbolina
p. 858, iStock.com/mbolina
p. 859, iStock.com/deimagine
p. 860, iStock.com/deimagine
p. 861, iStock/Spanishalex
p. 862, iStock/Spanishalex
p. 863, iStock.com/mbolina
p. 864, ©iStock.com/Rawpixel
p. 865, MCT/Tribune News Service/Getty Images
p. 870, ©iStock.com/Rawpixel
p. 871, iStock.com/peepo
p. 872, iStock.com/peepo
p. 873, ©iStock.com/Rawpixel
p. 874, ©iStock.com/fergregory
p. 878, ©iStock.com/fergregory
p. 879, iStock.com/Orla
p. 880, iStock.com/Orla
p. 881, iStock.com/Brostock
p. 882, iStock.com/Brostock
p. 883, ©iStock.com/fergregory
p. 884, iStock.com/Pratchaya
p. 888, iStock.com/Pratchaya
p. 889, iStock.com/eskaylim
p. 890, iStock.com/eskaylim
p. 891, iStock.com/Hohenhaus
p. 892, iStock.com/Hohenhaus
p. 893, iStock.com/Pratchaya
p. 894, iStock.com/Izabela Habur
p. 898, Josh Vertucci/Disney ABC Television Group/Getty Images
p. 899, iStock.com/Izabela Habur
p. 900, iStock.com/DNY59
p. 901, iStock.com/DNY59
p. 902, iStock.com/Martin Barraud
p. 903, iStock.com/Martin Barraud

p. 904, iStock.com/Izabela Habur
p. 905, iStock.com/Yagi-Studio
p. 913, iStock.com/Yagi-Studio
p. 914, iStock.com/janrysavy
p. 915, iStock.com/janrysavy
p. 917, iStock.com/Hohenhaus
p. 918, iStock.com/Hohenhaus
p. 919, iStock.com/Yagi-Studio
p. 920, iStock.com/AndrewSoundarajan
p. 924, @iStock.com/mcbrugg
p. 927, @iStock.com/mcbrugg
p. 928, iStock.com/Andrey_A
p. 929, iStock.com/Andrey_A
p. 930, @iStock.com/mcbrugg
p. 931, iStock.com/AndreaObzerova
p. 948, iStock.com/AndreaObzerova
p. 949, iStock/Spanishalex
p. 950, iStock/Spanishalex
p. 951, iStock.com/AndreaObzerova
p. 952, iStock.com/hanibaram, iStock.com/seb_ra, iStock.com/Martin Barraud
p. 953, iStock.com/Martin Barraud
p. 955, CBS Photo Archive/CBS/Getty Images
p. 957, iStock/homeworks255
p. 958, iStock/benzoix
p. 959, NBC Universal Archives
p. 959, iStock/TomekD76
p. 961, CBS Photo Archive/CBS/Getty Images
p. 963, iStock.com/Mutlu Kurtbas
p. 966, iStock.com/BilevichOlga
p. 969, iStock.com/Martin Barraud
p. 971, iStock.com/Martin Barraud
p. 974, iStock.com/polesnoy
p. 977, iStock.com/Domin_domin
p. 980, iStock.com/tofumax
p. 983, iStock.com/Martin Barraud
p. 986, iStock.com/Zocha_K
p. 988, iStock/Vimvertigo
p. 990, iStock.com/Martin Barraud
p. 992, iStock.com/MicroStockHub
p. 992, istock.com/vgajic
p. 992, istock.com/michaelquirk
p. 992, istock.com/Image Source
p. 992, iStock.com
p. 992, istock.com/AleksandarGeorgiev
p. 995, iStock.com/MicroStockHub
p. 996, iStock.com/Ales_Utovko
p. 998, iStock.com/kyoshino
p. 1000, iStock.com/MicroStockHub
p. 1001, ©iStock.com/BonNontawat
p. 1002, istock.com
p. 1002, iStock.com/dima_sidelnikov
p. 1002, iStock.com/yacobchuk
p. 1002, istock.com/andresr
p. 1002, istock.com/RFarrarons
p. 1004, ©iStock.com/BonNontawat
p. 1005, iStock.com/BlackJack3D
p. 1007, iStock.com/kyoshino
p. 1009, ©iStock.com/BonNontawat

studysync

Text Fulfillment Through StudySync

If you are interested in specific titles, please fill out the form below and we will check availability through our partners.

ORDER DETAILS

Date:

TITLE	AUTHOR	Paperback/ Hardcover	Specific Edition *If Applicable*	Quantity

SHIPPING INFORMATION

Contact:

Title:

School/District:

Address Line 1:

Address Line 2:

Zip or Postal Code:

Phone:

Mobile:

Email:

BILLING INFORMATION ☐ *SAME AS SHIPPING*

Contact:

Title:

School/District:

Address Line 1:

Address Line 2:

Zip or Postal Code:

Phone:

Mobile:

Email:

PAYMENT INFORMATION

☐ CREDIT CARD

Name on Card:

Card Number:　　　　Expiration Date:　　　　Security Code:

☐ PO　Purchase Order Number:

StudySync Text Fulfillment, BookheadEd Learning, LLC
610 Daniel Young Drive | Sonoma, CA 95476